THE HISTORY OF
HIGHER EDUCATION

Major Themes in Education

Other titles in this series

Philosophy of Education
Major Themes in the Analytic Tradition
Edited by Paul Hirst and Patricia White
4 volume set

History of Education
Edited by Roy Lowe
4 volume set

Psychology of Education
Edited by Peter K. Smith and Anthony D. Pellegrini
4 volume set

Adult and Continuing Education
Edited by Peter Jarvis

Curriculum Studies
Edited by David Scott
4 volume set

Literacy
Edited by David Wray
4 volume set

Special Educational Needs and Inclusive Education
Edited by David Mitchell
4 volume set

Educational Management
Edited by Harry Tomlinson
4 volume set

Science Education
Edited by John Gilbert
4 volume set

Teacher Education
Edited by David Hartley and Maurice Whitehead
5 volume set

Early Years Education
Edited by Rod Parker-Rees and Jenny Willan
4 volume set

Media Literacies
Edited by Margaret Mackey
4 volume set

Forthcoming:

Educational Assessment and Evaluation
Edited by Harry Torrance
4 volume set

English Language Teaching
Edited by Patricia Hedge
6 volume set

Mathematics Education
Edited by Alan Bishop
4 volume set

Gifted and Talented Education
Edited by Deborah Eyre
4 volume set

Multicultural Education
Edited by James A. Banks
4 volume set

THE HISTORY OF HIGHER EDUCATION

Major Themes in Education

Edited by
Roy Lowe

Volume I
The origins and dissemination of the
university ideal

Routledge
Taylor & Francis Group

LONDON AND NEW YORK

First published 2009
by Routledge
2 Park Square, Milton Park, Abingdon, Oxon, OX14 4RN, UK

Simultaneously published in the USA and Canada
by Routledge
270 Madison Avenue, New York, NY 10016

Routledge is an imprint of the Taylor & Francis Group, an informa business

Typeset in 10/12pt Times NR MT by Graphicraft Limited, Hong Kong
Printed and bound in Great Britain by
MPG Books Ltd., Bodmin, Cornwall

British Library Cataloguing in Publication Data
A catalogue record for this book is available from the British Library

Library of Congress Cataloging-in-Publication Data
The history of higher education : major themes in education / edited by Roy Lowe.
p. cm.
Includes bibliographical references and index.
ISBN 978-0-415-37854-3 (set) – ISBN 978-0-415-38469-8 (vol. 1, hardback) –
ISBN 978-0-415-38470-4 (vol. 2, hardback) – ISBN 978-0-415-38471-1
(vol. 3, hardback) – ISBN 978-0-415-38472-8 (vol. 4, hardback) –
ISBN 978-0-415-38473-5 (vol. 5, hardback)   1. Education, Higher–History.
I. Lowe, Roy.
LA173.H584 2008
378.09–dc22
2008008884

ISBN10: 0-415-37854-0 (Set)
ISBN10: 0-415-38469-9 (Volume I)

ISBN13: 978-0-415-37854-3 (Set)
ISBN13: 978-0-415-38469-8 (Volume I)

Publisher's Note

References within each chapter are as they appear in the original
complete work.

Sheldon Rothblatt has, for many years, been at the forefront of those studying and writing about higher education. Beyond his being one of the pre-eminent historians of his generation, he has proved to be a true and loyal friend to me through thick and thin, an unfailing source of sound advice and encouragement. This collection is dedicated to him, with my thanks and appreciation for all the years he has enriched my life and those of a generation of students of higher education.

Roy Lowe

CONTENTS

Editor's acknowledgements   xvii
Acknowledgements   xix
Chronological table of reprinted articles and chapters   xxiii

General introduction   1
Introduction   5

1 **Excerpts from *History of Islamic Origins of Western Education, 800–1350***   9
   MEHDI NAKOSTEEN

2 **Antecedents (before 1900)**   40
   J. F. ADE AJAYI, LAMECK K. H. GOMA AND
   G. AMPAH JOHNSON

3 **The rise of the universities**   67
   GABRIEL CAMPAYRE

4 **Late medieval universities**   81
   A. B. COBBAN

5 **Excerpt from *The Universities of the Italian Renaissance***   87
   PAUL F. GRENDLER

6 **The origins of Oxford and Cambridge**   110
   V. H. H. GREEN

7 **Excerpt from *Universities: American, English, German***   116
   ABRAHAM FLEXNER

8 **Jefferson's educational legacy**   126
   JENNINGS L. WAGONER, JR

CONTENTS

9 Four colleges and their communities   143
   W. BRUCE LESLIE

10 Universities in the U.S.A.: secondary school characteristics   158
   RALPH E. LOMBARDI

11 The Scottish university tradition   164
   ANDREW LOCKHART WALKER

12 Excerpts from *Academe and Empire: Some Overseas
   Connections of Aberdeen University, 1860–1970*   180
   JOHN D. HARGREAVES

13 The growth of a system   220
   R. D. ANDERSON

14 Development in higher education in the United Kingdom:
   nineteenth and twentieth centuries   236
   ASA BRIGGS

15 The expansion of higher education   257
   GARY B. COHEN

16 Higher education in Poland   279
   B. SIMON

17 European rectors and vice-chancellors in conference   286
   J. W. BLAKE

18 Higher education in the British colonies   290
   WALTER ADAMS

19 The changing political economy: the private and public lives
   of Canadian universities   298
   DONALD FISHER AND KJELL RUBENSON

20 The universities of Australia   317
   J. D. G. MEDLEY

21 Excerpt from *The African University in Development*   324
   ASAVIA WANDIRA

22 University education in free India   345
   S. R. DONGERKERY

23 General features and problems of higher education   352
   FAHIM I. QUBAIN

24 Models of the Latin American university   363
    ORLANDO ALBORNOZ

25 The past and future of Asian universities: twenty-first
    century challenges   373
    PHILIP G. ALTBACH

26 Chinese higher education: the legacy of the past and the
    context of the future   391
    WEIFANG MIN

27 Japanese higher education: contemporary reform and
    the influence of tradition   418
    MOTOHISA KANEKO

28 Higher education and scientific development: the promise
    of newly industrializing countries   443
    PHILIP G. ALTBACH

VOLUME II THE NATURE OF THE UNIVERSITY

Acknowledgements   vii

Introduction   1

29 **Concept of a university**   4
    A. B. COBBAN

30 **What is a university?**   18
    HASTINGS RASHDALL

31 **Knowledge its own end**   36
    JOHN HENRY NEWMAN

32 **Loss and gain: John Henry Newman in 2005**   51
    SHELDON ROTHBLATT

33 **Excerpt from *The Essence of T. H. Huxley***   64
    T. H. HUXLEY

34 **T. H. Huxley's idea of a university**   74
    CYRIL BIBBY

CONTENTS

35 **The idea of a modern university**   86
ABRAHAM FLEXNER

36 **Adaptation to a democratic age**   106
ALBERT MANSBRIDGE

37 **An experiment in democratic education**   123
R. H. TAWNEY

38 **The nature and aims of a modern university**   139
BRUCE TRUSCOT

39 **Changing conceptions of the university's task**   150
WALTER MOBERLEY

40 **Excerpt from** *The Universities in Transition*   167
H. C. DENT

41 **The idea of the idea of a university and its antithesis**   178
SHELDON ROTHBLATT

42 **The changing functions of universities**   222
A. H. HALSEY AND M. A. TROW

43 **The university in the modern world: an address delivered
to the Conference of European Rectors and Vice-Chancellors
at Göttingen on September 2nd, 1964**   229
LIONEL ROBBINS

44 **Idea of a university**   241
ERIC ASHBY

45 **Mass higher education**   253
ERIC ASHBY

46 **Federal universities and multi-campus systems: Britain and
the United States since the nineteenth century**   261
SHELDON ROTHBLATT

47 **Functions – the pluralistic university in the pluralistic society**   286
CLARK KERR

48 **The idea of a multiversity**   306
CLARK KERR

49 **Ideas of the university**   329
A. H. HALSEY

50 **Pressures and silences**   359
HAROLD SILVER

VOLUME III UNIVERSITIES AND THE STATE

Acknowledgements   vii

Introduction   1

51 **Higher education and social change: some comparative perspectives**   5
    KONRAD H. JARAUSCH

52 **The university and the state in Western Europe**   36
    GUY NEAVE

53 **Conclusion [*The Universities and British Industry, 1850–1970*]**   49
    MICHAEL SANDERSON

54 **Community service stations: the transformation of the civic
    universities, 1898–1930**   57

55 **The admission of poor men**   77
    LORD CURZON OF KEDLESTON

56 **The universities & social purpose**   100
    ROY PASCAL

57 **Reflections on policy**   106
    SYDNEY CAINE

58 **Conclusion [*British Universities and the State*]**   121
    ROBERT O. BERDAHL

59 **Excerpts from *Grants to Students***   133
    MINISTRY OF EDUCATION AND SCOTTISH
    EDUCATION DEPARTMENT

60 **Excerpts from *Higher Education***   156
    [ROBBINS COMMITTEE]

61 **Some conclusions [*Government and the Universities in Britain*]**   166
    JOHN CARSWELL

62 **Pasts and futures**   175
    HAROLD SILVER

63 **The business university**   188
    E. P. THOMPSON

CONTENTS

64 *Towards an Independent University*   211
   H. S. FERNS

65 Funding in higher education and economic growth in France
   and the United Kingdom, 1921–2003   228
   VINCENT CARPENTIER

66 Professionalization and higher education in Germany   250
   CHARLES E. McCLELLAND

67 National Socialism and the German universities   267
   NOTKER HAMMERSTEIN

68 The commission on German universities   283
   LORD LINDSAY OF BIRKER

69 Excerpt from *The University Reform of Tsar Alexander I,*
   1802–1835   289
   JAMES T. FLYNN

70 The American State university today   310
   ALEXANDER KINGHORN

71 Affirmative action   320
   SHELDON ROTHBLATT

72 Blacks in higher education to 1954: a historical overview   344
   JOHN E. FLEMING

73 Apartheid in the South African universities   350
   JOHN REX

VOLUME IV   THE EVOLVING CURRICULUM

Acknowledgements   vii

Introduction   1

74 Of the subjects of university teaching   4
   WILLIAM WHEWELL

75 Christianity and scientific investigation: a lecture   29
   JOHN HENRY NEWMAN

CONTENTS

76 The need for the study of philosophy   43
    R. W. LIVINGSTONE

77 The cosmos of knowledge   54
    KARL JASPERS

78 Culture and science   66
    JOSÉ ORTEGA Y GASSET

79 Outlines of a possible solution   75
    ADOLPH LÖWE

80 The college-university: its development in Aberdeen and beyond   89
    JOHN M. FLETCHER

81 Change and resistance to change: a consideration of the
    development of English and German universities during
    the sixteenth century   100
    JOHN M. FLETCHER

82 Excerpt from *The Great Instauration: Science, Medicine
    and Reform, 1626–1660*   135
    CHARLES WEBSTER

83 The limits of 'reform': some aspects of the debate on university
    education during the English Revolution   144
    JOHN TWIGG

84 From oral to written examinations: Cambridge, Oxford and
    Dublin 1700–1914   159
    CHRISTOPHER STRAY

85 Curriculum and style in the collegiate university: Classics in
    nineteenth-century Oxbridge   208
    CHRISTOPHER STRAY

86 Experimental science in early nineteenth-century Oxford   239
    G. L'E. TURNER

87 Structural change in English higher education, 1870–1920   255
    ROY LOWE

88 Modern Greats   273
    T. D. WELDON

89 General education   281
    J. S. FULTON

CONTENTS

90 Higher education since the war: universities, CATS and
technical colleges; Robbins and after   288
E. E. ROBINSON

91 From technical school to technological university   310
PETER VENABLES

92 The basic ideas   330
WALTER PERRY

93 Modular systems in Britain   340
OLIVER FULTON

94 The Paris statutes of 1215 reconsidered   351
STEPHEN C. FERRUOLO

95 American higher education in the age of the college   364
JURGEN HERBST

96 The Committee on Social Thought of the University of Chicago   383
JOHN U. NEF

97 The American modular system   391
SHELDON ROTHBLATT

VOLUME V   ELITE FORMATION, SYSTEM BUILDING AND THE RISE OF THE STUDENT ESTATE

Acknowledgements   vii

Introduction   1

98 Elite and popular functions in American higher education   5
MARTIN TROW

99 The student and the university   24
ALLAN BLOOM

100 The pattern of social transformation in England   63
HAROLD PERKIN

101 The evolution of the British universities   77
A. H. HALSEY AND M. A. TROW

CONTENTS

102 Excerpt from *English Culture and the Decline of the Industrial Spirit, 1850–1980* 101
MARTIN J. WIENER

103 Universities and elites in modern Britain 112
R. D. ANDERSON

104 English civic universities and the myth of decline 133
ELIZABETH J. MORSE

105 English elite education in the late nineteenth and early twentieth centuries 156
ROY LOWE

106 The expansion of higher education in England 173
ROY LOWE

107 The diversification of higher education in England 196
SHELDON ROTHBLATT

108 Education and the middle classes in modern France 217
FRITZ RINGER

109 The students and the future 255
BRIAN SIMON

110 The student movement 273
ERIC ASHBY

111 The medieval students of the University of Salamanca 286
ANTONIO GARCÍA Y GARCÍA

112 Economists as experts: the rise of an academic profession in the United States, 1870–1920 297
ROBERT L. CHURCH

113 Donnishness 332
SHELDON ROTHBLATT

114 The academic role 354
SHELDON ROTHBLATT

115 Emerging concepts of the academic profession at Oxford 1800–1854 371
ARTHUR ENGEL

116 Women and men 415
A. H. HALSEY

CONTENTS

117 **Patterns of provision: access and accommodation**   **432**
    CAROL DYHOUSE

118 **Reconsidering a classic: assessing the history of women's
    higher education a dozen years after Barbara Solomon**   **470**
    LINDA EISENMANN

    Index   502

EDITOR'S
ACKNOWLEDGEMENTS

Over many years I have been indebted to a generation of historians and students of higher education with whom I have worked in one capacity or another and who have each enhanced my understanding and insight. Those who come to mind as having been particularly influential on my work include R. D. Anderson, Jim Albisetti, Noel Annan, Harry Armytage, Asa Briggs, Kenneth Charlton, Sol Cohen, John Fletcher, Oliver Fulton, A. H. Halsey, Peter Hennock, John Honey, Peter Lundgren, Tony Mangan, Bill Marsden, Elizabeth Morse, Detlef Müller, David Reeder, Fritz Ringer, Sheldon Rothblatt, Harold Silver, Brian Simon, Richard Szreter, Martin Trow and Don Withrington. Some of these are, sadly, no longer with us, but the memory of them, and their influence, lives on. Without the inspiration of all these scholars and the opportunity, to greater or lesser extent, to listen to them, to exchange ideas and to read their work, it would have been quite impossible to reach the point in my career at which I could undertake a collection of this kind. Sheldon Rothblatt, in particular, not only offered constant encouragement, but facilitated a period of research at the Centre for Studies in Higher Education at the Berkeley campus of the University of California. It was there that, for the only time in my career, I had the chance to work full-time on university history. He has remained an unfailing friend, and this collection is dedicated to him with my grateful thanks.

I have to thank also my publishers, Routledge, who have supported my writing throughout my career. The invitation to undertake this collection led to a fascinating library quest. They have been helpful at every turn and, in this instance, I have to thank in particular Anne Urbschat for her part in helping the manuscript through the press.

Finally, I thank my wife, who once again has made the completion of a major project possible and has given unstinting support. It would have been impossible to bring this collection of essays together without the help and participation, directly or indirectly, of all these people. The decisions made in selection, and the balance of the five volumes, remains entirely my responsibility. Their appearance comes as a way of thanking and marking my indebtedness to all the people I have mentioned above.

ACKNOWLEDGEMENTS

The publishers would like to thank the following for permission to reprint their material:

Ohio University Press and James Currey Publishers for permission to reprint J. F. Ade Ajayi, Lameck K. H. Goma and G. Ampah Johnson, 'Antecedents (before 1900)', in J. F. Ade Ajayi, Lameck K. H. Goma and G. Ampah Johnson, *The African Experience with Higher Education*, published by the Association of African Universities, Accra in association with James Curry, London and Ohio University Press, Athens, Ohio, 1996, pp. 1–27.

Taylor & Francis for permission to reprint A. B. Cobban, 'Late Medieval Universities', in A. B. Cobban, *The Medieval Universities: Their Development and Organization*, Methuen, London, 1975, pp. 116–121.

The Johns Hopkins University Press for permission to reprint Grendler, Paul F., *The Universities of the Italian Renaissance*, pp. 3–21. © 2002 The Johns Hopkins University Press.

Penguin Books Ltd for permission to reprint V. H. H. Green, 'The Origins of Oxford and Cambridge', in V. H. H. Green, *The Universities*, Penguin Books, Harmondsworth, 1969, pp. 13–20.

Oxford University Press for permission to reprint Abraham Flexner, *Universities; American, English, German*, Oxford University Press, London, 1930, pp. 311–327.

Thomas Jefferson Foundation for permission to reprint 'Jefferson's Educational Legacy', from *Jefferson and Education* by Jennings L. Wagoner, Jr. Thomas Jefferson Foundation, Monticello Monograph Series, 2004, pp. 127–146 and 159–162. Copyright © 2004 by Thomas Jefferson Foundation, Inc.

Transaction Publishers and W. Bruce Leslie for permission to reprint W. Bruce, Leslie, 'Four Colleges and Their Communities', in W. Bruce Leslie, *Gentlemen and Scholars: College and Community in the 'Age of the University,'*

1865–1917, The Pennsylvania State University Press, University Park, Pennsylvania, 1992, pp. 11–28.

Blackwell Publishing for permission to reprint Ralph E. Lombardi, 'Universities in the U.S.A.: Secondary School Characteristics', *Universities Quarterly* (now *Higher Education Quarterly*), Volume IX, 1954–55, pp. 66–72.

Polygon (an imprint of Birlinn Ltd.) for permission to reprint 'The Scottish University Tradition' from *The Revival of the Democratic Intellect: Scotland's University Traditions and the Crisis in Modern Thought* by Andrew Lockhart Walker, Polygon Press Edinburgh, 1994, pp. 22–37 and 321–323.

Cambridge University Press for permission to reprint R. D. Anderson, 'The Growth of a System', in R. D. Anderson, *Universities and Elites in Britain since 1800*, published by Macmillan Press for the Economic History Society, 1992, pp. 12–28.

Taylor & Francis for permission to reprint Asa Briggs, 'Development in Higher Education in the United Kingdom: Nineteenth and Twentieth Centuries' from *Higher Education: Demand and Response*, by W. R. Niblett (ed.). Copyright © 1969, Tavistock Publication, London. Reproduced by permission of Taylor & Francis Books UK.

Purdue University Press for permission to reprint Gary B. Cohen, 'The Expansion of Higher Education' from *Education and Middle-Class Society in Imperial Austria, 1848–1918* by Gary B. Cohen. © 1996 Purdue University Press. Unauthorized duplication not permitted.

Blackwell Publishing for permission to reprint Brian Simon, 'Higher Education in Poland', *Universities Quarterly* (now *Higher Education Quarterly*), Vol. VII, 1952–53, published by Turnstile Press, London, pp. 176–183.

Blackwell Publishing for permission to reprint J. W. Blake, 'European Rectors and Vice-Chancellors in Conference', *Universities Quarterly* (now *Higher Education Quarterly*), Vol. X, 1955–56, published by Turnstile Press, London, pp. 15–18.

Blackwell Publishing for permission to reprint Walter Adams, 'Higher Education in the British Colonies', *Universities Quarterly* (now *Higher Education Quarterly*), Vol. I, 1946–47, published by Turnstile Press, London, pp. 145–153.

Blackwell Publishing for permission to reprint J. D. G. Medley, 'The Universities of Australia', *Universities Quarterly* (now *Higher Education Quarterly*), Vol. 2, No. 2, February 1948, published by Turnstile Press, London, pp. 151–158.

Blackwell Publishing for permission to reprint S. R. Dongerkery, 'University Education in Free India', *Universities Quarterly* (now *Higher Education*

Quarterly), Vol. V, 1950–51, published by Turnstile Press, London, pp. 72–79.

The Johns Hopkins University Press for permission to reprint Fahim I. Qubain, *Education and Science in the Arab World*, pp. 48–60. © 1966 The Johns Hopkins University Press.

University of New Mexico Press for permission to reprint Orlando Albornoz, 'Models of the Latin American University', in Joseph Maier and Richard W. Weatherhead (eds), *The Latin American University*, University of New Mexico Press, Albuquerque, 1979, pp. 123–134.

The Johns Hopkins University Press for permission to reprint Altbach, Philip G. and Toru Umakoshi, eds, *Asian Universities: Historical Perspectives and Contemporary Challenges*. pp. 13–32, 53–83, 115–143. © 2004 The Johns Hopkins University Press.

Greenwood Publishing Group for permission to reprint Philip G. Altbach, 'Higher Education and Scientific Development: The Promise of Newly Industrializing Countries', in *Scientific Development and Higher Education: The Case of Newly Industrializing Nations*, Philip G. Altbach et al. (eds). Copyright © 1989 Praeger Publishers (a division of Greenwood Press). Reproduced with permission of Greenwood Publishing Group, Inc., Westport, CT.

Disclaimer

The publishers have made every effort to contact authors/copyright holders of works reprinted in *The History of Higher Education* (*Major Themes in Education*). This has not been possible in every case, however, and we would welcome correspondence from those individuals/companies whom we have been unable to trace.

Chronological table of reprinted articles and chapters

Date	Author	Article/chapter	References	Vol.	Chap.
1838	William Whewell	Of the subjects of university teaching	W. Whewell, *On the Principles of English University Education*, West Strand, London: John W. Parker, pp. 5–51	IV	74
1852	John Henry Newman	Christianity and scientific investigation: a lecture	J. H. Newman, *Discourses on the Scope and Nature of University Education*, reprinted London: J. M. Dent, 1915, pp. 235–59	IV	75
1893	Gabriel Campayre	The rise of the universities	G. Campayre, *Abelard and the Origin and Early History of Universities*, reprinted New York: AMS Press, 1969, pp. 46–69	I	3
1893	Hastings Rashdall	What is a university?	H. Rashdall, *The Universities of Europe in the Middle Ages*, ed. F. M. Powicke and A. B. Emden, Oxford: Oxford University Press, 1936, pp. 1–24	II	30
1909	Lord Curzon of Kedleston	The admission of poor men	Lord Curzon of Kedleston, *Principles and Methods of University Reform*, Oxford: Clarendon Press, pp. 42–75	III	55
1910	John Henry Newman	Knowledge its own end	John Henry Newman, *The Idea of a University Defined and Illustrated*, London: Longmans, Green and Co., pp. 99–123	II	31
1914	R. H. Tawney	An experiment in democratic education	*The Political Quarterly* (May): 62–84	II	37
1923	Albert Mansbridge	Adaptation to a democratic age	A. Mansbridge, *The Older Universities of England: Oxford and Cambridge*, London: Longmans, Green and Co., pp. 172–95	II	36
1930	Abraham Flexner	The idea of a modern university	A. Flexner, *Universities: American, English, German*, London: Oxford University Press, pp. 3–36	II	35

Chronological Table continued

Date	Author	Article/chapter	References	Vol.	Chap.
1930	Abraham Flexner	Excerpt from *Universities: American, English, German*	A. Flexner, *Universities: American, English, German*, London: Oxford University Press, pp. 311–27	I	7
1940	Adolph Löwe	Outlines of a possible solution	A. Löwe, *The Universities in Transformation*, London: Sheldon Press, pp. 21–47	IV	79
1943	Brian Simon	The students and the future	B. Simon, *A Student's View of the Universities*, London: Longmans, Green and Co., pp. 120–42	V	109
1943	Bruce Truscot	The nature and aims of a modern university	B. Truscot, *Red Brick University*, London: Faber and Faber, pp. 45–56	II	38
1944	José Ortega y Gasset	Culture and science	José Ortega y Gasset, *Mission of the University*, London: Kegan Paul, Trench, Trubner and Co., pp. 63–72	IV	78
1946–7	Walter Adams	Higher education in the British colonies	*Universities Quarterly* I: 145–53	I	18
1946–7	T. D. Weldon	Modern Greats	*Universities Quarterly* I: 348–57	IV	88
1948	J. D. G. Medley	The universities of Australia	*Universities Quarterly* 2(2): 151–8	I	20
1948–9	John U. Nef	The Committee on Social Thought of the University of Chicago	*Universities Quarterly* III: 678–86	IV	96
1949	Walter Moberley	Changing conceptions of the university's task	W. Moberley, *The Crisis in the University*, London: SCM Press, pp. 30–49	II	39
1949–50	Lord Lindsay of Birker	The commission on German universities	*Universities Quarterly* IV: 82–8	III	68
1949–50	Roy Pascal	The universities & social purpose	*Universities Quarterly* IV: 37–43	III	56
1950–1	S. R. Dongerkery	University education in free India	*Universities Quarterly* V: 72–9	I	22
1950–1	J. S. Fulton	General education	*Universities Quarterly* V: 41–8	IV	89

Year	Author	Title	Reference		
1952	R. W. Livingstone	The need for the study of philosophy	R. W. Livingstone, *Education and the Spirit of the Age*, Oxford: Clarendon Press, pp. 22–39	IV	76
1952–3	B. Simon	Higher education in Poland	*Universities Quarterly* VII: 176–83	I	16
1953–4	John Rex	Apartheid in the South African universities	*Universities Quarterly* VIII: 333–40	IV	73
1954–5	Ralph E. Lombardi	Universities in the U.S.A.: secondary school characteristics	*Universities Quarterly* IX: 66–72	I	10
1955–6	Cyril Bibby	T. H. Huxley's idea of a university	*Universities Quarterly* X: 377–90	II	34
1955–6	J. W. Blake	European rectors and vice-chancellors in conference	*Universities Quarterly* X: 15–18	I	17
1955–6	Alexander Kinghorn	The American State university today	*Universities Quarterly* X: 69–79	III	70
1958	Ministry of Education and Scottish Education Department	Excerpts from *Grants to Students*	Report of the Committee appointed by the Minister of Education and the Secretary for Scotland in June 1958, *Grants to Students*, London: HMSO, pp. 1–8 and 77–87	III	59
1959	Robert O. Berdahl	Conclusion [*British Universities and the State*]	R. O. Berdahl, *British Universities and the State*, Berkeley: University of California Press and London: Cambridge University Press, pp. 183–94	III	58
1960	Karl Jaspers	The cosmos of knowledge	K. Jaspers, *The Idea of the University*, London: Peter Owen, pp. 93–110	IV	77
1961	H. C. Dent	Excerpt from *The Universities in Transition*	H. C. Dent, *The Universities in Transition*, London: Cohen and West, pp. 15–28	II	40
1963	[Robbins Committee]	Excerpts from *Higher Education*	*Higher Education*, Report of the Robbins Committee, London: HMSO, pp. 4–10 and 365–7	III	60
1964	Mehdi Nakosteen	Excerpts from *History of Islamic Origins of Western Education, 800–1350*	M. Nakosteen, *History of Islamic Origins of Western Education, 800–1350*, Boulder: University of Colorado Press, pp. 1–4, 13–27, 50–6, 61–3	I	1

Chronological Table continued

Date	Author	Article/chapter	References	Vol.	Chap.
1966	Fahim I. Qubain	General features and problems of higher education	F. I. Qubain, *Education and Science in the Arab World*, Baltimore: Johns Hopkins University Press, pp. 48–60	I	23
1966	Lionel Robbins	The university in the modern world: an address delivered to the Conference of European Rectors and Vice-Chancellors at Göttingen on September 2nd, 1964	Lord Robbins, *The University in the Modern World*, London: Macmillan, pp. 1–16	II	43
1967	T. H. Huxley	Excerpt from *The Essence of T. H. Huxley*	Cyril Bibby (ed.) *The Essence of T. H. Huxley*, London: Macmillan and New York: St. Martin's Press, pp. 220–30	II	33
1968	E. E. Robinson	Higher education since the war: universities, CATS and technical colleges; Robbins and after	E. E. Robinson, *The New Polytechnics*, London: Cornmarket, pp. 13–33	IV	90
1968	Sheldon Rothblatt	Donnishness	S. Rothblatt, *The Revolution of the Dons: Cambridge and Society in Victorian England*, London: Faber and Faber, reprinted Cambridge: Cambridge University Press, 1981, pp. 181–208	V	113
1969	Asa Briggs	Development in higher education in the United Kingdom: nineteenth and twentieth centuries	W. R. Niblett (ed.) *Higher Education: Demand and Response*, London: Tavistock, pp. 95–116	I	14
1969	Sydney Caine	Reflections on policy	Sydney Caine, *British Universities: Purposes and Prospects*, London: Bodley Head, pp. 246–66	III	57
1969	V. H. H. Green	The origins of Oxford and Cambridge	V. H. H. Green, *The Universities*, Harmondsworth: Penguin, pp. 13–20	I	6
1969	Martin Trow	Elite and popular functions in American higher education	W. R. Niblett (ed.) *Higher Education: Demand and Response*, London: Tavistock, pp. 181–201	V	98

Year	Author	Title	Reference	Vol.	Page
1970	Eric Ashby	The student movement	E. Ashby, *Masters and Scholars*, London: Oxford University Press, pp. 25–49	V	110
1970	H. S. Ferns	*Towards an Independent University*	H. S. Ferns, *Towards an Independent University*, London: Institute of Economic Affairs, 27 pp.	III	64
1970	E. P. Thompson	The business university	E. P. Thompson, *Warwick University Ltd.*, Harmondsworth: Penguin, pp. 13–41	III	63
1971	A. H. Halsey and M. A. Trow	The changing functions of universities	A. H. Halsey and M. A. Trow, *The British Academics*, London: Faber and Faber, pp. 31–7	II	42
1971	A. H. Halsey and M. A. Trow	The evolution of the British universities	A. H. Halsey and M. Trow, *The British Academics*, London: Faber and Faber, pp. 38–64	V	101
1972	Michael Sanderson	Conclusion [*The Universities and British Industry, 1850–1970*]	M. Sanderson, *The Universities and British Industry, 1850–1970*, London: Routledge and Kegan Paul, pp. 389–97	III	53
1974	Eric Ashby	Idea of a university	E. Ashby, *Adapting Universities to a Technological Society*, San Francisco, Washington and London: Jossey-Bass, pp. 1–15	II	44
1974	Eric Ashby	Mass higher education	E. Ashby, *Adapting Universities to a Technological Society*, San Francisco, Washington and London: Jossey-Bass, pp. 134–44	II	45
1974	Arthur Engel	Emerging concepts of the academic profession at Oxford 1800–1854	L. Stone (ed.) *The University in Society*, Vol. I: *Oxford and Cambridge from the 14th to the Early 19th Century*, Princeton: Princeton University Press, pp. 305–51	V	115

Chronological Table continued

Date	Author	Article/chapter	References	Vol.	Chap.
1975	Robert L. Church	Economists as experts: the rise of an academic profession in the United States, 1870–1920	L. Stone (ed.) *The University in Society*, Vol. II: *Europe, Scotland and the United States from the Sixteenth to the Nineteenth Century*, Princeton: Princeton University Press and Oxford: Oxford University Press, pp. 571–609	V	112
1975	A. B. Cobban	Concept of a university	A. B. Cobban, *The Medieval Universities: Their Development and Organization*, London: Methuen, pp. 21–36	II	29
1975	A. B. Cobban	Late medieval universities	A. B. Cobban, *The Medieval Universities: Their Development and Organization*, London: Methuen, pp. 116–21	I	4
1975	Charles Webster	Excerpt from *The Great Instauration: Science, Medicine and Reform, 1626–1660*	C. Webster, *The Great Instauration: Science, Medicine and Reform, 1626–1660*, New York: Holmes and Meier, pp. 115–22	IV	82
1976	Walter Perry	The basic ideas	W. Perry, *Open University: A Personal Account by the First Vice-Chancellor*, Buckingham: Open University Press, pp. 1–9	IV	92
1976	Sheldon Rothblatt	The academic role	S. Rothblatt, *Tradition and Change in English Liberal Education*, London: Faber and Faber, pp. 174–94	V	114
1977	W. H. G. Armytage	Community service stations: the transformation of the civic universities, 1898–1930	W. H. G. Armytage, *Civic Universities*, New York: Arno Press, pp. 243–64	III	54
1977	Asavia Wandira	Excerpts from *The African University in Development*	A. Wandira, *The African University in Development*, Johannesburg, Ravan Press, pp. 8–36	I	21

1978	Peter Venables	From technical school to technological university	P. Venables, *Higher Education Developments: The Technological Universities*, London: Faber and Faber, pp. 1–34	IV	91
1979	Orlando Albornoz	Models of the Latin American university	Joseph Maier and Richard W. Weatherhead (eds) *The Latin American University*, Albuquerque: University of New Mexico Press, pp. 123–34	I	24
1981	John E. Fleming	Blacks in higher education to 1954: a historical overview	Gail E. Thomas (ed.), *Black Students in Higher Education: Conditions and Experiences in the 1970s*, Westport, Conn. and London: Greenwood Press, pp. 11–17	III	72
1981	John M. Fletcher	Change and resistance to change: a consideration of the development of English and German universities during the sixteenth century	*History of Universities* I: 1–36	IV	81
1981	Konrad H. Jarausch	Higher education and social change: some comparative perspectives	K. H. Jarausch (ed.) *The Transformation of Higher Learning, 1860–1930*, Stuttgart: Klett-Cotta, pp. 9–36	III	51
1981	Roy Lowe	The expansion of higher education in England	K. H. Jarausch, *The Transformation of Higher Learning, 1860–1930*, Stuttgart: Klett-Cotta, pp. 37–56	V	106
1981	Charles E. McClelland	Professionalization and higher education in Germany	K. H. Jarausch, *The Transformation of Higher Learning, 1860–1930*, Stuttgart: Klett-Cotta, pp. 306–20	III	66
1981	Harold Perkin	The pattern of social transformation in England	K. H. Jarausch, *The Transformation of Higher Learning, 1860–1930*, Stuttgart: Klett-Cotta, pp. 207–18	V	100
1981	Sheldon Rothblatt	The diversification of higher education in England	K. H. Jarausch, *The Transformation of Higher Learning, 1860–1930*, Stuttgart: Klett-Cotta, pp. 131–48	V	107

Chr□logical Table continued

Dat	Author	Article/chapter	References	Vol.	Chap.
198	Martin J. Wiener	Excerpt from *English Culture and the Decline of the Industrial Spirit, 1850–1980*	M. J. Wiener, *English Culture and the Decline of the Industrial Spirit, 1850–1980*, Harmondsworth: Penguin, pp. 16–24	V	101
198	John Twigg	The limits of 'reform': some aspects of the debate on university education during the English Revolution	*History of Universities* 4: 99–114	IV	83
198	John Carswell	Some conclusions [*Government and the Universities in Britain*]	J. Carswell, *Government and the Universities in Britain: Programme and Performance, 1960–1980*, Cambridge: Cambridge University Press, pp. 159–68	III	61
198	Stephen C. Ferruolo	The Paris statutes of 1215 reconsidered	*History of Universities* V: 1–14	IV	94
198	Roy Lowe	English elite education in the late nineteenth and early twentieth centuries	W. Conze and J. Kocka (eds) *Bildungsbürgertum im 19. Jahrhundert*, Teil I, Stuttgart: Klett-Cotta, pp. 147–62	V	105
198	Guy Neave	The university and the state in Western Europe	D. Jaques and J. T. E. Richardson (eds) *The Future for Higher Education*, Proceedings of the 19th Annual Conference of the Society for Research into Higher Education, 1983, Guildford: SRHE and NFER-Nelson, pp. 27–40	III	52
198	Fritz Ringer	Education and the middle classes in modern France	W. Conze and J. Kocka (eds) *Bildungsbürgertum im 19. Jahrhundert*, Teil I, Stuttgart: Klett-Cotta, pp. 109–46	V	108
198	Allan Bloom	The student and the university	A. Bloom, *The Closing of the American Mind: How Higher Education Has Failed Democracy and Impoverished the Souls of Today's Students*, New York: Simon and Schuster, pp. 336–82	V	99

Year	Author	Title	Source	Vol.	Page
1987	Roy Lowe	Structural change in English higher education, 1870–1920	Detlef K. Müller, Fritz Ringer and Brian Simon (eds) *The Rise of the Modern Educational System, 1870–1920*, Cambridge: Cambridge University Press, pp. 163–78	IV	87
1988	James T. Flynn	Excerpt from *The University Reform of Tsar Alexander I, 1802–1835*	J. T. Flynn, *The University Reform of Tsar Alexander I, 1802–1835*, Washington DC: Catholic University of America Press, pp. 1–25	III	69
1988	Jurgen Herbst	American higher education in the age of the college	*History of Universities* VII: 37–59	IV	95
1989	Philip G. Altbach	Higher education and scientific development: the promise of newly industrializing countries	P. G. Altbach et al. (eds) *Scientific Development and Higher Education: The Case of Newly Industrializing Nations*, New York and London: Praeger, pp. 3–29	I	28
1989	G. L'E. Turner	Experimental science in early nineteenth-century Oxford	*History of Universities* VIII: 117–35	IV	86
1990	Harold Silver	Pasts and futures	H. Silver, *A Higher Education: The Council for National Academic Awards and British Higher Education, 1964–89*, London: Falmer Press, pp. 260–72	III	62
1991	R. D. Anderson	Universities and elites in modern Britain	*History of Universities* X: 225–50	V	103
1991	Oliver Fulton	Modular systems in Britain	R. O. Berdahl, G. C. Moodie and I. J. Spitzberg (eds) *Quality and Access in Higher Education: Comparing Britain and the United States*, Buckingham: SRHE and Open University Press, pp. 142–51	IV	93
1991	Antonio García y García	The medieval students of the University of Salamanca	*History of Universities* X: 93–105	V	111

Chronological Table continued

Date	Author	Article/chapter	References	Vol.	Chap.
1991	Clark Kerr	Functions – the pluralistic university in the pluralistic society	C. Kerr, *The Great Transformation in Higher Education, 1960–1980*, Albany: State University of New York Press, pp. 47–67	II	47
1991	Sheldon Rothblatt	The American modular system	R. O. Berdahl, G. C. Moodie and I. J. Spitzberg (eds) *Quality and Access in Higher Education: Comparing Britain and the United States*, Buckingham: SRHE and Open University Press, pp. 129–41	IV	97
1992	R. D. Anderson	The growth of a system	R. D. Anderson, *Universities and Elites in Britain since 1800*, London: Macmillan for the Economic History Society, pp. 12–28	I	13
1992	John M. Fletcher	The college-university: its development in Aberdeen and beyond	J. J. Carter and D. J. Withrington (eds) *Scottish Universities: Distinctiveness and Diversity*, Edinburgh: John Donald, pp. 16–25	IV	80
1992	W. Bruce Leslie	Four colleges and their communities	W. B. Leslie, *Gentlemen and Scholars: College and Community in the "Age of the University", 1865–1917*, University Park: Pennsylvania State University Press, pp. 11–28	I	9
1992	Elizabeth J. Morse	English civic universities and the myth of decline	*History of Universities* XI: 177–204	V	104
1992	Sheldon Rothblatt	Federal universities and multi-campus systems: Britain and the United States since the nineteenth century	J. J. Carter and D. J. Withrington (eds) *Scottish Universities: Distinctiveness and Diversity*, Edinburgh: John Donald, pp. 164–87	II	46

1994	John D. Hargreaves	Excerpts from *Academe and Empire: Some Overseas Connections of Aberdeen University, 1860–1970*	J. D. Hargreaves, *Academe and Empire: Some Overseas Connections of Aberdeen University, 1860–1970*, Quincentennial Studies in the History of the University of Aberdeen, Aberdeen: Aberdeen University Press, pp. 5–32 and 114–17	I	12
1994	Andrew Lockhart Walker	The Scottish university tradition	A. L. Walker, *The Revival of the Democratic Intellect: Scotland's University Traditions and the Crisis in Modern Thought*, Edinburgh: Polygon Press, pp. 22–37	I	11
1995	Carol Dyhouse	Patterns of provision: access and accommodation	C. Dyhouse, *No Distinction of Sex? Women in British Universities, 1870–1939*, London: University College Press, pp. 11–55	V	117
1995	A. H. Halsey	Ideas of the university	A. H. Halsey, *Decline of Donnish Dominion: The British Academic Profession in the Twentieth Century*, Oxford: Clarendon Press, pp. 23–57	II	49
1995	A. H. Halsey	Women and men	A. H. Halsey, *Decline of Donnish Dominion: The British Academic Professions in the Twentieth Century*, Oxford: Clarendon Press, pp. 216–34	V	116
1995	Clark Kerr	The idea of a multiversity	C. Kerr, *The Uses of the University*, Cambridge, Mass.: Harvard University Press, pp. 1–34	II	48
1996	J. F. Ade Ajayi, Lameck K. H. Goma and G. Ampah Johnson	Antecedents (before 1900)	J. F. Ade Ajayi, Lameck K. H. Goma and G. Ampah Johnson, *The African Experience with Higher Education*, Accra: Association of African Universities, in association with James Curry, London and Ohio University Press, Athens, Ohio, pp. 1–27	I	2

Chronological Table continued

Date	Author	Article/chapter	References	Vol.	Chap.
1996	Gary B. Cohen	The expansion of higher education	G. B. Cohen, *Education and Middle-Class Society in Imperial Austria, 1848–1918*, West Lafayette, Ind.: Purdue University Press, pp. 75–94	I	15
1997	Linda Eisenmann	Reconsidering a classic: assessing the history of women's higher education a dozen years after Barbara Solomon	*Harvard Educational Review* 67(4): 689–717	V	118
1997	Sheldon Rothblatt	The idea of the idea of a university and its antithesis	S. Rothblatt, *The Modern University and its Discontents*, Cambridge: Cambridge University Press, pp. 1–49	II	41
1998	Donald Fisher and Kjell Rubenson	The changing political economy: the private and public lives of Canadian universities	Jan Currie and Janice Newton (eds) *Universities and Globalisation: Critical Perspectives*, Thousand Oaks, Calif. and London: Sage, pp. 77–98	I	19
2000	Christopher Stray	Curriculum and style in the collegiate university: Classics in nineteenth-century Oxbridge	*History of Universities* XVI(2): 183–218	IV	85
2002	Paul F. Grendler	Excerpt from *The Universities of the Italian Renaissance*	P. F. Grendler, *The Universities of the Italian Renaissance*, Baltimore: Johns Hopkins University Press, pp. 3–21	I	5
2002	Harold Silver	Pressures and silences	H. Silver, *Higher Education and Opinion Making in Twentieth Century England*, London: Woburn Press, pp. 252–65	II	50
2003	Notker Hammerstein	National Socialism and the German universities	*History of Universities* XVIII(I): 170–88	III	67
2004	Philip G. Altbach	The past and future of Asian universities: twenty-first century challenges	P. G. Altbach and Toru Umakoshi (eds) *Asian Universities: Historical Perspectives and Contemporary Challenges*, Baltimore: Johns Hopkins University Press, pp. 13–32	I	25

2004	Motohisa Kaneko	Japanese higher education: contemporary reform and the influence of tradition	P. G. Altbach and Toru Umakoshi (eds) *Asian Universities: Historical Perspectives and Contemporary Challenges*, Baltimore: Johns Hopkins University Press, pp. 115–43	I	27
2004	Weifang Min	Chinese higher education: the legacy of the past and the context of the future	P. G. Altbach and Toru Umakoshi (eds) *Asian Universities: Historical Perspectives and Contemporary Challenges*, Baltimore: Johns Hopkins University Press, pp. 53–83	I	26
2004	Jennings L. Wagoner, Jr.	Jefferson's educational legacy	J. L. Wagoner, Jr., *Jefferson and Education*, Monticello Monograph Series, Monticello, Va.: Thomas Jefferson Foundation, pp. 127–46	I	8
2005	Christopher Stray	From oral to written examinations: Cambridge, Oxford and Dublin 1700–1914	*History of Universities* XX(2): 76–130	IV	84
2006	Vincent Carpentier	Funding in higher education and economic growth in France and the United Kingdom, 1921–2003	*Higher Education Management and Policy* 18(3): 1–22	III	65
2006	Sheldon Rothblatt	Loss and gain: John Henry Newman in 2005	Ann Lavan (ed.) *The University and Society: From Newman to the Market*, Conference Proceedings, UCD College of Human Sciences, University College Dublin, pp. 15–29	II	32
2007	Sheldon Rothblatt	Affirmative action	S. Rothblatt, *Education's Abiding Moral Dilemma: Merit and Worth in the Cross-Atlantic Democracies, 1800–2006*, Oxford Studies in Comparative Education, Oxford: Symposium Books, pp. 277–300	III	71

GENERAL INTRODUCTION

The rationale of the collection

These five volumes are an attempt to bring together and to summarise that vast field of scholarship which has devoted itself to the development and changing social functions of higher education. Higher education in general, and the universities in particular, have played a vital role in shaping the contemporary world. The writings I have chosen in this selection are, therefore, intended to illustrate some of the main themes of study, and at the same time to showcase work which is, in my view, particularly significant or worthy of putting before a wider audience.

The identification of these themes is, of itself, far from straightforward, and necessarily arbitrary. I have identified five and these are addressed separately in each of the five volumes of this collection. First, I have focused on work which shows the ways in which concepts of higher education have spread around the globe, so that there is today no part of the inhabited planet in which the population does not at least aspire to higher education and to some degree make it available to its citizens. There are important questions about how this dissemination of an ideal took place and about how common, how truly shared, are the concepts of what does and should go on in institutions of higher education and universities as well as the practices followed. Thus, an important criterion in compiling this first volume was that of geographical range. This collection is intended to show how widespread is the phenomenon of higher education and, more particularly, how it has evolved on a world scale.

This volume begins with the suggestion that it may be necessary to look back beyond the European university foundations of the early-modern period to prototypes in the Muslim world and in Africa to identify the origins of the university, and suggests, at least, linkages which go as far back as the Academy at Athens which was closed down in 529AD. It illustrates too the ways in which this ideal of higher education has been transmuted as it spread around the globe, ending with some very recent examples of university development in the so-called 'tiger economies' of South-East Asia.

Volume II brings together some of the best-known pronouncements on the nature of the university, illustrating the ways in which the call for specialisation, the need for a research base and the necessity to link with economic and social changes have been articulated at different times. The medieval and the nineteenth-century view of what constituted a university provides a context for recent and contemporary accounts of the universities at the start of the twenty-first century, focused on such phenomena as federalism and the rise of the multiversity, or as Clark Kerr identifies it, 'the pluralistic university'.

The third theme of the collection is the interplay between universities and the state. A cluster of questions underlie Volume III. To what extent should the universities in particular, and institutions of higher education in general, be answerable to political forces and in what ways? Is one of the central functions of the universities essentially political? In which ways, if any, should university curricula link to economic and political developments? Who should fund the universities and to what extent should they be autonomous institutions? What role should they play in shaping society and in determining entry to political, to economic and to social elites? Whilst there is no suggestion that the essays brought together here provide a comprehensive answer to these complex questions, each relates closely, in one way or another, to these issues.

Volume IV focuses on the curriculum. What should be taught? How should it be taught? What is the role of specialist subjects? How have modular systems emerged during the twentieth century? How broad should the education of young adults be within the universities? How best to examine students in the higher education sector? Should all students, to some extent at least, follow a common curriculum, or is out and out specialism the best route to a full education? These are questions which have confronted those running the universities throughout time and they remain as significant today as when they were first addressed. The essays assembled here attempt to show some of the answers offered to these problems and to illustrate how these answers have been modified over time.

The final volume deals with issues that are closely interrelated: the role of higher education in elite formation, the slow evolution of 'systems' of higher education and the issues around the selection of students and of staff. Not least, some of the essays in this volume focus on the role of the universities in gendering society. Essentially, what distinguishes the essays in this volume are the ways in which they throw light on the social functions of higher education from within, by focusing on staff, on students and on the experience of a university education. Thus, Volume V offers a slightly different perspective (but a vital one) on questions that have been raised elsewhere in the collection, or which are implicit in some of the earlier essays.

As is always the case when one is assembling a collection such as this, these issues are not discrete. Most of the writings selected for inclusion would sit comfortably in more than one of the volumes; some might have appeared in two or three. But the broad typology I have outlined here is intended to make possible a collection of readings which makes sense. My hope is that, by drawing from particular parts of this collection at different times, it will be possible for the reader to gain a much fuller grasp of these questions which are central to any understanding of what higher education in general, and the universities in particular, are for, and how they link with the changing needs and demands of wider society. Further, it is my intention that these essays might help towards an understanding of how these issues have developed over time, so that the reader may gain a historical perspective on what is going on in contemporary higher education and, through that, deeper insights into the role of higher education today within a global economy. If this collection comes close to fulfilling these interlinked aims, it will have succeeded.

INTRODUCTION

The essays in this volume have been selected to show the development of universities, both over time and around the world. They are intended to offer insights into some of the significant moments and periods which have shaped higher education and to illustrate the ways in which what has happened in one part of the world, or at a particular time, is necessarily linked to developments in other places and at other periods.

The antecedents of the medieval universities of Europe, which are widely considered to have been the first true universities in the sense that we understand the term, were explored in a significant but not widely known work by Mehdi Nakosteen, published in 1964. He argued that the true origins of the university ideal were to be found in the Muslim world and before that in the Persian Empire. It was at Jundi-Shapur, at Baghdad and in cities such as Fez and Cairo that the learning of the ancient world was preserved, translated, taught and passed on to later generations, Nakosteen argues, emphasising that the institutions established there should be considered universities because of both the scale of their operations and the range of their curriculum. The extract reprinted here as Chapter 1 summarises the key elements in his argument. Alongside this, there have been one or two public statements which suggest that it is to Africa that we must turn for important antecedents, most notably to Alexandria and Timbuctou. Chapter 2, by Ajayi, Goma and Johnson, provides a neat summary of this argument and should be read alongside the first chapter. It also contains a useful bibliography of important work that is not widely known.

Five extracts follow which deal with the origins and early development of universities in Europe. The first overview of the coming of universities in late-medieval Europe (Chapter 3) was written by Gabriel Campayre in the late nineteenth century, and the extract chosen illustrates the breadth and range of his scholarship and shows how quickly the idea of a university spread throughout Europe at this period. A. B. Cobban remains one of the best-known British historians of the medieval universities, and Chapter 4, an extract from his seminal book, focuses on the tensions between clerical and secular control during a formative period. By contrast, Paul Grendler's work on Bologna (Chapter 5), as a prototypical example of an early Italian university, focuses on the recruitment of faculty staff and on student numbers to illustrate how this pioneering institution became a template for many later colleges, fixing the university as a secular institution, with law and medicine at the heart of its curriculum. In contrast again, V. H. H. Green's account of the origins of Oxford and Cambridge universities (Chapter 6) portrays them as having far more random origins, as 'haphazard growths rather than planned foundations'. He paints a picture of institutions which, although essentially ecclesiastical in character, were responsive to the major changes taking place in secular society and were ready to play a key part in advancing some of the reforms that marked the English reformation. Another view of the origins of European universities was posited by Abraham Flexner in his enormously influential work on American, English and German universities, published in 1930 (Chapter 7). Flexner, writing about universities in Germany, argues that, although the German universities originated in the Middle Ages, 'for our purposes they began with the nineteenth century'. He then goes on, in the extract chosen here, to identify the particular characteristics of the nineteenth-century German university, involving both research and teaching, but with research pre-eminent. For Flexner, a degree of independence from secular or any external influence, the autonomy of the university teacher, a freedom to teach what he thought appropriate, and a tradition of itinerant staff and students were all key marks of the German universities at this time.

No account of the dissemination of the university ideal would be complete without some coverage of developments in North America, and Jennings Wagoner Jr.'s account of the origins of Jefferson's University of Virginia (Chapter 8) features a historian who is one of the most significant commentators on the early American colleges, writing about the early years of the college which was, arguably, to have the greatest impact on later developments in the United States. If this extract stresses the dependence of the American university on local funding from the outset, then W. Bruce Leslie's account of the foundation of four colleges, in Chapter 9, highlights the extent to which they struggled to break away from teaching at secondary level and were creatures of, and remained answerable to their local communities even though the stresses of the mid-nineteenth century were leading towards a major redefinition of their roles. The distinctiveness of the American university is underlined by Ralph Lombardi's essay (Chapter 10), reprinted from the *Universities Quarterly* 1954–5, and therefore written with an English readership in mind. This essay focuses on the extent to which and the ways in which American universities struggled to break from the traditions and mores of the secondary school, even into the period following the Second World War.

Two contributions on higher education in Scotland deal with significant characteristics of an emergent system of higher education which has been ferociously debated and whose nature remains contested to this day. On the one hand are those who claim Scotland to have been the home of the 'lad o' pairts', where even the poorest could aspire to some kind of higher education, and on the other are those who see higher education in Scotland as mirroring in many ways the development of elite institutions in other parts of Europe. Two authors have been selected to illustrate aspects of these debates. In Chapter 11 Andrew Lockhart Walker argues that the modernisation of Scotland's universities is directly attributable to the reforms associated with John Knox and the Scottish reformation. In Chapter 12 the work of John D. Hargreaves is deployed to show how pervasive was the Scottish influence on a world scale, and particularly within the nineteenth-century British Empire. This is an important reminder of the extent to which it was the travel patterns of the university graduates themselves that did much to plant the ideal of a university, and in many cases a sense of Britishness to go with it, in far flung corners of the globe.

Two contributions highlight key features of the development of universities in England during the late nineteenth century and the early twentieth-first century. In Chapter 13 R. D. Anderson illustrates the distinctiveness of British developments, stressing the importance of elite institutions whose styles and curricula were widely imitated by the newer universities and colleges. Asa Briggs, in Chapter 14, underlines the extent to which this may be seen as the birth of a system of higher education, offering a typically lucid and succinct account of developments at this time.

Two essays have been chosen to illustrate developments in other parts of Europe. Gary B. Cohen's work on Imperial Austria (Chapter 15) shows how the final years of the Austro-Hungarian Empire generated a university system which was markedly different from that of newly unified neighbouring countries. Here the continuing growth of the system eroded the ability of a weakening central government to control developments. In contrast, the final contribution on higher education in Europe is a brief article by Brian Simon, another major commentator on educational and social change. In Chapter 16, published in the *Universities Quarterly* 1952–3, Simon's determination to describe educational advance within a Communist framework is apparent, as is his determination to eulogise developments in Eastern Europe at the height of the Cold War. This piece serves as a reminder of the extent to which all writing in this field is, to some extent at least, informed by political persuasion. It brings into focus too the postwar emphasis on reconstruction, which was a shared characteristic of countries in both East and West Europe.

John Blake, during his brief tenure of the principalship at the newly founded University College of North Staffordshire, was in attendance in July 1955 at a meeting which was to prove portentous. Rectors, vice-chancellors and principals from different European countries met at Cambridge to discuss collaboration. This was to prove the starting point for the Conference des Recteurs Europeens, which in a relatively short time became one of the engines of European collaboration, anticipating schemes for students to move between universities in different countries and interlinking with the more general political movement towards European collaboration. Blake's essay (Chapter 17) describes that first gathering.

It would be a mistake, in any collection focused on the spread of the university ideal around the world, to overlook the role of the British Empire, latterly the Commonwealth of Nations, as an agency for the dissemination of a particular Anglo-centred view of the nature and purposes of the university. Walter Adams' article on higher education in the British colonies (Chapter 18), published immediately after the Second World War, is a glimpse into the late-Imperial psyche. His patrician account of the ways in which the universities of the British Empire were to be shepherded towards independence blends right-mindedness and patriarchy in a way that perhaps only members of the British ruling elite could do at that time.

The following six contributions have been chosen to illustrate the extent to which the growth of universities is a shared phenomenon around the world. In Chapter 19 Donald Fisher and Kjell Rubenson highlight the recent drift of Canadian universities towards privatisation. J. D. G. Medley's Chapter 20 is a reminder both of the fact that there was a system of higher education in Australia immediately after the Second World War but also of the difficulties it faced during the years of postwar austerity. Asavia Wandira picks out some of the characteristics of more recent developments in higher education in Africa in Chapter 21. S. R. Dongerkery's précis of the main points in the 1949 Commission on Indian University Education (Chapter 22) reminds us of the challenges faced by a newly created nation immediately after Partition, whilst, in a wide-ranging extract, Fahim I. Qubain identifies some of the enduring characteristics of universities in the Arab world (Chapter 23). A similar overview of the origins and growth of universities in Latin America is offered by Orlando Albornoz in Chapter 24.

Finally, four extracts identify some of the key characteristics of emergent university systems in different countries in Asia. In Chapter 25 Philip G. Altbach gives his overview of the challenges facing Asian universities at the start of the twenty-first century. Weifang Min gives an account of recent and contemporary issues confronting universities in China in Chapter 26. Motohisa Kaneko illustrates the tensions between reform and tradition in modern Japan (Chapter 27), and, finally, in Chapter 28 Philip G. Altbach shows the intimate linkages between scientific and technical development and university reform in the tiger economies of South-East Asia.

1

Excerpts from
HISTORY OF ISLAMIC
ORIGINS OF WESTERN
EDUCATION, 800–1350

Mehdi Nakosteen

Source: M. Nakosteen, *History of Islamic Origins of Western Education, 800–1350*, Boulder: University of Colorado Press, 1964, pp. 1–4, 13–27, 50–6, 61–3.

THE CULTURAL, POLITICAL, AND RELIGIOUS SETTING[1]

The intellectual life of the medieval period, particularly from the ninth century through the thirteenth, is marked by developments which took place in five recognizable geographic areas—the Sino-Japanese world (or should we say Chinese and Japanese worlds?), India, Greek Christendom, Latin Christendom, and Eastern and Western Islam. The Hebrew culture, though it maintained its identity throughout this period, had been incorporated politically within the Christian and Muslim domains. By adhering to its own faith and yet adapting itself politically, linguistically, and culturally to both societies, Hebrew scholarship proved itself an invaluable instrument of cultural exchange in both Muslim and Christian intellectual circles. We shall note later how much Latin schoolmen owed the Hebrews in transmitting the substance of the Greco-Muslim learning to the West by translations from Arabic into Latin and Hebrew, or into Latin from Hebrew translations of Arabic works.

The five areas may be looked upon geographically as two grand cultural worlds—India, China, and Japan in the East, and the Christian and Muslim worlds in the West. The two worlds—East and West—were separated by distance as much as by ideals, and any intellectual association between them was too small during the medieval period to bridge the wide gap which geography had imposed upon them. It is true that the art of manufacturing paper and the use of gunpowder and the compass may have reached Europe from China through the Muslims; and the Persians, Syrians, and Arabs transmitted Hindu medical, mathematical, and astronomical knowledge) It is true also that certain elements of Greek science reached India during the Alexandrian period, as they may also have reached China through Khiva. But such contacts between East and West were too infrequent and their influence too sparse to constitute any penetrating East-West cultural intercourse. Islam, as we shall see later, constituted nonetheless the bridge, however narrow, over which cultural traffic and exchange between East and West were maintained.

The Muslim and Christian worlds on the other hand, though each defined and maintained its own identity on religious and political grounds, shared in various degrees and for different purposes some common cultural elements. They were both sustained at different times and through different channels by the intellectual life of the Greco-Hellenistic world, and they claimed a common religious heritage from Judaism. They shared a religious basis for life and society. Also, in relations between religious and temporal powers certain similarities existed between the two cultures. In the Christian world two opposing trends developed: In Eastern, or Greek, Christianity the emperor appointed the patriarch of Constantinople and had the power to reduce or remove his jurisdiction. In Western, or Latin, Christianity the two centers of power, the pope and the emperor, competed for supremacy, the pope maintaining the upper hand throughout the Middle Ages. In Islam, too, the caliphs, and later the sultans, played the role of defenders of the faith, allowing the religious leaders a degree of autonomy in civic and religious matters but reducing their powers when they exceeded predetermined limits. But spiritual leadership in Islam was never centralized as in the Roman papacy, nor was it brought under political jurisdiction as in the Byzantine world. That is perhaps why religious stability was of such short duration in Islam, and gave way to politico-religious nationalistic identifications, such as Persian-Islam, Egyptian-Islam, and Hispano-Islam, while it remained of long duration in the Christian world, particularly in the Latin West.

The factors which kept Islam and Christianity apart and mutually ignorant of each other were far stronger than common elements which may have brought them together. The barriers of language, political rivalries and conquests, and of religious conflicts were formidable and moved each faith to use its intellectual facilities to destroy or misrepresent the other. The crusades were politically wasteful for both Islam and Christianity and bred the inevitable obstacles of ignorance, suspicion, fear, force, and bloodshed. For centuries the Muslims resisted the political power of the West in Italy, Sicily, Spain, and North Africa, and for the same number of centuries the Byzantines resisted the power of the Muslims in the East. As the crusades exhausted both the Muslims and the Christians, the Latin West expanded deep into Europe, the Greek East into southern and eastern Slavic areas, the Nestorian and Monophysite religious factions eastward into Arabia, Persia, and some of the fringes and centers of Asia. During this period the Muslims moved deep into Afro-Asia while remaining loosely on the edges of the three continents of Europe, Asia, and Africa.

On the intellectual plane the three powers and cultures—Latin, Greek, and Muslim—remained perpetually suspicious of each other, and suspiciousness led to mutual indifference and ignorance. Greek Christianity broke away from the Roman and was in turn divided into antagonistic religious sects of which Nestorianism proved the most formidable. Latin Christianity also isolated itself gradually but decisively from Greek orthodoxy, from Islam, and from the Hellenistic heritage which Eastern Christianity kept alive, mainly through Nestorian and Monophysite scholarship. Both Eastern and Western Islamic cultures, though founded upon Greco-Hellenistic, Persian, and Indian knowledges and skills, remained out of touch with the Latin Christian world for several centuries, save for contacts with Syriac Christianity in Eastern Islam and with certain elements of Christianity in Western Islam, mainly in Sicily and Spain.

Both Latin and Greek Christianity looked upon Muslims as infidels and upon Islam as a pagan faith. It took Western Europe until the twelfth century, or five hundred years after the birth of Islam, to develop respect for Muslim scholarship, and it took an additional five hundred years for the Muslim world to begin to examine the intellectual consequences of the European Renaissance, which their own intellectual contributions had largely initiated. The factors which kept Muslim and Christian cultures apart are evidenced in some of the views of Greek and Latin Christian writers of Islam and its prophet Muhammad.[2] John of Damascus calls Muhammad, to whom he refers as Mamed, a false prophet.[3] Theophanes Confessor, the Byzantine historian, refers to him as the prophet Mouamed, a poor epileptic, who indoctrinated the Arabs in immoral and foolish fables about man and the hereafter.[4] As late as the thirteenth century Bartholomew of Edessa writes about Mouchamet, (as Bartholomew called him), "a voluptuary, defiled to the very core, a brigand, a profligate, a murderer and a robber."[5]

The Latin world, which read its first text of the *Qur'an* (*Koran*) in the translation by Peter of Cluny in 1141, was hardly more charitable toward Islam than were the Byzantine writers. Eulogius of Cordova, martyred in 859, relates that Muhammad's corpse was devoured by dogs after his death, and that his soul "descended to hell," after the angels abandoned him.[6] Ginbert of Nogent (died 1124) tells us that Muhammad's body was devoured by pigs while he was in one of his epileptic fits. In *Chanson de Roland* Muhammad is confused with Allah, suggesting that the Muslims were the heathens who prayed to many gods, mainly to their God Muhammad.[7] With this error, Latin ignorance of Islam reached its lowest low! Even while the bulk of Muslim writings were reaching the schoolmen of Latin Europe, William of Tripoli could write a work on Islam in 1273 entitled *Tractate on the State of the Saracens, Muhammad The False Prophet, Their Law and Their Faith!*

The Muslims, on the other hand, were more charitable toward the Christians. For one thing, they had derived the substance of their own faith largely from Judaism and Christianity. Both Christians and Jews were accepted as *Ahl al-Kitab*, or the People of the Book, meaning the Old and New Testament. They accepted all the Judaeo-Christian prophets from Adam to Jesus, though they rejected the doctrine of Christ's divinity, as they also renounced the concept of the Trinity as polytheistic and therefore contrary to the belief in the absolute oneness of God.

Educated Muslims respected Jewish and Christian scholars during the formative and maturing centuries of their cultural development. Nestorian scholars, including medical theorists and practitioners, held positions of respect at the courts of the Muslim caliphs. From them the caliphs and their subjects received, in part, their first knowledge of Greek learning. To Nestorians they delegated the extensive task of translating classical works into Arabic, and remunerated them handsomely for the service. They accepted Nestorian leaders as teachers, heads of hospitals and medical academies, interpreters, and creative writers. They gave them freedom of faith and, with understandable limitations, freedom of action.

It was this Muslim attitude of limited charity which in the end well repaid both Muslim and Christian cultures. It opened the treasures of classical knowledge to creative minds within the culturally heterogeneous Muslim world. When the forces of hatred, isolation, and ignorance gradually gave way in the Latin West to an era of understanding, the substance of this classical learning, preserved and advanced by the Muslims, reached Latin Europe to pave the way for the Renaissance of the fifteenth and sixteenth centuries.

[. . .]

CLASSICAL FOUNDATIONS OF MUSLIM EDUCATION

The conquests of the Arabs during the earlier centuries of Islam (Umayyad and Abbasside) brought them into close contact with some of the great civilizations of the world. The old theory that the early Muslims were enemies of learning and science and that except in their own *Qur'an* and tradition they showed no tolerance of the beliefs and intellectual treasures of other nations is without historical basis. It is true that one could point out a particular person or age and charge him or it with intolerance, as happened with the burning of libraries by the early Muslim conquerors in Egypt and in Iran. But such exceptions or early short-sightedness should not conceal the spirit of inquiry and creativity which characterized the early centuries of Islam, particularly under the Abbassides. The Muslims of the Arab world, as well as those of Persia, Spain, Egypt, India, Afghanistan, Transoxiana, and so forth, produced great scholars who were not blind to the wealth of science and literature of each other and of the Hellenistic and Christian worlds. The famous al-Jahiz (869), speaking of the nature of these influences, especially Grecian, writes in the following manner:

> Did we not possess the books of the Ancients in which their wonderful wisdom is immortalized and in which the manifold lessons of history are so dealt with that the past lives before our eyes, did we not have access to the riches of their experience which would otherwise have been barred to us, our share in wisdom would be immeasurably smaller, and our means of attaining a true perspective most meager.[8]

Factors in transmission of classical culture

The transmission of Greek learning, Hellenic and Hellenistic, to the Muslim world was brought about by unusual historic factors. Among them, the following are of importance:

1. One important factor lies within Christian orthodoxy, which persecuted and excommunicated schismatic bodies separated from the mother church for reasons of doctrinal differences. Among such schisms in the Eastern church, the Nestorian and Monophysite dissenting sects should receive special attention. As these sects were persecuted, they were forced to migrate to more friendly cultures where they received protection and opportunities for self-perpetuation. Upon moving from centers of Nicene orthodoxy—Nestorians to the Persian empire, Monophysites to Persia and the Arab world—these hostile sects carried with them the Greco-Hellenistic heritage of learning, particularly in medicine, mathematics, astronomy, technology, and philosophy, and helped preserve them in foreign hands. This heritage was later returned to European schoolmen through Muslim channels.

When Muslim Arabs invaded the Roman and Persian empires, these minority sects welcomed the conquering Arabs as liberators and established friendly contacts with them from the very beginning. Unlike the Mongolian hordes of the thirteenth century, the Muslim invaders were tolerant of regional customs, religions, and cultures of the peoples they subdued; they left the traditions of learning undisturbed and protected them against internal persecution. Thus it seems obvious that orthodox persecutions within the Byzantine world led to the preservation and eventual transfer of the Greco-Hellenistic learning to the West in two ways: (a) By continuing this tradition in non-Christian cultures, particularly in the Zoroastrian-Sassanian cultures of Persia; and (b) by furthering it within the Byzantine and Persian world under Muslim protection and patronage during the early Muslim centuries.

Interest in neo-Platonism and Aristotelianism, though interpreted in Christian terms and adapted to Christian doctrines, nonetheless kept the Nestorians and Jacobites on a higher level of general education than the "Latin-speaking Christians of the West." With the Nestorians in particular, this Hellenistic interest was sustained for centuries, thanks to the protection given it first by the Sassanian Persians and later by Islam until the eleventh century and the ascendancy of the Turks. Indeed it was through the Nestorians that important elements of Greek thought, namely Aristotelian, were preserved in Greek and Syrian translations to become the backbone of Persian and Islamic intellectual life.[9]

Transmissions from classical cultures to the Muslims through these channels were largely of the following seven basic types: (a) Materials directly translated from Greek into Arabic; (b) materials translated into Pahlavi, amalgamated with Zoroastrian-Hindu (Buddhist) thought, and then transmitted through translation into Arabic; (c) materials translated from Hindu to Pahlavi, then into Syriac, Hebrew, and Arabic; (d) materials written within the Islamic period by Muslims but in effect borrowed from non-Muslim sources, with the line of transmission obscure; (e) materials which were mere commentaries or summaries of Greco-Persian works; (f) materials which were advances over pre-Islamic learning, but which would not have been developed in Islam except for the pre-Islamic foundations in Hellenistic, Syrian, Zoroastrian, and Hindu learning; and (g) materials which appear to arise purely from individual genius and national or regional stimulation, which would have developed regardless of pre-Islamic learning, although the form these original creations took might have been different if they had developed in a non-Islamic context or frame of reference.

2.   Another important factor lies within the conquests of Alexander the Great and his successors, who spread Greek learning into Persia and India, where Greek science and philosophy were enriched with native ideas.

3.   The third important factor, and the most significant, was the Persian empire's Academy of Jundi-Shapur, which developed a curriculum of studies patterned after the University of Alexandria and during the sixth century synchronized Indian, Grecian, Syriac, Hellenistic, Hebrew, and Zoroastrian learning. Jundi-Shapur encouraged translations of significant Greek classics in science and philosophy into Pahlavi and Syriac and became, in the early centuries of Islam, the central clearing house of ancient learning, transferring it to the Muslim world and the West, until this task was taken over by Baghdad in Eastern Islam and Sicily and Cordova in Western Islam.

4.   The scholarly work of the Jews was another important factor. Hebrew translators were powerful instruments of this transfer because of their skill in languages, both in early Islam, when they translated Greek works into Hebrew and Arabic, and in the thirteenth century, when they translated these and other works from Arabic into Hebrew and Latin, or into Hebrew and from Hebrew to Latin.

The Syrian-Nestorian background

The classical writings and teachings of Greek philosophers such as Aristotle and Greek scientists such as Galen and the whole complex of neo-Platonic learning and mysticism reached the Muslims largely by way of Nestorian and Jacobite teachers, Zoroastrian scholars of the Academy of Jundi-Shapur in Khuzistan, and the pagan teachers of Harran, whose beginnings and identity remain somewhat obscure. Nestorian and Jacobite interests in Hellenistic-neo-Platonic science and philosophy were sustained more by the support that Aristotelian logic gave to the theological doctrines of these two eccentric Christian groups than by an objective and detached interest in science and philosophy as such. Says H. G. Wells:

> The Nestorian Christians . . . seem to have been much more intelli-
> gent and active-minded than the court theologians of Byzantium, and
> at a much higher level of general education than the Latin-speaking
> Christians of the West. They had been tolerated during the latter
> days of the Sassanids [Persians], and they were tolerated by Islam
> until the ascendancy of the Turks in the eleventh century. They
> were the intellectual backbone of the Persian world. They had
> preserved much of Aristotle both in Greek and in the Syrian trans-
> lations. They had a considerable mathematical literature. . . .[10]

In the year 363, which ended a long and relatively useless, indecisive war between the Persian and Byzantine empires, the city of Nisibis was handed over to the Persians as one of the conditions of peace. The School of Nisibis, the intellectual pride of that city, was as a result of this political transfer moved to Edessa within the Byzantine empire soon to become the rallying place for the Nestorian schism against the doctrinal decisions of Ephesus. But Emperor Zeno in 439 closed the School of Edessa because of its Nestorian support and forced its members, led by Barsuma, to migrate to Persia, where the Persian monarch, Piruz, guaranteed them religious and intellectual freedom and protection.[11]

The School of Nisibis was re-opened under Nestorian control, and from there a Nestorian version of Christianity spread into the Middle East. There also the Nestorians developed a unique Christian theology, emphasizing the humanity of Jesus. Translations of Greek authorities were made into

Syriac to sustain Nestorian versions of Christian theology and philosophy. In this manner the works of Aristotle and the neo-Platonists were translated into Syriac, and later through Nestorian translators into Arabic to become a part of the heritage of the Muslim world. But Hellenism remained more provincial than creative in Nestorian hands, producing an extensive educational system but showing no appreciable creative development.[12] D. L. O'Leary says:

> If we regard the main test of educational efficiency as being in its research product and not simply the promulgation of material already attained, then Nestorianism was not an educational success; and it seems that this should be the supreme test, for knowledge is progressive, and so the smallest contribution toward further progress must be of more real value than the most efficient teaching of results already achieved.[13]

Whether or not we are willing to agree completely with this statement, the fact is that Nestorians as translators and transmitters became, through the Syriac versions, an important medium through which Hellenistic learning was modified and channeled to the Muslim world.

The Alexandrian background

During the Christian centuries, before the invasion of the Persian and Byzantine world by the Muslims, Alexandria had developed into a Christianized center of Greek learning. Schoolmen, such as Paul of Aegina (flourished in 625), Alexander of Tralles (525–602), Aetios of Arnida (flourished in 550), and Theophilos Protos-Patharios, had been expositors of Greek philosophy and science, particularly mathematics and medicine. They had written commentaries on the works of Aristotle, Ptolemy, Galen, Hippocrates, Archimedes, and others. But Alexandria abounded in occultism and mysticism, lacking scientific creativity and independent philosophic inquiry. The Greek tradition of dispassionate exploration and unhampered investigation was no longer an intellectual force. This task was assumed, as already noted, by Syrian scholars in Edessa and Nisibis, and at the Academy of Jundi-Shapur under Sassanian rulers of the fourth, fifth, and sixth centuries.

The academy of Jundi-Shapur

Before the advent of Islam, Hellenistic, Alexandrian, Syrian, and Hindu philosophy and science had spread out to the Sassanian centers of learning within the Persian empire. When the tradition of Greek education had all but faded away in Europe in the early Christian centuries, when the Academy of Athens was closed in 529 by Emperor Justinian, and when the Nestorians were being driven from cities and academies that were under orthodox Christian domination, it was in Sassanian Persia under King Anushirwan the Just that Syrian, Alexandrian, and Jewish scholars found refuge. There they preserved these traditions, improved upon and added to them, and later passed them on through Islamic scholarship to European educators. Among these Persian centers of learning were Salonika, Ctesiphon,[14] Nishapur, and most particularly Jundi-Shapur.

It should be borne in mind that even in the pre-Sassanian centuries Persia had acquired a wealth of the sciences of Babylonia and India and had made important advancements in areas of mathematics and music. The libraries of Zoroastrian temples included many scientific and ethical books written in the Pahlavi (Middle Persian) language, many of which were later translated into Arabic, centuries later into Latin, and still later into other important languages in Europe. The Sassanian king, Ardeshir, commissioned special experts to India, Mesopotamia, and nearby Byzantine cities to gather works of learning, an effort which was continued by his successor, Shapur. These works were translated into Pahlavi under the patronage of these kings.[15]

Some authors, such as ibn-Khaldun, go so far as to say that it was perhaps through Persia that the Greeks had learned their first lessons in science and philosophy. Dr. Thabih-Allah Safa states (using ibn al-Ibri as his authority) that Shapur, the son of Ardeshir, brought Greek physicians to Persia to study medicine. It was also under him that many Greek works were translated and preserved in the library of the Academy of Jundi-Shapur, among them works on philosophy and logic.[16]

During its early centuries, a number of eminent Persian scholars were converted to Christianity. Some of them, as Farhad (Aphraate) and Pulis Irani (Paul the Persian), achieved high ecclesiastical positions within the Christian church in Persia and elsewhere. These Persian Christian converts wrote interpretive works in Syrian for Khosru Anushirwan. Many returned to their homeland toward the end of the fifth century as a result of orthodox Christian persecutions and opened schools in Persian cities. One of them, the great scholar Narsi, opened a large academy at Nisibis in 457. It was through this school, and after orthodox Christian opposition to Nestorians was wiped out by armed assistance from the Persian monarch Firuz (459–483), that Nestorianism gained strength within the Persian empire and extended its religious and educational influences as far east as Herat, Marv, and Samarkand; but the main center was Jundi-Shapur. These educational Nestorian influences were mostly in the form of Hellenistic or Hellenized Syriac translations into Pahlavi. Many Nestorian scholars attached themselves to Persian academies as teachers and translators, largely of Aristotelian (Alexandrian) works. Nestorian, Syriac, and Hellenistic influences were further advanced as Nestorian teachers founded churches and schools in various Persian cities, developing Hellenized centers of learning.[17]

One of the important centers of Nestorian-Persian learning was *Beit Ardeshir* (The House of Ardeshir), known also as *Riv-Ardeshir*, or *Rishahr*, where special attention was given to translations and interpretations of the works of Aristotle as well as works in medicine, astronomy, and other sciences. There were other similar centers of learning, such as Ctesiphon, but none reached the fame and influence of the great Academy of Jundi-Shapur to which European medieval education owes a great debt as the first important channel of preservation and eventual transmission of Hellenistic, Hindu, and Persian learning to the Western world.[18]

The Academy of Jundi-Shapur was located in the city bearing that name in southeastern Persia (actually east of Shush or Saisanna, southeast of Dizful and northwest of Shushtar) where the present village of Shah Abad is located. It was referred to by Nestorians as the *Beit Labat* (House of Learning). The Arabs later called it Jandi-Sabur, or Jundaysabur, Arabized as Gundi-Shapur.[19]

The city of Jundi-Shapur was founded by Shapur I (241–271), who, according to tradition, used Roman prisoners of war to lay the foundation of the famous city. The same tradition credits Shapur I with having ordered collections of Greek scientific-philosophic works and their translations into Pahlavi for the library of Jundi-Shapur. He also made the city the center of Hellenistic medical science.

Al-Ghafti relates a tale regarding the city which is of passing interest. In the *Akhbar-al-Hukama* (*The History of Men of Learning*, Cairo, 1326 Lunar Year, p. 93), he says:

> When the daughter of Caesar travelled to that city [Jundi-Shapur] there were quite a number of artisans representing various crafts whom she brought along from her own country, and whose skills she needed. Among them were learned physicians who established themselves in that city and began to instruct students, whose number kept constantly increasing.[20]
>
> ... When Shapur, the son of Ardeshir, won victory over Syria and Antioch, he asked to marry the daughter of the Roman emperor. The emperor obliged and agreed to send his daughter to Shapur. Shapur built a city for her designed after Constantinople and that city is Jundi-Shapur.[21]

The city was invaded several times during the reign of Shapur II (310–379), who made it his headquarters.

Jundi-Shapur, unlike Edessa, was cosmopolitan both in taste and in the range of its intellectual interests. According to one unverified tradition, it had its origins in antiquity, being first known as the *Genta Shapirta* (the Beautiful Garden). However, it assumes historic significance from the reign of Shapur I (241–271), who rebuilt the city after the sack of Antioch and the defeat of the Roman Emperor Valerian by the Persian king. Shapur I romanized the city after his marriage with Aurelian's daughter.

When the city surrendered militarily to Islamic forces in 636, the university remained undisturbed. It continued a center of learning even after Baghdad had attracted its teachers as well as its intellectual traditions to that new Islamic city. Mention of Jundi-Shapur is made by Muslim writers, such as ibn Hawqal in 976, Yaqut, the encyclopaedist (died 1228), and al-Qazwini, as late as 1340.

From 531 to 579, during the reign of Anushirwan-i-Adel (the Just), the academy reached the peak of its development, bringing together for comparison and synchronism Hindu, Greek, Judaic, Syriac, Christian, and Persian learning. It became an important medical center. The hospital attached to the medical studies of the academy became a model for many built in the subsequent centuries throughout the vast cultural empire of Islam. This medical school survived until the end of the tenth century, and from the latter half of the eighth it exerted wide influence upon the science of medicine.[22] Jurjis ibn Bakhtishu (771), dean of the Jundi-Shapur hospital, and his descendants followed a brilliant medical tradition in Baghdad for some two and a half centuries.[23]

It was perhaps through Jundi-Shapur also that Hindu literary-ethical works were translated into Pahlavi. For example, *The Fables of Bed Pai* was translated from Sanskrit into Pahlavi during Anushirwan's reign. Both the original Sanskrit version and the Pahlavi translation were lost after the work was translated from Pahlavi into Arabic under the new title, *Kalila wa-Dimna*, by ibn al-Muqaffa, himself a Persian. Most of the original Sanskrit fables have also been preserved with many additions in the Hindu work *Panchatantra*. The Arabic *Kalila wa-Dimna* was translated into some forty European and other languages, including one in Icelandic and another in Malay.

One of the astronomical works of the period of Jundi-Shapur was a novel calendar which divided the year into twelve months of thirty days and each month into two seven-day and two eight-day weeks; then five intercalary days were added at the end of the year.[24]

Jundi-Shapur's contributions to Western education

The Academy of Jundi-Shapur is of interest to the historian of Western as well as Muslim education for two important reasons. First, the academy became an intellectual sanctuary in the sixth century for some of the great scholars of Greece and Syria who, in association with Hindu, Jewish, Persian, and perhaps even Chinese thought, carried on important elements of scientific (especially medical) and philosophical learning of classical cultures. Out of this scholastic association of minds a scientific synchronism arose which in many ways improved upon the scientific-philosophic conclusions of the separate cultures. The intellectual center of learning, which was once in Edessa (al-Ruha) and Harran and then transferred to Nisibis, was in the first half of the sixth century centered in this academy, which became the greatest institution of higher learning in the world.[25] In translating great scientific works, such as medical, mathematical, and astronomical works from Hindu and Greek into Pahlavi and Syriac (Aramaic) and by employing notable Syrian, Jewish, and Persian scholars and linguists to translate these works, the academy carried on, preserved, and improved upon these traditions.

The Greek teachers, who left the academy in Athens in 529, were Justinianos, Athenius, Proclus, Damascius, Simplicius, Eulamius, Priscianus, Diogenes, Isidorus. Among these, Priscianus was the monarch Anushirwan's favorite, with whom he carried on many inquiries in questions and answers. A partial translation of their Pahlavi original is preserved to the present day. The work contains discussions on psychology, care of the body, natural philosophy, astronomy, and natural history. An essay by Damascius has also survived.

Some interesting facts about the teachers of the Academy of Athens who taught briefly at Jundi-Shapur may be noted here.[26]

Damascius, formerly the head of the Academy of Athens from 511 until it was closed in 529, stayed at Jundi-Shapur from 531 to 533. He was a disciple of Proclus and author of a highly controversial work (*First Principles*), a biography of Isidorus, and some commentaries on Plato. Some have also ascribed to him the *Fifteenth Book of Euclid*.[27]

Simplicius, born in Sicilia, lived in Athens until 529 and stayed at Jundi-Shapur until 533. He was a student of Damascius and Anirnonius. He wrote several books on Aristotle, mostly commentaries, and a *Commentary on Book I of Euclid*. He was also a creative philosopher in his own right, explaining "the stability of the celestial bodies by the excess of their impetus over their gravity."[28]

Priscianus of Lydia remained at Jundi-Shapur until 533. Khosru Anushirwan engaged him in many discussions on philosophical questions, which are preserved as a collection of the philosopher's answers to the king's questions. Priscianus also wrote a commentary on Theophrastus' work on the senses. Unfortunately, his original *Greek Collection of Answers* is lost; however, a Latin translation of it appeared in the ninth century, ascribed to the philosopher John Scotus Erigena, known as *Solutiones Eorum de Quibus dubitavit Chosroes Persarum rex.*

Another Greek physician, Theodorus, lived from 309 to 379 in the Persia of Shapur II. He wrote a compendium of medicine in Pahlavi, which was translated later into Arabic and mentioned in ibn al-Nadim's *Al-Fihrist*.[29]

Anushirwan also welcomed scholar-refugees, mainly Nestorians from Edessa, who found Jundi-Shapur a cosmopolitan center of learning. During his reign (531–579), he encouraged Nestorians and neo-Platonists to use Syrian translations of Greek works in Jundi-Shapur and had Persian translations of the Syrian versions of Plato and Aristotle made under his personal supervision.

So great was Jundi-Shapur as a center of scholarship in philosophy, mathematics, astronomy, and medicine that after the Muslim conquest of Persia in the seventh century the academy flourished as an extensive intellectual reservoir having much influence on Islamic learning until the early eleventh century.[30]

The second reason for the interest of the historian of education in the Academy of Jundi-Shapur is that it continued as the scientific center of Islam throughout the Umayyad period (661–749). From this academy scholars, educators, and physicians went to the then Muslim capital, Damascus, and gave to Islam its first acquaintance with classical cultures. From it, or its alumni, the first Hindu, Persian, Syrian, and Greek works began to be translated into Arabic, a tradition which was transferred at the rise of the Abbassides in Eastern Islam about 750 to the new Muslim capital in Baghdad, where Islamic education and scholarship attained their highest peak. And to the extent that this new learning, this renaissance of translation, assimilation, and creative improvements and additions to the prevailing knowledge can be shown to have been stimulated and furthered by the example and contributions of the scholars of Jundi-Shapur, to that extent its importance for historians of Western education should be obvious. For Muslim scholarship preserved and enriched classical education and scholarship (mainly Greek, Syrian, Persian, and even Hindu) and transmitted it to Western schoolmen through Latin and Hebrew translations of Arabic works.

Insofar as the initial contributions of Jundi-Shapur are concerned, it is important to record that translations of Greek (and Hindu) classics into Arabic were resumed during the rule of the second Abbasside Caliph al-Mansur (754–775), mainly at the Academy of Jundi-Shapur. It was from the academy's famous hospital that Bakh-Tishu, its chief physician and dean, was summoned in 771 to the court of Abbasside Caliph al-Hadi (died 786) and the great Harun-al-Rashid (died 809).[31]

Bakh-Tishu is essential in any educational assessment of Jundi-Shapur because this Christian doctor's family produced distinguished physician-scholars for Islam for better than seven generations. It was through this family that the tradition of Greco-Persian-Hindu medical knowledge was conveyed to Islam, to be enriched and extended by its own scholars (mostly Persians, such as al-Razi from Rayy, Avicenna from Hamadan, and Haly Abbas the Magician) before its transmission to Europe.

The Academy of Jundi-Shapur disappeared as the center of intellectual influence in Islam in the late 880's, as scientific works which predominated in the Syriac and Pahlavi languages in the first half of that century gave way to more advanced scholarship in Baghdad and Samarra and still later to renewed Umayyad scholarship in Cordova and other Spanish and Sicilian academic communities.

During this long period of translation, which ended more or less about 900 A.D., Muslim science, particularly medicine, though both extensive in scope and intensive in substance, was founded nonetheless firmly upon Greek science and Persian and Indian thought and "experience." It produced great works formidable in scholarship but on the whole lacking originality. From the tenth century, however, Islam begins to rely more upon its own resources and to "develop from within" until the twelfth century. The sciences, particularly medicine, now pass rapidly from the hands of Christians and Sabians into the possession of Muslim scholars, mostly Persians.[32]

Elgood states in *The Legacy of Persia* that the first academic language employed in the hospital, medical school, and university of Jundi-Shapur was probably Sanskrit, and that Hindu medical knowledge flourished there until after 439, when the school of Edessa (al-Ruha) was closed in 439, bringing a large influx of Greek and Syrian teachers to the Persian scholastic center. The student of medical education interested in the traditions of his discipline would find the medical theory and practice at Jundi-Shapur hospital and school of medicine an interesting and important link in the chain of Greco-Hindu and Perso-Islamic medical innovations and development and the contributions of this medical synchronism at Jundi-Shapur to the development of medical education in both Eastern Islam and the West.

Buzurjmihr, the great court physician of Anushirwan the Just and tutor of his son, Hormuz, known to Western writers as Perzoes, was also one of the significant contributors to the medical school of Jundi-Shapur. On orders of the monarch, he went to India to secure a copy of the famed *Fables of Bed Pai*. Of special interest to the historian of education is the autobiography of Perzoes reproduced in the introduction of ibn al-Muqaffa's translation of the *Fables*.

A further incident may throw some light on the cosmopolitanism of Jundi-Shapur's medical school. Another royal physician of the court of Anushirwan, one Irian Durustpat, a Nestorian (and later Monophysite) Christian, also known as Jibra'il (Gabriel), is said to have cured the monarch's Christian wife, the favorite Shirin (Sweet), of sterility, and after Shirin bore a male child Jibra'il used his influence with the king to meddle in Nestorian church affairs.

Translations of classical works into Arabic

The Sassanian kings were patrons of learning. Even before them, the Hakhaminians had facilitated the assimilation and adaptation of Babylonian and Indian sciences—particularly mathematics, astronomy, and music — as well as the intellectual heritage of other Eastern cultures. However, Sassanian monarchs were more deliberate and systematic in their efforts to advance learning within their domains. Ardeshir Papakan, for example, sent learned men to India and the Roman Empire to procure scientific and philosophic works. He subsequently ordered their translation into Pahlavi, a task which was continued by his son, Shapur. Masudi concurs that the Persians were acquainted with some of the Greek philosophies and religions through similar communications with them.[33] Shapur himself, according to ibn al-Ibri, brought Greek physicians to his court to teach him medicine, perhaps at Jundi-Shapur, and ordered translations of Greek medical and other works into Pahlavi.[34]

In the fifth and sixth centuries many Zoroastrian scholars, who had adopted the Christian faith, kept Grecian science and philosophy alive in Sassanian and Syrian schools, particularly in the Persian school at Edessa. Among them were Farhad (Aphraate), who wrote in Syriac; Maraba the First, a Zoroastrian who, after adopting Christianity in 536, remained active in the Christian church; Paul (Paulus) the Persian of Nisibis, who wrote a book on Aristotelian logic in Syriac for Anushirwan. When the Persian school at Ruha was closed in 489, many of its scholars returned to Persia. They opened new schools within the Sassanian empire, advancing Greek (Aristotelian) and particularly Syrian philosophy and science and making new translations of them in Pahlavi.[35] All these resulted in new institutions of learning in important Persian cities, such as Jundi-Shapur. Outstanding among these new schools was Beit Ardeshir (Riv-Ardeshir, or Rishahr), whose dean's (Maana Beit Ardeshiri, a native of Shiraz) translations of Syrian works were known even in India.[36] According to Yaqut, the historian, Maana's school developed into a prominent center of Hellenistic, Syrian, and Zoroastrian scholarship. Another such school opened near Ctesiphon with Maraba as its dean.

There is no doubt, however, that the focal point of Sassanian learning, insofar as Western education is concerned, was the Academy of Jundi-Shapur. It should be apparent that, prior to the advent of Islam, Sassanian education had achieved a high degree of maturity. There were important schools all over the empire; great teachers had established them or had been attracted to them. These were centers of translation of Greek and Hindu works of science and philosophy into Pahlavi, and it was also from these schools that some of the most important translations of Sanskrit, Pahlavi, Syrian, and Greek into Arabic emerged.

Most famous and productive among these Persian translators were the following:

> George the son of Bakh-Tishu and his family of translators;[37] Abu Zakariyya Yuhanna ibn Musa, a physician of Jundi-Shapur who, during and following the reign of Harun al-Rashid, made important translations in Baghdad as head of the Dar al-Hikmah (the House of Learning);[38] Rabban al-Tabari of Marv (also called Sahl al-Tabari), who translated the Almagest into Arabic for the first

time;[39] ibn al-Muqaffa, translator of Pahlavi works into Arabic;[40] Naubakht of Ahwaz, translator of Pahlavi mathematical works into Arabic;[41] Abu Sahl Khorshaz-Mah, translator of mathematical works into Arabic; Abu Hafz Umar ibn Farrukhan al-Tabari, head of a school of translators;[42] Ibrahim ibn Habib-al-Fazari, translator of the famous fifth century Hindu mathematical works (*Siddhanta*)— completed, according to Biruni, in 770–71;[43] Muhammad al-Fazari Ibrahim's son, translator of mathematical works from Indian into Arabic, including parts of the *Siddhanta*;[44] Musa ibn Khalid the Tarjuman (or "the great translator"), who translated Pahlavi and Greek works into Arabic, including Hunayn's Syrian version of Galen's works;[45] Isa Ben Chahar Bokht (or Sahar Bokht [meaning *Four Fortunes*]) of Jundi-Shapur, who also translated Galen into Arabic; Yusuf (Joseph al-Naqil), "The Story Teller" of Khuzistan, who made medical translations into Arabic; Ali ibn Ziad al-Tamimi, translator of mathematical works from Pahlavi into Arabic;[46] Istiphan al-Qadim, translator of works on chemistry at request of Khalid ibn Yazid ibn Muawiya (850); Maserjis, translator of the works of Aaron of Alexandria.

Abu Yahya al-Batriq translated Greek medical and philosophical works, particularly those of Aristotle and Hippocrates. His *Serrul Asrar (Secret of Secrets)* is an Aristotelian work on administration of government. This work, better known as *Secretum Secretorum*, he translated into Syriac at the beginning of the ninth century. Another translation of this work into Hebrew was made by Judab al-Harizi.[47] His translation of Ptolemy's *Quadripartium* is equally important. He was employed by al-Mansur to carry on the tasks of translation. His treatise on *Death* by Hippocrates and his *Meteorology* of Aristotle are among his basic translations.[48]

Hunain ibn Is'haq (died 264) was the greatest of all translators of classical works into Arabic. Among his translations were *Timaeus* of Plato; *Story of Sahlman and Isaal; The Aphorisms;* the important works of Galen; *Prognostics* and *On the Nature of Man* as well as other works of Hippocrates.[49]

Ghasta ibn Luka (Luke) al-Ba'labaki was another translator of Greek medical and mathematical works.[50] Among them were studies by Diophantus, Theodosius, Autolycus, Hypsicles, Aristarchus, and Heron. Later other translations were made into Spanish and Latin by Stephen Arnaldus.

Hubaish ibn-al-Hasan al-A'asam al-Damashqi translated Syrian and Greek works (Galenic) in medicine.[51] In addition to these, he completed a *Quaestiones Medicales* of Hunain.[52]

Thabit ibn Qurra al-Harrani (826–900) of Harran made many translations of Greek works on medicine and mathematics,[53] including the works of Apollonius, Archimedes, Euclid, Theodosius, Ptolemy, Galen, and Eutocius. The founder of a school of translators, he published solar observations and works on mathematics and anatomical and medical materials, and on astronomy.[54] Still other translators are Istiphan ibn Basil, a student of Hunain ibn Is'haq, translator of Greek medical books (Galenic works); Kanka the Hindu, translator of Hindu mathematical and medical works in the latter part of the eighth century and the first decades of the ninth; ibn Dehn, also from India, who made translations of Hindu medical works;[55] Theophilus of Edessa (known also as ibn Thuma and as Thomas of Edessa; died 785) who translated one of Galen's works into Syriac and perhaps some Greek or Syrian into Arabic;[56] ibn al-Tabari, a Jewish scholar from Tabaristan and one of the greatest theologian-scholars of the late decades of the eighth century and the early decades of the ninth who translated many books on medicine and mathematics from Syrian and Greek into Arabic;[57] Abu Zakariyya Yuhanna (or Yahya) ibn-al-Batriq, translator of medical and philosophical works during the reign of Caliph Ma'mun (813–833), including translations from Hippocrates and Alexander Tralles;[58] Hajjaj ibn Yusuf ibn Matr (or Matar) who made mathematical translations from Euclid during the reign of Harun-al-Rashid and Ma'mun; Isa ibn Asid al-Nasrani, a pupil of Thabit ibn Qurra, who made translations from Syrian into Arabic; Abu Is'haq Ibrahim al-Ghuwairi, who wrote commentaries in Arabic on Aristotle; Hilal ibn Abi Hilal al-Himsi, translator of the first four books of Apollonius from Greek into Arabic for Ahmad ibn Musa ibn Shakir; Isa ibn Yahya ibn Ibrahim, who translated various Galenic works, made a partial translation of Aribasius, and wrote some original medical works; Qawamal-din (al-Fat'h ibn Ali ibn al-Fat'h al-Isfahani), who translated the *Shah Namah* of Firdawsi into Arabic for al-Mu'azzam, the Ayyubid ruler of Damascus (1218–1227); Yusuf al-Khuri, who translated Archimedes' lost work on triangles and Galen's *De Simplicium Temperamentis et Facultatibus* from Syriac versions into Arabic; ibn Sahda, translator of *De sectis* and *De Pulsibus Aditirones* into Syriac.

Other ninth- and tenth-century translators were[59] Zurba ibn Majuh al-Na'ami al-Himsi, Halal ibn Abi Halal al-Himsi, Abu al-Fath Isfahani (mathematics), Fethyun (or Fethum) al-Tarjuman, Abu Hasrawi (Kasrawi?) ibn Ayyub, Basil al-Mutran, Hairun (or Jairun) ibn Rabetch, Tazars' al-Sanghal, Abu Yusuf al-Katib (translations from Hippocrates), Gatha al-Rahawi, Mansur ibn Banas, Abdishu ibn Bahriq Mutram, Salam al-Abrash (translated some works from Aristotle), Ayyub, Sam'an, Abu Ruh al-Sabi (translated works from Aristotle), Abu Umar Yuhanna ibn Yusuf (translated from

Plato), Ayyub ibn al-Qasim al-Rahhi (translated *Isagogue* from Syrian into Arabic), Marlahi,[60] Abu Suhail Vikan ibn Rustam al-Kuhi, and Abdullah ibn Ali (translated the Hindu *Book of Sirak* into both Pahlavi and Arabic).[61]

Translations of Persian works

It was first in Jundi-Shapur and later in Baghdad under al-Ma'mun and others that translations of many Persian scientific, moral, historical, and proverbial treatises were made into Arabic, which ultimately were transmitted through the Arabs to the Western world as part of the heritage of Western education.

Among the early patrons of Persian and other non-Arabic learning in Islam was the Shu'ubiya Party (the "Partisan of the Gentiles"), a society of many diverse peoples who combined their efforts in loosening the fibers of Arabian political and cultural supremacy in the Muslim world by reviving ancient cultures and standards. Although their chief war cry was *back to the Persian*, there were among the Shu'ubiya Party many Jews, Egyptians, Greeks, and even Spaniards. The society had many opponents, primarily the Arabs. Baghdad was the center of the Shu'ubiya activities, and their principal objectives were to demonstrate how much the Arab-Muslim culture owed to the contributions made to it by other races and nations, particularly to Persian models, and the Shu'ubi writers, with the Zoroastrian priest as their source of information. It was in him that the best of Iranian culture was preserved. Thus the Shu'ubiya Party promoted learning and played a vital role in the development of Muslim education.

In the last half of the tenth century, this zeal for Iranian revival was dimmed because of political disturbances, but the literary materials which the Shu'ubiya Party produced were preserved for a later renaissance. Translations were made into Arabic from Parsi sources by older circles of Muslim civilization sympathetic to Persian culture.

Some of the Persian educational writings of this century and the next which were either translated into Arabic or written in that language are the following:

Adab-al-Arab-i Wal-Ajam (*The Manners of the Arabs and the Ajam*; i.e., Persians). The works of the tenth and eleventh centuries contain a list entitled *The Manners of the Arabs and the Persians*, written by ibn Mushkuya, a Persian philosophical writer who was the treasurer and a close friend of the Buide Adud al-Dawla. Ibn Mushkuya used as the source of his work the three Persian treatises on manners called *Javidani Khirad* (*Eternal Wisdom*), *Pand-Namah* (*The Book of Advice*), and *Andarz* (*Advice*). In this period there were other works of this character such as maxims, proverbs, fables, morals, and the like.

Ibn al-Muqaffa, another great translator of Persian works into Arabic, whose important translation was the famous *Kalila wa-Dimna*, which introduced this set of Eastern stories to the Western world. (Of this book and the *Arabian Nights*, we shall speak later.) He translated also into Arabic other Persian works, written on the basis of Persian sources, such as: *Khudai Namah* (the official chronicle of Sassanian times), *Ain Namah* (the institutes of the time), *The Book of Mazdak, Book of Taj* (political), two books on *Adab* (manners), and *Al Yatima* (on morals in politics of the Sassanians).

Aban al-Lahiki, a poet who versified many Persian works into Arabic—for example, *Kalila wa-Dimna, The Book of Barlaam and Josaphat, The Book of Sindbad, The Book of Mazdak, The Book of the Acts of Ardeshir*, and *The Book of the Acts of Anushirwan*.

Taifur (Ahmad ibn Tabir Taifur) who wrote a treatise entitled *Book of Hormoz, Son of Kisra Anushirwan*, a Persian Sassanian emperor.

The family of Naubakht. Naubakht was Persia's leading astronomer of his time, and his son and grandson followed him in the profession with books on astronomy and jurisprudence.

Musa and Yusuf, brothers, sons of Khalid, who wrote treatises on astronomy.

Baladhuri, translator of the *Book of the Counsel of Ardeshir*.

Jabala ibn Salem, who wrote the book of *Rustam and Isphandyar* and translated the Persian history, *Khoday Namah*.

Tamimi (Abu al-Hasan Ali ibn Ziad), translator of *Zick al-Shah-riyarvi* (*The Tables of Shahryar* [the king]).

Al Farrukhan (Omar ibn), who lived at the time of al-Ma'mun and Jafar Barmaki and was in close association with them. He translated *Kitab al-Mahasin* (*Book of Good Manners*). Others followed his example and wrote similar books, such as *Kitab al-Mahasin* (*Book of Good Manners*) by ibn Qutaiba, *Kitab Mahasin al-Akhlagh* (*Book of Good Morals*) by al-Ayashi, *Kitab al-Mahasin* (*Book of Good Manners*) by ibn al Hazm, *Kitab Mahasin Wal Masawi* (*Book of Good Manners and Their Likes*) by al Baihaqi, and *Kitab Mahasin Wal Azdad* (*Book of Good Manners and Their Opposites*) by Jahiz.

Is'haq ibn Yazid, translator of the *Khudai Namah*.

[. . .]

The university

The crown and glory of "medieval" Muslim schools were the universities, or research centers. We have already discussed the great University of Nizamiyyah in the section on Nizamal-Mulk, but let us take as another illustration of the character of Muslim universities the great research center of *Mustansiriyyah*.

The Mustansiriyyah University came into existence to compete with and overthrow the Nizamiyyah. Of the origin and development of this university, the writer of *Baghdad During the Abbasid Caliphate* speaks as follows:[62]

Within the precincts and, as seems probable, immediately south of the Gharabah Gate [occupying some of the area formerly covered by the older Hasani Palace, for one of its walls was washed by the Tigris stream], stood the great College of the Mustansiriyyah. Of this college the ruins still exist [1900], while of the adjoining palaces of the Caliphs hardly a trace remains; but unfortunately, as the college was only completed in 631 [A.D. 1234], no mention of it occurs in Yakut, who had finished his great geographical dictionary shortly before this date, and therefore we do not know for certain on what grounds of the older precincts the college was actually built. Mustansir was the penultimate Caliph of the house of Abbas and the father of Mustasim, whom Hulagu put to death, and this Madrassah of the Mustansiriyyah was founded by him with a view to supplant and eclipse the celebrated Nizamiyyah College, which Nizam-al-Mulk had built nearly two centuries before.

We are told that in outward appearance, in stateliness of ornament and sumptuousness of furniture, in spaciousness and in the wealth of its pious foundations, the Mustansiriyyah surpassed everything that had previously been seen in Islam. It contained four separate law-schools, one for each of the orthodox sects of the Sunnis, with a professor at the head of each, who had seventy-five students [*Fakih*] in his charge, to whom he gave instruction gratis. The four professors each received a monthly salary, and to each of the three hundred students one gold dinar a month was assigned. The great kitchen of the college further provided daily rations of bread and meat to all the inmates. According to Ibn-al-Furat there was a library [*Dar-al-Kutub*] in the Mustansiriyyah with rare books treating of the various sciences, so arranged that the students could easily consult them, and those who wished could copy these manuscripts, pens and paper being supplied by the establishment. Lamps for the students and a due provision of olive oil for lighting up the college are also mentioned, likewise, storage places for cooling the drinking water; and in the great entrance hall [*Aywan*] stood a clock [*Sanduk-as-saat*, 'Chest of the Hours,' doubtless some form of clepsydra], announcing the appointed times of prayer, and marking the lapse of the hours by day and by night.

Inside the college a bath house [*Hammam*] was erected for the special use of the students, and a hospital [*Bimaristan*], to which a physician was appointed, whose duty it was to visit the place every morning, prescribing for those who were sick; and there were great store-chambers in the Madrasah provided with all requisites of food, drink, and medicines. The Caliph Mustansir himself took such interest in the work of the institution that he would hardly let a day pass without a visit of inspection; and he had caused a private garden to be laid out, with a belvedere [*Manzarah*] overlooking the college, whither it was his wont to come and divert himself, sitting at a window—before which a veil was hung—and which opened upon one of the college halls, so that through this window he could watch all that went on within the building, and even hear the lectures of the professors and the disputations of the students.

A century after its foundation, Ibn Batutah, who visited Baghdad in 727 [A.D. 1327], dilates on the magnificence of the Mustansiriyyah College, which had fortunately escaped destruction during the Mongol siege; and he describes it as situated at the further end of the Tuesday Market [*Suk-ath-Thalathah*], which was the commercial centre of Baghdad in his days. The law-schools in the Mustansiriyyah were then still frequented by students of the four orthodox Sunni sects, each sect or law-school having its separate mosque, and in the hall the professor of law gave his lectures, whom Ibn Batutah describes as 'seated under a small wooden cupola on a chair covered by a carpet, speaking with much sedateness and gravity of mien, he being clothed in black and wearing a turban; and there were besides two assistants, one on either hand, who repeated in a loud voice the dictation of the teacher.'

The Persian geographer Hamd-Allah, writing a dozen years later than Ibn Batutah, also refers to the Mustansiriyyah Madrasah as the most beautiful building then existing in Baghdad; and it appears to have stood intact for many centuries, for the ruins of the college, as already mentioned, still exist [1900], occupying a considerable space of ground immediately below the eastern end of the present Bridge of Boats. Mustansir likewise restored the great mosque of the palace [Jami-al-Kasr], originally built by the Caliph Ali Muktafi, and Mustansir set up four platforms [*Dikkah*] on the right or western side of the pulpit, where the students of the Mustansiriyyah were seated and held disputations on Fridays after the public prayers. The remains of this mosque also exist, at the present day occuying part of the Suk-al-Ghazl [the Thread Market], at some little distance to the eastward of the ruins of the Madrasah. When Niebuhr visited Baghdad in 1750 he found that the ancient kitchen of the Mustansiriyyah College was clearly to be recognized, being used in his day as a weighing house; and Niebuhr copied here the inscription which gives the name and titles of the Caliph Mustansir, with the statement that this Madrasah had been completed in the year 630 [A.D. 1233]. A similar inscription [also extant] was seen by Niebuhr in the ruined mosque, with the date of 633 [A.D. 1236], doubtless when the restoration by Mustansir was finished, for, as already said, the foundation walls in all probability are far older than this date, and belong to the great mosque of the Palace of the Caliph.[63]

This rather elaborate description of the Mustansiriyyah is fortunate for us today, not so much for what it tells us of the magnificence of an Islamic university at its best as for the fact that such universities shone like the morning star in the early part of the thirteenth century. It is perhaps of interest to compare Mustansiriyyah University with the oldest Christian universities of Bologna, Paris, Montpellier, and Oxford in the twelfth century for comparative merits and demerits, their similarities and differences, and their influences on one another.

In Spain the development of higher education began in the tenth century. The Moors (Berbers), and following them the Arabs, entered Spain in 712. By 756, the Umayyad Prince Abd-al-Rahman had defeated the army of the Abbasside Caliph al-Mansur and was made the Amir of Cordova. This initiated another Islamic golden age in southern Spain under the Umayyads which continued to the eleventh century. Meanwhile, the tenth century was the apex of intellectual development in Muslim Spain with Cordova as its center, and Seville, Toledo, and Granada less important by comparison. Al-Makkari's *History of the Muhammadan Dynasties* in Spain contains a long list (some sixty pages) of this period's men of letters.[64]

Colleges provided higher education in Cordova (which was actually a university), Granada, Toledo, Marcia, Almeria, Seville, Valencia, and Cadiz. Elementary schools, charging tuition in contrast to schools in Eastern Islam, were open to large numbers of boys and girls, although some, as those patronized by Hakam II, were tuition free. Libraries were numerous—some seventy are known—attracting to them students and scholars in almost every field, be it art, music, literature, theology, philology, rhetoric, grammar, the sciences, or philosophy, indicating the varieties of informational materials in these libraries.

The curriculum of Muslim schools

The curriculum of Muslim education at that time reminds us in its extensive and intensive nature of curricular programs of modern advanced systems of education, particularly on higher levels of education. It was not unusual to find instruction in mathematics (algebra, trigonometry, and geometry), science (chemistry, physics, and astronomy), medicine (anatomy, surgery, pharmacy, and specialized medical branches), philosophy (logic, ethics, and metaphysics), literature (philology, grammar, poetry, and prosody), social sciences, history, geography, political disciplines, law, sociology, psychology, and jurisprudence, theology (comparative religions, history of religions, study of the *Qur'an*, religious tradition [*hadith*], and other religious topics). They offered advanced studies in the professions, for example, law and medicine.

Their vocational curriculum was varied and founded on the more general studies; in fact, it appears generally to have been as comprehensive as their education was universal. The extent and depth of Muslim curriculum can be detected by references to a number of encyclopaedias of general knowledge and specific disciplines, among them the celebrated *Encyclopedia of the Ikhwan al-Safa* (the *Brethren of Purity* or *Sincerity*), which was known to and respected by European schoolmen.

Another indication of the extent of Muslim curriculum is manifested in the fact that one Arabic dictionary contained sixty volumes, with an illustration for each definition.[65] Again, its richness may be determined by its practical and useful consequences, leading to such ventures as calculating the angle of the ecliptic, measuring the size of the earth, calculating the procession of the equinoxes, inventing the pendulum clock, explaining in the field of optics and physics such phenomena as "refraction of light, gravity, capillary attraction and twilight," using the globe in teaching the geography of a round earth, developing observatories for the empirical study of heavenly bodies, making advances in the uses of drugs, herbs, and foods for medication, establishing hospitals with a system of interns and externs, improving upon the science of navigation, introducing new concepts of irrigation, fertilization, and soil cultivation, discovering causes of certain diseases and developing correct diagnoses of them, proposing new concepts of hygiene, making use of anesthetics in surgery with newly innovated surgical tools, introducing the science of dissection in anatomy, furthering the scientific breeding of horses and cattle, and finding new ways of grafting to produce new types of flowers and fruits. In the area of chemistry, the curriculum led to the discovery of such substances as potash, alcohol, nitrate of silver, nitric acid, sulphuric acid, and corrosive sublimate. It also developed to a high degree of perfection the arts of textiles, ceramics, and metallurgy.

On the curriculum of Muslim higher education in the Abbasside period, the summation given by Abu Yahya Zakariyya is of interest.[66] It included such legal subjects [*shariyyat*] as jurisprudence, exegesis, and tradition; literary studies [*adabiyyat*] in philology, syntax, rhetoric, prosody, composition, reading, and history; mathematics [*riyadhiyyat*] including geometry, astronomy, arithmetic, algebra, music, politics, ethics, and domestic economy; rational [*aqliyyat*] studies in logic, dialectic, dogmatic theology, metaphysics, natural science, medicine, and chemistry; and such miscellaneous subjects were approved as surveying, veterinary, agriculture, phrenology, dream interpretation, astrology, and magic.

The greatest calamity which came to Muslim learning was the cataclysm of the Mongol invasion in the thirteenth century. The Mongols destroyed most of the great institutions of learning in Khurasan and Baghdad—the mosques, the universities, the libraries. After the Mongols, these Islamic universities never regained their old spirit and beauty.

Fortunately we have some definite information on the range and scope of Islamic learning in the latter part of the tenth century from three authentic sources. These are (1) the *al-Fihrist-al-Ulum* (*Index of the Sciences*) by ibn al-Nadim, 988; (2) the works of the Society of Encyclopaedists, known better as Ikwan al-Safa (Brethren of Purity), and (3) the *Mafatih al-Ulum* (*Keys of the Sciences*) by Yusuf al-Katib of Khwarizm (976).

In the treatises of the Ikhwan al-Safa which flourished in Basra in the second half of the tenth century, we have the following information compiled by Friedrich Dieterici from the fifty-one *Treatises* published by the fraternity:

> *Mundane studies:* Reading and writing, lexicography and grammar, calculation and computation, prosody and poetic art, the science of omens and portents, the science of magic, amulets, alchemy and legerdemain, trades and crafts, buying and selling, commerce, agriculture and cattle farming, and biography and narrative.
>
> *Religious studies:* Knowledge of the Scriptures (i.e., the *Qur'an*), exegesis of the Scriptures, the science of tradition, jurisprudence, and the commemoration of God, admonition, the ascetic life, mysticism (Sufiism), and the ecstatic or beatific vision.
>
> *Philosophical studies:* Mathematics, logic, numbers, geometry, astronomy, music, arithmetical and geometrical relations; natural science and anthropology; matter, form, space, time and motion; cosmogony; production, destruction, and the elements; meteorology, mineralogy; the essence of nature and its manifestations; botany; zoology; anatomy and anthropology; sense-perceptions; embryology; man as the microcosm; the development of the soul (psychical evolution); body and soul; the true nature of psychical and physical pain and pleasure; diversity of languages (philology); psychology—understanding, the world soul, etc.; and theology—esoteric doctrine of Islam, the ordering of the spirit world; the occult sciences.

In the *Mafatih al-Ulum* (the *Keys of the Sciences*) of al-Katib, we find a somewhat similar scope but different grouping of knowledge, excluding the mundane studies. The sciences, "which are for the most part Greek or Persian," are divided into two main branches, as follows:

> *The Indigenous Sciences: Jurisprudence* (*Fiqh*), principles and (*Furu'*) applications, such as legal purity, prayer, fasting, alms,

pilgrimage, buying and selling, marriage, homicide, wounding, retaliation, compensation and bloodwit, etc. (eleven sections); scholastic philosophy (*Kalam*) "the various schools and sects of Muslims, Christians, Jews and Gentiles (Persians, Indians, Chaldeans, Manichaeans, Marcionites, Bardesanians, Mazdakites, Sophists, etc.), Arabian heathenism, and the first principles of religion" (seven sections); grammar (*Nahw*) (twelve sections); the secretarial art (*Kitabat*) . . . including explanations of all the technical terms employed in the various government offices (eight sections); prosody and the poetic art (*Arieth and Shi'r*) (five sections); history (*Akhbar*) "the history of Ancient Persian, Muhammadan history, pre-Muhammadan history of Arabia, especially Yaman, and the history of Greece and Rome" (nine sections).

The Exotic Sciences: Philosophy (*Falsafa*) (three sections); logic (*Mantigh*) (nine sections); medicine (*Tibb*)—anatomy, pathology, materia medica, therapeutics, diet, weights and measures (eight sections); arithmetic including algebra (*Hisab, Arithma'tighi*) (five sections); geometry (*Handasa, Jumetriya*) (four sections); astronomy (*Ilmu n'nujum*)—"planets and fixed stars; the composition of the universe according to the Ptolemaic system; judicial astrology" (four sections); music (*Musighi*) (three sections); mechanics, hydrostatics (*Ilmu'lhiyal*) (two sections); and alchemy (*Kimiya*) (three sections).[67]

There is no doubt that in the Islamic educational curriculum the religion of Islam and the religious book (the *Qur'an*) stood at the center of all learning activities, as stated by ibn Khaldun. Next to religion, a language proficiency was essential (as it is considered today), but then it was to achieve a better understanding of religion. This language was, of course, Arabic. In fact, the *Qur'an*, writing, and some arithmetic were the only studies considered in the elementary schools, or *maktabs* (writing schools).

Medical education in early Islam

The medical profession and medical education in the early centuries of Islam followed the pattern and standards of the Greeks, particularly as they were maintained and improved upon at the medical school of the Academy of Jundi-Shapur. The Greek educational influences through this medical school in Iran may be traced beyond the Sassanian period to the Achaemenians. The standards and traditions of the school of medicine of the Academy of Jundi-Shapur were transferred and developed further in Baghdad under the Abbasside caliphs, and many of the teacher-physicians of the school of Jundi-Shapur, mostly Nestorian Christians and Jews, carried the tradition to the Muslim hospitals in Baghdad where the foundations of Muslim medical education were laid.

Medical education began early in a student's academic career, usually between his fifteenth and seventeenth years, although ibn Sina began at eleven, and Hunain ibn Is'haq had already completed his basic medical education at Jundi-Shapur when he was seventeen.

Studies in music, astronomy, and geometry were among optional pre-medical courses: Music to develop appreciation for the "subtleties of the human pulse; astronomy to determine lucky and unlucky times; geometry to determine the shape of wounds, for round wounds heal with ease."[68]

Students learned medical theory and practices interdependently in small classes and, as a rule, under a senior practitioner. The most basic aspect of training was clinical instruction in hospitals, including attendance at operations "and of those things that are incumbent upon the profession."[69] In addition to observation and internship, students attended lectures given by senior practitioners in their homes or in public places. Students questioned their masters on minute medical and surgical points with complete freedom, even to pointing out any fallacies in the master's theory. When so cornered, the teacher was often forced to revise his outlook or write treatises proving his position against objections.[70] One such treatise, the *Cure Within an Hour*, was written by Barr'-al-Sa'at after being challenged by hecklers in his class for stating that "it was possible to disperse the *materies morbi* of certain diseases within one hour." The methodology of instruction and learning stated here regarding medical students was, with some modifications, the methodology of higher education in all branches of study in Islamic colleges and universities.[71]

In lecture rooms, in the practitioner's home, or at the mosque, students took their seats according to academic seniority, the advanced students being seated together and closer to the lecturer. These lectures were always based on some written medical document and were immediately open to questions for clarification of obscure points, or definition of medical terms used during the lecture and indication of their correct pronunciation. Lectures were held sometimes during the evening hours, particularly during the *Ramadhan*, the month of fasting. Students gathered around famed lecturers from all over the Muslim world, with complete freedom to go from center to center to listen to other important lecturers, or to move to another teacher when the first one's professional "lemon was squeezed dry," or seemed dehydrated from the outset. Some of these international gatherings of students were quite large; usually the more famous a professor, the larger his classes.[72]

The most frequently used medical texts and references were the following: *Aphorisms*, Hippocrates; *Questions*, Hunain ibn Is'haq; *Guide*, Razes; also his book of al-Mansuri, *Continens; Commentaries*, Abu Sahl al-Nile; *Treasury*, Thabit ibn-Qurra; *Aims*, al-Jurjani; *Hidaya* (*Guide*), Ajwini; *Kifaya* (*Sufficiency*), ibn Faraj; *Treatises*, Galen; *Liber Regius*, Haly Abbas; *Hundred Chapters*, Abu Sahl; *Canon*, ibn Sina; *Thesaurus*, al-Jurjani. It should be noted here that the bulk of this list, when translated into Latin during the twelfth to fourteenth centuries, constituted the basis for the medical curricula of European medical schools, such as that of the University of Paris.[73]

[. . .]

Some Muslim contributions to education

Before concluding this brief summary of "medieval" Muslim education, it may be well to point out some of its basic contributions to educational theory and practice, and state also its basic shortcomings.

1.   Throughout the twelfth and part of the thirteenth centuries, Muslim works on science, philosophy, and other fields were translated into Latin, particularly from Spain, and enriched the curriculum of the West, especially in northwestern Europe.

2.   The Muslims passed on the experimental method of science, however imperfect, to the West.

3.   The system of Arabic notation and decimals was introduced to the West.

4.   Their translated works, particularly those of men such as Avicenna in medicine, were used as texts in classes of higher education far into the middle of the seventeenth century.

5.   They stimulated European thought, reacquainted it with the Greek and other classical cultures and thus helped bring about the Renaissance.

6.   They were the forerunners of European universities, having established hundreds of colleges in advance of Europe.

7.   They preserved Greco-Persian thought when Europe was intolerant of pagan cultures.

8.   European students in Muslim universities carried back new methods of teaching.

9.   They contributed knowledge of hospitals, sanitation, and food to Europe.

The strength of the Muslim educational system lay in the following areas: It produced great scholars in almost every field. It developed literacy on a universal scale when illiteracy was the rule in Europe. It transmitted the best features of classical cultures to the West. It led the way in the development of libraries and universities. Its higher education in its creative centuries was open to rich and poor alike, the only requirements being ability and ambition. It held teachers and books in reverence, particularly on higher levels of instruction. The teacher, the book, the lecture, the debate —these were the nerve centers of its educational system.[74]

The curriculum, which was in the early centuries balanced between sectarian and secular studies, became in the later centuries scholastic, making all or practically all secular studies subject to religious and theological approval. The curriculum became formal, fixed, traditional, religious, dogmatic, backward-looking. It encouraged static minds and conformity. It became authoritarian and essentialist.

Whereas in its early centuries Muslim education encouraged debates, experimentation, and individualism, in its later stages it encouraged formal methods, memorization, and recitation. A system which was in its early stages rather spontaneous and free, encouraging individuals to pursue learning and inspire others to enlightenment, lost in the later stages this sense of intellectual adventure and its direction became superimposed from the top (the state and church) rather than inspired by the people. This led in time to an elite and aristocratic concept of education, replacing its early democratic educational spirit. Muslim education did not, and with its scholastic disciplines could not, take advantage of the tools of science and experimentation which it had inherited and improved upon. Rather, it passed on these tools to European men of science, who utilized them effectively after the Renaissance and thus initiated and developed the modern world of science.

Notes

1 All dates refer to A.D. unless otherwise specified.
2 Incidentally, the many spellings and pronunciations of Muhammad's name throughout Christian Europe's Medieval period indicate unfamiliarity with Muslim sources in Latin writings. He is referred to, among other names, as Moameth, Mahomet, Mahoun, Mouamed, Mouchamet, Moamed, and Mehmet.
3 Von Greenbaum, Gustave E., *Medieval Islam*, Chicago: University of Chicago Press, Third Impression, 1957, p. 43.
4 *Ibid.*, pp. 44–45.
5 *Ibid.*, p. 45.
6 *Ibid.*, p. 47.
7 *Ibid.*, p. 48.
8 Arnold and Guillaume, *The Legacy of Islam*, pp. 239–240.
9 Wells, H. G., *Outline of History*, 1931, pp. 629–630.
10 *Ibid.*, p. 629.
11 Barsuma was a pupil of Ibas, the great teacher of the School of Edessa. Died 457.
12 O'Leary, *Arabic Thought and Its Place in History*, p. 34.
13 *Ibid.*, p. 34.
14 Ctesiphon was built on the left bank of the Tigris, 25 miles southeast of Baghdad. The city is mentioned by Polybius as early as 220 B.C. Ctesiphon was for a time the winter residence of the Parthian Arsacids after they conquered the region in 129 B.C., until it revolted from the Parthians in the first century A.D. With the founding of the Sassanian dynasty in the next century, the city developed into a metropolis with many impressive buildings. It was captured and plundered by Arabs in 637. When Baghdad became the capital of the Abbassides, Ctesiphon died away, save for a few surviving walls and a magnificent arch.
15 al-Nadim, *Fihrist*, pp. 333–334.
   Masudi, *Murawinij-u'Zhahab of Masudi*, p. 210.
   Safa, *Tarikh Ulum Aqli*, pp. 94–95.
16 *Ibid.*, p. 95.

17 Christensen, Arthur, *L'Iran Sous les Sassanides*, p. 427.

18 Safa, *Tarikh Ulum Aqli*, pp. 96–98.

19 The origin and meaning of the phrase are somewhat obscure. According to Safa, the original name of this academy and of the city in which it was located was Weh-*Andev*-Shapur, which literally means better-than-Antioch-Shapur, or the-city-of-Shapur-which-is-better-than-the-city-of-Antioch, the word *Andeve* being the Pahlavi word for Antioch. Antioch (or Antakyyah) was a model city with well-engineered, straight streets. Other cities tried to surpass Antioch in engineering and beauty, and whether or not they succeeded in doing so, they boasted of their town as better-than-Antioch. So in naming their towns, they pre-faced the names with the phrase, better-than-Antioch; hence the label *wehandev i Shapur*, or better-than-Andev, or Antioch-Shapur; later called Gundi-Shah-Pur, and finally Jundi-Shapur, or Kundi-Shapur. *Ibid.*, p. 98, using authority of *Mojmal-ut-Tavarikh*, p. 256; and Estakhri's *Masalik-ul-Mamalik*, p. 93. This method of naming cities was quite in fashion among the Sassanian Persians. Another example is that of a town built by Anushirwan called *Beh-az-andiv-i-Khasra*, or the-city-of-Khasra-better-than-andiv (Antioch). *Ibid.*, pp. 98–99.

20 *Ibid.*, p. 93.

21 Ghafti, *Akhbar-al-Hokama*, or *Annals of Learned Men*, p. 93. Translated from Persian as quoted by Safa, p. 99.

22 Browne, *Arabic Medicine*, p. 23; Sarton, Vol. 1, pp. 435–436; Sykes, Sir Percy, *History of Persia*, Vol. I, 1915, pp. 40–41; Durant, pp. 246–258.

23 Hitti, *History of the Arabs*, p. 309.

24 O'Leary, *Arabic Thought*, pp. 41–42.

25 Edessa was the intellectual headquarters of Christian-Syrian and Harran of non-Christian-Syrian, Sabians, or Sabi'uns.

26 Safa, *Tarikh Ulum Aqli*, p. 103; Safa, *Hellenic Learning (Sciences) Among Sassanians*, pp. 27–28. In Persian.

27 Heath, Th. L., *The Thirteen Books of Euclid's Elements*, Vol. III, Cambridge: 1908. Cited by Sarton, Vol. I, p. 421.

28 Sarton, *Introduction to the History of Science*, Vol. I., p. 423. According to Sarton, "The Berlin edition of *Greek Commentaries of Aristotle* includes the following by Simplicios: In Vol. 2 *de anima*, edited by Nich Hayduck (375 pp., 1882); Vol. 7, *de Coelo*, edited J. L. Heibert (796 pp., 1895); Vol. 8, *Categories* edited Carl Kalbfleisch (1907); Vol. 9–10 *Physicorum libri* edited Hermann Diels (2 vols., 1,500 pp. 1882–1895)." Sarton, Vol. I, p. 423.

29 *Ibid.*, Vol. I., p. 372; Browne, E. G., *Arabic Medicine*, p. 20.

30 *Ibid.*, p. 23; Sykes, M., *History of Persia*, Vol. I, pp. 40–41. Browne, E. G., *A Literary History of Persia*, Vol. I, p. 4.

31 Hitti, *History of the Arabs*, pp. 308–309.

32 Arnold and Guillaume, *Legacy of Islam*, pp. 315–319.

33 al-Nadim, *Fihrist*, pp. 333–334; Masudi, *Murawwij-ul-Thabab*, Cairo: p. 210.

34 Safa, *Tarikh Adabiyyat*, p. 95.

35 *Ibid.*, pp. 96–97.

36 *Ibid.*, p. 97.

37 Safa, *Tarikh Ulum Aqli*, pp. 52–56.

38 *Ibid.*, pp. 61–62.

39 Sarton, *An Introduction to the History of Science*, Vol. I, p. 565.

40 Safa, *Tarikh Ulum Aqli*, pp. 56–58.

41 *Ibid.*, pp. 58–59.

42 *Ibid.*, pp. 87–88.

43 *Ibid.*, p. 63.

44 Sarton, Vol. I, p. 530.

45 *Ibid.*, p. 613.
46 Safa, *Tarikh Ulum Aqli*, p. 60.
47 Sarton, Vol. I, p. 556.
48 Safa, *Tarikh Ulum Aqli*, p. 62.
49 *Ibid.*, pp. 63–71.
50 *Ibid.*, pp. 71–73.
51 *Ibid.*, pp. 73–74.
52 Sarton, Vol. I, p. 613.
53 Safa, *Tarikh Ulum Aqli*, pp. 75–79.
54 Sarton, Vol. I, pp. 599–600.
55 Safa, *Tarikh Adabiyyat*, pp. 108–114.
56 Safa, *Tarikh Ulum Aqli*, p. 85.
57 *Ibid.*, p. 60.
58 *Ibid.*, p. 63.
59 The following Hellenistic authors were translated into Arabic during this period: Alexander of Aphrodisias, and Alexander of Tralles, Anazarbas, Apollonius, Archigenes, Archimedes, Aristarchus, Aristotle, Asclepius, Autolycus, Damascius of Damascus, Diophantus, Dracon, Erophile, Erasistratus, Euclid, Eudemus, Eutocius of Ascalon, Galen, Gregory of Nysse, Hipparchus, Heron of Alexandria, Hippocrates, Iambilichus, Jasides, Claudius of Alexandria, Theodosius, Theon of Alexandria, Theophrastus, and Thessalus.
60 Sarton, Vol. I, pp. 562, 598, 600, 613; Vol. II, Book III, p. 686; Safa, *Tarikh Ulum Aqli*, pp. 79, 86.
61 Safa, *Tarikh Ulum Aqli*, pp. 89–91.
62 Yaqut, *Dictionary of Learned Men*, Vol. V, p. 231. Vol. VI, p. 343.
63 Le Strange, O., *Bagdad During the Abbasid Caliphate*, Oxford, 1900, 240–266.
64 Makkari, *History of the Muhammadan Dynasties in Spain*, trans. by de Cayangos, London, 1840, 2 v., VII, pp. 139–200.
65 Shalaby, 217.
66 *Al Lu'lu Al-Nazim fi Rawm al-Ta' Allum Wal-Ta'lim*, referred to in *Ahlwardt Verzerchmiss der Arabischen Haudschriften*, Vol. I, p. 28c. See Totah, p. 56.
67 Browne, Vol. I, 377–390.
68 Elgood, Cyril, *A Medical History of Persia*, Cambridge University Press, 1951, 234–235.
69 *Ibid.*, 236.
70 *Ibid.*, 240.
71 *Ibid.*, 244.
72 Hunayn, "The Examination of the Doctors" in *Mu'Allem al-Kubra* (*The Great Teacher*) by ibn al-Ukhawwa. Chapter 45. Geble Memorial Edition, cited in Elgood, *Medical History of Persia.*
73 Elgood, Cyril, *A Medical History of Persia*, 234–260.
   Browne, G. E., *Arabic Medicine.*
74 Haskins, *Medieval Science.*
   Coulton, G. C., *Medieval Panorama.* Cambridge University Press, 1940.

References

Arnold, Sir Edwin and Alfred Guillaume, eds., *The Legacy of Islam*, London: Oxford University Press, 1931.

Browne, Edward Granville, *A literary History of Persia*, 4 vols. Cambridge (Eng): The University Press, 1908, reprinted 1909. Vol. I, *From the Earliest Times Until Firdawsi*, 1906, reprinted 1915. Vol. II, *From Firdawsi to Sa'di*, 1920, reprinted

1928. Vol. III, *Tartar Dominion*—1265–1502, 1924, reprinted 1928. Vol. IV, Modern Times—1500–1924.

Browne, Edward Granville, *Arabic Medicine*, Cambridge (Eng.): The University Press, 1921.

Christensen, A., *L'Iran Sous les Sassanides*, Copenhagen: Ejnar Munksgaard, 1944.

Durant, Will, *The Age of Faith*, New York: Simon and Schuster, 1950.

Elgood, C., *A Medical History of Persia and the Eastern Caliphate*, Cambridge (Eng.): The University Press, 1951.

Ghafti, *Akhbar-al-Hokama*, (Annals of Learned Men), Cairo: no publ mentioned, 1325 Shamsi Hejira (in Persian).

Haskins, C. H., *Studies in the History of Medieval Science*, Cambridge: Harvard University Press, 1927.

Hitti, Phillip K., *History of the Arabs*, 6th ed., London: Macmillan Co., 1956.

Masudi, *Murawinij-u'Zhahab*, Cairo: no publ or date.

Nadim, abu-al-Faraj, Muhammad ibn-Ishaq, *Kitab al-Fihrist*, ed. by G. Flugel, Leipzig: Vogel, 1871.

O'Leary, Delacy L., *Arabic Thought and Its Place in History*, New York: Dutton, 1922.

Safa, Dr. Dhabih Allah, *Danish-hayi Yunani dar Shahan Shahi Sassani*, (Greek Science in the Sassanian Empire), Teheran: Rangin Press, 1330 Shamsi Hejira (in Persian).

Safa, Dr. Dhabih Allah, *Tarikhi Adabiyyat dar Iran*, (Literary History of Iran from the Middle of the Fifth Century to the Beginning of Seventh Century Hejira), Vol. II, Teheran: Elmiyyah Islamiyyah Press, 1339 Shamsi Hejira (in Persian).

Safa, Dr. Dhabih Allah, *Tarikh Ulum Aqli dar Tamadduni Islami*, (History of Rational Sciences in Islamic Civilization), Vols. I and II, Teheran: Danishgah Press, 1336 Shamsi Hejira (in Persian).

Sarton, George, *Introduction to the History of Science*, Baltimore: The Williams and Wilkins Co., Vol. I, 1927; Vol. II Part I and II 1931; Vol. III Part I and II, 1948.

Shalaby, Ahmad, *History of Muslim Education*, Beirut: Dar al-Kashshaf, 1954.

Sykes, Sir Percy M., *History of Persia*, 2 vols., London: Macmillan, 1930.

Totah, K. A., *The Contributions of the Arabs to Education*, New York: Columbia University Press, 1926.

Wells, H. G., *The Outline of History*, New York: Garden City Books, 1949.

Yaqut, *Dictionary of Learned Men*, ed. D. S. Margoliouth, Cairo: no publ mentioned, 1907.

2

ANTECEDENTS (BEFORE 1900)

J. F. Ade Ajayi, Lameck K. H. Goma and
G. Ampah Johnson

Source: J. F. Ade Ajayi, Lameck K. H. Goma and G. Ampah Johnson, *The African Experience with Higher Education*, Accra: Association of African Universities, in association with James Curry, London and Ohio University Press, Athens, Ohio, 1996, pp. 1–27.

Introduction

We in Zambia are immensely proud of our University. This pride is not simply that this is our first and only University. It is also because the university of Zambia is our own University in a very real sense. The story of how the people of this country responded so enthusiastically to my appeal for support is a very thrilling one. Humble folk in every corner of our nation – illiterate villagers, barefooted school children, prison inmates and even lepers – gave freely and willingly everything they could, often in the form of fish, or maize or chickens. The reason for this extraordinary response was that our people see in the University the hope of a better and fuller life for their children and grand children. (President Kenneth Kaunda, at the Chancellor's Installation Banquet, July 12, 1966, in *Addresses at the Installation . . .*, University of Zambia, 1966, p.28).

President Kaunda's after-dinner address captured the sense of communal pride and identity which everywhere initially greeted the coming of the University to Africa. In responding so enthusiastically to the University, and pinning so much hope on it for "a better and fuller life for their children and grand children", what picture of the University did the "humble folk", "the illiterate villagers", have in their minds? In what "real sense" was the University their very own? Again and again, the people dance to welcome the University and bring their fishes and best wishes on the day of inauguration but, if they ventured to show up at the gates on the day after inauguration, they find that no one there knows their name or understands their language.

The debate about what constitutes the African University, and how to make the University in Africa the "very own" University of African peoples, is central to the African experience with higher education. This debate is one of a species of intellectual arguments which rage or ebb from time to time about what constitutes African Christianity, African Islam, African philosophy, African Science or African University; or whether such concepts are in fact contradictions and convey little meaning in practical reality. For example, Islam is universal in its doctrine and centered on Mecca in its practice. Its core message as revealed in the Koran is not even allowed to be translated into languages other than Arabic. Nevertheless, in the practice of the religion, in the rise of different schools of Islamic Law, and the operation of different brotherhoods in the daily life of Muslims, cultural differences are clearly observable. However, is African identity something that Islam in non-Arab Africa should acquire or try hard to get away from? Is Islam in Timbuktu after nine or ten centuries African?

Similarly, the central doctrine of Christianity is in the Bible and is universal. The interaction of English culture and Christianity was such, especially since the Reformation, that the "Church of England" which missionaries brought to Africa in the 19th century, was not just the Church in England. Yet missionaries from that Church could still argue that organizing the Church in Africa into an African Church does not imply the possibility of African Christianity as a concept. Is it, then, possible to adapt African culture to Christianity and still remain African, or adapt Christianity to African culture and still remain Christian?

If it is not easy to separate practice from doctrine in religion, should it not be easier to separate methodology or form from content in branches of knowledge? Though musicology as a universal "science" may be controversial, African music provokes little controversy; it is distinguished from European music not only in content, but also in structure and form. Why, then, has there been so much debate about African philosophy? Many African philosophers insist that it is methodology, not the content, that defines philosophy as a branch of knowledge; that it is the thought of individuals when it conforms to certain methodological criteria that constitutes philosophy and, as such, anthropological summation of the thinking within a community about God or governance or social relations does not constitute philosophy.

The concept of African philosophy has been so controversial partly because of the close link between philosophy and religion, and the fear that African philosophy promotes the idea of African Christianity. Sometimes, the objection is to the lack of precision or definition in the concept of "African". Is it a geographical or a cultural concept? Does it cover the whole continent or just the land of Black people South of the Sahara, or even of Africans in the diaspora? Is it a summation of all the cultures or an analysis of the presumed "African" factor common to all? Thus, many people who have no problem with the concept of Western thought or Western education argue that while you could have Luo or Ewe philosophy or culture, African culture or philosophy is too much of an abstraction. Advocates of the concept of African philosophy have therefore responded by studies of African sagacity, the thoughts of individual African sages or wise men, analyzed within the framework and the methodology acceptable to Western philosophy.

With specific reference to higher education, some people argue that, even though it is possible to distinguish indigenous and Islamic traditions of higher education from the Western tradition, the modern University is exclusively within the Western tradition. This was the view initially taken by Ashby in the 1960s: that indigenous systems of education were "inward looking, conducted by members of the extended family, directed to ensuring conformity with social custom and acquiescence in the hierarchy of the community"; that Islamic traditions of education relied on "the technique of learning by rote" and transmitting truths which "rested on authority and not on observation or enquiry"; and therefore, while it could be adapted to be more responsive to African needs and environment, the University is "essentially a mechanism for the inheritance of the Western style of civilization". (Ashby, 1966 pp.147–8; 1974 p.2). Even after further research has shown that indigenous education did more than socialize and that Islamic education, especially secular disciplines in Islamic education, promoted observation and enquiry, Philip Altbach warned in 1982 that it is not easy to create "indigenous" academic models: the "institutional patterns, pedagogical techniques and, perhaps most important, the basic structure of knowledge" in our Universities are Western in origin. (Chideya, 1982, Altbach on p.47, Mazrui *cit.* on p.24). As Ali Mazrui put it, in opposition to other scholars like Robin Horton, the very rationality that we employ in our universities is of Western origin. How, then, are the Universities to be made African: how do we adapt the University to African culture so it can provide African development, not westernization? To what extent can a review of attitudes to knowledge in traditional societies or a survey of precolonial models of higher education provide useful insights into the intricacies of the problem?

Indigenous education

Studies of sagacity have drawn attention to the role of the sage in traditional African societies. (Oruka, 1991). The sage is recognized as a philosopher, an original thinker whose words of wisdom and advice are widely sought both by private individuals and public officials. He is reputed as a person very knowledgeable about traditional history, laws, customs and folklore, whose testimony is needed in resolving disputes and litigation over issues such as succession to office or property, land, inter- and intra-kinship relationships. He may also be knowledgeable about the properties of different plants and animals, and become a healer or a rain-maker. He may practise as a diviner, arbitrator or consultant. His wisdom may have come as a result of unusual personal experience interpreted as revelation, or from special anointing or possession by a deity associated with wisdom. He is treated with respect and awe because profundity of knowledge was generally viewed as signifying access to supernatural powers. Because of the high status of the man of knowledge in society, there may be an element of individual craving for knowledge and wisdom, and, therefore, self-education. More often, the sage as a leader of thought is a product of the formal or informal processes of indigenous higher education.

It is now clear that indigenous education involved far more than an inward-looking process of socialization. There were no clear-cut gradations, but it is possible to speak of an elementary level where, besides basic moral education and socialization into the kinship group and the larger community, the child learnt from the mother and other adults within the household to talk, to count, and appreciate subtleties of the language. The method is largely informal, between mother and child, but also communal for children of the same age grade within the household, through riddles and conundrums, games, fables and story-telling. At the second level, the child is educated partly through an informal system of apprenticeship to one or more adults to acquire skills in an occupation and the knowledge relevant for the pursuit of that occupation. There was also more formal training in educational establishments organized usually at puberty rites or within age grade associations, sometimes by the state, sometimes by secret societies such as the Poro or Bundo in the Upper Guinea area, about the traditions and values of the community, necessary to get the teenager acceptable as an adult member of society.

Forms of higher education existed primarily for training rulers and priests. Selection of candidates was rather complex, including membership of particular families and some evidence of special vocation or calling by the divinities concerned. Essentially, the training was through attachment and apprenticeship. Favoured children accompanied parents or grandparents to meetings where they learnt the art of public speaking and observed customary ways of dealing with issues. Acolytes were initiated into orders of priesthood and trained to progress from one degree to another. They learnt sacred chants and other esoteric knowledge, varieties of ritual dance and other aspects of religion and folklore. The system of education remained predominantly oral, eclectic and even esoteric. There was keen observation, collation and analysis of the properties of things. But its epistemology placed emphasis not so much on rationality as on the deeper meaning and the power of words, particularly the names of things. Sometimes, the knowledge of sacred chants and traditions acquired by an acolyte was tested at public ceremonies. There were opportunities for retreat and reflection and various exercises during which the divinities were expected to "possess" and teach the acolytes. Although indigenous education was, thus, permeated by traditional religion, and was therefore specific to each culture and language community, occasionally the sage practising as a diviner or healer, acquired such reputation as transcended the local community and could, thus, attract students from a wide region. In this and other ways, knowledge spread from one community to another. Thus indigenous higher education produced and transmitted new knowledge necessary for understanding the world, the nature of man, society, God and various divinities, the promotion of agriculture and health, literature and philosophy.

The man of knowledge or sage often had to earn his living within the household from the occupation prevalent in the community such as farming, hunting or fishing. As he became better known, he may begin to concentrate on specialist occupations as healer, diviner, court historian, judicial advocate or assessor, or several combinations of these. He thus needed recognition and patronage from the community. Those knowledgeable in history, literature and philosophy often made their reputation from "performing" during festivals, sometimes on a competitive basis. Thus, the community in general, and rulers in particular, through their patronage promoted the search for knowledge and skills, for example in healing particular diseases. They conferred titles and various privileges including gifts of land and farming estates on noted men of knowledge, or heads of the guild of court drummers, *griots,* diviners or healers. Yet such groups in their literary compositions and public performances also acted as social critics and conscience of the people. This sometimes bred tension, if not open conflict, with the authorities. Rulers have been known to show their annoyance when diviners failed to divine what the rulers wanted to hear, or if the *griots* became uncomfortably critical.

The legacy of Alexandria

The roots of the University as a community of scholars, with an international outlook but also with responsibilities within particular cultures, can be traced back to two institutions that developed in Egypt in the last two or three centuries B.C. and A.D. One is the Alexandria Museum and Library, and the other is the monastic system.

The Ptolemies in the 3rd Century B.C. decided to build their capital in Alexandria with its excellent harbour and nodal point of routes connecting the Mediterranean with the Red Sea and the Indian Ocean. They also built there the famous Museum and Library with the aim of assembling in one centre, through purchase or systematic copying of manuscripts, the whole of contemporary knowledge. Soon, more than 200,000 volumes were collected. The Library became known as the greatest cultural repository of its time. It attracted all the leading scholars from the Egyptian, North African, Greek, Roman, and Jewish worlds. Illustrious specialists were appointed on fellow-ships to manage the collection of books and guide the younger scholars within a collegiate system:

> Scientists and men of letters lived in this institution. They were housed and fed and were able to give themselves up entirely to their research and studies, with no menial duties to perform. Its organization was similar to that of modern universities, except that the resident scholars were not required to give lectures.
>
> (Riad, 1981, p.192)

Some of the most advanced intellectual work of the period was done in Alexandria. For example, Eratosthenes, the father of scientific geography who measured the circumference of the earth, an African from Cyrenaica, was Librarian there; Strabo, the Greek geographer, the last of whose 17-volume treatise is on Egypt, our best source on the Museum; and there were other famous scholars in cosmography and astronomy; Euclid, Archimedes and others in mathematics, especially geometry; Manetho, the Egyptian scholar-priest, one of the most important sources on ancient Egypt, even though his *Aegyptica* survives only in fragments; poets, historians and other literary men to whom we owe the survival of the tragedies of Aeschylus, the comedies of Aristophanes, the odes of Pindar and Bacchylides, and the histories of Herodotus and Thucydides; Theophratus, the founder of scientific botany; Herophilus, Erasistratus and other pioneers of human anatomy and physiology. The Library suffered damage when Julius Caesar set fire to ships in the harbour of Alexandria. Gradual decline set in during the instability of the period of Roman rule: instability in Rome and the consequent inability to defend the outlying province from attacks from Asia Minor. The scholars scattered and many of the books found their way to Rome, but the legacy of Alexandria remained:

> ... the fascination of the ancient Alexandria lies in the fact that it was at the root of a remarkable scientific movement which remained unrivalled until modern times. For well over a millennium, the scholarly achievements of ancient Alexandria served as guiding lights for the great humanists of the European Renaissance. It is perhaps legitimate to say that before the Alexandrian era, knowledge had been to a great extent regional, but with the creation of the Alexandrina as the first universal library in the history of mankind, knowledge too, became at once universal.
>
> (El-Abbadi, 1990, pp.15–16)

It was because of the strength of the intellectual foundations laid by the Library and Museum that Alexandria played such a notable role in the doctrinal controversies of the Early Christian Church. It was the unique contribution of Alexandria, through the work of St. Clement, "a man of prodigious erudition" and his pupil Origen, "under whom philosophical speculation and philological interest reached their summit", and other scholars to situate the message of Christianity within classical tradition and attempt to reconcile them. Secondly, the Patriarchs of Alexandria, notably St. Athanasius and St. Cyril, played a prominent role in the Arian controversy of the 4th and 5th centuries. This was a theological debate on which the unity of the Latin and the Greek Orthodox or Byzantine Church foundered. The Council of Chalcedon eventually ruled that Christ was one person with two intimately united natures, whereas the Patriarchs of Alexandria held fast to the belief that Christ had but one nature, a divine nature, and that the apparent human nature was but an outward show. This is the doctrine of Monophysitism which has remained central in the theology of the Egyptian and Ethiopian Coptic Church. (Donadoni, 1981).

The spirit of resistance and local patriotism thus symbolized by Alexandria bred the monastic system. Monophysite Christianity together with the spirit of resistance spread fast among the peasants of Egypt on whom Roman taxes fell so heavily. It is said that the practice developed of many peasants abandoning their farms and fleeing into the desert to make a new life as hermits away from tax gatherers. Soon, this developed a religious dimension, of people leaving as a group not only to escape tax gatherers but in fact to escape from the world, to seek contemplation, and mystic union with God. They were called anchorites (tax evaders) in derision. They often pooled their resources, lived communally and frugally, cultivated farms and traded their produce jointly. In their search for contemplation, they attracted teachers and religious guides. Thus arose the monasteries, with leaders emerging later to found different monastic orders to regulate the monastic way of life. Monasteries developed not only within Christianity but also Islam and became models for communal living favouring the search for knowledge as a joint enterprise.

Islamic education

By contrast with indigenous education, Islamic education operated within a unified structure, based on the written word of the Koran which had to be comprehended in Arabic. Teachers could therefore migrate from one place to another, and the pattern remained the same. There were teachers who made their living from teaching children rudiments of Arabic and the Koran usually in the open verandahs of their own homes. They received alms and gifts from the children's parents, while the children also helped with various occupations on the side, such as farming, leather work and various crafts, including even buying and selling. The informality of the system ensured that the children were brought up within particular cultures. The local particularities, however, diminished the higher the student climbed towards the sophistication of universal Islamic culture. A few of the teachers were qualified to take on more advanced pupils at the secondary level in introductory courses to Arabic philosophy, exposition of the Koran, and the life of the Prophet. Alternatively, some mosques organised *madrasas* or colleges along monastic lines for such advanced students, and supplemented the teaching by public colloquia, especially during the month of Ramadan. Some of the madrasas attracted enough reputable teachers and the courses of instruction were organised more formally like universities, with princely endowment, adequate libraries, and curricula built around one or more of the schools of Islamic law, advanced philology, Hadith, History, and Geography. More usually, the most reputable teachers were engaged in a variety of other activities as judges, diplomats, etc. and attracted students to study at their feet in a range of authorities and move on to other reputable teachers. The itinerant scholar, therefore, remained an important feature of Islamic higher education.

Thus, Islamic education, like the indigenous pattern of education, was rooted in religion. Particularly in the case of Islam, learning was an aspect of religious life. As Islam spread in Africa, – in Egypt and the Nile Valley, North Africa, the Maghreb and Western Sahara, from those centres to the Western and Central Sudan, and from Arabia to the Coast and islands of East Africa, – Islamic education spread with it. Islam spread initially through conquest and colonization, and the warring leaders patronized Islamic education as a weapon of state building. Later, Islam spread more through commercial and missionary activities followed by periodic reforms through jihads, with Muslim teachers and scholars rather than rulers taking the initiative. There were, thus, two major factors in the expansion of learning and scholarship within Islam. The first was the need of rulers to use scholars in their administration, especially in building up Islamic arts and culture in urban centres. The rulers employed learned men as diplomats, imams of mosques, judges, jurists, advisers on governance, law and taxation. The more prosperous the regime became, the more the rulers built not only palaces but also mosques and madrasas, and the more they attracted scholars from far and near. Thus a community of scholars ('ulama) grew up, often international, but also usually with a core of local scholars who had themselves travelled and studied at the major international centres of Islamic higher education. The second factor was the need of pious Muslims seeking contemplation. There were holy men who sought retreat in desert oases or fortified centres (ribat). More often the seat of the holy man develops into a monastery where mysticism is combined with advanced study in theology or jurisprudence. The monasteries became centres of learning which may or may not have developed formally into madrasas or organised colleges or universities.

The oldest Islamic University in Africa is Karawiyyin founded in 859 in the Old City of Fez around the Mosque by the Idrisids, a Sharifin dynasty, one of the many struggling to conquer the Maghrib, and hold it, if possible, as part of the wider Muslim empire. The Idrisids brought in Arab merchants and scholars from Kayrawan in Tunisia and Cordoba in Spain to establish an urban centre, propagating Sunni Islam in the midst of the Kharijite heresy of the Berbers, and upholding the supremacy of Arab and Berber Muslims in the midst of non-Muslim Berber groups resisting such domination. Fez thus became a centre for propagating Arab orthodox Islamic culture. The assemblage of scholars around the Karawiyyin Mosque became a powerful tool in that endeavour. The Idrisids endowed the University well. But as empires rose and fell – the Almoravids, the Almohads, the Marinids, etc. – the community of influential scholars acquired a certain independence of their own and became an important prize that awaited whoever controlled the capital city of central Morocco, but whose favour and loyalty also had to be specially courted. Karawiyyin University thus became a major force in the history of Islamic scholarship not only in the Maghrib, but also in the Sahara, and the Western Sudan. It played a notable role in the spread of the Maliki Code, the blending of the cultures of the Maghreb and Andalusia, and the rise of a distinctive Moroccan impact on Islam, especially Sufism and religious Brotherhoods, with their Shaykhs and marabouts. (Talbi, 1988).

The Fatimids founded the city of Cairo in 969 and decided to make it the capital of a Caliphate in succession to the Abbasids of Bagdad. They at once built barracks for their army, a palace and a mosque named Al-Azhar. Religious ideology played a prominent role in the contest to build a stable Caliphate: between Sunni and Shiite, between dynasties originating in the Hejaz, and those originating from Ifriqiya, or even further West in Berber country. The Fatimids were soon replaced by competing Ayyubid princes and they in turn soon lost power to the Mamluk garrison – white Turkish slaves, recruited early into the army, trained and exercised in the wars of the Crusades. They were stationed in Egypt to protect important trade routes and the Holy Land. With the divisions among the Ayyubids, they began to select the Sultan from among their own leaders and they maintained stability and prosperity in Egypt from 1250–1517 when they lost power to the Ottoman Sultan in Istanbul. Much of the trade and financial administration was in the hands of Christians and Jews. Thus with Mamluk nobles controlling the administration both in the capital and the provinces, they welcomed the community of scholars at Al-Azhar who concentrated on training students, promoted Sunni orthodoxy, and attracted an international staff from Andalusia, the Maghreb, Syria, the Hejaz, etc., that made Al-Azhar so famous and influential throughout the Islamic world, especially in Africa. Among the most famous teachers was Ibn Khaldun, the historian and sociologist, who arrived in Cairo in 1382 and lived there till his death in 1421. It was in Cairo that he did most of the work on his *Universal History*, and he was appointed again and again the grand Kadi of Maliki law. At the same time, while preserving their international character, the 'ulama of Al-Azhar fulfilled the important function of creating a specifically Egyptian stamp on Sunni orthodoxy, and they began to make themselves spokesmen of the Egyptian people, protesting against the luxury and exploitative practices of the Mamluk nobility. (Garcin, 1984).

Because of its location on the southern edge of the desert and at a strategic point on the routes linking the trading cities of the Niger Bend to the trade routes southwards to the gold producing areas, Timbuktu rose in the 12th and 13th centuries as a cosmopolitan urban centre which the different hegemonic powers – Mali, Mossi, Songhai, Bambara and even Morocco – tried to control. In fact, the foreign merchants there came to enjoy a high degree of autonomy. Partly for this reason, it also attracted scholars and students from far and near. Timbuktu became famous as a holy city of many Muslims distinguished by their piety and their quest for learning. The scholars became the greatest defenders of Timbuktu's claim to be a "little state within a state". (Hunwick, 1966, p.313). In the 14th and 15th centuries, the trend was for rulers of Mali or Songhai going on pilgrimage to import scholars from Al-Azhar, or for Sudanese students to go to Fez or Al-Azhar and surprise their teachers with their great ability. By the 16th century, the bulk of the teachers and holders of such offices as imams, kadis and khutabs, not only in Timbuktu but also in the other major centres like Walata, Jenne and Gao were Sudanese. Accounts of visitors to the Sudan suggest that the population of Timbuktu was about 80,000; that in the 16th century, there were about 180 koranic schools, and thousands of students from all parts of the Sudan and the Sahel who lived with their teachers or as lodgers.

The University of Timbuktu was not as centralized as al-Karawiyyin of Fez or Al-Azhar of Cairo, but consisted of a number of independent schools ("of transmission") of which those around the Mosque of Sankore (Sankara) were the best known. The scholars did not receive regular stipends, but some of them lived in communities or monasteries where their material needs were taken care of by the Mosque and they could devote their attention to their teaching. The best known "schools" were loose associations of outstanding scholars and their circle of friends, relations and students, differentiated from others in their curricula depending on the preferences of their masters. This tendency to differentiate curricula was counterbalanced by the integrative role of the Mosques, especially Sankore, where the courses of study offered were essentially open to all students who could qualify.

It has been said that in the 16th and 17th centuries, the intellectual life of Timbuktu was in fact dominated by three families of which the best known was the Aqit family. The school financed itself from patronage, and from official positions of the master and other prominent members of the school. The student attached himself to a particular scholar of repute, and not only attended the lectures and tutorials of the master, but also acted as his assistant and secretary, and was present at his audiences at all times. (Saad, 1983, chapter 3). The courses of instruction covered the usual ones of theology, exegesis, traditions, Malikite jurisprudence, as well as grammar, rhetoric, logic, astrology, astronomy, history and geography. Science and mathematics was very little developed. Malikite jurisprudence was a particular speciality. The method of instruction was essentially exposition and commentaries on texts and authorities in the scholastic fashion.

In spite of the constraints of this methodology, it is unlikely that the initially international staff could have been transformed to a predominantly Sudanese one without leaving a distinctly Sudanese imprint on their scholarship. Moreover, the 'ulama were actively involved in the expansion of Islam to the Central Sudan and other parts of West Africa. They contributed to the development of other notable centres of learning, especially in Kano, Katsina and Ngazargamo. Yet, Cisoko's verdict that through the University of Timbuktu "Sudanese humanism became a fundamental part of worldwide Islam" (1984, p.208) has to be balanced with the views of Dramani-Issifou that "Islamo-centrism made the universities of Timbuktu seem less brilliant than black Africans today would wish, as they can discern in those universities, as far as our present knowledge goes, hardly a trace of their cultural past". This, he added, was because the Muslim scholars belonged to a fairly closed world and were a small minority group facing a mass of adherents of African traditional religion whom they thought themselves duty bound to convert. (1988, p.112). The issue then is whether their passion for Islam and their operating within a closed system of universal Islam meant that they had lost all traces of Sudanese culture.

Unfortunately, little of the writings of the scholars at the University of Timbuktu survived the vandalism of the Moroccan invaders in 1591. The two outstanding works that we have – Al-Sadi's *Tarikh al-Sudan* (History of the Sudan, 1655) and the *Tarikh al-Fattash*, (Chronicles of the Researcher, 1664) compiled by Mahmud Ka'ti from various notes recorded by different members of his family – show clearly that the Sudanese scholars might have written completely within the traditions of Islamic scholarship and historiography, but they were certainly not remote from local oral traditions of the peoples and cultures of the Sudan.

Afro-Christian and Western education

In Ethiopia, education was the exclusive preserve of the Orthodox Church which organised and supported a wide range of educational establishments which dominated the cultural, religious, literary, artistic and even scientific life of Ethiopians. However, while Koranic schools tended to become universal in Muslim communities, especially in the urban areas, because of the necessity for every mature Muslim to comprehend the message of Islam in Arabic, only the children of the ruling class and others aspiring to be monks or priests went to school in Ethiopia. Traditionally, there were three levels of schools: the *Nebab Bet* (School of Reading) at the elementary level; at the secondary level were the *Quedasse Bet* (School of Holy Mass) and the *Quine Bet* (School of Poetry); and a variety of institutions of higher education referred to collectively as the *Metshafit Bet* (School of the Holy Books or Scriptures).

This pattern went back to the Zagwe period (c. 1100–1270), but it became more widespread and established during the expansion and consolidation of the Solomonid dynasty from the late 13th to the early 16th centuries. The emperors preferred to retain the arrangement by which the Bishop at the head of the Ethiopian Church was chosen from the Coptic Church in Egypt, which required the cooperation of the Mamluk Sultans. Sometimes the cooperation was not easy to obtain – there was no Bishop between 1458 and 1480 and therefore no ordinations, with the consequent shortage of priests. The emperors put up with the situation because of the strong links with the traditions of Alexandria, and the Egyptian connection was the main guarantee of contact with the outside Christian world, through Alexandria to the Byzantine Church, the Holy Land and even the Latin Church. With such an arrangement, the educational system of the Church was a vital factor in the development of an indigenous culture and outlook.

The pillar of the system was the monastic school that Iyesus-Mo'a established on Lake Hayk, and others patterned after it, including Debre Libanos. Later, two monastic orders rose to establish and regulate life in the monasteries. The monasteries were generally located in remote areas, initially for people seeking contemplation and personal salvation, and this tended to encourage the autonomy of each institution. But the more successful ones also began to attract scholars and train students for the priesthood and administrative and other state functions. The monastic schools thus became an essential "preparatory ground for national leadership. Apart from being born into a rich and powerful family, gaining meritorious distinction as a religious scholar was the most reliable way of joining the Christian elite". (Tadese Tamrat, 1984, p.441). There was the special monastery on the inaccessible Mount Geshen where all eligible princes were confined so as to simplify the process of succession. The princes were kept fully engaged there on the study and practice of Ge'ez poetry, Sacred Music, Church History, and Exegesis of Holy Scriptures, away from any possible intrigue. If a vacancy occurred, the selected prince was sent for to ascend the throne.

The emperors gave generous grants of land to the monasteries, but could not always effectively control them. In return, the monasteries produced candidates for ordination as priests who were to preside over different congregations, manage elementary schools and lead the Church into newly conquered areas. The aim of the highly elaborate system of education in the Orthodox Church was, thus, to conserve and to extend an existing culture, rather than to change it. Nevertheless, as an Ethiopian educationist reminds us:

> the notion of prescribed school curricula varying from one level of schooling to another, administration of examinations to test the completion of prescribed curricula, ceremonial manifestations marking graduation ceremonies, the awarding of a diploma with a seal affixed to it, and other aspects of present day formal education had existed for many centuries, especially in the northern provinces of Ethiopia.
>
> (Habte, 1976, p.116)

The expansion of Islam and Arabic influence succeeded in choking up the Latin Church in North Africa, reduce the Coptic Church in Egypt to a minority sect and the Church in Ethiopia into a beleaguered one. The Latin Church eventually made contact with West, Central and Southern Africa from the 15th Century onwards in the era of the slave trade. The Portuguese voyages of exploration and trade were sent out under royal charter, and monastic orders, notably the Benedictines and later the Jesuits, were invited to send missionaries and establish schools. Other European countries soon joined in the trade, – the British, Dutch, Danes, French – usually through chartered companies. As a result, small colonies of Europeans, mulattos and Africans developed at the main trading stations, notably in St. Louis and Goree in Senegal; Cape Coast, Elmina and Accra on the Gold Coast, Benin and the Kingdom of the Kongo. For the needs of these colonies some form of elementary schools began to be established to teach reading, writing and accounting in the different European languages. To provide teachers for such schools, boys were sent abroad for further education. Some of them became famous scholars abroad like Anton Amo from the Gold Coast who became a philosopher at the Martin Luther University in Halle, Germany, or Jacobis Capitein and Philip Quaque who returned as teachers, pioneers of an increasing number of Africans who went abroad for higher education.

The overall effect of the slave trade, especially the trans-Atlantic slave trade in the period 1600–1850, was profoundly disruptive of African social and intellectual life. The competition among European powers to control the trade, and the increasingly dehumanized capitalist mode adopted, promoted depopulation of youths, able-bodied men and women of child-bearing age on a scale that no society could contain without severe damaging effects. It strengthened some communities along the coast who, in self-defence, preyed on their neighbours until they themselves became victims of the internecine conflict. It encouraged the growth of slavery as the preferred mode of production. It disrupted intellectual life, the arts, crafts, manufacturing, agricultural production, peaceful trade and all notions of communal solidarity. The focus of the trade, and periods of worst disruption, shifted from place to place – Senegambia, Upper Guinea, Volta Region, Niger Delta, the Congo Basin. In the 19th century, the trans-Atlantic trade merged with the Arab trans-Indian Ocean trade with devastating effect in Central and East Africa. The movement for the abolition of the trade thus involved the need for rehabilitation of the peoples and reconstruction of a badly battered continent, and the renaissance of African civilization.

In the circumstances, the demand for Western education was certainly growing in Africa by the nineteenth century. The French mission to Egypt under Napoleon Bonaparte demonstrated some of the advances that scientific and industrial revolution were making in Europe. Several rulers in Africa, like Muhammad 'Ali in Egypt and Tewodros in Ethiopia, wanted Western schools as precursors of such changes, especially in military technology. Muhammad 'Ali certainly achieved considerable success in setting up a network of secular Western elementary and secondary schools and research institutes, side by side with the traditional koranic schools, madrasas and al-Alzhar. He also sent several students to France, Italy, Britain, Austria and other places in Europe to train as teachers, return to replace the initial international staff, and train the next generation of teachers within the new system of Western education.

However, most of the initiative for stimulating this demand came from Christian missionaries who saw in the campaign for the abolition of the slave trade and the promotion of Western education their most effective weapons for the propagation of Christianity. They did their best to attract children to school for religious instruction and to learn to read and write, usually in European languages. At the same time, they organised Sunday schools and Bible classes for adult converts and candidates for baptism to learn to read the Bible, if possible in African languages. Many of the missionary societies also realized that, if they wished to promote rapid evangelization, they could not ignore some form of training for African teachers and pastors either locally for larger numbers, or abroad at greater expense for a limited few. The missionaries had a fair measure of success in parts of West and South Africa. Their most spectacular success, however, was in Madagascar. There, because of competition between the Protestant London Missionary Society and the Roman Catholics, involving rivalry between Britain and France, and the Malagasy response of trying to play Britain against France, and shifting policy from active encouragement to outright proscription of missionary activities, Christianity took firm root on the central plateau of Imerina. When the Hova oligarchy seized power, a major plan in their reforms of 1869–70 was to organize a universal and compulsory system of state-run elementary schools, a little ahead of similar reforms in Britain. The success in Sierra Leone was also notable, if not so spectacular.

Both Sierra Leone and Liberia originated from the philanthropic venture of catering for the welfare of freed slaves who were viewed as constituting a social problem in Europe and America and were, therefore, repatriated to the West Coast of Africa. The British government took over Sierra Leone as a Crown Colony in 1808 so that it could be used as a base for the activities of the Royal Navy in its determination to enforce the abolition of the trans-Atlantic slave trade. That campaign became the motive force for British activities in West Africa leading eventually to the establishment of colonial rule towards the end of the nineteenth century. In the task of rehabilitating the freed slaves brought from Europe and North America, or freed in the course of the abolitionist campaign, the British depended very much on the cooperation of various missionary bodies, notably the Church Missionary Society and the Methodists.

Apart from a few who sought for commercial opportunities in Freetown, most of the recaptives were settled in various agricultural villages around Freetown under magistrates who were usually missionaries. Evangelization among the adults, and western education for the young, were the basic weapons of acculturation in creating the Creole society. This produced a network of elementary schools that compared with, and sometimes surpassed, what was available in most parts of rural England. The high mortality rate among European missionaries and officials encouraged the CMS to go further in the 1840s to develop two secondary schools, one for boys and another for girls. Both the CMS and Methodists also took steps to improve the training of teachers and pastors locally and to encourage the brighter candidates to study abroad. They encouraged as many of the affluent parents as could afford it to send their children to Britain for professional courses, especially in law and medicine. In one such project, the CMS encouraged the Royal Navy to sponsor four graduates of the Freetown Grammar School to go abroad and study medicine. Two of them, Africanus Horton and Broughton Davies, qualified and were employed as medical officers in the Navy. It was then that the issue of higher education in Sierra Leone became a matter of public debate: local training versus overseas training; the relevance of African culture in African higher education; and what kind of higher education was most relevant to African development.

The Freetown debate, 1872–73

Fourah Bay College, founded in 1826, was the main Church Missionary Society (CMS) institution for training its African auxiliaries. It began as a trade school inculcating the virtues of hard work. Gradually its literary content began to be improved. As the grammar schools began to function, the level of Fourah Bay was also raised to the level of an institution of further education for the products of the boys' Grammar School interested in becoming teachers or candidates for ordination as pastors. In 1859, the CMS authorities in London observed that in all the previous ten years, the College had trained only 10 students at a cost of nearly 800 pounds sterling and decided to close it down "as a collegiate establishment" until the demand for it improved. This raised controversy in Freetown as many people saw the closure as a retrograde and hostile action, arguing that the demand was low because the quality was poor and the range of subjects covered was too narrow.

Various African leaders, like Africanus Horton in 1861 and again 1862, put forward suggestions as to how the College could be made to broaden its appeal, but the suggestions were ignored. The College was reopened in 1863, but by March 1871, the newly appointed Principal, the Revd. Metcalfe Sunter, complained that there were only a handful of students, the buildings had fallen into disrepair, and the grounds were overgrown. To facilitate revival of the College, Sunter and Bishop Cheetham conceived the idea of throwing the College open to fee-paying children of wealthy parents who could at least benefit from a few years there on preliminary studies prior to going abroad for professional courses. There was little enthusiasm at the CMS Head-quarters in London even for such limited reforms. Henry Venn who usually favoured progressive pro-African projects was cool: he did not like the idea of mixing lay fee-paying students with the Society's theological students.

That was how the leaders of the educated elite in Freetown turned the discussion about the future of Fourah Bay College into a public debate in which the case for a secular African-controlled university was made. Africanus Horton, himself a product of Fourah Bay College who, as mentioned above, had been sponsored under CMS auspices to study medicine in Edinburgh, was then practising with the British Navy as Assistant Surgeon at Cape Coast. There, he lived in close contact with the Fante and later became a champion of Fante nationalism and self-government for the Fante Con-federation. A prolific writer and entrepreneur, he had suggested in 1862 that the British government should take over Fourah Bay and endow various chairs, especially in the sciences – Botany, Chemistry, Mathematics, Mineralogy, Engineering, Architecture. He repeated this in 1868, but in 1873, he added his voice to those demanding a government or public financed university located in Africa, emphasizing Science and Technology to develop the resources of Africa. It was by promoting such development that the university would become an instrument for restoring to Africa its lost place of glory in the world:

Africa, in ages past, was the nursery of science and literature; from thence they were taught in Greece and Rome, so that it was said that the ancient Greeks represented their favourite goddess of Wisdom – Minerva – as an African princess . . . Origen, Tertullian, Augustin,

Clemens Alexandrinus, and Cyril, who were fathers and writers of the Primitive [i.e. Early Christian] Church, were tawny African bishops of Apostolic renown . . . Herodotus describes them as 'wooly-haired blacks, with projecting lips'. . . And why should not the same race who governed Egypt . . . who had her churches, her universities and her repositories of learning and science once more stand on their legs and endeavour to raise their characters in the scale of the civilized world?

(cit. Thompson, 1930, pp.54–6)[1]

One of the most vocal in the debate was James Johnson, a product of both the Grammar School and Fourah Bay College, at the time without any overseas experience. By 1870, he was emerging as an introverted, puritanical, passionate and dedicated Anglican pastor. He knew and appreciated the extent to which African development depended on the missionary enterprise, but he was a radical critic of missionary education which he said laid "a fetter on our minds". In a letter to the Acting Governor of Sierra Leone in December 1872, published in *The Negro* in January 1873, he said that the missionaries had ignored the history, culture and "peculiarities" of the African people, and proceeded in every way to give them a foreign model to copy. The result, he said, was that "we as a people . . . have lost our self-respect and our love for our own race, are become a sort of nondescript people . . . and are in many things inferior to our brethren in the interior countries." (cit. Blyden, 1896).

The coordinator of the debate and most widely recognised spokesman of the radical group was Edward Blyden. Born in the Dutch West Indies, and singled out as unusually gifted in languages, he was sent to be educated in the United States. Refused admission into Rutgers University, he migrated to Liberia where, at Alexander High School in Monrovia, he received a good basic education in the classics. After a period as a journalist, teacher and Presbyterian Minister, he was appointed professor of classical languages at the foundation of Liberia College in 1862 by the Board of Trustees for Donations for Higher Education in Liberia, a philanthropic group based in Boston. Besides Latin, Greek and Hebrew, he took particular interest in Arabic and, as Secretary of State for Liberia, he was able to visit Beirut in 1866. He left Monrovia in 1871 in the tumult that led to the death of President Roye. He went to London where the CMS offered him the job of professor of Arabic at Fourah Bay and evangelist to the interior Muslim communities in Futa Jallon. He was discharged when the CMS learnt of the scandal in Monrovia involving him and the wife of President Roye, but with a recommendation to the government in Sierra Leone to profit from his undoubted skills, especially in making contact with the Muslim communities in the interior. James Johnson, who was very particular about such things, said he had investigated the allegations and found no fault with Blyden.

This situation allowed Blyden, for a while, to practise as a free-lance journalist, editing a newspaper which he christened *The Negro*. The proposed University of West Africa was the most important of the causes he took up. In December 1872, he exchanged a series of remarkable letters with John Pope Hennessy, the Irishman who was Acting Governor and who, to the embarrassment of the Bishop and the resident missionaries, responded sympathetically to the radical criticism of missionary education. Blyden, with Hennessy's agreement, published the letters. Because of the support which *The Negro* gave to the state subsidy to the work of the Anglican Church, the Methodist authorities championed a rival newspaper, *The Independent,* which attacked Blyden's views, thus widening the area of debate.

Edward Blyden's criticisms of missionary education were similar to James Johnson's, namely, that it was narrow, sectarian and stifling. Liberal education, Blyden said, "has, with very few exceptions, been substituted by the narrow and dwarfing influence of ecclesiastical dogmatism." What was needed, he added, was education that would first unfetter the African mind and then enlighten it. To do this, it was necessary to promote race consciousness in the African. He did not separate the ill effects of missionary education from the cumulative effects of the slave trade. However, by praising the moral character of interior peoples who had suffered from the slave trade but not from missionary education, in contrast to that of the coastal people who had suffered from both, Blyden gave the impression that missionary education – slavery of the mind – was worse than slavery of the body. About the slave trade, he said:

> Europeans owe us a great debt, not only for the unrequited physical labours we have performed in all parts of the world, but for the unnumbered miseries and untold demoralization they have brought upon Africa by the prosecution for centuries of the horrible traffic to promote their own selfish ends . . .
>
> (cit. Ashby, 1966, p.455)

Therefore, as a form of restitution, he urged the Acting Governor to take the initiative in seeking approval and funds for a secular, government-financed, well-established African University,

> in keeping with the advancing spirit of the age and adapted to the inherent necessities of the race . . . an Institution with able African teachers brought, if necessary, from different parts of the world – even a Negro Arabic Professor from Egypt, Timbuctoo or Futah – would have great influence in exposing and correcting the fallacies upon which our foreign teachers have proceeded in their utter misapprehension and, perhaps, contempt of African character.
>
> (ibid. pp.453, 52)

In his exchange of letters with Hennessy, perhaps for reasons of strategy, Blyden did not specify details of curriculum reform that would achieve the general objectives. He tackled this in an inaugural lecture he gave in 1881 to the Liberia College, entitled *The Aims and Methods of a Liberal Education for Africans*. His basic approach was to avoid the study of modern European civilization, the period when "the trans-Atlantic slave trade arose and those theories – theological, social and political – were invented for the degradation and proscription of the Negro." Rather, he would concentrate on the Classics which he said were capable of providing intellectual "nourishment . . . without . . . race poison". To the Classics, he would add Mathematics as well as Arabic and major African languages. The great value of Arabic and African languages that he emphasized was that they would open up communication with the peoples of the interior from whom a fount of African culture and traditions would come with which to reinvigorate the creativity of the coastal peoples. We must listen, he said,

> to the songs of our unsophisticated brethren as they sing of their history, as they tell of their traditions, of the wonderful and mysterious events of their tribal or national life, of the achievements of what we call their superstitions; we must lend an ear to the ditties of the Kroomen who pull our boats, or the Pesseh and Golah men who till our farms; we must read the compositions, rude as we may think them, of the Mandingoes and the Veys.
>
> (Blyden, 1882)

This echoed James Johnson's reference to "our languages enriched with traditions of centuries; our parables, many of them the quintessence of family and national histories; our modes of thought, influenced more or less by local circumstances, our poetry and manufactures which, though rude, had their own tales to tell . . ." However, how the University was to utilize this treasure of African culture to foster regeneration and creativity, neither Blyden nor Johnson could tell, since neither of them spoke any indigenous African language nor, up to that time, had any close contact with indigenous African people. It was not until 1876 when James Johnson, who was born in Freetown, was transferred to Lagos where he was able to make contact with his father's Ijesha and mother's Ijebu people, that he could speak more authoritatively about African culture.

Fourah Bay College, 1876

John Pope Hennessy forwarded the exchange of letters to London with a covering letter addressed to the Earl of Kimberley, supporting the demand for a Government-financed University which was responsive to the cultural needs of Africans. He added that he had a long conference in Freetown with the Hon. William Grant, African member of the Legislative Council and thirteen African pastors of the Church of England on the subject, and he had discussed it with others in Lagos and Elmina. He predicated his views on the Report of the Parliamentary Committee of 1865 that the aim of the British Government should be to train the peoples of the West African Coast to be self-governing. It was therefore necessary to have a University so as to reduce the necessity for sending people to Europe at a tender age, at the risk of their health, their morals, and continuity with their historical traditions. It is painful, he said,

> to notice the contrast between such young men, who ought to be the natural leaders of public opinion in their own country, and the Chiefs and people from the Interior who have been untouched by Europeans. The latter have a manly bearing, a natural courtesy, a very keen intelligence and a frank and honest disposition. The negroes who have been educated in Europe, or who have been forced here into a sort of Semi-European mould, are the very reverse of all this . . .

> I think a West African University founded on a very humble basis ought to be established, where not only the sons of rich Africans could be educated but where, like in the early Irish Universities and some of the Continental Universities of our own times, even the poorest youths who had talents and a real taste for knowledge might by sizarships or fellowships have an opportunity of cultivating learning.
>
> (cit. Ashby, 1966, p.457)

The response in the Colonial Office was sympathetic but cautious. If education in Europe was the cause of the degeneration, what of the large numbers educated locally who were reported to be degenerate? And if they were degenerate, why should their views be accepted? The main worry voiced out, however, was whether there was enough demand. Lord Kimberley decided to remit the matter to the substantive governor to give his "careful attention" to the matter and conduct a feasibility survey.

The reaction of the CMS authorities both in Freetown and in London was very hostile to what they called the Hennessy-Johnson-Blyden fever. They were not impressed by the arguments about the need for race consciousness or for regarding "African culture and traditions" as a treasure house, a source of intellectual invigoration and creativity. The official reply of the CMS to the Freetown debate appeared in the *CMS Intelligencer* of 1873: Concerning the charge that missionary education Europeanized the African, "the answer might be, what else could ever be done? We have already shown that Africa has no past . . . How, then, were race instincts [i.e. culture] to be respected which either had no existence or which [if it existed at all] were fatal and soul-destroying to the Negro?" They regarded the views of Blyden and others as impractical, due to mere fancy, and arising from sheer ingratitude for all that the missionaries had done or were doing. On the specific issue of "race sentiment", Bishop Cheetham said, using the controversial term "Negro" that Blyden had adopted to refer to all Africans:

> national feeling & so forth is not finding expression in the *Negro* but the Negro is spreading it on thick before the people are ready ... patriotism & national feeling etc. are plants that grow with a nation's growth & here there is not a nation yet, only a collection of persons of different tribes who heartily hate & distrust one another: & in the present condition of Soc^y. to write about race sentiment is understood to mean by the commonfolk – be good haters – hate well – everybody else but yourself.
>
> (cit. Ashby, 1966, p.464)

The Methodist establishment who were bitter rivals of the Anglicans because of the controversy over the state subsidy, were similarly incensed at the disparagement of missionary work and played their part separately in frustrating Government support for the proposed University.

The CMS further saw Pope Hennessey's influence as that of a dogmatic Catholic out to destabilise Protestants. They objected to the idea of a secular, Negro-controlled University where, at best, "Mohammedanism" would be placed on an equal pedestal with Christianity or, at worst, would be a "Godless University". Bishop Cheetham advised the new Governor that the Hennessey-Johnson-Blyden scheme would be too expensive; that it was better for government not to take the initiative, but to help the Africans only to the extent that they were able to help themselves. Then, in a confidential letter, he urged the CMS to move quickly to frustrate the scheme ...

> I would so open Fourah Bay & announce it open, as to cut to the ground the plea of necessity for another college: I would for a long time to come keep in my own hands, if I were you, the Higher Education of the Coast using Governors' names & all the rest of it for ornament and patronage but you being at the base.
>
> (*ibid.* pp.463–4)

Up to June 1873, Sunter was still of the opinion that "the time has not yet arrived ... for the establishment of a University, unless 'White Man's money' should not only establish it but also maintain it: the time has not yet arrived for the establishment of a College in affiliation with an European University: but the time has arrived, I think, when we may fairly begin to look forward in the direction of the latter and prepare for it . . ." However, the Parent Committee appreciated the need to move fast. They invited James Johnson to visit London to advise on the University project and other matters. Thus they heightened his loyalty to the CMS and diverted his attention away from a secular University towards a reform of Fourah Bay College. Soon after, they transferred him away from Freetown to face fresh challenges in Lagos.

The Parent Committee decided in November 1873 to proceed with the idea of opening up Fourah Bay to fee-paying students desirous of education "in advance of what has been hitherto given in our Grammar School." The religious and missionary character must be preserved and observed by all students. A Theological department for training youths for missionary work must be maintained. "For some time yet", Europeans should remain in charge. These proposals were endorsed by the missionary Conference in Freetown in June 1874. The initial intention was to approach London for affiliation, but when it was known that Durham had just granted affiliation to Codrington College in Barbados, an approach was made to Durham and affiliation became effective in May 1876. The curriculum was drawn up in Durham. Durham teachers were to set the papers and mark the scripts. For both the B.A. (pass) degree and the Licentiate of Theology, the needs of candidates for the Ministry of the Church of England dictated the contents of the course – Biblical Studies, the Classics, English History up to the Conquest, and Mathematics. The only adaptation that was possible was to supplement it with a non-examining course in Arabic and Islamic Studies. Proposals for Law, Medicine, Science, Agriculture, Economics, Engineering and Architecture, not to mention African Studies, were washed off.

Thus, the University institution at Fourah Bay, affiliated to Durham University, was a pale shadow of the Blyden-Johnson-Hennessy proposed West African University. The Revd Metcalfe Sunter, who was not a university graduate, remained Principal till 1882. He shouldered the bulk of the teaching. A converted Jewish Rabbi, Alexander Schapira, taught Hebrew and Arabic, while a German missionary and linguist, C.A.L. Reichart was in charge of Classics. Of the two African Assistants, N. S. Davis was himself a candidate and the first person to obtain the B.A. under the Scheme of affiliation in 1878.

Perhaps James Johnson became reconciled to the idea of Fourah Bay College, or his new pastoral and evangelistic duties in Lagos were enough to divert his attention from the problems of higher education. Africanus Horton turned to the idea of private sponsorship of higher education. When he died suddenly in 1883 at the age of 48, he left his house, Horton Hall as a bequest in his will for a Horton Collegiate High School for the advanced study of science to the level where it would be accepted in affiliation to an English University. It was the failure of his business ventures in mining and banking that left no funds to support his many bequests that killed the proposal. Edward Blyden continued to explore official channels to take the initiative and attract private funds. Eventually, he secured employment as Director of Muslim education throughout British West Africa and as such remained an influential adviser on education generally. In 1896, he suggested to the Governor of Lagos a plan for the Lagos Training College and Industrial Institute, based on joint sponsorship by government and the business community, the College being a centre of higher education "with an emphasis on the Classics, Mathematics, Mental and Moral Philosophy and Natural Science." The Governor and the Colonial office were attracted because of the emphasis on the vocational training Institute, but the plan was dropped because of the "apathy" of Lagos businessmen for whom colonial rule meant declining opportunities, revenues, prospects, and capacity to sponsor such projects. His 1899 proposal for a university level "Central Training Institution for Muslims", anticipating the Gordon Memorial College of Khartoum as a centre to give Muslim/Arabic teachers good grounding in English and Western education so as to make them useful agents of British imperial rule in the Western Sudan, did not receive adequate official support.

Fourah Bay College remained the only University institution in West Africa until 1948. Its one attraction was the opportunity to obtain a university degree without leaving West Africa. Its fortunes continued to fluctuate as before the time of affiliation, partly because of its unexciting quality, partly because of shortage of funds from the CMS to subsidize its work, and partly because of discrimination against educated Africans in the Sierra Leone public service. Its most distinguished alumni tended to be students from Nigeria who became well known as Principals of schools or made their mark in the Church ministry. In 1908, the College announced that it might have to close down its Collegiate section, but it managed to carry on until 1918 when negotiations for Methodist cooperation in the running and funding of the College eventually yielded some fruit. The degree course was lengthened to three years. The B.A. pass degree in Theology was instituted to replace the L.Th. In particular cases, with the support of part-time teachers, it was sometimes possible to arrange for the B.A. in Law, but down to the Second World War, very little had changed at Fourah Bay.

Towards African renaissance

The 19th century was a period of rapid and multiple changes in the Western world. The history of Fourah Bay College reflects two of these changes which were of particular importance to Africa. The first was the growth of imperialism, the European desire for overseas empire, particularly in Africa and South-east Asia. This began as part of the social reforms consequent upon the growth of industrialism – improved education, increase of parliamentary democracy, rise of an urban industrial working class, Evangelical revival, the missionary enterprise and abolitionist movement. The settlement in Freetown was an offshoot of the abolitionist movement. When FBC was founded in 1827, it was to train evangelists not only in theology but also in habits of labour as part of the effort to develop export crops as alternatives to the slave trade. By the time Blyden and others were demanding an African University, and the CMS decided to use the affiliation of FBC to Durham to frustrate it, the desire to stop the export of unpaid African labour across the seas was already being transformed into a desire to acquire territories in Africa where the land, the human and mineral resources could be exploited with African labour for the benefit of Europe. Some educated Africans co-operated with this European desire in the belief that colonial rule might prove a necessary step to African development. Colonial rule proved to be both an opportunity and an obstacle to African development.

The second change reflected in the history of FBC was the transformation of higher education in Europe and America. The Medieval university which grew out of the monastic traditions of Alexandria shared various aspects of indigenous African higher education described earlier – the oral, eclectic and sometimes esoteric character, not to mention the affinity of some kinds of knowledge in African epistemology to magic. Since the 17th century, the scientific revolution had been reducing these areas of congruence. There were also similarities with Afro-Christian and Islamic universities in the religious basis of higher education, the reliance on a number of set texts, the pursuit of vocational and professional training, – beyond law, medicine and theology, – in institutions other than the universities. It was the industrial revolution that brought scientific research, and vocational and professional training, more and more into the universities. Much of the reform of the universities in the mid-19th century – to have regular lectures, systematize research, promote national languages etc. – was taking place under the auspices of the state which showed increasing interest in relating the universities to the economic, military and managerial effectiveness of the nation. The clamour of Blyden and others for an African university was, in fact, partly a reflection of similar clamour in Europe and America for reform of education as a factor in national invigoration. Durham University, the third University in England following after the medieval Colleges of Oxford and Cambridge, was founded in 1832 four years before University College, London. In 1861, there were only 41 students in the University of Durham. It was a royal commission that initiated reforms which improved its quality in the 1870s and made it possible for the C.M.S. to consider affiliating Fourah Bay College to it. Thereafter, new universities and university colleges were established in London, Manchester, Bristol, etc. and, therefore, development was rapid.

In the early 20th century, the clamour for universities in Africa was muted as people learnt to cope with colonial rule. By the 1920s, the debate was resumed, and the usual theme was the regenerative power of universities, provided they were modern universities which reflected the reforms of the 19th century. Thus, Nnamdi Azikiwe of Nigeria, on his return from studying in the US, published a book in 1937, entitled *Renascent Africa* in which he took up the issue of the nature and function of the African University. Universities, he said,

> have been responsible for shaping the destinies of races and nations and individuals.. The universities of Europe and America have been responsible for the great movements in the national history of these continents . . . Give the Renascent African a university, . . . With twelve million pounds there is no reason why the best libraries, laboratories, professors cannot be produced right here, and this continent can become overnight "A Continent of Light".

Universities, he added, are mirrors "which reflect (the) particular sociological idiosyncrasies". An African graduate of European or American universities, "unless he has developed his individuality, is nothing short of a megaphone, yea a carbon copy of these societies". Yet, in his description of the African University, his emphasis was not on the factor of cultural heritage but of ownership and commitment: "an indigenous university sustained through African initiative . . . maintained at (African) expense". If such universities had existed in Africa, he said,

> they could have had their curricula filled with important divisions of knowledge which would have hastened their intellectual emancipation, and would have enabled them to make scientific researches into some of the quackeries which some of them are wont to elevate into an unmerited apogee by calling them a phase of 'Super-Science'.
>
> (cit. Fafunwa, 1971, pp.179–80)

In other words, the African University is to be defined not merely by its historical continuity with the African past, but even more by its commitment to the renaissance of Africa. Renaissance could not be achieved by merely reflecting the "quackeries" of the past. Rather, there must be intellectual emancipation from both the limitations of the past and the shackles that colonialism placed not only on the mind, but also on the freedom of choice.

Note

1 Compare the Speech of the Public Orator, C. J. Potter, at the Inauguration of the University College, Ibadan in November 1948:

The continent of Africa has a great and long tradition of learning. The valley of the River Nile was the very nurse and cradle of scientific research. The Library of Alexandria was among the wonders of the ancient world. At the time when the imperium of Rome extended to this continent, its northern shores were the home of many learned men. When the glory that was Greece and the grandeur that was Rome had become but memories in Europe, the tradition of learning was still alive on the banks of the Niger . . . So, the Secretary of State has come to inaugurate not the first, but the latest of the houses of learning in these regions. As his aeroplane crossed the coastline of Africa, it must have passed close to the place where one of the greatest African scholars of all time spent many years of his life – Saint Augustine, Bishop of Hippo, whose writings have profoundly influenced the thoughts of Europe. He loved to quote a phrase from an earlier inhabitant of Alexandria which might be borne in mind today – *Multitudo sapientum sanitas est urbis terrarum.*

(*University Herald*, Ibadan, March 1949)

References

Ashby, Eric (1966): *Universities: British, Indian, African*: A Study in the Ecology of Higher Education. Weidenfeld and Nicolson, London.

Ashby, Eric (1974): Adapting Universities to a Technological Society (San Francisco, Jossey-Bass Publishers).

Blyden, E. W. (1896): The Lagos Training College and Industrial Institute (Lagos).

Bray, Mark., Clarke, Peter B., Stephens, David, (1986): Education and Society in *Tropical Africa* (Edward Arnold, London).

Chideya, N. T., Choikomba, C. E. M., Pogweni, A. J. C. and Tsikirayi, L. C. (eds.) (1982): *The Role of the University and Its Future in Zimbabwe International Conference Papers* (Harare Publishing House).

Cissoko, S. M., (1984): "The Songhay from the 12th to the 16th Century" in *Africa from the Twelfth to the Sixteenth Century*, Unesco GHA, vol. IV, (ed.) D. T. Niane (Heinemann Educational Books, London).

Donadoni, S., (1981): "Egypt under Roman Domination in Ancient Civilizations of Africa", Unesco GHA, vol. II, (ed.) G. Mokhtar, Heinemann Educational Books, London).

El-Abbad, Mostafa (1990): *Life and Fate of the ancient Library of Alexandria* (UNESCO/UNDP, Paris)

Fafunwa, A. B. (1971): *A History of Nigerian Higher Education* Macmillan (Nigeria), Lagos

Garcin, J. C., (1984): "Egypt and the Muslim World" in Africa from the Twelfth to the Sixteenth Century, Unesco GHA, vol. IV (ed.) D. T. Niane (Heinemann Educational Books, London).

Habte, Aklilu (1976): "The Public Service Role of the University: the Ethiopian University Service, a Service/Study experiment" in *Higher Education for Development in Africa.*

Oruka, H. Odera (ed.) (1991): *Sage Philosophy: Indigenous Thinkers and Modern Debate on African Philosophy* (African Centre for Technology Studies, ACTS Press, Nairobi).

Riad, H., (1981): "Egypt in the Helenistic Era" in *Ancient Civilizations of Africa*, Unesco General History of Africa, v.II (ed.) G. Mokhtar, (Heinemann Educational Books, London).

Saad, Elias N. (1983). *Social History of Timbuktu: the role of Muslim Scholars and Notables, 1400–1900* (Cambridge University Press).

Talbi, M., (1988): "The Independence of the Maghrib" in *Africa from the Seventh to the Eleventh Century*, Unesco GHA, vol. III (ed.) M. El Fasi and I. Hrbek (Heinemann Educational Books, London).

Tamrat, Tadesee (1984): "The Solomonids in Ethiopia and the States of the Horn of Africa" in *Africa from the Twelfth to the Sixteenth Century*, Unesco GHA, vol. VI (ed.), D. T. Niane.

Thompson, T. J., (1930): *The Jubilee and Centenary Volume of Fourah Bay College* (Freetown).

University of Zambia (1966): *Addresses at the Installation of his Excellency the President as First Chancellor of the University of Zambia* (Zambia Information Services, Lusaka).

3

THE RISE OF THE UNIVERSITIES

Gabriel Campayre

Source: G. Campayre, *Abelard and the Origin and Early History of Universities*, New York: AMS Press, 1969, pp. 46–69. Originally published 1893.

> I. Various and irregular origins of the universities — Denifle's classification — Papal or royal institution — The universities often grew and were not founded — Chronological list of the universities erected in the thirteenth, fourteenth, and fifteenth centuries — The university movement in the following centuries — II. The university-mothers: Paris, Bologna, Oxford, and Salamanca — The successors of Abelard — The age of Robert Grosseteste in England — Roger Bacon — Bologna and Irnerius — The University of Salamanca — III. Influence of the University of Paris — Universities of Germany — Of England — Of Spain — Of Portugal — Influence of the University of Bologna — International exchange of scholars — Peter Lombard — Peter of Blois — John of Salisbury — Beginnings of the University of Cambridge — The United States of mediaeval universities.

I

To give a complete idea of the origin of the universities, one should be able to relate the particular history of each of them, and to enter into details incompatible with the plan of this treatise. I must be content with certain general views, and set aside the particulars which abound, and which permit me to say that, during the thirteenth and fourteenth centuries at least, no two universities were founded under identical conditions. It is only in the fifteenth century that the formalities of institution for new universities were regulated. The civil power, a king, an emperor, or some nobleman, took the first steps, and solicited the pontifical power for a bull of erection. This bull, which was never refused, authorized the creation of the university, conceded privileges to it, and determined the number of faculties. Then the civil power intervened anew and confirmed the organization of the university by a definite act.

But in the thirteenth and fourteenth centuries, in the period of hesitancy and of laborious births, we must not expect to find this precision and this regularity of form. Sometimes, and most frequently, it was the pope who took the initiative; sometimes it was the head of the state. Thus John XXII founded the University of Cahors in 1332, and it was only in 1368 that the Prince of Wales, and in 1370 that Louis, Duke of Anjou and lieutenant of the king of France in Languedoc, conferred upon it the favor of a civil institution.[1] By an inverse proceeding, other universities were created by royal decree and waited years for the pontifical consecration. Salamanca was legally established in 1243, by privilege of Ferdinand III, king of Leon and Castile; and did not receive a bull from Pope Alexander IV, approving the foundation, until 1254.[2] So likewise the English University of Cambridge had been already recognized by royal authority in 1217; it is from this year, in fact, that its "earliest authentic legal instrument" is dated, an edict of the king, Henry III, addressed to all clerks of Cambridge; but it was only a hundred years later, in 1318, that Pope John XXII accorded to Cambridge formal recognition as a *studium generale*. Sometimes the civil and the ecclesiastical authorities were not wholly in agreement. For example, Clement V erected the University of Orleans in 1306, through a sentiment of gratitude toward the schools of that city, where he had studied law; and 1312, the King of France, Philip the Fair, issued letters-patent which, while maintaining the University of Orleans, profoundly modified the privileges granted it by the pope.[3]

It is far from true, moreover, that all of the universities have had the double institution; many of them had to be content, some with a papal bull, others with a royal or imperial decree. There are even some, and among the number the most important and the most ancient, which erected themselves, so to speak, and which cannot exhibit in their *chartularium* any written act of institution. "The earliest universities," says Laurie, "grew and were not founded."

This is so true that Père Denifle, in his learned work on the universities of the Middle Ages,[4] has adopted as his principle of classification for the universities, and the basis of his labor, this diversity of origin. He distinguishes, in effect, four categories of universities: 1. The high schools, which organized themselves, without a written act of erection (*ohne Errichtungs-briefe*), — for example, Salernum, Oxford, Cambridge, Angers, Padua, etc.; 2. Those whose establishment was decreed by the pontifical will, — Rome, Pisa, Toulouse, Montpellier, Avignon, Cahors, etc.; 3. Those founded by a king or emperor, — Arezzo, Palencia, Naples, Orange, Salamanca, etc.; 4. Those, finally, and they were the least numerous during the period studied by Père Denifle, — that is to say, up to 1400, — which had the double investiture, — Prague, Vienna, etc.

Very few at the beginning, the universities rapidly multiplied themselves with a prodigious fecundity; and by the end of the fifteenth century there were already nearly eighty institutions of the sort presiding over the intellectual movement of Europe. It is to be remarked, moreover, that during three hundred years this movement went on accelerating from century to century. In the twelfth century there had been but a single official institution, — that of Bologna, in 1158; in the thirteenth century we reckon nineteen or twenty, most of them between 1200 and 1250; in the fourteenth, more than twenty-five; in the fifteenth century, thirty. Here is the list, with the description of their foundation:[5] —

Thirteenth century

1200, *Paris;* privilege granted by Philip Augustus.

12—, *Oxford;* whose university constituted itself without any official sanction; the first royal recognition, a charter from Henry III, is dated in 1258.[6]

12—, *Cambridge;* which sprang from Oxford, and developed spontaneously like Oxford; letters-patent from Henry III in 1217 and 1231; a bull from Pope John XXII in 1318.

12—, *Arezzo;* which likewise dates from the first half of the thirteenth century; imperial recognition from Charles IV in 1355.

1212, *Palencia;*[7] in Spain, founded by Alfonso VIII, King of Castile.

1222, *Padua;* which arose from an emigration of Bolognese professors.

1224, *Naples;* Frederick II, Emperor of Germany.

1224–1228, *Verceil;* which arose from an emigration of professors from Padua.[8]

1229, *Toulouse;* Pope Gregory IX.

1243, *Salamanca;* Ferdinand III, King of Castile and Leon; confirmation in 1254 from Pope Alexander IV.

1244, *Curia Romana;* Pope Innocent IV; this school followed the popes to Avignon.

1245, *Valencia;* in Spain; James I, King of Aragon.

1248, *Plaisance;* in Italy; Innocent IV; the Duke of Milan, Galeazzo II, confirmed its privileges in 1398.

1254, *Seville;* Alfonso X, the Wise, King of Castile and Leon.

1288, *Lisbon;* Denis, King of Portugal; Pope Nicholas IV transferred it to Coimbra in 1308.

1289, *Montpellier;* Pope Nicholas IV.[9]

1289, *Gray;* Otho IV, Count of Burgundy; transferred to Dêle in 1423 by Philip the Good.

1293, *Alcala;* Sancho IV, King of Aragon.

1295, *Pamiers;* Pope Boniface VIII.

Fourteenth century

1300, *Lerida;* James II, King of Aragon and Sicily.

1303, *Rome;* Pope Boniface VIII.

1303, *Avignon;* Pope Boniface VIII.

1306, *Orleans;* Pope Clement V; in 1312, King Philip the Fair.[10]

1307, *Perouse;* Clement V; in 1355, the Emperor Charles IV.

1308, *Coimbra,* already organized toward the close of the thirteenth century, in 1279; successor to the University of Lisbon.

1310, *Dublin;* Pope Clement V.

1332, *Cahors;* Pope John XXII.

1339, *Grenoble;* the Dauphin, Humbert II; Pope Benedict XII.

1343, *Pisa;* Pope Clement VI.

1346, *Valladolid;* Pope Clement VI.

1347, *Prague;* Pope Clement VI; in 1348, the Emperor Charles IV.[11]

1349, *Florence;* confirmed in 1364 by Charles IV.

1349, *Perpignan;* Peter IV, King of Aragon; confirmed in 1379 by Clement VII.

1354, *Huesca;* Peter IV, King of Aragon; re-established in 1464 by Pope Paul II.

1357, *Sienna;* from 1321, emigration to Sienna of professors from Bologna; privileges conceded, 1357, by the Emperor Charles IV.

1361, *Pavia;* Charles IV; in 1389, Boniface VIII.

1365, *Vienna;* the Emperor Rodolphus IV; Pope Urban V.

1365, *Geneva;* the Emperor Charles IV.

1365, *Orange;* Charles IV.

1365, *Cracovia;* Casimir III, King of Poland; Urban V.

1367, *Fünfkirchen,* in Hungary; Urban V.

1367, *Angers;* Louis II, Duke of Anjou.[12]

1379, *Erfurt;* Pope Clement VII.

1385, *Cologne;* Pope Urban VI.

1385, *Heidelberg;* Pope Urban VI.

1389, *Ofen;* Boniface IX.

1391, *Ferrara;* Boniface IX; this university had been established by municipal statutes since 1263.

Fifteenth century

Würzburg, 1403; *Turin,* 1405; *Aix,* in Provence, 1409; *Leipsic,* 1409; *St. Andrews,* Scotland, 1412; *Rostock,* 1419; *Dôle,* 1423; *Louvain,* 1426; *Poitiers,* 1431; *Caen,* 1436; *Bordeaux,* 1441; *Catana,* 1445; *Valence,* in France, 1452; *Treves, Glasgow,* 1454; *Freiburg, Greifswald,* 1456; *Basel,* 1459; *Nantes,* 1460; *Besançon,* 1464; *Bourges,* 1469; *Ingolstadt,* 1472; *Saragossa,* 1474; *Copenhagen,* 1475; *Upsala,* 1476; *Tübingen, Mayence,* 1477; *Parma,* 1482.

Who could deny, after merely glancing over this long enumeration, the importance of the university movement in the last three centuries of the Middle Ages? Doubtless among these universities many remained obscure or had no effective existence. Occasionally they were but the ephemeral adornment of over-ambitious cities which did not possess the resources necessary to make great schools prosper. Some of them, born of the favoritism of popes or kings, or owing their existence to a sort of local vanity, have inscribed their modest titles for a few years only in the history of the universities. But, on the other hand, how many have remained glorious, and maintained to our own day, while undergoing a transformation, their useful and laborious existence?

In the sixteenth century the creations did not slacken. The age of the Renaissance saw the birth of more than thirty universities, among them some which have left a mark in the history of letters and sciences; for example, Aberdeen (1506), Königsberg (1542), Jena (1552), Leyden (1575), Edinburgh (1582). Two special causes were added during the sixteenth century to those general ones which, in that epoch of renovation, were bound to multiply scholastic foundations. On the one hand, the Reformation gave rise to the institution of Protestant universities — the first was that of Marburg, in 1527; on the other, the creation of the Society of Jesus, among other pedagogic consequences, had that of the establishment of Jesuit universities — for example, that of Messina,[13] which Ignatius of Loyola organized in 1547 by sending several members of his order thither; and that of Pont à Mousson, also, which dates from 1572.[14]

Between 1600 and 1700, although most of the cities that were able to support universities were already provided with them, we see twenty-one more created, chiefly in Germany and Holland, — France and Italy having long since attained the maximum that they were capable of reaching. Finally, in the eighteenth and nineteenth centuries, without speaking of transatlantic universities, of those which in America have constituted themselves the fortunate rivals and the vigorous imitators of the universities of the Old World, more than forty new universities have seen the light of day in Europe.[15]

II

But I must go back and keep within the limits of my subject. From the thirteenth century, England with Oxford, Spain with Salamanca, France with Paris, Italy with Bologna, leaving unmentioned the universities of less importance, had each a focus of instruction whose brilliancy streamed afar. Germany was behindhand, — it is true that it has caught up very well since, — and it was not until the fourteenth century that it followed the movement. The first German university, that of Prague, dates, in fact, from 1347. It will be interesting to review rapidly the history of the origins of those great universities of the thirteenth century — which one might call the mother-universities, because from them nearly all the others originated — and to show that similar circumstances presided at their formation.

At Paris the movement created by Abelard survived him. The influx of students from every nation was prodigious during the second half of the thirteenth century, and we are told that it was one of the causes which determined Philip Augustus to enlarge the circumference of Paris.[16] Men who had a great reputation in their time continued Abelard's instruction. Among the number was Gilbert de la Porrée, who taught theology. He also was a heretic, and was persecuted in his turn by St. Bernard, who procured his condemnation by the Council of Rome in 1148.[17] After him I may cite Peter Lombard[18] and Maurice de Sully, who succeeded Peter Lombard as Bishop of Paris in 1150; and who arrived as a mendicant, begging his bread, in the city where he was afterwards to teach philosophy and theology with so much renown, and to occupy its highest ecclesiastical dignity.[19] Popes Adrian IV (1154–1159) and Innocent IV (1198–1216) studied at Paris during this period. An English historian enumerates no fewer than thirty-two eminent Oxonians who had also studied at Paris, and among them Robert Grosseteste and Roger Bacon.[20] The schools of Mount Ste. Geneviève and of St. Victor had their *clientèle*, and the cathedral school of Notre Dame continued to flourish. And it was not from the ancient palatine school, long before dispersed, but "from the reunion of the schools of logic established on the mountain with the school of theology that was in the cloister of Notre Dame, that the University of Paris was formed."[21]

Bologna, like Paris, laid claim to very ancient beginnings, and in Dezobry's *Dictionnaire de biographie et d'histoire* (1857) one may read: "The University of Bologna owes its origin to a school of law founded by Theodosius II, in 425, and revived by Charlemagne." More enterprising still, certain historians of the University of Cambridge trace back the foundation of their university to the fourth century before Jesus Christ. "The year 375 B.C.," wrote, in 1574, an adventurous author, "a son of the king of Spain, named Cantaber, landed in England, founded the town of Cambridge, and there instituted a university, composed at first of philosophers and astronomers whom he had brought with him from the city of Athens."[22]

Something must be abated from these pretensions to antiquity. As a school of law, Bologna does not appear to date earlier than the twelfth century. In the commencement of that century the professors of jurisprudence occupied an important position there. From 1123 they composed one of the three sovereign assemblies of the city of Bologna, — that which was called the Council of Credence (Consiglio di Credenza). It was in 1137 that Irnerius taught there, and he was the true founder of this university, as we shall see later on.[23]

In England, for the mother-university, that of Oxford, there was a slow and progressive preparation. Here we have not to go back to the remote beginnings, to the influence exercised in the eighth century by the celebrated Bede,[24] of whom an English writer has said that, "in his tomb science was enshrouded during four centuries"; nor to the part played by Alfred the

Great, and the efforts to regenerate studies in his realm, which he made in the ninth century in imitation of Charlemagne. I need only say that at that epoch Oxford possessed flourishing schools. They were twice pillaged and destroyed by the Danish invasions, but by the eleventh century they had regained their old position. The rhetoric of Cicero and the logic of Aristotle were studied there.[25] After having suffered further loss at the time of the Norman conquest, Oxford, thanks to the protection of Henry I, third son and second successor of William the Conqueror, again became a centre of studies. Undoubtedly there were then none of those scholastic palaces which arose there in the course of time. It is related that the lecture-halls and the houses where the students lodged were built of wood and thatched with straw, and were thus at the mercy of the fire which devoured them in 1130. But students flocked thither none the less. More than elsewhere, perhaps, the protection of the higher clergy was gained in England for the rising universities; and, on the other hand, the religious orders, the Franciscans and Dominicans, played a great part in the revival of studies.

One man who has left many memories of himself in his own country, Robert Grosseteste (1175–1253), contributed particularly toward this movement. The first half of the thirteenth century in England has been designated "the age of Robert Grosseteste,"[26] just as, in France, the first half of the twelfth century might be called the age of Abelard. "He was," says Laurie, "a patriot and a scholar and a humanist."[27] He had studied at Oxford, at Cambridge, and at Paris. After becoming Bishop of Lincoln, he did not cease to foster learning: by his writings he popularized the works of Aristotle. And it was not merely Greek books, in the form of translations, that he introduced into the English schools; Mullinger affirms that he sought to attract Greek scholars to England.

One name will serve to show what the intellectual development of England was in the thirteenth century, — that of the monk Roger Bacon (1214–1294). Roger Bacon, before studying in Paris, had studied at Oxford; then he established himself in England. By the freedom of his researches and the boldness of his experiments he aroused the fanaticism of his contemporaries, and was accused of magic. At the same time, uniting a love of antiquity to a taste for investigation in the natural sciences, he collected the masterpieces of classic literature at great expense, and, for his time, became a Humanist of the first rank.

The University of Salamanca was the queen of Spanish universities. Founded about the year 1200, it did not receive its official charter until 1243, from the hands of Ferdinand III, King of Castile and Leon. But from its very beginning it took its place in the first rank, among the great centres of instruction. It took part in drawing up the celebrated astronomical tables of the King of Castile, Alfonso X, the Wise. Like the University of Paris, it was mixed up with the great religious quarrels of the age, and took part in the schism of the West by pronouncing for the popes of Avignon.[28] It must not be forgotten that, later on, in the fifteenth century, it lent a courageous support to Christopher Columbus, that it alone had faith in the success of his great adventure, and that in the Convent of the Dominicans of St. Stephen, whose house is still in existence at Salamanca, the project of navigation to which the fifteenth century owed the discovery of America, was discussed and approved. In the sixteenth century the University of Salamanca was teaching the Copernican system, while Galileo was in prison. More than once it gave professors to Bologna and to Paris.[29] The bachelors of Salamanca remained celebrated up to the eighteenth century. All through the Middle Ages, more than four thousand students pursued there a course of instruction as complete and as various as that imparted at Paris.

The question has been much discussed in Spain as to whether or no the University of Salamanca was derived from that of Palencia, which was founded some years earlier, in 1212.[30] What is certain is that in the twelfth century there were important schools in Salamanca, schools which, like those of Paris, were installed in the cloister of the cathedral. It is also established that, from the beginning, medical studies took an important place in the University of Salamanca; and that the inspiration of these schools came from Arabian physicians. In the tenth century, Gerbert, before becoming Pope Sylvester II, went to seek in the Mohammedan academies in the south of Spain more thorough instruction than he had been able to find in the Christian schools of France. The presence of the Moors and the brilliancy of Arabian science, the philosophy of Averroes, and the medicine of Avicenna, exercised a manifest influence on the development of studies at Salamanca. Here, then, as elsewhere, there was a scholastic movement which preceded royal ordinances; although the individual action of sovereigns particularly favorable to the sciences, of a king who was a mathematician and astronomer, for example, like Alfonso the Wise, may have contributed much to the development of the University of Salamanca.

III

The example once given by the "mother-universities," the foundation of other universities was merely a question of imitation. Paris especially was imitated. "The Universities of Oxford and Cambridge in England, of Prague, Vienna, Heidelberg, and Cologne in Germany, derived their formal constitution, the tradition of their education, and their modes of instruction from Paris. The influence of this university has indeed emboldened some writers to term her 'the Sinai of instruction' in the Middle Ages."[31]

When the Emperor Charles IV organized, in 1348, the first German university, that of Prague, which had been authorized in 1347 by a bull of Clement VI, he drew upon his memories as a former student of the University of Paris. As Döllinger says, "in memory of his student life in the Rue de Fouarre, he wished to have a copy of the University there in his hereditary kingdom of Bohemia."[32] So, too, in 1385, when Pope Urban VI organized the University of Heidelberg, still so flourishing, the pontifical bull states that the new *studium generale* would be established according to the hallowed formula, *ad instar studii Parisiensis.*[33] Vienna, for its part, whose university dates from 1365, claimed to continue the traditions of Athens, of Rome, and of Paris.[34] Paris had succeeded to the literary capitals of the ancient world. Paris, said St. Bonaventura, is the source whence the streams of science spread over the whole world.

In England, French influence shone with no less brilliancy. Oxford, which according to Laurie "was entitled to the name 'Universitas' about 1140,"[35] and which in any case comprised a great number of students at the end of the twelfth or the beginning of the thirteenth century, since in 1209, says a contemporary chronicler, when an emigration to Cambridge occurred, *recesserunt ab Oxonia tria millia clericorum tam magis-trorumquam discipulorum,*[36] — Oxford was several times stimulated and improved by the coming of foreign professors from Bologna, and especially from Paris. It was Vacarius, a Bolognese, who in 1149 tried to install the study of Roman law there; but it was a former student of Paris, an Englishman by birth, moreover, Robert Pulleyne, who in 1130 "endeavored to revive the teaching of theology, and succeeded in infusing a higher spirit into the Oxford schools."[37] Later, in 1228, when, after a students' riot and the reprisals provoked by it, the masters and students of Paris emigrated in great numbers, it was not only in the studious towns of France, in Angers, Orleans, and Rheims, that they took shelter, but also in Oxford and Cambridge. Henry III, King of England, had invited them thither in a letter the text of which has been preserved: "*Duximus vestrce Universitati significandum quod si vobis placeat ad regnum nostrum Angliae vos transferre . . . civitates, burgos vel villas quascumque velitis eligere vobis ad hoc assignabimus.*"[38] This appeal was listened to. The migrating masters repaired in part to Oxford, and, says Laurie, "they would carry the genius of Paris with them."

It is hardly necessary to say that the provincial universities of France have been, for the most part, faithful copies of the University of Paris; Montpellier must be excepted, since it drew its inspiration partly from Bologna. It is true that, in the papal bulls relating to the universities, it is almost invariably written that they should be organized *ad instar studii Tolosani.* But the University of Toulouse itself, the most ancient after Paris, was modelled after the great Parisian school; the privileges were the same, and, due allowances being made, the studies were similar. Through Toulouse, then, it was Paris which was copied everywhere, at Orleans, Angers, Poitiers, Caen, Bordeaux, etc.

Even in Spain, where, nevertheless, Bologna and Montpellier had much influence, a strictly French influence made itself felt. When the King of Aragon, James II, established the University of Lerida in 1300, he affirmed in his decree that "the Holy See granted to the new *studium* the same indulgences, immunities, and favors already granted to the *Studium* of Toulouse."[39] In the previous century, Alfonso VIII, King of Castile, had constituted the University of Palencia by inviting "masters of theology and the liberal arts from France and Italy, to whom, in order to retain them, he assigned large salaries" (*Sapientes e Gallia et Italia convocavit, quibus magna stipendia est largitus*).[40] So, too, it was the privileges of the University of Toulouse that Pope Nicholas V conceded in 1450 to the University of Barcelona. When Pope Paul II restored the University of Huesca in 1464, he gave it Toulouse, Montpellier, and Lerida as models. Finally, in the bull of Sixtus IV, in favor of the University of Saragossa (1474), it is said that the *studium generale* would be founded there *ad instar* of the Universities of Paris and of Lerida.

It was from France, again, that Portugal borrowed in part the first elements of university organization. At the close of the thirteenth century, King Alfonso III, who had travelled in France, brought back with him two scholars, Domingos Jardo, a Portuguese, but a doctor of canon law in the University of Paris, and Aymeric d'Hébrard, a nobleman of Quercy.[41] It was with the aid of these two advisers that the kings of Portugal proceeded to the establishment of their national university, installed successively at Lisbon and at Coimbra.

Next to Paris, the University of Bologna had most imitators. The universities of Italy, that of Naples excepted, sprang directly or indirectly from Bologna. That of Padua, in 1222, was founded by a colony of professors from Bologna; so was that of Sienna, in the fourteenth century. "The intellectual movement of the northeast of Italy," M. Renan has said, "is altogether connected with that of Padua. Now the Universities of Padua and Bologna were really only one, at least as far as the philosophical and medical instruction was concerned. The same professors migrated nearly every year from one to the other, to obtain an increase of their salaries."[42] Bologna, however, extended its influence to foreign countries: in France, the Universities of Montpellier and Grenoble were copied after Bologna. It was Placentin, a Bolognese, who introduced the study of law at Montpellier.[43]

The multiplication of universities would have been impossible without these mutual loans and exchanges. Throughout the entire Middle Ages, there was a perpetual passing to and fro of masters and students from one country to another, — from France to England, from Italy to France, and back again, — or, in the same country, going in turn from one city to another city, from one school to another school. I may cite some examples. Peter Lombard, the *Master of the Sentences*, as he is called, the uncontested chief of theological instruction in the Middle Ages, whose classic work enjoyed so great an authority that, according to Crevier, — who had counted them, — it has had 244 commentators — almost as many as Aristotle; Peter Lombard studied successively at Bologna, Rheims, and Paris. The successor of Abelard, but more circumspect than he in the application of dialectics to

theology, Peter Lombard did not wholly escape the criticism of the orthodox, — of theologians who were alarmed by the freedom of his logic, and
who claimed that the subtleties of dialectics were "like a fine and minute
dust, blinding the eyes of those who stir it up."[44] Twenty-six erroneous
articles are counted up in his doctrines, — making him quite a "heretic." He
maintained that "Jesus Christ, in so far as he was man, was nothing," — a
proposition from which sprang the sect of "nihilists." One was a "nihilist"
on easy terms in those days. So, too, a writer justly celebrated in the twelfth
century, Peter of Blois, first studied letters and philosophy at Tours and at
Paris, then went to Bologna, about 1160, to follow the lectures on law, and
afterwards returned to Paris to take up theological studies. He finally ended
his career in England.[45] This example is particularly striking, because it
shows how, before the foundation of universities which later reunited in the
same city and in one centre all sorts of studies, a man eager for learning was
obliged to go seeking, from city to city and in special schools, the different
branches of human knowledge. John of Salisbury is another example of
how these learned peregrinations were then obligatory for all students. Born
about 1100, at Salisbury, in England, we have found him in Paris, in 1136,
an enthusiastic auditor of Abelard. He spent not less than twelve years in
the schools of France, exercising himself in theology, under the direction of
Robert of Melun (an Englishman who was teaching at Melun), in grammar
with William of Conches (himself a pupil of Bernard of Chartres), and in
mathematics and rhetoric under other masters. He taught in Paris about
1145; but he afterwards returned to England, where he was for some time
attached to the church of Canterbury. Then he travelled in Italy, and finally
returned to France, where he died, Bishop of Chartres, in 1180.

The beginnings of the University of Cambridge show plainly how the dis-
placements and migrations of nomadic professors or members of religious
orders, travelling from one country to another, scattered the seed of science
on fresh soil. Montalembert thus describes the origin of Cambridge: "Four
Norman monks, transplanted from Saint Evroul, in France, to Croyland, in
England, with the eloquent and learned Abbot Joffride, formerly professor
at Orleans, concluded to open a public course of lectures in a granary which
they hired near the gate of the town of Cambridge. But, as neither this
granary nor other still larger edifices were able to contain the throng of men
and women who soon hastened to listen to them, the monks of Croyland
conceived the notion of organizing the instruction given by the professors,
on the plan of the monastic exercises of the order. Thus, Brother Odo was
deputed to teach grammar, according to Priscian and Remy, at daybreak;
at Prime, Brother Terric taught Aristotle's logic with the comments of
Porphyry and Averroes; at Tierce, Brother William, the rhetoric of Cicero
and Quintilian; while, on every holiday, Brother Gislebert, the most learned
member of the community, explained the Sacred Scriptures to the priests
and to the scholars, and, moreover, preached every Sunday to the people, in

spite of his unfamiliarity with the English language. Such was the beginning of the University of Cambridge, — a feeble rivulet, which soon became, according to the expression of a French monk, Peter of Blois, a great stream which fertilized all England."[46]

Even after the universities had been constituted, the international exchange of students and of masters did not cease. The papacy, which protected the universities because it counted on directing them, aided by its universal domination in facilitating their relations and the reciprocal services they rendered to each other. It was in vain that certain cities, through self-love and local interests, sought to isolate their universities: Florence, for example, prohibited Florentines to study anywhere but at Florence, under penalty of heavy fines. A current stronger than national rivalry reunited all the universities of Europe in a sort of federation. There was then, in spite of incessant wars, in spite of invasions, in spite of the hatreds between peoples, there was above all the frontiers a European alliance of all the superior schools, a something like the United States of universities. And in this assemblage of almost similar schools, it was Paris that held the leadership. Even at Bologna, the college of theology, annexed to the university by Pope Innocent IV in 1362, was formed on the model of the theological faculty of Paris. Parisian professors were called to the German universities of the fourteenth century. The first rector of the University of Heidelberg, Marsilius de Inghen, had been rector of the University of Paris. It was not a pious illusion, it was truth itself, which inspired Duboulay, when, in the title of his book, he described most of the other universities as daughters of the University of Paris: *quœ ex eadem communi matre excesserunt.*

Notes

1 Fournier, *op. cit.*, t. ii, pp. 553–558.
2 Vicente de la Fuente, *op. cit.*, t. i, pp. 90, 312.
3 Bimbenet, *op. cit.*, p. 15 *et seq.*
4 *Die Entstehung der Universitäten des Mittelalters bis* 1400, Berlin, 1885.
5 I omit a certain number of *studia* which appear to have claimed, unsuccessfully, the title of university; for example, in Italy, Reggio, where a school of law flourished toward the end of the twelfth century; Modena, which, after obtaining from Honorius III and Frederick III (1225 and 1226) the concession of privileges, was unable to stand the competition of Bologna, and soon disappeared. It was the same with Vicena (1204), etc.
6 Laurie affirms that Oxford had been "a true university" from 1140, and Cambridge from 1200; but he admits that "their university *organization* took its form about 1230, after the Paris migration." Laurie, *op. cit.*, p. 242.
7 The university of Palencia had but an ephemeral existence. St. Dominic studied there.
8 Verceil was never very important, and soon disappeared. On all the Italian universities, see Savigny, *Geschichte des römischen Rechts.*
9 Montpellier had flourishing schools long before 1289. By 1220, the statutes for the teaching of medicine had been drawn up by a papal legate. In 1230 St. Louis regulated by an ordinance the promotions of the faculty of law.

10 Orleans had been a university of civil law a hundred years before the formal recognition of 1306.

11 Charles IV took the initiative, and asked the pope to institute this university.

12 Angers had flourishing schools in the first half of the thirteenth century.

13 The University of Messina was instituted, on paper, in 1459 by King John of Sicily. But it was not until 1550 that Pope Paul III, at the request of Loyola, granted the bull of erection. The Jesuits multiplied in Sicily, and in the eighteenth century they were the masters of instruction throughout the island.

14 The University of Pont à Mousson in Lorraine was instituted by Duke Charles III, and Pope Gregory XIII. See, concerning this university, various opuscules by M. Favier, Nancy, 1878, 1880.

15 Among this number are Berlin, 1810; Christiania, 1811; St. Petersburg, 1819; Brussels, 1834; London, 1836; Athens, 1836. In France the Revolution and the Empire suppressed the ancient universities, and at the present time the law which proposes to reestablish them is being discussed in the French Senate.

16 Juvenal des Ursins, in 1435, affirmed that there had been from 16,000 to 20,000 students in Paris the previous year. Their number must have been still more considerable in the thirteenth century, when the universities were not yet multiplied.

17 Gilbert de la Porrée (1070–1154).

18 See chapter v.

19 Maurice de Sully (1105–1196).

20 Mullinger, *op. cit.*, p. 134.

21 Thurot, *op. cit.*, p. 7.

22 Concerning these legends, see Mullinger, *op. cit.*, p. 450. The fabulous tradition related above proceeds from the English doctor, John Caye.

23 See Part III, chap. iii, where I shall have occasion to return to the founder of the University of Bologna.

24 Bede, an English monk and historian (673–735).

25 Vallet de Viriville, *Histoire de l'instruction publique en Europe*, 1869, p. 100.

26 Mullinger, *The University of Cambridge*, 1873, p. 84.

27 Laurie, *op. cit.*, p. 239.

28 Henry VIII, King of England, consulted it in 1527 concerning his divorce from Katharine.

29 In the sixteenth century, a canon of Salamanca, Peter Cizuelo, taught mathematics at Paris; and, at the same epoch, Bologna borrowed Ramos de Pareja, who passes for the inventor of modern music, from Salamanca.

30 Vicente de la Fuente, *op. cit.*, t. i, p. 76.

31 Mullinger, *op. cit.*, p. 74.

32 Charles IV, says an author of his time, ordained that "*Studium Pragense ad modum et consuetudinem studii Parisiensis, in quo olim ipse rex in puerilibus constitutus annis studuerat, in omnibus et per omnia dirigeretur et regeretur,*" Denifle, *Die Entstehung der Universitäten*, etc., p. 588.

33 Denifle, *op. cit.*, etc., p. 382.

34 Denifle, *op. cit.*, etc., p. 605.

35 Laurie, *op. cit.*, lecture xiii, Oxford and Cambridge.

36 Denifle, *op. cit.*, p. 242.

37 Robert Pulleyne wrote a book of *Sentences*, which is thought to have suggested that of Peter Lombard, which became the handbook of theology in the schools of the Middle Ages.

38 *Chartularium Univ. Paris.*, t. i, p. 119. The University College was founded at Oxford four years later, in 1232. In 1240, Robert Grosseteste ordered the professors of theology at Oxford to conform, in their lectures, to the usages followed at Paris. *Ibid.*, p. 169.

39 Vicente de la Fuente, *op. cit.*, t. i, p. 304.
40 Denifle, *op. cit.*, p. 474. The *stipendia*, the appointments, naturally played a great part in the prosperity of universities. An inscription, which may still be seen at Salamanca, says of the university of that city: *illa deficientibus stipendiis defecit,* — until it was reorganized by Alfonso X.
41 Aymeric d'Hébrard was the preceptor of the son of Alfonso III, Denis the Liberal, who founded the University of Lisbon. From 1130 it was customary at Coimbra to send certain canons of the Order of St. Augustine to study in France.
42 Renan, *Averroés et l'Averroisme*, 1852, p. 258.
43 See Part III, chap. iii.
44 Crevier, *op. cit.*
45 Peter of Blois died about 1198, in England, where he had become an important personage. See the *Histoire littéraire de la France*, t. xv, p. 341 *et seq.*
46 De Montalembert, *Les Moines d'Occident*, t. vii, p. 650.

4

LATE MEDIEVAL UNIVERSITIES

A. B. Cobban

Source: A. B. Cobban, *The Medieval Universities: Their Development and Organization*, London: Methuen, 1975, pp. 116–21.

The history of the later medieval universities, which followed the period of spontaneous university creation, has yet to be written.[1] It is an area of study which forms an uncertain mosaic wherein broad generalizations co-exist uneasily with the findings of monographic research. A reason for past neglect of this subject has been the assumption that the later universities were watered down and inferior versions of Europe's archetypal *studia* and manifested the symptoms of organizational and intellectual decline. But difference is not necessarily decline: and the readiness with which the later universities adapted to meet changing social needs suggests that the university movement continued to be a vibrant force and not a petrification of a once living ideal. Contemporaries would probably not have viewed the universities of the fourteenth and fifteenth centuries as exhibiting marks of decay just because they failed to emulate the position attained by Bologna, Paris, Oxford, Padua, or Montpellier in the early phase of university development when scarcity value led to easier distinction. If there were between fifteen and twenty universities functioning in 1300, there were about seventy in 1500,[2] which, by any criterion, was a sign of buoyant optimism in the university condition. Even allowing for substantial redistribution of the student population of the older *studia*, this massive university expansion presupposes a sizeable increase in Europe's student numbers[3] and teaching force. This rising academic stake in the community was reflected in the growing splendour of university buildings which were being designed to have a prestigious permanence: solidly enmeshed in their urban environments, the later medieval universities could not easily employ the threat of migration; and this marks a fundamental departure from the era when instability was the hallmark of university life and intermittent nomadism one of the perils of the academic profession. The diffusion of intellectual talent over so many widely dispersed *studia* broke the monopolistic sway of the old-established universities; but the fragmentation of these cosmopolitan academic concentrations did not necessarily mean a lessening of university standards: it may only have resulted in a levelling over a broad geographical canvas. Although these matters are beyond measurement, one should avoid the automatic assumption that because the archetypal *studia* suffered population and intellectual reverses, the new universities must have partaken in a corresponding diminution.

There is a rich profusion of documentation for the study of the later universities and some of it is different in kind from that available for the older *studia*. The main interpretative lines for the history of the archetypal universities, at least in their formative stage, were based largely upon the official documents such as statutes, charters, bulls and the like and combined with intellectual assessments of the outstanding schoolmen. For the new universities there is more material of an administrative and business nature including records of university government, books of account, and matriculation and degree lists. These are supported by collegiate records, letters, sermons, and legal, ecclesiastical, state and municipal categories of archive which, directly or indirectly, have a bearing on universities and can perhaps provide a better insight into university life at the average level than is obtainable from the records of the thirteenth-century *studia*. But the examination and publication of this material is very far from complete and synthesis is not yet possible.[4]

The majority of the fourteenth- and fifteenth-century universities were founded by secular rulers or by municipalities and confirmed by the papacy: Treviso (1318), Pavia (1381), Orange (1365) and Prague (1347–8) were imperial foundations, although Prague was nevertheless submitted for papal approbation.[5] While considerations of prestige loomed large among the motives for foundation, unless the proposed university was rooted in real need and was favourably sited, its chances of survival were not good. The University of Grenoble, founded in 1339, was badly placed in the Dauphiné whose territory was disputed between the Empire and the French monarchy; it never prospered and was eventually replaced by the University of Valence in 1452.[6] Moreover, there was often a long gap separating the initial foundation step and the time when the university came into active being. For example, a university was projected at Nantes, with papal backing in 1414, and again in 1449; but it was not until 1461 that a university was actually opened.[7] In addition, a number of stillborn or entirely paper universities were projected which were sanctioned by papal bulls conferring *studium generale* status. In most of these cases, the reasons for abortive growth are unclear. Among this category of *studia* are included the proposed universities of Dublin, Lucca, Orvieto and Gerona.[8]

The multiplication of universities in Italy, France, Spain, Portugal, Germany, Scotland and Scandinavia radically altered Europe's university geography. There was now far greater opportunity for students to attend

a local university and this helped to accentuate the position of the universities as agents of secular government. Just as Paris and Bologna in the later
medieval period succumbed to increasing state control, so the new foundations, from the circumstances of their inception, were accommodated to
national, regional or municipal interests from the start. The celebrated
exodus of 1409 from Prague University of the German masters and students,
who comprised a majority of the academic population, following the altera-
tion of the constitution by King Wenceslas to ensure the Bohemian masters
a rigged commanding voice in all university assemblies, is only an outstanding instance of the way in which nationalistic concerns began to infiltrate
the European *studia*.[9] Universities lost their supranational character and
were increasingly regarded as integral parts of political territorial units,
designed to serve the needs of national institutions and to be of benefit
to those living in the locality. In the late medieval German universities, for
example, many of the masters approximated to the rank of state officials,
and this led to a close fusion of the professional intellectual ethos with that
of the professional civil servant.[10] By definition, a cosmopolitan academic
gathering, especially one wherein the foreign element was noticeably large,
was held to be at odds with the centralized pattern of secular government
which was so pronounced a trend in the late middle ages. There is nothing
to indicate that the universities exhibited organized resistance to their rôle
as protégés of secular authority: they must long since have realized that
academic freedom, in any purist sense, was a chimera and that society would
not tolerate or financially support academic groupings without exacting some
kind of quantitative return.[11] In these circumstances, it is not surprising that
the proportion of lay masters and students was augmented appreciably,
especially in the *studia* of Italy and southern France where there had always
been a significant lay tradition.[12]

If the later medieval universities were trapped within the orbit of secular
control, they were far freer than their predecessors from ecclesiastical
dominion. This is particularly true of the fifteenth-century *studia*. For
by that time the hard-fought struggle with the ecclesiastical authorities
had been won and the 'commonwealth' episcopal era begun.[13] Most of the
fifteenth-century French *studia* such as Aix (1409), Dêle (1422), Poitiers
(1431), Valence (1452, 1459), Nantes (1460) and Bourges (1464) were almost
entirely free from attempts by local ecclesiastical powers to infiltrate and
control the university corporation. Likewise, episcopal dominion is not
really a live issue in the universities of Germany, Bohemia, and the Low
Countries of the late fourteenth and fifteenth centuries. Many of these, such
as Prague (1347–8), Vienna (1365), Heidelberg (1385) and Leipzig (1409)
owed their inception to the actions of the local rulers.[14] Others such as
Cologne (1388) and Rostock (1419) were brought to fruition as a result of
municipal enterprise. Würzburg (1402) was an episcopal foundation, and it
was fairly common practice in this group of universities to appoint a bishop

or archbishop as chancellor. But where this was done, the chancellor's authority was to be largely nominal and his jurisdictional powers were, from the start or at a conveniently early stage, conferred upon the governing body of the university, usually represented by a rector.[15] The universities of Germany, Bohemia and the Low Countries were thus conceived in an intensely secular milieu, and this provided a solid limitation to the exercise of ecclesiastical authority. In Scotland, as previously mentioned,[16] episcopal initiative in university foundation was a wholly benevolent force, and one entirely compatible with an inevitable advance towards independent status. As far as one can judge, the same holds true for the situation in fifteenth-century Scandinavia.[17]

[. . .]

The archetypal universities of Bologna and Paris formed the models upon which the twofold pattern of late medieval university organization was based, the former giving rise to the notion of the student university and the latter to that of the masters' university. Generally speaking, the north European *studia* followed the framework of Paris and those of southern Europe the direction of Bologna. But few universities reproduced these patterns without adaptations. Even the German universities, which were closely influenced by the Paris model, show important departures. The earliest of these, Prague and Vienna, initially allowed scope for student participation, although these Bologna elements were later phased out.[18] The position of rector ceased to have much significance in the German situation. It lost its Parisian connections with the faculty of arts and the rector could be chosen from any quarter. Sometimes the office was accorded to a young aristocrat on a largely honorary basis as it was to the advantage of many German universities to encourage aristocratic patronage.[19] Several universities evolved features of such a hybrid nature that they formed a third constitutional category whose inspirational base was a combination of Bologna and Paris. Some of the French provincial *studia* were cast in this mould. The institutional permutations were manifold; and the chain of archetypal borrowing, adaptation and borrowed adaptation becomes so complex that it is not always possible to work out the constitutional pedigree of several of these later *studia*. Nation groupings were usually less important in the later universities than in those of the thirteenth century, presumably a symptom of the diminishing international university order.[20] In some universities, for example Orange, Dêle, Caen, Cahors, Perpignan, Nantes, Bordeaux, Erfurt and Cologne, there was no system of nations at all,[21] and in other *studia* such as Heidelberg they were quickly abolished.[22] Where nations survived, they did so primarily as administrative units and not as governmental or educational organs. The artificial and formal nature of the nations in the late medieval period represents a compromise between respect for a fundamental pioneer force in university development and a progressive need to fade out the nation unit as a central feature of the academic landscape. The nations had become something of an albatross: they were democratic embarrassments from a bygone age. Their centrifugal character could not be allowed to deflect from the more unitary style of university government that was emerging in the late middle ages.

Notes

1 For the later medieval universities see e.g. S. d'Irsay, *Histoire des universités* . . . , cit., i; Rashdall, *Universities*, ii; J. Verger, *Les universités au moyen âge*, cit., pp. 105 ff.; H. Koller, 'Die Universitäts-Gründungen des 14. Jahrhunderts' *Salzburger Universitätsreden*, no. 10 (Salzburg, 1966).

2 See the 'university map' in Rashdall, op. cit., i, p. xxiv and in V. H. H. Green, *Medieval Civilization in Western Europe* (London, 1971), pp. 264–5. The problem of computing numbers of universities is complicated by the fact that it is not always possible to know if some universities were functioning at a particular point in time, or even if they had progressed beyond the stage of paper foundation.

3 E.g. Verger, op. cit., p. 105.

4 See the remarks of Verger, ibid., pp. 106–9.

5 See Rashdall, *Universities*, ii, pp. 43–4, 51–3, 184–6, 213 ff.

6 Ibid., ii, pp. 183–4; Verger, op. cit., pp. 140–1.

7 Rashdall, op. cit., ii, pp. 203–5.

8 'Paper universities' are discussed ibid., ii, appendix i, pp. 325 ff.

9 For the Czech-German struggle at Prague see ibid., ii, pp. 222 ff. and H. Kaminsky, 'The University of Prague in the Hussite Revolution: The Role of the Masters', *Universities in Politics*, cit., pp. 79 ff.

10 See L. Boehm, 'Libertas Scholastica und Negotium Scholare: Entstehung und Sozialprestige des Akademischen Standes im Mittelalter' in op. cit., p. 47.

11 See the highly utilitarian and changeable attitude adopted by the Florentine Signoria towards the University of Florence in G. A. Brucker, 'Florence and the University, 1348–1434' in *Action and Conviction in Early Modern Europe*, cit., pp. 220 ff.

12 E.g. Verger, op. cit., p. 111.

13 See Cobban, 'Episcopal Control in the Mediaeval Universities', art. cit., esp. pp. 13–14.

14 Leipzig owed its foundation to Frederick and William Landgraves of Thuringia, who invited a section of the German scholars who migrated from Prague in 1409 to establish a *studium* in this city.

15 E.g. at Prague the archbishop was chancellor and exercised considerable authority in the early years. In 1397, however, the university obtained a complete exemption from all episcopal and archiepiscopal jurisdiction (Rashdall, ii, pp. 218, 220). At Würzburg (1402) the bishop became chancellor but, by the founder's charter of privileges of 1410, both spiritual and temporal jurisdiction over all students were conferred on the rector (Rashdall, ii, p. 257). The bishop of Merseburg was made chancellor at Leipzig (1409) and delegated jurisdiction over the students to the rector at an early stage; here, degrees were usually conferred by a vice-chancellor (Rashdall, ii, p. 259). The chancellor at Rostock (1419) was the bishop of Schwerin, but by 1468 the rector had acquired extensive jurisdictional powers from the bishop (Rashdall, ii, p. 261 and n. 2).

16 See above, p. 76.
17 See the accounts of the universities of Upsala (1477) and Copenhagen (1478) in Rashdall, op. cit., ii, pp. 298–300.
18 On the nations of Prague and Vienna see Kibre, *The Nations in the Mediaeval Universities*, pp. 167–76; Rashdall, op. cit., ii, p. 281.
19 Rashdall, op. cit., ii, p. 281; see J. M. Fletcher, 'Wealth and Poverty in the Medieval German Universities' in *Europe in the Late Middle Ages* (ed. J. R. Hale, J. R. L. Highfield and B. Smalley, London, 1965), pp. 410 ff.
20 For the nations in the later medieval universities see Kibre, op. cit., chs. iv, v.
21 Ibid., pp. 156, 177.
22 Ibid., p. 177.

5

Excerpt from
THE UNIVERSITIES OF THE ITALIAN RENAISSANCE

Paul F. Grendler

Source: P. F. Grendler, *The Universities of the Italian Renaissance*, Baltimore: Johns Hopkins University Press, 2002, pp. 3–21.

BOLOGNA AND PADUA

The Middle Ages created the university, the period's most magnificent and enduring achievement after the Christian Church. But the definition of *university* is not always clear. And Italian universities differed in important ways from their northern European counterparts, especially those of Paris and Oxford.

The Italian university

A functioning, whole Italian university had two complementary parts. It possessed a papal or imperial charter authorizing it to confer license and doctoral degrees recognized throughout Christendom. A local college of doctors and the chancellor of the university, often the bishop or his representative, usually exercised the power bestowed by the charter. Possession of a papal or imperial charter permitted a commune to claim that a *studium generale* (university empowered to grant degrees) existed in the town.[1] But this did not necessarily mean that it was a whole university. A university also had to offer advanced instruction in law, arts, medicine, and sometimes theology. A complete, if small, functioning Italian university had a minimum of six to eight professors teaching civil law, canon law, medicine, logic, natural philosophy, and usually rhetoric, but not necessarily theology, in regular classes at an advanced level. Only the combination of charter and teaching made a university.

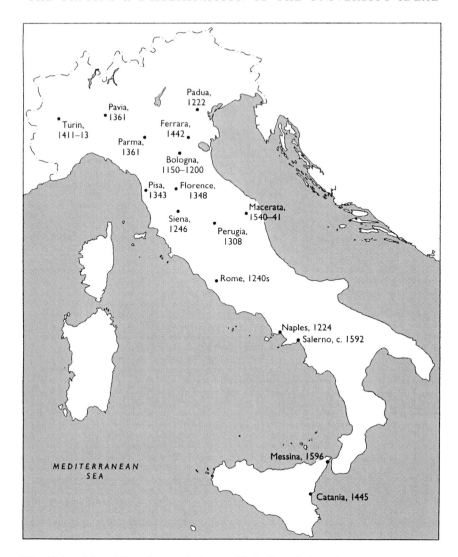

The Universities of Renaissance Italy and Their Foundation Dates.

Providing advanced teaching in a variety of disciplines was considerably more difficult to accomplish than acquiring the right to award degrees. Popes and emperors handed out university charters practically for the asking, especially if a sum of money accompanied the request. A visiting emperor might present a university charter to his communal hosts as an expression of good will. A pope might award one in exchange for support against an antipope. A charter encouraged the commune to create a university, but that was all. It resembled a hunting license authorizing prince or

88

commune to seek professors and the money to hire them. Raising money, hiring professors, and attracting students were difficult tasks. Lack of funds and internal or external political opposition often prevented a town from turning a charter into a functioning university. Communes with charters to award degrees but without advanced instruction were "paper universities," not teaching universities.[2]

Sometimes a commune with a charter achieved part of its goal. A number of Italian communes and courts appointed an advanced teacher of law or medicine, or both. A commune with one, two, or three men teaching some university subjects at an advanced level did not have a university, whether or not it possessed a charter. It might have an incomplete university.[3] The largest and best-known incomplete university in Italy was the Collegio Romano, founded by the Society of Jesus in 1551. It had many scholars who taught grammar, rhetoric, humanities, Greek, logic, natural philosophy, mathematics and astronomy, and theology at every level from elementary to advanced. Pope Paul IV in 1556 conferred on the Jesuits the power to award doctorates in arts and theology (but not law and medicine) to students of the Collegio Romano.[4] But it was not an Italian university, because it neither taught nor awarded degrees in law and medicine. It lacked the complete curriculum of an Italian university.

Italian universities differed from those in northern Europe and in Spain in several ways. They concentrated on law and medicine; arts and theology had less importance than in ultramontane universities. Italian universities granted doctoral degrees but almost never awarded bachelor's degrees. Most students at Italian universities were eighteen to twenty-five years of age, somewhat older than students at northern universities.[5] The majority of Italian professors were married laymen, rather than members of the clergy. Instruction at Italian universities occurred at "public" lectures, that is, lectures open to all, delivered by professors appointed and paid by the civil government. By contrast, much teaching at the universities of Paris and Oxford took place in colleges, which combined residence and teaching, especially for younger students. Clergymen were often college teachers in northern Europe. And instruction inside the college was not necessarily open to nonmembers of the college. By contrast, teaching colleges did not exist in Italian universities.

In this study the term *Italian university,* or just *university,* means a teaching institution that awarded doctorates and had a minimum of six to eight professors. Paid by the commune, the professors offered advanced instruction in the core subjects of law, medicine, and arts, which defined Italian universities. The host commune possessed a papal or imperial charter authorizing the conferral of license and doctoral degrees bearing the university's name.

Italy had sixteen universities between 1400 and 1601.[6] Bologna was the first.

Bologna: second half of the twelfth century

Bologna vied with Paris for the honor of being the first European university, and it provided the model for all others in southern Europe. The traditional account states that sometime in the late eleventh century students began to gather at the feet of lawyers who looked to Roman law as the guide to creating legal principles that enabled society to sort out the confusion between imperial claims, communal authority, and citizens' rights.[7] The most famous of these jurists was the Bolognese Irnerius (c. 1055–c. 1130), a practicing lawyer and judge involved in cases concerning imperial authority in northern Italy. He glossed (made detailed comments on) Justinian's *Corpus juris civilis* of the sixth century, and especially the *Digest,* in an effort to derive legal principles useful to medieval society. Others gathered to hear him, although it is not clear if he taught in a formal academic setting.

Other legists soon followed his example. About 1140 Gratian, a monk with legal experience living in a Bolognese monastery, made a compilation of church council decrees, papal letters, and extracts from patristic writings. He organized them so as to illustrate legal principles appropriate to the church and to ecclesiastical issues. Gratian's work became the basis for the study of church legislation, although he probably did not teach.

Nevertheless, a number of men did begin to teach civil and canon law at Bologna, attracting a growing number of foreign (non-Bolognese) students to the city. Since these students had little or no legal existence away from their homes, they created a student association in order to assert certain legal rights. They were law students, after all. An imperial document of 1158 recognized such an association (*universitas*), although nothing else is known about the student organization at this time.

The combination of structured teaching and student associations marked the origin of the University of Bologna. In the nineteenth century the leaders of the University of Bologna decided that this had happened in 1088, so that there might be a grand celebration in 1888. Bologna then celebrated its nine-hundredth anniversary in 1988. But it is not likely that enough instruction and organization existed to merit the term *university* before the 1150s, and it might not have happened before the 1180s.[8]

The presence of teaching legists probably encouraged teachers in other fields to come to Bologna. *Ars dictaminis,* grammar, logic, philosophy based on Aristotle, mathematical arts, and especially medicine were taught there by the middle of the thirteenth century. Taddeo Alderotti (c. 1210–95) of Florence, who adapted Aristotelian natural philosophy to the needs of medicine, began to teach in Bologna about 1260.[9] He soon raised medicine to a prestigious position in the university. Recognizing the contribution of Alderotti and his pupils, the commune extended scholarly privileges and tax exemptions to them between 1274 and 1288. About this time a college of physicians composed of teachers began to examine candidates for medical degrees. A student organization for arts comparable to that of the law students developed at the end of the thirteenth century and in the first years of the fourteenth at Bologna. Like the law student *universitas,* it hired professors and imposed pedagogical conditions on them.

For the better part of the thirteenth century the Bolognese student associations exercised powers of which students everywhere dream: they appointed, paid, and dismissed the professors. The students' greatest strength lay in the threat to migrate to another town, taking with them the considerable income that wealthy foreign students brought to a host city.

However, the commune began to pay law professors' salaries in the 1220s, stopped in the 1230s, a high point for the student *universitates,* but resumed payments in 1280.[10] The commune also began to pay salaries to medical professors, possibly to Alderotti, certainly to his successors in the first decade of the fourteenth century. It is likely that the commune did so because paying academic salaries almost guaranteed the stability of the university. As professors stayed in one place in order to receive regular salaries, students did as well, unless they could find another group of professors to teach them. And if students left, a stationary corps of teachers would attract new students. The decision to pay professorial salaries showed that the city viewed the university as an asset to the community, rather than as a group of wealthy young men who drove up housing costs, disturbed the peace, and violated women. The commune recognized that the university earned prestige for the city and poured income into the pockets of merchants, landlords, servants, and others. Bologna became a communally financed and ruled university by 1350.

The decision of the commune of Bologna to wrest control of the university from the students by paying professors was probably the most important decision in the early history of Italian universities. The civil government appointed professors and opened or closed the university. Student power did not completely disappear; the student organizations and many of their privileges remained, as did the regulations they imposed on professors, which the commune now enforced. But paying professorial salaries decided the issue of control. Every other Italian university followed the Bolognese example. Commune or prince ruled all Italian universities.

Pope and emperor, the twin towers of medieval authority, played no substantive role in the birth of the University of Bologna. The papacy entered only in 1219, when Honorius III decreed that the archdeacon of Bologna, an official of the Bolognese church, had to approve the granting of the *licentia docendi,* the license to teach.[11] This seems to have been only a claim, because teachers already conducted examinations and awarded degrees. A division of responsibilities developed, even though few records survive to document the process. A college of doctors examined a candidate who, if successful, received a degree sanctioned by the church, represented by the local bishop as chancellor of the university. The papally sanctioned degree gave the recipient the right to teach anywhere in Christendom. This permission became accepted as the right of the pope (later the emperor as well) to issue a charter authorizing the establishment of a *studium generale* with the authority to award degrees recognized throughout Christendom. In future centuries a city or prince wishing to create a university obtained a charter from pope, emperor, or both.

The first surviving faculty rolls of the University of Bologna come from the mid-fourteenth century. The commune of Bologna paid salaries to 17, 23, and 17 professors, respectively, the majority teaching law, in the three academic years 1351–52 through 1353–54.[12] However, these may not be complete rolls. The next surviving faculty roll comes from the academic year 1370–71, followed by almost all faculty rolls through the eighteenth century, the most complete set of surviving rolls for any Italian university. Bologna had the largest faculty in Italy throughout the Renaissance.

After growing steadily until reaching an average size of 97 in the decade of the 1440s, the number of teachers stabilized at 85 to 110 until the 1530s, when it fell to about 80. Bologna had more legists than artists until the decade 1510–19, when the artists temporarily dominated. Then from the 1540s through the end of the century, Bologna had more artists than legists. The reasons are twofold: Bologna added more professors of medicine and arts, as some subjects (e.g., anatomy, medical botany, and the humanities) grew in importance. Moreover, professors of theology and Scripture were added. By contrast, law declined because the university sharply reduced the number of canonists (see Ch. 13) and because student lectureships in law were seldom filled in the second half of the sixteenth century. Student lectureships in arts continued to be filled.

Examination of the distribution of professors by subject offers a more detailed picture of the faculty. In 1370–71 the university had 11 professors of civil law (called civilians), 7 professors of canon law, 3 professors of medical theory ("the philosophy of medicine and principles of physiology and pathology"), 2 of medical practice ("the specifics of diagnosis and treatment"),[13] 1 professor of surgery, 1 professor who taught both medicine and natural philosophy, a logician, an astrologer, a rhetorician, and a professor of notarial art, for a total of 29.[14] The university continued to grow. The roll of 1388–89 numbered 15 professors of canon law, 18 for civil law, 16 for theoretical and practical medicine and surgery, 5 natural philosophers, 2 moral philosophers, 3 logicians, 4 astronomers, 1 rhetorician, and 3 who taught notarial art, for a total of 67.

The faculty grew mostly through the addition of more professors in the traditional subjects in the fifteenth century. For example, the roll of 1426–27 listed 25 canonists, 28 civilians, 11 professors of medical theory, 10 for medical practice, 3 professors of surgery, 1 for orthopedics (*Ad lecturam dislocationum et fracturarum ossium*), 4 professors of natural and moral philosophy, 3 astrologers, 3 logicians, 4 professors of rhetoric and poetry, a

Table 1 Average Annual Number of Professors at Bologna, 1370–1599.

Years	Law	Arts & Medicine	Total
1370–79	18	13	31
1380–89	27	24	51
1390–99	43	30	73
1400–1409	33	24	57
1410–19	31	26	57
1420–29	46	33	79
1430–39	45	28	73
1440–49	59	38	97
1450–59	68	42	110
1460–69	54	36	90
1470–79	49	37	86
1480–89	50	35	85
1490–99	57	35	92
1500–1509	49	39	88
1510–19	44	47	91
1520–29	47	53	100
1530–39	43	37	80
1540–49	37	39	76
1550–59	38	41	79
1560–69	35	45	80
1570–79	28	49[a]	77
1580–89	30	56[b]	86
1590–99	34	52[c]	86

Source: Dallari, 1888–1924, 1, 2, and 4: *Aggiunte;* plus Zaoli, 1912 and 1920.

Note: The professorship (occasionally with two men) of notarial arts was listed in the arts faculty until 1458–59, when it moved to the law faculty. It is always classified as law in the table above, because it was closer to law than arts. The table includes one to three teaching student rectors of law and arts, when these positions were filled, which was less often after 1550. It includes the competitive student lectureships, which totaled eleven (six law, five arts and medicine) when all were filled. This was frequently not the case, which helps explain the fluctuation in numbers. A small number of incomplete rolls have not been included in the averages. The majority of rolls, especially after 1450, also list preuniversity teachers who taught beginning reading and writing, Latin grammar and reading, rhetoric, and arithmetic and geometry (i.e., abbaco) in different quarters of the city (see Grendler, 1989, 26–29, for further explanation). These teachers have been excluded. The small number of cases in which it is not clear whether a grammarian taught at the university or preuniversity level do not affect the overall averages.

[a] This includes an average of 1.5 professors of theology and Scripture, listed in the arts rolls.
[b] This includes an average of 2.5 professors of theology and Scripture, listed in the arts rolls.
[c] This includes an average of 4 professors of theology and Scripture, listed in the arts rolls.

professor of Greek, and a professor of notarial art, making a total of 94.[15] Although this was an early peak, Bologna still averaged 79 professors through the 1420s.

The distribution of faculty changed little in the course of the century. The rolls of the 1470s usually listed about 17 canonists, 23 civilians, 1 notary professor, 8 professors of medical theory, 3 or 4 professors of medical practice, 2 or 3 surgeons, 5 natural philosophers, 2 moral philosophers, 2 or

3 astronomers, 5 logicians, 4 professors of rhetoric and poetry, a professor of Greek, and 1 for Hebrew, an innovation. In addition, 2 student rectors and 5 to 11 unpaid student lecturers taught.

Having decided to pay professorial salaries, the commune created a civil magistracy to rule the university directly and to serve as a buffer between *studium* and the higher ranks of government. In or about 1376 the commune appointed four citizens—a senator, a noble, a knight, and a merchant—to oversee the university.[16] Called Riformatori dello Studio (Reformers of the University), this magistracy negotiated with professors, determined stipends, compiled the annual roll, fixed the teaching schedule, and regulated the university in every way except the legal privileges of the students. The Riformatori reported to the highest council of the commune. Other cities and princes followed the Bolognese example by establishing a civil magistracy, often also called Riformatori dello Studio, to oversee the local university. In 1463 the Riformatori appointed a *punctator,* an official charged with visiting classes daily to make certain that professors delivered lectures, taught the required one or two hours, and had a minimum of five students in attendance. A professor deficient in any of these categories suffered financial penalties.[17] Other universities followed the Bolognese lead with similar legislation.

The University of Bologna flourished amid political instability. The city had a population of 32,000 in 1371, making it one of the five or six largest in Italy and clearly one of the wealthiest.[18] But Bologna did not enjoy political peace. A free commune throughout the university's formative period, Bologna maintained its independence under the overlordship of the papacy in the early fourteenth century. Communal strife intensified in the second half of the fourteenth century because no individual, faction, or outsider was strong enough to hold the city for long. Hence, Bologna alternated between free communal government, more or less direct papal rule through a legate, and princely rule by an outsider in the last half of the fourteenth century.

Constant strife and frequent change of office prompted the leading citizens in 1393 to concentrate authority in a council of patricians called the Sedici Riformatori, who would serve for life.[19] But instead of creating unity, the council served as a launching pad for men with princely ambitions, especially members of the Bentivoglio family. In addition, factions of patricians occasionally invited the papacy to exercise direct rule through a legate, invitations that the papacy eagerly accepted.

The pattern continued into the following century. The Bologna underwent a major political change in 1445. After several abortive attempts, the Bentivoglio succeeded in becoming de facto "first citizens." Sante Bentivoglio (b. 1424) became prince of Bologna in everything but name in 1445 and remained so until his death in 1463. Giovanni II Bentivoglio (1443–1508), a second cousin, immediately succeeded him as "first citizen" and lasted until 1506.

The Bentivoglio still had to contend with the papacy. In 1447 Pope Nicholas V and Sante Bentivoglio created a mixed constitutional state.[20] The key provision was that the highest civil magistracy and the papal legate had to concur; the actions of one were invalid without the consent of the other. In other words, oligarchic commune dominated by the Bentivoglio and pope shared power; commune and legate would act in unison. This seemingly impossible arrangement worked because the papacy and the Bentivoglio, who dominated the Sedici Riformatori, wanted it to work. "First-citizen" members of the Bentivoglio family and papal legates supported each other for the next sixty years. The Bentivoglio dominated civic affairs, while the papacy determined foreign policy.

During the latter part of the century Giovanni II Bentivoglio increasingly became patron and prince of the university. In particular he drew the university humanists, who were Bolognese natives, into his orbit. Francesco da Pozzo (called Puteolano), Filippo Beroaldo the Elder, Antonio Urceo (called Il Codro), and Giovanni Garzoni, humanist and professor of medicine, tutored Bentivoglio children, praised the "first citizen" in their works, and enjoyed Bentivoglio patronage. As always, princely patronage had a price: losing the prince's favor meant dismissal for some professors.[21] The Bentivoglio also insisted that the university award a few degrees for political reasons.

The concord between Bentivoglio and papacy helped the university when Pope Nicholas V sent Cardinal Bessarion to be his legate (1450–55). The learned Bessarion immediately proposed improvements for the university which Nicholas V, who had taken an arts doctorate at Bologna in 1420 and had been bishop of the city, implemented through a bull. However, his attempt to add a professorship of music did not succeed.[22]

In 1384–85 the forty-four teaching professors received a total of about 4,900 lire bolognesi, a modest average salary of 111 Bolognese lire, paid quarterly.[23] Salary expenses then rose to 10,000 to 13,000 Bolognese lire annually in the second and third decades of the fifteenth century. Two or three law professors earned very high salaries, but the average was a modest 165 to 195 Bolognese lire, the equivalent of about 83 to 117 Florentine florins or Venetian ducats.[24] In addition, university statutes of 1405 permitted professors to collect small fees (sometimes called "bench money") from students attending their lectures. Doctoral examination fees and fiscal immunities increased professorial incomes.

Bologna financed the university through tax revenues.[25] In 1416 the commune assigned the revenues from several taxes, including that on pepper, to the university. This apparently proved inadequate. Hence, in 1433 the papal governor (Bologna having temporarily returned to direct rule by the papacy) assigned the revenues of a tax on all saleable goods coming into the city. Pope Eugenius IV confirmed this in 1437 and promised additional funds if needed. This tax financed the university through the rest of the century.

The College of Civil Law conferred 1,427 known combined licentiates and doctorates, or licentiates only, in civil law, or civil and canon law together (*utroque iure*), between 1378 and 1500. This was an average of 11.6 degrees per year.[26] Since there are some lacunae in the records, and because such records seldom included all recipients, the actual number is probably higher. Moreover, it is likely that Bologna awarded at least 5 canon law degrees and at least 7 arts and medicine doctorates annually. Hence, Bologna awarded a minimum of 24 degrees annually in the fifteenth century; the real number was undoubtedly higher.[27]

The geographical distribution of the civil law degree recipients demonstrates the international character of the student body. About 73 percent of the civil law and *utroque iure* degrees went to Italians and 26 percent to non-Italians.[28] Of the foreigners, the largest number came from France (29%), Germany (28%), Spain (21%), and England (11%). Students from what are now Austria, Belgium, Greece, the Netherlands, Poland, and Portugal also received civil law licentiates and doctorates between 1378 and 1500. Because the number of non-Italians acquiring civil law degrees was much greater after 1450 than earlier, it appears that the student body became more international in the course of the century.

But localism ruled in the faculty. Prominent Bolognese family names dominated every faculty roll of the fifteenth century. Indeed, son sometimes followed father into university teaching. A few political leaders held teaching posts. Antongaleazzo Bentivoglio took a degree in civil law in 1414 and held an ordinary professorship of civil law from 1418 to 1420 at a salary of 300 Bolognese lire, the third highest salary in law.[29] He then ruled the city for six months of 1420 before being driven into exile. Members of leading Bolognese families opposed to the Bentivoglio also held faculty positions. Bologna did not often hire foreign—that is, non-Bolognese—professors at this time, and they did not stay long.

Other communes countered faculty provincialism to a limited extent by hiring a few prominent foreign scholars at higher salaries. Pope Nicholas V in 1450 attempted to limit the salaries of Bolognese citizen professors to 600 Bolognese lire in an effort to accumulate money that could be used to attract distinguished foreigners.[30] But his decree had little effect on appointments or salaries. The vast majority of both Bolognese and foreign professors earned considerably less than 600 Bolognese lire before 1450 and remained far below this figure later. In the academic year 1470–71, seventy-two professors received a total of 14,535 Bolognese lire. One professor received 1,200 Bolognese lire, and two received 1,000. The next highest salary was 400, and the average stipend was 202 Bolognese lire.[31]

Certainly 14,500 Bolognese lire for university salaries was a large commitment of resources. But Bologna chose to hire numerous professors, mostly local men, at modest salaries, rather than fewer but more eminent professors, including expensive outsiders. Certainly the Bolognese policy had advantages. A large faculty meant that students could always find instruction on a particular subject or text. And because most locally born professors taught at Bologna their entire careers, the faculty had great stability.

Many professors bearing local names were able scholars, but few were commanding figures in their fields. An exception was Alessandro Achillini (1461/63–1512), a native of Bologna. Achillini took his degree at Bologna in 1484 and immediately began teaching there: logic until 1487, natural philosophy from 1487 to 1494, morning ordinary professor of medical theory from 1494 to 1497, and afternoon ordinary professor of natural philosophy from 1497 to 1500. Achillini then held both ordinary positions simultaneously: morning professor of medical theory and afternoon professor of natural philosophy, from 1500 until the fall of 1506. This meant that he delivered two lectures daily, which was very unusual. As a warm supporter of the Bentivoglio, Achillini left for Padua in early November 1506, when Giovanni II Bentivoglio lost power. After having taught for two years a t Padua, he returned to Bologna in September 1508 to reclaim the same two positions in medicine and philosophy, which he held until his death in 1512. In 1509–10 Achillini received a salary of 900 Bolognese lire, the third highest after two legists.[32] He published many works in medicine, anatomy, and philosophy. He may have discovered, and he certainly was the first to describe, the small bones of the ear and the ileocaecal valve connecting the small and large intestines. As a philosopher Achillini maintained an Averroist interpretation of Aristotle.

The University of Bologna prospered in the fifteenth century despite the sharp and sometimes bloody competition for political power in the city. Commune and papal legate worked together to ensure that the university sailed serenely through choppy political seas. The commune did not reduce the university appropriation in time of difficulty, and it maintained the size of the faculty when one regime replaced another. The papacy in its capacity as overlord and supranational authority issued bulls to support student and faculty privileges, encouraged foreign students to attend, and worked to strengthen the university.

Bologna in the sixteenth century

The Bolognese kept the papacy at a distance through the fifteenth century despite recognizing papal authority and making annual payments. But the papacy always viewed concessions granted to the commune as temporary. When Giovanni II Bentivoglio lost support within Bologna in the first years of the sixteenth century, Pope Julius II marched on the city. Giovanni II fled rather than face certain defeat, and papal troops entered the city in November 1506. Although he and other members of his family attempted to regain power in the next few years, their rule had ended.

But papal triumph did not signal Bolognese subjugation. After the death of Julius II in 1513, papacy and commune reinstated the terms of the agreement of 1447 under which they shared power. A Senate of forty (later fifty) life members drawn from the leading noble families of Bologna replaced the Sedici Riformatori. When a vacancy occurred, the pope chose a replacement from a group of four nominees presented by the Senate. The Senate later became hereditary. Communal legislative and fiscal structures remained in place. As before, Senate and legate had to act in accord under the principle that "the legate can do nothing without the Senate, and the Senate can do nothing without the legate."[33] The Bolognese mostly governed themselves in internal matters. And like a sovereign state, Bologna had a small armed force under the joint authority of Senate and legate and maintained a resident ambassador at the papal court. Bologna and its *contado* (the surrounding countryside under direct rule of the commune) remained a largely self-governing aristocratic republic within the papal state until the unification of Italy in the nineteenth century.[34]

Governance and fiscal support for the University of Bologna continued as before under the direct authority of the commune. Julius II confirmed in 1509 that the tax on goods coming into the city to be sold (called *grossa gabella*) would finance the university. It yielded income of slightly more than 25,000 Bolognese lire for the university in 1509–10 and similar or larger annual amounts in the next twenty years. Subsequent popes confirmed this financial arrangement in 1567 and 1586.[35] The Riformatori dello Studio chose the professors and determined stipends. A representative of the Senate and the legate ratified the actions of the Riformatori.

With increased funding the university had a large faculty. Bologna continued a policy of appointing three to six or more concurrent professors for the major professorships, such as the ordinary morning professor of civil law and ordinary morning professor of medical theory. But only the stipends, which were not published, indicated which person was considered to hold the first position. In the 1520s the faculty numbered 100, including the 6 student lecturers in law and 5 in arts, divided between 47 legists and 53 professors of arts and medicine. The law faculty now typically included about 24 professors of civil law, 21 professors of canon law, and 2 professors of notarial art. The arts and medicine faculty had approximately 18 professors of medical theory, 5 of medical practice, 5 professors of surgery, 5 natural philosophers, 2 metaphysicians, 5 logicians, 4 astronomers, 7 professors of rhetoric and poetry or humanities, a professor of Greek, and one to teach Hebrew or Hebrew and "Chaldean" (i.e., Aramaic). This large faculty received about 25,000 Bolognese lire in 1523–24 and 30,000 Bolognese lire in 1526–27. The average salary in 1526–27 was about 306 Bolognese lire.[36] University expenses remained at this high level. The commune spent a little more than 31,000 Bolognese lire on the university, all except about 1,000 of the amount for faculty salaries, in 1552–53. The star civilian Mariano

Sozzini the Younger received 5,200 Bolognese lire, more than one-sixth of the total. The commune spent about 17,400 Bolognese lire for arts and medicine salaries alone in 1563–64.[37]

The Riformatori dello Studio took advantage of the ill fortune of the University of Padua in order to pursue the most famous philosopher of the day, Pietro Pomponazzi of Mantua (1462–1525). Pomponazzi had taught at Padua since 1488, with the exception of three years of private study. When war closed the University of Padua in 1509, Pomponazzi fled to Ferrara. When the Venetians did not immediately restore the Studio Padovano, the Bolognese persuaded him to come to Bologna to hold the position of ordinary professor of natural philosophy at a salary of 200 gold ducats (worth about 700 Bolognese lire at this time), less than he had earned at Padua.[38] Pomponazzi began teaching at Bologna either during the academic year 1511–12 or in the autumn of 1512.

The Bolognese had to pay considerably more to keep Pomponazzi. In 1514–15 he held two posts, ordinary professor of natural philosophy and extraordinary professor of moral philosophy with the obligation of lecturing on holidays. The Bolognese offered him a four-year contract at 400 ducats (1,250 Bolognese lire) to continue these two posts. But the Florentine government then offered him 500 florins to teach natural philosophy at Pisa. When the University of Pisa did not open for the academic year in the autumn of 1515, the Florentine authorities invited him to lecture at Florence. The Bolognese responded by using every means at their disposal to hold Pomponazzi. They took the high ground of begging Pope Leo X and Cardinal Giulio de' Medici to dissuade the younger Medici princes in Florence from pursuing him. They took the low road of denying Pomponazzi permission to move his effects out of Bologna. In October 1515 Pomponazzi signed a four-year contract with Bologna. However, the Florentines continued to pursue him. The Bolognese countered with an offer of an eight-year contract for 600 ducats (2,100 Bolognese lire), which Pomponazzi signed in late December 1518. Throughout this academic tug-of-war, Pomponazzi taught large classes and wrote his most famous book, *De immortalitate animae*, which was printed in 1516. He taught at Bologna until illness forced him to stop in 1524; he died in 1525.[39]

The Bolognese took further advantage of Paduan difficulties by hiring the eminent Carlo Ruini of Reggio (c. 1456–1530), who had also been teaching at Padua. Bologna appointed him its major afternoon ordinary professor of civil law in 1511 at a stipend of 3,000 Bolognese lire (about 857 gold ducats), a figure later raised to 4,320 Bolognese lire (about 1,234 gold ducats).[40] After Ruini's death the Bolognese pursued other famous non-Bolognese legists.

Although Bolognese legists taught *mos italicus*, the traditional legal method, a famous name was more important than methodological consistency. Hence, Bologna turned to the leading representative of the new humanistic jurisprudence, Andrea Alciato of Milan (1492–1550). Alciato agreed to come from Pavia to Bologna for 1,200 gold scudi per annum plus 200 scudi for moving expenses. He taught civil law at Bologna for four years, 1537 through 1541. However, pressure from Emperor Charles V, overlord of Lombardy, forced Alciato to agree to return to the University of Pavia at the end of 1541.[41] Bologna continued to pursue famous law professors throughout the century.

As the example of Alciato demonstrated, the commune had begun to hire a few eminent non-Bolognese professors. In 1513 the Senate decreed that the university might have four non-Bolognese professors on its rolls, one each in law, philosophy, medicine, and the humanities.[42] The commune did its best to ensure that these four would be the most famous scholars that money could buy. The commune was not just interested in scholarship; it wanted eminent foreigners in order to attract students, especially ultramontanes. Nor did the university limit itself to four; it appointed some professors, especially in arts and medicine, from other parts of Italy.

Still, the non-Bolognese faculty constituted only a small fraction of the total. Law was almost exclusively staffed by local men through the rest of the century. Fortunately, Bologna and its territory had a strong intellectual tradition that produced many good scholars, especially in medicine. For example, Giulio Cesare Aranzio of Bologna (c. 1530–89) took a degree at Bologna in 1556 and taught surgery from 1556 to 1570 and anatomy from 1570 to 1588 there, making important discoveries about the human fetus.[43] Gaspare Tagliacozzi of Bologna (1545–99) took his degree in medicine at Bologna in 1570, was appointed to the newly established anatomy professorship, taught at Bologna until his death, and was a pioneer in plastic surgery. The Bolognese Ulisse Aldrovandi (1522–1605) developed natural history during his long teaching career (1553–1600).

Thanks to talented native sons and a few outsiders, Bologna achieved a level of scholarly eminence above all other Italian universities with the exception of Padua. The two institutions competed throughout the century; indeed, a significant number of well-known scholars taught at both.

As table 1 indicated, Bologna had 80 to 85 professors and student lecturers in the last third of the sixteenth century. The civilians numbered 20 to 23, and the canonists had dropped to 7 to 10. The faculty of arts and medicine of 45 to 50 persons had 9 professors of medical theory, 7 for practical medicine, 4 for surgery, and 1 for medical botany. There were about 8 natural philosophers including Aldrovandi, who taught "fossils, plants, and animals." Two astronomers, 1 mathematician, 3 humanists, 1 professor of Greek, 2 metaphysicians, and 1 or 2 logicians made up the rest. A professorship of Hebrew (sometimes Hebrew and Aramaic) came and went. The student rector of arts sometimes taught, as did up to 5 student lecturers, 1 each in medicine, natural philosophy, astronomy, rhetoric, and logic. Finally, the arts roll listed 1 to 4 professors of theology and Sacred Scripture, a new departure for Bologna (see Ch. 10, "Universities Reluctant to Teach Theology").

The university acquired its own quarters through the efforts of the papal legate. Classes had met in rented rooms throughout the city, but especially in the center. Stimulated by the example of the University of Padua, where all classes met in the university building by 1530, the papal legate agitated for a home for the Bolognese *studio*. Pope Pius IV, aware of the need from his student days at Bologna (he took a law degree *in utroque iure* in 1525), issued a bull in 1561 ordering the erection of a building. The Bolognese Senate strongly opposed the measure, as did the professors, who feared that part of their salaries would be diverted to construction costs. The legate prevailed, and the professors' fears were realized. Construction of the Archiginnasio building very near the cathedral of San Petronio in the center of the city began in March 1562. The city and the faculty bore the construction costs of 64,000 Bolognese lire. The building was completed in time for the opening of the academic year in October 1563. The Archiginnasio had seven lecture halls for law, six for arts and medicine, space for a permanent anatomical theater (added after 1595), and two additional rooms for other purposes. Classes met in the Archiginnasio until 1803; it now houses the Biblioteca Archiginnasio, the city's major library. Numerous crests of student rectors, professors, and students decorate the walls.[44]

Bologna conferred a large number of degrees in the sixteenth century. It awarded an average of 25 doctorates in arts and medicine annually between 1550 and 1559, the decade with the highest number of known degrees in arts and medicine. In law, Bologna awarded an average of 55 degrees annually between 1583 and 1599.[45] It is likely that the total number of doctorates was greater than this sampling indicates, because documentation for university degrees is seldom complete.

Since Bologna boasted the largest faculty in Italy, it is likely that its enrollments were the highest. Bologna may have had average annual enrollments of 1,000 students from 1400 to 1450, about 1,500 for 1450–99, and 1,500 to 2,000 between 1500 and 1550. Enrollment probably held at about 2,000 at midcentury and then declined to 1,500 in the last years of the century. These are only estimates, because no precise information is available.[46] Enrollments could fluctuate considerably from year to year.

The city's population and physical size could accommodate a large student body. The inhabitants probably numbered slightly fewer than 40,000 at the end of the fourteenth century and possibly about 50,000 at the end of the fifteenth century. The sixteenth century saw steady growth to 62,000 in 1569 and 72,000 in 1587. Recession and famine then lowered the population to about 65,000 in the 1590s, and it remained at this level through the first two decades of the following century.[47]

Students frequently disturbed the peace. They commonly wore swords, and some carried firearms in the late sixteenth century. Clashes between students of different nations, or between students and the communal police force, could be bloody. When fighting produced a fatality, the Bolognese commune often executed the alleged killer, despite student claims of immunity from local prosecution. And the commune acted swiftly and brutally against any perceived threat of insurrection. In 1520 it decapitated a student accused of writing treason against the commune. On the other hand, the city sometimes bent over backward to avoid antagonizing the students as a whole, fearing that they would leave for another university or overwhelm the city's small police force. When in 1560 a fight between students and police led to the death of a student, the authorities appeased the students by hanging a policeman who had allegedly thrown a rock at them.[48]

The University of Bologna sailed relatively serenely through the sixteenth century. Its large faculty of numerous local sons and some eminent outsiders seemed to satisfy students. The Riformatori dello Studio became a little more aristocratic in composition, as its four members typically included two nobles. Then in the 1520s the Bolognese Senate established its own subcommittee to deal with extraordinary university matters. Called the Assunteria di Studio, this committee of four senators gradually assumed control over the most important matters, such as professorial hiring and salaries. The Riformatori were reduced to scheduling and keeping track of missed lectures.[49]

The Bolognese consulted with their papal overlords about major university matters more often than previously, especially when attempting to appoint a distinguished foreign scholar. Then the Assunteria di Studio contacted the Bolognese ambassador to the Holy See, who would enlist the help of influential cardinals. Popes often helped in the recruitment of leading scholars.[50] Both commune and pontiff strove to maintain the university at the highest level. Indeed, the papacy put the interests of the University of Bologna ahead of those of other universities (Perugia, Macerata, Ferrara after 1598, and Rome itself) in the papal state.

Many future university scholars studied or took degrees at Bologna. So did five popes, Nicholas V (1447–55), Alexander VI (law degree in 1456; pope 1492–1503), Pius IV (1559–65), Gregory XIII (1572–85), and Gregory XV (1621–23). Nicholas V (Tommaso Parentucelli) took an arts degree in 1420.[51] The Bolognese-born Gregory XIII (Ugo Buoncampagni) took a law degree *in utroque iure* in 1530 and taught civil law at Bologna from 1530 to 1540 before moving to a curial post in Rome. Many future papal diplomats, curialists, bishops, and cardinals also studied at Bologna. Most of them took degrees in law, because law, rather than theology, positioned a clergyman for advancement in the Renaissance church. The Protestant Ulrich von Hutten also studied law at Bologna, in 1516–17.[52] Nicolaus Copernicus (1473–1543), who studied law and astronomy at Bologna from 1496 to 1501 (see Ch. 12, "Professors of Astrology, Astronomy, and Mathematics"), may have been Bologna's most famous student.

Bologna awarded the second known doctorate to a woman, who then became the first female professor. The Bolognese Laura Maria Caterina

Bassi (1711–78), the daughter of a professor of medicine, studied privately. She then participated in a public disputation with five professors on these in logic, metaphysics, and physics before an assemblage of senators, professors, and the cardinal archbishop on April 17, 1732. So impressed were they that a doctoral examination was arranged. Bassi passed the examination on May 11, 1732, and received her degree on May 12. The commune then offered her a teaching position at 500 Bolognese lire. Her name appeared on the roll for the rest of her life, from 1732–33 through the academic year 1777–78 as a professor *Ad universam philosophiam* with the freedom to lecture on texts of her choosing ("ad beneplacitum"). However, she apparently did not lecture in the university building but at home. Although some male professors also taught at home, this seems to have been a concession to those who objected to the appointment of a woman. In later years Bassi also conducted physical experiments for advanced students, lectured frequently at the local academy of science, corresponded with Voltaire and Alessandro Volta among others, and received Emperor Joseph II, who admired her physical experiments.[53]

The Studio Bolognese was the first Italian university and set the pattern. When the commune began to pay faculty salaries and make appointments, it fixed the character of the Italian university as a civic enterprise teaching the secular subjects of law and medicine. The commune appointed citizens and residents of the city and its territory to the majority of teaching posts, a policy followed by most Italian universities. By 1400 the Studio Bolognese was a large institution attracting students from the entire European world. Political turbulence had few negative effects on the university. Although commune and papacy contested each other for political control of the city, they collaborated for the benefit of the university. So far as is known, it never closed between 1400 and 1600, a remarkable record for the times. Although Bologna began by teaching law, arts and medicine were equally important, perhaps more significant, in the sixteenth century. Bologna had the largest number of professors and probably the highest student enrollment among Italian universities. Overall, Bologna competed with Padua for the title of Italy's leading university.

Notes

1 Verger's explanation of *studium generale* is worth quoting: "A *studium generale* was an institution of higher education founded on, or, at any rate, confirmed in its status by, an authority of a universal nature, such as the pope or (less frequently) the emperor, whose members enjoyed a certain number of rights, likewise universal in their application, which transcended all local divisions (such as towns, dioceses, principalities, and states). . . . Titles awarded in the universities were guaranteed by the founding authority and therefore regarded as being universally valid. This meant that the licenses (*licentiae docendi*) granted by the universities were licenses *ubique docendi*, entitling the holder to teach throughout

Christendom. . . . As for the titles of doctor or master, the holding of them was regarded as a sign of the very highest intellectual competence and of equivalent value in all circumstances, no matter which university had granted them; and, as a consequence, they were supposed to allow access everywhere to the offices and honours reserved for the holders of this high rank." Verger, 1992, 35–36.

Verger's explanation assumes that *studium generale* meant that both the right to confer degrees and advanced teaching existed. But this was not always the case. Contemporary documents often used the terms *studium generale* and *studium* (*studio* in Italian) when a charter, but not a complete teaching university, existed. Modern historians faithfully following the documents use these terms, sometimes leaving the impression that teaching universities existed when they did not. Local pride in the institution encourages this tendency. The following pragmatic definition of an Italian university attempts to clarify a blurred picture.

2 Rashdall (1936, 2:325) defines *paper universities* as "universities for which Bulls were granted, but which never came into actual existence." I define a *paper university* as one that had a charter and awarded degrees but did not teach.

3 *Incomplete university* is my term.

4 Villoslada, 1954, 33–36.

5 Marc-Antoine Muret's description of the ideal progress of studies (written 1572–85) clearly states that the student should begin university studies at the age of eighteen. Muret, 1737, 1:302–7; Renzi, 1986, 267–70. Abundant evidence from the lives of students and the ages when doctoral degrees were conferred supports Muret.

6 From this point onward, *university* means "a complete teaching university," unless otherwise indicated. See Chapter 4 for some paper and incomplete universities. Occasionally *studium* and *studio* are used for the sake of variety.

7 The following is based on Rashdall, 1936, vol. 1, ch. 4; Sorbelli, 1940, chs. 1–4; Stelling-Michaud, 1955, chs. 2 and 3; Hyde, 1972; Bellomo, 1995, 58–63, 65–68; and Southern, 1995, chs. 8 and 9, esp. 274–82. Although there is much more bibliography, these works are essential.

8 Hyde (1972, 34–37) and Southern (1995, 312–17) suggest the 1150s; Verger (1992, 47–49) prefers the 1180s; and Rüegg (1992, 4–6), the last years of the twelfth century. But all scholars recognize that the creation of the University of Bologna was an evolutionary process.

9 The following is based on Rashdall, 1936, 1:233–42; Siraisi, 1981, 13–24; and Sorbelli, 1940, ch. 4.

10 Rashdall, 1936, 1:210–11; Hyde, 1972, 44.

11 Rashdall, 1936, 1:221–24, 231–32; Sorbelli, 1940, 92; and Trombetti Budriesi, 1988, 140–53. The last includes much additional bibliography.

12 Sorbelli, 1912. The information comes from communal payment records, is somewhat confusing, and may be incomplete. The total annual amount may have reached 2,000 Bolognese lire.

13 Quoted from Siraisi, 1990, 73.

14 Dallari, 1888–1924, vol. 4: *Aggiunte*, 3–4.

15 Ibid., 51–53.

16 Simeoni, 1940, 11–12. There is no study of this body.

17 ASB, Riformatori dello Studio, Appuntazioni dei lettori, 1465–1526, 1531–37, provides evidence that the *punctator* discharged his duty.

18 Salvioni, 1890, 45.

19 Ady, 1969, ch. 1, for this and the following paragraph.

20 Ibid., 37–41.

21 Ibid., 144–45, 161–63.

22 For Nicholas V's degree, see Piana, 1966, 118–19. The roll of 1451–52 listed a professorship *Ad lecturam Musice* without a holder. Dallari notes that a name had been erased from the original document. Nothing more is heard of the music professorship. Dallari, 1888–1924, 1:32. There were no professors of music in Italian universities. The University of Pavia listed as a professor the musical theorist Francesco Gaffurio in the late fifteenth century, but he taught music at the Milanese court. See Ch. 3, "Pavia, 1361."

23 Dallari, 1888–1924, 1:3–5. Unlike most rolls, this one included salaries that totaled 3,415 Bolognese lire and 900 florins pegged at 33 soldi. Since the Bolognese lira was worth 20 soldi, the florin pegged at 33 soldi was worth 1.65 Bolognese lire. Hence, 900 florins can be converted to 1,485 Bolognese lire and added to 3,415 lire to get the total salary expenses of 4,900 Bolognese lire.

24 Zaoli, 1912, 136–50; Zaoli, 1920, 196–97, 202–5, 226–44. The Bolognese lira was worth 50 to 60 percent of the florin and ducat at this time. As always, such figures should be treated as approximate. Salvioni, 1890, 57–60; Spufford, 1986, 72–79. The Bolognese lira decreased in value against the florin and ducat in the sixteenth century.

25 This aspect of the university has been little studied. The following paragraph is based on ASB, Assunteria di Studio, Bu. 95, fascicle 1, which summarizes the decrees dealing with finances; plus Zaoli, 1920, esp. 201–5, and Zaccagnini, 1930, 46, 48, 50.

26 Trombetti Budriesi, 1988, 165–79.

27 Unfortunately, only limited records for arts and medicine degrees for the fifteenth century survive. Piana (1966, 113–74) located 92 arts degrees (7 per year) awarded between 1419 and 1431. And Bronzino, 1962, 1–7, based on a seventeenth-century source, lists 139 degrees in arts and medicine, an average of 7 per year, awarded from 1480 to 1499. Alidosi Pasquali (1980; first published in 1623) lists arts, medicine, and theology degrees, 1000–1623, in alphabetical order along with bits of biographical information for the recipients. But his information is incomplete.

28 Trombetti Budriesi, 1988, 172–75.

29 Zaoli, 1912, 146.

30 Zaccagnini, 1930, 50; Sorbelli, 1940, 235.

31 ASB, Riformatori dello Studio, Appuntazioni dei lettori, 1465–1526, 1531–37, a salary list of Nov. 2, 1470, no pag. The roll for 1470–71 in Dallari, 1888–1924, 1:82–85, lists 83 professors including 11 student lecturers who did not receive stipends.

32 See B. Nardi, 1958, 179–279; B. Nardi, 1960; Dallari, 1888–1924, vol. 1; and ASB, Assunteria di Studio, Bu. 92, roll of 1509–10, for his salary. Even though Dallari (1:198) lists him as teaching medicine at Bologna in 1507–8, B. Nardi (1958, 259) demonstrates that he did not return until September 1508.

33 Nulla può il Legato senza il Senato, nulla il Senato senza il Legato. Quoted in Fanti, 1978, 216. This work and Colliva, 1977, provide good accounts of Bolognese politics and government after 1500.

34 Gleason, 1993, 277; Hughes, 1994, 9–11.

35 ASB, Assunteria di Studio, Bu. 95, fascicle 1, and ibid., Bu. 92, Diversorum. Lettori e collegi, secc. XVI–XVIII, fascicle 8, with fiscal rolls of 1509–10, 1523–24, and 1526–27.

36 ASB, Assunteria di Studio, Bu. 92, with fiscal rolls of 1523–24 and 1526–27.

37 Cavina, 1988, 437–40 (for 1552–53); Simili, 1956, 391–93 (1563–64).

38 Professorial contracts and correspondence between commune and professors indicated that the value of a gold ducat, a Florentine florin, and the scudo ranged between 3 and 4 Bolognese lire in the sixteenth century and may have

been about 3.5 Bolognese lire at this time. By 1580 the scudo had risen to more than 4 Bolognese lire. McCuaig, 1989, 61–62.

39 Costa, 1902–3b, with numerous letters; also see ASB, Assunteria di Studio, Bu. 52, fascicle 36, with several letters to and by Pomponazzi.

40 For a short biographical and bibliographical sketch, see Belloni, 1986, 180–82. For his salary, see ASB, Riformatori di Studio, Minute dei rotoli 1515–44, ff. 2^r, 6^r, 30^r; ASB, Assunteria di Studio, Bu. 53, Requisiti dei Lettori. Lettere R, vol. 24, fascicle 42; and ASB, Assunteria di Studio, Bu. 92. fiscal rolls for 1523–24 and 1525–26.

41 Costa (1902–3a) describes the pursuit of these legal scholars. Alciato's Bolognese salary is found in ASB, Assunteria di Studio, Requisiti dei Lettori, Bu. 30, fascicle 42, letter of Aug. 29, 1537. Incidentally, because war broke out in Lombardy in early 1542, Alciato did not immediately return to Pavia but went to Ferrara for 1,350 ducats.

42 Costa, 1902–3a, 330 n. 24, Senate decree of 1513, repeated in 1540 and 1578; Zaccagnini, 1930, 146–47.

43 Mondella, 1961.

44 Simeoni, 1940, ch. 2.

45 Bronzino (1962) provides a list of arts and medicine degrees, 1480 through 1800, based on university archival records. Simeoni (1940, 65) provides a count of law degrees, 1583–99, and arts degrees (the number a few less than Bronzino located), 1506–1600, based on the same records. Neither used notarial records, which might include additional doctorates.

46 See the Appendix for estimates of student enrollments for all universities. Simeoni (1940, 63) suggests a maximum student enrollment of "several thousands" at Bologna. Brizzi (1977, 444) estimates 2,000, and Fanti (1978, 228) suggests more than 1,000.

47 Salvioni, 1890, 72–77; Ginatempo and Sandri, 1990, 85, 100, 254–55.

48 Zaccagnini, 1930, 187–91.

49 Simeoni, 1940, 11–12, who does not give a precise date for its establishment. I have found Assunteria records beginning in the mid-1520s. Comparing the surviving documents of Assunteria and Riformatori shows clearly that the former was the more important agency by the third quarter of the sixteenth century.

50 See the numerous letters concerning the recruitment of professors in ASB, Assunteria di Studio, Bu. 75, Lettere dell'ambasciadori agli Assunti, 1571–1694, and ibid., Bu. 79, Lettere di diversi all'Assunteria, 1575–1691.

51 His degree is recorded in Piana, 1966, 118–19.

52 Knod, 1970, 225.

53 The bibliography on Bassi is too extensive to list here. See Comelli, 1912; Findlen, 1993; and Dallari, 1888–1924, vol. 3, pt. 1, pp. 336, 341, 346, 350, 355; vol. 3, pt. 2, pp. 5, 11, 16, 21, 26, 31, 37, 42, 47, and passim, 205, 211, for the rolls listing Bassi.

References

Archival

Bologna, Archivio di Stato (ASB)
  Assunteria di Studio
  Riformatori dello Studio

Printed works

Primary sources, collections of documents, and summaries of documents

Alidosi Pasquali, Giovanni Niccolò, 1980. *I dottori bolognesi di teologia, filosofia, medicina, e d'arti liberali dall'anno 1000 per tutto marzo del 1623*. Bologna: Nicolo Tebaldini, 1623; rpt. Bologna.

Bronzino, Giovanni, 1962. *Notitia doctorum sive catalogus doctorum qui in collegiis philosophiae et medicinae Bononiae laureati fuerunt ab anno 1480 usque ad annum 1800*. Milan.

Dallari, Umberto, 1888–1924. *I rotuli dei lettori legisti e artisti dello Studio Bolognese dal 1384 al 1799*. 4 vols. Bologna.

Muret, Marc'Antoine, 1737. *Orationes, epistolae, et praefationes*. 2 vols. Roboreti, Ex Typographia Berniana.

Secondary sources

Ady, Cecilia M., 1969. *The Bentivoglio of Bologna: A Study in Despotism*. Oxford, 1937; rpt.

Bellomo, Manlio, 1995. *The Common Legal Past of Europe, 1000–1800*. Translated by Lydia G. Cochrane. Washington, D.C.

Belloni, Annalisa, 1986. *Professori giuristi a Padova nel secolo XV: Profili bio-bibliografici e cattedre*. Frankfurt am Main.

Brizzi, Gian Paolo, 1977. "Le istituzioni educative e culturali: Università e collegi," in *Storia della Emilia Romagna*, edited by Aldo Berselli. Vol. 2: *L'età moderna*. Bologna, pp. 443–461.

Cavina, Marco, 1988. "Ricerche su Agostino Berò, canonista e consiliatore bolognese (1474 ca.–1554)," *Studi senesi* 100:385–440.

Colliva, Paolo, 1977. "Bologna dal XIV al XVIII secolo: 'Governo misto' o signoria senatoria?" in *Storia della Emilia Romagna*, edited by Aldo Berselli. Vol. 2: *L'età moderna*. Bologna, pp. 13–34.

Comelli, Giambattista, 1912. "Laura Bassi e il suo primo trionfo," *SMUB*, vol. 3, pp. 197–256.

Costa, Emilio, 1902–3a. "Andrea Alciato nello Studio di Bologna," *Atti e memorie della R. Deputazione di storia patria per le provincie di Romagna*, ser. 3, 21:318–42.

——, 1902–3b. "Nuovi documenti intorno a Pietro Pomponazzi," *Atti e memorie della R. Deputazione di storia patria per le provincie di Romagna*, ser. 3, 21:277–317.

Fanti, Mario, 1978. "Bologna nell'età moderna (1506–1796)," in *Storia di Bologna*. Bologna, pp. 197–282.

Findlen, Paula, 1993. "Science as a Career in Enlightenment Italy: The Strategies of Laura Bassi," *Isis* 84:441–69.

Ginatempo, Maria, and Sandri, Lucia, 1990. *L'Italia delle città: Il popolamento urbano tra Medioevo e Rinascimento (secoli XIII–XVI)*. Florence.

Gleason, Elisabeth G., 1993. *Gasparo Contarini: Venice, Rome, and Reform*. Berkeley, Los Angeles, and Oxford.

Hughes, Steven C., 1994. *Crime, Disorder and the Risorgimento: The Politics of Policing in Bologna.* Cambridge.

Hyde, J. K., 1972. "Commune, University, and Society in Early Medieval Bologna," in *Universities in Politics: Case Studies from the Late Middle Ages and Early Modern Period,* edited by J. W. Baldwin and R. A. Goldthwaite. Baltimore and London, pp. 17–45.

Knod, Gustav C., 1970. *Deutsche Studenten in Bologna (1289–1562): Biographischer Index zu den Acta nationis Germanicae universitatis Bononiensis.* Berlin, 1899; rpt. Aalen.

McCuaig, William, 1989. *Carlo Sigonio: The Changing World of the Late Renaissance.* Princeton, N.J.

Mondella, Felice, 1961. "Aranzio, Giulio Cesare." *DBI,* 3:720–21.

Nardi, Bruno, 1958. *Saggi sull'aristotelismo padovano dal secolo XIV al XVI.* Florence.

———, 1960. "Achillini, Alessandro." *DBI,* 1:144–45.

Piana, Celestino, 1968. "Lo Studio di S. Francesco a Ferrara nel Quattrocento: Documenti inediti," *Archivum Franciscanum Historicum* 61:99–175.

Rashdall, Hastings, 1936. *The Universities of Europe in the Middle Ages.* Edited by F. M. Powicke and A. B. Emden. 3 vols. Oxford.

Renzi, Paolo, 1986. "*Magna populi calamitas est uxorius princeps:* Educazione marziale e insegnamento della storia nel Cinquecento," in *Profili di donne: Mito immagine realtà fra Medioevo ed età contemporanea,* edited by B. Vetere and Paolo Renzi. Galatina, pp. 257–301.

Rüegg, Walter, 1992. "Themes," in *Universities in the Middle Ages,* pp. 3–34.

Salvioni, Giovanni Battista, 1890. "La popolazione di Bologna nel secolo XVII," *Atti e memorie della R. Deputazione di storia patria per le provincie di Romagna.* ser. 3, 8:19–120.

Simeoni, Luigi, 1940. *Storia della Università di Bologna.* Vol. 2: *L'età moderna (1500–1888).* Bologna.

Simili, Alessandro, 1956. "Gerolamo Cardano lettore e medico a Bologna," *L'Archiginnasio* 61:384–505.

Siraisi, Nancy G., 1981. *Taddeo Alderotti and His Pupils: Two Generations of Italian Medical Learning.* Princeton, N.J.

———, 1990. *Medieval and Early Renaissance Medicine: An Introduction to Knowledge and Practice.* Chicago and London.

Sorbelli, Albano, 1912. "Gli stipendi dei professori dell'Università di Bologna nel secolo XIV," *L'Archiginnasio* 7:313–19.

———, 1940. *Storia della Università di Bologna.* Vol. 1: *Il medioevo (secc. XI–XV).* Bologna.

Southern, R. W., 1995. *Scholastic Humanism and the Unification of Europe.* Vol. 1: *Foundations.* Oxford.

Spufford, Peter, 1986. *Handbook of Medieval Exchange.* With the assistance of Wendy Wilkinson and Sarah Tolley. London.

Stelling-Michaud, S., 1955. *L'Université de Bologne et la pénétration des droits romain et canonique en Suisse aux XIII et XIV siècles.* Geneva.

Trombetti Budriesi, Anna Laura, 1988. "L'esame di laurea presso lo Studio bolognese: Laureati in diritto civile nel secolo XV," in *Studenti e università degli studenti dal XII al XIX secolo,* edited by Gian Paolo Brizzi and Antonio Ivan Pini. *SMUB,* n.s., vol. 7, Bologna, pp. 137–91.

Verger, Jacques, 1992. "Patterns," in *Universities in the Middle Ages*, pp. 35–74.

Villoslada, Riccardo G., 1954. *Storia del Collegio Romano dal suo inizio (1551) alla soppressione della Compagnia di Gesù (1773)*. Rome.

Zaccagnini, Guido, 1930. *Storia dello Studio di Bologna durante il Rinascimento*. Geneva.

Zaoli, Giuseppe, 1912. "Lo Studio bolognese e Papa Martino V (Anni 1416–20)," *SMUB*, vol. 3, pp. 105–88.

——, 1920. "Di alcuni 'rotuli' dello Studio della prima metà del secolo XV. (Contributo alla storia dello Studio dal 1420 al 1455)," *SMUB*, vol. 4, pp. 191–249.

6

THE ORIGINS OF OXFORD
AND CAMBRIDGE

V. H. H. Green

Source: V. H. H. Green, *The Universities*, Harmondsworth: Penguin, 1969, pp. 13–20.

For many years legend as unhistorical as it was picturesque enshrouded the origins of the universities of Oxford and Cambridge; 'moonshine,' as one writer frankly admitted, 'and like many erudite disputations, where men reason without data, or even understanding their own terms, not worth a straw'. How the universities came into being remains obscure. They seem to have been an accidental by-product of geography and history. Oxford, a nodal centre of communications, was the home of religious houses and frequently visited by the royal court, and foreign scholars, attracted to English shores by the prospect of royal or archiepiscopal patronage, were teaching there as early as the reign of King Stephen. The groups of young men who congregated around these and other distinguished teachers were the nucleus of the future schools. But many another English town already housed a school of repute and could just as easily have become the site of a university.

If we cannot now know exactly why Oxford was chosen, we do know that factors at work in the late twelfth and early thirteenth century made the foundation of a university in England inevitable. There was everywhere in Europe at this time a tremendous flowering of the intellect, an enthusiasm for the acquisition of knowledge and an unprecedented concern with logical inquiry into the nature of things; the zeal for scholarship which invaded every court and country spawned cathedral schools and generated eminent teachers at whose feet eager young men sat to imbibe the new learning. Greater prosperity and the increasing flow of wealth provided the endowments needed to foster religion and scholarship for the benefit of both church and state. Paris was the first and for a long time the foremost community of teachers and scholars to which the name of university was freely given. England, though in some respects isolated from the intellectual currents running so strongly through European life, could not escape the influence of the continent with which it was under its Angevin kings politically and spiritually conjoined.

The quarrel between King Henry II and Archbishop Thomas Becket, leading to a temporary ban on English scholars studying in France (for the French King had given the arrogant if dedicated Archbishop refuge from Henry's iron wrath), may have served to enlarge the small community of scholars living at Oxford. The cluster of teachers slowly increased in number, drew more and more students to listen to their lectures, and acquired a rudimentary organization as its size grew with its reputation. By the early years of the thirteenth century the university of Oxford was a recognizable institution, with a chancellor (the office has been filled in unbroken succession certainly since 1221), proctors, doctors and masters,[1] faculties and lectures; it was acquiring property, slowly winning benefactors, lending money from its university chests to poor students and awarding degrees.

There may well have been a similar group of scholars at the fenland town of Cambridge, perhaps connected with the rich abbeys of the neighbourhood, but the event which could have transformed a school if such existed into a university was a migration of students from Oxford in 1209. The reason was a quarrel between the students and the townfolk, the first of many such, caused, so it was alleged, by the execution of a scholar in revenge for the murder of a townswoman by another student. Although Cambridge attracted less attention than Oxford, at least until the fifteenth century, neither in its character nor in its curriculum did it differ much from the older foundation. It too had acquired a chancellor by 1226, developed an organization very similar to that of Oxford, and won benefactors. Oxford and Cambridge had become the chief centres of learning in England by the middle of the thirteenth century, supplying the country with its leading clerics and administrators – the two were virtually synonymous at this period – and creating a pool of scholarship and ideas which undoubtedly influenced the increasing number of literate laity, whether they actually studied at the university or not.

These two medieval universities were haphazard growths rather than planned foundations, benefiting from precedent, especially from that of the highly reputed university of Paris, and created by experience. To function with a minimum of friction, they required rules of some sort: the ultimate pattern of their constitutions was as complex and intricate as the constitutional machinery of the medieval church. In the end a compromise between the hierarchical organization and the relatively democratic republic of doctors and masters provided a framework flexible enough to allow for the future development of the universities, and forged a bond of community which made them into a genuine *studium generale*. Neither Oxford nor Cambridge have ever completely lost their medieval impress, though at recurrent crises their character has been reorientated by external pressures.

*   *   *

The medieval university was not initially a collegiate institution. The majority of students lived in one of the many private licensed halls run by a master of the university. It was, however, realized that it would be more convenient and comfortable for serious graduates to live in common in a college than in the hurly-burly of a hostel. Thus the history of Oxford and Cambridge was punctuated by the foundations of colleges which were ultimately to become coterminous with the university. University College, Oxford, accredited by misinformed legend with King Alfred as founder, probably came into existence as a result of a benefaction from William of Durham who died in 1249. In the 1260s John de Balliol and his wife Devorguilla agreed to support a number of students at Oxford. Between 1262 and 1264 Walter de Merton, Chancellor of England, made over his estate at Maldon in Surrey to a community of scholars which by 1270 had settled permanently at Oxford. At Cambridge Hugo de Balsham, Bishop of Ely, founded Peterhouse in 1284. These colleges were intended primarily for poor scholars who were already graduates; those who were in possession of a benefice or of a private income were normally debarred from becoming members of the foundation though they were welcome to take rooms and to share in the common life as paying guests. Although the number of colleges steadily increased, they housed only a small fraction of the university population and had as yet little influence in the moulding of university policy.

For the universities to prosper they had to win favour from the established order. At all stages of their history their studies have been more or less closely correlated to the national needs. If the modern university sees its task as supplying the country with civil servants, administrators and technologists, the medieval university existed to train churchmen, canonists, monks and friars, schoolmen and schoolmasters. Its scholarship, like that of the modern university, was not an indigenous growth but a by-product of its social setting. Yet if the medieval universities required government patronage, they also needed, as do their modern counterparts, sufficient autonomy to be free of municipal or other external pressures. They needed the power to order their own affairs freely. In their early stages they wanted the backing of the Crown, which was usually generously given, to support the authority of their own officials over their own often unruly students, and against the townspeople, with whom for centuries they were to be engaged in a running dog-fight, as well as to give them protection against undue interference by the local bishop. Document after document testifies to their relentless determination to win jurisdiction over their undergraduates and to prevent exploitation by the townsfolk, more especially in the matter of rents and prices for food.

The universities represented then the training schools for the established order, even if the number of laymen educated there was only a fraction of the whole. The population of medieval Oxford and Cambridge was a motley one; there were travelling scholars, intellectual dilettantes, academic hangers-on, 'beatnik' clerics, hard-bitten threadbare men fascinated by glimpses into the sophisticated world of medieval philosophy. There were the scions of noble families, hardly a conspicuous group but never negligible; rumour asserted that King Henry V had studied at Oxford and his brother Humphrey, Duke of Gloucester, a leader of fashion and devotee of learning, proved a notable benefactor. Nonetheless the average student was either in holy orders or intending to take them. The episcopal registers are full of dispensations for nonresidence granted to beneficed clergymen so that they could follow a course of study at the universities. With what relief must Sir Walter Strolringer, the rector of Wootton Courtenay in Somerset, given leave of absence by his bishop to study at a university for three years in September 1448, or Sir Philip Puttenham, the rector of Newton St Loe, given similar leave to study at Oxford in 1462, have left their boorish peasant flock for the intellectual stimulus and lively, if sometimes violent, life of a university town. In addition to the secular clergy, there were a number of monks and friars, residing at the special houses which their orders had established in Oxford and Cambridge, lecturing and learning before they moved to other monasteries or friaries in England or on the Continent.

The universities were clerical brotherhoods but they were colourful, often unruly and rich in their assortment of personalities. They were neither uniform in appearance and dress nor harshly ascetic. In some respects they were less class conscious then than later. Obviously the number of those who could study at the university was to some extent circumscribed by financial considerations. The student had to pay fees for his lectures, to buy his food, to pay his heavy degree fees, to clothe himself for a number of years and to purchase books and writing paper. His expenses were proportionally smaller than at a later date but they were not negligible. Many an undergraduate ran into debt. Many a graduate, temporarily short of money, had to borrow from the university chest and leave his books as a guarantee of future repayment. But bishops were often generous to would-be scholars; lay patrons supported poor students. In 1419 Thomas Langley, the Bishop of Durham, gave William Ingleby an annuity of 100s. 8d. to keep him at Oxford. The interest in learning diverted many a benefaction from a monastic house to the university, and for some scholarship was a handsome investment which repaid the earlier mortgage.

All in all, the medieval universities reflected an aspiration to intellectual achievement which conditioned contemporary scholarship and helped to mould the manner of thinking of cleric and layman alike. To a later generation the atmosphere and scholarship of early Oxford and Cambridge may seem remote and antipathetic, but the scholastic philosophy of the period, the finest flower of its intellect, was itself an integrated aspect of the existing social order. Its influence declined not merely vis-à-vis the newly fashioned humanism of the Renaissance scholars but because it became less and less suited to a society that was increasingly lay in character and shaped by a competitive commercialism.

* * *

For the first two centuries of their existence Oxford and Cambridge had been firmly in the intellectual mainstream, gradually replacing the intellectualized Augustinianism which had been the fodder of university teaching in the middle of the thirteenth century with the coherent Thomistic philosophy; then, as fashion demanded, moving with the fourteenth-century modernists in the direction of nominalism. The best minds of the medieval university continued to grapple with a basic problem, though they would not have phrased it in this way, that of reconciling the received truths of religion with intellectual integrity. The renaissance of the twelfth century, to which the universities owed their birth, had made the conservatives aware that intellectual achievement could offer a challenge to revealed faith. There was no possibility, given the social and intellectual circumstances of the period, that the religious concepts which sustained the life and learning of western Europe could be abandoned or even directly questioned; but at least they could be brought into harmony with progressive thinking. That the solutions which were offered were not ultimately accepted casts no reflection on the importance of what was attempted or indeed achieved.

In the late fourteenth century the comparative academic calm of Oxford scholasticism was disturbed by the teaching of John Wyclif, who was for a short time master of Balliol College and subsequently continued to lecture in the university, and by the appearance of Lollards among the dons who followed him. Wyclif's preaching, especially in his later years – he died in 1384 – with its stress on the literal interpretation and authority of the Scriptures and its repudiation of so much of the teaching of the contemporary church, its sacramental theology and its ecclesiastical hierarchy, made him and his followers appear to be the nucleus of a revolutionary movement. In fact although Wyclif seemed to be a progressive thinker, his original teaching stemmed from a philosophical conservatism, a reaction against the prevailing school of nominalist philosophy in favour of ideas which would have been more popular a century earlier. Paradoxically, philosophical conservatism cradled religious radicalism. For twenty years or so the Lollard movement sprouted at Oxford, finding some support among the seniors; but the university quickly repented of this flirtation with his ideas on discovering his supposed heterodoxy, though the danger to the orthodox appeared greater than it actually was. The prominence of Lollardy at Oxford may have contributed to the rise in the reputation of Cambridge, which in the fifteenth century came to challenge the predominant position that Oxford had held hitherto in the scholastic life of the nation.

Lollardy was, however, a solitary regression in the forward development of the universities. In general they were in the forefront of intellectual movements, centres of lively and exciting discussion. They often housed scholars of original temper, whether the eccentric friar Roger Bacon in the thirteenth century or the thoughtful group of scientists and mathematicians who resided at Merton College, Oxford, in the early years of the next century. By the middle of the fifteenth century individual scholars at both Oxford and Cambridge were beginning to be aware, though in a cautious and conservative spirit, of the classical revival that was taking place in Italy. They brought back books and manuscripts to their libraries by the Cam and the Isis; they copied the ancient writings, improved their prose style and aped rather than adopted the fashions of their *avant-garde* contemporaries. The revived interest in Greek learning led to a fresh insight into the meaning and relevance of the New Testament, sowing the seeds of a new intellectual outlook, even though the Aristotelian tradition remained as strongly entrenched as ever. As the sixteenth century opened the universities no less than the church and state were on the verge of some revolutionary changes.

By 1500 Oxford and Cambridge, two and a half centuries old, had established an order and curriculum which were to remain substantially the same for years to come. But in other aspects of university life change was inescapable. Economic and social factors diversified the personnel of the universities, and led eventually to the establishment and dominance of the colleges. The universities were still ecclesiastical in character and still designed to meet the needs of the church, yet they became more lay in spirit than they had been before. The Protestant Reformation effected a revolution in their lives and brought them more closely under the control of the Crown. Although the universities of the sixteenth and seventeenth centuries were strongly rooted in their medieval past they were very different institutions.

Note

1 The title of doctor was for some time interchangeable with that of master or professor; later the title master or magister was used for members of the faculty of arts while that of doctor was used to distinguish members of the superior faculties such as divinity or law.

7

Excerpt from
UNIVERSITIES: AMERICAN,
ENGLISH, GERMAN

Abraham Flexner

Source: A. Flexner, *Universities: American, English, German*, London: Oxford University Press, 1930, pp. 311–27.

[THE ORIGINS OF THE GERMAN UNIVERSITIES]

III

The German universities originated in the Middle Ages; but for our purposes, they began with the nineteenth century. They have maintained their outer form, precisely as have Oxford and Cambridge; even the new universities at Cologne, Hamburg, and Frankfurt have assumed the same form as the others. But on the founding of the University of Berlin new wine was poured into the old bottles; and the old bottles burst. Never before or since have ancient institutions been so completely remodelled to accord with an idea. The process had of course been long in fermenting; in the result, looking back, one discerns the influence of Leibnitz, Kant, Goethe, and others — all of those who participated in the creation of the national culture. But the new era is concretely associated with a later group — Hegel, Fichte, Schleiermacher, and Humboldt; and the occasion was the protest of spirit against the domination of brute force.

The helplessness of a Germany, splintered into small states and lying prostrate beneath the armies of Napoleon, was defiantly answered by the Hegelian philosophy of the unified state as the embodiment of reason. Paradoxically enough, this conception was embraced by the divided nation, despite its continuing division; and, if I may anticipate, the theory is still accepted, though particularism continues to make itself felt. Within the ideally unified state, Hegel and his successors saw the university as offering unhampered opportunity for the complete development of the individual. A state constituted of developed personalities — this was Hegel's conceptual contribution to the renascence of Germany.

The creation of the University of Berlin, heralded by preliminary steps at Halle, Göttingen, and Jena, was a deliberate break with academic tradition. Freedom in the modern sense could not have characterized the mediaeval university; it emerged only with the development of rationalism in the late eighteenth century. The new University was intended primarily to develop knowledge, secondarily and perhaps as a concession, to train the professional and the official classes, at the level at which knowledge may be promoted. Humboldt conceived the salvation of the German nation as coming from the combination of teaching and research, and time has proved him right. To be sure, the philosophers of previous centuries had laid the foundation; to be sure, the soldiers and statesmen of the nineteenth century made an indispensable contribution to German intellectual unity. Though Bismarck and the first William appear not to have been particularly intimate with the universities, the second William gloried in them, precisely as he gloried in the German army and in German commerce: he knew and aided scholars and scientists; they were evidences of success in the empire of thought, as the army and commerce were evidences of success in the arena of action. It would, however, be a serious misinterpretation to represent the professor as seeking imperial favour though as wholes the universities were gradually permeated by the monarchical spirit. The monarchy affected the universities in some such way as business now affects them in the United States. Social Democrats were excluded from the highest academic posts; honours, decorations, and attentions were freely showered upon professors, though always a few like Paulsen, preserving to the last their democracy and simplicity, refused to crook their knee to the court.

"Blood and iron" were then only partly the makers of United Germany. The real Germany was not only the Germany of Bismarck and his generals and his emperors, but the Germany of Goethe, Schiller, Fichte, Schleiermacher, Carl Schurz, Paulsen, and Virchow — a Germany in the making of which originally philosophy, literature, science, and war all coöperated. After a detour, brilliant, dazzling, but of relatively short duration, in which the warlike element was greatly exaggerated, Germany has now returned to the main road: returned — but with a difference. For without entirely eliminating German particularism, Bismarck welded Germany into a unified, though fortunately not uniform, political entity. His ruthlessness persuaded the German states that they must hang together; so much good at any rate came from their military career; but German education — the *Gymnasium* and the universities, despite profound social, philosophical, and political differences — welded Germany into the intellectual unity that was originally signified by the word "*Kultur*"[1] to which the War attached such sinister and inappropriate significance.

The Hegelian philosophy, with its rounded personalities, seems to conflict with the development of science, requiring, as it does, ever increasing specialization. But, as Rathenau maintained, experience may be regarded as a circle, from any point on the circumference of which an educated man can make his way towards the centre. The individual is intellectually saved in Germany, as he is often saved in England and rarely in America, by his excellent secondary education and the rich cultural tradition into which he is born. That is why English and German scholars and scientists so frequently strike one as better educated or more highly cultivated than their American colleagues; that is certainly why neither English nor German universities tolerate the weeds that grow so rankly in American institutions.

Changes have followed in the wake of the Revolution, to some of which I have already alluded. The partial demoralization of secondary education, due to the sudden collapse of the Empire and the sudden rise to power of the working classes, has, for the moment, by lowering the standard and excessively varying the types of the secondary school, lowered to the same extent the plane of the university. The overcrowding of the university, due partly to the lack of employment and partly to the naïve desire of the heretofore repressed to "taste the fleshpots of Egypt," has operated to the same end. Here and there, vocationalism or quasi-professionalism has won a precarious foothold. The increase in the number of students who must "work their way" has damaged the non-profitable subjects in favour of subjects that promise a return in the shape of a ready livelihood. The professors, whose savings have been destroyed, have been compelled to take on extra burdens for no other purpose than the earning of paltry sums. Rehabilitation and improvement of building and equipment have been gravely hindered. The wonder is not, however, that temporarily the university has slipped: the wonder is the clearness with which its original function is still on the whole perceived, the steps that have been taken to bring it into closer touch with present-day realities, and the high quality of the permanent administrative staff, who, frankly admitting past errors and present shortcomings, are endeavouring to adhere to the historic idea.

The German university has for almost a century and a half fruitfully engaged in teaching and research. As long as those two tasks combine in fertile union, the German university, whatever its defects of detail, will retain its importance. It has stimulated university development in Great Britain; from it has sprung the graduate school of the new world; to it industry and health and every conceivable practical activity are infinitely indebted. Neither utility nor even practical professional training is of its essence. Indeed, from time to time, it has been more open to criticism on the ground of indifference than to criticism on the ground of worldliness.

IV

There are, including the *Technische Hochschulen*, thirty universities in Germany,[2] externally the same, and within limits kept fairly well to the same general standard, partly by the influence of the Reich through various *Staatsexamen*, partly by competition, partly by constant migration of students and teachers, partly through the interchange of views at the annual[3] *Hochschule* Conference. Yet there are subtle differences, due to historical or geographical factors. We have seen how the founding of Berlin in the early years of the nineteenth century shook the entire system, with the result that essentially mediaeval universities made all possible haste, one after another, to modernize themselves in accordance with the Berlin idea. Prussia took the lead at that time; its size and the number of its universities have given it a kind of hegemony ever since. But it would be incorrect to assume that the other federal states have subordinated themselves. The larger states, such as Saxony and Bavaria, not to mention the smaller, have, within the same general framework, preserved and exercised liberty of action. Thus with all its tremendous influence, at no time has Prussia been slavishly copied; other states have experimented, and since the Revolution, even more independently than formerly, on lines quite remote from Prussian example. German culture is thus fruitfully individualized as one passes from Vienna to Munich, Freiburg, or Hamburg. Bonn and Cologne feel a peculiar responsibility for maintaining the cultural flavour of the Rhineland; the new University of Hamburg casts its eyes overseas. Breslau is distinctly conscious of East-Europe; Königsberg of East-Germany. The new universities, staffed mainly from the old, cannot, however, wander too far afield; and fundamental ideals are too deeply imbedded to be uprooted.

The German university is ultimately governed by a central authority, the education ministry of each of the eight federated states. The ministry, whatever its precise title, is charged with oversight of education, art, the theatre, and the opera — the state thus assuming a direct responsibility for the upholding of the cultural level; but our present concern is with education only.

The minister of education is a member of parliament — occasionally, like Becker, a scholar in his own right. The several divisions of the ministry are usually headed by men trained in the universities and are usually forced by the competition of other states to go forward. Administration causes much less distraction than in the United States: the business affairs of the university are looked after by the local *Kurator* both through subordinates on the ground and through his own immediate contact with the ministry; the confidential representative of the government, he likewise is the trusted representative of the university in its dealings with the administration. The revolving *Rectorat*, lasting only a single year, neither spoils a scientist nor makes continuity of policy impossible: for faculties and ministry follow well-worn paths, sometimes, indeed, too well worn; and the *Kuratorium* acts as a "shock-absorber" in respect to minor matters of detail. The faculties — philosophy (equivalent to arts and sciences), medicine, jurisprudence, theology — are distinct, autonomous, and, as a rule, equally prominent and equally developed. Business is transacted by committees of the faculty, who through their deans negotiate with the proper division of the ministry. Progress is sometimes slow, committees and conferences abound, and talk prolific; and yet, though local dissatisfaction is at times great, no other country made equal advances in respect to equipment, finance, and expansion during the seventy-five years preceding the War.

I select as of outstanding importance four features of university life. I begin with *Lehr-* and *Lernfreiheit*. The German teacher, whether *Privatdozent* or professor, selected in the way I shall shortly describe, pursues his own course, unhindered. He is perfectly free in the choice of topics, in the manner of presentation, in the formation of his seminar, in his way of life. Neither the faculty nor the ministry supervises him: he has the dignity that surrounds a man who, holding an intellectual post, is under no one's orders. His function is the double one that I began by ascribing to the university — that of conserving and of advancing knowledge: teaching and research. There is a common notion that the German professor is from the very nature of the university interested only in research — that he takes teaching lightly. The error arises doubtless from the fact that in teaching he avoids spoon-feeding. His students do not require any such method; he himself is above it. From Humboldt's conception that the university should combine teaching and research the university has never departed. The recently published partial bibliography of the more important publications of Wilamowitz covers almost eight closely printed pages;[4] to foreigners he is the typical German "*Gelehrter*" — the productive scholar at his best. Yet, looking back upon his career, Wilamowitz speaks of his books as "the cast off slough of my (his) development. . . . In Germany one is only a scholar in a subsidiary sense: the chief duty is the professorship, and I have always treated it as of paramount importance."[5] Three forms of instruction and work are commonly employed: the lecture to large groups (*Vorlesungen*); practical exercises (*Übungen*), in which assistants coöperate; the seminar, reserved for the elect — nowadays, alas, not quite elect enough, inasmuch as "*Zwang*" (compulsory) seminars are at times employed, and a superseminar privately arranged for the really able. The necessity of presenting to his students his subject in its entirety requires that the professor's scholarship be broad in scope; the necessity of conducting a seminar for advanced students requires that he be active in production. Of course, the balance is not always perfectly struck. But it is surprising how often great investigators are reputed to be conscientious and inspiring teachers. From recent times, one may mention Virchow, Mommsen, Cohnheim, Ludwig, Erich Schmidt, Harnack, Friedrich Müller, Wilamowitz; they attached to themselves groups of devoted students; they formed schools of disciples, who, one by one, carried new ideas into old chairs; and in the general lectures covering their respective subjects in broad outlines they inspired large masses, the scientist often attracting humanistic students, the humanist often attracting students of science and philosophy. Poor teachers exist; trivial and pedantic essays and theses are of course not unknown. Heine's ridicule has not even yet lost its point entirely. Carlyle's gerund grinder may still be found. But even so, German pedantry rests upon scholarship: the philologian or philosopher who spends a lifetime on a trifle after all knows his Plato and Aristotle. And the pedantries which may attach themselves to the Early Fathers are assuredly different from the trivialities that attach themselves to the making of ice cream or the duties of a school janitor. One of the ablest of the younger German administrators writes officially:[6]

> "The university is a seat of research, but also the training ground of those who govern. Just as a people is interested in theoretical problems, so at present especially it must train men competent to apply learning at the university level — quite aside from the stimulus that science can procure from the realities of life."[7]

And again:

> "Specialization that looks to a vocation simply dazes the German student. This is a point that concerns all faculties equally: for it is not the business of the university to introduce the student to all future and possible details, but to train him in fundamentals so that he can later solve his own problems."

Theoretically the student is equally free. His credentials being recognized at face value, he can go where he pleases — thus, if he will, overcrowding Berlin, while Tübingen might do better by him. He selects his own teachers; he wanders from one university to another; he may waste his time in fencing or drinking; he may forego vacations in order to work as "*Famulus*" in a laboratory or clinic. In the professions where a logical order of studies prevails, he may take advice or neglect it at his peril. He is treated like a man from the day he matriculates.

In practice, however, the student who contemplates passing an examination is less free than theory would indicate. There are two distinct examinations, that of the state, which is the gateway to a calling, that of the university, which leads to the doctorate. While professors figure in the former or are consulted regarding them, the university itself conducts and regulates the latter, which is, as a matter of fact, taken by only a minority of the students. Prescription and compulsion thus creep in. Sometimes prescription lies in the very nature of the subject: for example, one cannot pursue physiology in ignorance of anatomy, or physics in ignorance of mathematics. In such matters, the subject itself abridges *Lernfreiheit*. But *Lernfreiheit* is further and harmfully abridged by the examinations. Strong efforts, too often successful, are made to increase the number of separate subjects in which students, especially professional students must be examined,[8] either by the state or the university or both. Fortunately attendance is not, as a rule, rigidly "controlled." The student may be industrious or idle; may accomplish his purpose in the minimum number of semesters or may consume more; may stay in one place or go elsewhere. Neither dean nor professor has him on his conscience. He is regarded as competent to care for himself and he takes the full consequences. Finally, he has, when he himself thinks the moment has come, to submit to an examination. No calendar tells him when or precisely on what. As to the number of examinations, one hears it said that there is observable a tendency to divide Germans into two classes: those who examine and those who are examined. Unquestionably, the more the student is examined, the more restricted become his opportunities to pursue his own thoughts and work out his own salvation — the very essence of university work. But it must not be forgotten that neither the German nor the English student can obtain a degree or qualify for examination by arithmetical accumulation of points or hours or credits: he is examined, when he himself thinks he is ready, and he is exposed to any line of questioning that his examiners regard as germane.

I place second the selection of the full professors, which starts with the suggestion to the faculty of three candidates by a committee of the faculty. This list the faculty is free to modify before it is submitted to the minister. Here is a strong bulwark in the university against the danger of encroachment on the part of the state. And it works both ways — holding both university and ministry up to high standards. The faculty, keen to preserve its prerogatives, must beware of giving the ministry a pretext for appointing an outsider: its list will therefore as a rule be good; and good suggestions having emanated from the faculty, the minister cannot easily justify himself in ignoring them. He is free to appoint one of the three, or, if he so please, an outsider. It happens occasionally that the minister disregards suggestions emanating from the faculty; or refers its nominees back for further considerations, but his power to do so discourages, without of course entirely preventing, internal cliques. Almost invariably the three persons named by the faculty have attained prominence in some other university. Writing, however, of his Greifswald days, half a century or more ago, Wilamowitz in his recent memoirs objects that important personages at Berlin at times prevailed upon the minister to dictate to the faculties of the less conspicuous universities. "Virchow," he writes, "had assistants to find places for, and Mommsen, when I complained, openly said, 'We had no use for him.' So he was good enough for Greifswald." Thus the young and brilliant Erich Schmidt was once passed over for someone who enjoyed the favour of

Minister Falk. "That in a small university youth preponderates gives it a special stamp; but it is deplorable when a man remains permanently, just because he should never have been appointed at all."[9]

In Saxony, since the advent of the present government, the ministry has more than once overridden the suggestions of a conservative university. In Jena, more recently, an appointment, widely regarded as unfit, was forced upon the university by the ministry. But it has never been impossible for strong individuals to be passed over or to find themselves uncomfortable. "The unity of teaching and research," writes the present *Ministerialdirektor* of the Prussian Education Ministry, "signified during the last century that a scholar could usually reach his goal, if he became a member of a university faculty. But the fate of Schopenhauer, Nietzsche, Dühring, Hartman, Robert Mayer, Freytag, and others, who either knocked in vain at the portals of the universities, or profoundly disillusioned turned from them — that, alas, is still possible. Science must not fail to recognize what it might gain from such spirits."[10] Personal, political, and racial considerations thus mar the ideal working of the German scheme.

Since the War, the more progressive states have had to press more strenuously, on account of the generally conservative attitude of the faculties. At the present moment, a conflict between the ministries and the faculty of law, which is widely criticized, is in prospect. Generally speaking, the German arrangement works best when a strong *Ministerialdirektor* or ministry negotiates with a strong faculty: both being strong, deliberation takes place, and out of deliberation between equals, a sound result usually emerges. If, on the one hand, the ministry is weak, a university clique may prevail; if, on the other hand, the faculty is weak, the ministry may get an unfair advantage. Althoff, the ablest personality in the Education Ministry of Prussia during the last fifty years, undoubtedly antagonized the universities at times; but to his judgment of men and his vigour in action the promotion of men like Ranke, Harnack, and Helmholtz, who had already shown their quality, the creation of research institutions, and the amazing development of medicine were largely due. Undoubtedly, so strong and self-willed an individual may make trouble and evoke resistance. Wilamowitz tells us that Althoff preferred to find things out for himself and liked best curators who resembled "messenger boys"; on the other hand, he freely admits Althoff's great reverence for the universities and the immense efforts which he made to raise them to a high level. "His work remains; one who visits his grave in the Botanical Garden should know that there rests an honest and loyal man."[11] On the whole, one may infer from results that the strength of the universities and their great prestige are sufficient proof that, generally speaking, legitimate considerations have prevailed as frequently as is humanly possible.

The third point I have in mind is the "wandering" of the university instructor. Though there is a family likeness throughout the German, Swiss, and Austrian universities, they are not locally inbred; a man will get his degree and become *Privatdozent* in Munich after having studied previously at two or three other universities; he will be called as *Extraordinarius* (reader or lecturer, as the English would say, associate professor, as one would say in America) to Tübingen or Graz; he will next be called as professor to Bonn; thereafter, if he continues productive, to Leipzig, and perhaps finally to Berlin or Vienna, though some of the ablest men, despite calls to the metropolis, cling to the smaller universities, on account of their "*Gemütlichkeit*." The progress and the financial welfare of the university depend on a severe nation-wide competition, in the winning of which the main factors are two — fame as a teacher, distinction as an investigator; the lack of either element is likely to be fatal to promotion.

A still more effective guarantee of both freedom and scholarship is to be found in the "*Privatdozentur.*" The docents are the recruits from among whom the professors are ultimately obtained. The ministry has a veto, even the possibility of initiative, in the choice of the professor; it has no voice whatsoever in granting "the licence to teach" which is wholly the prerogative of the faculty. But the "*Privatdozentur*" is more than a bulwark of academic freedom and security. In its pre-War form it was a large group of persons who entered a severe and unpaid novitiate in the hope of making an academic career. There could be no better proof of the esteem in which the universities were held. The German student had won his doctorate on the basis of a thesis, presumably showing some capacity to do original work, and an examination, presumably showing a competent knowledge of the literature of his subject. He wanted to make a career in scholarship or science. Did he get a university appointment which at the crucial moment of his development made him comfortable and overloaded him with teaching routine? Not at all. He got an unsalaried licence to teach, became, as they say, *Privatdozent*, offered a lecture course or two, and in any one of a variety of ways attached himself to a laboratory, a clinic, or a library, in order that he might continue his productive work. The *Privatdozenten* formed the nursery from which, as I have said, the German university selected its *Extraordinarii* on the basis of teaching ability and scholarly productivity; from the *Extraordinarii* of all Germany and German-speaking countries in the fashion above described, the *Ordinarii* were selected; at every stage the two factors counted; the candidate must have been able to expound his subject, he must have produced. It was a severe system: often the *Privatdozent* had for years hard sledding, especially if the *Ordinarius* was indifferent or hostile to him, as might happen. Thus it resulted in a learned proletariat, sometimes unhappy; but in every field — in science, in the humanities, in law, in medicine, and in theology — it developed a host of workers, a supply for the universities, for the secondary schools, for the governmental services, and for industry. As a well thought-out institution for the doing of certain definite and difficult things, the German university — the essential features of which I have just described — was a better piece of mechanism than any other nation has as yet created.

Finally, the German student is, like the professor, a wanderer, though, for financial reasons, less so nowadays than formerly. The loyalty which marks the Harvard man in the United States, the Oxford man in England, is unknown in Germany, except perhaps to the extent of a sentimental attachment to the university in which the student spent his first semester. There is no such thing as a Berlin man, a Greifswald man, a Vienna man. Unquestionably, this indifference is costly: it costs some of the personal and institutional attachments that add to the amenities of life in English-speaking countries. It costs something from the standpoint of the student as human being. None the less, whatever the personal or social loss, intellectually the German gains far more than he loses through wandering. It has its disadvantages: for example, it enables an indifferent student to seek his degree wherever it is most easily attained. But what is more important, it enables the able student to go where his subject is most vigorously prosecuted, and it stimulates the professor to do his best in order to attract the most competent students; for on the quality of his students depend the fame of seminar and laboratory and to some extent the professor's income.

Notes

1 Becker maintains that German unity came, in consequence of Bismarck's policy, to be too largely a military, too little a cultural achievement. C. H. Becker, *Kulturpolitische Aufgaben des Reiches* (Leipzig, 1919), p. 3.
2 In their classical form, best described by Friedrich Paulsen in *The German Universities* (translated by Frank Thilly and William W. Elwang, New York, 1906), and by W. Lexis in Vol. I of *Die Universitäten im Deutschen Reich* (Berlin, 1904).
3 The Weimar Constitution established an Imperial Committee for this purpose, but it is ineffective.
4 The bibliography is printed not in the original German edition, but in the English translation (London, 1930), pp. 391–99.
5 Ulrich von Wilamowitz-Moellendorf: *Erinnerungen, 1814–1914* (Leipzig), *Vorwort*. My subsequent references are to the German edition, not to the English translation.
6 Unpublished memorandum.
7 See what I have previously said regarding Pasteur, Haldane, etc., pp. 131–32, 256.
8 The moment a branch is included in the examinations, the student must register and pay a special fee.
9 *Loc. cit.*, p. 187.
10 Werner Richter, *Die Organisation der Wissenschaft in Deutschland*, p. 4.
11 *Loc. cit.*, pp. 199, 251. He remarks, further, that during his $13\frac{1}{2}$ years at Göttingen only once did the ministry appoint a professor not proposed by the university, viz., a case in which the faculty had no expert; the choice was universally accepted as admirable. (*Ibid.*, p. 250.)

8

JEFFERSON'S EDUCATIONAL LEGACY

Jennings L. Wagoner, Jr.

Source: J. L. Waggoner, Jr. *Jefferson and Education*, Monticello Monograph Series, Monticello, Va.: Thomas Jefferson Foundation, 2004, pp. 127–46.

This institution will be based on the illimitable freedom of the human mind. For here we are not afraid to follow truth wherever it may lead, nor tolerate any error so long as reason is left free to combat it.
— THOMAS JEFFERSON TO WILLIAM ROSCOE, DECEMBER 27, 1820[1]

When the first students began to enroll at the University of Virginia on March 7, 1825, they became the initial beneficiaries of Thomas Jefferson's educational legacy. That legacy, however, included far more than a stately group of classical buildings neatly arranged around an open space soon to be covered with grass and lined with trees. Jefferson's legacy was framed by a philosophy of education that was reflected in much more than the buildings and layout of his "academical village." It further encompassed his views regarding the broad range of advanced studies, mode of organization and governance, qualifications and expectations of faculty and students, and secular orientation of his university. Perhaps most significantly, the Jeffersonian legacy incorporated larger social and political purposes to which he pledged the university *and* the elementary and secondary institutions that were always a vital component of his conception of a complete system of education.

As noted when describing earlier phases of Jefferson's evolving educational plans, specific details changed over time. He made both academic and architectural adjustments as useful advice, advancing knowledge, altered circumstances, and his assessment of economic and political realities of the moment dictated. Jefferson was entirely consistent, however, in defining the broad outlines of his plans and purpose. To Jefferson, education should equip *all* citizens of the new nation with the skills and sensibilities that would enable each to become self-sufficient, able to pursue happiness, and capable of maintaining a republican society. From the outset, Jefferson's vision for education in Virginia included an entire system, not only erudition for a leadership class. It is significant in this regard to note that in composing the Rockfish Gap Report, Jefferson took into consideration not only the direct charge to the commission of determining the site for the university, but stressed again that a solid precollegiate system was essential for the creation and advancement of an educated republican citizenry. In that report he specified the objectives of the "primary" or basic levels of education as follows:

- To give every citizen the information he needs for the transaction of his own business;
- To enable him to calculate for himself, and to express and preserve his ideas, his contracts and accounts, in writing;
- To improve, by reading, his morals and faculties;
- To understand his duties to his neighbors and country, and to discharge with competence the functions confided to him by either;
- To know his rights; to exercise with order and justice those he retains; and to choose with discretion the fiduciary of those he delegates; and to notice their conduct with diligence, with candor, and judgment;
- And, in general, to observe with intelligence and faithfulness all the social relations under which he shall be placed.[2]

Neither the passage of time, scores of blue ribbon commissions since Jefferson's day, nor the pronouncements of a growing line of claimants to the title of "the education president" have resulted in a better set of goals for the instruction of the public at large. Surely Jefferson's title as "the first" education president is uncontested in terms of both time and substance, even though it was not until many decades after his death—indeed, after the Civil War—that Virginia put into place a statewide system of universal elementary education.

So strongly did Jefferson feel about the relationship between literacy and citizenship that he once considered denying the privileges of citizenship to those who were illiterate. While urging the passage of his revised education bill in 1817, Jefferson not only stressed the duty of the state to provide for the education of all of its citizens, but reflected as well on the reciprocal obligations that citizens had to the state. Although reluctant to have the state make attendance compulsory, he did insert a provision in this new bill stating that "no person unborn or under the age of twelve years at the passing of this act, and who is compos mentis, shall, after the age of fifteen years, be a citizen of this commonwealth until he or she can read readily in some tongue, native or acquired." While recognizing that it might be better to "tolerate the rare instance of a parent refusing to let his child be educated" than to force a child to attend school against the wishes of a parent, Jefferson's reasoning was clear: "If we do not force instruction, let us at least strengthen the motive to receive it when offered." As it happened, Jefferson need not have agonized over this issue, for Cabell prudently struck this provision and others likely to distract from the chief purpose of the education bill before submitting it to the legislature. Even so, the bill met with defeat.[3]

Jefferson's view of the public "pursuit of happiness" as well as the private benefits of education underlay his advocacy of libraries and a free press as well as a system of publicly supported schools. "The basis of our government being the opinion of the people, the very first object should be to keep that right; and were it left to me to decide whether we should have a government without newspapers, or newspapers without a government, I should not hesitate a moment to prefer the latter," wrote Jefferson in 1787. He hastened to add, however: "But I should mean that every man should receive those papers and be capable of reading them." Jefferson's aphorism points yet again to his fundamental belief that in a free society, "the people are the only censors of their governors" and the best guardians of their own liberties.[4]

Jefferson's advocacy of public support for the education of the mass of the population was in many ways an exception to his general premise that government should interfere as little as possible with the natural functioning of society. As historian Peter Onuf observed, "Spending on education constituted the grand and significant exception to Jefferson's minimal state, for this was precisely the kind of public investment that would foster the welfare of the rising generation without wasting its future prospects." Jefferson stated the matter directly in a letter to Madison: "I am not a friend to a very energetic government. It is always oppressive." Yet in an expanded version of the same letter sent to another correspondent, Jefferson stated that providing the public with access to information "is the most certain, and the most legitimate engine of government. Educate and inform the whole mass of the people," he continued. "Enable them to see that it is [in] their interest to preserve peace and order, and they will preserve it. [And] it requires no very high degree of education to convince them of this. They are the only sure reliance for the preservation of our liberty."[5]

In the same report in which Jefferson spelled out the aims of education for the general population, he was no less specific when it came to defining the educational purposes for those who would be recipients of more advanced education and thus would likely be called into service as governors of the citizenry. Here again his list of objectives for university education bears quoting:

- To form the statesmen, legislators and judges, on whom public prosperity and individual happiness are so much to depend;

- To expound the principles and structure of government, the laws which regulate the intercourse of nations, those formed municipally for our own government, and a sound spirit of legislation, which, banishing all arbitrary and unnecessary restraint on individual action, shall leave us free to do whatever does not violate the equal rights of another;
- To harmonize and promote the interests of agriculture, manufactures and commerce, and by well informed views of political economy to give a free scope to the public industry;
- To develop the reasoning faculties of our youth, enlarge their minds, cultivate their morals, and instill into them the precepts of virtue and order;
- To enlighten them with mathematical and physical sciences, which advance the arts, and administer to the health, the subsistence, and comforts of human life;
- And, generally to form them to habits of reflection and correct action, rendering them examples of virtue to others, and of happiness within themselves.[6]

These were the goals set for what Jefferson at times called "the natural aristocracy . . . [of] virtue and talents" or "the most precious gifts of nature"— those individuals drawn from every rank in society who should compose the professional class from which some would be drawn and entrusted with the highest offices and responsibilities in the society. Although Jefferson firmly believed that everyone was endowed with a shared moral sense and that a plowman could determine right from wrong as easily or perhaps even better than a professor, he also held that offices of public trust should go to those who had pursued learning to the highest levels. It was on this very point that Jeffersonian Democrats differed so markedly from their successors, the Jacksonian Democrats.[7]

The features that Jefferson put in place at the University of Virginia to bring these goals within reach gave a distinctive character to the institution that notably separated it from other seats of higher learning of the day. The University of Virginia was a maverick institution. It established a new pattern for American higher education, albeit one that was only slowly incorporated into the nation's leading universities.

Among the significant departures from tradition that marked the university's opening was Jefferson's insistence that the professors recruited be "of the first order of science" in their academic fields. The prevailing faculty pattern at most colleges and universities was characterized by hiring a few classically trained generalists, often assisted by young tutors, to lead students through a set of standard texts employing a recitation format. Jefferson wanted professors who, as experts in specific fields of knowledge, would lecture on subjects that, in his familiar words, were "useful to us at this day, and in their *highest* degree." He was aiming to create a university much more akin to modern graduate and professional schools than to the more limited collegiate institutions of the day. It is for this reason that the university did not offer bachelor's degrees until long after Jefferson's death. The diplomas he and the initial Board of Visitors authorized were of two grades, "the highest of doctor, the second of graduate."[8]

As early as 1800 Jefferson had suggested to Joseph Priestley that the university he was contemplating would probably have to turn to Europe at the outset for professors of the highest standing, but when he began to cast about for professors for Central College, he first looked to Americans. In addition to Samuel Knox and Thomas Cooper, in 1818 Jefferson extended an offer to Nathaniel Bowditch, whose mathematical and navigational acclaim had earlier prompted invitations from Harvard and West Point, both of which he had declined. Likewise, Jefferson's projected offer of $2,000 and a rent-free pavilion with a garden also failed to draw him southward from Massachusetts, where his income as president of Essex Fire and Marine Insurance Company was considerably higher than Jefferson could offer. Jefferson then turned to Harvard linguist George Ticknor, with whom he had enjoyed a steady correspondence for several years. While studying at the University of Göttingen, Ticknor had extolled the academic freedom and the stimulating climate of scholarship that professors in Germany experienced, points that were not lost on Jefferson as he contemplated his own university's features. However, neither Jefferson's description of his university plans nor the enticements of Virginia's "genial climate" could entice Ticknor to abandon Cambridge for Charlottesville.[9]

When these overtures failed, Jefferson became all the more convinced that he would have to turn to Europe to find academics of the highest caliber. As the buildings around the Lawn were nearing completion in the spring of 1824, the Board of Visitors went on record as agreeing with Jefferson in the opinion that "to obtain professors of the first order of science in their respective lines, they must resort principally to Europe." On behalf of the board, Jefferson enlisted Francis Walker Gilmer, a young Charlottesville lawyer and son of an esteemed Jefferson friend, to undertake the mission of going abroad in search of professorial talent. Recognizing that European scholars of the absolute top rank would hardly be inclined to give up their posts to come to an as-yet unfinished university, Jefferson reasoned that Gilmer should aim to recruit the top scholars' protégés, young men who, as the historian Phillip Bruce phrased it, might be "treading impatiently on the heels of the veterans." Jefferson paved the way for Gilmer by giving him a letter of introduction to, among others, Richard Rush, the American minister in London. Jefferson explained Gilmer's mission to Rush and asked for the ambassador's assistance in making contacts with Great Britain's leading scholars. Universities in England, Scotland, and Ireland were deemed logical recruiting grounds in that scholars there would share with Americans a "common language, habits, and customs"—or at least Jefferson hoped that would be the case.[10]

It is somewhat ironic that the first scholar to sign a contract with Gilmer was George Blaettermann, a German by birth and education who was then living in London. Blaettermann had corresponded with Jefferson regarding an appointment in 1823 and had been recommended to Jefferson by Ticknor. Gilmer met with Blaettermann in London and offered him a contract as professor of modern languages at a salary of $1,000 plus a tuition fee of $50 for every pupil who pursued his courses only, $30 for those who would attend another professor's lectures, and $25 from each student who would attend two other "schools," or professors. Whether because of Blaettermann's strong accent or other reasons, Gilman's decision to offer this German scholar a base salary of $1,000 plus student fees was less than the maximum of $1,500 plus fees that had been authorized and would be offered other professors he recruited. Nonetheless, the range of languages Blaettermann agreed to teach was impressive: French, Spanish, Italian, German, and Anglo-Saxon, along with the history and geography of each country. Blaettermann also announced that, if students were interested, he was prepared to give lessons in the vernacular languages of Denmark, Sweden, Holland, and Portugal![11]

Gilmer faced difficulties in trying to persuade some other promising scholars of the advantages to be had in casting their lot with the novel American university being built in a decidedly non-cosmopolitan part of Virginia. He was disappointed in not finding anyone at the University of Edinburgh willing to transplant himself to Virginia, but finally was able to accomplish his mission by signing five foreign professors. In addition to Blaettermann, Gilmer received an enthusiastic acceptance from Thomas Key, a graduate of Trinity College who had studied medicine at Guy's Hospital in London and had just received a master's degree from Cambridge University. As mathematics professor, Key was expected to teach algebra, trigonometry, plane and spherical geometry, mensuration, navigation, conic sections, differential calculus, and military and civil architecture. He was joined by a classicist from the same university, George Long, who was recruited as the professor of ancient languages. The 1824 curriculum set by the board specified that the "higher grade" of Latin and Greek would be Long's responsibility, along with Hebrew, rhetoric, belles-lettres, and ancient history and geography. Charles Bonnycastle, who had been educated by his father, a noted mathematician at the Royal Military Academy, became the professor of natural philosophy. Included in his domain were mechanics, statics, hydrostatics, hydraulics, pneumatics, acoustics, optics, and astronomy. Dr. Robley Dunglison became professor of anatomy and medicine, specialties that included surgery, the history of medicine, physiology, pathology, material medica, and pharmacy. Dunglison, a Scot, had obtained medical degrees in London and Germany and had a diploma from the Society of Apothecaries.

These appointments were soon augmented by the addition of two Americans, both of whom had become naturalized citizens: John Patton Emmet, who had been born in Ireland, became the professor of natural history, and George Tucker, a native of Bermuda, was appointed professor of moral philosophy. Emmet had attended West Point and had earned a medical degree from the College of Physicians and Surgeons in New York. His assignment included botany, zoology, mineralogy, chemistry, geology, and rural economy. Tucker was a graduate of the College of William and Mary, a noted author, and congressman. His teaching duties included "mental science generally, including ideology, general grammar, logic and ethics."[12]

The visitors had a more difficult time identifying the person to fill the final vacancy, the professorship of law. Above all others, this was the position that Jefferson considered it vital for an American to occupy. The post was first offered to George Gilmer, who, after considerable thought, declined. William Wirt, attorney general of the United States from 1817–1829 and the chief prosecutor in the conspiracy trial against Aaron Burr, was another candidate. The board, against Jefferson's wishes, so wanted Wirt that he was offered the presidency of the university along with the law professorship, but he declined both appointments. Thereafter the board agreed to abide by Jefferson's wish that the university be governed by the visitors and the faculty as a whole under a rotating chairmanship, and that there not be a chief executive officer other than the rector—a system that prevailed until 1904. Not until July 1826, a full year after classes had begun in the other schools, did the board finally secure the services of John T. Lomax, a Fredericksburg attorney who satisfied all the requirements deemed necessary for the position. His nativity and his political views were in accord with the wishes of Jefferson and the Board of Visitors.[13]

The qualifications set for professors included more than the potential for eminence in their respective areas of learning. When it was once suggested by Cabell that Jefferson consider an attorney who was a relative for the law professorship, Jefferson replied: "The individual named in your letter is one of the best, and to me the dearest of living men." But Jefferson reminded Cabell that they had, "from the beginning, considered the high qualification of our professors as the only means by which we could give to our institution splendor and pre-eminence over all its sister seminaries." Jefferson then set forth the primary dictum that was to guide the visitors in making appointments: "The only question, therefore, we can ever ask ourselves, as to any candidate, will be, is he the most highly qualified?" Jefferson then pointed to other considerations as well, noting that "a man is not qualified for a professor, knowing nothing but merely his own profession. He should be otherwise well educated as to the sciences generally; able to converse understandingly with the scientific men with whom he is associated, and to assist in the councils of the Faculty on any subject of science on which they may have occasion to deliberate." Jefferson further made it clear in framing the governance of the university that professors were expected to be fully committed to their teaching and studies and thus "shall engage in no other pursuits of emolument unconnected with the service of the University without the consent of the Visitors."[14]

Perhaps the most striking feature of the Jeffersonian educational legacy was his dedication of the University of Virginia to the principles of intellectual freedom. At a time when conformity to doctrinal positions of sponsoring denominations was still expected on the part of faculty in both English and American institutions of higher learning, Jefferson launched his university with the promise that scholars at Virginia could enjoy the "illimitable freedom of the human mind." In recruiting professors, Jefferson assured candidates that, given the liberal character and tolerant disposition of members of the board, they would in effect have lifetime tenure in their posts and would be unfettered in their teaching. Unlike institutions at which the board of trustees determined books that might be used in various classes, the Virginia trustees concurred with Jefferson that the choice of texts should be left with the individual professors since they would be much more knowledgeable about their respective fields than would any member of the board.[15]

This is not to say that there was not a disconnect between Jefferson's professed high *ideals* and his own conception of practical restraints regarding free expression at his university, however. While he could in good conscience proclaim that "I have sworn upon the altar of God eternal hostility against every form of tyranny over the mind of man" with respect to religious bigotry, he was decidedly more cautious when it came to political persuasions and sectional controversies, especially in his latter years. On matters related to government, his institution was in actuality to be dedicated to the principles of Republicanism as Jefferson understood those principles. Madison agreed with Jefferson that the best safeguard against the intrusion of heretical political theories was the selection of "an able and orthodox professor" in the fields they considered most critical to the continuance of the principles of 1776, law and government. Before the visitors appointed a professor for the school of law (in which government would also be taught), therefore, special conditions were placed on the person who would hold that office. Not only should the professor be an American, but he should insure that his students were well acquainted with democratic-republican scripture. Thus, while all other professors at the university were given total freedom in the selection of books to be used in their courses, an exception was made in the case of the professor of law. Jefferson and Madison, with the consent of the board, believed that on the matter of law and government, they were in fact likely to be more knowledgeable than some as-yet unidentified professor. Accordingly, they determined that the visitors should identify certain texts that should form the basis of the curriculum in law and government. The texts included the Declaration of Independence, John Locke's *Treatises on Government*, Algernon Sidney's *Discourses On Government, The Federalist Papers*, and Madison's Virginia Report of 1799 on the Alien and Sedition Laws. Madison suggested that George Washington's first inaugural and farewell addresses be added to the list, a suggestion that Jefferson heartedly endorsed. Madison also cautioned that the prescribed texts should be viewed as a guide or a standard "without requiring an unqualified conformity to them, which indeed might not in every instance be possible." The board approved the list at its meeting on March 4, 1825.[16]

That Jefferson was somewhat uncomfortable in specifying any texts was evidenced in the fact that he cautioned Cabell several weeks before the board meeting to hold the pending resolution in confidence, for "the less such things are spoken of before hand, the less obstruction is contrived to be thrown in their way." It is important to emphasize, however, that the list adopted by the Board of Visitors for study in the school of law was *pre*scriptive, not *pro*scriptive in nature. Adoption of these fundamental treatises did not preclude the use of other texts. The intent was to insure that the students received grounding in the "correct" principles of American government. Dumas Malone commented in this regard that complete consistency cannot be rightly claimed for Jefferson, but that "it is safe to say that no other American of his generation did more to remove shackles from the mind." Malone observed further: "And, judged by contemporary standards, the institution he had planned was to be one of notable liberality."[17]

Although the term was not then in vogue, the academic freedom Jefferson thought important for professors applied to the university's students as well. A basic ingredient in student freedom was total election of studies. Jefferson informed Ticknor of his intentions in this regard by writing, "I am not fully informed of the practices at Harvard, but there is one from which we shall certainly vary, although it has been copied, I believe, by nearly every college and academy in the United States. That is, the holding the students all to one prescribed course of reading, and disallowing exclusive application to those branches only which are to qualify them for the particular vocations to which they are destined. We shall, on the contrary, allow them uncontrolled choice in the lectures they shall choose to attend, and requiring elementary qualification only, and sufficient age." Accordingly, in regulations adopted on October 4, 1824, the visitors specified that "Every student shall be free to attend the schools of his choice, and no other than he chooses."[18]

The elective system, today a feature of almost every college and university in the land, spread only slowly and in limited degrees to other colleges before the Civil War. Ticknor pressed for changes at Harvard, but not until the administration of Charles W. Eliot (1869–1909) did Harvard energetically adopt an elective format. Although typically given credit as being the father of the elective system, Eliot recognized Jefferson as the one who first implemented and "preach[ed] with the utmost persistence the underlying doctrine of the elective system." He wanted every student, said Eliot, "to follow the line of his inclination in the selection of his course of study."[19]

In yet another respect students at Virginia were given liberties that were denied at other higher education institutions of the day. Compulsory chapel attendance, a bedrock requirement elsewhere, received no sanction at Virginia. Jefferson suggested that students and faculty might hold worship services in a room in the Rotunda, but construction of a separate chapel he deemed unnecessary and potentially a source of sectarian friction. Here again other institutions did not follow the university's lead in terms of voluntary worship until after the Civil War and, at many denominationally sponsored institutions, chapel attendance remained compulsory until deep into the twentieth century.

Jefferson's insistence that students be free to worship (or not) as they pleased merely added fuel to the fire for those who opposed the secular—or "Godless"—orientation of Mr. Jefferson's University. While Jefferson had made provision for a professor of theology in his 1814 curricular proposal sent to Peter Carr and the Central College trustees, he later followed the suggestion of Thomas Cooper when devising plans for the University of Virginia and dropped that chair from his proposed professorships (as he had done earlier as governor when attempting to reform William and Mary). Jefferson emphasized, however, that religion would be taught as a natural component of courses in Hebrew, Greek, and Latin and in the study of history that would accompany instruction in those languages. Moreover, studies in moral philosophy and ethics that developed "those moral obligations in which all sects agree" would be, he stated in an 1822 annual report, both constitutionally and academically appropriate.[20]

On behalf of the board, Jefferson labored to stem the tide of public opinion that saw in this latitudinarian approach a hostility toward religion. In the 1822 report he insisted that "the relations which exist between man and his Maker, and the duties resulting from those relations, are the most interesting and important to every human being, and the most incumbent on his study and investigation." To have no instruction in religion would create "a chasm" at the university, he stated. Incorporating an idea that Samuel Knox had outlined in his essay presented to the American Philosophical Society in the mid-1790s (see chapter 4), Jefferson proposed that each religious sect establish seminaries adjacent to the university. This, he said, would give the seminarians "ready and convenient access" to studies at the university and at the same time would enable students at the university to attend worship services with others of their own particular denomination. "Such an arrangement," Jefferson wrote, "would complete the circle of useful sciences embraced by this institution, and would fill the chasm now existing on principles which would leave inviolate the constitutional freedom of religion, the most unalienable and sacred of all human rights."[21]

Jefferson claimed to be a Christian "in the only sense in which he [Jesus] wished any one to be; sincerely attached to his doctrines, in preference to all others," yet his denial of the divinity of Jesus Christ and his lifelong criticism of narrow-minded ministers and "corruptions of Christianity" made him an inviting target for adherents to doctrinal orthodoxy. Moreover, his failure to provide for a professor of divinity, his rejection of compulsory chapel, and his earlier move to hire the free-thinking Thomas Cooper as one of the first faculty members of Central College combined to arouse considerable controversy and opposition. Jefferson refused to back away from his support of Cooper and persuaded a reluctant board of the newly chartered University of Virginia that it should respect the earlier offer made to him. John Holt Rice, both a Presbyterian minister and an early supporter of the university, led a campaign against Cooper. This placed the institution in an embarrassing situation until Cooper, aware of the resentment against him, removed himself from candidacy in 1820. Jefferson branded Presbyterian clergymen as the loudest and "most intolerant of all" sectarian leaders and asserted that they opposed the university because "they wish to see no instruction of which they have not the exclusive direction." But Presbyterians were not alone in questioning Jefferson's beliefs and decisions with respect to religion—and Cooper—at the university. Madison did not agree with Jefferson regarding Cooper's appointment, nor did fellow visitors John Hartwell Cocke, Chapman Johnson, and Joseph Cabell. As Cocke put the dilemma, "I think our old friend went a little too far . . . [but] we must stand around him . . . and extricate him as well as we can." It is understandable then that his invitation to the leading denominations to erect seminaries near (but not on) the university grounds naturally was suspect in the minds of many. To religious critics of the university, the institution deserved the "Godless" reputation being imputed to it. This charge of infidelity was only somewhat softened under Madison's rectorship several years later when the faculty began inviting ministers to hold Sunday services in the Rotunda.[22]

There was yet another aspect of Jefferson's university that was unusual—and for a time, at least—unworkable. Jefferson's belief in freedom caused him to steer a liberal course when it came to student discipline. He was fully aware of the problems associated with a large body of young men brought together over an extended period of time. He confessed anxieties in this regard to Cooper after the latter had become a professor and then president of the University of South Carolina. Upon hearing of some student disturbances at South Carolina, Jefferson wrote, "The article of discipline is the most difficult in American education. Premature ideas of independence, too little repressed by parents, beget a spirit of insubordination, which is the great obstacle to science with us, and a principle cause of its decay since the revolution. I look to it with dismay at our institution, as a breaker ahead, which I am far from being confident we shall be able to weather."[23]

Although concerned, Jefferson determined to institute a system of student government that would encourage students to assume responsibility for their conduct. "Pride of character, laudable ambition, and moral dispositions are innate correctives of the indiscretions of that lively age," he had explained in the Rockfish Gap Report. Believing that "the affectionate deportment between father and son offers in truth the best example for that of tutor and pupil," Jefferson's plans called for a student-run Board of Censors to act as the principal judicial body. Professor Robley Dunglison called Jefferson's scheme for student self-government a "fanciful" idea, but the faculty had no choice but to abide by the founder's wishes.[24]

Although some years later this progressive concept evolved into a student-run honor system at the University of Virginia, Jefferson found to his great disappointment that at least some of the students in Charlottesville were not prepared by temperament or prior education to accept the academic demands and associated freedom of the university. A few "vicious irregularities" during the early months of the university's existence climaxed with the first of a succession of major disturbances by the fall. After the first riot, Jefferson assembled the students, faculty, and visitors in the Rotunda and began to admonish the students for their misconduct. Choked with emotion and unable to go on, the eighty-two-year-old Jefferson yielded the floor to Visitor Chapman Johnson, who rebuked the students and asked for the leaders of the disturbance to confess their guilt. Fourteen stepped forward in admission of the part they had played in the riotous behavior, one of whom was one of Jefferson's grandnephews. Upon seeing a member of his own family admit guilt, Jefferson could not disguise his grief. With the collapse of Jefferson's plan for student self-government crumbled also one of his most cherished convictions. Disillusioned, he encouraged the Board of Visitors to appeal to the General Assembly for authority to tighten regulations within the university. In the years that followed Jefferson's death, the faculty and visitors multiplied the rules as the students multiplied their offenses. The tide began to turn back towards Jefferson's idealistic vision of student self-government when, in 1842, two years after the murder of a popular professor by a drunken student, Virginia students adopted an "Honor Code" which contained the essence of Jefferson's belief in individual integrity and self-discipline. It remains as one of the most distinctive and significant features of the university—and a point of continuing tension.[25]

To give a full account of Jefferson's educational legacy, we must also acknowledge that while his educational plans proved to be bolder and more progressive than many of his contemporaries could appreciate, he was less bold and progressive than we today might wish, limited by his own and his society's assumptions. This is true in varying degrees with respect to his opinions on the education of women, African Americans, and Native Americans.

Although Jefferson's plan of 1779 and later renditions called for the education of girls through the elementary grades, he did not envision *public* support for the education of women beyond that point. He did, however, favor the continuing education of women within the family circle for reasons of both utility and ornamentality. Reflecting the accepted definition of the "woman's sphere" in the early American social order, Jefferson reasoned that, as future wives and mothers, young women needed instruction in household economy as well as in other realms. Jefferson's letters to his two daughters who survived childhood and to his granddaughters stressed the importance of learning French, Spanish, and Latin, as well as gaining proficiency in their own language. While living in Paris, he enrolled his daughters in the Abbaye Royale de Panthemont, a convent school considered the most genteel in Paris. Throughout their youth, he encouraged them in the fine arts, recommended books, established rigid schedules for their studies, and filled his letters with advice on manners and morals. He pointed to the lasting value of education for women, as it was for men, in a letter to his daughter Martha in 1787: "The object most interesting to me for the residue of my life, will be to see you both [daughters Martha and Maria] developing daily those principles of virtue and goodness which will make you valuable to others and happy in your selves, and acquiring those talents and that degree of science which will guard you at all times against ennui, the most dangerous poison of life. A mind employed is always happy. This is the true secret, the grand recipe for felicity."[26]

While Jefferson saw the education of women, however circumscribed, as an activity to be encouraged, he was far less open-minded in his opinions about the education of black slaves. While his sweeping scheme for publicly supported education was closed to African Americans and he seems to have made no efforts to provide private opportunities for his own slaves, several slaves at Monticello and Poplar Forest did learn to read and write. Surviving letters and accounts written to and by Jefferson's slaves indicate a fair degree of functional literacy and numeracy, at least among some domestic servants and those in skilled crafts. On a larger scale, a surviving fragment of a letter to Quaker activist Robert Pleasants suggests that Jefferson *may* have been at least willing to entertain the notion of educating slaves. Considering Pleasants's plan for the education for slaves, Jefferson somewhat passively replied that his own plan for publicly supported education could perhaps be modified to include black children. Practically speaking, however, Jefferson seems to have taken no active role, privately or publicly, in advancing opportunities for furthering formal education among enslaved or free blacks—except for purposes of their return to Africa.[27]

A conviction that "deep seated prejudices" held by whites, "ten thousand recollections" of abuse on the part of blacks, and "the real distinctions that nature has made" foreclosed in Jefferson's mind the possibility of the two races ever living in harmony. When working on the revisal of Virginia laws in the late 1770s, Jefferson prepared for the Virginia legislature a plan for the gradual emancipation of slaves. He proposed as an amendment to a bill defining the status of slaves that all children of slaves born after a certain date be offered training at public expense in farming, the arts and sciences, or other fields according to their abilities. Upon arriving at adulthood, women at eighteen and men at twenty-one, these descendants of slaves were to be provided with arms, tools, household implements, and domestic animals and then colonized in Africa as "a free and independent people" in alliance with and initially under the protection of the United States. To replace the expatriated slaves, Jefferson recommended the importation of white indentured servants from Europe. Jefferson's plan was neither adopted by the Virginia legislature nor acted upon by Jefferson himself.[28]

Jefferson was less ambivalent about the equality of Native Americans with whites: he considered Native Americans to be equal in intelligence, physical strength, and moral sense to *Homo sapiens Europeaneus*—in essence, they were white people who wore moccasins and breechcloths. With respect to the education of Native Americans, Jefferson preferred that the federal government rather than religious denominations or private societies "civilize" them. Good deist as he was, he feared the influence of Christian missionaries among the Native Americans and compared the evangelists to tribal medicine men—enemies of progress, bent upon keeping Indians in ignorance. As with his reform of the Indian School at William and Mary, Jefferson wanted individuals with the sensitivities and respect of anthropologists to take the lead in dealings with the American aborigines.[29]

Any summary of Thomas Jefferson's educational legacy must thus take into account the context of the times *and* the negative as well as positive judgments that might be made by those of our own and succeeding generations. While Jefferson was in some ways a product of his time, he was most significantly the prophet of later times. His labors on behalf of the education of citizens showed him to be far in advance of the thinking of his day. His lack of sustained attention to the education of those who, in his time and place, were outside the realm of citizenship is understandable even though lamentable.

Jefferson died on July 4, 1826, justly proud of his achievement as the Father of the University of Virginia, a university that he set on a distinctive course far in advance of other institutions of higher education. If his struggle for over four decades on behalf of publicly funded elementary and secondary schools might be reckoned a failure, it was a failure embedded in the limited vision of those whose religious, social, and political views thwarted his numerous attempts to bring such a system into existence. His plans were not perfect, nor his judgment always unclouded, realities that

Jefferson certainly understood. Yet, whatever his personal or philosophical shortcomings as judged by later standards, Jefferson's insistence for nearly half a century on the necessity and justness of public support for the education of all citizens places us in his debt. It may well be, as Dumas Malone once observed, that had Jefferson's educational plan of 1779 (or its later iterations) been enacted and proven effective in practice, "it probably would have been listed with the statute for religious freedom among his greatest achievements."[30]

In the final analysis, perhaps Jefferson's most enduring legacy is the dictum that the current generation must chart its own course in matters educational as in other ways. He warned against ascribing to men of the previous ages a superhuman wisdom. As successive generations endeavor to adjust their educational goals and structures to the demands of their time, his advice penned in an 1816 letter seems appropriate to bear in mind: "Laws and institutions must go hand in hand with the progress of the human mind. As that becomes more developed, more enlightened, as new discoveries are made, new truths disclosed, and manners and opinions change with the change of circumstances, institutions must advance also, and keep pace with the times. We might as well require a man to wear still the coat which fitted him as a boy, as [for] civilized society to remain ever under the regimen of their barbarous ancestors."[31]

Notes

1 TJ to William Roscoe, December 27, 1820, Thomas Jefferson Papers, Library of Congress (hereafter LC).
2 Rockfish Gap Report, Honeywell, 249–50.
3 A Bill for Establishing a System of Public Education, 1817, Honeywell, 234–35; Wagoner, "Jefferson, Justice and the Enlightened Society," 27–28.
4 TJ to Edward Carrington, January 16, 1787, in Merrill D. Peterson, *Thomas Jefferson Writings*, (New York: The Library of America, 1984) (hereafter *Writings*), 880.
5 Onuf, 119; TJ to James Madison, December 20, 1787, in Julian P. Boyd, *et al.*, eds., *The Papers of Thomas Jefferson* (Princeton: Princeton University Press, 1950–) (hereafter *Papers*), 12:442; TJ to Uriah Forrest, with Enclosure, December 31, 1787, *Papers*, 12:478.
6 Rockfish Gap Report, Honeywell, 250.
7 TJ to John Adams, October 28, 1813, Cappon, 2:388; TJ to Peter Carr, August 10, 1787, *Papers*, 12:15.
8 Regulations Adopted by the Board of Visitors of the University of Virginia, October 4, 1824 (hereafter Regulations); Honeywell, 272; Malone, 6:417. Prizes of medals and books were awarded to graduates who might be termed "honorable mention" but less than "highly meritorious" students.
9 TJ to Joseph Priestley, January 18, 1800, *Writings*, 1071; TJ to Nathaniel Bowditch, October 26, 1818, LC; George Ticknor to TJ, October 14, 1815, LC; TJ to Ticknor, October 25, 1818, LC.
10 Bruce, 1:340; TJ to Richard Rush, April 26, 1824, LC.

11 TJ to George Blaettermann, April 26, 1824, LC: Bruce, 1:341, 359; 2:90.

12 Malone, 6:409–10; 416. Board of Visitors, "Organization and Government of the University," April 7, 1824, Honeywell, 269.

13 TJ to Joseph Cabell, April 21, 1826, in Nathaniel F. Cabell, ed., *Early History of the University of Virginia as contained in the Letters of Thomas Jefferson and Joseph C. Cabell* (Richmond, VA: J. W. Randolph, 1856) (hereafter *Letters*), 377; Bruce, 2:101–105; Honeywell, 106–33.

14 Joseph Cabell to TJ, January 29, 1824, and TJ to Cabell, February 23, 1824, *Letters*, 288–290 and 291–92; Honeywell, 281, 270.

15 See, for example, TJ to Nathaniel Bowditch, October 26, 1818, LC; TJ to Joseph Cabell, February 3, 1825, *Letters*, 339.

16 TJ to Benjamin Rush, September 23, 1800, LC; TJ to James Madison, February 1, 1825, in James Norton Smith, ed., *The Republic of Letters: The Correspondence between Thomas Jefferson and James Madison, 1776–1826* (New York: W. W. Norton & Co., 1995) (hereafter Smith), 3:1995; TJ to Joseph Cabell, February 3, 1825, *Letters*, 339; TJ to Madison, February 8, 1825 and February 12, 1825, Smith, 3:1924–26; University of Virginia Board of Visitors Minutes, March 4, 1825, U.Va.; Malone, 6:417; Peterson, *Thomas Jefferson and the New Nation*, 986.

17 TJ to Joseph Cabell, February 3, 1825, *Letters*, 339; Peterson, ibid., 986–87; Malone, 6:418. A more critical appraisal is offered by Leonard W. Levy, *Jefferson and Civil Liberties* (Cambridge: Harvard University Press, 1963).

18 TJ to George Ticknor, July 16, 1823, in Andrew A. Lipscomb and Albert Ellery Bergh, eds., The Writings of Thomas Jefferson (Washington, D.C.: Thomas Jefferson Memorial Foundation, 1905) (hereafter L&B), 15:455; Regulations, October 4, 1824, Honeywell, 272.

19 Charles W. Eliot, "Address at Southwestern Association of Northern Colleges, San Antonio," San Antonio *Express*, February 27, 1909, clipping, Eliot Papers, Harvard University, Box 273. TJ credited William and Mary with employing a system of free election in a letter to his grandson, Francis Wayles Eppes, November 17, 1821, Betts and Bear, eds., *Family Letters*, 441.

20 Board of Visitors, To the President and Directors of the Literary Fund, October 7, 1822, *Letters*, 474.

21 Ibid., 474–75; Honeywell, 168.

22 TJ to Benjamin Rush, April 21, 1803, L&B, 10:380; TJ to William Short, April 13, 1820 and October 19, 1822, LC; John Hartwell Cocke to Joseph Cabell, March 1, 1819, and Joseph Cabell to Cocke, March 6, 1819, Cabell Papers, U.Va.; Addis, *Jefferson's Vision for Education*, 68–87; Bruce, 2:366–69, 370–71; Malone, 6:376–77.

23 TJ to Thomas Cooper, November 2, 1822, LC.

24 Rockfish Gap Report, Honeywell, 257; Robley Dunglison, "The Autobiographical Ana of Robley Dunglison, M.D.," *Transactions of the American Philosophical Society*, Samuel X. Radbill, M. D., ed., (1963) 53:29–30. On Jefferson's views of paternal affection in education, see Hellenbrand, *The Unfinished Revolution*.

25 Jennings L. Wagoner, Jr., "Honor and Dishonor at Mr. Jefferson's University: The Antebellum Years," *History of Education Quarterly*, 26 (Summer, 1986), 155–180.

26 TJ to Martha Jefferson, May 21, 1787, Betts and Bear, eds., *Family Letters*, 41; Wagoner, " 'That Knowledge Most Useful to Us,' " 123–25.

27 TJ to Robert Pleasants, undated fragment [August 27, 1796], LC; Lucia Stanton, *Slavery at Monticello* (Charlottesville, Va.: Thomas Jefferson Foundation, 1993), 40.

28 TJ, *Notes on the State of Virginia*, William Peden, ed. (Chapel Hill: University of North Carolina Press, [1787], 1954) (hereafter *Notes*), 137–139, 162–63; A Bill Concerning Slaves, *Papers*, 2: 470–473; TJ, Autobiography, L&B, 1:72–73.
29 John Chesterton Miller, *The Wolf by the Ears* (Charlottesville: University Press of Virginia, 1991), 72. For a good example of Jefferson's written communications with American Indians, see TJ to the Chiefs of the Cherokee Nation, January 10, 1806, L&B, 19:146–149.
30 Malone, 1:280.
31 TJ to Samuel Kercheval, July 12, 1816, *Writings*, 1401.

References

Addis, Cameron, *Jefferson's Vision for Education, 1760–1845*. New York: Peter Lang, 2003.

Betts, Edwin M. and James A. Bear, Jr., eds., *The Family Letters of Thomas Jefferson*. Charlottesville: University Press of Virginia, 1966.

Bruce, Philip Alexander, *History of the University of Virginia 1819–1919*, 5 vols. New York: The Macmillan Co., 1922.

Cappon, Lester J., ed., *The Adams-Jefferson Letters*. Chapel Hill: University of North Carolina Press, 1959.

Hellenbrand, Harold, *The Unfinished Revolution: Education and Politics in the Thought of Thomas Jefferson*. Newark: University of Delaware Press, 1990.

Honeywell, Roy J., *The Educational Work of Thomas Jefferson*. Cambridge: Harvard University Press, 1931.

Malone, Dumas, *The Sage of Monticello*. Vol. 6 of *Jefferson and His Time*. Boston: Little, Brown and Co., 1981.

Onuf, Peter, *Jefferson's Empire: The Language of American Nationhood*. Charlottesville: University Press of Virginia, 2000.

Peterson, Merrill D., *Thomas Jefferson and the New Nation: A Biography*. New York: Oxford University Press, 1970.

Wagoner, Jennings L., Jr., "Jefferson, Justice, and the Enlightened Society," in Deborah A. Verstegen and James Gordon Ward, eds., *Spheres of Justice in Education*. New York: HarperCollins, 1991, 11–33.

——, "That Knowledge Most Useful to Us': Thomas Jefferson's Concept of Utility in the Education of Republican Citizens," in James Gilreath, ed., *Thomas Jefferson and the Education of a Citizen*. Washington, D.C.: Library of Congress, 1999, 115–133, 333–338.

9

FOUR COLLEGES AND THEIR COMMUNITIES

W. Bruce Leslie

Source: W. B. Leslie, *Gentlemen and Scholars: College and Community in the "Age of the University," 1865–1917*, University Park: Pennsylvania State University Press, 1992, pp. 11–28.

Founding a college in nineteenth-century America required courage and vision, if not foolhardiness. There was no European precedent for creating numerous small institutions of higher education; this was truly an American enterprise. Many colleges were doomed to fail or become secondary schools; a surprising number succeeded. Survival depended on attracting varied sources of support: local, denominational, ethnic, and governmental. The emotions that inspired support also produced conflict: those who cared enough to pay expected colleges to conform to their vision. These extraordinary ventures reflected the aspirations of many different Americans.

A variety of forces shaped the four colleges in this study after the Civil War. To understand the constraints and opportunities they faced after 1865, we must analyze the groups that founded the colleges, the clientele that supported them, and the structures and practices already in place.

One of the nine colonial colleges, Princeton had a long history and national reputation that gave it potential support unavailable to the other three colleges. But by the 1860s, sectional and denominational schism eroded these advantages.

Princeton was the first college of the Great Awakening, born of the Old Side and New Light controversy that split Presbyterianism in 1736. Unwelcome at Old Side Yale and out of place at Harvard and at William and Mary, New Light ministers from the Synod of New York and New Jersey established the College of New Jersey, conventionally called Princeton College, in Newark.

Founded to train Calvinist ministers, its mission and clientele soon broadened. Scotch-Irish New Light Presbyterians in Pennsylvania attached themselves to the new college. The royal governor of New Jersey offered

Figure 1 Nassau Hall, the College of New Jersey, ca. 1860.

support in exchange for places on the board of trustees for himself and four members of his council. Both groups insisted on a more central site than Newark. Princeton outbid New Brunswick and, in 1756, opened Nassau Hall, the largest building in colonial America.

This impressive edifice reflected Princeton's expanded base. In religiously heterogeneous New Jersey, sectarianism would have been suicidal. Although Presbyterians dominated the board of trustees, it included Anglicans, Quakers, and non-Presbyterian Calvinists. Princeton was not legally tied to the synod, which, in turn, contributed little financially. Most donations came from individuals and were earmarked for liberal rather than ministerial education. New Jersey contributed occasional grants. Thus Princeton had neither formal governmental nor denominational ties; it was a spiritually denominational college with a public purpose. Most faculty were Presbyterian; students and supporters belonged to various Protestant denominations.

Princeton had a broad geographic base. Almost half of Princeton's eighteenth-century students came from New England and the South; only about one-quarter came from New Jersey. Financial support came from all sections of the country and even from overseas; contributions for Nassau Hall came from England, Ulster, and Scotland.[1]

The cosmopolitan contacts of the struggling college were enhanced by recruiting the Rev. John Witherspoon from Scotland as president. He became the only Scottish signer of the Declaration of Independence. During Witherspoon's presidency (1768–95), the institution produced many political leaders; its alumni constituted 16 percent of the Constitutional

Convention, including James Madison. Later in Witherspoon's tenure and under his successor, Samuel Stanhope Smith, the production of ministerial candidates dropped precipitously. Smith's theological and disciplinary liberalism made enemies for him in the denomination. When students torched Nassau Hall in 1802, the trustees stepped in.[2]

Over the next sixty years denominational influence grew. After another campus riot in 1807, the Presbyterian General Assembly decided that contact with undergraduates contaminated ministerial candidates and built a separate seminary nearby. Although legally discrete, the seminary strongly influenced the wayward college. Of sixty-four trustees elected to the board at Princeton College between 1812 and 1868, thirty-six were also connected to Princeton Theological Seminary.[3]

The college's fortunes sank in the 1810s and 1820s. Presbyterian philanthrophy was diverted toward the seminary. Smith's successor showed that the iron hand did not stop student disruptions—but it did effectively reduce enrollment. By the late 1820s there were only seventy students, and the president considered closing the institution. But Professor (later President) John Maclean repaired the financial base by organizing the alumni association as a new source of revenue and reformed the curriculum. The result was a financial and intellectual renaissance. Enrollment more than tripled between 1829 and 1839, and talented new faculty were hired. The departure of three of the ablest in the mid-1840s, including physicist Joseph Henry, who went to Washington to become the first director of the Smithsonian Institution, ended the intellectual revival. As Maclean aged, he became increasingly concerned with the faculty's piety and bequeathed his successor an undistinguished, solidly Calvinist faculty.[4]

By the late 1860s Princeton was drawing its students from the narrowest geographic range in its history. Princeton had lost its appeal in New England with the reconciliation of the New Light and the Old Side a century earlier. For almost a century Princeton drew primarily on the Middle Atlantic states and the South. Many border-state Scotch-Irish were disaffected when the Presbyterian schism of 1837 left the college in the anti-evangelical Old School camp. Then the sectionalism of the 1850s evaporated the southern student pool. After the Civil War about two-thirds of the students came from the Middle Atlantic states, and most of the remainder from the border states. Its clientele had become regional rather than national.[5]

While its geographic base and academic reputation were shrinking, Princeton's potential for raising money grew. The spectacular growth of New York City was particularly helpful. A railroad connected the college to both New York and Philadelphia in the early 1840s, making it accessible to two sources of urban wealth. In the 1850s Princeton raised $60,000 for scholarships and quickly got the funds to repair Nassau Hall after a fire. In the midst of the Civil War the college raised $100,000, primarily from New York businessmen.

The long and sometimes distinguished history of the college gave it credibility with the wealthy of New York and Philadelphia, particularly among Scottish and Scotch-Irish Presbyterians. The central New Jersey corridor was the center of early Scottish settlement and culture in North America. A number of Presbyterians involved in the founding of Princeton were Scots or Scotch-Irish. Scottish trading houses in New York, Perth Amboy, and Philadelphia linked with Scotland and Ulster to create a transatlantic Scottish culture. Although initially many Scots and Scotch-Irish were not Presbyterians, and many Presbyterians were English, Scottishness and Presbyterianism became increasingly synonymous in America. With that convergence, in Thomas Wertenbaker's words, "Nassau Hall became the religious and educational capital of all Scotch-Irish America."[6] For all of its problems, Princeton retained the loyalty of many wealthy Presbyterians in the Middle Atlantic states. The growing prosperity of Scots and Scotch-Irish in New York and Philadelphia gave Princeton considerable potential for the future.

Franklin and Marshall College also enjoyed a period of internationally recognized intellectual achievement. But it served a small ethnoreligious group with a much more limited social and financial potential than Princeton. Franklin and Marshall was formed in 1853 by a merger of two institutions. Franklin College predated the Constitution, and its founders included several of the framers. Marshall College was one of the most remarkable intellectual successes among the "hilltop colleges" of the early republic.

Franklin College was founded in 1787 by Benjamin Rush and several other prominent Philadelphians to assimilate the heavily Germanic population of southeastern Pennsylvania into the republican values and English-speaking culture dominant in the eastern end of the state. The new college in Lancaster, then the largest inland town in the United States, promoted Americanization with the country's first collegiate bilingual program.

The college's orientation soon changed. Its charter established a board of trustees composed of fifteen Lutherans, fifteen German Reformed, and fifteen without denominational restriction, the first legally stipulated church-college relationship. But the real divisions followed geographic lines. The Philadelphians lost interest, thereby allowing Reformed and Lutheran Lancasterians to gain control and reorient the college toward promoting German culture and language. Few students appeared, and the college closed without conferring degrees, later operating fitfully as a secondary school.[7]

Higher education did not return to Lancaster until the town lured a college that successfully combined German ethnicity with the denominationalism of the Calvinist German Reformed church. A product of the Reformation, the Reformed church thrived in the Palatinate until the Thirty Years' War and succeeding conflicts ravaged the area, driving Mennonites, Lutherans, and Quakers as well as Reformed north to Holland and England.

From there many were drawn by the religious tolerance and fertile lands of southeastern Pennsylvania. German Calvinists initially were affiliated with the Dutch Reformed church before establishing the German Reformed church in 1793.[8]

German immigration following the abortive revolutions of 1830 and 1848 increased church membership from about 20,000 in the 1820s to over 100,000 by the Civil War. In the late 1830s, the church began to develop the denominational apparatus of Sunday schools, missionary societies, journals, and colleges. The fivefold increase in pastorates and the denomination's belief in highly educated clergy compelled it to make formal provisions for higher education.[9]

Given the Lancasterians' failure to sustain Franklin College, the initiative for German Reformed education fell to a small group that moved from one southern Pennsylvania town to another like medieval scholars for twenty-five years. In 1825 Dr. Lewis Mayer opened a seminary to train German Reformed ministers in Carlisle, attached to the Presbyterians' Dickinson College and funded by European contributions. Friction with Dickinson authorities soon led Mayer to York. Since many students did not intend to enter the ministry, a "High School of the Reformed Church" was attached to the seminary in 1832. Financial troubles forced another move, this time to Mercersburg, a small mountain town in southern Pennsylvania.

Spurred by the Lutheran's recent founding of Gettysburg College, the synod decided to add a collegiate branch to the Mercersburg institutions. The Pennsylvania legislature responded by incorporating Marshall College and granting it twelve thousand dollars. The Mercersburg community raised another ten thousand dollars. The name "college" was quickly translated into reality by a talented faculty shared with the theological seminary.[10]

Marshall College evolved from European forms toward an ethnically distinct American denominationalism. While there were classes in German language and literature, most instruction was in English. The German-speaking sections of the literary societies ceased functioning in the 1840s. The contact with German universities was crucial to the remarkable intellectual success of this small institution in an unlikely American setting. Former Heidelberg professor and later Marshall College President Frederick A. Rauch wrote *Psychology* (1841), one of the first works to bring the new German psychology to America. Professors John W. Nevin and Phillip Schaff epitomized the Anglo-German atmosphere. Schaff was brought from Germany to teach at the theological seminary. Nevin, Scotch-Irish and originally a Presbyterian, trained at Princeton Theological Seminary before being hired by Marshall College and converting to the Reformed church. They published two of the most influential theological journals of the period, the *Mercersburg Review* and *Die Kirchenfreund*.

Despite the intellectual achievements and fruitful blending of two cultures, the Mercersburg institutions did not have unified Reformed support.

Schaff and Nevin's "Mercersburg Theology" was an internationally respected defense of high church practices, but it split the German Reformed church. The controversy flared up in 1843 when Dr. Nevin attacked revivalism in "The Anxious Bench." A year later Schaff's inaugural address portrayed Protestantism as an outgrowth of, rather than a departure from, Catholicism. At a time of fervent revivalism and anti-Catholicism, the Mercersburg Theology divided the denomination and drove some members toward more evangelical sects.[11]

By the late 1840s the Mercersburg institutions were financially troubled. Reformed congregations in Ohio and North Carolina created separate colleges, and many Pennsylvania congregations refused to contribute to the college or the seminary. The German Reformed church had created the typical institutions of American denominationalism but lacked the wealth or unity to support them comfortably. Marshall College was having difficulty maintaining its high standards; events in Lancaster offered a solution.

In the 1840s Lancaster enjoyed an economic boom. A mercantile city in a fertile agricultural area, Lancaster was the fifteenth largest city in the United States in 1800. Its economy stagnated with the decline of artisanal crafts, but Lancaster became an industrial center after the arrival of the railroad. Most of the successful industrialists were of German extraction; many were German Reformed. Most leading non-Germans were also Calvinists, Scotch-Irish Presbyterians.[12] Lancaster was a booming small city that lacked an important civic institution: a college.

The vestige of Franklin College, operating as a secondary school, offered a solution. Its officers proposed a merger with financially troubled Marshall College, whose trustees accepted despite a sense of betrayal among Mercersburg residents. The German Reformed synod approved the merger in January 1850. The Lutherans, who already controlled Gettysburg College, agreed to sell their one-third share of Franklin College.

The Pennsylvania legislature granted a charter uniting Franklin College and Marshall College in 1850. For three years the German Reformed church raised the seven thousand dollars owed to the Lutherans, while the citizens of Lancaster raised twenty-five thousand dollars for the endowment that Marshall College demanded before moving. That done, Marshall College combined its students, faculty, and scholarly reputation with the resources of Lancaster in 1853.[13]

In the next few years an impressive neo-Gothic main building was constructed, along with matching side buildings for the literary societies. But the new college could not escape the Mercersburg Theology controversy. The trustees selected a president who had not been involved in the recent conflicts, but he soon proved to be a Mercersburg Theology partisan. Former Marshall College faculty and their Mercersburg Theology controlled the college, the seminary, and the denominational publications but alienated many in the small denomination.[14] The Civil War aggravated the crisis; the

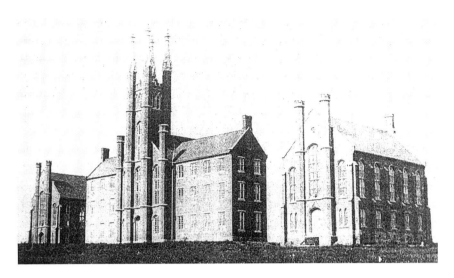

Figure 2 Old Main and the Diagnothian and Goethean Literary Societies, Franklin and Marshall College, 1860.

class of 1866 numbered only six. The financial condition of the school was desperate. In addition, opponents of the Mercersburg Theology founded a rival college (ironically called Mercersburg College) that further divided Reformed support.[15] Franklin and Marshall College entered the post–Civil War era tied to a small, divided ethnic denomination with a tradition of highly educated clergy. Despite its earlier international prestige, its survival now depended on students and money from south-central Pennsylvania, and especially Lancaster.

Like Franklin and Marshall, Bucknell University owes its existence to the unique American combination of denominationalism and boomtown boosterism. But while it seemed strange for a city of Lancaster's size not to have a college, founding Pennsylvania's first Baptist college in Lewisburg, a small town far up the Susquehanna River, was brashly optimistic.

As evangelicals, Baptists accepted the concept of a highly educated clergy more slowly than the high church Presbyterians and German Reformed. But by the 1820s Baptists, particularly in the North, were attracting a wealthier clientele and developing denominational organizations and a professionalized clergy. The rapidly growing demand for ministers led Baptists in many states to found colleges in the 1820s and 1830s. However, the New Jersey and Pennsylvania Baptist organizations, including the influential Philadelphia Baptist Association, failed in their attempts to create a college. In the early 1840s, the New Jersey and Pennsylvania Baptist education societies still sent their ministerial candidates to colleges in New York state.[16]

The opportunity to build an institution commanding the loyalty of New Jersey and Pennsylvania Baptists was seized by a small group in Lewisburg, a town of two thousand on the Susquehanna River in north-central Pennsylvania. In 1840 the Northumberland Baptist Association, composed of Lewisburg area congregations, had only 267 members, and there was no Baptist church in Lewisburg. A revival bolstered membership, and in late 1843 Baptists in Lewisburg began planning for a church and, improbably, a university. Two years later the Northumberland Baptist Association endorsed the audacious project and formally proposed to Pennsylvania's Baptists "that a Literary Institution should be established in Central Pennsylvania, embracing a high school for male pupils, another for females, a college, and also a theological Institution, to be under the influence of the Baptist denomination."[17]

A committee drew up plans, purchased land, and hired an agent, Stephen Taylor, who had recently resigned from Madison (now Colgate) University. He secured legislative approval of the charter creating the University of Lewisburg, which was to be governed by a board of trustees with general powers and a board of curators to oversee academic affairs. All of the trustees and a majority of the curators were to be Baptists.

The charter placed the institution under the "patronage, supervision and direction" of Baptists but also stipulated that "no religious sentiments are to be accounted a disability" in the selection of faculty or students. The charter also required the backers to raise $100,000. The *Lewisburg Chronicle* supported the venture, and residents from various denominations quickly raised $12,000. The demand for Baptist ministers had created an extraordinary opportunity for a small town.

This interdenominational support reflected the economic base of Lewisburg. The construction of the eastern branch of the Pennsylvania Canal in the late 1820s spurred a commercial boom. The two canal builders, a Presbyterian and a Baptist, were founders of the college. The leading merchant was a Lutheran and a prominent college supporter. Lewisburg was the market town for the fertile Buffalo Valley, and by the 1840s it had foundries, gristmills, tanneries, and other industries. Members of its elite were willing to back any institution that would advance their civic ambitions. But a population of less than two thousand was a modest base for an institution of higher learning.[18]

The Lewisburg community and the Northumberland Baptist Association pledged about one-third of the requisite $100,000. Taylor then approached the Philadelphia Baptists. He convinced the pastors and congregations to support this unlikely venture, then a three-day journey from the metropolis. They pledged another third of the required sum. Among the leading contributors were two men whose names grace the two institutions later spawned by the University of Lewisburg: John P. Crozer and William Bucknell.

Figure 3 Old Main, the University of Lewisburg.

Classes started in Lewisburg while two Baptist ministers canvassed Baptist congregations in the rest of Pennsylvania, Delaware, and New Jersey for financial support. It took them three years to collect the remainder of the $100,000; the University of Lewisburg was then offically incorporated in 1849. Three wealthy Philadelphians (William Bucknell, John P. Crozer, and Dr. David Jayne) had donated a total of $25,000, while 4,481 others contributed the other $75,000.

From its inception, the university was a multipurpose institution. Since only one of the twenty-two original students knew Latin and Greek, the studies were necessarily preparatory. In the second year, a few students began collegiate work. When this group became the first graduating class in 1851, enrollment in the four college classes numbered sixty-one, a figure that remained relatively stable for forty years. This first collegiate section was dwarfed by the 186 students in other sections of the university: the academic department (i.e., college preparatory), the English division, the female division, and the primary department. The last was soon handed over to a local schoolmaster, but the other three divisions remained part of the university for over sixty years, and a theological seminary was soon added.

Taylor became professor of mathematics and natural philosophy and built a solidly Baptist faculty for the collegiate department. For reasons that remain unclear, Taylor was passed over for the presidency in favor of the Rev. Howard Malcom, a Baptist educator whose antislavery stance had recently cost him a college presidency in Kentucky. Malcom's tenure in Lewisburg was also stormy. His combination of liberal curricular ideas and stiff pietism discomforted some trustees and led to his resignation in 1857.

The university was soon torn by the tension of being situated in Lewisburg while drawing on Philadelphia for a major share of its students and funds.

In 1856 John P. Crozer offered fifty thousand dollars if the institution moved to Chester, twenty miles south of Philadelphia. The trustees declined the offer by a 10–4 vote, with Crozer and William Bucknell in the minority. The division resurfaced in the search for a new president. The nominating committee proposed a prominent Philadelphia pastor, but a Lewisburg resident and son of one of the founders nominated University of Lewisburg professor Justin Loomis. After fourteen ballots Loomis became the president, at the cost of alienating some Philadelphia trustees.[19]

The geographic schism and other problems plagued the university during Loomis's presidency. Minor disputes angered important supporters, including several of the founders, and weakened the university's appeal in some Baptist congregations. Financial limitations put faculty pay in arrears and delayed dormitory improvements, leading to the death of three students from tuberculosis. These problems and the disruption caused by the Civil War reduced the enrollment to thirty-five in 1862. President Loomis averted disaster by raising $100,000 in the last years of the war. The major contribution, $20,000, came from John P. Crozer. Conspicuous by his absence from the list of major donors was William Bucknell.

The University of Lewisburg entered the postwar years renewed. Collegiate enrollment in 1865–66 reached a record eight-six, and the academy was booming. Local Baptists had to be gratified to be running a large institution that served local needs for secondary education as well as offering baccalaureate degrees and graduate theological studies for Baptists in Pennsylvania and New Jersey. By 1865 the institution could also claim the loyalty of many Philadelphia clergy who were alumni or trustees. On the other hand, some former supporters, including William Bucknell, had been alienated by the factional disputes. Localism, denominationalism, and chance had conspired to bring a large educational institution to an unlikely spot on the banks of the Susquehanna.[20]

The evolution of Swarthmore College is one of the more unusual sagas in the history of American higher education. Swarthmore is a nationally prestigious college that Burton Clark labeled a "model of undergraduate education."[21] But Swarthmore developed along a unique path that contradicts most assumptions about nineteenth-century denominational colleges. Many of its Quaker founders were uncomfortable with intellectual endeavors and ambivalent about education beyond the secondary school. Swarthmore was rooted in traditional piety, yet it was a curricular innovator and one of the first coeducational colleges in the Northeast. Its curriculum emphasized science, downplayed the classics, and had an elective system before Charles Eliot's famous speech at Harvard.

For five decades after it opened in 1869, Swarthmore College was torn between its distinctive Quaker tradition and more worldly pressures. The demanding Quaker life-style and beliefs originated in the religious turmoil of seventeenth-century England. Discomforted by Stuart elegance and Cromwellian authoritarianism, Quakers challenged both with a "plain" life-style and pacifism. The resulting persecution drove many members of the Religious Society of Friends to William Penn's colony. After actively participating in Pennsylvania affairs into the 1750s, most Quakers withdrew into "Quietism."

Friends exhibited as much nonconformity in education as in politics. Their aversion to legal, political, and clerical professions made much of traditional education irrelevant or repugnant to them. The clerical faculty and denominationalism of most colleges alienated Quakers. They valued training for teaching, commerce, and agriculture, subjects that were not taught in most colleges.

Quaker emphasis upon practical knowledge dicated a utilitarian education. George Fox, founder of the movement, wanted schooling restricted to the "civil and useful," a view shared by most Friends. To provide vocational training within the context of "guarded education" and prevent common schools from luring away young Friends, a number of Yearly Meetings established boarding schools in the early 1800s.[22]

Dissatisfaction with Quietism led to denominational schism in 1827. A restive group desiring a more activist approach gained control of the Philadelphia Meeting. A dominantly Quietistic group seceded to form a separate meeting, dubbed "Hicksite." Similar splits occurred in the New York, Baltimore, Ohio, and Indiana meetings. The ideological split partially followed urban/rural lines. This was particulay pronounced in the Philadelphia Meeting, where the Orthodox outnumbered Hicksites in the city by 3,000 to 1,500 but had a mere 5,000 followers in the surrounding environs, where there were 14,500 Hicksites.[23]

The Orthodox included most wealthy urban Friends who could finance denominational activities. They started a journal seventeen years before the Hicksites created their *Friends Intelligencer*. The Orthodox also seized the initiative in education. Having retained control of most Quaker schools, they added new academies and founded Haverford College and Earlham College in the 1850s.[24]

Hicksites were composed of three main groups. The largest was made up of rural Friends who resented the wealthy urban Orthodox leaders. A second group consisted of urban artisans who were threatened by the Industrial Revolution and wanted to cling to traditional ideas. The third group, and the one that later financed much of Swarthmore's work, represented established wealth that viewed the Orthodox leaders as nouveau riche. Hicksite Quietism discouraged denominational activism and stunted educational progress. But a non-Quietist minority who valued the Hicksite movement more for its tolerance than for its Quietism and traditional life-styles became increasingly anxious to have a college under Hicksite auspices.[25]

In 1860 several members of the Hicksite Baltimore Yearly Meeting proposed establishing a boarding school and a teacher training institute to provide "additional facilities for the guarded education of Friends' Children, and especially for the supply of suitable teachers in membership with us to whom to entrust our children in our neighborhood Schools."[26] The Baltimore Yearly Meeting approved the proposal and soon procured assistance from the Philadelphia and New York meetings. The three Yearly Meetings published a joint appeal for financial support in early 1861, but national events intervened.

The contributors elected sixteen male and sixteen female Hicksite Friends to a board of managers and authorized it to start classes when fifty thousand dollars had been subscribed. In 1864, the Pennsylvania legislature chartered Swarthmore College, named for George Fox's home. The following year land was purchased outside Philadelphia, and a president selected. Four years of fund-raising lay ahead before Swarthmore could open its doors.[27] The Hicksites developed their denominational mechanisms, including their college, late and ambivalently. But their purpose was clear: to defend a distinctive denominational life-style.

When the Civil War ended, these four institutions were very different from what they would be when the United States entered World War I.

Figure 4 Main Building (later Parrish Hall) under construction, Swarthmore College, 1869.

Each could depend on denominationalism and localism for modest support. But each suffered from divisions within those groups. All four were constricted by limited resources, albeit the financial potential of their supporters differed considerably.

Although their existence was modest, the mere survival of these institutions and hundreds like them showed a remarkable commitment to advanced education, though the four-year college was just one part of a broader commitment. Only the College of New Jersey stood alone. At Bucknell and at Franklin and Marshall, secondary education appeared first and continued to be a major part of the institution, and the founders of Swarthmore were more interested in secondary and normal education than higher studies. These were multifunctional institutions rather than the freestanding colleges of the twentieth century. They were also surprisingly popular institutions that were not isolated from antebellum American society.

Denominational ambitions were essential to the creation of each college, and most faculty and trustees were members of the sponsoring denomination. But the phrase "denominational college" obscures the complex nature of support. In two cases denominationalism also conveyed ethnicity, and in a third a unique life-style. Only Bucknell was the product of a relatively undifferentiated American Protestant denominationalism. In all cases the colleges depended on local boosterism for financial support as well as for students, regardless of denomination. State and local public funds mixed with private. Formal denominational fund-raising brought in only modest sums; the largest donations came from wealthy New Yorkers, Philadelphians, and Lancasterians, most of whose donations were induced by denominational loyalty.

In 1865 higher education was not yet a national enterprise. Historians have wondered why a modernized academia with a professionalized professoriate based on national organizations and shared values did not emerge more quickly. But as Bucknell, Franklin and Marshall, and Princeton emerged from the Civil War and Swarthmore planned to open its doors, none faced a strong demand to heed reformers' calls to promote research and stop giving moral guidance. Indeed, it would have been strange for these schools to have done so—strange and disloyal to their roots. These four colleges were staffed by, and served, members of communities to whom university reform had little relevance. The colleges shared an intellectual tradition but developed within the context of local, regional, and denominational communities whose values would be challenged by rapid social change after Appomattox.

Notes

1 Thomas J. Wertenbaker, *Princeton, 1746–1846* (Princeton: Princeton University Press, 1946), 1–47; Howard Miller, *The Revolutionary College: American*

Presbyterian Higher Education, 1707–1837 (New York: New York University Press, 1976), 60–75.

2 In the classes of 1753, 1763, and 1773, 49.2 percent of the graduates became ministers; in the classes of 1783, 1793, and 1803, only 8.9 percent entered the ministry. Princeton University, *General Catalogue, 1746–1896* (Princeton: Princeton University Press, 1896), 42–151; Miller, 68; Wertenbaker, 116. For excellent intellectual histories of the Witherspoon-Smith years, see Douglas Sloan, *The Scottish Enlightenment and the American College Ideal* (New York: Teachers College Press, 1971), chaps. 3 and 4; and Mark A. Noll, *Princeton and the Republic, 1768–1822* (Princeton: Princeton University Press, 1989).

3 Varnum L. Collins, *Princeton*, American College and University Series (New York: Oxford University Press, 1914), 119–27; Wertenbaker, 118–52, 238–39.

4 Collins, 127–64; Wertenbaker, 153–289; Princeton College, *Plan for a Partial Endowment of the College of New Jersey* (1853); Stephen Alexander, *Address at the Laying of the Cornerstone of the Astronomical Observatory* (Newark, N.J., 1867); Princeton College, *Catalogue of the College of New Jersey* (1866/67).

5 Proportions were calculated from the catalogs and class publications. Wertenbaker, 175–81; Patricia Graham, *Community and Class in American Education, 1865–1918* (New York: John Wiley & Sons, 1974), 183–84.

6 Wertenbaker, 113; Ned C. Landsman, *Scotland and Its First American Colony, 1683–1765* (Princeton: Princeton University Press, 1985), 3–13, 175–79.

7 David W. Robson, *Educating Republicans: The College in the Era of the American Revolution* (Westport, Conn.: Greenwood Press, 1985), 196–205; Jurgen Herbst, *From Crisis to Crisis: American College Government, 1636–1819* (Cambridge: Harvard University Press, 1982), 200–201; Miller, 136; Owen S. Ireland, "The Crux of Politics: Religion and Party in Pennsylvania, 1778–1789," *William and Mary Quarterly* 42 (October 1985), 453–75.

8 The name was changed to "Reformed Church in the United States" (not to be confused with the Dutch Reformed church, which became the "Reformed Church in America"). The German Reformed church merged with the Evangelical church in 1934 and the Congregational church in 1957, creating the United Church of Christ. Winthrop S. Hudson, *American Protestantism* (Chicago: Chicago University Press, 1961), 158–59; Robert T. Handy, *A History of the Churches in the United States and Canada* (New York: Oxford University Press, 1977), 98, 151; James I. Good, *History of the Reformed Church in the United States in the Nineteenth Century* (New York: Board of Publications of the Reformed Church of America, 1911).

9 Glenn Weaver, "The German Reformed Church and the Home Missionary Movement Before 1863: A Study in Cultural and Religious Isolation," *Church History* 22 (December 1953): 298–313.

10 Ibid., 307–11; Joseph Henry Dubbs, *History of Franklin and Marshall College* (Lancaster, Pa.: Franklin and Marshall Alumni Association, 1903), 151–78. An indication of Mercersburg's extraordinary intellectual achievement is that three of the faculty of this tiny college (Rauch, Nevin, and Schaff) are noted in a major survey of American intellectual history: Lewis Perry, *Intellectual Life in America: A History* (New York: Franklin Watts, 1984), chap. 5.

11 James H. Nichols, *Romanticism in American Theology: Nevin and Schaff at Mercersburg* (Chicago: University of Chicago Press, 1961), 1–4, 192–235, 281–311; George W. Richards, "The Mercersburg Theology—Its Purpose and Principles," *Church History* 20 (September 1951): 42–55; Handy, 206–7; Dubbs, 179–202; *Dictionary of American Biography* (New York: Scribners' Bros., 1934), 13:442–43, 16:417–18; Perry, 212–23, 249–52.

12 John W. Loose, *Heritage of Lancaster* (Woodland Hills, Calif.: Windsor Publications, 1978), 1–49; Thomas R. Winpenny, *Industrial Progress and Human Welfare: The Rise of the Factory System in Nineteenth-Century Lancaster* (Washington, D.C.: University Press of America, 1982), 1–19, 41–44.

13 Dubbs, 141–47, 237–47; H. M. J. Klein, *History of Franklin and Marshall College, 1787–1948* (Lancaster, Pa., 1952), 61–63.

14 Nichols, 221–35; Dubbs, 255–81, 302–14; Good, 298.

15 Dubbs, 302–14; Klein, 93–101; Franklin and Marshall College, Board of Trustees, Minutes (Franklin and Marshall Archives), 7 and 8 July, 1868.

16 J. Orin Oliphant, *Beginnings of Bucknell University: A Sampling of the Documents* (Lewisburg, Pa.: Bucknell University Press, 1954), 11; Robert G. Torbet, *A Social History of the Philadelphia Baptist Association, 1707–1740* (Philadelphia, 1944), 72–76. There is an outstanding account of antebellum Baptist ventures in higher education, including Bucknell: David B. Potts, *Baptist Colleges in the Development of American Society, 1812–1861* (New York: Garland Press, 1988).

17 Oliphant, *Beginnings*, 24. For the history of Lewisburg, see Lois Kalp, *A Town on the Susquehanna, 1769–1975* (Lewisburg, Pa.: Colonial Printing Co., 1980), which integrates town and gown particularly well. There is also a county history that sheds light on the origins: Charles M. Snyder, *Union County, Pennsylvania: A Bicentennial History* (Lewisburg, Pa.: Colonial Printing House, 1976), 90–94, 106–9.

18 Bucknell is blessed with two excellent institutional histories that describe the founding very well. J. Orin Oliphant, *The Rise of Bucknell University* (New York: Appleton-Century-Crofts, 1965), 3–35; and Lewis Edwin Theiss, *Centennial History of Bucknell University, 1846–1946* (Williamsport, Pa.: Grit Publishing Co., 1946), 11–55.

19 Potts, 134–61; Oliphant, *Rise*, 29–87; Theiss, 39–89, 142–43; Sanford Fleming, "American Baptists and Higher Education" (Unpublished manuscript, American Baptist Historical Association, Rochester, N.Y., 1965), 184–85.

20 Theiss, 67–68, 114, 136–41, 154–75; Bucknell University, *Quinquennial Catalogue* (Lewisburg, Pa., 1900).

21 Burton R. Clark, *The Distinctive College: Antioch, Reed, and Swarthmore* (Chicago: Adams Publishing Co., 1970), 172.

22 A standard history of Quakerism is Sydney V. James, *A People Among Peoples* (Cambridge: Harvard University Press, 1963). John M. Moore, ed., *Friends in the Delaware Valley: Philadelphia Yearly Meeting, 1681–1981* (Haverford, Pa.: Friends Historical Association, 1981) has important essays; those by J. William Frost and Edwin B. Bronner are particularly relevant to this study. See also Homer D. Babbidge, Jr., "Swarthmore College in the Nineteenth Century: A Quaker Experience in Education" (Ph.D. diss., Yale University, 1953), 18–30.

23 Robert W. Doherty, *The Hicksite Separation* (New Brunswick, N.J.: Rutgers University Press, 1967), 67–89, provides a sociological analysis of the schism.

24 On the first two Orthodox colleges, see Opal Thornburg, *Earlham: The Story of the College, 1847–1962* (Richmond, Ind.: Earlham College Press, 1963); and Gregory Kannerstein, ed., *The Spirit and the Intellect: Haverford College, 1833–1983* (Haverford, Pa.: Haverford College, 1983).

25 Doherty, 67–89; Babbidge, 33–41; Moore, 59–102.

26 "Proceedings in Baltimore," Edward Parrish, Presidential Papers (Friends Historical Library), 2 October 1860; Babbidge, 42–53.

27 Babbidge, 50–68; Swarthmore College, Board of Managers, Minutes (Friends Historical Library), 2 December 1862–5 December 1865.

10

UNIVERSITIES IN THE U.S.A.
Secondary School Characteristics

Ralph E. Lombardi

Source: *Universities Quarterly* IX (1954–5): 66–72.

There are about 1,400 degree-granting colleges and universities[1] in the United States (1,900 if the two-year junior or community colleges are included) and they vary so much that it is difficult to generalize about them. However, one fact is clear: they are, to a great extent, simply extensions of American high schools. The jump from high school to university is small, for many university practices and customs are similar to high-school practices and customs. Let us examine some of them in order to understand better why and how American universities differ from European universities.

First of all, the American undergraduate does not penetrate as deeply into his 'major field' as does his British counterpart. He often is not sufficiently grounded in such basic subjects as English and history to be able to devote all his time (or even a large part of it) to the subject that interests him most. Another reason is that he must take a great variety of subjects. There has been an increasing tendency to broaden the subject requirements owing to a popular belief that the 'well-rounded man' is needed more than the dyed-in-the-wool scholar. Hence in American universities the first two years are largely a continuation of high school with a smattering of English grammar and literature, history, languages, and perhaps some science and mathematics. Specialization does not usually begin until the third year. Therefore most sincere scholars become postgraduates before they feel that they are digging below the surface of their major subject.

Admission standards differ to a certain extent. Most universities are willing to admit the 'average' high-school student, and at least two have declared that any graduate of a high school can enter! Hardly more than half of the undergraduates get satisfactory grades in enough courses so that they may receive a degree. Hence many undergraduates who should not have been admitted are forced to leave with the knowledge of having already had a serious failure in life.

Some of this wastage may consist of students transferring to another university, but some undergraduates fail so many courses that they are no longer eligible to receive a degree, others may lose interest or drop out because of a personal reason. Often part-time work competes with studying. A small percentage of students receive scholarships and student costs are high. Admission standards to graduate schools are higher, but even here mistakes are made.

Not only does a student take many different subjects, but he also has a varied list from which he chooses those subjects which satisfy the university's requirements and his own interests. Some of the standard subjects are Contemporary Civilization, American History, Introductory Chemistry, English Literature, College Algebra, Introduction to Sociology, Introduction to Economics, and Beginning French. Some universities offer degrees (including the Ph.D.) in such subjects as swimming, home economics, speech, radio, dramatics, photography, nursing, library service, journalism, industrial management, and television.

Usually a student must accumulate at least thirty credits in his major subject (about one-fourth of the total number required for a degree) and about twelve or eighteen credits in a minor subject. The minor may be closely related to the major, or it may be completely different. Opinions differ widely on what the relationship between major and minor subjects should be.

In universities where agricultural and technical courses predominate, such subjects as history and literature often suffer, for they are considered as 'service' courses and their teaching is on an inferior level most of the time so that a 'reasonable' number can pass the course. As is generally true in high school and university courses, if an instructor holds closely to his conception of what the standards of his course should be, many of his students may fail it. Then he will become unpopular, his classes will diminish in size, and he may get into difficulties with the university authorities. This is also true in some of our best-known universities. Few Americans are aware of this problem or the dangers involved.

Arts courses are frequently frowned upon by the majority of students, who are more interested in 'practical' studies which may earn them money later on. It is a commonplace that science and mathematics students appear more serious and work harder. On the other hand much language teaching is on an elementary or intermediate level and few students ever learn a foreign language well.

The elective system was introduced by President Eliot of Harvard towards the turn of the century in a more general way than it had ever been used before. It permits a great freedom of choice in courses, but its benefits are still controversial. Students are often confused when trying to choose from the maze of course titles. They often do not know what to take. Hence such considerations as the time the course is given, whether or not the instructor is 'easy', and the difficulty of the subject itself often determine their choice. This is one practice which does not come from high school, but it has been introduced in some modern high schools. It is clear that Thomas Jefferson's liberal conception of a university had much influence on the development of the American university and we are more German than English in our emphasis on the freedom of the student.

Student supervision ranges from imitations of the Oxford-Cambridge tutorial system (e.g., at Harvard and Princeton) to a minimum of supervision by the faculty and deans. Often an instructor is designated as a student's advisor. Or there may be an educational specialist who is trained in advisement. In small colleges the head of each department may advise students 'majoring' in his field. In a few places students who work for honours get closer attention. Freedom is restricted more than the students indicate by their gay exterior and active social life. Such practices as taking attendance, reprimands for missing class, required reading designated by chapter and verse, early curfews for freshmen, punishment for cheating at examinations, and so forth, are popular.

The number of tests or examinations in each course is determined by the instructor. Students usually prefer quizzes once a week to exams which may require the ability to retain information over a long period. Only postgraduates are allowed to go as long as an academic year without examinations.

Reference to what the student 'likes' may seem strange, but this factor has a great influence on the curriculum and teaching in America. Sometimes the teacher is evaluated by the students! This is more possible in state universities where it may or may not be compulsory. The results are usually revealed only to the instructor. Many naturally dislike this innovation.

Grading ordinarily breaks down into five categories: A is excellent, B good, C fair, D passing, and E or F failure. Credit is not given for a D or failing grade. Honours given to students with high average grades do not have the importance they have in Britain, and are seldom ever mentioned. Students do not aim for honours or 'pass'.

Classes run from eight to sixteen weeks, and from one to five (usually three) hours a week. The student may attend a course three days a week for one hour, and at the end of term he receives a grade which goes down on his transcript (the registrar's record) of grades and which determines whether he receives credits for the course. Three credits will probably be given for this course, and when the student accumulates 120 or 130 or so credits he receives the bachelor's degree, provided his grades are satisfactory and he has fulfilled the requirements of his department. The student normally takes four or more courses a term, two terms a year, for four years. Again, we have a practice that is similar to high-school procedure.

Lecturing is not as common as in British universities, although it is used to a great extent by the large universities. Even where there are lectures, however, the lecturer is often interrupted by questions, and an informal atmosphere prevails. Large classes are sometimes broken up into smaller groups headed by assistants to the professor. In this way the professor may lecture once a week and the assistants will meet their groups several times a week to lead discussions and answer questions. Teaching methods similar to those used in high school are often employed. The term 'classroom' is more common than 'lecture hall'. There is note-taking at lectures and often professors give the same lectures every year so that notes of former students can be used to advantage. The practice of mimeographing notes and selling them to other students has occasionally arisen.

Tests often take the character of high-school tests. They may consist of true and false questions, multiple-choice questions, 'fill-in blanks', or some other form of factual quiz. Teachers who give 'essay questions' are often unpopular.

Unfortunately there are no U.S. government scholarships (except the 'Fulbrights' for overseas students) and no system of scholarships that discovers and trains an intellectual élite the way the British system does. The high cost of tuition forces many students into part-time work during the academic year and full-time work during the long vacation. The natural result is that too much time is taken away from studies. Often students begin working when in high school and simply continue this practice through their university career.

Many students live 'off the campus' (especially in the redbrick universities), but they do not lose the social advantages of university life, for they engage in clubs, athletics, etc. Extracurricular activity, as in high school, causes studies to be neglected until tests are imminent when a great deal of 'cramming' is done. Hence instructors try to increase the frequency of tests.

American students want a degree so they can get a better job, improved social standing, prestige, and so on, and they are encouraged by parents, teachers, and others to think this way. Few are scholars in the traditional sense. Anyone interested in truth for its own sake or an academic subject for its own sake is looked at with great curiosity.

Throughout the educational system there is less emphasis on effective writing of English than there is here. Few essays are written. Postgraduate students in literature or social studies often find themselves handicapped because of their inability to write well.

As in high school, classes are sprinkled through the day so that a student may spend almost a full day alternating classes with study hours or other activities.

After the war the universities expanded rapidly to permit the large backlog of students to enter along with the war veterans who were aided by a generous allotment from the government. The immediate result was a fall in standards, for classes became too large and teaching was often inferior. Many high-school teachers moved up into university teaching to fill the need.

Most instructors teach too many hours a week. Some universities limit the number of hours to fifteen or less but the instructors constantly seek other sources of income through extension lecturing, evening schools, special lectures, and so forth. Moreover, an instructor may be asked to teach a wide variety of courses at the same time. A good example might be: American history, Russian history, contemporary world politics, and a seminar in Pacific-American relations—all in the same term.

Faculty members endeavour to be 'popular' with the students so their classes will be large and they will be esteemed highly by the university community. Students seldom take a class without first investigating the reputation of the teacher to discover whether he is 'easy' or 'hard', formal or informal, gives frequent quizzes or none at all, speaks well, etc. The importance of being 'liked' which is so common in American business society is therefore carried over into the classroom and lecture room.

High school and university teachers usually strive to be objective and impartial in their lectures and comments. This is often due to a fear of being labelled politically, religiously, or philosophically. The result often is that professors profess nothing.

Usually every campus organization, such as international relations clubs, debating societies, and the like, has an instructor as moderator or advisor. University radio stations are common and serve as excellent training grounds for potential writers and actors as well as reporting and entertaining media for the university community.

There is keen competition among students for the title of 'Big Man on Campus' or 'The Most Popular'. A 'B.M.O.C.' is usually a big man physically who is extremely competent in athletics and is well-known and liked. He may or may not be a scholar. Usually he is not.

There is a big gap between the serious student and the rest who strive to be 'friendly all-round Joes'. The serious student is often labelled a 'grind' and may be ostracized by the others. This tends to reduce the number of 'grinds', for few wish to be unpopular. This, too, grows out of high school. There is much drinking among students, but most of it is not very dangerous. They often congregate in neighbourhood taverns to consume large quantities of beer and sing college songs.

Although a certain amount of lip-service is given to the importance of good conduct there is more stress on the development of character in British universities. In America the educated man is often confused with the well-informed man. This is true even in graduate schools, where instruction is superior to undergraduate instruction (seminars and classes are conducted well). There is too much emphasis on 'research' and not enough on thought.

162

This helps to increase the number of large dissertations that are read by no one except the examining board. The lectures and books of university teachers reveal this tendency towards factual and statistical work. Moreover, attempts to supplement their income by writing articles for popular publications often result in fewer original contributions to the academic field.

Often students will leave the university without having considered the fundamental problems of life or having come to any consistent philosophy of life, for the prospect of a true and false quiz the next day does not stimulate meditation on deeper problems. In this important respect most American universities must be considered a failure. However, there is an encouraging movement towards courses in civilization, group discussions of 'great books', and so on, which may improve the situation. Small church colleges are often better than large universities in this respect. Mr. Robert Hutchin's *The Higher Learning in America* exemplifies the trend among thoughtful educators towards what Sir Walter Moberly calls classical humanism, especially in his attack on material objectives in universities.

Underneath all these factors which make American institutions of higher education so different from the universities of other countries lies the theory that society has the obligation to educate each person. The assumption that everyone can be educated is the root of American educational philosophy. Hence the attainment of diplomas and degrees, speedily and efficiently, has become the main goal of many Americans.

Note

1 In this article I use the term *university*, for convenience, to cover all degree-granting institutions. This is not illogical for the systems are extremely alike although the academic standards vary.

11

THE SCOTTISH UNIVERSITY TRADITION

Andrew Lockhart Walker

Source: A. L. Walker, *The Revival of the Democratic Intellect: Scotland's University Traditions and the Crisis in Modern Thought*, Edinburgh: Polygon Press, 1994, pp. 22–37.

"It has been shown that, from a very early period, schools of various kinds existed over the greater portion of Scotland, and that, in the more important towns, there was more or less complete provision for advanced education."[1] To give just one example, Ayr Burgh School was founded in 1233, that is 150 years before Winchester, England's oldest public school, and 82 years before Robert the Bruce was crowned king of Scotland at a national parliament held in St. John's Church in Ayr in 1315.

So where did the young Scots go, who wanted a higher education, before St. Andrews was founded in 1411? A few went to Oxford and Cambridge, which began their careers as full universities in the thirteenth century, but the great majority went to universities on the Continent, mostly in France. They formed part of the famous wandering scholars of the Middle Ages, a practice that still exists in Germany. Indeed, the number of Scottish students in Paris in the fourteenth century was so great as to attract the attention of the authorities, and the Bishop of Moray found it necessary to found a Scots college in Paris in 1326. The words Collège des Ecossais can still be seen on a frontage in the Rue Cardinal Lemoine. Other Scots colleges were set up at Oxford: Balliol College founded by Sir John de Balliol in 1293; Douai 1576; Ratisbon (Bavaria) 1515 in the Scots monastery of St. James, founded at the beginning of the twelfth century; Rome, 1600; Madrid, 1627; Valladolid, 1770, still functioning; Montpellier, founded by Patrick Geddes in 1924 after failing to resuscitate the Collège des Ecossais in Paris – it is still flourishing.

It is hardly surprising that the authorities were forced to take note of the Scots since the students led a pretty wild life in Paris. "This life, curiously compounded of hardship and kindliness, was doubtless useful in teaching

164

them to face and overcome difficulties, but the freedom of it and the self-reliance it fostered, almost necessarily created a habit of mind impatient of restraint and strict discipline when they reached the precincts of the university."[2] This independent life of the students, with the universities having no responsibility for them, no status *in loco parentis*, was ever after to be the normal practice at Scottish universities, as different as could well be imagined from the cloistered, cosseted life of students at Oxford and Cambridge, with proctors and bulldogs hemming them in. An amusing example of this six centuries later is given by the late John Mackintosh MP:

> Professor Grierson, who once held the Chair of English at Edinburgh, used to commence lecturing each year by trying for five minutes to be heard above the uproar. When he failed he would shriek: 'Send for the police!' A group of burly constables who had been waiting outside rushed in, seized the leading troublemakers and threw them outside on the pavement, after which there was some semblance of order.[3]

The students were treated like any ordinary members of the public; they had no special penalties to face and no special immunities.

Since Scotland was a very poor country the number of young men who could afford to study abroad in this way must have been limited, though numerous enough as we have seen. Many of those who had profited from the "advanced education available in the more important towns" would have been unable to do it. "The astonishing thing", says Sir James Irvine,[4] a former Principal of the University of Edinburgh, "is that a small, poor and sparsely populated country produced scholars in suffiency to justify the bold educational experiment made by the little band of Masters and Doctors who, in 1410, commenced lectures in St. Andrews". The university received its charter from Bishop Henry Wardlaw on 27 February 1411. Even more astonishing, of course, was the fact that by the end of the century there were two more universities in Scotland: Glasgow, set up by Bishop William Turnbull in 1451, and Aberdeen, founded by Bishop Elphinstone in 1494. The demand was quite clearly there, so that by the end of fifteenth century, and before the creation of Edinburgh nearly a century later, Scotland already had one more university than England.

In its early period Scottish university education benefited from the talents of a few very able and very wise men, Bishop Elphinstone being one of the first for he held the view that "Scotland's greatest educational need was the provision of trained university teachers, and that more purposes could be served by a university than merely guaranteeing a succession of recruits for the Church".[5] One of the greatest of these men was Andrew Melville who, like so many able Scots of the period, taught in the universities of Europe. Aberdeen's first Principal had been a professor in the University of Paris; Melville had been a student at Paris, a regent (i.e. lecturer) at Poitiers, and a Professor at Geneva. On his return from Geneva he reorganized the University of Glasgow so that within a few years "there was no place in Europe comparable to Glasgow for a plentiful and good cheap market of all kinds of languages, arts and sciences".[6] These references to what can only be described as academic market forces should not worry the contemporary reader too much. They reflect the fact that Scotland's universities followed the medieval tradition of being "largely vocational schools . . . The universities, overwhelmingly orientated towards the professional needs of society, became increasingly reflective of the establishment which they served."[7] It turned out to be a healthy tradition, as we shall see in the eighteenth and nineteenth centuries especially, since it meant that the distinction between the academic and the vocational, between the gentlemen and the players, was never as strong in Scotland as in England, where it did great damage by creating deep-rooted and restrictive elitist instincts throughout the education system.

In Scotland it was otherwise. "From the beginning the Scottish universities have been among the most democratic in the world – duke's son and cook's son sat on the same student benches and shared the same fare at the common table."[8] The most important feature of all was the "ouverture aux talents": "From the humblest of Scottish homes there was now a direct connection through the schools to the class-rooms of the College, and the ladder of learning – rudely fashioned and with uneven steps – had become a reality."[9] There was to be no such ladder of learning in England till four centuries later. Here was born the reality of the 'lad o' pairts' – no myth or legend, as some contemporary scholars have sought to show. True, it became the Scots' favourite image of their educational tradition, but that is entirely to their credit. It is surely infinitely preferable to the shibboleths of such contemporary pundits as Sir Christopher Ball, who calls for the reduction of Scottish university courses to three years instead of four, and for students of "imaginative and creative minds to devote themselves to . . . the more immediate and pressing issues of making and selling".[10] Or Dr. John Ashworth, Director of the London School of Economics, who also calls for the reduction of Scottish university courses to three years, and makes much play with fashionable jargon terms like 'quality assurance'.[11] The records give convincing proof that the longing for learning was and is something real in Scotland, shared by rich and poor alike.

The three earliest universities had many points in common. They were all based more or less completely on the medieval universities of the Continent. Indeed, the older Scottish universities are now the only true continuators of the medieval organization, for they recognize the following elements as constituting the 'university': 1) the students; 2) the graduates (or *magistri non regentes*; 3) the professors (or *magistri regentes*); 4) the Rector; and 5) the Chancellor.[12] Papal authority was required to give them as learned communities self-government, immunity from taxation, power to give degrees and the freedom to teach. Owing to the poverty of Scotland and the selfishness of the nobility the only support they could count on was that given them by church dignitaries who took an interest in them. Their development was greatly hindered by international struggles. Indeed, in 1560 they were to be all but wiped out at the time of the Reformation. One of the reasons that so many young Scots went to France rather than England for a university education was that during the split in the Papacy Paris and Scotland supported Pope Clement in Avignon, whereas England supported Pope Urban in Rome. So young Scots were not welcome at Oxford and Cambridge.

Indeed, it would not be an exaggeration to say that no other country underwent an ordeal so prolonged and so destructive of the social peace necessary for the progress of the universities. During the latter part of the sixteenth century and the whole of the seventeenth century, every twenty years there would be a change in the religious authority in power: stern and moderate Presbyterian, spurious and genuine episcopacy. "At each stage a fresh Commission would adapt the conditions in the universities to the wishes of the Church for the time in the ascendant. Confusion and the destruction of discipline was inevitable and steady progress impossible."[13]

Yet, already before the Reformation, in 1496, the first compulsory Education Act recorded in history was passed in Scotland. And Hume Brown could say, in his *Life of Buchanan*, another in the line of great Scottish educators: "There is excellent reason for believing that, with the exception of the Netherlands, no country in Europe was better provided than Scotland with schools for what was then primary and secondary education."[14] Morgan shows how the early Celtic Church of Columba and his followers, and then the Roman Catholic Church, created schools all over Scotland, both within the monasteries, abbeys, priories and in neighbouring burghs, and even controlled schools in distant towns and parishes. Thus there were abbey schools in Dunfermline, Arbroath, Cambuskenneth, Paisley, Melrose and Kinross, and outside schools at Dundee (to which William Wallace went), the Canongate School, the Royal High School, Haddington, Stirling, Abernethy, Roxburgh, Perth, etc. "In this manner, before the end of the fifteenth century, all the principal towns in Scotland, and many that have since fallen into obscurity, had grammar schools in which the Latin language was taught."[15] Morgan refers also to universities, saying that we should "gratefully acknowledge that it was to the Roman Church that we owe the great universities which have always continued so natural in their character and have afforded during the centuries the opportunities of a liberal education to the poorest of the people".[16]

The democratic intellect again. Have all our educational historians been wrong about this, as some contemporary authors would have it? The fifteenth century in Scotland was a time of great literary achievement, which, as Hume Brown tells us, "no country except Italy surpassed or even equalled".[17] Yet much of that literature – prose, poetry and historical writing – was written in the language of the people and was addressed to them, as witness Sir David Lyndsay:

Whairfor to coilyearis, carters and to cuikis,
To Jok and Tam my ryme shall be direckit,
With cunning men howbeit it will be lackit[18]

Whatever the critics thought, it is clear the colliers, carters and cooks could read and appreciate literature. Yet Scotland had only 250,000 inhabitants. This popular love of literature was to be the seedbed for the genius of Robert Burns three centuries later.

It is not therefore so surprising that three universities should have been set up in the fifteenth century. A well-educated populace needed local institutions of higher education, rather than having to travel to the Continent. It is an extraordinary fact that at the end of the fourteenth century nine out of twenty-one students in the 'English' nation at the University of Paris (which was composed of the British Isles, Germany and Scandinavia) should have been Scots; all of them became bishops in Scotland.

How then was teaching and learning conducted in the Scottish universities? "The business of instruction was not confined to a special body of privileged professors. The university was governed, the university was taught, by the graduates at large. Professor, master, doctor, were originally synonymous. Every graduate had an equal right of teaching publicly in the university the subjects competent to his faculty and to the rank of his degree; nay, every graduate incurred the obligation of teaching publicly . . . for such was the condition involved in the grant of the degree itself."[19] Thus Sir William Hamilton, one of Scotland's greatest professors of philosophy, in the eighteenth century, speaking of Glasgow University in its early years. Its Charter was modelled on that of Bologna, the student-run university, but it also imitated Louvain, because Louvain's Rector was a Scotsman, John Lichlin.

The teachers were called Regents and would take a class through the four years of the Arts degree, *in all subjects*. The degree courses, based on the classical trivium: grammar, rhetoric, dialectic; and the quadrivium: astronomy, music, mathematics, natural philosophy thus consisted of seven different classes, taught for four years by the same man. So the teachers had to be something of a walking encyclopedia, and they had pastoral duties to the students as well. A Master of Arts on graduating was obliged to teach for two years, but then escaped. For many years no salary was attached to the post, and the regents were dependent on the students' fees, which were very small, and indeed were waived altogether for poor students (as they were at Paris). Scotland being such a poor country, there was a great lack of printed books, so much time was taken up by the dictation, or 'diting', of notes. Morgan calls this "a cramping system that still lingers in some of the excessive note-taking of today". His view is that little real advance of knowledge was possible as long as teaching was tethered to textual exposition.[20]

Laurie, on the other hand, says that, though intellectual activity had to limit itself to dictation and exposition of the definitions and propositions of the recognised authorities; this was not a fruitless exercise. No doubt these discussions gave rise to much dialectical absurdity as well as subtlety, but it would be wrong to despise this as some do, quite lacking a sense of historical perspective. "For such dialectic, even in its crudest form, was in marked and significant contrast to the dead conformity of the Church preceding the universities, and familiarized the minds of the students to a quasi-independence in speculation . . . When Thomas Aquinas had written and Duns Scotus speculated theology tended to pass more and more into metaphysics. Scotus Erigena had at last triumphed."[21]

The want of books also gave great opportunities to regents who were good teachers. It compelled students to do much memory-work and to reflect on the lessons dictated to them, and was thus a very effective producer of mental discipline. This was further developed by the oral side of the students' work, which was highly organized in the form of 'disputations'. These come directly down from the Greeks, and especially from Aristotle. "The practice was coeval with the Scottish universities, and it appeared to suit the temperament of the people for it increased as time went on and may have helped to develop what is often regarded as a feature of the Scottish character – 'the scholastick itch of disputing all things'."[22] At fixed times students would come together in a group to debate a thesis set beforehand on the basis of the work done in class. Some of the students would have been told to 'impugn', i.e. attack, the thesis, others to 'prepugn' or defend it. There can be no question that this exercise developed the students' dialectical skills. Indeed, one wonders whether this long-lasting pedagogic practice (it was still going strong in the nineteenth century) has had anything to do with the superior debating skills of the students of Glasgow University who have so often won the Observer Mace for debating. The main test on graduation was a public disputation on a lengthy thesis based on the student's four-year course. In the forenoon each student defended his thesis; and in the afternoon warded off the arguments of those who attacked it. All this was in Latin, and the candidate must on no account show resentment when refuted.

Much must have depended, as always, on the teaching skills of the regent, but the method of teaching, so far as it went, was admirable. Indeed, some of the more modern teaching methods in today's universities are harking back to these rhetorical skills, which must have produced very articulate students. An interesting sidelight is thrown on the work of the regents by one author who says that the Scottish universities followed quasi-professional courses, keeping literary culture to a minimum, and were scarcely influenced by the social ideal of the gentleman prevalent at Oxford and Cambridge, with the exception perhaps of St. Andrews. They concentrated on subjects like logic and metaphysics "in a more professional, perhaps more rigid mould than was the case in England. There was all the difference in the world between the haphazard appearance of an English student's notebook and a Scots student's, the one deriving from an informal tutorial system, the other, systematically laid out, following the dictates of a lecturer, the 'regent'. . . The students' notebooks of the Restoration period reveal an impressive concern to come to grips with the problems presented by the 'new philosophy', and the range of reference was much wider than any English equivalent during the period."[23] The 'new philosophy' was the ideas of Descartes, Gassendi, Hobbes, Boyle and Bacon.

So the abolition of regenting was not an unmixed blessing. It severed the close teaching relationship between master and student, so that one of its first effects was to lead to irregularity of studies and to a great decline in the numbers graduating in Arts, since students now went only to classes that met their needs. Only at Aberdeen's two separate colleges did this not happen, they being the very last to abolish regenting.[24] The method did not, however, go far enough for Andrew Melville when he took over at Glasgow in 1577 and cleared the decks with his *Nova Erectio*. He was the right man at the right moment and his six years at Glasgow marked an epoch in Scottish higher education. His first aim was to abolish the regenting system which in his view made scholarship worthy of a university imposs-ible. He allowed an assistant to carry on in the old way while he trained a selected group of young men for teaching under the new system, where a teacher specialized in one subject. This involved an exacting six year course in which he undertook all the teaching with the assistance of his nephew James Melville. Scottish higher education owes a very great debt to Andrew Melville, for it was he who first created the idea of the specialist teacher. His Nova Erectio was well ahead of its time and "it contained the most progres-sive and enlightened ideas regarding university teaching and administration to be found at the period in Europe. It ushered in an epoch of great reform in all the Scottish universities."[25]

The one great weakness of his proposals, many maintained, was in dropping metaphysics and relegating philosophy to a subordinate place in the curriculum. These had been at the heart of Scottish university teach-ing from the beginning. It will be remembered that the University of Paris was renowned as a great specialist school of philosophy, and that it had a very great influence on the curricula of Scotland's ancient universities. So throughout the centuries the prominence given to philosophical studies was a feature of the Scottish university curriculum. At Edinburgh, up to the Second World War, philosophy was the one subject that had to be studied by every MA candidate. The historian of Europe's medieval universities

Hastings Randall lays great stress on this feature of Scottish university education and merits quotation at some length: "The consequences of the retention of the old medieval curriculum in the Scotch universities, and the subsequent evolution of distinct chairs of philosophy out of it, have been of the utmost importance, not only in the history of Scotch education, but in the history of British and even European thought. Scotland gained from an education at once stimulating and practical, however grave its deficiencies on the score of sound preparation and classical discipline; while to the seemingly accidental circumstance that the Scotch universities provided philosophers not merely with chairs, but with classes to teach, Europe probably owes in no small measure the development of an important School of Philosophy. Between the time of Francis Hutcheson and John Stewart Mill, a majority of the philosophers who wrote in the English language were professors, or at least alumni, of Scotch universities."[26] This is a question of central importance in the development of Scottish universities both in the past and in the future. We shall return to it at length in a subsequent chapter.

Melville's ideal of replacing regents with specialist subject teachers, the forerunners of the professoriate, took a long time to implement in full. It was to be only at the beginning of the eighteenth century that opinion would move strongly in favour of specialization of teaching and the harnessing of each regent to a particular subject. Thus regenting was only finally abolished at Edinburgh in 1708; Glasgow in 1727; St. Andrews in 1747; Marischal College, Aberdeen in 1753; and King's College, Aberdeen not till 1798 (Aberdeen had two universities for centuries). This, however, was well ahead of other universities. Morgan notes[27]: "The widening of the intellectual horizon, and the progress of science in all directions owing to the rise of the inductive philosophy, made the 'ambulatory' system no longer suitable." This again is a matter of great moment in the development of the universities and of Western thought as a whole. It has now reached its apogee with the extreme specialization and fragmentation of knowledge. We shall discuss its effects on the universities in a later chapter.

A few years before Andrew Melville returned to Glasgow occurred the most important event in the whole history of Scottish education. This was the publication of the *First Book of Discipline* in 1560, a document which enshrines the essential spirit of democratic intellectualism despite, or perhaps because of, the auspices under which it was written. Its authors were the 'six Johns', but there is no doubt that its principal author was John Knox. It was in effect the constitution for the governance of the newly created Presbyterian Church and it was laid before the Church's General Assembly in 1560. The chapter on schools and universities must be one of the greatest manifestos on education ever written. It proposed that there should be:

1   In the country parishes elementary schools open to all children from 5 or 6 to 8 years of age;

2   In "towns of any repute" grammar schools where town children would learn the rudiments and then, together with country children, Latin grammar from 8 to 12;
3   In important towns high schools where selected pupils of 12 to 16 would learn the other classical languages, along with logic and rhetoric.

The best scholars, able to pass the entrance qualification, would then advance to university to study for eight years (a three year 'Arts' course, including mathematics and moral and natural philosophy, then five years of professional study in medicine, the law or theology). They would receive a bursary if necessary, for there were to be bursaries for the 'clever poor': seventy-two for St. Andrews and forty-eight each for Glasgow and Aberdeen. Only people entirely lacking a sense of historical perspective could fail to see what a progressive proposal this was for the period. It was a continuation of the tradition at Paris and Bologna and was to continue right down to the twentieth century. And there would be ten 'superintendents' "appointit to visit scholles for the tryall of their exercise, proffit and continewance." HMIs in short. Interestingly, too, it proposed that there be a different teacher for each subject at the universities some seventeen years before Andrew Melville. Both were a century ahead of their time.

This plan has been, and continues to be today, of the greatest importance in Scottish education. It proposed a system covering the whole nation, and was by far the most comprehensive national education scheme in Europe. It saw education as the right of all children, and, appreciating as they did its enormous value, it was to be compulsory. Girls are not mentioned, but in fact the parish schools were co-educational from the start. It placed great stress on the moral and spiritual culture of the child. It preserved the family and community influence (most Scottish students still live at home). There was to be a national organization of the universities, without snobbery or special privileges for the rich. As James Scotland says[28]: "In the event more poor boys got to the universities in Scotland than in any other country before the late nineteenth century development in the United States." This in a small, desperately poor country.

The scheme was highly practical; indeed one could say that it was largely a rationalization of what already to a considerable extent existed. All it required was money, but of course it didn't get it; the rapacity of the nobles saw to that by plundering the wealth of the Church. But it has shone like an inspiring beacon of advanced educational thought through the centuries and still does now. Its fundamental ideas have still not been fully implemented, so we can still learn from it. These ideas were that Scotland should have a complete national system of education forming a highway from the primary school to the university; and that there should be close coordination between the different grades: primary school, secondary school and university. The condition of admission to the university should be a favourable report from the schoolmaster. Education must be compulsory and a boy should continue at school till the special talent is discovered by which he can best serve the community. Education is not the privilege of a class but the common need and right of all, and there should be free scope for the upward movement of ability at every level of society. Finally the poor but clever student should be maintained by the State.

The epilogue of the chapter on schools and universities of the First Book of Discipline reads as follows: "If God shall grant quietness and give your Wisdoms grace to set forward letters in the sort prescribed, ye shall leave wisdom and learning to your posterity, a treasure more to be esteemed than any earthly treasures ye are able to provide for them; which, without wisdom, are more able to be their ruin than help or comfort." These words have a powerful resonance today as we look around at our greedy consumerist societies, the starvation and destitution in the Third World, and our incredible despoliation of the biosphere. Carlyle, in his rectorial address at the University of Edinburgh, said: "Knox was heard by Scotland, the people heard him and believed him to the marrow of their bones; they took all his doctrine to heart and they defied principalities and powers to move them from it."[29] One cannot, alas, say as much for those who direct educational affairs in Scotland today.

It can truly be said that most of the progress in Scottish education has consisted in advancing towards Knox's ideals, and Hume Brown even says that the First Book of Discipline is the most important document in Scottish history. Its proposals and guiding spirit have moulded the Scottish character and instincts, in relation to education, for more than four centuries. Of course the reality, because of lack of resources, never fulfilled these noble aspirations, but their enormous, lasting influence gives the lie to those who today, for whatever reason, dismiss the idea of the 'lad o' pairts' as a romantic myth and that of the democratic intellect as the eccentric brainchild of George Elder Davie.

Some scholars seem at a loss to explain how there could be such sophisticated educational thinking and modern, advanced teaching in Scotland's universities. Speaking of the fifteenth century, one of them says: "The cultural climate in Scotland in the fifteenth century was curiously and inexplicably rich, fostering native writers and poets who have not ceased to be read. It is difficult to account for this resurgence of culture in a country which was in so many ways still disordered, primitive and poor . . ." Proceeding, he exclaims how astonishing it is that they (Scotland's universities) "should have continued to produce scholars of such quality that, at least in the eighteenth century . . . they cast Oxford and Cambridge into the shade . . . The progress made in mathematical and scientific studies was the more impressive when contrasted with the state of affairs at the English universities . . . It is not easy to explain the exuberance of Scottish culture at this time. It must surely reflect the excellence of the parish and high schools fostered by legislation in 1646 and 1696." He gets it in one. It was precisely those embodiments of the democratic intellect, those rungs on the ladder for the 'lad o'pairts', that provided the well-educated youngsters the universities so thrived on. They served to create, as he puts it, a society that was "literate, mobile and, if spiritually authoritarian, socially democratic". It was probably also, he suspects, due to "the vitality of urban life sustained by an interchange between academic and mercantile society not to be found at Oxford and Cambridge." At any rate the climate of the Scottish universities in the eighteenth century was secular and liberal, the prevailing tone being set by the moral philosophers with David Hume, Adam Smith and Thomas Reid in the van. They even tended to support the French Revolution, with the celebrated lawyer John Millar presiding over a dinner to celebrate the event, and Professor John (Jolly Jack Phosphorus) Anderson (whom we shall meet again) presenting the French with his shock-absorbing gun carriage and balloons to carry messages. St. Andrews, *horribile dictu*, even presented a medical degree to Jean-Paul Marat!

Our author was impressed by the fact that the Scottish professor was more likely to be a specialist than the tutor who was responsible for teaching all subjects at Oxford and Cambridge. He concludes by saying that the conditions provided fertile ground for the ideas of Bacon, Newton and Locke – indeed Newtonian physics were taught in Scotland before they were taught at his own university, Cambridge. There was also a lively interchange with the celebrated universities of Holland, especially Leyden and Utrecht, so that in the eighteenth century "the universities of Scotland, except St. Andrews, became more adventurous and dynamic, while their counterparts in England were suffocating under the weight of tradition."[30]

Green also provides some figures which make an interesting comparative social comment on the features of the Scottish universities he has been discussing. Between 1740 and 1839 13% of the students at Glasgow University came from the families of the nobility and landed gentry, by comparison with 35% at Cambridge between 1752 and 1849; 11% at Glasgow came from industry and commerce, as compared with 8% at Cambridge. Whereas there were virtually no working-class children at Cambridge, at Glasgow one third, i.e. $33^{1}/_{3}$, came from labouring families. That non-existent democratic intellect again! Glasgow was particularly dynamic and had scholars of European reputation: R. C. Jacob in Classics, and Edward Caird who later became the Master of Balliol College, Oxford. Above all there was William Thompson, Lord Kelvin, who became professor of natural philosophy in 1846, a chair he held for 53 years. He set up the very first chair in experimental natural philosophy (i.e. physics) in 1855, and the BSc degree was established in 1872.

Two centuries earlier the gradual abolition of regenting had enabled men like James Gregory, who came to Edinburgh from St. Andrews as professor of mathematics, to concentrate on specialized mathematical teaching and research. His *Optica Promota* of 1663 is remarkable for its description of the first reflecting telescope. He was the first to introduce the work of Kepler, Galileo and Descartes to a Scottish university, and he was responsible for the first observatory in Britain, at least two years before the establishment of the Royal Observatory at Greenwich. Sadly, he died in the prime of life in 1675, "having anticipated his friend and correspondent Isaac Newton in the solution of some of the most abstruse problems of mathematics and physics."[31]

Thus by about 1730 the Scottish universities had succeeded in developing a wide range of subjects taught for the most part by specialist teachers who were alive to the latest developments in their field, yet (and this is central to an understanding of the Scottish university tradition) "still retaining a sense of the inherent unity of the education system in which they were comprehended."[32] The view was generally held that the proliferation of academic centres in Scotland – five, including Marischal College in Aberdeen – was an inherent part of the notion of an educated community. The remarkable thing is how widely these new ideas and teaching methods were distributed and the peaks of intellectual distinction reached by men heavily involved in teaching large numbers of young students. "What must never be forgotten is that the belief that education and intellectual achievement should have breadth of involvement as well as height of virtuosity was the great gift to Scotland of the Renaissance and the Reformation . . . an inheritance furthermore that would ensure that the Scottish form of the Enlightenment would be protected against the kind of brittle elitism that too often predominated elsewhere."[33] These attitudes were prevalent at all levels of education. As R. H. Campbell points out, "By the modest standards of what was being achieved elsewhere, the record, in lowland rural Scotland art least, is undeniable, whether tested by the extent of the provision or by the standard of instruction. Many of those who made the greatest contribution to the intellectual achievements of the Enlightenment in Scotland were themselves the product of that education system."[34]

What were the values, the principles of action, that led to these remarkable educational achievements in a small, poor country with a fiercely turbulent history? One was certainly a collectivist attitude imposed on them by that history; here Scotland has similarities with other small peoples. "It is interesting to note that of all the European peoples who seem to excel in educational achievement, the Jews, the Scots, the Czechs (who have the highest rate of university education in Europe) and the Finns, seem to have developed their 'love of learning' as oppressed national or religious minorities."[35]

But collectivism is also a mode of status allocation, and status in Scotland has usually come from identification with public rather than private ventures. Thus the great individual benefactions in Scotland have been made to education, as in the case of Andrew Carnegie, and, unlike England, have been made to the public system. There were many smaller benefactions to support poor university students – up to one third of the students at one university in the 1840s.[36] The aim of this generosity was also to make education publicly accessible as a matter of social policy. So higher education in Scotland, as Andrew McPherson makes clear, was highly collectivist in all three dictionary senses of that term: an assertion of nationality; a mode of status allocation; a type of social policy.

The accent throughout the centuries in Scotland's universities has been facilitating access in three senses: geographically, numerically and socially, i.e. availability to different social classes. It was justified by reference to the traditional model, that of John Knox in the *First Book of Discipline*; to principle, i.e. the ideal of individual upward social mobility; and to expedience, in that it favoured general economic prosperity. As the (Argyll) Education Commission was later to show (in 1868), this policy paid off handsomely. One in 205 of the Scottish population went to public secondary schools, and one in 1000 went to university. The corresponding figures in England were one in 1300 and one in 5,800. The Argyll Commission Report explained the thinking behind these figures. "The theory of our school system as originally conceived was to supply *every member of the community* with the means of obtaining for his children not only the elements of education, but such instruction as would fit him to pass to the Burgh school, and thence to university, or directly to the university from the parish school. The connexion between the parochial and Burgh schools and the university is therefore an essential element in our scheme of National Education."[37]

No such ladder of educational opportunity existed in England. McPherson makes the point: "Scotland's emphasis, relative to England, on contest mobility (i.e. more young people are given a chance for longer) is attributable to a value that has been consciously and consistently held over a considerable period of time."[38] As a result, in the 1860s something over 20% of students in Scottish universities had manual origins; Aberdeen had as many as 33%. McPherson calls this an 'open doors' policy. It is interesting to compare these figures with the situation today. Nor are they surprising when one knows what was being done in the schools. The Glasgow presbytery in 1700 proposed that pupils in 'English schools' should be taught "to write weel and to read write (i.e. handwriting as well as print); and to count also; some of the plainest and usefulest parts of Geometry and Geography; and music, at least the common tunes; and History, especially of our own Church and State." Those who went on to grammar schools were to go through this course beforehand. Able children went to a four or five year public Latin school, where they did Greek and Hebrew in their fifth year. In addition, they studied Greek and Roman antiquities, a compendium of trades and sciences, and the Janua and Atrium of the great seventeenth century Czech educationist Comenius. They also had to acquire some knowledge of geography "both by the globe and plain chart . . . which was very profitable for schools and helpful to the understanding of history and reading it with pleasure; also some elements of chronology, all which may be rendered easie and delightful by Tables, draughts and pictures."

D. J. Withrington, from whom this information is taken,[39] says this is remarkable because "this desire to widen and make relevant the curriculum was supposed only to have happened in the later eighteenth century. Yet here we have doubts about the classical languages even before the Union. The newer subjects, including navigation and mensuration, should be taught to the classical scholars as well." Only today, with the publication of the Howie Report on the upper classes in secondary school, but with a divisive academic/vocational split, are we cautiously approaching ideas which were the subject of discussion and practical application all but three centuries ago. For example, Ayr Burgh School in 1746 transformed itself into a school which had three sections: Classical; English subjects; Arithmetic, book-keeping, geometry, navigation, surveying, algebra, other parts of mathematics and parts of natural philosophy. It was an exceptionally comprehensive curriculum in a single publicly-run institution which included all post-elementary schooling: Classical, English and 'scientific'.

This first hint that a narrow, purely classical education, as at the English public schools and Oxford, was not the best education in a country begin-ning to feel the throes of the industrial revolution, was to become a major leitmotif of the higher education commissions and debates that took up most of the nineteenth century from 1826 onwards. On this subject our national poet laid about him in his usual inimitable style:

> A set o' dull, conceited hashes,
> That tease their brains wi' college classes,
> They gang in stirks and come oot asses,
>   Plain truth to speak,
> And syne they think to climb Parnassus
>   By dint o' Greek.

A telling criticism of the purely classical curriculum. Francis Jeffrey, advo-cate, co-founder of the *Edinburgh Review*, wielded a more skillfully forensic rapier:

I admit, on the whole, the justice of the reproach levelled against our general national instruction, namely, that though we have a greater number of all ranks who possess considerable information, there are fewer who are completely learned – that our knowledge, in short, though more general, is more superficial than with our neighbours in England. That is quite true, and our system of educa-tion leads to it; but I think it is a great good on the whole; for many of those who leave college very imperfectly instructed, supply the

177

defects by their own study afterwards, in a manner they could not have done, but for that superficial training and initiation by their teachers.[40]

Lyon Playfair was to make a telling, and by implication similar, point near the end of the great debate in 1876: "Oxford and Cambridge have exalted the preparatory pedagogium, or Arts Faculty, to be the end instead of the beginning of the universities and thus have cut themselves off from the professions."[41] This, of course, made them odd man out in Europe and cut them off also from the medieval tradition.

So the great educational battle was joined, with Scotch critics and Edinburgh reviewers on one side and affronted Oxbridge dons on the other. The issue at stake: a general education before professional specialization, and democratic intellectualism, as in Scotland's universities, versus a refined, narrow, elitist, classical or mathematical education at Oxford and Cambridge. Utility versus knowledge for its own sake. Breadth versus cultivation of the intellect. The 'open door' policy versus finishing-school for the sons of the rich and influential. Secular, liberal education versus ecclesiastical domination. Sir William Hamilton versus William Whewell.

However, before we can enjoy this debate we must take a straight look at the opposition in the blue corner: Oxford and Cambridge.

Notes

1 John Kerr (1910), *Scottish Education: School and University from Early Times to 1908*, Cambridge University Press, p. 28.
2 Ibid., p. 34.
3 *Times Education Supplement for Scotland (TESS)*, March 22, 1968, p. 97.
4 Sir James Irvine, CBE (1942), *The Scottish Universities* (pamphlet), Edinburgh, Oliver & Boyd, p. 8.
5 Ibid., p. 34.
6 Ibid., quoted on p. 147.
7 A. B. Cobban, *Student Revolutions, Ancient and Modern, Times Higher Education Supplement (THES)*, 28 March 1975.
8 Irvine, op. cit., p. 12.
9 Ibid., p. 16.
10 *Time to cut our longer courses, The Scotsman*, 30 October 1991, p. 20.
11 *Academics wary of separate funding, The Scotsman*, 11 December, 1991.
12 S. S. Laurie (1886), *Lectures on the Rise and early Constitution of Universities*, London, Kegan Paul, Trench & Co, p. 193.
13 John Kerr, op. cit., p. 113.
14 Alexander Morgan (1927), *Rise and Progress of Scottish Education*, Edinburgh, Oliver & Boyd, quoted on p. 36.
15 Ibid., p. 25.
16 Ibid., p. 34.
17 Hume Brown, *Life of George Buchanan*.
18 Quoted in Morgan, op. cit., p. 36.
19 Sir William Hamilton, *Dissertations*, quoted in Kerr, op. cit., p. 70.

20 Alexander Morgan (1933), *Scottish University Studies* (SUS) Oxford University Press p. 59.
21 Laurie, op. cit., pp. 273–47.
22 Morgan, op. cit., p. 593.
23 H. F. Kearney (1970), *Scholars and Gentlemen: Universities and Society in Pre-industrial Britain, 1500–1700*, London, Faber, p. 154.
24 H. M. Knox (1953), *250 Years of Scottish Education, 1696–1946* Edinburgh, Oliver & Boyd.
25 Morgan, op. cit., p. 1394.
26 Hastings Rashdall (1936), *The Universities of Europe in the Middle Ages, Vol. 2* (Oxford University Press), pp. 322–3.
27 Morgan, op. cit., pp. 72–3.
28 James Scotland (1969), *The History of Scottish Education*, 2 vols, London, University of London Press.
29 Both quotations from Morgan, *Rise and Progress of Scottish Education*, pp. 50–53.
30 V. H. H. Green (1969), *The Universities*, Harmondsworth, Pelican, pp. 77–92.
31 Ronald G. Cant, 'The Universities' in R. H. Campbell and Andrew Skinner, eds (1983), *The Origins and Nature of the Scottish Enlightenment*, John Donald p. 45.
32 Ibid., p. 55.
33 Ibid., p. 59.
34 R. H. Campbell, 'The Enlightenment and the Economy', in *The Origins and Nature of the Scottish Enlightenment*, p. 15.
35 Andrew McPherson, *Selections and Survivals: A Sociology of the Ancient Scottish Universities in Knowledge, Education and Cultural Change*, Richard Brown, ed. (1974), p. 167.
36 Ibid., p. 168.
37 Ibid., Note 25, p. 190.
38 Ibid., p. 169.
39 D. J. Withrington 'Education and Society in the eighteenth Century' in *Scotland in the Age of Enlightenment* (1970), eds N. T. Phillipson and R. Mitcheson, Edinburgh, EUP, p. 172.
40 From his evidence given to the 1826 Commission on the Universities and Colleges of Scotland.
41 Lyon Playfair (1876), quoted in Green, op. cit., p. 118

12

Excerpts from
ACADEME AND EMPIRE

Some overseas connections of Aberdeen University, 1860–1970

John D. Hargreaves

Source: J. D. Hargreaves, *Academe and Empire: Some Overseas Connections of Aberdeen University, 1860–1970*, Quincentennial Studies in the History of the University of Aberdeen, Aberdeen: Aberdeen University Press, 1994, pp. 5–32 and 114–17.

EMPIRE AND OPPORTUNITY:
OVERSEAS CAREERS OF ABERDEEN
GRADUATES 1860–1955

During the years 1858–60 most Aberdeen professors were no doubt pre-occupied with implementing the union of the colleges required by the new Universities (Scotland) Act. But other events during these years were to prove hardly less important for the new university. The publication of Darwin's *Origin of Species* in 1859 and, in the same year, the establishment of the General Medical Council may be taken to signal two developments – the expansion of scientific studies and the professionalisation of careers – whose relevance was no doubt evident to the more far-sighted academics. Not all would show the same interest in such distant events as the act which transferred responsibility for the government of India to the Crown, the establishment of British Columbia and Queensland as separate British colonies, preparations for the annexation of Lagos in West Africa, treaties imposed on China after her defeat by Britain and France. Yet in coming decades British expansion – in the 'informal empire' of influence, trade and culture as well as in the formal empire of rule – would open important new frontiers to alumni seeking employment, whether trained in scientific disciplines or in the older humanist tradition of Scottish universities.

The reception and demarcation of new fields of study in Aberdeen had already begun; the union of the colleges was marked by the establishment of four new chairs – one in botany, three in the medical disciplines of obstetrics, physiology and materia medica. More thorough revision of the map of learning had to await the Universities (Scotland) Act of 1889, when a separate faculty of science was established, and there was considerable diversification in the arts curriculum.

The priority given to medicine derived largely from the establishment in 1859 of the General Medical Council, with responsibility for registering practitioners who had satisfied the examiners in approved teaching institutions. Previously, under the Apothecaries Act of 1815, medical graduates of Scottish universities – though for the most part equipped with a better scientific education than their English contemporaries – had been precluded from practice in England and Wales without prolonged apprenticeship. (They were, however, permitted to practise elsewhere in the territories of the Crown, and so were already well represented in the medical services of the East India Company, the army and the navy.[1]) Since under the Medical Registration Act of 1858 the major providers of training were London teaching hospitals and Irish and Scottish Universities, Aberdeen's reorganised medical school became an imperial centre, training many doctors for overseas service, and attracting increasing numbers of students domiciled abroad.

It was not only in medicine that government action was extending the use of academic examinations as the mode of access to professional careers. Although the Scottish MA provided a badge of intellectual achievement for clergy and other professional persons it never served as a vocational qualification. But the appointment of the Northcote-Trevelyan Commission in 1853 heralded the introduction of competitive examination for the public service; as the Master of Pembroke pointed out in 1854, the Civil Service examiners now had the potential to become 'an Imperial University, which will mould every college and school in the land'.[2] Though the new principle was introduced only gradually, from 1855 it was applied to administrative and medical appointments in India, a country in which Aberdeen alumni were already giving distinguished service. If the united university was to retain its stake, it would eventually have to take such examinations seriously.

Other manifestations of the epidemic of examinations introduced as conditions for professional registration – as pharmacists (1868), dentists (1878), accountants (1880), chartered secretaries (1891), civil engineers (1897)[3] – affected Aberdeen University indirectly. The Victorian middle classes, whose numbers and wealth were rapidly increasing, often sought to provide their children with economic security, social status, or personal fulfilment through a professional education. In the longer run, this move towards professionalism provided incentives for universities to develop vocationally useful studies. More immediately, growing competition at home meant that more alumni, from the arts as well as the medical faculties, would need to look towards overseas careers, inside or outside the British empire. Figures in the Appendix to this volume indicate the scale on which they did so, the careers they pursued, and the regions of the world in which, at different periods, they chose to work. This chapter will attempt a preliminary survey of these career patterns, analysed in cohorts according to the period of first graduation.

1860–1900

One feature which emerges strongly from our data for the forty years following the union of the colleges is the high proportion of medical graduates pursuing overseas careers. Whereas about a quarter of arts graduates worked abroad, well over a third of medical graduates did so. This may reflect the expense of establishing a private practice in the UK, and the low salaries of the junior hospital appointments available to young doctors. Over half of those who went overseas, about 400, set up in independent practice or took salaried posts with private companies. South Africa and Australasia were favoured destinations, but there was a fair sprinkling of Aberdeen doctors in the Americas and in eastern Asia. A second group, numbering about 262, were directly employed in imperial service. The largest number were in the Indian Medical Service, which a few graduates entered in most years, but by the end of the century many went to the West African Medical Service, or to other parts of the expanded empire. About 75 (one in eight of these two groups of doctors) were returning to work in their countries of birth. The next chapter will examine these overseas students more closely. Substantial numbers of medical graduates also served in the army (86), the navy (51) or the merchant marine (11, not counting many who signed on for a voyage or two while saving to establish themselves in practice).

Some of these emigrant doctors engaged in medical teaching overseas, and several made notable contributions to the developing science of tropical medicine. Foremost among them was Patrick Manson (MB 1865), who was largely responsible for founding a medical college in Hong Kong, carried out fundamental work on the transmission of malaria, and, as Medical Adviser to the Colonial Office from 1897, exercised an important though sometimes controversial influence on the development of tropical medicine. Kenneth Macleod (MA 1867, LLD 1892) carried out veterinary research while in the IMS and was head of its medical school from 1897 to 1902. W J R Simpson (MB 1876), after twelve years as Medical Officer of Health in Calcutta, became a key figure in the London School of Tropical Medicine and Hygiene, which Manson had helped to found, and the leading government expert on tropical epidemiology. Aberdeen's contribution to the development of medical education in Ceylon, as well as

1 Patrick Manson as a student, 1864.

the work of some medical teachers in North America, will be considered in Chapter 3.

Among the 79 Aberdeen graduates of the period who worked abroad as Christian missionaries, 13 were doctors, the most notable being Robert Laws of Livingstonia. This group also includes teachers and other lay workers; only a minority of the clergy who worked abroad did so as missionaries. At least 97 clergy went to minister to established congregations – 47 in Australia and New Zealand, 19 in North America, 11 in continental Europe, 8 in South Africa, and 12 distributed from China to Argentina. Fifteen others held colonial chaplaincies, 11 of them in India. In addition, 12 of the sample of non-graduating students analysed in Table VIII worked as ministers overseas, and one (E Leal, class of 1865–9) as a missionary of the Catholic Apostolic Church.

It was in the years 1870–90 that missionary vocations seem to have been most strongly felt: 22 graduates of the 1870s and 32 of the 1880s worked as missionaries, compared with nine of the 1860s and 16 of the 1890s. Of this total of 79, the Free Church provided 35; 21 worked with the Church of Scotland; two with the United Presbyterians, and 11 with the Presbyterian churches of England (with their strong missionary work in China); three were Episcopalians, and seven worked for other churches. India was evidently the most attractive region, and this is reflected in surviving minute books of the student Missionary Association: 37 Aberdeen graduates worked there, and contributed greatly to the work of the Christian colleges. This will be discussed in Chapter 3. From the late 1870s, east-central Africa also became an important Scottish mission-field. Of the 12 graduates, six of whom were doctors, five worked at the Free Church mission of Livingstonia, five with the Church of Scotland near Blantyre, and two elsewhere in the region. Rather surprisingly, ten graduates worked as missionaries to the Jews in Europe, or the Turkish empire in Asia, compared with nine in China (plus one in Tibet). Four worked in the New Hebrides, the same number as in South Africa; there were two in Jamaica and one in Calabar.

Table IV may exaggerate the number of those who went abroad bent an educational careers. Apart from the medical and missionary teachers already discussed, some graduates seem to have found a teaching post a good base from which to start in agriculture or business. Probably less than two-thirds of the 184 graduates shown under 'Education' in Table IV emigrated with the primary intention of teaching non-medical subjects in secular schools or colleges. From the 1870s South Africa was a popular destination; in all 49 educationalists went there, 24 of them graduates of the 1890s. Sixteen teachers went to Canada, six to the USA, 22 to Australia or New Zealand. Most eminent of the five who taught in Europe was Eugène De Faye (MA 1881), son of a French Protestant minister by Catherine Henderson of Caskieben, a notable Patristic scholar who held a chair at the Sorbonne.[4] W S Wilson (MA 1884) became professor of English in Imperial

St Petersburg; after imprisonment during the Revolution, he returned to teach in Riga. Seventeen graduates held posts in India, most of them in the Indian Education Service established in 1889. Formal educational services in the Crown Colonies were organised only in the twentieth century; but four graduates of this cohort taught in Africa outside the Union, one in Demerara, and one in the Falklands. William Craigie (MA 1870) taught English to Japanese engineers.

As the colonies of British settlement discovered new needs for special-ised leadership they established their own colleges of higher education, which aspired to recognition as universities whose degrees would command international respect. These offered new opportunities to enterprising Scots graduates. Although the number of Aberdonians in such posts in the nineteenth century is not large, some played formative roles in particular colleges, as will be shown in Chapter 3. In Canada, Aberdeen's closest links were formed with Queen's University, Ontario, founded in 1843. Aberdonians were not prominent in the early years of Australian univer-sities, but John Shand (MA, Kings, 1854) and Duncan MacGregor (MA 1866) both held chairs when Otago University opened in the Scottish settle-ment of Dunedin in 1871. Several Aberdonians taught in South African colleges during the later nineteenth century; William Ritchie (MA 1873), a contemporary of Cecil Rhodes at Oxford, became professor of classics in South Africa College, Cape Town in 1882, and was one of the moving spirits behind the act of 1916 which established the modern South African university system. In India, missionary teachers at the Christian colleges of Madras, Bombay and Calcutta made major contributions to the develop-ment of an Indian university system. One of the first women graduates in science, Alice Bain (MA 1899, BSc 1901) became professor of chemistry at Lady Hardinge College in 1916, and reader in Delhi University 1923–8.

As already explained, in Table IV the figure of 172 military careers over-laps largely with the medical total, and is inflated by some relatively short periods of service, for example as ships' doctors. But both medical and arts graduates and alumni are to be found serving (and too often dying) in the British Army and Navy, the Indian Army, or younger colonial units like the West African Frontier Force, in every major imperial campaign of the period. Peter Shepherd (MA 1864), author of a pioneer manual of first aid, died fighting the Zulus at Isandhlwana in 1879; a gold medal in surgery was awarded in his honour. At least 36 graduates (21 with no other overseas experience) served in the South African War of 1899–1902, including a son of Sir Alexander Ogston (MA 1865, MD 1866), professor of surgery since 1882, who was among those who died there. Ogston himself was a formidable critic of the army's surgical practice, drawing on personal experi-ence in the Sudan campaign of 1884–85, in South Africa, and (when in his seventies) of the Serbian and Italian fronts during the First World War. Perhaps the most striking imperial career was that of Major-General J R L

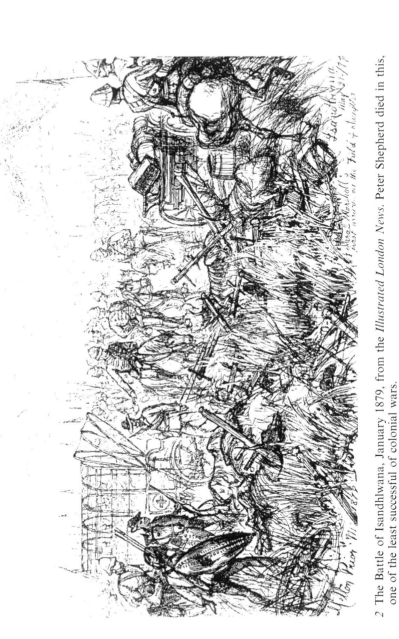

2 The Battle of Isandhlwana, January 1879, from the *Illustrated London News*. Peter Shepherd died in this, one of the least successful of colonial wars.

3 Major-General Sir J R L Macdonald RE.

Macdonald RE (alumnus 1877) who, in 1891–2, surveyed the route of the railway on which Britain's East African empire was based; acted as first Commissioner of the Uganda protectorate; served in China after the 'Boxer rebellion'; and commanded the escort of Francis Younghusband's mission to Tibet in 1903–4. Many officers ended honourable service as Lieutenant-Colonels or Surgeon-Commanders, but few approached the eminence of Field-Marshal Lord Milne (alumnus 1881), commander of the British force at Salonica in the First World War, and later Chief of the Imperial General Staff.

Table IV shows 70 careers in government, administration and politics. These form a rather varied group. For the university, the most significant element was the number of successes in the Indian Civil Service examination. Between 1856 and 1913 entry was achieved by 48 Masters of Arts, but also by 29 other alumni. For this intellectual elite, the ICS examination was the one that counted; in the years 1869–90 only seven out of 33 entrants went through the formality of graduation.[5] Some ways in which the ICS examination influenced university policies will be considered in Chapter 4.

4 Sir William MacGregor. This farmworker's son from Towie, on Donside, was successively Governor of British New Guinea, Lagos, Newfoundland and Queensland.

Eight graduates became student interpreters in China and one in Japan, mostly between 1861 and 1872, and several went on to hold consular appointments. Later a few alumni entered the civil services of Ceylon or the Straits Settlements; and John Anderson (MA 1877) crowned a distinguished Whitehall career by becoming Governor of each of these colonies. The organisation of a Colonial Administrative Service came after this period, but two colonial surgeons, Samuel Rowe (MA 1865) and William MacGregor (MB 1872), son of a Donside farmworker, transferred to administration and held important governorships.

The university offered no law degree until 1895, and most of those who obtained legal qualifications after graduation practised in Scotland. A few later emigrated to British colonies, however, and others obtained legal qualifications there. Three of the 30 men who took the BL degree before 1900 practised overseas, one in Malaya and two in South Africa, where Dutch influence on the law tended to favour Scots lawyers. Other graduates obtained legal experience and served in the expanding empire; A D Russell (MA 1885) was to hold senior judicial appointments in the Gambia and Trinidad, and J C Dove Wilson (MA 1885) became a judge in Natal. Few alumni seem to have been active in colonial politics, but the lawyer John Garland (MA 1882) was elected to the New South Wales Assembly and later became Australian Minister of Justice, and William Berry (MD 1861) was Speaker of the Cape Colony legislature. The controversial South African career of James Sivewright (MA 1866) will be considered in Chapter 3.

Beyond the traditional learned professions, British universities did not try to provide vocational education. Victorian pioneers of industry, agriculture and commerce prided themselves on learning in 'the school of experience', sometimes supplemented by formal apprenticeships or by classes in various institutions for technical and agricultural education, developed in response to locally perceived needs. But although only 2 per cent of all Aberdeen graduates of the period followed entrepreneurial careers abroad, this figure must be multiplied several times if all alumni are included. Many students who went out to seek their fortune as planters, traders, engineers or surveyors had first spent a year or two taking university courses in mathematics, natural history, or less evidently applicable subjects. J S Sinclair, future Earl of Caithness, attended the mathematics class of 1874–75 before embarking on land speculation in Dakota. Very wide research would be needed to measure the contribution of these 'educated adventurers' to the expanding 'informal empire' of investment, trade, and settlement.

Careers as planters have often attracted alumni who disposed of a little capital; their interest now tended to move from sugar to tea, coffee or rubber, and from the Caribbean to southern Asia. How far their success, when achieved, may have been attributable to their university studies is debatable. Others took up farming in temperate climates, with varied fortunes. David Ritchie of the class of 1881–85, who took an Oxford BA and an Edinburgh

BL before going to farm in New Zealand, went on to become professor of history and political economy in Wellington University College. Arthur and John Burnet-Craigie became ranchers in the Argentine, until Arthur was killed by lightning in 1899. Even more dramatic was the family history of William Benton (MA 1863), who owned a ranch near the Texas-Mexico border. His brother James (alumnus 1868–9) was murdered in 1875, and W S Benton (alumnus 1875–7), one of two cousins who engaged in silver-mining in the area, also met a violent death during the Mexican revolution of 1914.[6]

Two other brothers of William Benton had distinguished and less violent careers in India. While Alexander (MA Kings 1858) entered the ICS and became a judge in the Punjab, John Benton was one of four alumni in the class of 1866–70 to practise engineering overseas. After two years study of mathematics and natural philosophy, and a period at Edinburgh University, he entered the Indian Public Works Department by way of their College at Cooper's Hill, undertook important irrigation works in Burma and the Punjab and, as Inspector-General of Irrigation for India, was eventually knighted. One classmate in natural philosophy, Andrew Jamieson, who served an apprenticeship with Hall Russell, was, as chief electrician to the Eastern Telegraph Company, in charge of British naval communications during

5 Image of the Buddha: part of a collection presented to the Anthropological Museum by Sir J R L Macdonald after the Younghusband mission to Tibet, 1903.

the Russo-Turkish war of 1877–8; he later became professor of electrical engineering at Glasgow Technical College. David Simpson, who completed four years in the same class, trained in Boulton's office in Aberdeen and became divisional railway engineer in Sydney, while James Stewart worked as a ship's engineer. Four distinct patterns of engineering careers can thus be illustrated from the members of this single arts class.

Commercial careers of Aberdeen alumni were equally varied. G S Yuill (alumnus 1864–66), after some years in China, became general manager of the Orient shipping line in Australia, and later proceeded to an independent business career. W R MacBean (MA 1896), after distinguishing himself as a mathematician at Cambridge, was before his early death a successful businessman in South Africa, Australia and South America. J G Macgowan (MA 1866), managing director of the Bedford Petroleum Company, Paris, seem to have been the first of many graduates to enter the petroleum industry. Many alumni held more modest posts in commerce, banking and insurance throughout the world. F W Hardie (alumnus 1888–90) worked as a photographer in Australia and South Africa on behalf of the well-known George Washington Wilson, before returning to open his own business on Union Street, Aberdeen. Now as later, there was a substantial trickle of graduates into overseas journalism. Alexander Wilson (MA 1869) left a headteacher's post to edit the *New Zealand Times*, and Alan Shepherd (MA 1863) was sub-editor on *The Times of India*.

Late in the century a new overseas career as professional scientist began to emerge. Since the Scottish MA degree included courses in natural philosophy and natural history, sometimes taught by eminent authorities, important contributions to the natural sciences had often been made through the ordered observations of graduates travelling or working abroad. Recent examples included the geographical and botanical observations in eastern Africa by James Augustus Grant (alumnus Marischal 1841–44),[7] and the studies of polyzoa (sea-mosses) which P H MacGillivray (MA, Marischal 1851), son of a professor of natural history, carried out while in medical practice in Australia. Some notable contributions to botanical science by Aberdeen graduates in the Indian Medical Service will be considered in Chapter 3. From the 1890s a few specialised posts were created for government bacteriologists, or specialists in other medical sciences.

Aberdeen alumni also worked abroad as astronomers; in 1875 Charles Meldrum (MA, Marischal 1844), while teaching mathematics in Mauritius, became director of the observatory there. A more prestigious scientific appointment was that of [Sir] David Gill, a pupil of Clerk Maxwell at Marischal, to be H M Astronomer at Cape Town in 1879; Gill was to become a pioneer of geodetic survey in southern Africa. By the time Aberdeen awarded its first BSc degree in 1890 it was clear that new types of career opportunity were being created for professional scientists, in the empire as well as within the UK.

6 One of J A Grant's East African botanical sketches (National Library of Scotland, MS 17937).

1901–1925

After 1900 the number of students in Aberdeen University began to rise; despite fluctuations (especially during the First World War) the total of graduates for the 25 years of the second *Roll* is slightly higher than that for the previous 41.[8] There were, however, changes in the composition of the student body that affected the pattern of overseas careers. The number of men graduating in medicine each year continued to average about 50, but these were now augmented by an average of eight women. The proportion of male medical graduates working overseas dropped from 37 per cent to about 30 per cent: a fall more marked in the case of those going to private practice than for those holding appointments with colonial governments or the armed forces, or with private mining and plantation enterprises. The fall may be partially due to improved professional prospects at home, partly to the growth of medical schools in the older British dominions, a process to which Aberdeen graduates of the period continued to contribute. A W Falconer (MB 1901, MD 1907) left an Aberdonian imprint on the medical faculty in Cape Town, and Aberdeen physiologists were conspicuous in early Canadian medical schools.

Aberdonians also remained active in medical teaching in the tropical world, where it would usually be a matter of developing basic health care at pre-clinical levels. E W Cruickshank (MB 1910, MD 1920), before becoming professor of physiology in Dalhousie and in Aberdeen, had occupied chairs in Pekin and in Patna. Two IMS officers, W C Gray (MB 1901) and Duncan Coutts (MB 1905) also worked in medical education, and there was a sprinkling of Aberdonians at the growing number of young medical schools throughout the world. Robert Brown (MB 1905, MD 1907) taught anaesthetics at Cairo; T B Heggs (MB 1902, MD 1904) was professor of public health in Baghdad; H W Smith (MB 1901, MD 1912) became professor of psychiatry in the American University of Beirut; C F Simpson (MA 1906, MB 1910) professed surgery at Mukden, in the Manchurian mission-field. In 1932 J P Mitchell (MB 1907, MD 1911) became principal of the Uganda Medical School, which would eventually merge into Makerere University.

Almost a quarter of the women who graduated in medicine in this period went abroad. Many of these did so on marriage, and in some cases did not record having practised their profession abroad – though it is reasonable to assume that many did at least some part-time or voluntary work. Of the 37 who did practise, 16 worked in Christian missions, ten of them in India; this compares with some 14 medical missionaries among the much larger number of male graduates of the period. One of the most adventurous was Stella Henriques (MB 1923) who worked in the unpromising mission-field of Persia. Ten women doctors, mostly post-war graduates, held public appointments, including Catherine Anderson (MB 1904), a planter's daughter who became a lecturer in the Ceylon Medical College, and Leila Chatterji (MB 1922) who lectured in Delhi. The remaining 11 seem to have engaged in some form of private practice, including three who returned to their native South Africa.

The number of students graduating in the faculty of arts rose fairly steadily from 77 in 1901 to 149 in 1913: then, after sharp falls during the war, to an exceptionally high figure of 222 in 1925. A primary reason for this was increasing access to grants, both through the Carnegie Trust for the Universities of Scotland and through the support given by the Scotch Education Department to teachers in training. Grants for 'Queen's Students' at universities began in 1895, and from 1906 an honours degree became a prerequisite for admission to secondary teaching. This and other moves towards professionalisation made degrees more valuable, and students in good standing no longer omitted to graduate. In addition to this, most of the growing number of women students were in the faculty of arts; and for them, even more than for the men, teaching was the most widely intended career.[9]

This was equally true for the 240 female graduates of the period who worked overseas. If we deduct 105 women who went abroad on marriage and recorded no formal career (again, no doubt many of these did in fact do some teaching) two-thirds of this group had careers as teachers, many as headmistresses, in all parts of the empire. For the male arts graduates there were new opportunities in higher education, especially in young universities in the white Commonwealth. J R Elder (MA 1902, DLitt 1914), whose younger brother had gone to teach English at Kyoto Imperial University, Japan, left his lectureship in Aberdeen for the chair of history at Otago. [Sir] Robert Wallace, son of a blacksmith from Old Deer and professor of English at Melbourne 1912–27, became an energetically reforming Vice-Chancellor of Sydney University. There were prominent Aberdonians in the new South African university of Witwatersrand, as well as in Cape Town; others continued to serve in North American universities, notably Queen's.

Nine women missionaries, in addition to four of the 16 medical missionaries already noted, obtained the MA degree in this period. Most went to teach, though Janet Rankine (MA 1912) was later found performing plays in America and eastern Asia in the cause of Moral Rearmament. But overall there seem to have been fewer clerical vocations than formerly. Several male graduates served as chaplains, notably in India; others went to minister to established congregations, though increasingly overseas churches preferred to train their own clergy. E D Danson (MA 1902) became Episcopal Bishop of Labuan and Sarawak. A notable group of missionary teachers, lay or ordained, continued to serve the Indian Christian colleges.

As the number of students increased, arts graduates in particular became concerned about employment. Beyond the established professions of law

and medicine, teaching and the ministry, there were still varied opportunities for the enterprising, at home and abroad. A few MAs were still able
to enter careers which may be classified as scientific, as meteorologists for
example. Over a dozen graduates of the period worked abroad as journalists, with varying success. Hugh Adam (MA 1912) became editor of the
Melbourne Herald; P M Jack (MA 1920) gave up a chair of rhetoric at Ann
Arbor to write for the *New York Times*; P H Tough (MA 1911), David
Walker (MA 1913) and the novelist Eric Linklater (MA 1925) worked on
The Times of India. A few found openings in banking and insurance, especially in North America. As the teaching of modern languages developed,
posts as translators or interpreters in Europe became possible; these were
largely held by women graduates, who also found work abroad as secretaries
or librarians.

Nevertheless an increasing number of graduates were looking for careers
in the public service, and university authorities felt an obligation to advise
them on means of access to these. In 1899 Cambridge University established a high-level committee 'to see whether ability was running to waste';
its recommendations led to the establishment of an Appointments Board
in 1902.[10] Aberdeen responded similarly. In 1900 the Senatus established a
committee 'to assist graduates in obtaining educational or other appointments'; one of its four sub-committees was 'Colonial & Foreign', the others
dealt with Teachers, British government appointments, and Ladies. (Senate
Minutes, 13 January, 29 September 1900). Ladies were apparently outside
the remit of the Cambridge board. A list of ten possible careers which the
committee later drew up shows that a high proportion of such appointments
lay overseas, and increasingly within the formal empire:[11]

1. Indian and Colonial Universities, Training Colleges and Schools
2. The Indian, Straits Settlements, Federated Malay States, Hong
Kong and other Police Forces . . . specially suited for young men
combining good physique with sufficient attainments
3. Assistants in the British Museum . . . [&c]
4. Student Interpreterships for the Ottoman Dominions, Persia,
Greece and Morocco
5. Student Interpreterships in China, Japan, and Siam
6. General Consular Service . . .
7. Inspectors of Factories
8. Colonial Appointments generally
9. Indian Finance and Customs Appointments
10. Agricultural and Forestry Appointments

Some students did find work in most of these spheres. There were a few
entrants to the imperial police and to the consular (though not yet the
diplomatic) service. At the suggestion of the Scotch Education Department

a register was maintained of 'actual and prospective graduates who would be willing to accept educational appointments in India or the Colonies'. A special committee advised students hoping to enter the Indian and Home Civil Service; but in fact interest in the ICS fell off after the First World War, partly perhaps because of apprehensions that it might not long provide a lifetime career for expatriates. Seventeen graduates entered the service in the years 1901–14, but only seven in the inter-war period – the last of these, Sir Fraser Noble, later returning to Aberdeen as principal.

In the colonies proper, the administrative services of Malaya and Hong Kong continued to recruit by competitive examination; five Aberdeen graduates of the period entered the former and one the latter. At the other end of the hierarchy, Sir John Anderson left the Colonial Office in 1904 to become governor of Malaya, and later of Ceylon.[12] But the administrators of the new colonial empire continued to be recruited by a reformed patronage system. Within the Colonial Office selection was controlled by Sir Ralph Furse, an old Etonian who believed that the essential qualifications for imperial government were character, breeding, and physical vigour, rather than academic achievement. After an initial phase during which the African empire was largely governed by young military officers, Furse looked for public schoolboys with strong personal recommendation from trusted university tutors, mostly in Cambridge and Oxford. Only Scots from upper-class families who had by-passed the Scottish educational system were likely to secure Furse's approval. An analysis of 200 administrators who achieved the rank of governor shows only one 'indubitable Scot' who entered the service under this procedure, via Fettes and Edinburgh University.[13] During the inter-war period only three Aberdeen graduates seem to have entered the African service by this method, including David Edwards (MA 1912, LLB 1914) who became a distinguished judge. One or two did so by way of the legal or audit services. It is hard to believe that there were no others who might have served the new empire as well as their predecessors in the ICS. British colonial administration reflected both the merits and the limitations of men like Sir Ralph Furse.

After the First World War international organisations began to offer new openings for public service in Europe. George Mair (MA 1905), a former journalist, became Assistant Director of the League of Nations Secretariat, and later head of its London office. Some women were quick to take such oportunities. Marjory Geddes (MA 1910), after working for the Foreign Office, joined the staff of the ILO in 1924; Eva Tonochy (MA 1913) worked as a translator during the Versailles peace conference, and subsequently for the Reparations Commission; Harriet Berry (MA 1908) for many years worked for the Bank of International Settlements in Basle.

In other respects too war had widened the possibilities open to educated women. Grace McDougall (née Smith: alumna 1906–10), served with the First Aid Nursing Yeomanry throughout the war, escaping from German

His Excellency
Sir John Anderson G.C.M.G.K.C.B
Governor & Commander-
-in-Chief in and over the Island
of Ceylon with the dependencies thereof

May it please Your Excellency,
In Welcoming You as
President of the Board of Agriculture
we desire to express our earnest hope
that the work of the Board may continue
to Prosper during Your Excellency's
Regime as it has in the past under that
of your Distinguished Predecessors.

Signed on behalf of the Vice-
-Presidents and Members of the
Board of Agriculture.

[signature]	Vice President
[signature]	Vice President
[signature]	Vice President
[signature]	Vice President
[signature]	Secretary

7 Illuminated address presented to Sir John Anderson on his appointment as
Governor of Ceylon, 1916. The university archives hold a collection of such loyal
addresses, embellished with colourful vignettes and flowery language.

captivity in October 1914 and winning French and Belgian decorations; afterwards she went to farm in Southern Rhodesia. Elizabeth McHardy (MA 1906) spent three years in Poland doing post-war relief work for the Red Cross. Margaret Hardie (MA 1907) had worked as an archaeologist with her husband F W Hasluck; after his early death she learned Albanian (assisted by Wilson travelling fellowships), made a home in that country and, as one of the few British authorities on the country, was to direct the Albanian operations of GHQ Cairo during part of the Second World War.[14]

But apart from the new colonial education services, the most numerous opportunities which the new empire opened to Aberdeen graduates were for men (and later women) with scientific training.

Imperial politicians like Joseph Chamberlain justified colonial expansion in the name of scientific development. But at the start of the new century Aberdeen's teaching aimed 'to turn out well-educated men, with a good deal of general culture and knowledge',[15] rather than to train scientific specialists. Its BSc degree, first awarded in 1890, was initially an offshoot of the arts syllabus, where the principles of natural philosophy and natural history had long been an essential element; an MA who had chosen appropriate courses could add a BSc for relatively little extra work.[16] The zoologist J Arthur Thomson was the first eminent researcher to be appointed (in 1899) since the notorious decision to dispense with the services of Clerk Maxwell at the time of the union of King's and Marischal. So the Appointments Committee did not pay much attention to specialised scientific careers.

Of the 22 holders of the BSc who had first graduated before 1901 and worked abroad, some did so in non-scientific posts, and perhaps only the Arctic explorer Rudmose Brown (BSc 1900, DSc 1909) can be regarded as following a purely scientific career. Apart from two agriculturalists who will be considered later, only two of the group, both chemists, were employed by colonial governments: Charles Allan (BSc 1900) in Jamaica and later in India, and James Mair (MA, BSc 1897) in the Transvaal Mines department. W S Simpson (MA 1900, BSc 1904) became an explosives chemist in South Africa. Later other business opportunities appeared. Charles Allan re-applied his chemistry to a sugar-manufacturing concern in India, of which he became managing director, and Alfred Tingle (BSc 1896) left the University of Wisconsin for the Chinese Imperial Mint.

The science faculty did not undertake formal research training until after the First World War; although 265 men and 114 women received the BSc between 1901 and 1925, only 89 men and 11 women are recorded by Theodore Watt to be working as 'scientists'. By my calculation (which may use slightly different criteria) slightly under half of these went overseas. The interest in polar exploration was maintained by R S Clark (MA 1908, BSc 1911, DSc 1925), a biologist with Shackleton in 1914–16, and by James Marr (MA, BSc 1925) who, having also served with Shackleton before graduating, worked as a zoologist on several later expeditions. The growth of the oil

8 Albanian gypsy musicians, photographed by Margaret Hasluck, 1934.

industry offered new careers to chemists and geologists; the latter were taught in a separate department from 1898, with a professor from 1922. Half a dozen post-war graduates worked for oil companies in Iran, Iraq, Bornea and Burma; and H S M Burns (MA 1921, BSc 1922), a geophysicist who joined Shell in California in 1926, became president of its New York company in 1947.

As yet few science graduates went to academic posts abroad, except in medical sciences. But Harold Thompson (MA 1912, BSc 1920) directed fishery research laboratories at St John's, Newfoundland, and later at Sydney, and G A Currie (BSc 1923), having worked as a research entomologist in Canberra, went on to become Vice-Chancellor of universities in Western Australia and New Zealand. Laura Florence (MA 1907, BSc 1909), a pupil of J Arthur Thomson, after a distinguished research career in America became professor of bacteriology in a homeopathic medical college in New York. Thomson's own son David (MA 1921, BSc 1924) took his PhD at Cambridge and went on to develop the department of biochemistry at McGill.

Substantial contributions to knowledge were also made by scientists who went abroad in colonial service. The work of Sophia Summers (MA 1907, BSc 1909) as honorary entomologist in the medical research institute at Lagos (directed by her husband Andrew Connal) won her both a DSc (1929)

199

and an MBE. In 1945, W T H Williamson, after twelve years as chief chemist to the Egyptian ministry of agriculture, founded Aberdeen's department of soil science. J J Simpson (MA 1904, BSc 1906, DSc 1911) and D W Duthie (MA 1925, BSc 1927, PhD 1935) were among those who carried out significant research while working for the colonial agricultural service.

The growth of such specialised colonial services was to provide essential support for Aberdeen's attempts to develop scientific disciplines with direct application to the economy of northern Scotland. Since 1840 a small endowment bequeathed by Sir William Fordyce had supported a part-time lectureship in agriculture; among those who held the post was J S Brazier, who as professor of chemistry (1861–88) interested himself in agricultural problems at home and overseas, offering advice on fertilisers to one of the few Ceylon planters to take much interest in science.[17] But universities were slow to respond to the great crisis of British agriculture which began in the 1870s. Edinburgh established the first BSc course in the subject in 1886, but the essential stimulus came from the whisky money, raised by spirit duties in the 1890 budget and subsequently reallocated for the development of technical education. Aberdeen benefited less from this than it had hoped, but the lectureship was made full-time, and a degree of BSc (Agriculture) was inaugurated. Its syllabus indicated an intention to apply scientific principles to the practical problems of Scottish farmers.

Students were slow to appear. Practical farmers preferred to take the Diploma in Agriculture, thus avoiding the courses in basic sciences. Up to 1901 only two students graduated in agriculture (though 12 students obtained the Diploma) and both went abroad. W R Buttenshaw obtained government appointments in the West Indies and William Angus, after teaching the subject in England, became Director of Agriculture for South Australia. After 1904 the establishment of the North of Scotland College of Agriculture increased the number of students. The university was able to appoint more part-time lecturers (including one in Forestry), and in 1911 Lord Strathcona provided endowment for a chair. Its first holder, James Hendrick, obtained a small grant from the Development Commission for a research institute in animal nutrition. John Boyd Orr was appointed as first director, and after the war the donation of J Q Rowett enabled him to build up a centre of scientific excellence. Orr's imaginative programme of pure and applied research, which increasingly extended into the field of human nutrition, led to a wide extension of research work overseas. Four graduates of the mid-1920s carried out research in Kenya connected with the Institute's work, while Beatrice Simpson (MA 1913, BSc 1917) spent four years in New Zealand.[18]

The demand for scientifically trained agriculturalists at home seems to have remained limited: 22 of the 65 men who graduated in agriculture up to March 1914 went abroad. Four engaged in farming (two in Canada, one in Australia, one as plantation manager in Ceylon); one worked in Rome

Nr. *3*

Berlin den 2 NOV. 1913

D i e n s t v e r t r a g

----

für Herrn W a l t e r I n k s t e r .

....

Zwischen dem Kalisyndikat G.m.b.H., Berlin, einerseits
und Herrn W a l t e r I n k s t e r andererseits
ist heute nachstehender Vertrag geschlossen worden.

§ 1

Herr Inkster tritt in den Dienst des Kalisyndikats
als Propagandabeamter für Australien und wird zunächst Assi-
stent auf der dort bestehenden Geschäftsstelle des Kalisyndikats. Das Kalisyndikat behält sich vor, bei zufrieden-
stellenden Leistungen des Herrn Inkster ihm später einen
selbständigeren Wirkungskreis zu übertragen.

Herr Inkster hat die mündlichen und schriftlichen An-
ordnungen der Kalisyndikatsverwaltung strengstens zu beach-
ten und deren Weisungen unbedingt nachzukommen.

§ 2

Herr Inkster verpflichtet sich zur Ausübung einer Propaganda zu Gunsten der Kalisalze, die durch das Kalisyndikat
zum Vertrieb kommen, in den ihm zur Bearbeitung überwiesenen
Gebieten. Er hat zu diesem Zweck alle Massregeln zu treffen,
welche geeignet sind, diese ihm gestellte Aufgabe zu lösen.
Es wird besonders von ihm erwartet, dass er nicht nur nach
den ihm gegebenen Weisungen arbeitet, sondern selbständig
Mittel und Wege sucht und vorschlägt, die geeignet sind, die
Interessen des Kalisyndikats zu fördern.

§ 3

Herr Inkster ist verpflichtet, bei allen seinen Massnah-
men mit der Sorgfalt eines ordentlichen Kaufmannes zu handeln.
Er erhält eine Dienstanweisung, welche eine allgemeine An-
weisung für seine Tätigkeit enthält. Ausserdem erwarten die

9 Contract of Walter Inkster with the German Potash Syndicate, the most important employer of graduates in agriculture before the First World War.

for the International Institute of Agriculture; 13 held government appointments in India, Malaya, Sudan, Nigeria and other British dependencies. Some rose to senior office, like C C Calder, as Director of Calcutta's Botanical Gardens, or H G Burr, Superintendent of Agriculture for Nigeria. But the largest pre-war employer was the German Potash Syndicate, one of the earliest European cartels. Founded in 1881 and based on the natural monopoly of supply which Germany enjoyed until the First World War, the Syndicate was well placed to compete internationally for agricultural chemists.[19] The university archives contain a contract which Walter Inkster (MA 1911, BSc (Ag) 1912) signed in Berlin on 26 November 1913. As *Propagandabeamter* (rendered on his visiting card as 'Advisory Agriculturalist') for Australia, Inkster bound himself zealously to promote the Syndicate's interests, in return for the generous salary of 10,000 marks (£500).[20] After the war he returned to a university lectureship. Other employees of the Syndicate included two London managers, H M Will (MA 1898, BSc (Ag) 1905) and G A Cowie (MA 1904, BSc 1907), as well as A G Howitt (BSc (Ag) 1910), their representative in South Africa, and Alfred Hill (BSc 1909, BSc (Ag) 1911) who was caught in Germany in 1914 and interned throughout the war.

Agricultural industries at home do not seem to have offered comparable opportunities. After the war agricultural scientists continued to emigrate, to posts in colonial agricultural departments or to Asian plantations. More students enrolled for agriculture degrees, but 57 of the 118 graduating between 1914 and 1925 went abroad. This may lend some support to the view that British businessmen were slow to offer opportunities to those scientists whom British universities were at last beginning to educate.[21]

But it also reflects the growth of organised agricultural and forestry services in the colonial empire. Furse's prejudice in favour of extrovert public schoolboys did not extend to the 'scientific branches'; he delegated responsibility for these to colleagues, taking advice from, among others, Sir David Prain (MA 1878, MB 1883), director of Kew Gardens. Though the scale of recruitment fluctuated with the economic climate, the new services proved a vital outlet for Aberdeen graduates in agriculture, and still more so in forestry.[22]

Forestry had been taught in the agriculture department since 1908; a separate degree was established by ordinance in 1914 but nobody graduated until 1919. Although the intention was to serve the needs of Scottish forestry the university wished to see the degree recognised as a qualification for colonial service. The policy of the Indian government was to concentrate specialised training for well educated men, whom it had already selected, in Oxford, where Robert S Troup (alumnus 1891–4) became director of the Imperial Forestry Institute.[23] Some Aberdeen graduates entered the Indian Forestry Service by this route, but it was a matter for relief when in 1923 the Colonial Office, having taken the advice of the Forestry Commission, agreed that the new degree ranked with those of Oxford, Cambridge and Edinburgh, and that its graduates were eligible for colonial appointments.[24] Almost half of the 183 men who graduated before 1946 worked overseas; and though about half of these went as planters in the tropics, or as foresters in the old Commonwealth, the remainder entered colonial service, though some were required to take the Oxford course first.

1926–1955

Conclusions about the overseas experience of those first graduating during the years 1926–55 are in some respects more tentative. The data in the third volume of the *Roll of Graduates* is less complete. Even when updated with information from the Supplement to the fourth volume of the series, published in 1982, it does not cover the full working life of post-war graduates; and in any case alumni of the period were already less conscientious in providing the editors with information. Moreover these figures understate the range of overseas experience acquired on national service before, during, or after the period of study. As with earlier wars, this has not been included, except in a few cases where officers in the RAMC or other specialists undertook long-term responsibilities towards overseas populations; but if national service were taken into account it would surely show that this generation of graduates enjoyed wider overseas experience, both geographically and in range of duties, than their predecessors.

Since Mackintosh's *Roll* provides no annual breakdown of graduate numbers, the figures in Table III of the appendix do not distinguish the overseas experience of those taking particular degrees, or of those graduating before, during, and after the war. This might have been illuminating. Economic depression meant that student numbers fell fairly steadily between 1926 and the outbreak of war, reflecting what was probably an even sharper decline in employment opportunities. Since the depression was world-wide, this decline was apparent abroad as well as at home; there is no evidence of a strong move towards overseas careers during the 1930s, and in fact many graduates of this period first went abroad only after the war. A breakdown according to date of first employment overseas (rather than of first graduation) might well show that it was not until about 1950 that significant new patterns of graduate emigration began to take shape. During the immediate post-war years there were many posts to be filled in the UK, by returning service folk as well as by new graduates; from 1950 there was more competition for these, and perhaps more disillusionment with continued post-war austerity. In such conditions, opportunities overseas, in particular those offered by the government's drive to develop the material and human resources of the colonial empire, may well have seemed more attractive. But the methods employed in the present analysis do not permit verification of such hypotheses.

Subject to these qualifications, it seems that the proportion of those graduating in this period who worked overseas, fell slightly to 20.8 per cent of the total. Compared with the 1901–25 period the proportion of male graduates fell, from 31.9 per cent to 23.75 per cent, but the proportion of women graduates rose, from 14.75 per cent to 16.0 per cent. However, while 43.75 per cent of women emigrating in the earlier period were married, and recorded no overseas employment, the comparable figure for 1926–55 graduates is only 17.35 per cent. To some extent the white man's burden was being taken over by white women.

Table V makes it possible to compare the numbers of 1926–55 graduates pursuing particular careers overseas with those in the earlier generation. It must be remembered that while the total of overseas careers has increased, these are drawn from a total graduate population some two-thirds larger. Thus though the number of male doctors working abroad is fairly static it represents a proportionate decline, while for women the comparable figure represents a proportionate as well as an absolute increase. These figures must be related to the introduction of the National Health Service in 1948, which provided full employment for British doctors, if not on terms satisfactory to all of them. A broadbrush analysis of the figures in Table V (ii) suggests a progressive reduction in appointments to colonial medical services, as these became more fully staffed by local doctors; and also a fall in the number of doctors holding regular or short-service commissions in the armed services. (Many more, of course, served overseas during national service.) The largest numbers of medical migrants seem to have gone – sometimes for relatively short periods – to private practice or to specialist hospital or university appointments, especially in North America and Australasia; at certain periods of discontent about pay, conditions and prospects in the National Health Service there was talk nationally of a medical and scientific brain drain. Among Aberdeen graduates, psychiatrists and pharmacologists appear to have been among the specialists in most demand abroad.

In a period when many developing countries and colonial territories were, subject to economic constraints, building up new educational systems, it is not surprising to find a continuing increase of teaching careers overseas. The figures in Table V (ii) also include a number of graduates serving in the new educational branches of the armed forces. As some regional studies in Chapter 3 suggest, more men were finding university posts abroad (and there is some overlap here with the figures for medical careers), but the striking growth in the number of women is largely made up of schoolteachers. It is also notable that, while the number of men serving the church overseas declined, the number of women working as medical or educational missionaries increased.

The education figure also overlaps with the rather spectacular increase in careers classified under 'science'. These reflect the early growth of postgraduate teaching in the faculty of science, and to a limited extent the return to their home countries of overseas students. It seems reasonable to assume that, in both respects, figures for those first graduating after 1955 would show still more notable increases. Substantial numbers of those included in this total were employed in full-time research posts, or as scientific specialists with foreign or colonial governments. But many industrial chemists and petroleum geologists employed by multi-national corporations have been classified under 'business'; this borderline is a particularly arbitrary one, and the total number of science graduates utilising their training is certainly greater than the figures suggest. Although the number of agriculturalists abroad seems to have fallen slightly, perhaps reflecting reduced opportunities on private plantations, forestry graduates now began to find careers in both temperate and tropical countries.

The growing number of graduates employed in business is striking. As already suggested, it largely reflects new opportunities for science graduates and engineers. The number of these working for oil companies or other multinational corporations (and often serving successively in different regions of the world) is particularly notable among post-1945 graduates. There was some small increase in the number of arts and law graduates finding posts in commerce, banking and insurance, particularly in North America; but the university failed to develop any special capacity in such fields. Encouraged by the Aberdeen Chamber of Commerce, after the First World War it did institute a Bachelor of Commerce degree, but this was allowed to lapse after the Second World War: student demand, initially promising, seems to have fallen away in the 1930s because of limited opportunities at home during the depression. Of the 128 holders of this degree 34 worked abroad, but some as teachers, or in other noncommercial posts. The number of journalists included in the 'business' group was now slightly swollen by graduates working for radio or television, one of the most notable being H A (Sandy) Gall (MA 1952), a future rector of the University.

Engineers make up the largest single group of 'business' careers in this period. The total includes, besides those working for private contractors, those who were employed, on contract or on the permanent establishment, by the Public Works Departments of overseas governments. As Table III shows, about a quarter of all Aberdeen's engineering graduates of the period worked overseas. In view of the reluctance of the UGC to provide the university with funds to develop the department during this period,[25] this raises interesting questions. Did Aberdeen engineers emigrate because employers judged them less suitable for employment at home? Or, more probably, was the capacity to train efficient professional engineers little prejudiced by the alleged weakness of the departmental research base?

A final feature for comment in Table V (ii) is the small increase in the number of graduates holding posts in government or public administration. The honourable line of entrants to the Indian Civil Service came to an end with T A Fraser Noble in 1940, but the post-war expansion of the colonial service was more widely based than in Furse's heyday, and 15 post-war graduates held administrative posts in Africa. Others served in legal or police appointments, or with locally based civil services. Some students continued to find careers with international organisations, including N D Begg (MB 1929), European regional director of the WHO from 1951. And, for the first time, Aberdeen graduates began to rise to senior posts in the diplomatic service: Donald Gordon (MA 1944) was Ambassador to Vienna, 1979–81; (Sir) Iain Sutherland (MA 1948), Ambassador to the USSR 1982–85; and (Sir) John Thomson (MA 1947) concluded his career as permanent representative to the United Nations. As the possibilities of employment in the service of the British empire dwindled, opportunities began to open for new generations of students to pursue a variety of challenging careers in what was becoming known as the developing world.

CONCLUSION: ABERDEEN UNIVERSITY AND THE BRITISH EMPIRE

This study has attempted to trace the significance of the nineteenth-century expansion of the British empire (and the less formal expansion of the economic and political influence of the British state) for the development of Aberdeen University. The world beyond Europe has provided graduates and alumni with wide opportunities for employment and enterprise; to an increasing degree it has supplied the university with students of varied cultural backgrounds; and (though perhaps to a lesser extent than might have been expected) it has influenced the content and direction of teaching and research carried out in Aberdeen.

To proceed to ask complementary questions about the place of the university in the history of the British empire may at first seem absurdly pretentious. Aberdeen alumni constitute only a tiny proportion of those settlers, entrepreneurs and government agents who populated the overseas empire; and, although some individual careers of distinction have been noted, few of them reached the commanding heights of imperial power. Yet it is precisely through consideration of this subordinate role that it may be possible to identify the specific contribution which a provincial and Scottish university could make to the processes of imperial expansion, and to those of transformation and dissolution which followed.

The clue may be found in the very impressive recent study of *British Imperialism* by P J Cain and A G Hopkins.[26] Drawing on research by social and economic as well as imperial historians, they interpret the expansion of the British state since 1688 as the fruit of an alliance, forged over three centuries, between old landed property and successive injections of new money, derived essentially from the provision of financial and other services rather than from direct participation in manufacturing industry. Naturally the exact nature of this alliance, the means by which it exercised its hegemony, and the objectives of its overseas activities, varied greatly over time; but there was a continuity of underlying structure, to which Cain and Hopkins give the name of 'gentlemanly capitalism'.

The base of gentlemanly capitalism was the City of London and the English home counties. That is not to say that Scots were excluded; indeed, it becomes increasingly clear that opportunities for Scottish gentry and entrepreneurs to participate in the development of the expanding empire were among the principal reasons why such persons accepted and sustained the Union of 1707.[27] But increasingly, during the period studied in this volume, Scots who aspired to share in the exercise of power at the summit found it expedient to shift their activities southwards: to establish bases in the City, to exercise influence in Whitehall and Westminster, to send their children to English-type public schools and to the Universities of Oxford or Cambridge. Cain and Hopkins may underestimate the extent to which Edinburgh retained some autonomy as a financial and cultural, if no longer a political, metropolis; but the virtues and the limitations of Aberdeen were clearly those of a provincial city, with a provincial university. Similar cities elsewhere in Britain, and the manufacturing and agricultural industries which sustained them, drew many benefits from empire, and on occasion their representatives might influence policy; but when the interests of provincial business and metropolitan finance clashed, it was the gentlemanly capitalism of the City which prevailed.

Acceptance of the general thesis of Cain and Hopkins, however, by no means reduces the importance of studying provincial contributions to the extension of British power and influence in the world. Not only was the capital on which the City of London drew created largely by the enterprise of provincial manufacturers and merchants, but so was the human material out of which new colonial societies were formed. Every quarter of the United Kingdom provided some quota of settlers, emigrant artisans, soldiers for imperial armies and police forces, and could celebrate the courage and enterprise of some local hero of empire. But educated persons were also needed to provide specialised services and leadership in the new communities, and graduates had crucially important roles to play in forming their culture. Here Scottish universities, which in the eighteenth century enjoyed national and international pre-eminence, had more than merely provincial contributions to make.

In the century after the Union, before the alliance of old landed estates with new money had completed its reform of British government, the systems of patronage fortified by Dundas allowed Scots full access to power and wealth within the empire; and Scottish universities provided education and ideologies for many members of the ruling elite. As Victorians reformed the institutions of the state on the basis of professionalisation and competitive examinations, Oxford and Cambridge, together with the English or English-modelled public schools, largely took over their roles as educators of imperial statesmen and administrators, and as prime guardians of a new imperial ideology and culture. Old connections were strong enough for the Scottish universities to retain a substantial share of appointments to the Indian public service, at least until the new regulations of 1892. But in the new empire that share was, as a matter of policy, reduced. The major imperial role of the Scottish universities now became – to a greater degree than in the new English foundations – the education of the professional specialists – physicians, engineers, scientists, teachers – who were increasingly recruited by colonial governments working to transform and modernise conditions under which their subjects lived.

Study of other Scottish universities – notably Edinburgh? – might provide a slightly different picture; but the contribution of Aberdeen University seems broadly clear. Its medical school, though relatively late in modernising its teaching, became a significant provider of physicians and surgeons for the United Kingdom and the empire as a whole. At certain times, the university community inspired clergy (as well as lay missionaries and teachers) with the challenge of overseas service; their dedication helped to spread the influence of the British state, as well as of the Christian Gospel, in India, Africa, China and many other countries. In the twentieth century the science faculty began to train some of the applied scientists – agriculturalists, foresters, engineers – to whom the imperial government looked for enterprises now known as 'development' or 'nation-building'. From the 1920s the university, largely through the associated research institutes, became a centre of research in such evidently applicable fields as soil science, fisheries, and nutrition. The Cain-Hopkins thesis suggests a perfect metaphor to embrace all these roles; Aberdeen University was training physicians, chaplains and tutors for the households, and later factors and foresters for the estates, of the gentlemanly capitalists who were directing the destinies of an expanding empire.

Yet what these educated expatriates were doing, and often believed themselves to be doing, was of broader historical importance than such neat slogans might suggest. They were not merely serving imperial governments. They changed the lives of colonial peoples. It seems probable that all but the most cynical at some stage in their work shared some sense of a personal mission, which individuals might define with primary reference to Christian evangelism, to the spread of European civilisation, or to economic modernisation. These differing motivations each reflected elements within the continuing purposes of the imperial rulers.

For colonial empire was not, as angry critics sometimes argue, simply a system of oppression and exploitation. Even when it seemed most autocratic, oppressive or exploitative, there was at least a latent belief in London that formal rule would not be permanent. The politically correct terminology spoke of an evolutionary progress towards self-government, often qualified, in the case of the Asian and African dependencies, by warnings about the necessity of very lengthy periods of preparation. Intelligent imperialists always knew that foreign rule could not last for ever, in Nigeria any more than in New Zealand. A continuing purpose of British policy – and there seems no reason to regard it as a sinister one, even though it was often ineptly pursued – was to encourage the formation of free-standing societies, in Asia and Africa, as well as in America and Australasia, whose interests and values would become congruent with those of the United Kingdom. The political expression of these hopes in the twentieth century was the Commonwealth ideal of continuing collaboration among a varied group of independent nations who would retain, from their imperial experience, at least some common values and common interests.

If this was indeed the underlying purpose of empire, the role of educational institutions, above all universities and colleges of higher education, was clearly primordial, whether their leaders recognised it or not. One theme which recurs in all the regions briefly surveyed in Chapter 3 is the work of doctors, teachers and clergy in creating new educational structures, and eventually new universities. Aberdeen's contribution to the development of medical education in Ceylon provides an early example of cultural reproduction taking place without any conscious initiative on the university's part. Back in Aberdeen University the extension of British values overseas was not always explicitly considered as a corporate objective. Yet from the union of the colleges a few Asian and African students were received in Aberdeen, and the work of Aberdeen graduates abroad was often recognised by the award of honorary degrees.

After the Second World War British universities were formally invited to participate in new policies directed towards a rapid transformation of colonial empire. The number of overseas students in Aberdeen grew, while teachers from the university accepted short and long-term missions to assist the proliferating growth of new universities within the Commonwealth.[28] Aberdeen graduates were now progressively working themselves out of many of the jobs which their predecessors had pioneered. But new roles – as consultants, advisers, volunteers – continued to present themselves; the university in the later twentieth century has become a more cosmopolitan place than at any time since the foundation. By the time of the sescentenary new patterns in Aberdeen's relationships with the post-imperial world will surely have become apparent.

Notes

Abbreviations

AUL   Aberdeen University Library
AUR   *Aberdeen University Review*

CMC   Ceylon Medical College
DAAD   Deutsche Akademische Austausch Dienst (German Academic Exchange
           Scheme)
DES   Department of Education and Science
ICS   Indian Civil Service
ILO   International Labour Office
IMF   International Monetary Fund
IMS   Indian Medical Service
IUC   Inter-University Council
MOH   Medical Officer of Health
NOSCA   North of Scotland College of Agriculture
PRO   Public Record Office
RAMC   Royal Army Medical Corps
SED   Scottish Education Department
SRC   Student Representative Council
UGC   University Grants Committee
WHO   World Health Organisation

1 N and J Parry, *The Rise of the Medical Profession* (London, 1974), 115. Ch. VII
  of this work provides a general background to these changes.
2 PP 1855, vol XX, Papers relating to the Reorganisation of the Civil Service,
  1855, p. 50, Dr Jeune to Northcote and Trevelyan, 14 March 1854.
3 F Musgrove, *The Migratory Elite* (London, 1963), 10–11.
4 *AUR*, XVII (1929–30), 125–31.
5 List of entrants, 1856–1913, in *AUR*, II (1914–15), 250–53. See also Ch. 4, xxx.
6 *AUR* I (1913), 299; III (1915–16), 279.
7 See R C Bridges, *James Augustus Grant in Scotland* (National Library of Scotland,
  1979); also Robert Ralph, *William MacGillivray* (London, 1993).
8 Robert Anderson, *The Student Community at Aberdeen, 1860–1939* (Aberdeen,
  1988), Figure 2, p. 131.
9 Watt, *Roll of Graduates*, App. A & B; Anderson, *Student Community, 56–61*. See
  also Lindy Moore, *Bajanellas and Semilinas* (Aberdeen, 1991).
10 H A Roberts, 'Careers for University Men': four articles in *The Cambridge
   Magazine*, 27 April–25 May 1912.
11 *Aberdeen University Calendar*, 1913–14, pp 136–7.
12 On Anderson, see obituary in *AUR*, VI (1918–9). AUL MS 2965 contains an
   interesting collection of Loyal Addresses presented to Anderson.
13 F Nicolson and C A Hughes, 'A provenance of pro-consuls: British colonial
   governors, 1900–1960', *Journal of Imperial & Commonwealth History*, IV (1975).
   Aucuparius: Memoirs of a Recruiting Officer (Oxford 1962) is revealing, especially
   Ch. 3. See also R Heussler, *Yesterday's Rulers: the Making of the British Colonial
   Service* (Syracuse 1963).
14 See the appreciations in *AUR*, XXXIII (1949), 157–60.
15 George Pirie, professor of mathematics 1878–1904: *AUR*, XXXVIII (1960), 368.
16 James Hendrick, dean of science, commending a new ordinance to the General
   Council, 11 October 1920, *AUR*, VIII (1920), 70.
17 T J Barron, 'Science and the nineteenth century Ceylon coffee planters', *Journal
   of Imperial and Commonwealth History*, XVI (1987), 19.
18 James Hendrick, 'The Early history of agricultural education in Aberdeen';
   'Agricultural research in Aberdeen', *AUR*, XXV (1937–8), 7–12, 103–10; J B Orr,
   'The Rowett Research Institute', *AUR*, XI (1923–24), 37–48.
19 G Stolper, K Hauser, K Borchardt, *The German Economy, 1870 to the Present*
   (NY 1967).

20 AUL, MSS 3306/1.
21 D S L Cardwell, *The Organisation of Science in England*, 2nd edn (London, 1972), 204–9.
22 Furse, *Aucuparius*, 66–70. His appendix gives interesting figures for annual intakes to the different services.
23 R Symonds, *Oxford and Empire: The Last Lost Cause* (London, 1966), 132–69.
24 PRO, CO 877/2/7196/1923: correspondence with H J Butchart, April 1923.
25 I G C Hutchison, *The University and the State: The Case of Aberdeen 1860–1963* (Aberdeen, 1993), 92–3.
26 P J Cain and A G Hopkins, *British Imperialism, I, Innovation and Expansion, 1688–1914. II, Crisis and Deconstruction, 1914–1990* (London, 1993).
27 E.g. C A Bayly, *Imperial Meridian: The British Empire and the World, 1780–1830* (London, 1989), chs 4 and 5.
28 J D Hargreaves, 'Universities and Decolonization: British Experience in comparative perspective, 1945–1960'. Paper presented to the international colloquium, *Les Décolonisations comparées*, Aix-en-Provence, October 1993.

Appendix

A note on statistics

Aberdeen University is fortunate in possessing four large volumes which record names, degrees, and varying amounts of biographical information for every graduate of the years 1860–1970. A project now in hand aims to enlarge this splendid database to include all who studied in the university (including, eventually, the pre-union colleges); to amplify the biographical information to the greatest possible extent; and to record all data in a form which will facilitate computer analysis.[1] In some years time this should permit, among other things, a more thorough, accurate and complex statistical analysis than a single scholar can at present attempt. With such a prospect in view, it was decided that the present survey should attempt its broad analysis of graduate employment overseas without benefit of modern information technology – a decision which has limited the possibilities for elaboration, and which the author has often felt inclined to regret.

Hence the figures on which the argument of this volume depends represent orders of magnitude rather than definitive statistics. They deal primarily with graduates, as distinct from alumni; they rely on the necessarily incomplete information in the four *Rolls of Graduates*; the analysis is therefore, in places, based on certain more or less arbitrary assumptions, which may not be entirely consistent. (Was this teacher also working as some sort of missionary? Should this geologist be seen as engaged in science or in business – or in both? Was this period of overseas study or service long enough to count?) If taken to indicate lifetime careers overseas, these figures will give an exaggerated impression; but they may under-estimate the number of Aberdeen graduates with significant experience abroad. The introductory notes which follow attempt to clarify some of the limitations in the data.

The four volumes in question, which will be cited by the names of their editors, are:

William Johnston, *Roll of the Graduates of the University of Aberdeen, 1860–1900*. (Aberdeen, 1906)

Theodore Watt, *Roll of the Graduates of the University of Aberdeen, 1901–1925. With Supplement 1860–1900* (Aberdeen, 1935)
John Mackintosh, *Roll of the Graduates of the University of Aberdeen, 1926–1955. With Supplement 1860–1925* (Aberdeen, 1960)
Louise Donald & W R Macdonald, *Roll of the Graduates of the University of Aberdeen, 1956–70. With Supplement 1860–1970* (Aberdeen, 1982)

Biographical data on any individual may not, of course, extend beyond the publication date of the volume in which his first graduation in Aberdeen is recorded. In many cases later careers are dealt with in the Supplements referred to in the titles of the later volumes; but many graduates failed to supply updated information to the General Council, on whose records the entries are based. This has become increasingly so in recent years, when attachment to the *alma mater* seems generally to have become more short-lived. Only in the case of those proceeding to a further degree in Aberdeen is there certain to be some record of later career. For 35 per cent of those graduating between 1956 and 1970, and for a still higher proportion of overseas students, only names and degrees are recorded in the Donald volume; the data are so incomplete that I reluctantly decided not to attempt to compile figures for those first graduating after 1955.

One further difficulty in the historical interpretation of these statistics should be noted. They relate to the year of first graduation in Aberdeen and not to the dates of overseas employment, which cannot always be ascertained, but in some cases may be several years later.

Imperfect though they may be, however, these figures for graduate employment overseas are the fullest currently available for any British university. In attempting to evaluate them, the shortage of comparative data has been a source of great frustration. Sanderson gives figures showing that of 181 Glasgow graduates of 1850–1900 working in business, 54 went overseas.[2] A published edition of the Register of the London School of Economics for 1895–1932 provides data on 1,840 out of 2,428 persons receiving degrees, diplomas, or certificates in this period; it shows 10 per cent working in the British empire, 6 per cent in foreign countries; but as a high proportion of non-respondents were probably overseas, these figures have little comparative value.[3] Richard Symonds gives figures showing the percentage of matriculates of three Oxford Colleges known to have worked in the British empire as just under 22 per cent for 1874–1914 and 18 per cent for 1918–1938.[4] These relate to the formal empire only (and include Balliol College, which was especially imperially-minded); and it must be remembered that Oxford offered no medical qualification. Less complete data from five women's colleges suggest that perhaps 10 per cent of pre-1914 Oxford alumnae may have worked in the empire. A tentative conclusion is that the proportion of Aberdeen graduates working abroad (though not the pattern of their careers) has been comparable to that of Oxford, but probably higher than in many other British universities.

I Numbers of graduates working overseas, by period of first graduation

a 1860–1900

Figures for this period are based on 4,085 entries in Johnston's *Roll*, upated from the Supplements to later volumes. (The 275 Honorary Graduates who did not already hold a post-1860 degree from the University of Aberdeen are deducted from Johnston's grand total of 4,360.) Only four women graduates of this period went overseas, three on marriage.

The total number of Aberdeen medical graduates 1860–1900 is 2,056 (Johnston, pp.678–9); but the overseas total below includes a few who graduated MA or BSc before 1900 and took medical degrees later. Where a post-1860 medical graduate already held an MA from Kings or Marischal these earlier degrees are included in my calculations. I include among the 'double graduates' in arts and medicine those who obtained only one of these degrees from the University of Aberdeen. Figures of medical graduates include a few who took the MD as first degree, as well as those with the new qualification of MB ChB.

On this basis the number of persons whose first degree from Aberdeen University was taken between 1860 and 1900, and who at some time worked or lived abroad, is 1,223, or 29.98%. This is compatible with the decennial estimates for graduates working in the 'Rest of the World' (including Ireland) obtained by D I Mackay on an extensive sample; the figures on p.94 of his *Geographical Mobility and the Brain Drain* (London, 1969) yield totals of 28.2% for 1860s graduates, 31.7% for the 1870s, 31.1% for the 1880s and 27% for the 1890s.

It is sometimes difficult to distinguish between those who worked abroad for short periods, and those whose whole career was overseas. In general I omit those who worked abroad for short periods, for example for study, as *locum*, or on retirement, without recording this in the *Roll*.

b 1901–1925

Watt's *Roll* shows a total of 4,539 persons graduating in this period, 2,912 men and 1,627 women; but if the 406 men and 1 woman who received Honorary degrees are deducted this is reduced to 4,132. My calculation of the numbers working overseas

Table I

Of the 1,223: 436 held the degree of MA only (or with BD,BL &c)
   627 held medical degrees only
   140 held arts and medical degrees
    22 held science degrees (1 MA, DSc: 13 MA, BSc: 2 MB, BSc:
     6 BSc only) (But 5 of these were conferred after 1900).

Approximately 25% of MAs, 37% of medical graduates, and 34% of pre-1901 science graduates thus served overseas.

Notes
Honours and Ordinary degrees are not distinguished.
Employment in Ireland, North or South, is excluded.

Table II Numbers of those first graduating 1901–25 who worked overseas.

Total MA	(Men)	1575		Overseas	354	22.4%
	(Women)	1423			198	13.9%
Total Medical	(Men)	1251		Overseas	374	29.9%
	(Women)	199			48	24.1%
Total BSc	(Men)	265		Overseas	58 or more	
	(Women)	114			15	
Total BSc Agri		183 (incl 1 woman)		Overseas	80	43.7%
Total BSc Forestry		17		Overseas	9	53.0%
Total BCom		57		Overseas	21	36.8%
Total Law (LLB + BL)		115		Overseas	20	17.4%
Total BD		106		Overseas	15	14.1%

totals 1,039: 799 men and 240 women. This represents just over 25% of all graduates: 31.9% of men, 14.75% of women.

Table II shows the percentage of those holding particular degrees who first graduated from Aberdeen in this period and worked abroad. In recording overseas careers I did not make double entries for those who held the degree of BSc in addition to that of BSc in agriculture or forestry, and so no percentage for the former degree is shown

A number of graduates of this period who worked overseas took higher degrees, including 8 PhD, 8 DSc, and 1 DLitt, but as in many cases these were conferred after 1925 comparisons with totals of these degrees conferred in this period would be pointless.

c 1926–1955

Unfortunately Mackintosh, unlike his predecessors, does not provide consolidated statistics for the total of first graduations in 1926–55. By my count this volume contains 7,527 entries: 4,652 men and 2,875 women. My calculation of the number of these who worked overseas is 1,566: 1,105 men and 461 women. This represents 20.8% of all graduates: 23.75% of men and 16.0% of women. But the number of incompletely recorded careers is certainly greater for this than for earlier periods, and so the real figures may be higher.

The numbers of those holding particular degrees who worked overseas are given in Table III. I have counted the total numbers taking the vocational degrees of BSc (Agriculture), BSc (Forestry), BSc (Engineering) and BCom, and these figures are compared with those for overseas employment of those taking such degrees.

II Careers

Calculations based on particulars in the *Rolls* involve many assumptions and approximations. Not only is information about the exact nature of work often incomplete, but, as noted below, increasingly arbitrary classification is necessary. In general I have double-counted not only those who changed careers but many with a double vocation, such as medical missionaries, missionary teachers, professors of medicine. I have made some arbitrary assumptions about the nature of overseas

Table III Numbers of those first graduating 1926–55 who worked overseas.

Degree of MA:	292 men and 340 women	
MB ChB:	384 men and 82 women	
BSc (all types):	391 men and 40 women	
incl Agriculture	66 men	out of 259 = 25.5%
Forestry	69 men	out of 166 = 41.5%
Engineering	101 men	out of 407 = 24.8%
BCom	10 men and 3 women	out of 61 = 21.3%
BD	14 men and 1 woman	
EdB	10 men and 1 woman	
Law degrees	31 men	
Higher degrees		
MEd	2 men and 1 woman	
MSc	1 man	
MD/CM	24 men and 3 women	
PhD	66 men and 14 women	
DSc	13 men	
DLitt	1 man	

careers, notably that medical graduates who simply recorded an overseas address usually engaged in some form of practice. A sample of Class Records confirms that this was indeed frequently the case. I do not however make this assumption in the case of women who went abroad on marriage and did not record their own careers.

I exclude military service in the two World Wars, and National Service after 1945, except in a few cases of appointments which clearly carried important civil responsibilities. I do, however, include in regional totals short periods of service in nineteenth-century colonial campaigns. Thirty-six graduates recorded service in the South African War of 1899–1902; 15 of these had other overseas experience; the remaining 21 are included in the general military total. I also include in military totals medical graduates who recorded in the *Roll* service as a ship's doctor, though others may have spent a year or two in this way before buying a practice.

III Regional analysis

For this purpose I have classified the regions of the world where graduates were employed as follows:

Table IV Careers of Aberdeen graduates 1860–1900 serving overseas.

Medicine (practice, missions, company employment)	401
Medicine (IMS, Colonial, or other government service)	262
Church & mission work	191
Education (including one woman)	184
Military (incl. 147 medics: 86 Army, 51 Navy, 10 ships' doctors	172
Government, Administration and Politics	70
Business and Engineering	39
Agriculture	32
Scientists	18
Other: (including 3 women going overseas on marriage.)	9

Table V Overseas careers of men & women graduates 1901–25 and 1926–55.

	1901–25		*1926–55*	
Medical practice &c	159 men &	27 women	234 men &	63 women
Medical services	134	10	92	10
Church & mission	65	23	53	31
Education	145	84	215	220
Military	92	1 [78 medic]	79	5 [58 medic]
Government &c	48	5	71	19
Business	75	1	201	11
Agriculture	75	2	65	1
Forestry	12	–	63	–
Science	44	5	101	25
Law	12	–	19	–
Library, Trans, Sec &c	1	6	5	24
Married, unknown	7	105	12	80

Notes

'Science' represent a relatively modern career designation; 12 of the 18 so identified in Table I graduated in the 1890s. Later there is more difficulty in deciding how scientific specialists should be classified. I have tended to class a plant pathologist working for a colonial Agriculture department under 'Agriculture', a geologist employed by an oil company as 'Business'. But there is a little double-counting.

A comparable difficulty in drawing distinctions leads me to classify Engineers as 'Business', even if they were working for government Public Works Departments. Before Aberdeen established its chair of engineering in 1924, this is a minor problem; in Table I only 8 of the 33 shown under 'Business' can be regarded as engineers. Journalists, of whom there was a significant sprinkling in each period, are also classified as 'Business'.

The degree of BL was not conferred in Aberdeen until 1895; but a few arts graduates obtained qualifications elsewhere and practised abroad. In Table IV they have been classified with 'Government'.

Figures for education include graduates who worked abroad on exchange programmes for periods of at least one year; but not the overseas residence requisite for students of modern languages. But the data do not permit complete consistency.

IND: India, Pakistan, Burma
CEY: Ceylon
AS: Rest of Asia
[ME: Middle East; included in Asian totals]
AUS: Australia, with Papua, Fiji, and Pacific Islands
NZ: New Zealand
SAF: Union of South Africa, Zimbabwe, Botswana, Lesotho, Swaziland, Namibia
AFR: The rest of Africa, including Mauritius and islands, Aden
BNA: Canada, including Newfoundland
USA: USA
EUR: Continental Europe: including Polar exploration
BWI: British West Indies, Guyana, Belize, Bahamas, Bermuda
LAM: Rest of American continent, including Falklands

I have re-classified the data of the *Rolls* to indicate changes in areas of work according to the following historical periods: 1860–80; 1881–1900; 1901–1920; 1921–45; 1946–55. It must be remembered that these are dates of first graduation in Aberdeen, not of emigration. This analysis is further developed in Chapter 3.

I have double-counted those who worked in more than one region. However, after 1945 careers tended to become more mobile; engineers, scientists and consultants,

216

Table VI Numbers of graduates employed in overseas areas (Women shown in brackets).

	1860–80 [490]	1881–1990 [674]	1901–20 [712]	1921–45 [984]	1946–55 [879]
IND	132	113 [2]	162 [32]	117 [33]	21 [8]
CEY	24	25	16 [6]	14 [5]	3
AS	43	59	94 [13]	149 [36]	91 [22]
[ME	3	6	19	32	24]
AUS	88	96	59 [13]	70 [12]	82 [17]
NZ	39	43	25 [9]	36 [15]	33 [18]
SAF	59	143 [1]	109 [19]	98 [23]	59 [15]
AFR	18	56	88 [13]	213 [63]	207 [38]
BNA	23	50 [1]	74 [28]	110 [50]	188 [54]
USA	26	23	36 [15]	47 [9]	71 [25]
EUR	16	20	28 [10]	63 [36]	61 [29]
BWI	13	29	9 [2]	47 [5]	48 [13]
LAM	10	17	12 [6]	30 [11]	18 [3]

Table VII Proportion of overseas careers in different regions.

	1860–80	1881–1900	1901–20	1921–45	1946–55
IND + CEY	31.8%	20.5%	25.1%	13.2%	2.7%
AS	8.8%	8.8%	13.2%	14.8%	10.3%
AUS + NZ	25.9%	20.5%	11.8%	10.7%	13%
SAF	12.2%	21.2%	15.3%	10%	6.8%
AFR	3.7%	8.3%	12.4%	21.3%	23.5%
BNA + USA	10%	10.8%	15.4%	15.7%	29.4%
EUR	3.2%	3.0%	4%	6.3%	7%
BWI + LAM (other American)	4.5%	6.8%	2.8%	7.7%	7%

and even colonial officials, might have significant experience in many different areas. In these cases I have recorded only those areas which seem to have been most important.

Table VI shows the number of persons working in each region in each period. The number of women included is shown in brackets. Military service is included only when it involved a significant appointment in one specific region.

Table VII, grouping together certain of the regional figures, shows these totals in proportion to the total number of overseas careers recorded (which is of course greater than the total of persons involved). This table forms the basis of the accompanying histogram.

IV A note on non-graduating alumni

The overseas careers of those members of nineteenth-century arts classes who for any reason failed to graduate in the University of Aberdeen seem to have followed different patterns. During this period students entering the university together felt

PROPORTIONS OF ABERDEEN GRADUATES
FOLLOWING CAREERS IN DIFFERENT REGIONS

	1860-1880	1881-1900	1901-1920	1921-1945	1946-1966
	AM 4.5%	AM 6.8%	AM 2.8%	AM 7.7%	AM 7%
	EU 3.2%	EU 3.3%	EU 4%	EU 6.3%	EU 7%
	AF 3.7%	AF 8.4%	AF 12.4%	AF 21.3%	AF 23.5%
	SA 12.2%	SA 21.2%	SA 15.3%	SA 10%	SA 6.8%
	NA 10%	NA 10.8%	NA 15.4%	NA 15.7%	NA 29.4%
	AU 25.9%	AU 20.5%	AU 11.8%	AU 10.7%	AU 13%
	AS 8.8%	AS 8.7%	AS 13.2%	AS 14.8%	AS 10.3%
	IC 31.8%	IC 20.5%	IC 25.1%	IC 13.2%	IC 2.7%
TOTALS:	490	674	712	994	880

KEY: AM America (except Canada and the USA)   NA Canada and the USA
EU Europe   AU Australasia
AF Africa (except South Africa)   AS Other parts of Asia
SA South Africa (with Southern Rhodesia)   IC India and Ceylon

Table VIII

Class	Total	Ab. Grad	Gr/Os	Non-G	Non-G/Os	HE
1865–69	113	46	11	67	26	[8]
1866–70	134*	63	20	66	24	[11]
1870–74	137	75	19	62	29	[12]
1872–76	140	83	26	57	19	[7]
1880–84	148	97	18	51	11	[5]
1881–85	156*	97	26	59	20	[7]
TOTALS	825	466	110	362	129	[50]

* Adjusted for 3 persons also included in previous year's Record.

strong corporate solidarity, and they often maintained it by periodic reunions and the preparation of records of individual careers.[5] As a sample, I have examined six of the most thoroughly kept 'Class Records' of the period 1865–85. These show that 362 out of 828 students failed to graduate in Aberdeen. About 50 of these, however, appear to have completed their higher education. Some graduated elsewhere, or took vocational courses in subjects like engineering; others, including some who had already passed the Indian Civil Service examination, simply failed to appear for examination, or to pay the graduation fee. These appear in the HE column of Table VIII, which shows the totals of Aberdeen graduates and of non-graduates in these classes and the numbers in each category who worked overseas.

The career patterns of the 129 persons who did not graduate in Aberdeen and so are not included in the *Rolls of Graduates* differ from those examined in Section II above.

Business 39	Agriculture 22	Education 21	Church 13
Engineering: 14	Govt & Law: 18	Medicine: 6	Military 4

Their regions of service, though broadly consistent with those of graduates, show a somewhat greater preference for Australasia and North America.

IND: 31	AUS: 27	SAF: 20	USA 20	NZ: 18	BNA: 17
BWI: 8	CEY: 7	AS: 4	AFR 4	EUR: 3	LAM: 1

After university education in Scotland was restructured by the Act of 1889 it became less usual for students in good standing not to graduate. Moreover as the arts classes became less homogeneous, class records were produced less regularly. Six exist between 1901 and 1909, but there are difficulties in comparing these with earlier examples. That for 1909–13 appears to include graduates only; that for 1901–5 explicitly excludes 36 who left before the end of the second year; that for 1906–10 gives names of 14 who attended for one or two years, but biographies for only three. Out of 761 students included in these class records, there is information on only 49 who did not graduate, and only 12 of these (as compared to 164 graduates) appear as working abroad.

219

13

THE GROWTH OF A SYSTEM

R. D. Anderson

Source: R. D. Anderson, *Universities and Elites in Britain since 1800*, London: Macmillan for the Economic History Society, 1992, pp. 12–28.

The notion of three phases of long-term development in higher education is a useful starting-point, provided that chronological subdivisions are also allowed for. The first phase may be seen as lasting until the 1870s, the second from then until the 1950s. The first phase was 'traditional', in that the demand for university education remained limited, but it also saw innovations: the foundation of modern rivals to Oxford and Cambridge, from around 1830, and the reform of the ancient universities themselves, which gathered speed from 1850. By the 1870s Oxford and Cambridge had been modernized and launched on a new career of success, and the foundation of 'civic' universities in English provincial cities led to rapid expansion of numbers. By 1889 the state was prepared to intervene with subsidies, and by 1914 there was something like a national university system. The Scottish universities, which had previously gone their own way, took large steps towards assimilation, and university education was founded in Wales. By 1914, too, deliberate if limited policies of equality of opportunity were being pursued. The First World War had significant effects on student numbers, but the inter-war period was one of stagnation, and it took another war to stimulate further expansion. This took off in the 1950s and 1960s, and inaugurated a third phase in which universities had to share their position with other institutions, and in which participation reached levels which pointed to, if they have not yet reached, the qualitative shift from élite to mass higher education.

Few countries have had universities as confined to the élite as England in 1800, and the new century was unlikely to leave Oxford and Cambridge untouched. While most European universities (including the Scottish ones) combined general education with vocational preparation for the professions or the bureaucracy. Oxford and Cambridge had turned their backs on professional education, and offered a narrow curriculum based on classics at

Oxford and mathematics at Cambridge. Their students were sons either of the aristocracy and gentry, for whom the university was a social finishing school as much as an intellectual experience, or of the clergy. So far as the universities had a vocational task, it was to supply the clergy of the Church of England, of which they were an integral part. There were religious tests which confined their benefits to anglicans, and most of the teachers were in clerical orders.

These features, and the heavy expense required by an aristocratic lifestyle based on residential colleges, made the universities largely irrelevant to the needs of the new middle classes, many of whom were nonconformist. There was a demand, if a limited one, for cheaper and more modern alternatives, and around 1830 this coincided with utilitarian attacks on Oxford and Cambridge as corrupt corporations misusing resources which ought to belong to the whole nation. If the English bourgeoisie had been stronger, they might have taken the universities over and reformed them in their own image to form a new, modern élite recruited on principles of talent and merit rather than birth and privilege, as happened in France after the revolution [145]. But in England the landed and anglican establishment was too powerful, and early attempts to open up Oxbridge failed. The alternative strategy was to found new colleges, and the first appeared as the 'University of London' in 1828. It was renamed University College London (UCL) in 1836, when a new University of London was founded to grant degrees to its students and those of King's College London, opened in 1831 as an anglican riposte.

UCL and Owens College Manchester, founded in 1851, are usually seen as the most significant developments of this period, both being non-denominational, and offering new subjects not available in the fossilized Oxbridge curricula. Manchester was, after all, the symbolic capital of the provincial, entrepreneurial, nonconformist middle class. However, while it is convenient to see nonconformity as a kind of ideological expression of capitalism, by no means all the rising bourgeoisie were nonconformist. The other new university of these years, Durham (1832), was anglican, as was Queen's College at Birmingham (1843), which as a later component of the University of Birmingham has as good a claim as Owens to pioneering status. In fact religion was a major source of cultural division in England, and tended to dominate debate on university questions. Anglicans refused to abandon the view that religious and secular education were inseparable, and that universities should be moral and religious as well as intellectual communities. Behind the stubborn defence of the privileges of Oxford and Cambridge lay the persisting ideal of a national élite with common values and experiences, which secularization would destroy.

The most striking feature of the new foundations was their limited success. Durham struggled to survive, and Owens College found no immediate imitators in other cities. The colleges found a niche in teaching new subjects like modern languages, science and economics, but attempts to set up general degree curricula found few takers. An Oxbridge degree had well-understood social advantages, but otherwise formal graduation had little career value, and university education remained ill-defined and not clearly distinguished from secondary schooling. Roman catholics, for example, satisfied their need for higher education through classes attached to secondary schools, and a catholic university founded in London in 1875 collapsed after a few years [79]. Even at Oxford, numbers were stagnant until the 1860s [142].

This weakness of demand contrasted with the economic dynamism of an industrializing Britain, suggesting that for most of the entrepreneurial class, industrialists or merchants, university education was simply irrelevant. In principle, there should have been more demand for professional training, as professional status came to depend on formal qualifications and examinations. But even here there were problems. Medicine led the way: medical schools were founded in London and leading provincial cities in the 1820s and 1830s, and the Act of 1858 which set up a medical register also created a unified system of medical education. Universities and degrees played an important part in this, but only alongside the royal colleges and other qualifying bodies. Other professions like law and engineering, while taking steps to raise their professional status, resisted moves towards academic exclusivism. Most of the new colleges set up courses in these subjects, but had to contend with a strong British prejudice in favour of learning through personal experience and apprenticeship to established practitioners [Engel in 63]. It was only in the 1850s that examinations began to multiply, and that pressure intensified on parents to invest in education to secure their sons' future [107].

That pressure was felt first in the schools. The deficiencies of secondary education had been another source of weakness for the new colleges. Oxford and Cambridge could draw on the ancient public schools, which kept boys until 18 and took classics to a high level. But the ancient network of grammar schools, teaching the classics to local boys and connected with the universities by scholarships, had for various reasons fallen into decay. The middle class instead used private schools, most of which concentrated on commercial and practical subjects, ending at 15 or 16. In London, both UCL and King's founded their own schools to act as feeders, but for the most part the new colleges had to take their students young and start at an elementary level: often students simply used them as staging-posts towards Oxford or Cambridge.

The best documented development in English secondary education is the reform and expansion of the public schools, following Thomas Arnold's work at Rugby. The growing middle class found the reformed schools to their taste, many new ones were founded, and the new model triumphed over possible alternatives. The grammar schools were revived after legislation in 1869, but this was too late to challenge the position of the public schools, and a true system of state secondary education had to await legislation in 1902. Public schools, as boarding institutions, were relatively expensive, but they offered a solid education to the professional and business élite, and pointed them naturally towards Oxford and Cambridge, whose links with the public schools became the foundation of their late Victorian prosperity. Thus although the middle classes did succeed in founding alternative university institutions, in secondary education there was a compromise which adapted the institutions of the old élite to new needs. Once the serious reform of Oxford and Cambridge began, the same compromise could be worked out there, and their opening to a new clientele satisfied a large part of the demand for higher education. Whether this represented a takeover of the old institutions by the middle class, or a takeover of the middle class by the old élite, is a question to which we shall return.

The reform of the old universities, accelerated by state intervention after 1850, has stimulated much scholarship. Interest has switched from the traditional constitutional and religious aspects [147] to the reform of the curriculum and the 'revolution of the dons' which produced a secular, professionalized teaching body [47; 139; 116; 23; 58; 40; 51]. Reform retained the college system, with teaching through tutorial methods rather than professorial lectures, but also remodelled the curriculum to admit modern subjects like history and science. Recent work has stressed that there were many changes even before 1850; but these had concentrated on developing a rigorous examination system, which encouraged the best students to compete for honours. This was perhaps originally designed as a means of social discipline, or to strengthen the aristocratic élite to meet the challenges of a revolutionary age [Rothblatt in 142; Stone in 98], but it soon became especially attractive to students with professional advantages in mind [22]. Here were the origins of the specialized degree, with classified honours, which remains characteristic of the British system. And with the reshaping of the ideal of 'liberal' education, university examinations assumed a new role as the guarantee of professional status.

The nineteenth century saw a notable debate (well covered by historians) on liberal education and on the most appropriate education for the social élite in a newly scientific and industrial world [123; 117; 44; Lyons in 98]. At first Oxbridge intellectuals responded to utilitarian attacks by expounding the unique virtues of classics or mathematics in forming the mind and character, a tradition given its finest expression in J. H. Newman's lectures of the 1850s which became *The Idea of a University*. Others in the 1860s and 1870s like John Stuart Mill, Lyon Playfair or Thomas Huxley, put forward a more comprehensive ideal in which science would take its rightful place. The most influential figure – or at least, the one generally regarded as symbolic – was Matthew Arnold, whose *Culture and Anarchy* (1869), though not directly concerned with universities, popularized the notion of general culture. For Arnold culture was chiefly literary, but one outcome of this debate was to detach the idea of liberal education from its previous association with the classics: now it could be embodied by any subject if taught in a 'liberal' way. This fitted in well with the specialized, single-subject degree and the research ideal, but it also encouraged a bias against the purely vocational.

The Arnoldian ideal was part of a characteristically Victorian complex which tied together liberal education, the concept of the 'gentleman', the public schools, the examination system, the professional and public service ethos, and preference for 'all-rounders' over specialists. A classic example was the competitive civil service examination, first suggested in the Northcote-Trevelyan report of 1853, and applied to most of the senior civil service in 1871. This was both a form of professionalization, substituting impartial selection methods for personal patronage, and a move towards meritocracy. But since the examinations were based on those of the universities, the effect was to open the civil service to the middle class, using liberal education as a social filter and a guarantee of gentlemanly character, rather than drawing talent from all social classes. At Oxford, Balliol College under Benjamin Jowett became renowned for producing an academic élite imbued with the ethic of public service. But although Jowett and others wished to widen the university's social base, this aspect of reform had limited success.

In universities as in public schools, the liberal ideal stressed the moral side of education, for which the socializing experience of residence was thought indispensable. Universities were to be communities, where the intangible benefits of character formation and the personal influence of teachers were as important as the lecture-room [117]. This pastoral concept of the university was not unchallenged – in 1858 London University threw its degrees open to any individual, regardless of institutional affiliation, thus defining university education simply as the mastery of a body of knowledge – but over the years it has profoundly marked the British tradition of higher education.

The university reforms can be interpreted as a conservative social strategy, against a background of growing democracy (the vote was extended to working men in 1867), state-supported popular education, and the decline of religion as an integrating force. The aim was to strengthen the influence of the educated classes, to form a 'clerisy' giving the nation intellectual and spiritual leadership. Once free from their exclusive connexion with anglicanism (the tests for students had been abolished in the 1850s), the universities were restored to a central position in national life, able to absorb and civilize the new bourgeoisie and blend it into a single élite [106; 58; 73; Rothblatt in 63]. Even if this programme was not fully achieved, it is especially significant for university history that the revival of the old universities took place before the expansion of the new ones really began, making it difficult for the latter to challenge their values, and attracting away the richer provincial élites.

Owens College was virtually refounded in 1870–1, and by 1881 it had been joined by university colleges (full university status often came considerably later) at Newcastle, Leeds, Sheffield, Birmingham, Liverpool, Nottingham and Bristol. Later additions, in less industrial towns, were Southampton. Reading and Exeter. Sometimes there were gifts or legacies from wealthy individuals, but in all cases it was local business and professional men who took the initiative and superintended development. Colleges often started with a strong practical emphasis related to local industry, but there were also roots in the long-established medical schools and in the 'extension' lectures by which the older universities, especially Cambridge, had sought to take liberal education to the provinces. By the 1900s the 'civic' or 'redbrick' colleges were offering a wide range of subjects, and more of their students were taking full courses leading to degrees – in the early years, there had been much work at a lower level, and much part-time study in evening classes. This standardization of the pattern was partly to meet the conditions laid down by the state for awarding grants or the prized royal charters which gave degree-granting powers.

The state played a more active role in university development than is often recognized. Annual grants to university colleges began in 1889, and legislation of the same period on technical education gave elected local authorities an active role. Sometimes their funds went into direct support of the local college – Nottingham was founded and directly controlled by the city council: more often, they built up technical colleges which had some work of degree standard, and which entered into cooperative relationships with the university – at Manchester, for example, the municipal technical college became its Faculty of Technology. By 1914 colleges on the grant list got about a third of their income from the state, and another 15 per cent from local authorities.

Universities also profited from the organization of state secondary education after 1902. New or reorganized grammar schools were strongly oriented towards academic subjects and university entrance: senior pupils worked for university 'matriculation' examinations (coordinated from 1917 as the School Certificate), and Oxbridge scholarships were their blue riband. The policies of Robert Morant (the civil servant at the head of the Board of Education) have been much criticized for stifling practical alternatives and relegating technology to an inferior role, but they reflected the view (also found in the contemporary adult education movement) that extending opportunity to the working class meant a right to share in liberal education of the highest form. From 1907 the introduction of 'free places' ensured that scholarship children from elementary schools sat in the grammar schools alongside middle-class children whose parents paid fees. But it was significant for the future, and a point which distinguished Britain from other countries, that the machinery of state-sponsored opportunity was developed within a second-rank system, rather than by opening up the public schools which gave direct access to the élite.

Training graduate teachers for secondary schools became a large part of the work of arts and science faculties. Universities also acquired a share in training elementary teachers. Training colleges, mostly run by the churches, went back to the early nineteenth century, and were always an important channel of social mobility. From 1890 universities were allowed to set up their own 'day training colleges', which brought an influx of working-class students financed by the state. Later developments allowed them to graduate before starting the professional part of the course.

Schoolteaching was the main occupation chosen by women students, whose admission to universities was another feature of the period after 1870. Academic secondary schools for girls, with the same curriculum as for boys, began to develop in the 1850s [26]. The universities helped by opening their 'local' examinations for school-leavers to girls, and by the late 1860s many towns had lectures of university level for women. The pressure for admission to proper university study was reinforced by the campaign for women's medical education, and achieved success, in the 1870s. The new university colleges were open to women from the start, and London University degrees from 1878. At Oxford and Cambridge, the collegiate system made it relatively easy to found women's colleges, though numbers were small and equal academic status was denied for many years. In London, UCL opened to women on equal terms, but there were also women's colleges, including 'King's College for Women' on a separate site from the original college. By 1900, when girls' secondary schools were everywhere a normal part of middle-class life, women university students had also consolidated their position, though their numbers were limited by the scarcity of outlets. Training in social work and in domestic subjects (a speciality of King's College for Women) were curricular innovations which sought to respond to women's needs.

Why had the state taken a new interest in universities? One reason was growing international economic and great-power competition, especially from Germany; education was identified as a field where Britain was falling behind. This mood intensified after the Boer war of 1899–1902, and was expressed in the 'national efficiency' movement, which looked to vigorous state action to exploit Britain's human resources. This included the more efficient discovery and selection of merit, and the free places of 1907 were part of a deliberate Liberal policy of extending educational opportunity. Sanderson has emphasized that 'this brief period of the 1900s was of profound significance in the development of access to education' [125, *25*].

According to Sidney Webb, 'nothing is more calculated to promote National Efficiency, than a large policy of Government aid to the highest technical colleges and universities' [cited in 48, *182*]. Sidney and Beatrice Webb founded the London School of Economics in 1895 to apply scientific principles to business and public administration, and they were not the only political figures active on the educational scene. Others were Joseph Chamberlain, patron of Birmingham University, and Richard Haldane, who was involved in many enterprises, including a major reorganization of

London University in 1898, and the foundation of Imperial College London (1907), which amalgamated several existing science colleges and was Britain's answer to the German 'technical high schools' [19].

Between 1870 and 1914, and especially after 1889, English universities not only expanded, but came to form a system with common ideals and standards, to which other British universities were increasingly assimilated. There were various pressures behind this: the common requirements of the professions and public services, the prestige of the internationally-accepted research ideal, the development of an academic profession which circulated freely throughout the system [54]. But not least there was the Oxbridge model, and it is widely accepted that the original dynamism and distinctiveness of the civic universities gave way to imitation – according to Jarausch, they 'altered their entire mission from higher technical training towards the traditional university function' [63, *19*].

The fullest account of this, within the framework of 'systematization', is by Roy Lowe. He argues that the system became hierarchical, with Oxford, Cambridge and London at the top, the civic universities second, and (looking at higher education as a whole) technical and teacher training colleges as a third layer. By shedding their part-time and non-degree work, the civics were as anxious to distinguish themselves from the layer below as they were to adopt the university model. The outcome was that they gave the same sort of education as the élite universities, but with less prestige and for a local rather than a national clientele. Thus there emerged 'an educational system which by the time of the First World War had become segmented at various levels, the better to serve the needs of a differentiated society'. While Oxbridge remained aloof and protected from change, at the second level there was 'a reversion from the modernism of the late nineteenth century towards a more prestigious "humane" education' [Lowe in 92, *177*; cf. Halsey in 53; 54; 105; Lowe and Rothblatt in 63]. The common tendency of institutions founded for practical or specialist purposes to abandon them for activities of higher prestige has been called the 'generalist shift' by Ringer, 'academic drift' by others.

This view of Oxbridge dominance is so familiar as hardly to need stressing. British cultural history is often told in terms of university cliques and influences [15], and since so many of the political, literary and artistic élite were educated at Oxford or Cambridge, they figure in countless memoirs, biographies and novels – including novels of university life which, so argues Ian Carter [29], have further reinforced the image of the ancient universities and endorsed their conservative values. In other universities, professors recruited from Oxbridge brought their ideals and prejudices with them, and subjects like classics or history, developed as part of the education of a governing class [132; 133; 136; 137; 138], were taught in the same way to prospective schoolteachers. Civic universities began to develop halls of residence and tutorial systems, university histories celebrated the triumphant

227

Table 1 Student numbers, 1861–1901.

	1861	1871	1881	1891	1901
Oxford and Cambridge					
No.	2400	3690	4710	5100	5880
per cent increase		54	28	8	15
Other English					
No.	985	1840	5963	10913	11959
per cent increase		87	224	83	10
England					
No.	3385	5530	10673	16013	17839
Per 1000 population	0.2	0.2	0.4	0.6	0.5
Scotland					
No.	3399	3984	6595	6604	6254
per cent increase		17	66	0	−19
Per 1000 population	1.1	1.2	1.8	1.6	1.4

Sources: [63, 45; 9, 467].

march to chartered status, and student life took on new corporate forms inspired by the collegiate ideal [11]. Yet the capitulation to Oxbridge values can be exaggerated, and there are counter-arguments which will be examined in Chapter 3.

By 1900, Oxbridge accounted for only a third of English students. This is shown in Table 1, which compares statistics compiled by Lowe for England (many of them estimates) with those for Scotland. The table shows the percentage increase in each decade, and the number of students per 1000 total population, a crude but useful means of comparison. Once population growth is allowed for there was little real expansion in Scotland, which already had some 2850 students in 1800 (1.8 per 1000), at a time when Oxford and Cambridge together had about 1150. Within the existing assumptions about the social function of university education, Scotland reached the limits of expansion early and could not go beyond them; the figures thus cast doubt on the notion of 'seismic' growth resulting from industrialization. In England, there was plenty of leeway to catch up, but once this happened the pace fell off. The most dynamic decade in both countries was the 1870s, which suggests that this was the period when graduation became accepted as a standard professional aspiration.

Table 2 shows student numbers after 1900. There was significant growth before the First World War, and a leap in numbers after it. Enrolments remained on the new plateau, but then stagnated or declined. The 1930s were a difficult decade for universities, especially since the depression and the cuts in public expenditure after 1931 made schoolteaching an unattractive career. This particularly affected the recruitment of women: the percentage

Table 2 Student numbers, 1900–1938.

	1900	*1910*	*1920*	*1930*	*1938*
England					
No.	13845	19617	33868	33808	37189
per cent women	15	18	23	25	22
Wales					
No.	1253	1375	2838	2868	2779
per cent women	38	35	28	33	27
Scotland					
No.	5151	6736	11746	11150	10034
per cent women	14	24	26	32	27
Great Britain					
No.	20249	27728	48452	47826	50002
per cent women	16	20	24	27	23

Source: University Grants Committee reports.

of women students reached a peak at the end of the 1920s, but then declined, and remained stuck at 23–24 per cent until the 1960s. For recent periods, it is also possible to calculate the 'age participation ratio' (APR), the proportion of the age-group which attended university. This was about 0.8 per cent for Great Britain in the 1900s (and thus perhaps 1.5 per cent in Scotland), 1.5 per cent in 1924, and 1.7 per cent in 1938 (1.5 per cent in England and Wales, 3.1 per cent in Scotland). If other forms of higher education were included, the 1938 figure would be 2.7 per cent, but university education remained very much a minority experience [109, *16*; 105, *229–30*].

The two world wars are usually seen as catalysts for social change, but their effects on higher education were not the same. The First World War followed a period of active expansion, and reconstruction plans were based on the pre-war policies of the Liberal government [128]. The dynamism of the pre-war period was carried over into the 1920s, but then petered out. In 1939, by contrast, higher education was stagnant: the war itself seems to have created a new mood of social expectation, and post-war policies led into a continually rising curve of growth.

The 1918 Education Act (like that of 1944) was not directly concerned with universities, but the war was followed by significant changes. In 1919 the University Grants Committee (UGC) was created to unify administration of grants in England, Wales and Scotland, and introduced an element of central planning: Oxford and Cambridge were now brought into the grant system. New university colleges were founded at Leicester and Hull. Local authority scholarships multiplied, and a limited number of national state scholarships was introduced. Subjects like modern languages, engineering, science and commerce expanded, and the idea of universities leading to business careers gained ground. But their fundamental association with the professions remained, and if there was a new influx of scholarship students it hardly changed the social atmosphere. Oxford and Cambridge retained their upper-class image and their bond with the public schools. In retrospect, it may seem that investment in higher education, especially in science and technology, would have prepared Britain for recovery from the depression. But neither contemporary governments nor the cautious-minded UGC thought in such terms [16].

The experience of the Second World War, however, gave new prestige to science and planning, and reconstruction plans accepted that university numbers would have to expand by at least 50 per cent. There was also a new emphasis on equality of opportunity, as part of the post-war 'welfare state' settlement which aimed to break down class divisions and extend the social rights of citizenship. The English Act of 1944 abolished fees in secondary schools (this had been done in Scotland in 1918), and introduced 'secondary education for all'. But this was to follow the 'tripartite' organization of grammar, technical and modern schools, and only the grammar schools, recruited selectively through the '11+' examination and taking about a fifth of the age-group, led to universities. Nevertheless, systematic selection replaced the arbitrary scholarship 'ladder', and the expansion of qualified school-leavers stimulated by this reform created a wholly new demand for higher education.

Stress on technology was also characteristic of the post-war years, though opinion was divided on whether to put resources into universities or into building up selected technical colleges. Ten of the latter were eventually designated as Colleges of Advanced Technology (CATs), and in the 1960s these were given full university status, along with two Scottish equivalents. But there were also new foundations devoted to the liberal ideal. North Staffordshire (later Keele) was an experimental university founded in 1949, and in the 1950s plans were laid for a series of 'green field' sites. Sussex opened first in 1961, and was followed by York, East Anglia, Essex, Lancaster, Kent and Warwick. These residential (in some cases collegiate) universities were a striking triumph of the pastoral ideal. They would hardly have been possible without another significant development, the introduction of uniform, 'mandatory' student grants in 1962, following the Anderson report. Any school-leaver accepted for a place now had a right to have living expenses away from home paid as well as fees. This broke the link between civic universities and their localities, and with the creation of a unified admissions procedure turned British universities for the first time into a single system with national recruitment.

All this preceded the Robbins report (1963), which 'could do little more than legitimise what by then had become inevitable' [77, *172*]. Its significance lay partly in its proclamation of the 'Robbins principle' ('courses of higher education should be available for all those who are qualified by ability and attainment to pursue them and who wish to do so' [109, *8*]), partly in its statistical work, which seemed to make the case for expansion irrefutable, and partly in looking at 'higher education' as a whole. The report aroused a remarkable degree of political support, and provides a prime example of the 'post-war consensus' on social reform (which did not extend to secondary education, where the selective grammar schools were now coming under attack). Successive governments, believing that higher education was a key to economic growth, found resources to meet the targets for expansion.

But Robbins's administrative proposals, for a unitary structure with universities in a coordinating role, found less favour. Instead the 1964 Labour government's 'binary' policy divided higher education between a university sector under the UGC and a 'public' sector consisting mainly of local authority colleges. There were no more new universities in England (though Scotland acquired one at Stirling), apart from the Open University, teaching adults by distance learning. Nevertheless, the Robbins period left Great Britain with over 50 universities – over 70 if the colleges of London University were counted separately. Within the public sector, there were many amalgamations, and colleges of education (as training colleges had been renamed) lost their specialized character. In England and Wales, some thirty larger colleges were developed as 'polytechnics'; in Scotland, the binary system took a different form, with the leading colleges under the direct control of the Scottish Education Department. In the 1990s, however, the dual structure in place since the 1960s was scheduled to disappear, with polytechnics gaining university status, and separate 'funding councils', covering the whole of higher education, for England, Wales and Scotland. All these arrangements (like most of the statistics below) excluded Northern Ireland, which had never come directly under the UGC, or under the scrutiny of Robbins; developments there followed similar lines, but the binary line broke down sooner when the polytechnic at Belfast was merged with the New University of Ulster founded at Coleraine in the 1960s.

In 1962 the Robbins committee found 216,000 full-time students in higher education in Great Britain; 118,000 in universities. 55,000 in teacher training, 43,000 in 'advanced further education' (technical colleges). Its projection of 558,000 places in 1980 was not quite met – there were to be 301,000 in universities and 223,000 in the public sector [56, *270, 275*]. But the public sector then expanded more rapidly, and by 1990 there were about 650,000 full-time students in the United Kingdom, 340,000 in universities, 310,000 in colleges: if part-time and Open University students were included, the total was nearly a million. The result of this expansion was that the university APR, still only 3.4 per cent in 1955 and 4 per cent in 1962, rose to about 8 per cent by the mid-1980s, when for higher education as a whole it was 14 per cent [56, *270*; 141, *278*].

Numerical expansion was accompanied by formal equalization of standards, as three or four year degrees replaced the diplomas or certificates to which much college work had formerly led. But in one respect the Robbins projections were not met: the demand for humanities and social science subjects proved stronger than for science and technology, where places fell well short of the targets. As Carswell has argued [28], this was partly because there was no corresponding reform of schools, partly because women accounted for a significant part of the Robbins expansion. In 1958, only 21 per cent of university students were women, but the proportion rose to 28 per cent in 1968, 38 per cent in 1980, and 40 per cent in 1984 [141, *279*]. By 1989 it was 44 per cent – still lower than in many comparable countries. The rise was due predominantly to wider changes in society, especially the increasing career opportunities for women in business and the professions: but there were also controlling factors within education itself, as Cunningham [33] has shown for Scotland, where a less segmented school system was one reason for consistently higher women's participation rates.

What was the historical significance of the post-war expansion? While scholarly inquiry has begun to tackle the inter-war period [130], for the years since 1945 it remains at the stage of provisional synthesis [77: 141]. Otherwise we are dependent on contemporary analyses, or the recollections and reflections of participants. The commonest theme has been the survival of the liberal ideal despite the move towards a mass system. The traditional model was endorsed by Robbins, and the academic ethos reigned supreme [14; 15; 127; 28]. The binary system protected the status of the universities, and can be seen as a further example of 'segmentation' reflecting social inequalities [77]. While in principle all higher education enjoyed parity of esteem, the diversion of new students into cheaper and less prestigious institutions allowed the universities, old and new, to retain such élite features as residence and the single-subject degree. The latter was indeed encouraged by the specialized Advanced Level examination introduced in the 1950s (though not in Scotland) to replace the broader-based School Certificate, and by a grant system which favoured the full-time student coming straight from school. Expansion thus changed the character of the universities less than the conservative authors of the educational 'Black Papers' in the early 1970s feared, or than some reformers hoped. Polytechnics and colleges had a different ethos which stressed vocational subjects, retained links with the local community, and welcomed part-time students. But even they (like the CATs before them) were tempted by 'academic drift' to expand into arts and pure science.

British development seemed to diverge in this period from that in other countries. In the 1900s or the 1930s, participation rates were not out of line with comparable countries, but in the 1950s Britain began to lag notice-ably behind, and this was one of the arguments for expansion used by Robbins [125]. By the 1980s, while British participation rates rose towards 20 per cent for all higher education, the western European norm was becoming 30–40 per cent, and it was higher still in America or Japan. Other

European countries generally retained open university entry for all who passed the qualifying school examinations, so that the democratization of secondary schooling brought huge increases, with consequent problems of overcrowding, impersonal teaching and high drop-out rates. But Britain chose a more expensive form of growth, with residential universities, mandatory grants, and intensive teaching supported by high staff-student ratios. This tied state funding to specific student numbers, and inhibited the transition to a true mass system. By the 1970s, strains were appearing, as the social pressures for university expansion continued but governments became less willing to provide the resources, The 1980s saw moves to replace grants with loans and attract private funding by making universities more responsive to market forces.

It is difficult to say whether alternative policies were seriously considered in the 1960s. It seems more likely that the traditional university model was simply taken for granted, as one more example of the London-Oxbridge axis in British life [129]. The ideals of the redbricks or the technical colleges failed to impose themselves on the debate, and in practical terms open entry would not have been compatible with the special position of Oxbridge and its collegiate system. Thus the weight of the past determined the direction of progress, and for the same reason it seems unlikely that the abolition of the binary division will remove the hierarchy of prestige and function which British higher education displays. Every country, indeed, has such hierarchies: but it is history which dictates the form they take.

Bibliography [edited]

[9] Anderson, R. D., 'Education and Society in Modern Scotland: a Comparative Perspective', *History of Education Quarterly*, XXV (1985).

[11] ——, *The Student Community at Aberdeen, 1860–1939* (Aberdeen, 1988).

[14] Annan, N., 'British Higher Education, 1960–80: a Personal Retrospect', *Minerva*, XX (1982).

[15] ——, *Our Age: Portrait of a Generation* (London, 1990).

[16] Argles, M., *South Kensington to Robbins: an Account of English Technical and Scientific Education since 1851* (London, 1964).

[19] Ashby, E. and Anderson, M., *Portrait of Haldane at Work on Education* (London, 1974).

[22] Becher, H. W., 'The Social Origins and Post-Graduate Careers of a Cambridge Intellectual Elite, 1830–1860', *Victorian Studies*, XXVIII (1984–5).

[23] Bill, E. G. W., *University Reform in Nineteenth-Century Oxford: a Study of Henry Halford Vaughan, 1811–1885* (Oxford, 1973).

[26] Bryant, M., *The Unexpected Revolution: a Study in the History of the Education of Women and Girls in the Nineteenth Century* (Windsor, 1979).

[28] Carswell, J., *Government and the Universities in Britain: Programme and Performance, 1960–1980* (Cambridge, 1985).

[29] Carter, I., *Ancient Cultures of Conceit: British University Fiction in the Post-War Years* (London, 1990).

[33] Cunningham, S., 'Women's Access to Higher Education in Scotland', *World Yearbook of Education 1984* (London, 1984).

[40] Engel, A. J., *From Clergyman to Don: the Rise of the Academic Profession in Nineteenth-Century Oxford* (Oxford, 1983).

[44] Garland, M. McM., *Cambridge Before Darwin: the Ideal of a Liberal Education, 1800–1860* (Cambridge, 1980).

[47] Green, V. H. H., *Oxford Common Room: a Study of Lincoln College and Mark Pattison* (London, 1957).

[48] ——, *British Institutions: the Universities* (Harmondsworth, 1969).

[51] Haig, A. G. L., 'The Church, the Universities and Learning in Later Victorian England', *Historical Journal*, XXIX (1986).

[53] Halsey, A. H., Floud, J. and Anderson, C. A., *Education, Economy and Society: a Reader in the Sociology of Education* (London, 1961).

[54] Halsey, A. H. and Trow, M. A., *The British Academics* (London, 1971).

[56] Halsey, A. H. (ed.), *British Social Trends since 1900: a Guide to the Changing Social Structure of Britain* (London, 1988).

[58] Harvie, C., *The Lights of Liberalism: University Liberals and the Challenge of Democracy, 1860–86* (London, 1976).

[63] Jarausch, K. H. (ed.), *The Transformation of Higher Learning, 1860–1930: Expansion, Diversification, Social Opening and Professionalization in England, Germany, Russia and the United States* (Chicago, 1983). [essays on England by R. Lowe, S. Rothblatt, H. Perkin, A. Engel]

[73] Knights, B., *The Idea of the Clerisy in the Nineteenth Century* (Cambridge, 1978).

[77] Lowe, R., *Education in the Post-War Years: a Social History* (London, 1988).

[79] McClelland, V. A., *English Roman Catholics and Higher Education, 1830–1903* (Oxford, 1973).

[92] Müller, D. K., Ringer, F. and Simon, B. (eds), *The Rise of the Modern Educational System: Structural Change and Social Reproduction, 1870–1920* (Cambridge, 1987). [essays on general themes by Müller, Ringer; on English higher education by Simon, R. Lowe]

[98] Phillipson, N. (ed.), *Universities, Society and the Future* (Edinburgh, 1983).

[105] Ringer, F. K., *Education and Society in Modern Europe* (London, 1979).

[106] Roach, J. P. C., 'Victorian Universities and the National Intelligentsia', *Victorian Studies*, III (1959–60).

[107] ——, *Public Examinations in England, 1850–1900* (Cambridge, 1971).

[109] [Robbins Report], *Higher Education: Report of the Committee Appointed by the Prime Minister under the Chairmanship of Lord Robbins, 1961–63* (Report and 5 Appendices, London, 1963).

[116] Rothblatt, S., *The Revolution of the Dons: Cambridge and Society in Victorian England* (London, 1968).

[117] ——, *Tradition and Change in English Liberal Education: an Essay in History and Culture* (London, 1976).

[123] Sanderson, M., *The Universities in the Nineteenth Century* (London, 1975). [a selection of source material with commentary]

[125] ——, *Educational Opportunity and Social Change in England* (London, 1987).

[127] Scott, P., *The Crisis of the University* (London, 1984).

[128] Sherington, G., *English Education, Social Change and War, 1911–20* (Manchester, 1981).

[129] Shils, E., 'The Intellectuals. I: Great Britain', *Encounter*, IV (1955).

[130] Shinn, C. H., *Paying the Piper: the Development of the University Grants Committee, 1919–46* (Lewes, 1986).

[132] Slee, P. R. H., *Learning and a Liberal Education: the Study of Modern History in the Universities of Oxford, Cambridge and Manchester, 1800–1914* (Manchester, 1986).

[133] ——, 'Professor Soffer's "History at Oxford" ', *Historical Journal*, XXX (1987).

[136] Soffer, R., 'The Modern University and National Values, 1850–1930', *Historical Research*, LX (1987).

[137] ——, 'Nation, Duty, Character and Confidence: History at Oxford, 1850–1914', *Historical Journal*, XXX (1987).

[138] ——, 'The Development of Disciplines in the Modern English University', *Historical Journal*, XXXI (1988).

[139] Sparrow, J., *Mark Pattison and the Idea of a University* (Cambridge, 1967).

[141] Stewart, W. A. C., *Higher Education in Postwar Britain* (London, 1989).

[142] Stone, L. (ed.), *The University in Society. Volume I: Oxford and Cambridge from the 14th to the Early 19th Century* (Princeton, 1975).

[145] Vaughan, M. and Archer, M. S., *Social Conflict and Educational Change in England and France, 1789–1848* (Cambridge, 1971).

[147] Ward, W. R., *Victorian Oxford* (London, 1965).

235

14

DEVELOPMENT IN HIGHER EDUCATION IN THE UNITED KINGDOM

Nineteenth and twentieth centuries

Asa Briggs

Source: W. R. Niblett (ed.) *Higher Education: Demand and Response*, London: Tavistock, 1969, pp. 95–116.

I

It is only during the course of the last few years that it has become possible to talk meaningfully – if, even then, somewhat uncertainly – about a 'system' of higher education in Britain. 'There can be no serious doubt', one writer put it in 1944, 'that there is a great need to rethink and replan our university system, if it may be called a system';[1] and although the first pages of the Robbins Report on *Higher Education* (1963) refer specifically to 'a system of higher education,' the Report states flatly that

> even today it would be a misnomer to speak of a system of higher education in this country, if by system is meant a consciously co-ordinated organization. . . . Higher education has not been planned as a whole or developed within a framework consciously devised to promote harmonious evolution. What system there is has come about as the result of a series of particular initiatives, concerned with particular needs and situations, and there is no way of dealing conveniently with all the problems common to higher education as a whole.[2]

Most changes in British history have to be explained in this way, although attention has recently been paid – rightly – not only to 'particular initiatives', separated in time, but to cumulative and self-generating processes

236

within the history of administration itself. In the history of British universities since the early nineteenth century, it is necessary to separate out four related aspects of history – first, changes within the universities themselves, mainly though not solely the product of inner forces, some intellectual, some organizational; second, changes within society affecting the demand for university places; third, changes within society affecting attitudes to universities and ideas about universities; and, fourth, changes in the pattern of resources, institutional and governmental, upon which universities can draw.

Each aspect of history can be treated separately, and each aspect has its own complexity. Thus, for example, it is not always easy in examining the internal history of universities to plot the relationship between intellectual changes and organizational changes. The key to understanding, in my view, is to examine the succession and interplay of generations and the modes of intellectual and social transmission as yesterday's students become today's teachers and administrators. Likewise, a study of the demand for university places leads at the same time to a study of other educational institutions – schools in particular – and to a study of professions and graduate occupations. The number of related variables is immense. At the same time, generalization is not easy in Britain because of the diversity within the pattern. Oxford and Cambridge for centuries prided themselves on their differences rather than on their similarities: within each of them different colleges emphasized their own identity. One of them, indeed, Balliol, very different from the rest, made the bold claim on one occasion that 'if we had a little more money we could absorb the University'.[3] The world of 'Redbrick', superficially much the same everywhere, reveals, on a closer examination, at least as much variation, and variation of more than style. British cities in the nineteenth century, out of which Redbrick institutions emerged, were strikingly different from each other in social structure and in cultural drive;[4] and although during the twentieth century there have been many tendencies making for increasing standardization, even the most casual visitor to the universities of Nottingham and Leicester, for instance, is struck with the differences between them.

This paper inevitably simplifies, therefore, and the most that it can hope to do is first to set in perspective some current preoccupations, including those concerned with the sense of a university 'system', and second to show that the study of a selected number of earlier episodes in university history in England may be as illuminating as a study of what is happening here and now. It was Lord Acton who suggested that the study of history not only should ensure that we should understand our own times better, but should deliver us from thraldom to them. The paper is concerned almost exclusively with England, not with Britain, since the Scottish tradition in education, that of what has been called 'the democratic intellect', is different from that of England. Even though persistent efforts were made during the nineteenth century to narrow the differences and to assimilate the Scottish tradition with its European background within the English tradition, it emerged, if not unscathed, at least not destroyed.[5] In its turn the Scottish tradition has influenced, usually obliquely, some features of twentieth-century English university history.

II

Any simple narrative account of the development of English universities during the nineteenth and twentieth centuries – and not only is there no adequate simple narrative account in existence but most general histories of England during this period include few references to them – would probably concentrate on a number of episodes widely separated in time, 'the particular initiatives' mentioned in the Robbins Report. Among them, the first of the landmarks that stand out, is the founding of University College London in 1826, 'the radical, infidel college' which broke the centuries-old duopoly, reinforced by religious tests, of Oxford and Cambridge and provided for the first time in British history the country's capital city with the beginnings, in 1836, of what was to become by British standards a quite exceptionally large and complicated university. Henry Brougham, who was one of the most active of the founders, believed not in one new university, but in several – to make higher education more accessible, or, in his own characteristic words, 'come-at-able by the middle classes of society'.[6] He did not secure that extension of his purpose in 1826. It was not until later in the nineteenth century that the newly-chartered civic universities – the term was coined by R. B. Haldane – came into existence, the origins of which can be traced back to the founding of Owen's College in Manchester in 1851, the year of the Great Exhibition. Leaving in the background Durham, of clerical foundation, each of these ventures was an initiative of private enterprise – and the grants of charters (the Victoria University, Manchester, led the way in 1880) followed sustained local pressure on the Privy Council. The ideal behind the nineteenth-century civic university was unmistakably Victorian, and, like the ideal of the Victorian city itself, it was best expressed by Joseph Chamberlain. 'To place a university in the middle of a great industrial and manufacturing population', he proclaimed at the first meeting of the Court of Mason University College, Birmingham in 1898, 'is to do something to leaven the whole mass with higher aims and higher intellectual ambitions than would otherwise be possible to people engaged entirely in trading and commercial pursuits.'[7] Ideal and reality were thus placed in uneasy relationship to each other.

Nine years before this declaration, however, the government had taken what in retrospect seems to be just as important a step as the local sponsors of new university institutions had taken in Manchester, Birmingham, Liverpool, and Leeds. The Salisbury Government decided in 1889 to distribute

£15,000 per annum from Treasury funds to the civic universities and appointed a committee to advise on the disbursement of the grant; Manchester received, incidentally, £1,800 from it. In 1904 the total grant, which then stood at £27,000, was doubled, again by a Conservative government. Once the decision to make such government grants was taken there could be no going back.

In 1919, when the University Grants Committee was formally established, Oxford and Cambridge for the first time accepted grants. The task of the new UGC, which included a majority of academics and was made directly responsible no longer to the Board of Education but to the Treasury, was that of 'enquiring into the financial needs of university education in the United Kingdom and advising the Government as to the application of any grants that may be made by Parliament towards meeting them.' From 1915 onwards, four years before the setting up of the UGC, there were other government grants which extended the range of public provision, for in the heat of the First World War it had been decided – Haldane was involved behind the scenes in the making of this decision also – to set up the Department of Industrial and Scientific Research (DSIR) with an initial grant of £25,000.[8] The same man, Sir William McCormick, was part-time Chairman both of the new UGC and of DSIR: already since 1909 he had been chairman of the committee advising the Board of Education on the distribution of university grants, a committee which on the eve of the First World War was already visiting English universities and meeting, incidentally, with resentment from some of them concerning its modes of inspection.[9]

The next landmark in the story was 1935, when Sir Walter Moberly, former Vice-Chancellor at Manchester University, became full-time Chairman: he was to stay in the post until 1949, spanning the Second World War. By then Parliament was granting slightly over £2 million each year to the universities, a figure which remained more or less the same throughout the inter-war years and during the Second World War, when there were never more than 50,000 full-time university students in the country. In 1945, after a further burst of pressure for university expansion during the war – as one expression of a greater pressure for post-war social reconstruction[10] – the recurrent grant was greatly increased until it reached £6.9 million in 1946–7. The UGC itself hailed the increase as 'initiating a new era' in the financial relations between the university and the State.[11]

It is interesting to note how, in 1947, the UGC went on to express the relationship between what was happening in the universities and what was happening in society. 'The contributions which the universities were able to make in many fields of war-time activity won for them a new prestige and a place in the national esteem which it will be their ambition to retain in the period of reconstruction which has just now begun. Within the academic sphere itself, the intermingling of institutions of contrasting types brought advantages which went some way to counterbalance the inconveniences of evacuation.'[12] The UGC was encouraged in its plans for expansion not only by the record of the immediate past but by projections of the future, which began to play an increasingly important part in university history, and particularly by the recommendations of the Barlow Committee, which had been appointed in December 1945 to examine problems of scientific manpower and its use. This Committee reported the willingness of the civic universities to increase their numbers by 86 per cent in ten years – it described this figure as 'an appreciable underestimate of what could be done'[13] – and while stating firmly that it was in the national interest to double the output of graduates in science and technology, it also – and this was important – urged an increase in the number of graduates in arts and social studies. The UGC referred to the Barlow Report as giving 'authoritative expression . . . to the demand for university expansion'[14] and set a target of 90,000 students in 1948–9. It asked all universities in the light of this recommendation to revise their estimates of possible expansion ignoring financial considerations, and consequently produced a revised total of 88,000. It admitted that 'these recommendations involve changes at the universities which can only be described as revolutionary'.[15]

It should be clear even from this very brief history of landmarks that by 1947 the UGC had already changed its role from a distributor of money to an agent of planning, even though the planning was of the simplest kind, depending on collecting estimates from universities and comparing them with 'targets' set out in official papers. In fact, the doubling of numbers of students in science and technology was reached in two years rather than in the ten years envisaged by the Barlow Committee. The problem of the divergence between projection and accomplishment – the accomplishment being determined by hundreds of 'micro'-decisions in particular universities – was henceforth to become of major importance in university history. The UGC, not surprisingly, had its terms of reference widened in 1946 to read 'to inquire into the financial needs of university education in Britain; to advise the Government as to the application of any grants made by Parliament towards meeting them; to collect, examine and make available information on matters relating to university education at home and abroad; and to assist, in consultation with the universities and other bodies concerned, the preparation and execution of such plans for the development of the universities as may from time to time be required in order to ensure that they are fully adequate to national needs.'[16] Lord Murray of Newhaven, who was to serve as Chairman of the UGC from 1953 to 1963, has described this statement as 'the first open recognition that national needs should be a factor in the development of universities'[17] in Britain.

When the UGC went on in 1947 to make its first non-recurrent grants to universities to meet their capital needs and their needs for scientific equipment – and the power to decide on the distribution of these capital grants clearly increased the influence of the UGC – the Vice-Chancellors'

Committee, a body which had first come into existence very informally in 1918, welcomed the new dispensation. 'The universities entirely accept the view that the Government has not only the right, but the duty to satisfy itself that every field of study which in the national interest ought to be cultivated in Great Britain is in fact being cultivated in the university system and that the resources which are placed at the disposal of the universities are being used with full regard both to efficiency and to economy.'[18]

We seem to be very near to our own times with this statement. Yet it is doubtful whether it would have been subscribed to in 1947 by most academics other than vice-chancellors or even whether most vice-chancellors would have regarded it as more than a concession to expediency at that time. Moreover, the firmness of the statement concealed some doubt as to its exact meaning. Certainly our own times seem so different from those of Moberly that at the recent jubilee dinner of the Vice-Chancellor's Committee, a recently re-modelled body, it was rightly said that the last ten years had seen bigger changes than the previous forty. Moreover, Sir John Wolfenden, the present Chairman of the UGC, remarked recently that 'if Moberly came to Park Crescent [the present HQ of the UGC] tomorrow morning, he would quite simply – for all his great wisdom and experience – not have a clue. The UGC has changed a good deal over the past twenty years and, indeed, over the past ten or five. It has changed, not because there was anything wrong about the way it did its job, but because the job has changed, in size and in complexity if in no other ways.'[19]

In this most recent period statistics have seemed to count more than landmarks. The number of full-time university students increased in Britain from 77,000 in 1947 to over 94,000 in 1957 and to 169,486 in 1965–6. At the same time government expenditure on the recurrent grants to universities rose from £7 million in 1946–7 to £28 million in 1956–7 and £122 million in 1965–6. Non-recurrent grants rose sharply from £28 million in 1961–2 to nearly £80 million in 1965–6. These figures spoke for themselves, or at least appeared to do so to governments: marginal items of expenditure became politically significant items, posing questions both of absolute scale and of priorities within the educational system as it was beginning to be conceived.

At the same time, there have been several landmarks or, at least, what seemed at the time to be landmarks, in the recent history of universities. The first was the setting-up in 1949 of the new University College of North Staffordshire, an institution which deliberately set out to innovate, to look at university education in a new way. The second was the long sequence of decisions, first taken within the Ministry of Education in 1953, which led in 1956 to the designation as Colleges of Advanced Technology (CATS) of a number of local technical colleges of high standing, financed from 1962 onwards not by local authorities but by direct Ministry of Education grant. They were to be granted charters as full universities from 1964 onwards, thereby broadening the base of the community of universities and widening the scope of the UGC.

The third was the decision taken by the UGC in 1958 to sponsor seven brand-new universities, not upgraded institutions nor institutions subjected, like North Staffordshire, to an initial period of tutelage, but autonomous and free. It is the implications of this decision that have received most public attention. One new university would have been incremental, as North Staffordshire was; seven changed the dynamics of the system, indeed, helped to foster the sense of a system. It was a decision taken in steps without a debate in Parliament five years before the Robbins Report on *Higher Education* – and taken essentially on the same basis, to begin with, as the decision taken to increase university numbers after the Barlow Committee had reported in 1946. The steps were: inquiries to existing universities about the targets they wished to achieve; estimates of national 'shortfall'; determination about new provision. The Barlow Committee, indeed, had recommended the foundation of at least one new university and several university colleges, and it was only after the UGC had found in 1946 and 1947 that existing universities were able more or less to meet the need as defined by Barlow that it had decided then not to pursue this particular recommendation. The language was cautious, moreover, even if its argument was somewhat general. 'It is clear that the situation contemplated by the Barlow Committee does not immediately arise. In these circumstances the establishment of new institutions could no longer be regarded as a necessary means to the policy of expansion, and we have acted on the opinion that, in present circumstances, with shortages of qualified staff and with restrictions on building, greater progress can be made by concentrating the limited men and materials upon the development of existing institutions than by scattering them over a wider field.'[20]

In 1954 and 1955, when the UGC began to consider a shift in its policy, it could go back to the word 'immediately' in the first sentence of the earlier statement and use it in a way familiar to all members of committees, as a link word across time. The argument in 1957–8 for creating new universities looked simple. Existing universities together could not or were not willing to meet the demand for additional university places by 1970, 'irrespective of questions of finance'. It was assumed that they were quite free each separately to determine what their maximum rates of growth and maximum future targets would be, just as it was also assumed by 1957–8 that it was right that the UGC as a national body should assess future total demand for university places. The national assessment was based on demographic factors – 'Bulge' – and socio-educational factors – 'Trend' – and the demand for action was quickened when it became clear that the government itself was disturbed that unless more university places were provided a sizeable number of those qualified to go to university on current standards would not have a chance of securing a place.[21] Representatives of secondary education

on the UGC pressed the same point. Yet from 1954 onwards there was pro-
tracted debate inside the UGC (a very English debate) about the quantitative
estimates of 'Bulge' and 'Trend', about what lines of action to pursue to
speed up expansion, and about how speedy expansion should be. Even as
late as 1956, when it was decided to support proposals being made locally
in Sussex for a new university to be located in Brighton, there was no
commitment to a whole cluster of new universities. It was not until 1960
that York and Norwich were also accepted as new university sites, and the
Treasury was informed that three or four more new universities would be
necessary.[22] The setting-up of a UGC Sub-Committee on New Universities
in April 1959 enabled the UGC to examine and choose between local bids
for universities: it attached importance from the start to local enthusiasm
and interest.[23] In May 1961 Essex, Kent, and Warwick were approved, and
in November Lancaster.

The act of choosing sites took the UGC outside the realm of applied mathematics. So too did a concern for innovation which was already beginning
to be expressed in many circles. Yet one other point must be made about the
mathematics behind the critical decision, since it has never been made clear
to a certain number of commentators in Britain itself. It was assumed that
in the short run there could be only limited growth in the new universities
and that the main thrust of immediate expansion should be met in the
existing universities, some of which, notably Hull and Leicester, had grown
rapidly since 1945 (Hull 800 per cent by 1958, Leicester 1,100 per cent). 'We
did not face a choice between expansion of the existing universities and
creation of new ones', the UGC reported faithfully in 1964. 'It was clear to
us that both were needed.'[24] This was the last bit of mathematics, and qualitative as well as quantitative questions quickly entered into the argument:
indeed, they were part of the texture of the argument inside the UGC itself.
'We also had in mind the need for experimentation.'[25] After Southampton,
Hull, Exeter, and Leicester had passed from university-college status to full
university status between 1952 and 1957, the UGC recognized that an epoch
had ended, and that any new universities brought into existence should
start freer than North Staffordshire had done. The 'newness' of the institutions and the fact that they were not upgraded institutions with a history
was of their very essence. 'New institutions, starting without traditions with
which the innovator must come to terms, are more favourably situated for
such experimentation than established institutions.'[26] The formula that was
devised for the creation of new universities – local initiative; competitive
bidding to the UGC; formulation of academic plans by UGC-appointed
Academic Planning Committees; granting of charters – encouraged not only
innovation but diversity. Each new university appointed its own faculty,
devised its own curriculum, its own approach to teaching methods, its own
governmental organization, although the Privy Council (via the UGC) had to
approve of their charters and the UGC itself could influence their 'mix' of

subjects taught and the rate of growth. The diversity was accentuated by the fact that from the start the new universities never worked together as a *bloc* or attempted to bargain together to strengthen their position *vis-à-vis* older universities. Between 1961 and 1968 they moved on separate lines, although they obviously had common problems and sometimes, at least, produced common solutions.

The fourth recent landmark was the Robbins Report on Higher Education, which appeared in 1963. The Robbins Committee had been appointed in February 1961 'to review the pattern of full-time higher education in Great Britain and in the light of national needs and resources to advise Her Majesty's Government on what principles its long-term development should be based. In particular, to advise, in the light of these principles, whether there should be any changes in that pattern, whether any new types of institution are desirable and whether any modifications should be made in the present arrangements for planning and coordinating the development of various types of institution.'[27] This was the first occasion on which universities had been reviewed along with those other institutions of higher education in Britain that had their own separate histories and their own current group status – colleges for the education and training of teachers, started originally in the nineteenth century by voluntary bodies, mainly religious, but expanded in numbers by local education authorities, which were responsible in 1963 for 98 out of 146 institutions; local, area, and regional technical colleges; Colleges of Advanced Technology; colleges of further education; agricultural colleges; schools of art; and a small number of other institutions. The Report recommended that there should indeed be some changes in pattern, including the conversion of the CATS into new universities, that there should be an augmented Grants Commission dealing with the needs of all 'autonomous institutions of higher education' including non-university institutions, and that, as the basis of statistical projections, there should be sufficient expansion of numbers to permit 'courses of higher education to be available for all those who are qualified by ability and attainment to pursue them and who wish to do so'.[28] This was a new kind of statement in the history of higher education in Britain.

The Report, which reflected and to some extent stimulated greater interest in higher education than had ever been shown before, was clearly concerned more with student demand than with 'national need': perhaps for this reason it produced fewer results than had been anticipated. No new universities were created in its aftermath, nor was a new Grants Committee, although in February 1964 the UGC was transferred from the Treasury to the Department of Education and Science. Teachers' Training Colleges were renamed Colleges of Education, and subsequently B.Ed. degrees were introduced, but the colleges were not transferred directly into the university sector. By 1965 there was as much talk of sectors as there was of systems, and a confused public argument had started (and is still in progress intermittently) concerning a so-called 'binary system' involving the existence side by side of a university sector and a non-university or 'public' sector. The Secretary of State for Education gave a speech on the subject at Woolwich in April 1965 which is in its way something of a landmark: it was followed in May 1966 by the publication of a White Paper (Cmnd. 3006), vague in language and uncertain in intention, proposing the designation of 27 institutions as Polytechnics, very much *not* to be in the university sector. In April 1967 the 27 became 28, and the green light was flashed: the work in them was to lead to the granting of degrees administered not by particular universities but by a recently founded (September 1964) Council for National Academic Awards (CNAA) and to other national qualifications.

Public debate about the 'binary system' has been confused for three reasons. First, it was never made clear whether the system was considered to be an 'ideal' or an acceptance, largely for economic reasons, of historical fact, involving the 'systematization' of what had hitherto been unsystematic dualism or polycentrism in higher education. Second, the bare economics of the systematization were never clearly set out – relative costs, for example, in universities and polytechnics. Third, the implementation of policy was determined largely by civil servants in discussions with local authorities, and much that was happening was hidden from public view. Although a higher education planning group was set up within the Department of Education to consider the relation between the different parts of the system, its work has been confidential and its statistics have never been published. The Robbins Report had stated that the Committee initiated its own statistical inquiries and surveys because of 'the paucity of information on higher education in general' and that it hoped that 'the information here assembled will serve as the foundation for further observation and analysis'.[29] Yet there seems to have been a retreat since Robbins on this front, not an advance. The Robbins projections are becoming increasingly out of date, and there have been no open moves towards 'ten-year planning' as the Committee recommended.

At this point in time the economic determinants of global expenditure on university expansion and development of other educational institutions have obviously begun to be treated as imperatives. Controls have been tightened, and for economic reasons there has been little preparation for what Robbins anticipated would be a new wave of expansion during the mid 1970s. It was specifically stated in February 1965 that no further universities would be created during the next ten years,[30] and all recent official statements have suggested not increases in but curbs on university expenditure. The gap between aspirations and achievements has widened. The controls have taken different forms – UGC costing exercises, establishment of building and equipment 'norms',[31] limited rationalization of courses; and, in July 1967, the government's decision to give the Comptroller and Auditor-General power to inspect university accounts[32] and to report back to the Public Accounts Committee.

The Committee of Vice-Chancellors and Principals has in the meantime been seeking to carry out what internal reforms it can within the 'university system'. It has recognized that while there is now a greater measure of State involvement in university provision than any Victorian, radical or conservative, could ever have contemplated, universities in Britain have retained to the present day a substantial measure of autonomy and that, as the two English universities of 1800 have given way to the 36 of today, universities and government have seldom come into direct confrontation with each other. Between them as a group – and they are a disparate group – and the government there still stands the UGC. They know, of course, as Sir John Wolfenden has stated, that the UGC is a changing UGC and that if the present is cloudy the future is not clear. 'It is not easy', Wolfenden has also stated, 'to combine the proper autonomies of the universities with the proper attention to effective use of scarce national resources. It could well turn out that the degree of success with which the UGC and the universities conduct this (delicate) operation over the next few years will determine their whole future.' The arrangements depend on 'the continued observance of conventions', on 'reciprocal good will', and, not least, in crucial stages on particular personalities.[33] The issues have little, in my view, to do with party politics, which have themselves changed completely during the period since 1800, although they have much to do with opinion. More must be said of that later. Constitutional history and social history cannot be realistically studied in separation from each other, just as social issues cannot be divorced from economic issues, much as we should like to divorce them.

III

A number of points emerge from the bare outline of the story as I have told it so far. First, the history of university development has been one of fits and starts, with much of the *élan* concentrated into short sharp bursts. 'University education', Sir Richard Livingstone remarked in 1948, 'has grown up in the casual English way. It has never been viewed, much less planned, as a whole. A cynic might give a book on the subject the title of *Drift*.'[34] There has been much more 'planning' – a difficult term to apply to university policy-making – and much more 'system' since 1948, yet, as an educational journalist put it recently, Sir John Wolfenden's successor as chairman of the UGC, who takes up his unenviable post in January 1969, 'confronts a higher education in turmoil. Stop-go economics for the universities, confusion of purposes as Universities, polytechnics and even the Open University expand in directions that only cohere in some sublime pigeon-hole in the Department of Education, and revolting students will buffet him from all sides. Not the least of his problems is the inexorable rise in demand; a rise which, unless some new methods of financing are developed, is going to make higher education one of the Exchequer's biggest headaches in the 1980s.'[35]

Second, the pattern as it has emerged, down to the current question marks, is very similar to other patterns in English history – to that of the social services in general, for example. In other words the outline of university history is not unique within the general web of history. Development has owed much to particular individuals, it has been characterized so far by remarkable continuities more than by sudden reversals, it has depended on delicate conventions and obviated frontal conflict, it has left considerable margins of choice. Each university remains a separate unit, as universities were in the nineteenth century, but the UGC has developed a common system of financial provision and control which affects all universities, including Oxford and Cambridge – although to a limited extent Oxford and Cambridge retain a greater measure of autonomy because of their college endowments and independent finance. The element of competition within the 'system' has been curbed as it has in all other sub-systems of English society since there are more or less common pay scales in all universities and common formulae for dealing with building costs and services. Diversity, therefore, which was such a conspicuous feature of the British solution to the problem of university expansion during the 1960s, is diversity within set limits, and there is always a danger that *micro*-planning within the particular university will be handicapped or frustrated by *macro*-planning or the lack of it in the Department of Education and Science or the UGC.

Third, although the number of university students has increased sharply during the period I have been talking about, the proportion of the age-group attending a university institution in Britain remains small, by both American and European standards. Indeed, as the well-publicized UNESCO chart of 1957 showed, in the provision of university places per head Britain's parsimony was surpassed in Europe only by that of Ireland, Turkey, and Norway.[36] Throughout the nineteenth century and deep into the twentieth century, the assumption that university students constituted some kind of elite – there were differences of opinion about what kind of an elite – was as strongly held, usually without argument, as the assumption that universities were free and autonomous corporations holding property and administering their own affairs. There was a close association (to which we still cling) in the mid-Victorian debate about the university between the theory of the 'clerisy' as advanced by Coleridge – the theory of an endowed class 'comprehended of the learned of all denominations',[37] a theory with a religious pedigree – and the theory of the elite. The theory also had social implications, as strong as the social implications of twentieth-century theories of 'national need'. 'Obligation is a strong word in reference to going to college at any age,' F. D. Maurice wrote in 1837, 'but I do conceive that those who are destined by their property or birth to anything above the middle station in society, and intended to live in England, are bound to show cause why they do not put themselves in the best position for becoming what Coleridge calls the *Clerisy* of the land.'[38]

The main effect of the direct, although strictly limited, intervention of the State into the mid-Victorian affairs of Oxford and Cambridge was to stimulate a movement for internal reform which had gained ground before the State decided to intervene.[39] Colleges revived their community ideal and re-stated it in Victorian language, emphasizing its relevance to moral education and character formation.[40] Universities considered the role of the university as an institution for learning, comparing British with German institutions, and examining the implications of an increase in the number of professors and the encouragement of research.[41] Reformers inside Oxford and Cambridge in this key period were never in complete agreement with each other – nor were the academic reformers within the new civic universities – but their debate, a far more sophisticated debate than that conducted between radicals and conservatives in Parliament, touched on every relevant issue – the curriculum, which was transformed and extended; modes of teaching and examining; college and university organization; attitudes to the community outside the universities; and university 'extension', which meant in the first instance university expansion. In the often painful process of debate in Victorian England, when the theory of the elite was being given a new form, balances were struck. Colleges strengthened their tutorial system, more university professors were appointed. A new breed of 'dons' emerged, but they were still dons. Many of them, not least Mark Pattison, were disillusioned with the domestic effects of reform, but others were proud of the influence of the universities on public life – both on men of power, public servants as they thought of themselves, and men interested in social protest. Their own influence as dons, indeed, along with their status, was magnified by the influence of their pupils, and by the pull of the university as the minority communications system of the day. We find in the nineteenth century, when we see the debate about the university taking something like its modern form, a whole variety of response. Alongside Pattison's intellectual uneasiness we have to set Jowett's worldliness; we have also to take account of what in the 1880s, when the debates were beginning to shift yet again and a new generation was emerging, was called 'the new Oxford movement', a movement which developed, I think for the first time, an overall though limited view of the relationship between the university and society as a whole. 'The most living interest in Oxford [is] now that in social questions. Yes! Oxford has turned from playing at the Middle Ages in churches, or at a Re-Renaissance in cupboards; and a new faith, with Professor Green as its founder, Arnold Toynbee as its martyr, and various societies for its propaganda is alive among us.'[42]

Throughout the debate, however, university education remained an education for an elite, a social elite living alongside an educational elite. 'Dons did not expect unusual or sudden changes in . . . social structure; and none occurred, at least none that can support a causal explanation of reform': what statistical evidence there is points to 'a remarkable continuity in the social background of undergraduates'.[43] It was not merely a matter of working-class exclusion: industrial and commercial wealth was not represented significantly either. Even in the industrial cities, where there was access to new wealth, institutions languished for want of recruits. During the late 1860s, when Oxford and Cambridge were in the midst of spontaneous reform, Queen's College, Birmingham was in debt to the extent of £10,000 and its charter was repealed, while Owen's College, Manchester was fighting against what was called 'half-hearted sympathy and openly expressed contempt'.[44] In 1885 James Bryce, who had spent six years as a lecturer at Manchester between 1868 and 1874 before taking his chair in Oxford, pointed out that Germany, with a population of 45 millions, had 24,187 university places, while England, with a population of 26 millions, had only 5,500. 'Nothing', he asserted, 'could so clearly illustrate the failure of the English system to reach and serve all classes.'[45]

Pattison in Oxford and Seeley in Cambridge were only two of the distinguished Oxbridge men who were shocked by this state of affairs, yet essentially it persisted despite the emergence of new institutions in the late nineteenth and early twentieth centuries. It may be said, indeed, that throughout the nineteenth century the universities were influenced relatively little by the economic and social changes which were transforming the country industrially, that many people inside them thought that they stood for a way of life superior to that involved in 'the pursuit of wealth by industrious competition',[46] and that outside opinion, curious or critical, in relation to the universities – leaving aside the opinion of their own graduates, many of whom had figured also as masters in the public schools, with whom they had the closest links – had only an extremely limited influence upon them. While there were some reformers who wanted to introduce more scientists into the elite or to widen the basis of its social recruitment, there was little challenge to the conception of the university as a place where an extended 'clerisy' was not 'trained' but 'educated'. Most Victorians who knew about these things would have settled for something like John Stuart Mill's statement in his inaugural address at a Scottish university – St Andrews – in 1867: 'The proper function of a university in national education is tolerably well understood. At least, there is a tolerably general agreement about what a university is not. It is not a place of professional education. Universities are not intended to teach the knowledge required to fit men for some special mode of gaining their livelihood. Their object is not to make skilful lawyers, or physicians, or engineers, but equable and cultivated human beings . . . Men are men before they are lawyers, or physicians, or merchants, or manufacturers; and if you will make them equable and sensible men, they will make themselves capable and sensible lawyers or physicians.'[47] Mill had written earlier that he believed that universities had 'the especial duty . . . to counteract the debilitating influence of the circumstances of the age upon individual character, and to send forth into society a succession of minds, not the creatures of their age, but capable of being its improvers and regenerators'.[48]

This approach to university education – and it was broad enough to encourage research as well as teaching, the discovery of new knowledge as much as the transmission of existing knowledge – permitted or rather stimulated belief in what I would like to call a 'high' conception of the university as a special kind of institution within the constellation of educational institutions. Given the limitations both of undergraduates and of their teachers, given the fact that some at least among the elite might be attending the university for social reasons or, despite what Mill said, for the sake of professional advancement, the nineteenth-century university – the reformed university – should none the less offer the best to the best. The learner should become an explorer as well as a critic. The vision of learning was put most clearly by Mark Pattison when he exclaimed in a college sermon – note again the relationship with the religious background – that the university student should be placed in a position where 'his intelligence is not only the passive recipient of forms from without, a mere mirror in which the increasing crowd of images confuse and threaten to obliterate each other; it becomes active and throws itself out upon phenomena with a native force, combining or analysing them – anyhow altering them, imposing itself upon them . . . The point in time in our mental progress at which this change takes place cannot be precisely marked: it is a result gradually reached, as every form of life is developed by insensible transition out of a lower. As physical life passes into psychical life by a succession of steps in which there is no break, so does psychical life into spiritual. This is the life that the higher education aspires to promote, this is the power which it cherishes and cultivates, this is the faculty to which it appeals.'[49]

This statement of a philosophy of higher education is clearly very different from those twentieth-century statements about higher education which are primarily 'organizational' or quantitative in character. Yet it echoes through much twentieth-century writing in Britain and has influenced much English thinking within what may be called, not purely rhetorically, the English tradition. It lies behind the mathematics of the English staff-student ratios, and it has influenced some, at least, of the pioneers of new universities in a quite different phase of twentieth-century educational expansion. It has survived the fragmentation of the clerisy and the loss of the sense of a clerisy – the divisions of the academic community into several sections, each following its own way. For these reasons alone when one is talking about an elite, an excursion into Victorian history is relevant and worthwhile.

It is important to bear in mind, however, that Pattison and many men who thought like him envisaged what they regarded as the central experience of the university student in a broad context. Pattison, in particular, wanted 'the national mind' to work and live as its 'proper organization' in the university.[50] He was concerned deeply about the state of the nation. 'We have no system in anything;' he complained, 'our affairs go on by dint of our practical sense, a stupid precedent implying in all cases the want of method.'[51] He wanted universities to provide something more than a response to the practical needs of the time: to meet a national challenge by going beyond the practical sense, by creating an intelligent, highly-motivated elite, not in his case by underwriting social privileges. He anticipated therefore, in a nineteenth-century setting, the twentieth-century sense of national need.

IV

So long, however, as the social composition of the Oxford and Cambridge colleges remained unchanged and the role of the civic universities remained subordinate, limited, and inferior, the Victorian debate was very different from the twentieth-century debate as we know it. For a quite different view of the universities at the end of the nineteenth century, this time a view from outside, it is useful to turn to George Bernard Shaw's *Socialism for Millionaires* (1901) where he warned millionaires against endowing universities. 'Be careful,' he exclaimed, 'university men are especially ignorant and ill-informed. An intelligent millionaire, unless he is frankly an enemy of the human race, will do nothing to extend the method of caste initiation practised under the mask of education at Oxford and Cambridge. Experiments in educational method and new subjects of technical education are . . . abhorrent to university dons and are outside the scope of public elementary education, and these are the departments in which the millionaire interested in education can really make his gold fruitful . . . It is the struggles of society to adapt itself to new conditions which every decade of industrial development springs on us that really need help. The old institutions, in the interests of that routine, are but too well supported already.'

This seems to me to be an appropriate text on which to pin much of the experience of the twentieth century, the main landmarks which I have already tried to describe. There were, indeed, more university and college teachers in the United States when Shaw wrote (24,000) than there were university and college students in England, and the American story had already diverged sharply from that of Britain. The Shavian approach – and characteristically it was stated more basically, with less irony and with more crudeness, by H. G. Wells – has become a key factor in twentieth-century English experience for four main reasons – (i) a fundamental change in the provision of school education, elementary and secondary, influencing aspirations, expectations, and the possibility of realizing them; (ii) a growth in the demand for graduates – not surprisingly, the Cambridge Appointments Service was founded in 1899 (it became a Board, with full university provision three years later); (iii) the rise of scale and organization in business, industry, and government, each of which made demands on the universities as science institutions; (iv) an increasing expenditure on scientific and technological research, already on the way before DSIR started with its first small grants during the First World War.

Given these four factors alone, the consequent growth both in student numbers and in university expeditures and the increasing involvement of the State in the process have had about them an air of social inevitability, although in English history, at least, there have always been as many brakes as accelerators. The nineteenth-century echoes seemed to provide as many alarms as inspirations. 'Those who know our universities best', Ernest Barker, then Principal of King's College, London, wrote in 1932 – and he was a university man who spent much of his academic life in Oxford and Cambridge as well as in London – 'are haunted by the fear that a democratic enthusiasm, as genuine as it is ill-informed, may result in an attempt to increase the quantity of education at the expense of its quality.'[52] 'One cannot but depre- cate the attempts that are being made to found universities up and down the country,' another writer on what were then called 'the new universities' – the civic universities – had remarked four years before. 'If matters con- tinue as they are at present we are promised a spate of new universities. They will either lower the standard of education in the universities that are already in being, and widen further the breach which exists between the old and the new, or else they will form a new and surely unnecessary type, perhaps most like the American small town college.'[53] 'Narrow the gates of entry', the Vice-Chancellor of Birmingham warned his colleagues in 1930, telling them that the percentage of really good students was lower than 'indulgent universities' cared to assume.[54]

Although during the 1960s new voices were raised,[55] this line of argument was never broken. 'More means worse' was a familiar cry when the latest batch of new universities was brought into existence during the early 1960s. A few weeks ago a fellow of a Cambridge college generalized boldly that recent student unrest was explicable mainly in terms of quantitative expan- sion by itself. 'Any community that grew at a rate beyond its normal growth' – whatever that was – 'was in danger of losing its characteristic ethos.'[56]

It would be easy to end the story here were it not for the students themselves and for the changing communications system which not only influences some students across national frontiers in quite different univer- sity situations (and the wind blows both across the Atlantic and across the Channel) but also influences public attitudes towards universities – to an exceptional extent perhaps in England – through attitudes towards students. In England, as in other countries, universities have become news largely during the last ten years, and, while public policy is not made by headlines, public attitudes well may be. The anti-student movement is strong, and public reactions, particularly local reactions, to relatively minor forms of student disturbances have been disproportionate, even dramatic, and cer- tainly undiscriminating. Issues have been oversimplified in terms of discipline and authority, and the role of the mass-communications system has been simply to focus on temporary issues, which has made for misunderstandings, rather than what might be called public education about the central issues of the expansion of higher education in the country. If the universities were to be left in these circumstances to the mercy of local pressures – and there are signs that there has been a trend in this direction behind the scenes for some time – then we are in for a very tough fight indeed in the course of the next twenty or thirty years.

Given the limited resources available for British universities and given the relatively generous overall national and local support for students through grants[57] – these are not administered through the UGC but directly by local authorities – any increase in misunderstandings between the public as citizens and taxpayers and the universities as bodies dependent for 80 per cent of their income on the State could jeopardize not only further university expansion but, in Britain, the precarious maintenance both of the 'system' as it exists and of the traditions – particularly the teaching tradition – which survive and, in some cases, have been recently revitalized. A minority, indeed, wishes to see the system go (it does not like systems) and the traditions disappear (it is very uneasy about traditions) without having so far any ideas of how to replace the system or the traditions; and conflict situations – part of the struggle of society, doubtless, to adapt itself to new conditions – have already arisen which do not fit easily into the history of universities in England as I have described it. Such issues could influence the course of discussions not only about university finance but about the still unsettled relationships between universities and other institutions of higher education. The balances on which the English 'system' depend are as delicate as the individual universities themselves are fragile. So much is true also, of course, of all universities at the present time. As Karl Jaspers put it a few years ago, 'complex relationships are not resolved but destroyed by simple solutions, such as separating research from teaching institutes, liberal education from specialized training, the instruction of the best from that of the many'.[58] All this points to the fact that 1968, with its compressed debates, does not provide a very satisfactory vantage point for the historian from which to survey either the future or for that matter the past.

Notes

1 J. Macmurray, 'The Functions of a University', *Political Quarterly*, vol. XV, 1944.
2 Cmnd. 2154 (1963), §14, §18.
3 A remark of Benjamin Jowett, quoted in C. E. Mallett, *A History of the University of Oxford*, vol. III, 1927, p. 456.
4 See Asa Briggs, *Victorian Cities* (Penguin edition, 1968).
5 For a fascinating and controversial study, see G. E. Davie, *The Democratic Intellect: Scotland and her Universities in the Nineteenth Century*, Edinburgh, 1961.

6 See his *Observations on the Education of the People* (1824). See also C. W. New, *The Life of Henry Brougham* (1961), chs. XIX, XX.

7 J. Amery, *The Life of Joseph Chamberlain*, vol. IV (1951), pp. 209–21.

8 For a brief account of the background, see A. Marwick, *The Deluge* (1965), ch. 7. See also a lecture by H. Hetherington, *The British University System, 1914–1954* (1954).

9 See J. Simmons, *New University* (1958), pp. 41–2, for resentment at Leicester.

10 Lord Butler has claimed that the Education Act of 1944, which dealt with schools, had inevitable corollaries for higher education in the future. 'It was I who first recommended Robbins to write his report. And the Robbins Report is a kind of follow-up in higher education to what we did for secondary education in 1944' (*The Times Educational Supplement*, 19 May 1967). The British Association for the Advancement of Science produced a report in 1944 suggesting a doubling of the post-war Treasury grant to universities and an increase in the number of students to 50,000 (*Report of the Committee on Post-War University Education*, 1944).

11 UGC, *University Development, 1935–47* (1948), p. 11.

12 ibid., p. 16.

13 Cnd. 6824 (1946).

14 See H. C. Dent, *Universities in Transition* (1961), pp. 72ff. UGC, *University Development, 1935–47*, p. 26.

15 ibid., p. 28.

16 ibid., p. 11.

17 Quoted in A. Kerr, *Universities of Europe* (1962), p. 206.

18 Committee of Vice-Chancellors and Principals, 'A Note on University Policy and Finance' (1947).

19 Sir John Wolfenden, lecture on 'Universities and the State' (1967), p. 15.

20 UGC, op. cit., p. 42.

21 According to Sir Edward Boyle, the fact that 'the English sense of fairness came into play' was of considerable importance in the making of decisions. See M. Beloff, *The Plateglass Universities* (1968), p. 22. The government agreed to bigger targets on a short-term basis after discussions with the UGC. Thus in 1956 it agreed to 106,000 by the mid-1960s. The UGC stated in the same year that its 'minimum' figure for 1968 was 168,000. In the same year the government announced that authority had been given for capital expenditure to permit a doubling of building starts. 'Large though the increase is, the Government believes that the universities should be encouraged to expand even more. The UGC has advised us that a larger expansion would be desirable if resources can be made available. It would like to invite the universities to consider still further expansion to meet national needs' (quoted in UGC, *University Development 1957–1962* (1964), p. 71). The same process was repeated in 1957–8. It was in discussions about capital between the UGC and the Treasury that the UGC greatly strengthened its role in the planning process.

22 ibid., p. 100. By then the UGC had settled on a national target of 170,000 for the early 1970s.

23 For other criteria, see ibid., pp. 96–101.

24 ibid.

25 ibid.

26 UGC, *University Development, 1952–1957* (1958), p. 5.

27 Cmnd. 2154 (1963), p. iii.

28 ibid., p. 8.

29 ibid., p. 3.

30 One was created after the seven – Stirling in Scotland.

31 See Cmnd. 9 (1956); Cmnd. 1235 (1960).
32 For demands for tighter control, see the 'Fifth Report from the Select Committee on Estimates, 1951–52', p. xv; Special Report from the Committee of Public Accounts, 1966–7, 'Parliament and Control of University Expenditure'.
33 Wolfenden, loc. cit., p. 5, p. 8.
34 Sir R. Livingstone, *Some Thoughts on University Education* (1948), p. 13.
35 R. Bourne, 'Universities and the Public Purse', *The Guardian*, 11 Nov. 1968.
36 Beloff, op. cit., p. 23.
37 See S. T. Coleridge, on *The Constitution of Church and State According to the Idea of Each* (1837 edn), p. 49, for his definition – 'the clerisy of the nation, or national church in its primary acceptation and original intention, comprehended the learned of all denominations, the sages, and professors of law and jurisprudence, of medicine and physiology, of music . . . of the physical sciences . . . in short, all the so-called liberal arts and sciences, the possession of which constitute the civilisation of a country.'
38 F. Maurice, *Life and Letters of F. D. Maurice* (1885), vol. I, p. 224.
39 The more Conservative reaction was to claim that inquiry into Oxford and Cambridge constituted 'an unwarranted inquisition' into the affairs of 'venerable bodies'. James II's intervention in the seventeenth century was cited as a precedent.
40 See S. Rothblatt, *The Revolution of the Dons* (1968), ch. 7.
41 See J. Sparrow, *Mark Pattison and the Idea of a University* (1965), pp. 91ff., for Pattison's interesting and significant change of views on the relative position of college and university between 1850 and 1877.
42 *The Oxford Magazine*, 21 Nov. 1883, quoted in M. Richter, *The Politics of Conscience* (1964), p. 346. The attempt to associate the university or even to identify it with popular forces outside preceded the 1880s, and explains much, for example, of Frederic Harrison's sense of mission.
43 Rothblatt, op. cit., p. 86.
44 W. H. G. Armytage, *Civic Universities* (1955), p. 220.
45 Preface to J. Conrad, *The German Universities for the Last Fifty Years* (1885), pp. xiv–xxx.
46 See G. M. Young, *Victorian England, Portrait of An Age* (1936), p. 95, although Young's conclusion that 'the Universities broke the fall of the aristocracy by civilizing the plutocracy' is not borne out by university statistics. There was a Victorian gap here between aspiration and accomplishment, well brought out in Seeley's dream of 'a great teaching order which shall have its fixed lecture-rooms in every great town' seeking to raise 'the dead-level, insipid, barren, abject, shopkeeping life' of England (*A Midland University: An Address* (1887)).
47 Inaugural Address at St Andrews, printed in F. A. Cavenagh (ed.), *James and John Stuart Mill on Education* (1931), pp. 133–4.
48 Essay on 'Civilization' (1836), printed in G. Himmelfarb (ed.), *Essays on Politics and Culture* (1963), p. 55.
49 Quoted in Sparrow, op. cit., p. 129.
50 M. Pattison, 'Oxford Studies', in *Oxford Essays* (1855), p. 259. 'The University must be the intellectual capital of the country, attracting to itself not all the talent, but all the speculative intellect' (ibid., p. 254).
51 ibid., p. 284.
52 E. Barker, 'Universities in Great Britain', in W. M. Kotsching and E. Prys (eds.), *Universities in a Changing World* (1932), p. 118.
53 H. G. G. Herklots, *The New University, An External Examination* (1928), pp. 87–8.

54 Sir Charles Grant Robertson, *The British Universities* (1930), p. 75.
55 For a trenchant and controversial attack on the attitudes of universities, see an article in *The Economist*, 'Let Dons Delight', 1 March 1958, which attacked elitist views in Oxford and Cambridge, 'imitation' in Redbrick, and 'suave' suggestions that there should be no changes. 'Everything must change,' it went on, 'the varieties of degree, the methods of selection . . . and [the view that] the universities' main task is producing firsts in arts and science for the top jobs.'
56 Dr T. R. Henn, quoted in *The Times*, 4 Nov. 1968.
57 Relatively generous overall support that has substantially increased the proportion of students with working-class backgrounds as compared with students in European universities does not mean that there have not been sharp exchanges about the level of individual student's grants. For the effects of recent cheeseparing, see the interesting article by H. Johnson, 'The Economics of Student Protest', in *New Society*, 7 Nov. 1968.
58 K. Jaspers, *The Idea of a University* (1960).

15

THE EXPANSION OF
HIGHER EDUCATION

Gary B. Cohen

Source: G. B. Cohen, *Education and Middle-Class Society in Imperial Austria, 1848–1918*, West Lafayette, Ind.: Purdue University Press, 1996, pp. 75–94.

As elsewhere in Europe during the late nineteenth century, aspirations spread among broader segments of the Austrian population than before for careers in public service, medical and legal practice, and business management. Those ambitions fueled a growth in university and technical college enrollments between the 1850s and 1910 that was more than three times the increase in total population (see table 1). Not surprisingly, the growth in higher education came in waves that corresponded roughly to those in secondary school enrollments, allowing a lag for the time it took students to graduate from the secondary schools (see tables 1 and 2 in the appendix).[1]

Although functionally differentiated, the universities and technical colleges competed to some extent for the same students, much like the *Gymnasien* and *Realschulen*. One should not try to draw too sharp a distinction between the social appeals of university and technical college education, for at times total enrollments in the two tracks showed a clear reciprocal relationship.[2] Total attendance in the universities and technical colleges declined between 1851 and 1856 because of the aftereffects of economic crisis and political upheaval in the late 1840s, the introduction of the *Matura* for the universities, and the curricular reforms in secondary and higher education.[3] Once secondary school enrollments began to expand in the late 1850s and 1860s, the numbers of students in the universities and, to a lesser extent, the technical colleges began to increase rapidly. During the slight recession of the middle 1860s and the wars of German unification, Austria's technical colleges lost enrollments, while the universities gained. At the peak of the economic boom in the early 1870s, attendance in the technical colleges ballooned, while the numbers of university students declined somewhat.

The trends reversed during the next decade. Just as *Gymnasium* enrollments grew strongly at the expense of the *Realschulen* during the depression years of the 1880s, university attendance increased by half while the technical colleges lost nearly half their enrollments. Well into the late nineteenth century, the Austrian state continued to prefer university education, particularly in law, over technical studies for its higher functionaries.[4] In the 1880s, with straitened conditions in industry and commerce, greater numbers of Austrian youth than before chose university studies, apparently in preparation for state employment or careers in law, medicine, and secondary school teaching, as opposed to advanced technical education. Technical college enrollments also suffered in these years from the growing competition of industrial and trade schools and from the introduction in 1889–90 of more rigorous state examinations in the technical fields.[5]

Enrollments in the technical colleges recovered after 1890 as economic growth quickened. Indeed, while all higher education experienced unprecedented expansion during the next twenty-five years, technical college enrollments increased more rapidly in relative terms during each five-year period than did the number of university students. Besides the growing employment opportunities in industry after the mid-1890s, the rising formal status of the technical colleges helped make them more attractive to students than before. At the turn of the century, the Austrian educational authorities, like the German, recognized the growing importance of research in advanced technical and engineering fields and, after two decades of agitation by professors and alumni, approved doctoral degrees for the technical colleges. The more than doubling of technical college students between 1900 and 1910 caused critical overcrowding in many of the institutions in the Alpine and Bohemian lands.[6]

Enrollments in the Austrian technical colleges increased so strongly compared with the universities around 1900 that Austria had a much higher ratio of technical college students to university students in the last years before World War I than did Germany. It is commonly assumed that Germany, with its larger population, stronger economy, more-developed chemical and electrical industries, and eminent scientific institutes, had a stronger commitment to modern science and technology than did Austria. In fact, Austria had considerable accomplishments in the applied sciences and technology, and one comparative study of academic physics around 1900 has found that the Habsburg Monarchy as a whole had a smaller number of physicists in its universities and technical colleges than did Germany but spent almost twice as much on their work relative to national income as did Germany.[7] Larger percentages of the students in Austrian higher education, particularly in the Alpine and Bohemian lands, chose to attend technical colleges than was the case in Germany. In 1870, 18.9 percent of the matriculated students in Austrian higher education attended technical colleges, compared with 16.5 percent in Germany. In 1911, 30.6 percent of the matriculated students in Austrian higher education attended technical colleges, but only 17.5 percent in Germany.[8]

The rates of enrollment in higher education during the late nineteenth century showed many of the same inequalities among the various Austrian crown lands as did attendance in the academic secondary schools (see table 6). If the differences among the various lands were somewhat narrower for higher education than for secondary education, that was due largely to the more arduous screening, intellectual and social, that had to be endured in order to reach a university or technical college, regardless of a student's geographical origin. As in secondary education, Lower Austria and the Bohemian lands produced larger numbers of university and technical college students with respect to their populations than did any of the other larger crown lands for most of the period between the 1850s and 1914. In winter 1879–80, compared with total population, youth born in Lower Austria were enrolled in Austrian universities as matriculated and non-matriculated students at a rate nearly twice as high as for Upper Austrians and nearly 60 percent higher than for natives of Carniola or Dalmatia.[9] Obviously, natives of crown lands without universities or technical colleges and ethnic groups that lacked higher education in their mother tongue suffered serious disadvantages, but local economic conditions, social mores, and popular culture also mattered. Silesia, like Upper Austria, had no institutions of higher education within its borders in 1880; its youth had to travel to Vienna, Prague, or perhaps Krakow to study in a university. Nonetheless, Silesia, with its significant mining and industry, had a rate of university attendance relative to total population nearly 30 percent higher than Upper Austria's. Whatever the distances to the institutions, the less urbanized and less industrialized character of Upper Austria, Styria, and Carinthia and the continuing strength of the traditional culture of village, farm, and forest in those crown lands limited aspirations for higher education among their populations throughout most of the late nineteenth century.[10] Tirol shared many of the same characteristics, of course, but the size and vigor of the Catholic theological faculty in Innsbruck helped boost university attendance by Tiroleans above the norm for the more rural Alpine lands. In 1879–80 enrollment in technical colleges with respect to population was also significantly weaker for natives of the less-developed Alpine lands and Dalmatia than for Lower Austria, Bohemia, and Moravia.

By 1910 some of the gaps in rates of university and technical college attendance had narrowed between the less advanced Alpine lands and Lower Austria or the Bohemian lands, but there were still great differences among the crown lands. Between 1880 and 1910, Carniola, for example, with a population 94 percent Slovene, more than doubled the rate at which its natives were attending Austrian universities despite the fact that none of the institutions used Slovene as the language of instruction. Nonetheless, Carniola's 1910 rate of university enrollment for its nineteen- to twenty-two-year-olds

Table 2/6 Austrian University and Technical College Enrollments by Province of Birth Relative to Population, Winter 1879–80 and Winter 1909–10.

	Winter Semester 1879–80			
Province of birth	*Matr. & non-matr. univ. students per 1,000 pop. & per 1,000 19–22 yrs.*		*Matr. & non-matr. tech. col. students per 1,000 pop. & per 1,000 18–22 yrs.*	
Lower Austra	0.451	5.23	0.154	1.450
Upper Austria	0.238	3.74	0.101	1.272
Salzburg	0.263	3.96	0.088	1.067
Vorarlberg	0.467	7.10	0.029	0.352
Tirol	0.496	7.18	0.378	0.441
Carinthia	0.296	4.14	0.073	0.818
Styria	0.303	4.34	0.095	1.096
Carniola	0.283	4.38	0.071	0.871
Bohemia	0.369	5.41	0.206	2.431
Moravia	0.407	5.41	0.193	2.282
Silesia	0.307	4.33	0.118	1.331
Galicia	0.348	4.73	0.066	0.720
Bukovina	0.403	5.32	0.060	0.630
Maritime Lands	0.264	3.15	0.077	0.750
Dalmatia	0.286	3.68	0.064	0.671

	Winter Semester 1909–10			
Province of birth	*Matr. & non-matr. univ. students per 1,000 pop. & per 1,000 19–22 yrs.*		*Matr. & non-matr. tech. col. students per 1,000 pop. & per 1,000 18–22 yrs.*	
Lower Austra	1.080	13.12	0.471	4.57
Upper Austria	0.547	8.74	0.134	1.70
Salzburg	0.662	9.77	0.144	1.70
Vorarlberg	0.767	10.10	0.196	2.03
Tirol	0.787	10.04	0.120	1.26
Carinthia	0.597	8.12	0.212	2.33
Styria	0.783	11.61	0.220	2.59
Carniola	0.669	11.22	0.212	2.62
Bohemia	0.813	12.42	0.536	6.42
Moravia	0.853	13.78	0.574	7.24
Silesia	0.651	9.64	0.371	4.30
Galicia	1.010	15.65	0.190	2.31
Bukovina	1.323	19.44	0.114	1.33
Maritime Lands	0.679	7.68	0.243	2.25
Dalmatia	0.591	8.32	0.169	1.91

Sources: Statistisches Jahrbuch für das Jahr 1879; Öster. Statistik 2, no. 1 (1882); n.s., 7, no. 3 (1913); Urbanitsch 1980, 3, 1: 38, table 1.

was 81 percent that of Moravia. Upper Austria's rate of enrollment in universities that year was less than two-thirds the rate for Moravian-born youth (see table 2/6).

The appetite for higher education proved noticeably stronger among the populations of Moravia and Bohemia, both Czech- and German-speaking, than in the less-developed and more rural Alpine lands. In 1880, Moravia and Bohemia each had relatively more of their nineteen- to twenty-two-year-olds attending universities than did even Lower Austria. This was partly a matter of the historically strong development of secondary and higher education in the Bohemian lands before the nineteenth century. Beyond that, the rise of modern market-oriented agriculture, the slow decline of a rich craft tradition, and the development of a diverse modern industrial sector during the nineteenth century encouraged growing popular demand for advanced education in all forms. Czech educators during the 1860s introduced in Austria the concept of the *Real-Gymnasium* as a unitary secondary school, and *Realschulen* also enjoyed strong growth in Bohemia and Moravia after the 1850s. In higher education the populations of these two crown lands developed a particularly strong interest in engineering and the applied sciences. During much of the late nineteenth century, enrollments of Bohemian- and Moravian-born students in technical colleges with respect to total population or to the population in the prime age group far surpassed the rates for the other populous crown lands, even Lower Austria. In winter 1909–10, Moravia and Bohemia ranked just behind little Bukovina, Lower Austria, and Galicia in the numbers of their natives enrolled in universities compared with their total populations; and they still led all the Austrian crown lands in technical college attendance by their natives relative to total population or to eighteen-to twenty-two-year-olds (see table 2/6).

Besides economic development, political mobilization and popular commitments to social change also helped increase demand for higher education. In 1880, Galicia ranked just below Lower Austria and above Carniola, Styria, and Silesia in the number of Austrian university students born in the province compared with the province's nineteen- to twenty-year-old population. Galicia at that time had next to no modern industry, and its per capita income was among the lowest in Austria. Nonetheless, it had two universities, which, thanks to the political influence of Polish landowners, taught primarily in Polish after the 1860s.[11] In addition to the Galician-born students in the universities of Krakow and L'viv, significant numbers also attended the Vienna University, most of these Jewish. After 1875 some Galician students went to Chernivtsi as well. In the last decades of the century the offspring of Polish noblemen, some of the Polish and Ukrainian peasants and craftsmen, and Galicia's Jewish craftsmen and small business owners pressed into universities to prepare for careers in law, state or private administration, and secondary school teaching.[12] Compared with the nineteen-to twenty-two-year-old population, attendance in Austrian universities by the Galician-born more than tripled between 1880 and winter 1909–10. In the winter 1909–10 semester, Galicia's rate of university attendance actually exceeded the levels for Moravia and Lower Austria. Over those three decades the enrollment of the Galician-born in technical colleges compared with the eighteen-to twenty-two-year-old population also tripled, but Galician demand for higher technical education still lagged significantly behind that of the Moravian, Bohemian, and Lower Austrian populations.

Bukovina, like Galicia, also had a remarkably high rate of university attendance at the beginning of the twentieth century. Economically, Bukovina remained far less developed than the Alpine and Bohemian lands, and much of its population was extremely poor; but by 1900 this fairly compact territory was relatively well provided with secondary schools and a university. Jews and Romanians there took particular advantage of the educational opportunities, the Ukrainian inhabitants to a lesser extent. In 1909–10, Bukovina had the highest rates of university enrollments relative to both its total population and its nineteen- to twenty-two-year-olds of any Austrian crown land.[13]

In the expansion of Austrian higher education, unlike secondary education, the founding of wholly new institutions played no major part during the late nineteenth century. The central authorities were hesitant to found new universities and technical colleges, although they created many new professorial chairs and institutes as well as several new faculties to meet scholarly and professional needs and public demand for greater access. In the 1850s the Ministry of Religion and Instruction added professors and institutes to various universities, but, as already noted, the ministry acted to dissolve what remained of the old universities in Salzburg and Olomouc, leaving only free-standing Catholic theological faculties in those cities. Beyond establishing the University of Chernivtsi in 1875, the central authorities were willing to expand the university network only by dividing Prague's Charles-Ferdinand University into separate Czech and German institutions after 1882, adding a theology faculty in Innsbruck in 1857, and establishing medical faculties in Graz in 1863, Innsbruck in 1869, and L'viv in 1894. In 1904 the central government attempted unsuccessfully to open a new law faculty with Italian-language instruction in Innsbruck.[14] At the turn of the century, the central authorities resisted proposals for a new university in Salzburg, a new Czech university in Brno, or an Italian university in Trieste or Trento.

The Ministry of Religion and Instruction and the provincial governments, which operated most of the technical colleges until the early 1870s, followed similar policies for higher technical education. During the second half of the century, the ministerial and provincial authorities radically reformed the technical colleges in several phases, but they opened no new institutions except by the division of the technical institute in Prague into separate Czech and German schools in 1869 and the similar division of the technical college in Brno in 1900.

Compared with Germany's educational authorities, Austrian officials proceeded with great caution during the late nineteenth century in developing specialized *Hochschulen* in the arts or applied sciences. For the arts, only the Akademie der bildenden Künste (Academy of Fine Arts) in Vienna won the status of a *Hochschule* with its own rector in 1872. Up to 1918 the Ministry of Religion and Instruction never accorded that rank to the other arts academies and conservatories in Vienna and other cities.[15] After 1849 advanced schools of mining and metallurgy (*Montan-Lehranstalten*, later called *Bergakademien*) operated in Leoben, Styria, and Príbram, Bohemia, both with German-language instruction. Initially, they offered only two-year programs and had inferior status to the technical colleges. The two mining schools only gained the rank of *Hochschulen* in 1904 and the authority to grant doctoral degrees in 1906.[16] Many of the technical colleges carried on some instruction and research in agronomy. After the central government created a separate Ministry of Agriculture in 1867, however, it established in 1872 the College of Agriculture (Hochschule für Bodenkultur) in Vienna. Anyone with a *Gymnasium* or *Realschule Matura* could be admitted to it as a regular student, but only as late as 1911 did enrollments exceed 1,000.[17] No other independent agricultural college opened in Austria before 1918.

The cautious policies on institutional expansion resulted in Austrian university education being concentrated in a small number of institutions. Germany, with its traditions of *Landesuniversitäten*, had more than twenty universities at the end of the century. After 1882 the Austrian half of the Habsburg Monarchy had eight universities: in Vienna, Prague (Czech and German), Graz, Innsbruck, Krakow, L'viv, and Chernivtsi. By 1900 all had a full complement of four faculties except Chernivtsi, which lacked medicine. The rising enrollments in Galicia after the 1880s resulted in substantial growth for the University of L'viv, from only 1,091 matriculated students in winter 1889–90 to 4,309 in winter 1909–10, and the University of Krakow, from 1,113 in 1889–90 to 2,858 in 1909–10. Otherwise, the two oldest of the Austrian universities, Vienna and Prague, continued to attract the largest numbers of students throughout the late nineteenth century. Two-thirds or more of all the matriculated university students in Austria were enrolled in Vienna and Prague in the 1850s, 1860s, and 1870s. In winter 1909–10, the Vienna University with 7,579 students and the two Prague universities with 4,808 students still accounted for 54 percent of all the matriculated university students in Austria.[18] The universities in Graz and Innsbruck remained small, with only 1,643 matriculated students in the former and 1,006 in the latter in winter 1909–10.

At the beginning of the twentieth century, Austria had a larger number of technical colleges compared with population than did Germany. After 1900 there were seven Austrian technical colleges: in Vienna, Prague (Czech and German), Brno (Czech and German), Graz, and L'viv. Imperial Germany, with two and one-quarter times the population of Austria, had only eleven technical colleges in 1910.[19] As elsewhere in Central Europe, the individual Austrian technical colleges attracted smaller numbers of students than did most universities. Here, too, the institution in the imperial capital drew the largest enrollments. In winter 1909–10, the Vienna Technical College had 3,015 matriculated students. It was followed by the Czech Technical College in Prague with 2,854 students and the Technical College of L'viv with 1,660. In winter 1909–10 each of the other four colleges had fewer than one thousand matriculated students.[20]

The concentration of university and technical college students in a relatively small number of institutions made some of the Austrian schools unusually large by European standards. In 1910 only the Berlin University with its 9,700 matriculated students exceeded the Vienna University as the largest university in Central Europe, the Low Countries, and Italy. The Vienna Technical College and the Czech Technical College in Prague had the largest enrollments of any such institutions in Central Europe and Italy. Among individual faculties, the Vienna law faculty, with 3,418 matriculated students in winter 1909–10, easily surpassed the largest of its German counterparts in Berlin and Munich.[21] Officials in the Austrian Ministry of Religion and Instruction could defend on fiscal grounds their policies of keeping low the number of universities and technical colleges, but students repeatedly faced severe overcrowding in lecture halls, seminars, and laboratories from the late 1860s onward.[22]

The addition of new teaching positions, institutes, and programs in Austrian higher education during the late nineteenth century came roughly in three waves: as part of the Thun-Exner reforms of the 1850s, under the German liberal cabinets between 1867 and 1879, and during the great growth period for all public education after the mid-1890s. Despite limited financial resources, the ministerial authorities in 1848 and the 1850s aggressively recruited new professors and established new seminars and institutes in the universities to meet the new curricular requirements and replace some of the least able older professors.[23] Engelbrecht cites the philosophical faculty of the Vienna University as indicative of the substantial growth after 1848: from only 17 professors and *Privatdozenten* in 1848 to 47 in 1868 and 109 in 1888.[24] The number of professors in Austrian universities altogether nearly tripled between 1847 and the early 1870s.[25] Although university enrollments grew only modestly between 1870 and 1880 and economic growth slowed after the crash of 1873, the German liberal cabinets in the 1870s approved many new institutes, seminars, and clinics in a range of specialties from history and philology to all the natural sciences, law, and medicine. Some of the technical colleges, however, experienced slower growth in the numbers of teaching positions and institutes than did the universities between the 1850s and 1880s.

Nearly all of Austrian higher education shared in the new round of expansion that began in the 1890s. The great rise in enrollments provoked calls by student groups, professors, elected politicians, and popular organizations for more teaching personnel and expanded facilities in all the universities and technical colleges. A proliferation of new academic specialties also created pressure for the creation of new seminars and institutes, and the ministry generally responded as best it could. The smaller universities and technical colleges benefited along with the larger ones from the addition of new professorial chairs and institutes.[26] Educational expenditures, of course, had to compete with other urgent demands on the state budget; and the ministerial officials had to admit that, despite all they accomplished, they were not keeping up with the growing needs of higher education.[27]

Enrollment trends after the mid-nineteenth century in the various university faculties and in the particular schools within the technical colleges reflected shifts in popular demand and changing career opportunities. Already in the mid-1870s, government statisticians were commenting on the clear relationship of employment opportunities, the oversupply of newly educated professionals in some fields, and specific enrollment trends in the medical, philosophical, and theological faculties.[28] Nonetheless, some of the Austrian enrollment patterns also showed a stronger persistence of older attitudes regarding higher education and preparation for professional careers than was the case in Germany.

As in the German universities, the faculties of law and public administration (*Rechts- und Staatswissenschaften*) had the largest enrollments among the Austrian university faculties during the late eighteenth and early nineteenth centuries, and throughout the period from 1860 to World War I the law faculties continued to draw between 38 and 60 percent of all matriculated Austrian university students (see table 2 in the appendix). In the last years before 1914, though, Austrian youth were enrolling in the law faculties at more than twice the German rate. In 1910, the Austrian law faculties had 6.11 matriculated students per thousand inhabitants aged nineteen to twenty-two years, compared with only 2.75 law students per thousand inhabitants aged twenty to twenty-three years in Germany in 1911. In the latter year, the law faculties enrolled 51 percent of all the matriculated university students in Austria, compared with only 25 percent in Germany.[29]

In total numbers, enrollments in the Austrian medical faculties generally ranked second behind the law faculties from the mid-nineteenth century until after 1900, when the philosophical faculties overtook medicine. The medical faculties passed through several waves of expansion and contraction during the second half of the century (see figure 2 above and table 2 in the appendix). Increasing numbers of *Gymnasium* graduates in the late 1850s and 1860s, new medical faculties in Graz and Innsbruck, and the phasing out of the Josephs-Akademie after 1868 all contributed to strong increases in total medical faculty enrollments between 1860 and the early 1870s.[30] By 1870 many of the courses were badly overcrowded, and fears began to spread in the medical profession and the educational bureaucracy of a surplus of newly trained physicians. The cumulative costs and duration of medical training greatly exceeded those for the other learned professions. Overcrowding in the medical faculties and rising competition among new graduates for hospital appointments could easily discourage new enrollments. This and the uncertain economic conditions of the middle and late 1870s led to significant declines in the numbers of Austrian medical students.[31] Germany, which experienced many of the same economic and professional trends, also saw some decline in medical enrollments between 1872 and 1875.[32] The new, more demanding curriculum introduced in Austria in 1872 may have also had a dampening effect.[33]

During the 1880s Austrian medical enrollments recovered strongly along with university enrollments in general. Enrollments in the Vienna University's world-renowned medical faculty reached particularly high levels in the mid-1880s: in winter 1884–85, for instance, there were 2,291 matriculated students along with 164 nonmatriculated students.[34] The closing of the old surgical schools (*Wundärztliche Schulen*) in the 1870s sharply reduced the supply of medical practitioners from outside the universities and contributed, by the 1880s, to a widely perceived shortage of physicians. The largest cities might be well supplied, but small town and rural interests complained of inadequate numbers of practitioners. In 1891 the Society of Physicians in Vienna's First District, for instance, supported dropping the per-hour tuition fees (*Kollegiengeld*) for medical students and substituting lower flat fees to help supply more physicians to the countryside.[35] Germany's medical faculties had much the same experience as Austria's during the 1880s as their enrollments grew in response to rising demand for medical services and the continuing professionalization of medical training and practice.[36]

By the mid-1890s, a reaction set in to the increase in numbers of Austrian medical students and graduates so that medical enrollments declined significantly until around 1905. In Germany the reaction had already begun in 1889–90.[37] Medical enrollments rebounded in both countries after 1905 as the attraction of medical careers grew again in a period of strong economic expansion. In both Austria and Germany the numbers of medical students nearly doubled in the five years between 1905 and 1910.[38]

To some extent, the trends in enrollments in medical faculties throughout Central Europe during the late nineteenth century showed an inverse relationship to changes in the numbers of law students. In Austria, the law faculties grew strongly during the 1870s, while medicine lost significant numbers of students, and philosophy and theology declined modestly. The trends in medical and law enrollments reversed between 1885 and 1890, when the numbers of medical students increased by 25 percent and law students decreased by 4 percent. Between winter 1889–90 and winter 1904–5, the absolute numbers of matriculated law students in Austria increased by 75 percent, while the numbers of medical students fell by 58 percent. Enrollments in law and medicine also showed an inverse relationship in

Germany between the 1880s and 1905.[39] This inverse relationship suggests that legal and medical studies competed directly with each other for some segments of the student population. This will be borne out later by the analysis of the socioeconomic origins of students in the various faculties, which shows strong parallels between the law and medical students.[40] Probably few students changed from medicine to law or vice versa once they began university studies; the great differences in curricula made that difficult. Apparently, though, many youth during their studies in the *Gymnasien* envisioned as a general goal a career in a respected, secure profession and were choosing *between* law and medicine as they approached entry into a university.[41]

Enrollments in the philosophical and theological faculties were also governed to a great degree by popular estimations of career opportunities and the relative prestige and financial rewards of the professions those faculties served. Here, too, though, persisting older traditions of Austrian higher education played a part. The Austrian university reformers of the 1850s and 1860s gave great importance to improving and expanding the philosophical faculties, but those faculties drew few students compared with law and medicine until after 1900. Only 17 percent of all matriculated Austrian university students were enrolled in the philosophical faculties in 1861 and 1880 and only 15 percent in 1900. By winter 1909–10, however, that portion had risen to 24 percent. In Germany, by contrast, where philosophical faculties tended to split into separate faculties of humanities and natural sciences, enrollments in these faculties taken together grew from 33 percent of all university students in 1865–66 to fully 52 percent by 1910–11.[42]

Before the mid-nineteenth century, few Austrian students had gone to the universities to study in the humanities and natural sciences, and traditional preferences in this regard apparently persisted to a greater extent in Austria during the late nineteenth century than in Germany during the same period. Even after 1900, when enrollments in the Austrian philosophical faculties began to increase significantly as compared with the other faculties, those numbers grew more slowly than in Germany. This increase occurred in a period when throughout Central Europe employment in secondary school teaching was expanding, the humanities and natural sciences gained greater prestige, and more of the school-aged population was enrolling in higher education than ever before.[43]

Throughout the late nineteenth century, Austria's university-based theological faculties, all of them Catholic except for an Eastern Orthodox faculty in Chernivtsi, attracted fewer students than did the faculties of law, medicine, or philosophy. Germany's universities showed similar trends from the early 1870s onward.[44] In 1866 only 15 percent of all the matriculated Austrian university students were enrolled in theological faculties, compared with 26 percent of all university students in Germany. After the 1860s and 1870s, all of Austria's university-based theological faculties suffered significant declines compared with the other faculties except in Innsbruck. In 1910 the Austrian theological faculties enrolled only 6 percent of all matriculated university students, again lower than in Germany, where the Protestant and Catholic faculties together drew 8 percent of the university students.[45] Young men in Austria who wished to join the clergy could also study Catholic, Orthodox, or Protestant theology in diocesan seminaries, monastic institutions, and several independent theological faculties. Nonetheless, by 1900 the low attraction of theological studies and clerical careers resulted in generally low enrollments in the other institutions as well. In the winter semester 1904–5, for instance, all of Austria's Christian seminaries and independent theological faculties had an enrollment of only 2,076, compared with the 1,197 matriculated students in the university theological faculties, 16,416 in the secular university faculties, and 7,656 in the technical colleges.[46]

The preferences of Austrian technical college students for the various schools within the colleges fluctuated relatively little during the late nineteenth century. Overall, the schools of general engineering had the largest enrollments for nearly the whole period from the late 1870s to World War I. Chemical engineering with its related fields (the *Chemisch-technische Schulen*) gained strongly in the 1870s, but those schools lost students as did all the others during the depression of the 1880s. During the expansion of higher education between the early 1890s and 1914, the general engineering schools and the *Maschinenbauschulen* for mechanical engineering and related fields showed the strongest growth. The schools of civil and structural engineering (*Hochbauschulen*) consistently had the smallest enrollments within the Austrian technical colleges. This contrasted with the *Bauschulen* in many of Germany's technical colleges, which had relatively larger enrollments. The Austrian technical colleges, however, undertook little of architectural training, leaving the primary role to the Academy of Fine Arts in Vienna. Within the individual technical colleges, the distribution of students among the various schools tended to follow the general pattern except for the two Czech technical colleges in Prague and Brno. In those two institutions after 1900, as elsewhere, the general engineering schools led in enrollments; but they were followed in the Czech colleges by the "general departments," which taught diverse subjects such as applied mathematics, actuarial science, and some business specialties, and then by the mechanical engineering schools.[47]

Many forces caused Austria's academic secondary and higher education to expand and the student numbers to increase during the second half of the nineteenth century. The unevenness of growth over time and the variations among the various segments of the educational system suggest that no one factor had primacy. An expanding school-aged population was an obvious prerequisite for general growth in enrollments, but the increasing share of that population that pursued advanced education also represented qualitative changes in values and behavior. The ministerial authorities in Vienna controlled part of the process by deciding where and when to expand the educational institutions that the ministry funded, but one cannot say that the central government intended or even managed to control all the growth that occurred, because much initiative in expanding secondary education came from local governments and voluntary associations. In any case, the institutional expansion often failed to keep pace with the increasing student numbers. Once the central government had established the legal principle that those who earned the *Matura* from the appropriate secondary school, along with acceptable course grades, were entitled to admission to a university or technical college, it could not control the growth in enrollments in higher education except by introducing extraordinary numerical limits and risking public outcry.[48]

With regard to economic forces, the government authorities considered what educational initiatives seemed appropriate to assure growth and prosperity and what expenditures their budgets could sustain. Various officials, elected representatives, and educators differed, though, over what educational measures might best contribute to popular well-being. The neo-absolutist reformers of the 1850s thought that improving the quality of academic secondary and higher education, although not necessarily the quantity, was necessary to the general welfare of state and society. The German liberal ministers of the 1860s and 1870s pursued educational policies that both improved advanced education and broadened access to it, and until 1873 they benefited from an economic boom that recommended such action and made it affordable. The more conservative figures who framed policies in the 1880s and early 1890s faced straitened economic conditions, and they argued for increased vocational training and against expanding academic education. Nonetheless, they could not stop the growth during the 1880s of *Gymnasium* and university enrollments at the expense of the *Realschulen* and technical colleges that was motivated by reduced employment opportunities in industry and commerce and heightened interest in more traditional professions. Renewed economic development after the mid-1890s encouraged government officials to resume the expansion of educational facilities on a broad front, but they failed to keep up with the ballooning enrollments in the secondary schools, universities, and technical colleges.

In considering educational issues, Austrian government officials, like their counterparts elsewhere in Europe, might try to influence popular attitudes in hopes of stemming the growing appetite for advanced education. The ministerial authorities in Vienna attempted to reduce enrollments when they introduced the admissions examinations for secondary schools in 1870 and, as will be seen, they made additional efforts in the 1880s and 1890s.[49] Nonetheless, the state could do little to control the rising popular aspirations for secondary and higher education and for careers in learned professions. Indeed, the ministerial officials, along with the provincial and local governments, often helped encourage those aspirations by modernizing the curricula and expanding the institutions After the late 1850s, though, they were often only responding to growing popular demand as expressed in the overcrowding of facilities and calls by elected politicians and voluntary associations for more schools.

While economic trends and government policies helped fuel popular demand for educational opportunities, those popular aspirations had something of their own dynamic. It was no accident, of course, that the boom years of the 1860s and early 1870s and the new boom era around 1900 saw strong increases in enrollments, particularly in the more modern and technologically oriented segments of secondary and higher education. A developing economy encouraged beliefs that new opportunities were opening in industry, commerce, and finance as well as in the more familiar pursuits of higher state service, law, medicine, and secondary school teaching. The difficult economic conditions of the 1880s and the government's fostering of vocational education stopped for a decade the growth in the portion of all eleven- to eighteen-year-olds attending the academic secondary schools. Nonetheless, popular aspirations for advanced education and hopes for careers in a learned profession continued to increase during the 1880s, as the percentage of the nineteen- to twenty-two-year-olds who went on to universities continued to grow.

Social and political competition among Austria's various ethnic and national groups often focused on educational issues, and ethnic or national competition surely contributed to the growth in popular demand for advanced education. Czechs in the Bohemian lands and Slovenes in the southeastern portions of the Alpine lands raised demands for secondary and higher education in their mother tongues as part of their challenges to the historic dominance of German-speakers, just as did Ukrainians in their struggle with Polish elites in eastern Galicia. After the 1860s nationalist politicians often succeeded in winning increased educational opportunities for their peoples, but they typically used their peoples' educational aspirations only as part of broader efforts to mobilize them for social and political action. Nationalist leaders encouraged and exploited popular educational aspirations, but they seldom created them.

The spread of desires for advanced education and entry into learned professions to larger segments of the population than before the mid-nineteenth century was only another by-product of the larger transformation from the traditional economy and corporate society to a modern industrial market economy and class structure. That transformation also worked to spread modern national identities and provided the social fodder for the nationalist political movements themselves. In the Bohemian lands, for instance, there was an "educational competition" between Czechs and Germans, as Friedrich

Prinz puts it, which surely added to the development of the educational network and to increasing enrollments,[50] but these crown lands also experienced some of the most rapid economic and social development of any part of Austria during the nineteenth century. If ethnic competition worked as a critical independent factor in increasing both popular demand and access to advanced education in imperial Austria, then it would be hard to explain why Moravia consistently had relatively higher enrollments for its youth in secondary and higher education than did Bohemia, where the Czech-German conflict was more intense, or why secondary enrollments were particularly strong in ethnically homogeneous, but well-industrialized Vorarlberg (see tables 5 and 6). The Slovenes in Carniola, southern Styria, and southern Carinthia had as much reason as the Czechs to want to use education to help overcome the social dominance of ethnic Germans. Nonetheless, the poorer economic conditions and slower development of those lands, along with the Slovenes' smaller numbers, resulted in the Slovene national political movement and Slovene advanced education evolving more slowly than the Czech counterparts. Ethnic competition was only part of a complex, evolving social and political matrix that produced increases in school attendance and ultimately the growth of the professions.[51]

Whatever the force of government policies, economic conditions, and ethnic competition, those factors were refracted by popular perceptions in influencing the growing demand for advanced education. The individual calculations of youth and their parents and their beliefs about the value of education and the prospects for careers in educated pursuits determined who enrolled in the secondary schools, universities, and technical colleges. On the eve of World War I, advanced academic education still remained the province of an elite in simple numerical terms: in spring 1910, only 3.06 percent of all eleven- to eighteen-year-old males and females throughout Austria were attending academic secondary schools. In winter 1909–10, only 1.2 percent of the nineteen- to twenty-two-year-old males and females were matriculated students in universities with only 0.42 percent of all eighteen- to twenty-two-year-olds matriculated in technical colleges. Nonetheless, those rates of enrollment represented more than twofold gains for the secondary schools and universities over the rates in 1870 and a quadrupling in the rate for the technical colleges. Aspirations for advanced academic education, the privileges it conferred, and the professional careers to which it led were clearly increasing among the Austrian population, as elsewhere in Western and Central Europe during the late nineteenth century.

Many contemporary observers considered the increasing enrollments in secondary and higher education and the apparent broadening of access to the educated strata as signs of progress, but others were less sanguine. In Austria, already by the 1870s and increasingly in the 1880s and 1890s, conservative officials, politicians, and educators warned against producing larger numbers of people prepared for professions than society actually needed. Pessimists feared the raising of misplaced hopes among the lower classes for upward social mobility through education. In 1889 one anonymous commentator on Austrian education voiced such worries in particularly somber terms:

> This aiming high above one's status, often notwithstanding all conditions, is, in fact, a dark side of our social relations, for it accords with a basic misjudgment of the value and importance of a trained agricultural and craft element, a sad delusion about the good fortune of becoming something "better," a mistake which often must be paid for with the bitterest disappointment, a mongrel life, and the dire circumstances of pressing occupational responsibility and an increasing struggle for survival, and which raises up that multifarious proletariat in office garb that is worse off than the proletariat with the callused hands of labor.[52]

Such critics feared that expanding educational opportunities were bringing into the circles of the educated and semieducated too many from the lower middle classes and working classes, who might not be suited to professional callings, would not have careers up to their expectations, and in frustration might contribute to political radicalism and social unrest. These fears were shared by high officials in the Ministry of Religion and Instruction after 1879, when a conservative cabinet came to power. The central government after the early 1880s made repeated, although largely fruitless, efforts to limit the growth of secondary and higher education. Indeed, the pressures favoring the further growth and development of advanced education became so strong after the mid-1890s that the state authorities saw a gradual erosion of their powers to control change.

Notes

1 Statistics derive from Schimmer 1858, 7, no. 1: 26–27, 125; Schimmer 1877, 59, 65; *Statistisches Jahrbuch 1869* (1871), 334–35, 354–55; *Statistisches Jahrbuch 1874* (1877), 8–9, 14–15; *Statistisches Jahrbuch 1879* (1882), 10–21, 36–47; *Öster. Statistik*, 16, no. 2 (1887): 2–5, 14–17; 28, no. 4 (1892): 2–5, 14–17; 51, no. 1 (1898): 2–5, 15–17; 68, no. 3 (1903): 2–5, 16–19; 79, no. 3 (1908): 2–5; 14–17; and n.s., 7, no. 3 (1913): 2–5, 14–17.

2 See discussion of the social origins of university and technical college students in chapter 5 below. Ringer 1979, passim, emphasizes the social differentiation of the various segments of secondary and higher education in late-nineteenth-century Germany, but others, such as Lundgreen 1981, point out that the sons of all occupational groups in Germany preferred the classical *Gymnasien* over other secondary schools. In Lundgreen's view only the universities and technical colleges in Germany showed the social segmentation that Ringer claims.

3 See Schimmer 1877, 61; Otruba 1975, 77; Prinz 1969, 60; and Jílek and Lomič 1973, 444.

4 Megner 1985, 77.
5 See Stark 1906, 193–94; and Lomič and Horská 1978, 168–71.
6 On the introduction of doctoral degrees in the technical colleges, see Engelbrecht 1982–88, 4:254; and Lomič and Horská 1978, 269. On the limitation of enrollments, see Wurzer 1965–67, 48; and the ordinances reprinted in Jähnl 1916, 433–37. See further discussion of these emergency measures in chapter 3 below.
7 Forman, Heilbron, and Weart 1975, 6–8.
8 Calculated from statistics in Haan 1917, 161; and Titze 1987, 28–32, 70–71.
9 The primacy here of Lower Austria, including Vienna, was not simply the result of migration to Vienna by students, since the statistics on education published by the Austrian Statistical Central Commission analyzed students on the basis of birthplace or legal home residence (*Heimatrecht*), not current residence. The published statistics on the geographical origins of students did not distinguish between the matriculated students, who were pursuing diplomas and degrees, and nonmatriculated students.
10 See further discussion of the recruitment of students in secondary and higher education in chapters 4 and 5.
11 The Germanizing tendencies of the neo-absolutist regime during the 1850s led even to the introduction of German-language instruction in the University of Krakow after 1853, but reduced central control in the early 1860s allowed the Galician provincial authorities to begin the gradual establishment of Polish as the language of instruction in the universities of Krakow and L'viv, a process that was essentially complete by 1871. See Strakosch-Graßmann 1905, 283–84; and Urbanitsch 1980, 100–101.
12 See further discussion in chapter 4.
13 Haan 1917, 183, 189.
14 On the division of the Prague University, see Goll 1908; and Skilling 1949, 430–49. On the attempt to open an Italian law faculty in Innsbruck in 1904, see chapter 3.
15 See Haan 1917, 165; and Engelbrecht 1982–88, 4:256–59, 274–76.
16 See O. Frankl 1905–9; and Engelbrecht 1982–88, 4:263–65.
17 Engelbrecht 1982–88, 4:255–56.
18 Statistics in Schimmer 1858, 7, no. 1:26–27, 125; Schimmer 1877, 59, 65; *Statistisches Jahrbuch 1869* (1871), 334–35, 354–55; *Statistisches Jahrbuch 1874* (1877), 8–9, 14–15; *Statistisches Jahrbuch 1879* (1882), 10–21, 36–47; *Öster. Statistik*, 16, no. 2 (1887): 2–5, 14–17; 28, no. 4 (1892): 2–5, 14–17; 51, no. 1 (1898): 2–5, 15–17; 68, no. 3 (1903): 2–5, 16–19; 79, no. 3 (1908): 2–5; 14–17; and n.s., 7, no. 3 (1913): 2–5, 14–17.
19 See Haan 1917, 162, 167.
20 *Öster. Statistik*, n.s., 7, no. 3 (1913): 2–5, 14–17.
21 See Haan 1917, 170–73. In winter 1910–11 the largest technical colleges in Germany, in Munich and Berlin, had 2,452 and 2,150 matriculated students respectively. In the same semester the Berlin law faculty had 2,835 matriculated students and the Munich law faculty 1,625.
22 See, for example, the complaints from students in the Vienna University medical faculty in 1869, reported in Lesky 1976, 262. See further discussion of student experiences in the educational institutions in chapter 6 below.
23 See Lentze 1962, 31, 113–48.
24 Engelbrecht 1982–88, 4:235.
25 Ficker 1873, 245.
26 See Strakosch-Graßmann 1905, 315–18.

27 See Engelbrecht 1982–88, 4:227–38.

28 See Juraschek 1876, 333; and Schimmer 1877, 72–73.

29 Statistics calculated from table 2 in the appendix and from data on Germany in Haan 1917, 161; and Ringer 1979, 291.

30 See Widmann 1974, 202–17.

31 Pliwa 1908, 9–10.

32 Titze 1984, 104–5.

33 On the development of the reforms in the medical curriculum, see Lesky 1976, 261–73.

34 *Öster. Statistik* 16, no. 2 (1887): 2–3. See discussion of the trends in medical enrollments in Lesky 1976, 261.

35 AVA Wien KUM Praes. 1891, no. 13447, "Promemoria des Vereins der Ärzte des I. Bezirkes in Wien in Angelegenheit der Reformfrage der medicinischen Studienordnung," 20 June 1891.

36 See Titze 1984, 105–6.

37 On enrollment trends in Germany, see Jarausch 1982, 38–49, 145–48.

38 On the trends in Germany, see Titze 1984, 105–6.

39 See the statistics in Jarausch 1982, 136.

40 See discussion in chapter 5.

41 Late in life, Sigmund Freud reminisced about choosing during his *Gymnasium* years between future study of law or medicine, although he asserted he decided more on intellectual than professional grounds. See Freud [1935] 1950, 13–15.

42 Jarausch 1982, 136.

43 On these developments in Germany, see Jarausch 1982, 134–59.

44 See statistics in Jarausch 1982, 136.

45 See table 2 in the appendix for the Austrian statistics and for Germany, Jarausch 1982, 136.

46 *Öster. Statistik* 79, no. 3 (1908): 26–29. During the late nineteenth century Austria's traditional orthodox rabbis were trained in various yeshivas in Galicia and Hungary. Future rabbis from the Alpine and Bohemian lands who wanted more modern education typically studied first in a philosophical faculty and then completed their training in a rabbinical seminary in Germany or Hungary. A small Jewish theological institute was founded in Vienna in 1893. On Austria's seminaries and church-run theological schools, see Engelbrecht 1982–88, 4:265–68.

47 On general enrollment trends in the Austrian technical colleges, see Wurzer 1965–67, 60–66; and for Prague, Lomič and Horská 1978, 170–71, 380–88.

48 See chapter 3.

49 See chapter 3.

50 Prinz 1969, 50. Prinz balances this by placing the factor of national competition in the context of economic and social development in the Bohemian lands (pp. 49–66, passim). Turn-of-the-century commentators on Czech education tended to portray the rise of Czech secondary and higher education as part of the struggle for national rights. For examples, see Šafránek 1913–18; Šafránek 1898; and from an Austrian German perspective, Wotawa 1918.

51 On ethnic identification and nationalistic political mobilization in the Bohemian lands, see G. Cohen 1981; Stölzl 1971; and the somewhat more schematic interpretation in Urban 1978, 179–256, passim.

52 *Die vor- und nachmärzliche Mittelschule* 1889, 31–32; also quoted in Engelbrecht 1976, 45.

Appendix A

Table 1 Enrollments in Austrian Secondary Schools, 1851–1910*.

Academic yr.	Men's Gymn.	Realgymn.	Women's Gymn.	Total Gymn.	Realsch.	Total
1850–51	21,175			21,175	4,455	25,630
1855–56	19,958			19,958	6,662	26,620
1860–61	27,039			27,039	9,223	36,262
1865–66	31,969			31,969	11,866	43,835
1869–70	27,772	2,725		30,497	13,237	43,734
1874–75	22,686	11,451		34,137	21,552	55,689
1879–80	38,378	9,590		47,968	17,967	65,935
1884–85	43,775	9,459		53,234	16,327	69,561
1889–90	44,597	8,314		52,911	18,384	71,295
1894–95	49,842	6,310		56,152	23,600	79,752
1899–1900	59,649	4,998		64,647	31,267	95,914
1904–5	73,467	4,133	493	78,093	41,877	119,970
1909–10	—	91,546	2,732	94,278	46,267	140,545

Sources: Schimmer 1858; Schimmer 1877; Statistisches Jahrbuch für das Jahr 1874; Statistisches Jahrbuch für das Jahr 1879; Öster. Statistik 2, no. 1 (1882); 16, no. 2 (1887); 28, no. 4 (1892); 61, no. 1 (1898); 68, no. 3 (1903); 79, no. 3 (1908); n.s., 7, no. 3 (1913).

* Enrollments are the total number of matriculated ("public") and "private" students at the end of each academic year indicated.

Table 2 Matriculated Students in Austrian Universities and Technical Colleges, 1857–1910.

Winter sem.	Total univ.	Law	Med.	Phil.	Theol.	Total tech. col.
1856–57*	3,709	2,039	821	459	390	2,235
1864–65*	4,901	2,269	1,117	776	739	2,472
1869–70	7,904	3,038	2,376	1,515	975	1,699
1874–75	7,616	3,521	1,600	1,860	635	3,152
1879–80	8,114	4,364	1,544	1,384	822	2,988
1884–85	11,361	5,103	4,005	1,070	1,183	2,121
1889–90	12,421	4,922	5,234	939	1,326	1,608
1894–95	13,169	6,158	4,686	1,210	1,115	2,579
1899–1900	14,331	8,393	2,793	2,127	1,018	4,843
1904–5	17,613	8,621	2,214	5,581	1,197	7,656
1909–10	23,068	11,668	4,389	5,605	1,406	10,110

Sources: Schimmer 1858; *Statistisches Jahrbuch der öster. Monarchie für das Jahr 1865; Statistisches Jahrbuch für das Jahr 1869; Statistisches Jahrbuch für das Jahr 1874; Statistisches Jahrbuch für das Jahr 1879; Öster. Statistik* 2, no. 1 (1882); 16, no. 2 (1887); 28, no. 4 (1892); 61, no. 1 (1898); 68, no. 3 (1903); 79, no. 3 (1908); n.s., 7, no. 3 (1913).
* *The statistics for 1856–57 and 1864–65 do not include the universities of Pavia and Padua.*

References

Austrian governmental periodicals

Österreichische Statistik. 1882–1910; n.s., 1910–18.
Statistisches Jahrbuch der österreichischen Monarchie für das Jahr 1863 et seq. 1864–68; after 1867, *Statistisches Jahrbuch für das Jahr 1867* et seq. 1869–84.

Other printed sources

Cohen, Gary B. 1981. *The Politics of Ethnic Survival: Germans in Prague, 1861–1914*. Princeton: Princeton University Press.
Engelbrecht, Helmut. 1976. "Zur Organisation der österreichischen Sekundarschulen in der zweiten Hälfte des 19. Jahrhunderts." *Jahresbericht des Bundesgymnasiums Krems am Schlusse des Schuljahres 1975/76*, 5–46. Krems a. D.: Bundesgymnasium Krems.
———. 1982–88. *Geschichte des österreichischen Bildungswesens*. 5 vols. Vienna: Öster. Bundesverlag.
Ficker, Adolf. 1875. "Die österreichischen Mittleschulen in dem Vierteljahrhundert von 1850 bis 1874." *Statistische Monatsschrift* 1:97–118.
Forman, Paul, John Heilbron, and Spencer Weart, eds. 1975. *Physics circa 1900*. Supplement to *Historical Studies in the Physical Sciences*, vol. 5. Princeton: Princeton University Press.
Frankl, Otto. 1905–9. "Bergbaulehranstalten." In *Österreichisches Staatswörterbuch*, edited by Ernst Mischler and Josef Ulbrich, 1:484. 2d ed. rev. Vienna: Hölder.
Freud, Sigmund. [1935] 1950. *An Autobiographical Study*. Translated by James Strachey. London: Hogarth Press.

Goll, Jaroslav. 1908. *Rozdělení pražské university Karlo-Ferdinandovy roku 1882 a počátek samostatné university české* (The Division of the Charles-Ferdinand University of Prague and the Beginning of the Independent Czech University). Prague: Nakl. Klubu historického.

Haan, Hugo Freiherr von. 1917. "Statistische Streiflichter zur österreichischen Hochschulfrequenz." *Statistische Monatsschrift*, n.s., 22:155–208.

Jähnl, Wilhelm. 1916. *Vorschriften für die Technischen Hochschulen Österreichs.* Vienna: K. K. Schulbücherverlag.

Jarausch, Konrad H. 1982. *Students, Society, and Politics in Imperial Germany.* Princeton: Princeton University Press, 1982.

Jílek, František, and Václav Lomič. 1973. *Dějiny českého vysokého učení technického* (History of the Czech Technical College). Vol. 1, pt. 1. Prague: České vysoké učení technické.

Juraschek, Franz. 1876. "Der Besuch der österreichischen Universitäten in den Jahren 1861–1875." *Statistische Monatsschrift* 2:303–37.

Lentze, Hans. 1962. *Die Universitätsreform des Ministers Graf Leo Thun-Hohenstein.* Österreichische Akademie der Wissenschaften, Philosophisch-Historische Klasse, Sitzungsberichte, vol. 239, no. 2. Vienna: Böhlau.

Lesky, Erna. 1976. *The Vienna Medical School of the Nineteenth Century.* Translated by L. Williams and I. S. Levij. Baltimore: Johns Hopkins University Press.

Lomič, Václav, and Pavla Horská. 1978. *Dějiny českého vysokého učení technického* (History of the Czech Technical College). Vol. 1, pt. 2. Prague: České vysoké učení technické.

Lundgreen, Peter. 1981. "Bildung und Besitz—Einheit oder Inkongruenz in der europäischen Sozialgeschichte?" *Geschichte und Gesellschaft* 7:262–75.

Megner, Karl. 1985. *Beamte: Wirtschafts- und sozialgeschichtliche Aspekte des k. k. Beamtentums.* Studien zur Geschichte der Österreichisch-ungarischen Monarchie, vol. 21. Vienna: Öster Akademie der Wissenschaften.

Otruba, Gustav. 1975. "Die Universitäten in der Hochschulorganisation der Donau-Monarchie: Nationale Erziehungsstätten im Vielvölkerreich 1850 bis 1914." In *Student und Hochschule im 19. Jahrhundert*, edited by Christian Helfer and Mohammed Rassem, 75–155. Göttingen: Vandenhoeck & Ruprecht.

Pliwa, Ernst. 1908. *Österreichs Universitäten 1863/4–1902/3: Statistisch-Graphische Studie.* Vienna: F. Tempsky.

Prinz, Friedrich. 1969. "Das Schulwesen der Böhmischen Länder von 1848 bis 1939: Ein Überblick." In *Aktuelle Forschungsprobleme um die Erste Tschechoslowakische Republik*, edited by Karl Bosl, 49–66. Munich and Vienna: R. Oldenbourg.

Ringer, Fritz K. 1979. *Education and Society in Modern Europe.* Bloomington: Indiana University Press.

Šafránek, Jan. 1898. *Rozvoj českého školství: Památník na oslavu Padesatiletého Jubilea Františka Josefa I* (The development of Czech schooling: Commemorative volume for the Fiftieth Jubilee of Francis Joseph I). Prague.

———. 1913–18. *Školy české: Obraz jejich v voje a osud ů* (Czech schools: A portrait of their development and trials). 2 vols. Prague: Nakl. Matice česká.

Schimmer, Gustav A. 1858. "Statistik der Lehranstalten des österreichischen Kaiserstaates für die Studienjahre 1851–1857." Parts 1 and 2. *Mittheilungen aus dem Gebiete der Statistik* 7, no. 1; no. 4.

———. 1877. "Frequenz der Lehranstalten Oesterreichs von 1841 bis 1876, in Vergleichung zur Bevölkerung." *Statistische Monatsschrift* 3:53–74.

Skilling, H. Gordon. 1949. "The Partition of the University of Prague." *Slavonic Review* 27:430–49.

Stark, Franz, ed. 1906. *Die k. k. deutsche technische Hochschule in Prag 1806–1906*. Prague: Selbstverlag.

Stölzl, Christoph. 1971. *Die Ära Bach in Böhmen: Sozialgeschichtliche Studien zum Neoabsolutismus 1849–1859*. Munich and Vienna: R. Oldenbourg.

Strakosch-Graßmann, Gustav. 1905. *Geschichte des österreichischen Unterrichtswesens*. Vienna: A. Pichler.

Titze, Hartmut. 1984. "Die zyklische Überproduktion von Akademikern im 19. und 20. Jahrhundert." *Geschichte und Gesellschaft* 10:92–121.

———. 1987. *Das Hochschulstudium in Preußen und Deutschland 1820–1944: Datenhandbuch zur deutschen Bildungsgeschichte*. Vol. 1, pt. 1. Göttingen: Vandenhoeck & Ruprecht.

Urban, Otto. 1978. *Kapitalismus a česká společnost: K otázkám formování české společnosti v 19. století* (Capitalism and Czech society: On the questions of the formation of Czech society in the nineteenth century). Prague: Svoboda.

Urbanitsch, Peter. 1980. "Die Deutschen in Österreich: Statistisch-deskriptiver Überblick." In *Die Habsburgermonarchie, 1848–1918*, edited by Adam Wandruszka and Peter Urbanitsch, vol. 3, pt. 1:33–410. Vienna: Öster. Akademie der Wissenschaften.

Widmann, Eva S. 1974. "Idee und Wirklichkeit der Universität Wien im Spiegel autobiographischer Quellen des 19. Jahrhunderts." Ph.D. diss., Universität Wien.

Wotawa, August Ritter von. 1918. *Das tschechische Schulwesen: 10. Flugschrift der Deutschen Arbeit*. Prague: Verlag Deutsche Arbeit.

Wurzer, Rudolf. 1965–67. "Die Stellung der Technischen Hochschule Wien im Ablauf ihrer Geschichte." In *150 Jahre Technische Hochschule in Wien 1815–1965*, edited by Heinrich Sequenz, 1:11–157. 3 vols. Vienna: Technische Hochschule Wien.

16

HIGHER EDUCATION
IN POLAND

B. Simon

Source: *Universities Quarterly* VII (1952–3): 176–83.

A recent visit to Poland enabled me to make a study of the main developments in the Polish system of higher education since the war. Much of
my information was obtained from the Ministry of Higher Education, in
answer to questions I was asked to submit in advance, or in the course
of two long interviews at which I met the heads of seven departments of
the Ministry. The rest was obtained in the course of visits to a number
of colleges and institutes, at Gdansk, Warsaw and Cracow particularly. At
one of these colleges, I was received by the Pro-Rector, professors, lecturers,
and student representatives, and in the general discussion which followed
students and junior lecturers took a considerable part. At others I met
professors who had been university teachers for twenty, thirty, and, in one
case, forty years and the discussions were equally full and frank.

The key to the structural changes in the Polish system of higher education is its adaptation to meet the needs of an increasingly planned socialist
society. When the Six-Year Plan (1949–55) is completed, Poland will have
made the transition from a predominantly agricultural to a predominantly
industrial economy. This transition has made necessary a considerable
expansion and reorganization of higher education.

From 1946, a generous system of grants and scholarships has made possible the entry of many students from working-class and peasant homes,
either through the growing school system, or by means of special two-year
preparatory courses. The number of full-time students between the ages of
eighteen and twenty-three in institutions of higher education has grown
from 45,000 before the war to 110,000 in 1951, while the total population
has dropped in the same period from 32 millions to 24 millions. At the same
time there have been radical changes in the structure of the system to meet
the new conditions.

To-day the various institutions of higher education form part of a unified system, all being of equal status and having the power to grant similar degrees. With some exceptions, which will be detailed below, the Ministry of Higher Education and Science, set up in 1949, is responsible for their administration and development. Each type of institution has a clearly defined function.

Universities

The pre-war Polish universities, of which there were five, were, of course, the apex of the system of education. They normally had the four traditional faculties—philosophy, law, medicine and theology; technology was provided for in the famous higher technological colleges, particularly that of Warsaw, which had no connexion with the university. In general the principle of *Lehr und Lern Freiheit* obtained, professors lecturing on what subjects they liked, while the student, who attended only those lectures he wished to, was under no obligation to present himself for his degree examination in any particular year.

Reorganization has meant, first, the separation of the medical faculties from the universities and their establishment as independent academies under the aegis of the Ministry of Health. In addition, new medical academies have been set up in non-university towns, such as that at Gdansk with 3,000 students. The purpose of this change has been to ensure the effective integration of the system of medical education with the hospitals and health service.

In the same way, the few faculties of agriculture in existence (for instance, at Cracow and Poznan) are now being separated from the universities and linked with the independent higher agricultural colleges in a unified system of higher agricultural education. Again, new institutions of this kind are being developed, of which perhaps the most important is the college of Olzczyn for 5,000 students, all of whom are being housed in hostels in what will be a small university town. These agricultural colleges have close links with the Ministry of Agriculture, which is directly responsible for agricultural intermediate schools, though they are at present administered by the Ministry of Higher Education.

Other higher educational institutions, mentioned below, are also being developed. The position of the universities to-day, therefore, is that of *primus inter pares*. They no longer have the monopoly of degrees, and have been shorn of some of their former functions, but they remain the leading institutions for the fundamental study of the traditional humanistic and scientific subjects. Two new universities have been established, one at Lublin, the other at Lodz. The old faculty of philosophy has been divided into a faculty of humanities and a faculty of science, while the faculty of law remains at most universities, together with the faculties of theology at Warsaw and Cracow. (There is also a Catholic University at Lublin.)

There is an increasing demand for university graduates, both in arts and science. The expansion of industry and of research accounts for the latter, while the rapid development of secondary and higher education has meant a growing demand for arts as well as science graduates as teachers. Apparently there are several other avenues apart from teaching open to arts graduates, resulting particularly from the general development of cultural activities.

Technological, economics and art colleges

The greatest expansion has been, naturally enough, in higher technological education; from 9,000 students before the war to 52,000 to-day. There are now ten polytechnics, each of which has close links with the Ministries chiefly concerned with the employment of its graduates (*e.g.*, Heavy Industry, Transport, Shipping, etc.). The aim here appears to be to concentrate the study of particular specializations in one or two main institutions, large enough to provide for a wide range of teaching and research. There are, for instance, two main centres of mining technology: one at the Cracow School of Mining, which has 2,000 students, and the other at Gliwice.

The ten higher economics schools are largely new creations. The first to be organized, in 1949, was the Central School of Planning and Statistics at Warsaw, which now has about 2,000 internal and 2,000 external students in four faculties: planning of industry, planning of commerce, statistics, finance. This college has the specific aim of preparing entrants for the central planning institutions. After a year's experience of running this school, other economics schools were established in 1950, each designed to prepare economists, statisticians, and planners for work in particular sections of the economy. For instance, the schools at Katowice and Cracow are linked to heavy industry, those at Lodz and Warsaw to light industry that; at Sopot and Sczczecin to transport, and the school at Poznan to commerce and banking. At Warsaw there is also a higher school for diplomacy and foreign trade.

Apart from the medical academies, all the institutions already mentioned are administered by the Ministry of Higher Education, which, therefore, has four main departments: universities, technology, economics, agriculture. In addition, however, there are nineteen higher schools of art, music, sculpture, drama and choreography which come under the Ministry of Arts. Finally, the Ministry of Education is responsible for the six higher pedagogical schools. These are new four-year degree-giving institutions preparing teachers for the new secondary schools, where the pupils are in the 14 to 18 age range.

Planning

The Six-Year Plan, which covers social and cultural facilities as well as industry and agriculture, requires a definite and increasing number of trained specialists each year. The plan for higher education is closely linked with this national plan, and is drawn up in some detail each year at the Ministry. Preliminary discussions first take place with other Ministries, at which the number of specialists required in different branches of the economy is carefully assessed. The Ministry, in collaboration with the colleges, then draws up a general plan for submission to the Central Planning Council, which is responsible for co-ordinating all plans from different sections of the economy. The Council eventually passes back directives to the Ministry, incorporating the final requirements of the overall plan, and the Ministry is responsible, in co-operation with the various institutions of higher education, for carrying out these directives.

Planning of studies

This kind of planning presupposes an organized system of higher studies. One of the first steps was, therefore, to urge on students and teaching staff the necessity of organizing courses and completing them in the stated time. This involved both the working out of plans of study and the introduction of more disciplined methods of teaching and learning.

The planning of studies is the responsibility of the Central Council of Higher Education, which is attached to the Ministry and is, in fact, an essential part of the administration. It is composed of heads of colleges and professors, and is responsible for planning the reorganization of institutions and the establishment of new ones. The council has a number of sub-sections, one for each major subject of study, staffed also by leading professors and teachers from the different institutions. These are responsible for working out the syllabus for each different subject. Suggestions are regularly sent in at the close of each academic year, and the syllabus is modified accordingly. More than 800 members of staff take part in this work.

As a result, the basic courses in each subject are now similar in all colleges. This ensures a recognized standard, and lays certain obligations on staff as well as students to cover a course thoroughly in the way that general experience has found to be best. Over and above this, professors are free to lecture as they will, particularly to final year and post-graduate students.

A more recent innovation has been the introduction of a general course for all students in Marxist philosophy and political economy. The programme for this course is worked out in the usual way at the Central Council by the professors and lecturers concerned; it covers dialectical and historical materialism, and Marxist economics, and takes into account current problems in the economic and social life of Poland. In addition, all students normally take at least two foreign languages.

Student methods of work

So far as student methods of work are concerned, there have been important innovations. All students are guaranteed employment on graduation, and receive considerable material aid. They are, therefore, encouraged to think of their studies, not so much as a private and personal concern, but as a social obligation. It is their responsibility to make the most of their opportunities for learning, and to try to complete their courses in the normal time.

The long-standing university tradition has sometimes proved difficult to overcome, but the new methods of group work and responsibility introduced in the last two years, have been very successful. The initiative here has often been taken by the students themselves. In fact the new student body—it was everywhere admitted—has had a decisive influence in bringing about more disciplined methods of study throughout the higher educational system.

In each year the students now form subject groups, numbering from ten to thirty. Each group works as a unit for seminars and discussions, the more advanced students assisting the weaker with their individual work. A secretary is elected, and a university lecturer assigned as tutor. The whole group makes itself responsible for the work of each member, and takes a pride in its collective achievement.

The result has been that standards have risen and nearly all students now take their examinations at the normal time. I was told that the impetus behind this development comes to some extent from the members of the United Workers' Party and Union of Polish Youth among the students, who regard the improvement of the level of studies as an important social responsibility.

Faculties and "Chairs"

The new methods of work have been paralleled by changes in the internal organization of higher colleges. Within each faculty there are a number of chairs, a term now implying the collective departmental organization rather than a single professorship. Each chair usually consists of two or three professors, as well as assistant professors, lecturers, and "assistants" (of which there are three grades), and the students attached to it.

For example, the Chair of Political Economy at the Warsaw School of Planning and Statistics comprises four professors (one of whom is in charge), five assistant professors, and 33 assistants of all grades. Its function was described as lecturing, supervising the work of the students in group discussion and written work, assisting the research of staff members and post-graduate students, and training young members of staff. This particular chair had as many external as internal students, taking the new type of correspondence course, which involves the staff in a great deal of work.

Chairs in allied subjects are sometimes grouped together to form an Institute, which functions as a unit within the faculty, and which may have relations also with the newly-established Academy of Science. The director of such an institute is subject to the dean of the faculty. An example is the Institute of Chemistry at Cracow University, housed in a new five-storey building of three large wings; it has six professors, each of whom has four or five assistant professors and many junior assistants. The institute forms a unit for both teaching and research.

The members of a chair meet frequently for discussion of the work of the department. In the case of one institution I visited, all the staff of each chair meet once a week for approximately four hours. At this meeting the general trend of the work of the department is discussed, as well as the progress of the students, the impact of the teaching methods used, and efficiency of the teaching whether of professors or assistants. Similar meetings take place for the purpose of training lecturers, for which the latter prepare talks dealing with different aspects of the syllabus. A meeting is also held once a month for the general discussion of some topic relevant to the research work of members of the department. The discussion is opened by an assistant and prepared beforehand by the circulation of a summary of his thesis with references. Finally, each department organizes what are called subject circles, where the best students participate in the discussions.

The chair is, therefore, the basic teaching unit and opportunity is provided for all its members to submit criticisms and suggestions. Besides this, every faculty has a faculty council, while the senate, which governs the institution as a whole, has a wide basis of representation from professors to students.

Research

Developments in the planning of research can only be referred to briefly. Research is carried on both in the higher colleges and in research institutes. The new Academy of Sciences has, since 1952 had the task of drawing up a general plan of research at the highest level related to national needs, based on proposals from the institutes and from the chairs of colleges. It is also responsible for planning and building new research institutes where required. The Academy has 30 full members, leading scientists and scholars, as well as other forms of membership. It is organized in four sections, and covers the main fields of knowledge from philosophy and the humanistic studies to science and technology. Full membership carries with it an assured income for life, and academicians are freed from all undergraduate teaching so that they may concentrate on research and the training of research workers.

284

Two points made in connexion with this form of planning by Professor Infeld, professor of theoretical physics at Warsaw University and member of the Academy, are worth noting. First, such plans can only be drawn up by the scientists themselves, who alone know what forms of research are possible and which institutions are best equipped to undertake various projects. Secondly, planning of this kind does not imply concentration only on immediate and practical problems. On the contrary, the scientists are able to see that pure research takes its proper place, and plans for long term research form as important a part of the overall plan as more short-time projects.

Conclusion

The reorganization described in this article has apparently been achieved with the minimum of friction. The general recognition of the need for these changes can only be fully understood in relation to the terrible material and human devastation of the war years, and to the undeniable success with which plans for reconstruction and development have been fulfilled. It was this, I was told by many university people, which had convinced those who might otherwise have been opposed to all planning of this kind.

In addition, the actual reorgnization of higher education has been largely the work of university teachers themselves. They take part in policy discussions at all levels, from the chair and faculty to the Central Council. They have had, therefore, the chief responsibility for deciding the form that reorganization takes.

A leading part has undoubtedly been played by the United Workers' Party which, so far as the outside observer can see, functions in the same kind of way as the Russian Communist Party as described by the Webbs; though it is relatively considerably larger, having been formed by the fusion of the former Socialist and Communist parties. Members of the United Workers' Party in the universities apparently see their function as that of convincing their colleagues in the various committees, rather than imposing views upon them. This question is quite openly discussed, and it was pointed out that the imposition of views could only lead to hostility and opposition and so render the work of the universities ineffective.

Many of the university people I met had had first-hand experience of institutions in this country, America, or France; some had only recently returned to Poland. They seemed convinced that the present system functions effectively, and are fully co-operating in its development. I was everywhere told that all former university teachers who remained in Poland, or returned there after the war, retain their positions.

17

EUROPEAN RECTORS AND VICE-CHANCELLORS IN CONFERENCE

J. W. Blake

Source: *Universities Quarterly* X (1955–6): 15–18.

It would, I suppose, be true to say that few of the Rectors, Vice-Chancellors and Principals who took part in the Cambridge Conference during the fourth week of July 1955, quite knew what to expect when they arrived. Most of the United Kingdom delegates, having attended on the previous day the colourful and impressive Installation of the First Chancellor of the University of Hull, had already had a taste of the cosmopolitanism that was to be a feature of the Conference at Cambridge; for many of the Rectors from Western European universities, not least from Bologna, most ancient of all universities in Europe, had been able to make their way to Hull to pay their respects and present their congratulatory addresses. We knew that the conference was the outcome of long and careful preparation. Arising from Article III of the Brussels Treaty, wherein the Benelux signatories had agreed 'to promote cultural exchanges', preliminary meetings of Vice-Chancellors and others from the countries of the Council of Europe had in the autumn of 1953 recommended such a conference; an Organizing Committee had prepared an agenda and documentation at Clermont-Ferrand in September 1954; and the small British delegation at Clermont-Ferrand was already not unaware of some of the difficulties which such a conference as was envisaged would raise. But most of us, on our arrival at Cambridge, were, I think, a trifle over-awed by the occasion. After all, this would be a unique gathering. No conference of this kind had been held in Europe for over two hundred years. It would be an historic occasion. As the Rt. Hon. H. U. Willink, Vice-Chancellor of Cambridge, modestly put it in his Presidential Address, he was talking to an 'extraordinarily distinguished gathering'. For myself, inexperienced and innocent, I went as a lamb to the slaughter. But I was, like others, also curious, expectant and very flattered to be privileged to attend. What fruit would the Conference yield?

Mostly we came on the evening of Tuesday, July 19th, by car, coach or train, to be received at Trinity, at Magdalene, at Caius, at St. John's or at Clare. I travelled down by special coach, generously put at our disposal by the University of Hull, and I recall wondering whether that peaceful July evening was symbolical of Providence turning a favourable eye on the impending Conference. My coach colleagues, with one exception, were all drawn from continental universities. The babel of tongues had started. But for the time being we kept our counsel and did not mix much. It was like this the following morning when His Royal Highness the Duke of Edinburgh, Patron of the Conference, graciously opened our meetings in plenary session with frank and forthright references to leading university problems. As we sat that morning in Senate House, some of us fascinated with our ear-phone toys, and astounded at the speed and efficiency of poker-faced interpreters who gave us simultaneous versions in English and French, the official Conference languages, we were arranged in order as national delegations, the United Kingdom delegates taking the rear seats. As yet, we mixed briefly and rarely. It was like this in all plenary sessions. Of necessity they were formal, a little inflexible. I thought that the British delegates, perhaps conscious that the other national delegations tended to look to them for a lead, were particularly diffident. Later, in our Study Groups, on college lawns, in our rooms, at receptions, at high table in college, we began tentatively to mix more freely as individuals, and to make ourselves known better one to another across the national barriers.

Throughout the week that followed, if one gained many fleeting impressions, there was little time for reflection. We were caught up in what I might describe as a whirlwind programme, a round of receptions, a spate of talking, especially I observed from the Italians in Study Group A, which was concerned with the difficulties of maintaining a due balance in university curricula between specialization and general education; and we had to digest a mass of papers which the busy Secretariat, working very late, issued every day to the Conference. Looking back now, a month after the end of the Conference, I feel we were a little too engaged, a trifle over-organized. We needed, I think, just a little more leisure to develop the informal contacts with our colleagues from other lands.

What are the impressions which remain still with me? I want, I know, to bear witness to the generous hospitality of the University of Cambridge. If when first sounded a little reluctant, she excelled herself in the event throughout the Conference. I recall also how all of us, listening by candlelight in King's College Chapel, on the evening of July 23rd, were deeply and visibly moved by a most charming and beautiful rendering of Latin and English Church music. The Rector of Wurzburg, Bavaria, told me afterwards that it was a revelation to him. Emotionally stirred, he confessed to earlier doubts about coming to the Conference. These by now had been entirely dispelled. He was thrilled to be at Cambridge. King's College Chapel Choir had charmed away the last of his misgivings. But there was something deeper behind all this. The delegates as a whole seemed to become aware, as I thought rightly, of their privilege that quiet Saturday evening in being able to share in the rich cultural inheritance of Europe, an inheritance that was unique and without rival. I also remember, as a Humanist, that the inspired oration of Dr. Gilbert Murray, delivered on the evening of the first day of the Conference, had aroused a like and quite spontaneous response from them. In that oration—one of the great moments of the Conference— Dr. Murray, as an elder academic statesman, frank, wise, and steeped in the classical tradition, had talked to us of the dangers threatening our historic European civilization, of 'Democracy unlimited', of how numbers had always been against us, and of the responsibility which consequently rested on the universities to lead Europe back to sanity. 'For the universities', he had added, 'have more power than they mostly realize in directing the whole intellectual activity of their respective nations.' 'And so', he went on, speaking of the Western European nations, 'for mere security, as well as for higher reasons, they are forced to combine.' Here, I think, he struck the first real note of mutual confidence at the Conference. Everybody was conscious that the Chairman did not need to comment; the audience responded magnificently. I think it was Dr. Murray who first made us realize vividly that the Conference reflected the anxieties of the times in which we live, yet also the resolute determination of the peoples of Western European Union to grapple courageously with their problems. I shall long treasure the experience of that evening. It would be fair to say, too, that H.R.H. The Duke of Edinburgh made a great impression upon the continental delegates, not only by what he had to say, but by the informality and simple dignity of his presence: he joined the Conference for the rest of the opening day as a member of the audience in the Senate House.

Yet it would be untrue to suggest that all was always smooth-going at the Conference. In the Group meetings, even in the closing plenary sessions, the differences of academic attitude and intellectual approach, not only between national delegations, but also between individual delegates, were marked. The language barrier itself was shown in one or two instances to be almost insuperable: in Group A, which I mostly attended, the French and British delegations clearly did not always understand the same thing by the phrase 'an educated man', and it gradually emerged that 'Philosophy' as a formal discipline signified differently to Italians and to Englishmen. It was evident, too, that the complications of university curricula and university structures cannot always be easily explicable to an international audience; and, without that, progress in mutual understanding is scarcely possible. To my mind, therefore, without more detailed study and an infinity of time devoted to explanatory qualifications, the 26 Resolutions, which the Conference ultimately accepted, could be no more than general aspirations, even though they represented the highest common denominator of understanding and agreement.

I suppose I am right when I say that the real value of the Conference derived from the informal contacts that we were able to make with colleagues from other countries. Undoubtedly the Conference stimulated, if not always agreeably. We do not as a general rule like to be reminded of our defects or of the defects of the institutions to which we owe allegiance. But it is good that we should be provoked to be self-critical. It is also good that the universities of the countries of Western European Union have come together in this unique and historic fashion. Conference Resolution XXVI recommends 'that similar Conferences be convened periodically'. From what I saw of the Cambridge Conference, I am confident that Resolution XXVI should be implemented.

18

HIGHER EDUCATION IN THE BRITISH COLONIES

Walter Adams

Source: *Universities Quarterly* I (1946–7): 145–53.

The territories for which the Secretary of State for the Colonies has responsibility have a total population of possibly 60,000,000. These territories, with an area of over three million square miles, have four universities—three of which are located in very small units of the Colonial Empire. There is, for example, no university in the African Colonies and Dependencies which contain more than two-thirds of the total Colonial population; and there is none in the West Indies with a population of over two and a half million. The Royal University of Malta, constituted in 1769, has at present 233 students; but, because of the limitation of its resources, it can only admit new students every third year. The University of Hong Kong, founded in 1911, had before the war 538 students. The Hebrew University of Jerusalem, established in the early 'twenties of this century as a centre of research, has only in recent years developed undergraduate work, the total number of its students of all categories being between 500 and 600. The University of Ceylon, created in 1942, has nearly 1,000 students. On the assumption that Hong Kong University is restored to its pre-war size, the four existing universities represent a total student population of little more than 2,000.

Since the number of students from the Colonial Empire in the universities of the British Isles was 748 in March, 1946, and there were possibly less than half that number in universities elsewhere, the present position is that the ratio of university students to total population is 1 to 20,000 for the Colonies compared to 1 to 885 (the 1934–35 figure) in Great Britain. It may, of course, be argued that because the populations differ so completely in social and economic conditions, the comparison is pointless. Nevertheless, if the new vocabulary in Colonial policy of "trusteeship" and "partnership" is to be something more than words, we must be prepared to make such comparisons of fact and admit that the contrast disclosed is intolerable.

The need for educational advance

Great Britain is committed to a policy of development and welfare for its dependent peoples which will require for its execution in the next decades very large numbers of administrators, research workers, doctors, teachers, agriculturists, engineers and other technical experts and professionally quali-fied specialists. The home population, diminishing in total numbers, changing in age structure, and needing for its own tasks to double in the immediate future its output of scientists, cannot possibly supply more than a tiny fraction of the number required. The successful execution of the new policy will depend, therefore, not only on the services of a multitude of specialists, but also on understanding co-operation and participation by the dependent peoples themselves. This implies the creation of an educated public and of an informed political leadership, and the release and use of local potentialities on a scale at present almost unimaginable.

Thus the immediate task is a revolutionary advance in education in the Colonial Empire—an attack on mass illiteracy; a conservation of the adult education gains made among the troops during the war and a develop-ment of new forms of adult education in civil life; the expansion of school education for children (at present 17.7 per cent. of children of school age in S. Nigeria attend, 1.7 per cent. in N. Nigeria); the provision of technical and trade schools and of facilities for professional training. (There is, approximately, 1 doctor to 1,000 inhabitants in Great Britain; 1 to 100,000 in Nigeria.)

This educational campaign needs to be envisaged as a whole. Priorities may differ from place to place and time to time, but a co-ordinated advance along the whole front will always be required. The place of university educa-tion in this programme has been defined in terms of general principles in the report of the Asquith Commission[1] and in detail for four regions by reports on higher education plans for Malaya, East Africa, West Africa and the West Indies.[2]

Interdependence of higher and other forms of education

The Asquith Commission was fully aware of the interdependence of progress at the various levels of education. "On the one hand the facilities for instruc-tion at the secondary stage determine the number of students fitted for entry into institutions of a higher category; on the other the efficiency of higher education must govern the scope of instruction and determine the supply of qualified teachers in secondary schools." It did not regard the urgency of the needs for mass education as a reason for postponing, but rather as a reason for pressing on with, the provision of university education. "Where education as a whole is backward, effort is most rewarding when it is directed to the higher levels."

The Asquith Commission regarded the establishment of universities in the Colonies as an inescapable corollary of any policy which aims at the achievement of Colonial self-government. To universities

> we must look for the production of men and women with the standards of public service and capacity for leadership which self rule requires. It is the university which should offer the best means of counteracting the influence of racial differences and sectional rivalries which impede the formation of political institutions on a national basis. Moreover, universities serve the double purpose of refining and maintaining all that is best in local traditions and cultures and at the same time of providing a means whereby those brought up under the influence of these traditions and cultures may enter on a footing of equality into the world-wide community of intellect.

The university facilities must be provided locally in the Colonies, not only because considerations of cost and the congestion in existing universities make impossible the training elsewhere of the numbers involved, but also because as a matter of policy

> it is undesirable that the training of the entire professional class should be conducted remote from local conditions and out of range of local influences ... A university should become a focus for the intellectual self-expression of the people. By receiving their higher education together in their own country, Colonial students will be encouraged to direct their new knowledge and ideas to the understanding of the character and problems of the country in which they are working.

The commission, believing that "there is no fundamental antithesis between liberal and vocational education," considered that universities could better meet the needs of professional education than specialized training institutions, because they can provide the courses in arts or science which are the necessary preliminary to professional studies, can attract a staff of superior qualifications, and can prescribe higher standards of initial entry and of subsequent study. It is, however, significant that the report should add that

> it is not enough that a professional man should attain competence in his own subject; association with the life of a university will give him a larger range of interest and enhance his value both in pursuit of his profession and as a member of society. Our aim should be to produce not only doctors, but educated doctors; not only agriculturists, but educated agriculturists; and to this end universities minister far more effectively than specialized institutions.

Development of new universities

The recommendations of the reports involve the development as soon as possible of at least five or six new universities. In three or four cases they can be constructed on the basis of existing "higher colleges"; in two areas, Nigeria and the West Indies, they will have to be entirely new creations. In East Africa (including for this purpose, although it is not a Colonial territory, the Anglo-Egyptian Sudan), one will be founded on the existing Makerere College and the medical school near Kampala, which now provide for the three territories of Uganda, Kenya and Tanganyika higher education in the form of two year basic courses in arts or science, followed by professional training leading to a locally recognized diploma in education, medicine, agriculture or veterinary science. In the Anglo-Egyptian Sudan, the basis will be Gordon Memorial College at Khartoum. In West Africa, in addition to establishing an entirely new institution at Ibadan in Nigeria, it may be decided to develop the existing Achimota College in the Gold Coast to university status. In Malaya, the proposal is that the College of Medicine and Raffles College, both at present sited in Singapore, should be fused into a single college from which a university would ultimately develop.

The rate of progress towards independent university rank will vary in each case, not least because of the different degrees of maturity of local secondary education. It is envisaged that all will pass through an interim period as university colleges, in order to ensure that their degrees, when awarded, are of such standards that they secure ready acceptance as proof of high academic attainment, of sound intellectual training and of adequate preparation for professional work or for postgraduate work in British universities. After considering various alternatives, the Asquith Commission recommended that the colleges during this interim period should enter into a special relationship with the University of London which has been designed to remove such disadvantages of the "external" system as the divorce of teaching and examining, the imposition of a common syllabus insufficiently adapted to teaching needs and to local study material, and the exaggeration of the importance of the examination as an incident in university training. With the colleges qualifying for this special relationship, the University of London is prepared to make arrangements for close personal and academic co-operation, for consultation on syllabus requirements, for visiting examiners, and for association of teachers with the examining.

Central machinery

This special relationship with the University of London is only one of the practical proposals made by the Asquith Commission for ensuring the active co-operation of the home universities in establishing the Colonial universities on a sound basis. Among its other recommendations, three dealing with machinery and administration may be mentioned—the creation of an Inter-University Council, of a Grants Committee and of a system of temporary staff secondment. An "Inter-University Council for Higher Education in the Colonies" has now been established in London, on the initiative of the Secretary of State for the Colonies, as an autonomous body composed of one representative of each of the home universities and of the four existing Colonial universities, with power to co-opt. Its broad purpose is to canalize to the Colonial institutions the experience, expert advice and other forms of academic assistance available from the British universities. The council, which has elected Sir James Irvine as its chairman, will have to discover empirically the most effective means of fulfilling its purpose, but assistance in staff recruitment, the organization of visits to and from the Colonial institutions in order to remove their isolation, negotiations concerned with the recognition of local diplomas, and the encouragement of Colonial studies in the home universities will be among its many tasks.

A sum of four and a half million pounds has been allocated under the Colonial Development and Welfare Act as a contribution from Imperial funds towards the development of higher education. For advice on the expenditure of this sum, the Secretary of State is appointing a Colonial University Grants Advisory Committee on which, as the Asquith Commission recommended, there will be strong representation of university experience.

Staff secondment

The third proposal is perhaps the most important. It is suggested that the Colonial colleges should be staffed in part by members of home universities, seconded for periods of from one to three years, on agreements which protect them from loss of seniority or superannuation rights at home. Such "intellectual lend-lease" would make available to the colleges, in a continuous and intimate way, appreciation of British academic standards and experience; it would overcome the isolation of the Colonial institutions; it would create in the home universities an increasing group of men and women with personal knowledge of the Colonial Empire, of its needs and opportunities; it could lead to individual or co-operative research work. However close and helpful the relations may be between the University of London, the Inter-University Council, or the Grants Committee and the Colonial institutions, they will necessarily be less influential and constructive than the effect of an ever-widening pattern of personal friendships between the Colonial colleges and a growing number of university teachers at home who have personally shared in this educational adventure.

As the Colonial colleges develop towards full university maturity, they will be able to appoint to their staffs an increasing proportion of locally recruited members from among their own graduates and those of other colleges. For the next one or two academic generations, it is evident that the Colonial colleges will depend heavily on their ability to attract qualified staff from the United Kingdom, from the Dominions and, to a lesser extent, from other countries. It is within this period that the home universities must make their most decisive contribution, which can make or mar Colonial university education. They have both an opportunity and an obligation to ensure that the new universities achieve from the outset the highest stand-ards and that they learn from the experience and mistakes of the British universities.

General characteristics of the new universities

The Asquith Commission in fulfilling its terms of reference "to consider the principles which should guide the promotion of higher education, learning and research and the development of universities in the Colonies," has attempted to distil from home experience some of the general lessons which are relevant and some of the conclusions derived from investigations of such special subjects as the functions of universities in medical, agriculture and veterinary education and in teacher training. Thus, the commission emphas-izes the need for the autonomy of the Colonial colleges—their independence from governmental control, their need of the security provided by financial endowments and by the system of block grants over periods of years. It insists on the importance of the residential character of the new universities, not only because of the great distances from which the students would be drawn (the West Indies Committee report recommending that the transpor-tation expenses of the students travelling to and from the central university each year should be a charge on the university budget), but chiefly because of the educational value of community residences of students from all faculties. On many other points the commission gives advice derived from British experience—the necessity for an adequate range of subjects within the one institution to ensure that directly and indirectly the student acquires a general education and is not merely trained as a technician; the funda-mental importance of the universities being centres of learning, permeated with the spirit of fundamental research; the value of adequate libraries, of a long-term building programme, of extra-mural activities, of conditions of service for the staff appropriate to the special nature of university work.

However authoritative and immediately valuable the advice of these commissions may be, the members would be the last to claim that the blue-prints they have drawn are final. Hence the proposal to establish the Inter-University Council, whose task it will be continuously to review and assess the developing needs of Colonial higher education and to analyse the developing experience of home and other universities. The council will, no doubt, investigate the lessons to be learned from higher educational work in the French and Dutch Colonies, from such countries as India, Turkey and the U.S.S.R., which have attempted educational revolutions, and from the fertile experimentation in the U.S.A. In no sense, however, will the Colonial colleges be merely the passive recipients of advice and guidance from the Inter-University Council. They will have as much to teach as they have to learn. As living institutions adapting themselves to meet unique conditions and unprecedented problems, they will provide experience which may well challenge some of the assumptions and established habits of the home universities. They will raise questions which will call for a radical analysis and deeper self-knowledge by the British academic world. Is there a genuine principle behind the present distinction between "arts" and "science", or is it an organizational survival? Are the "humanities" in fact efficient instruments for humane education? Are we quite sure what we mean by "intellectual discipline" when we insist on classics or mathematics in organizing the subjects to be included in a degree course?

Probably in two particular spheres, the Colonial universities may most fruitfully contribute in this process of "reverse lease-lend". First, because of the desperate need for technically and professionally qualified specialists, and because the home conditions of students are such that the college will be almost the sole source of their cultural development, the Colonial colleges will be more squarely confronted than we at home by the problems of the relationship between vocational training and general education. In thinking through this question and experimenting in methods of solving the problems raised, the Colonial colleges will certainly have valuable experience to offer to the home universities. Secondly, the Colonial universities will not be able to evade a direct and explicit responsibility for the spiritual and moral development of their students. Although they will become increasingly the expression of their local cultures, they are, and must remain, instruments for the introduction of an alien culture into societies whose own moral and intellectual structure has already been shaken by contact with the West. The students, separated from some of the traditions and sanctions of their own societies, face greater problems of personal adjustment than do British students in the relative stability of their society and its moral and cultural assumptions. It would be as disastrous to encourage a hollow imitation of Western customs as it would be for the Colonial universities to ignore this central problem of human values. They may well discover methods which it would profit the home universities to adopt in tackling problems which at present they are inclined to ignore.

A challenging opportunity

The whole plan for the next stage of development of higher education in the Colonies is full of challenge to the British universities as well as to the Colonial peoples. To create several entirely new universities, whose graduates will be the leaders of their peoples' social, cultural, economic and political advance—to do so in full awareness of the dangers of imposing alien customs on other countries, while ensuring that we give of the best of our own experience, to do so at a time of acute shortage in academic manpower at home, and to do so in full intention that having assisted in their birth we should encourage the universities to achieve complete independence so that we can learn from them in their maturity—will make unparalleled demands on our university resources and statesmanship which we dare not fail to meet.

Notes

1 *Report of the Commission on Higher Education in the Colonies* (Cmd. 6647. June, 1945).
2 *Higher Education in Malaya* (Colonial No. 173. June, 1939).
Higher Education in East Africa (Colonial No. 142. September, 1937).
Report of the Commission on Higher Education in West Africa (Cmd. 6655. June 1945).
Report of the West Indies Committee of the Commission on Higher Education in the Colonies (Cmd. 6654. June, 1945).

19

THE CHANGING POLITICAL ECONOMY

The private and public lives of Canadian universities

Donald Fisher and Kjell Rubenson

Source: Jan Currie and Janice Newton (eds) *Universities and Globalisation: Critical Perspectives*, Thousand Oaks, Calif. and London: Sage, 1998, pp. 77–98.

The Canadian postsecondary system has developed a distinctive and unique character since the Second World War. The transition from an elite to a mass system has already taken place (Scott, 1995). In 1994–1995, Canada spent $15.9 billion on postsecondary education, which represents 2.09% of gross domestic product (GDP). Canada has consistently been at the top of the range in the Organization for Economic Cooperation and Development (OECD) when expenditures are calculated as a proportion of the GDP. Governments are the primary source, providing 76% of direct funding. The participation rates in 1994 among 18- to 21-year-olds and 22- to 25-year-olds was 40.3% and 22.8%, respectively. With these rates, Canada was at the top of the OECD table for the 18- to 21-year-olds and third for the 22- to 25-year-olds (Government of Canada, 1996, p. 3; OECD, 1996, pp. 61, 131). The commitment to egalitarianism rather than elitism is expressed in the relatively low fees charged to students. Similarly, the level of institutional autonomy is probably more pronounced in Canada than in any other OECD country. The system can be characterized as soft federalism. Although the federal government has, since the 1950s, shouldered a significant portion of the bill for universities, the constitutional responsibility has remained with the provinces. In 1994–1995, federal support to postsecondary education represented 52% of the total cost of postsecondary education in that year (Government of Canada, 1996, p. 3). The public monopoly over the binary structure (colleges and universities) accounts for the limited competition and the perceived equivalence between credentials across the country. This state public system is relatively homogeneous and, as a vestige of its roots in the United Kingdom, is still committed to the ethos of liberal education rather than vocationalism. However, strong external and internal pressures are currently pushing universities in the latter direction.

The intent of this chapter is to lay the groundwork for understanding the changing role of universities in Canadian society during a time of fundamental shifts in the relation between capital and labor and between the public and private spheres. Like all modern institutions in capitalist democracies, universities are involved in an exercise of mutual legitimation, as academics attempt to balance elements of *bildung* against the structural force of commodification. When trying to understand the operation of social forces in and through a university system, it is useful to divide the life of the system into its external and internal components (Clark, 1983), or expressed differently, the division between demand (for education, specialist training, research services of various kinds) and response (by the university system and individual institutions). These divisions help to focus attention on changes in university culture and the contents of the intellectual field (Bourdieu, 1969; Ringer, 1992).

Four objectives are of concern in this chapter. First is to describe and interpret the political economic trends that form the backdrop to current changes in the vocational contours of university education in Canada. Against this background, a brief historical account is provided of the gradual withdrawal of the federal government from funding the system. Second is an analysis of the new discourse on vocationalism at both the federal and provincial levels of government. This discourse is shaped by three overlapping social forces: the fiscal crisis of the state, the ideological dominance of neo-liberalism, and the perceived need for human resource development. Third is a case study analyzing the changes in the vocational role performed by universities in British Columbia. The conclusion locates the above discussion in a broader theoretical framework and speculates on the future implications of current trends.

Changes in Canadian political economy

The social demand that once directed the growth of the postsecondary education system is gradually giving way to a new, economically driven imperative that places importance on highly developed human capital, science, and technology to support Canada's needs for economic restructuring and greater international competitiveness. This economic imperative has been amplified by severe limitations on public expenditures and the emergence of the accountability movement, which is based on a general suspicion of public institutions and a belief in the greater efficiency of free market forces. In this section, we will look at the changing political landscape and the changing link between education and the economy.

During successive Conservative administrations between 1984 and 1993, the federal policy agenda was grounded on a neo-liberal ideology, with an emphasis on shrinking the Keynesian welfare state and freeing the market. The contradiction apparent in the United Kingdom is that whereas an activist and strong state is condemned in theory, in practice it is needed to carry out the policies. A privatization trend that cut across most OECD countries during this period meant the transfer of costs and responsibility from public or state control to private control. This involved selling off crown corporations to private investors and shifting from compulsory taxation to a voluntary, user-pay approach to public services (Stanbury, 1989, p. 274). According to the Conservatives, their approaches to social welfare and labor market policy can be justified on the grounds that the government has little or no choice. Not only does the nation-state lack the power to resist global economic forces, but the well-being of citizens is served if the country opens up to international market forces (Johnson, McBride, & Smith, 1994, p. 9).

Barlow and Cambell (1991) see the Canada–United States Free Trade Agreement (FTA) and the later North American Free Trade Agreement (NAFTA) as the cornerstones in the Conservative and corporate agenda to reshape Canada. The agreements prevent the reestablishment of an interventionist state and firmly establish a free market and entrepreneurial spirit in Canadian political culture. For the Conservative government, a free-trade solution was an alternative economic model to the Keynesian policy paradigm (McBride & Shields, 1993, p. 134). As a means of achieving a level playing field, free trade provided the justification for the neo-conservative agenda to reduce business taxes and various forms of social benefits. Having achieved political dominance in the 1980s, the Mulroney government and its business supporters then sought to insulate their achievements from the democratic processes during the 1990s (McBride & Shields, 1993, p. 169).

The need for Canada to become more competitive became the basis for Conservative economic and social policy housed in the free trade agreements (Abele, 1992). Policy initiatives such as training the labor force, overhauling the unemployment insurance system, and reducing the deficit and inflation were all promoted as measures to improve Canada's competitiveness. Yet, adoption of a New Right ideology as a response to fiscal crises came late in Canada, and policies of monetarism, deregulation, privatization, and reduced social expenditure were not as draconian as in Thatcher's England or Reagan's United States (Mullay, 1994). The Conservative government's approach was incremental and favored greater selectivity, setting ceilings on program costs and in some instances, making them self-financing. Despite tough talk about bringing down the deficit, the Conservative government was only partially successful in shrinking the federal state. This was in large part due to the cost of servicing the debt. As McBride and Shields (1993) point out, if program expenditures are considered in isolation from debt-servicing costs, the statistics show a major reduction. Program expend-itures shrunk from 19.4% of GDP in 1983–1984 to 16.0% in 1990–1991.

The Conservatives were replaced in 1993 by a Liberal government that had campaigned on job creation and debt and deficit reduction. In com-parison with other major industrialized countries, Canada, it was stressed, had the second-largest deficit and debt relative to GDP and, by a large margin, the highest level of foreign debt relative to GDP. The Liberals quickly set out to do what the Conservatives only marginally had been able to do—cut the deficit. Without the ideological overtures of neo-liberalism that characterized the former governments' policy rhetoric, more severe spending cuts were put in place. The 1995 budget introduced measures that will gradually reduce the deficit to 3% of GDP in 1996–1997 (half of the 1993 figure) and 2% the year after. A major part of the savings are coming from a drastic reduction of financial transfers to the provinces for income assistance, health, and postsecondary education. The Established Programs Fund (EPF) entitlement, the major educational transfer from the federal government to the provinces, will be entirely paid for in the form of taxes forgone. This will be a loss to the provinces of $14 billion (Government of Canada, 1996). The EPF and the Canada Assistance Plan have been com-bined into one single mechanism, the Canadian Health and Social Transfer (CHST). By 1997–1998, the federal government will have cut $4.5 billion from the cash component of the CHST. As a result of these cuts, the prov-ince of New Brunswick in 1995–1996, for example, faced a 17% reduction in federal transfer payments for social programs, including postsecondary education, from the previous year (Department of Finance, New Brunswick, 1996). The result of these changes in transfers to the provinces will likely lead to a balkanization of social programs and an abdication of the federal government's responsibility to ensure that all have access to a high-quality medicare, postsecondary education, and adequate social assistance.

Universities face further cuts in their budgets because the federal govern-ment decided in 1995 to cut 14% over three years to the major federal research councils, the Social Sciences and Humanities Research Council of Canada (SSHRCC) and the Natural Sciences and Engineering Research Council of Canada (NSERCC).

During the past fifteen years, the postsecondary system has had to accom-modate a very large increase in student numbers with moderate budget increases, resulting in substantial reduction in cost per student. The spending on postsecondary education per student has been reduced from $12,011 in 1975 to $9,190 by 1990 (Horry & Walker, 1994).

To make things worse, not only do the provinces have to accommodate large federal cuts, but they also have to cut their own debts and deficits. The combined impact of the fiscal crisis at both levels of the state has created enormous pressure to reduce public expenditures. In this climate, Ontario and Alberta have elected populist New Right governments that are not satisfied with scaling back the welfare state but want to see savage cuts in public spending and the abolition of the welfare state. The mentality is very much the same as could be found in New Zealand and England, with the introduction of workfare programs and draconian cuts in social assistance. Other provinces governed by less conservative parties are facing major cuts to their program expenditures and try to portray themselves as fiscal conservatives. It is in this fiscal climate that postsecondary education is being called upon to spearhead the new information economy and be an engine for increased competitiveness.

A new discourse on vocationalism

Federal and provincial policy documents see education and training as a way of making Canada more able to compete in a time of globalization and economic restructuring. A key statement in the discussion paper *Agenda: Jobs and Growth: Improving Social Security in Canada* (Human Resources Development Canada, 1994) is typical: "As the pace of global competition quickens and technological complexity intensifies, the fortunes of individuals and of nations turn increasingly on the skills they already possess or are prepared to acquire" (p. 39). The connection between learning and earning can be seen in titles such as *Lifelong Learning and the New Economy*, a 1994 report from the Ontario Premier's Council on Economic Renewal. The report states, "Lifelong learning, therefore, is the key link between our educational and economic strategies as the 21st century approaches" (p. 2).

Within the new economic imperative, the relationship between postsecondary education and work has become the key issue and a major battleground between competing ideologies and interests. The structure of universities, educational provisions and student options, the curricula, and the governance of the linkages between universities and work are being questioned. Recent policy documents express a strong need to establish closer ties with the labor market and "[to adapt] education to the real requirements of the labour market, . . . making it more relevant, and . . . easing the transition into the workplace" (Gouvernement du Québec, 1996, p. 54). This discussion is set within a broader context of the Canadian training deficit.

A key issue in the debate on education and training is the lack of private sector involvement. The Canadian Job Strategy (CJS), launched by the Conservative government in 1985, and its replacement, the Labour Force Development Strategy (LFDS) from 1989, emphasized market sensitivity and private sector involvement (Haddow, 1995). A cornerstone of CJS was making public funds, which traditionally had gone to community colleges through federal-provincial agreement, available to the private partners for "indirect federal training purchases." Canada Employment Centres could enter into training agreements with firms, private providers, nonprofit organizations, or sectorial committees. These groups might, if they so chose, purchase the education and training from a public education institution. The result was rapid growth in private sector training enterprises and, despite some entrepreneurial approaches by the college system, a reduction in federal training funds going to public institutions.

The LFDS, which was introduced to overcome the shortcomings of CJS, specifically its narrow preoccupation with lower-end skills, approached private sector involvement in a different way. Haddow (1995, p. 344) characterizes the CJS as a pluralist approach to private sector involvement; the LFDS was constructed around a corporatist approach. Following the creation of a federal LFDS board, some provinces set up similar boards. As training increasingly becomes a provincial responsibility alongside education, we see a merger of what traditionally has been two partly separate policy fields. This change has major repercussions on postsecondary education.

In British Columbia, the responsibility of the Labour Force Development Board (BCLFDB) was to provide the Minister of Education, Skills, Training, and Labour with strategic and tactical advice on labor force development, training, and adjustment. In its first report, *Training for What?*, the board presented an analysis of the future of work, skills that will be required, and how British Columbia could best organize its learning system to meet these skill needs (BCLFDB, 1995). Because BCLFDB is a major player in the policy arena, its conclusions cannot be taken lightly. The following conclusion has led to much controversy:

> First, the mix of education and training programs [does] not match labour market needs as well as it might. For example, while there is no gap in the capacity of the province's universities and university colleges to produce the number of university graduates that will be required, there appears to be a relative over-supply of graduates in academic programs and an under-supply of those in applied.
>
> (p. 43)

The changing political economy as reflected in the fiscal situation and policies, as well as human resource strategies to improve Canada's competitiveness, has caused concern about the ability of the postsecondary system to respond. Several provinces have or are presently undertaking reviews of their postsecondary system. The purpose here is to briefly review how the changing external factors are being reflected in the present policy discussions.

An overview of provincial policy

External differentiation

To meet the demands for rationalization and differentiation, either provincial intermediary bodies have been created or their powers to intervene have been strengthened (see, for example, Nova Scotia Council on Higher Education, 1995; University Program Review Panel, Saskatchewan, 1993). To meet the financial challenges, the Nova Scotia Council on Higher Education (1995) presented a series of goals and strategies. To increase responsiveness to social, cultural, and economic needs and opportunities, the council suggested a reexamination and a refocus of the institutional mission of universities. The purpose was to define the institutional relationship with the labor market, to improve means for ongoing liaison between stakeholder and university communities, and to promote programs addressing the needs of the economy and society. With these goals in mind, the council recommended consolidation of institutions and "structural changes that would make possible system-wide decisions on major policy and program issues" (p. 27). Teacher education has already been restructured, and currently other programs are under scrutiny. One of the principles underlying the proposed new funding formula for universities in Nova Scotia was to provide incentives for system effectiveness, including institutional differentiation and interinstitutional cooperation (Nova Scotia Council on Higher Education, 1996).

Similarly, recent reviews in Québec and Manitoba concluded that differentiation of university institutions was beneficial and necessary (Gouvernement du Québec, 1996; University Education Review Commission, 1993). The "major" universities in Quebec supported the plan that certain universities would specialize in research, whereas others would concentrate on undergraduate studies. Not surprisingly, the "other" universities were afraid of being left with reduced missions and were not willing to give up their research and graduate programs. As the commission noted, "The restructuring would also require changes in policy with respect to funding, faculty workloads, and faculty assessment to replace the current system that often results in an undue dispersal of funds" (University Education Review Commission, 1993, p. 13). The Manitoba commission concluded,

> In recent times, Manitoba's post-secondary institutions have explicitly defined the mission and roles to which they are committed. This commendable development, however, has taken place without the presence and articulation of the mission and roles of Manitoba's post-secondary system as a whole. The Commission has viewed this as a deficiency, in a context of an environment in which both interdependence and longer term planning for the future are so important.
> (p.11)

Ontario's response to fiscal pressures was to restructure the university system and to rationalize professional programs. This involved tightening new program-funding approval criteria, as well as cutting and merging existing programs (Ontario Council on University Affairs, 1995). The provincial legislature authorized the provincial auditor to examine the financial records of three of its universities. This task force issued 47 recommendations, all intended to make universities more accountable to the government and the public at large. Alberta has undergone a joint university-government exercise to eliminate program duplication. Attempts have been made to reduce government expenditures by instituting major transfer payment cuts following a government review. George and McAllister (1995) cite a March 1994 draft of a White Paper that includes as one of its goals "to ensure responsiveness and accountability [by universities] to learners and tax-payers" (p. 311). To fit within an accountability framework, postsecondary institutions in Alberta are required to provide key indicators of perform-ance on enrollment levels, graduation rates, costs per student, measures of student satisfaction, and employment outcomes.

Internal differentiation

The tensions between teaching and research are particularly visible in pro-fessional applied fields. From their inception, universities have been concerned with "vocational" issues. Alongside the provision of what has come to be called a liberal, classical education, universities took responsibility for teaching subjects intended to meet the intellectual requirements for the performance of certain practical professions. The development of the modern university is housed in and has contributed to the professionalization of society. The model of the late nineteenth century included the four traditional faculties: theology, arts, law, and medicine.

The professionalization of society has been mutually beneficial to uni-versities and the professions. While a university education justifies the professions' claims to a knowledge base and therefore to professional status, it also serves to screen entrants to the profession through means that may sustain and improve professional standards. Universities have expanded their client base by offering career-oriented courses and including areas of professional training that were previously outside the university's domain (Eraut, 1992). This is particularly the case in the fields of social work, education, and administrative sciences (business administration, commerce, and public administration). Since the early 1960s, the number of full-time, tenure-track faculty in English-speaking Canadian universities in these fields has expanded enormously. Between 1960 and 1990, the increase was from 58 to 274 (372%) in social work, from 290 to 1,611 (455%) in education, and from 81 to 1,484 (1,732%) in the administrative sciences (Commonwealth Universities Yearbooks). As these fields have reached for legitimacy within the academy, so faculty have emphasized scientific research and have run the danger of separating themselves from their pro-fessional communities. This is particularly the case in education where, over the past decade, "academic researchers" account for the large majority of appointments.

Internal differentiation lies at the heart of the strong concerns regarding quality of teaching and the balance between teaching and research. During the past 25 years, the reforms within higher education have concentrated on questions about the expansion and organization of higher education. At the same time, particularly since the early 1980s, there has been a lively discussion of research policies. However, Canadian universities were originally teaching institutions, and only after the Second World War did research become an integral part of their activities. Graham, Lyman, and Trow (1995, p. 12), when discussing the changing professoriate, note that as the research university became the most influential model for higher education, professors defined their work not as their teaching but more as their research. In the standard vocabulary of campuses, teaching was a "load," research an "opportunity."

Financial constraints that inevitably led to differentiation have had an impact on the discussion of the relationship between research and teaching. Several national and provincial reports conclude that the quality of teaching is a major problem and point to the underfunding of teaching in universities, resulting in deficiencies at the undergraduate level (New Brunswick Commission on Higher Education, 1993; Smith, 1991). During public hearings in Quebec, college and university students criticized the overuse of lectures (Gouvernement du Québec, 1996). The Ontario Council on University Affairs (1995) asked, in its Resources Allocation Review,

> Should the balance among teaching, research, and community service be altered? If so, what form of differentiation in roles would be appropriate? Should it be at the level of institution, academic unit, or individual faculty member? Should the funding allocation system be changed to enable any such shifts?
>
> (p. 72)

In its discussion paper, the council reviewed the empirical research and concluded that little evidence exists to support links between effective undergraduate teaching and research. The council suggested some caution in the interpretation. However, it seems obvious that without strong evidence for these links, the move toward differentiation at the level of individual faculty becomes more convincing. The concern with quality of teaching is used to frame a more explicit division of labor between teaching and research. At the same time, administrators seem convinced that with the inflation of credentials, the strongest vocational role for the modern research university is through an excellent undergraduate liberal arts program.

Changes in the vocational role of universities in British Columbia

Structural differentiation characterizes the relationship between and within the three older universities. Consistent with the historical development of the university system in British Columbia and elsewhere in Canada, each institution continues to carve out its own particular niche. Of the three universities, only the University of British Columbia (UBC) continues to claim the universal functions that go with being a major national research university. As the recipient of about 80% of the total external funding for research coming to British Columbia, UBC can quite properly claim the "right to be irrelevant." The security and status of being the only full medical/doctoral university in the province gives the institution the confidence to claim the traditional vocational ground that goes with the older professions. On the other hand, Simon Fraser University (SFU) and the University of Victoria (UVic) claim with confidence their relevance to community and provincial interests. Both institutions have consciously tried not to replicate existing programs and have attempted to identify unique programs they can develop.

Just as, in the province of Ontario, York University began life as the antithesis to the University of Toronto, so in British Columbia SFU continues to take pride in not being UBC. The focus is on innovation and interdisciplinarity. As one administrator put it, "the ethos of the institution is more open to thinking in different ways, in doing things differently" and developing "a sense of community responsibility." With its strong commitment to continuing and cooperative education and to serving the metropolitan region of Vancouver, SFU, not UBC, took the lead and established the downtown Harbour Centre Campus. Through this campus, the university serves a "bridging" function and has become accessible to the community by location, program/course, and, according to their mission statement, even spirit. Their initiative is perhaps best represented in the outreach degree-completion program designed for employees of B.C. Hydro and Canadian Pacific Rail, which began operation in 1995.

Similarly, UVic has developed a special expertise in cooperative education. UVic mounts the third-largest program in the country, running behind Waterloo and Sherbrooke. The cooperative philosophy permeates the culture and has become the defining characteristic of this campus. Co-op programs operate in over thirty-five departments. Some departments offer an optional program; others make it mandatory. The Faculty of Business Administration began life with a mandatory co-op component at both the undergraduate and graduate levels. In addition, the Faculty of Engineering, which dates back to the early 1980s, has from its inception had a mandatory component. As one administrator put it, "The thought was that in those applied fields of Business and Engineering it would be sensible for all our graduates to have had some work-based learning experience."

All departments at UVic, except anthropology, political science, and psychology, have some work-based learning opportunities, through either co-op, internships, or practicums. UVic's reputation for bridging the gap between the academy and the labor market was a key factor in the university's being chosen as the Canadian location of the Swiss-based program in hotel and restaurant management.

Analysis of policy documents reveals that commitment to adult and part-time study is strongest in the original mission statements of SFU and UVic. Both institutions are strongly committed to the maintenance of access for adult learners and the development of facilities and programs for part-time study. In its original statement of mission, UBC's commitment to adult and part-time study could, at best, be characterized as lukewarm. Not until the 1980s did UBC, in a series of revised and successive statements of mission, become theoretically committed to adult part-time study and lifelong learning. At SFU, continuing education is not so marginalized as it is in other universities, and it has become part of the wider ethos of the university. The faculty agree on the value of lifelong education and the outreach policy. For the group in continuing education, "liberal education is more than education for its own sake—it is education that is relevant to the general public interest." It follows that the MBA Executive program and the Downtown Eastside-City Program should exist side by side.

Although these approaches to vocationalism serve to distinguish the three universities, there exists substantial agreement among the three universities on their "real" vocational function. All three universities have over the past decade expanded to include more applied fields and programs. This trend is nowhere more pronounced than at UVic, which has self-consciously added many professional and applied programs and schools over the past twenty years. These additions were, according to one administrator, "all designed to address the problems of society." Law was added in 1973, followed by a number of programs (nursing, social work, public administration, child and youth care, and health information science) that are now housed in the Faculty of Human and Social Development. Engineering programs were added in the 1980s and computer science later joined the Faculty of Engineering. The addition of engineering was a controversial decision, causing massive division in the Faculty of Arts and Science and a profound split in the Senate. This debate was a turning point in the history of UVic, as the ideal and myth of the university as a liberal arts college were put to rest. Finally, the Faculty of Business Administration was added in 1991. The change has been both massive and drastic. As one faculty member put it, "The whole nature of its [UVic's] operation has changed. Now, with all the applied and professional programs, there's much more focus on students wishing to prepare themselves for specific professions when they leave university."

At UBC, the fastest-growing areas are commerce and computer science. A school of journalism opened in 1997. The new undergraduate programs in occupational hygiene and advanced wood processing were tailored to the needs of profession and industry, involving the cooperation and financial backing of government.

The pressure on universities to respond to external social forces can be observed in the debates on training versus education and the trend toward interdisciplinarity. A clear distinction is made between education and training. According to one administrator, training is, for many faculty, "a dirty word because it's not educational, not cognitive enough for them." The colleges, university colleges, and new universities (Royal Roads University and Technical University) are expected to fulfill training rather than education functions. Whereas the "academic drift" symbolized by the Malaspina Liberal Arts degree and the British Columbia Institute of Technology applied degree is recognized, the three older universities still retain their claim to liberal education. For most faculty, the arts and sciences are still the core of the university. As one faculty member put it,

> Universities are not here simply to train people for jobs. It is a fundamental tenet of universities that they exist to educate. Universities exist to provide people with an opportunity to explore the intellectual world as well as preparing people for the jobs and the workforce.

Senior administrators talk at length about the generic skills (flexibility, critical thinking, problem solving, independence, and the ability to communicate) that are learned as part of a classical liberal education. These skills are regarded as the vocational heart of any institution that claims to be a university and are symbols of the unity between theory and practice. One administrator declared that it was false to make "any distinction between pure and applied research, or between theoretical and vocational education." The Arts and Science One course is held up by UBC as the exemplar of modern vocational education. The liberal arts components of both the cooperative and outreach programs at SFU and UVic are similarly displayed as badges of vocational virtue. SFU is wedded in the broadest sense to the concept of liberal education. All undergraduates take a "general education" program in their first two years. At UVic, which began life as a liberal arts college, all programs have strong roots in the Faculty of Arts and Science.

In recent years, generic skills have received more attention, in part because of the continuing inflation of credentials and the concomitant expansion of graduate work. If specialized vocational preparation is a postgraduate experience, then space is left for a more traditional undergraduate education. This view converges with the conventional wisdom that employers want generalists who can learn on the job. Universities then quite properly should be providing broad, general liberal education not just for students in the arts and sciences, but also for students in professional, applied, and technological fields. According to this view, which is the mirror image of the position taken by the Conference Board of Canada, general education will produce trainable workers who can think critically, work in a team, and solve problems.

The trend across the system is toward more interdisciplinarity and more applied programming. At SFU, the tradition of interdisciplinarity has been extended into new graduate programs such as environmental toxicology, which are geared to provide people with certification or professional requirements for the local job market. UVic has a strong commitment to interdisciplinarity, which is demonstrated by the rise of the applied and professional fields referred to earlier and exciting initiatives such as the computer science master's degree in software engineering. Universities take accountability to the external world more seriously than they have done before. All three universities defined themselves as being more responsive, more willing to take the initiative and be proactive. Inevitably, administrators were aware of the political-economic pressure to change but were clear that neither government or industry had pushed them in a particular policy direction. Rather, financial stringency and government policy stressing the vocational role of the tertiary sector have created a climate for change. For the most part, universities have translated the signals and then taken the initiative, although at times, government direction has clearly been decisive. The Nursing School at UVic was a direct response to government overtures. Similarly, the Faculty of Business idea was renewed in the late 1980s by the government after the initial suggestion was rejected earlier in the decade. The faculty was established with line funding from the government. The best example at UBC is the advanced wood products program.

Although many of the changes have not been formulated as policy, we can identify clear shifts. The most obvious example is the move toward full cost recovery. This became policy at UBC for continuing education in 1995 and is under active consideration at SFU and UVic. The trend is toward strategic, money-making, diploma and certificate programs. The new climate explicitly rewards entrepreneurship. The boundary separating the academy and industry is much more permeable. As one administrator put it,

> Education is a door opener to industry. They're interested, and if you help them out with their education and training problems, you're going to get to know them better. They'll get to know you better, and then you can start talking about joint research ventures with them, so that your faculty get involved in joint research.

Although administrators would want to deny that their universities are "for sale," the trend toward sale of services and profit-taking is clear and consistent.

The professionalization of university culture has reached a critical stage in the 1990s, as our universities have become more corporate. At one level, administration has become a separate career, producing a culture at odds with the traditional, collegial definition of university life. The division between scholars and administrators is not new, but now the tensions are exacerbated in an extreme way by the external pressure to focus on relevance and accountability. The collegial model of governance continues to be undermined, and the uneasy truce between the two cultures has been broken. Many faculty, particularly within the most established arts and science disciplines, as well as students, are highly critical of these developments. Most faculty regard the work of professional and applied units as legitimate but are concerned about the current vocational trend. For many, our universities have crossed a line that challenges the fundamental autonomy of the university with its "particular character . . . and own institutional esprit de corps and raison d'être." The pursuit of learning, critical thinking, and basic research all come under threat, according to one faculty member, when instrumental and functional objectives displace the concern with autonomy and a separation of powers within society. As one student representative observed,

> The dominant political culture [on campus] has created a more atomized, individualistic, competitive kind of atmosphere on campus, and that cuts in so many different directions . . . student to student, faculty to faculty . . . people see each other as competitors rather than as people who are learning in a common environment . . . a market competition mentality.

Yet, against this background, senior administrators define the new relationships with industry and government as opportunities rather than threats.

The definition of professionalism is changing as fields such as commerce and forestry respond to external pressures and embrace praxis. For one administrator in commerce, professional schools should quite properly "link ideas and practical skills." The faculty is run as "a business on full cost recovery and then some," yet the belief is that the research mission has been strengthened. The "ivory tower" definition of the university has been replaced by a "society-problem-oriented" one where the university is connected to the external world in a hundred different ways. According to one administrator, the Faculty of Forestry has thoroughly embraced the new definition:

> We are a professional faculty. . . . if society did not have forestry problems, UBC would not have a forestry faculty, and so we see our destiny as being linked to the outside world, and, being a bridge between the outside world and the university to a degree.

Professional faculties that initiate and promote contact with external agencies provide the best indicator of what has become a "sea change" in university culture.

Conclusion

The foregoing analysis highlights seven overlapping changes in the external life of Canadian universities. First is the further softening of federalism. Less involvement will mean less regulation and will undermine the principle of universalism, which has been at the heart of the post-Second World War experience in Canada. Second is a further blurring of the vocational part of the boundary that has traditionally separated the universities and colleges. The education-versus-training labels will no longer characterize the binary structure of the postsecondary sector as in the past. On the surface, two contradictory trends seem to be at work: academic drift, as colleges become more like universities; and vocationalism, as universities take on more responsibility for training the highly skilled technical employees in, for example, computer science, and for retraining professionals. The increase in university transfer courses and the extension of degree-granting status to colleges are indicators of the former trend. The long-established trend toward vocationalism is exemplified by the expansion of commerce and business administration over the past two decades. On the boundary between these two sectors are the applied degrees offered by technical colleges or universities.

Third is the increasing differentiation and specialization within the university system. The hierarchy between institutions will become more pronounced. A small number of universities will qualify as national institutions. These elite corporate research universities will continue to attract both corporate and state funding as they become more specialized, yet still retain the character of the full university. Occupying the second rung are two parallel institutional categories that meet both provincial and specialized needs. The two categories are as follows: liberal arts undergraduate and provincial research universities. The third rung includes smaller provincial universities and the technical universities. The final rung is occupied by the relatively small number of university colleges and those with a religious affiliation.

The fourth change will be the higher level of competition for research funding and for students. The new academic industry liaison offices and research service units in our universities are but two indicators of this long-established trend. The new emphasis on marketing universities through the media with glossy brochures is the first major salvo in the new battle for student dollars. The international market seems particularly attractive. Fifth is the continuing decline of the public sphere. Universities will have less autonomy as they establish a closer and more accountable relationship with business and industry. The exchange relation between governments and universities has always been understated. As provincial governments become more directly responsible, we have noted obvious attempts at tighter control over university policy and more emphasis on the strategic needs of the province. Increasingly, profit will become a motive for action, as universities more consciously try to adapt to the needs of business and students. Sixth is the continuing bifurcation in the opportunity structure in the labor market. Universities will explicitly attempt to capture the "good jobs" market and the professional retraining market. The inflation of credentials will continue, so that more jobs will require a degree as a screen for entry. Finally, as a corollary to the previous point, universities will become more the preserve of the elites in our society. The existing relationship between socioeconomic status (SES) and participation in adult education will be reinforced (Fisher & Rubenson, 1992). We can expect to see a tightening of the tie between class and levels of participation in different levels of the system. The barriers to access will increase, so that people from lower SES backgrounds will be pushed into lower echelons of the system. The participation of females at the top of the hierarchy is in danger of dropping, as the lower-status semiprofessions such as nursing and teaching are pushed onto the lower rungs of the system. With less public regulation, the market will punish the weaker members of our society.

If we now turn to the internal life of Canadian universities, we can highlight four overlapping changes. First is a change in the culture of our university. Canadian universities are becoming more commercial and more entrepreneurial. The *bildung* part of our academic tradition, which emphasizes the cultivation of inward and external criticism and a "richness of mind and person," will be further undermined (Ringer, 1992). What might be called the "civilizing mission" of universities will be less central than in the past, except for a privileged elite. The current tendency of some university administrators to define liberal education as the vocational heart of the modern university might best be regarded as the modern version of "vocationalism of dominant groups" (cited in Wright, 1992, p. 219). It follows that the critical function of universities will also be threatened. The tradition of academic freedom has been tied to and colored by the profound distrust of utilitarianism and utilitarian forms of knowledge. With less "relative autonomy" guaranteed by the state, academics will take fewer risks.

Second is an intensification of the current trend toward organizational models that are bureaucratic, corporate, and directed to the market. As administrators become corporate managers and strive for more efficiency, we can expect certain costs. Our results confirm the conclusions drawn by Ball (1990), who claims that academics will experience the following changes in their work: an intensification of work practices, a loss of individual autonomy, closer monitoring and appraisal, less participation in decision making, and a lack of personal development through work. The division between administration and research will become wider. Third is an increase in the commodification of education leading to more internal differentiation by program. Differential fees, full cost recovery, and the establishment of programs for profit are all part of this trend. Finally, the increasing emphasis is on short-term individual experience at the expense of long-term collective contributions. According to the OECD (1993), this is the real danger of educational policy making in the 1990s, because the long-term contributions are often more indirect than direct and less easy to measure than by merely what it costs.

The most pronounced change in our universities is the continuing trend to more and more differentiation. This is occurring across the Canadian system between and within provinces. We can expect variations on the California Plan as the functions served by our higher education institutions are divided along lines of education and training, or "pure" versus applied/professional. The pressure to rationalize program offerings within the province will increase as provincial governments look for ways to save money. Although British Columbia is somewhat of an anomaly because provincial spending on the system has been maintained rather than reduced, we do see a very clear hierarchical division of labor. Similarly, we already see a greater degree of differentiation within our universities along the "teaching/research" divide. Universities have come to rely on part-time or sessional instructors to do much of the teaching work once done by tenure-track professors.

Privatization continues to be the overwhelming trend. Institutions are changing their practices to accumulate power. Our universities are becoming more corporate, more technocratic, more utilitarian, and far more concerned with selling products than with education. Jointly designing curriculum with private donors, the differentiation between teaching and research internally, and the reliance on nontenure-track sessional or part-time labor are already established trends. Full cost recovery is a major theme. The marketing of programs at profit-making rates to foreign elites will become the norm. In short, the very essence of the university in Canada will change in ways that undermine some of the best parts of the tradition that emphasized national norms and public service.

References

Abele, F. (1992). The politics of competitiveness. In F. Abele (Ed.), *How Ottawa spends, 1992–93*. Ottawa: Carleton University Press.

Ball, S. J. (1990). Management as moral technology: A Luddite analysis. In S. J. Ball (Ed.), *Foucault and education: Disciplines and knowledge* (pp. 153–166). London: Routledge.

Barlow, M., & Cambell, B. (1991). *Take back the nation*. Toronto: Key Porter.

Bourdieu, P. (1969). Intellectual field and the creative project. *Social Science Information, 8*(2), 89–119.

British Columbia Labour Force Development Board (BCLFDB). (1995). *Training for what?* Victoria: Author.

Clark, B. R. (1983). *The higher education system: Academic organization in cross-national perspective*. Berkeley: University of California Press.

Commonwealth Universities Secretariat. *Commonwealth Universities Yearbook* (Selected Years). London: Author.

Department of Finance, Province of New Brunswick. (1996). *Budget 1996–1997*. Fredericton: Queen's Printer for New Brunswick.

Eraut, M. (1992). Developing the knowledge base: A process perspective on professional education. In R. Barnett (Ed.), *Learning to effect*. Buckingham, UK: The Society for Research into Higher Education and Open University Press.

Fisher, D., & Rubenson, K. (1992). Polarization and bifurcation in work and adult education: Participation in adult education in British Columbia. *Policy Explorations*, *6*(3), 1–19.

George, P. G., & McAllister, G. A. (1995). The expanding role of the state in Canadian universities: Can university autonomy and accountability be reconciled?, *Higher Education Management*, *7*(3), 309–327.

Gouvernement du Québec. (1996). *The state of education in Quebec, 1995–1996*. Québec City: Author.

Government of Canada, Human Resources Development Canada. (1996). *Federal and provincial support to post-secondary education in Canada: A report to Parliament, 1994–1995*. Ottawa: Author.

Graham, P. A., Lyman, R. W., & Trow, M. (1995). *Accountability of colleges and universities*. New York: The Trustees of Columbia University.

Haddow, R. (1995). Canada's experiment with labour market neocorporatism. In K. Banting & C. Beach (Eds.), *Labour market polarization and social reform*. Ontario: Queen's University School of Public Policy.

Horry, I., & Walker, M. (1994). *Government spending facts two*. Vancouver, BC: The Fraser Institute.

Human Resources Development Canada. (1994). *Agenda: Jobs and growth: Improving social security in Canada*. Ottawa: Author.

Johnson, A. F., McBride, S., & Smith, P. J. (1994). *Continuities and discontinuities: The political economy of social welfare and labour market policy in Canada*. Toronto: University of Toronto Press.

McBride, S., & Shields, J. (1993). *Dismantling a nation: Canada and the new world order*. Halifax: Fernwood.

Mullay, R. (1994). Social welfare and the new right: A class mobilization perspective. In A. F. Johnson, S. McBride, & P. J. Smith (Eds.), *Continuities and discontinuities: The political economy of social welfare and labour market policy in Canada*. Toronto: University of Toronto Press.

New Brunswick Commission on Higher Education. (1993). *New Brunswick Commission on Excellence in Education*. Fredericton: Author.

Nova Scotia Council on Higher Education. (1995). *Shared responsibilities in higher education*. Halifax: Author.

Nova Scotia Council on Higher Education. (1996). *Government support of universities in Nova Scotia: A proposal for a new funding formula*. Halifax: Author.

Ontario Council on University Affairs. (1995). *21st annual report*. Toronto: Author.

Ontario Premier's Council on Economic Renewal. (1994). *Lifelong learning and the new economy*. Toronto: Queen's Printer for Ontario.

Organization for Economic Cooperation and Development. (1993). *Employment outlook*. Paris: Author.

Organization for Economic Cooperation and Development. (1996). *Education at a glance: OECD indicators*. Paris: Author.

Ringer, F. (1992). *Fields of knowledge: French academic culture in comparative perspective, 1890–1920*. Cambridge, UK: Cambridge University Press.

Scott, P. (1995). *The meanings of mass higher education*. Buckingham, UK: The Society for Research into Higher Education and Open University Press.

Smith, S. L. (1991). *Report on the Commission of Inquiry on Canadian University Education*. Ottawa: Association of Universities and Colleges of Canada.

Stanbury, W. T. (1989). Privatization in Canada: Ideology, symbolism, and substance. In P. W. MaCavoy, W. T. Stanbury, G. Yarrow, & R. J. Zekhauser (Eds.), *Privatization and state-owned enterprises: Lessons from the United States, Great Britain, and Canada* (pp. 273–329). Boston: Kluwer.

University Education Review Commission. (1993). *Post-secondary education in Manitoba: Doing things differently*. Winnipeg, Manitoba: Author.

University Program Review Panel. (1993). *Looking at Saskatchewan universities: Programs, governance, and goals*. Regina, Saskatchewan: Author.

Wright, P. (1992). Learning through enterprise: The enterprise in higher education initiative. In R. Barnett (Ed.), *Learning to effect*. Buckingham, UK: The Society for Research into Higher Education and Open University Press.

20

THE UNIVERSITIES OF AUSTRALIA

J. D. G. Medley

Source: *Universities Quarterly* 2(2) (1948): 151–8.

Australia is a Federation of six States with a capital city at Canberra. Each State has one university situated in its capital city and last year there was founded at Canberra a National University which is, in the first instance at all events, to devote its energies entirely to research. In addition, there is at Canberra a small University College which presents its students for Melbourne degrees, at Armidale in New South Wales a University College which trains for Sydney degrees and hopes soon to take independent rank as the University of New England, and at Mildura in Victoria a residential branch of the University of Melbourne which deals with first year work only in certain subjects. There are thus in the whole Commonwealth seven Universities proper, two University Colleges and one attached branch. They contain at the present time some 20,000 full-time students and about 10,000 others who are doing courses on a part-time basis—which means that about 1 in 400 of Australia's population is a full-time student as opposed to a pre-war (1939) figure of 1 in 1,000.

As is everywhere the case, this state of things is of course abnormal. Our Universities are swollen with entries from the services in addition to the usual civilian enrolment, and we are encountering those difficulties in the provision of staff, accommodation and equipment which are the common contemporary lot. For the next three years we must expect a continuance of the struggle, by which time we may hope that material resources will have become adequate to cope with reduced numbers—whatever the figure may be. In the meantime the Federal Rehabilitation scheme, which I do not propose to traverse in detail here, is undoubtedly having the effect of steering in the direction of the professions a considerable number of those who would not under normal circumstances have considered such a career, and the universities have somehow to do them justice.

Our difficulties are particularly great, for we do not in Australia exercise the degree of selectivity which is the rule in Great Britain and America. The University of Sydney is forced by the provisions of its University Act to accept every entrant who is formally qualified by matriculation for the Faculty of his choice. The University of Melbourne does refuse applications much in excess of the numbers it can adequately train, but it has to stretch its capacity beyond all reason and to proceed with the greatest caution. There is, I think, a twofold reason for this curious state of things. The number of our universities is limited and their distances from each other very great. It is not possible to say to a rejected applicant "We don't want you but after all there are other places which can give you what you want." To reject him damns his chances for good. And over and above that, a real appreciation of the importance of quality is not yet firmly implanted in Australia. There are no private Universities. All of them have always been and must now to an ever increasing extent continue to be dependent upon political sources for a large part of their annual income. It is right to put on record that Australian governments have used their power in this respect with the greatest self control and that the experience of our Universities over the vexed question of academic freedom has been on the whole very fortunate. But public opinion is sensitive upon the point, and I doubt very much whether it would tolerate the standards of selectivity which are invariably set by the great universities elsewhere.

My purpose is to give a general picture of our universities and not to dilate upon our present difficulties which are after all much the same everywhere. At the moment it is difficult to see the wood for the trees or to arrive at any but the vaguest estimates of what the general position is likely to be when some degree of 'normality' returns. But Australian universities have a reasonable stretch of history behind them—both Sydney and Melbourne will be celebrating centenaries within the next seven years; their performances, despite grave difficulties caused by poverty and isolation, have been comparable to those of far more fortunate institutions, and it is not probable that the immediate future will see any very radical changes in the pattern that has been evolved.

University finance

The self control exercised by Australian governments in their dealings with universities to which I referred earlier has unfortunately been extended into the financial field. One of the first things to strike an impartial observer would be the surprisingly small budgets upon which our universities operate. Income is derived as elsewhere from government grants, endowments and fees (except in the case of the University of Western Australia which is a 'free' University and charges nothing for tuition). Fees are very moderate: the cost of a university year in a three year arts course is about £A35; the total cost of a six year medical course is £A300.[1] There is talk about raising them but the expressed policy of most Australian governments is to work towards 'free' universities and it is very unlikely that appreciable budget relief will come from that direction.

As regards endowments, though there have been substantial gifts to universities notably in Sydney, Adelaide and Western Australia, the general picture is that income from this source is a comparatively minor item and is largely confined to special purposes. There are various reasons for this. There are few large aggregations of capital in Australia and a society whose money has been largely employed in the ups and downs of the pastoral industry is apt to be tenacious of its resources. It is only comparatively recently, moreover, that the universities have become really interested in the problem of their public relations and no serious attempt has as yet been made to capitalise the loyalty of alumni which is so prominent and profitable a feature of the United States. We have probably missed our chances in this field: it seems unlikely that under present taxation levels— even though gifts to universities are legitimate deductions—any substantial degree of salvation can be sought in this direction.

We are thus confronted, whether we like it or not, with the prospect of increasing dependence upon government grants and all that this implies. Before the war, State governments only were involved: under the constitution education at all stages was left as a State function. Beyond the annual provision of £30,000 for research in the physical sciences and the financing of a limited number of special Chairs, the Federal Government played no part in the university arena. But the last few years have produced radical changes. The Federal Government is now the sole income taxing authority: under the Rehabilitation Scheme it has disbursed some $1^1/_2$ million pounds to the universities for capital equipment and subsidies in addition to fee payments: as the result of a referendum held in 1946 it can now, if it so desires, constitutionally control social services, presumably including education. At the moment as the result of swollen numbers and inadequate staffs, the universities are more or less balancing their budgets. But during the next few years numbers will decrease (though to what extent is quite uncertain) as service men and women complete their courses, income will decrease, inasmuch as the service people will take with them not only their fees but a Federal subsidy of £ for £ on fees as well, and costs will most certainly not decrease proportionately.

All universities are thus faced with the prospect of a rapidly increasing gap between their income and their expenditure which can only be filled by a reduction in expenditure so drastic that standards will practically cease to exist, or an increase in government help on a scale which may well be beyond the capacity of State governments to achieve. The universities themselves would in all probability welcome the establishment of a Federal body on the lines of the British University Grants Committee, despite the very real difficulties of finding in Australia available persons of sufficient standing and knowledge to man it—provided it were given the same complete freedom of action that committee possesses and adequate funds to disburse. But all that can really be said at the moment is that the financial future of our universities is obscure and worrying, and that during 1948 there will be a great deal of three-cornered arguments on the subject between Federal and State governments and the universities themselves. In the meantime the University of Melbourne, with some 9,000 students, to take one example, can command from all sources annual receipts of about £500,000—almost exactly the same as the University of Birmingham with 2,600 students. No wonder Australian Vice-Chancellors grow prematurely old!

Disadvantages of homogeneity

I referred earlier to poverty and isolation as our two main handicaps. They are alike responsible for a striking feature of our universities—their complete homogeneity of type and the very limited amount of staff and student migration that takes place between them. There has never been enough money for bold experiment or enough competition to encourage variations in pattern. There is no Oxford or Cambridge in Australia to act as a magnet for the best brains and a refuge for the humanities: there are no liberal arts colleges designed to give a pre-professional training or to cope with the needs of those who do not intend to qualify for a profession. The average Australian student matriculates at the age of 17 $^1/_2$, comes up immediately to his own State university, goes into a professional school and proceeds to qualify for entrance to the earning arena in the minimum time possible. Our universities in short consist of a collection of professional schools and, save for such minor variations as the fact that there are as yet no medical schools in Western Australia or Tasmania, and that the teaching of Veterinary Science is largely centralised in Sydney, they all teach the same subjects, in the same sort of school, in very much the same kind of way.

They reflect the community in so doing. Australia is a large continent but, though experts profess to be able to distinguish between Victorians and Queenslanders at a glance, Australians wherever they live do in fact talk and think and look at life with very little variation of accent or attitude. It is easy to point to the defects of so exclusively professional a training, to stigmatise our universities, as their critics are fond of doing, as 'nothing but technical schools,' and to reinforce the criticism by reference to the fact that only a very small proportion of our students—not more than 10%—reside in colleges or hostels during their university life. Each university has affiliated to it colleges which are owned and managed by governing bodies appointed by religious denominations, and in some cases these colleges provide a tutorial system for their residents and play an important part in the affairs of the university. But at present it is not the declared policy of the universities to enter this field themselves and, if it were, it is most unlikely that money would be available to construct hostels on any large scale.

The exceptions to this statement are the New England University College at Armidale which is largely residential and the Melbourne experiment at Mildura where 560 first year students are housed in an Air Force camp in which, owing to distance from Melbourne and lack of local facilities, residence is compulsory. One year's trial, generously backed by the State Government of Victoria, has tended to show that the experiment is a success from most points of view and it may well encourage further developments on these lines in other parts of the country. But I think it safe to say that the majority of Australian students will continue to live either at home or in lodgings, and in theory of course this must militate severely against their enjoyment of a full university life. Many do undoubtedly regard their university purely as 'a shop'—a place to get into and get out of as quickly as possible. But it would be a grave error to dismiss Australian universities with a wave of the hand on this account. The admitted quality of good Australian students—and they are produced in large quantities—would alone suffice to confound the too caustic critic. What saves the situation is the fact that each university does get its full share of the best brains of its own State: there are no counter attractions elsewhere and our early age of matriculation compared with Great Britain has the result that even the small numbers of those whose ambition is to go abroad tend to do a course in Australia first.

Our universities are much more than technical schools. In all of them there is intense extra-curricular activity, which has tended in the recent past to take a largely political flavour but is now being increasingly reinforced by aesthetic and social developments. Student Representative Councils are very vigorous and co-operative and are represented in some cases upon university governing bodies. The general tone of all universities—particularly at present with the large influx of minds maturer than ordinary—is one of high seriousness and there is remarkably little of that kind of activity which has to be excused by a reminder that 'boys will be boys.' The Australian student can, if he so wishes, live a very full and exciting life and though critics of 'student apathy' are always with us, they have far fewer grounds for serious alarm than was the case a few years ago. It is sometimes said that only by an increase in the length of all courses, and the insertion of at least two pre-professional years of general subjects can a balanced university education be achieved in Australia. 'Had we but world enough and time' that might well be so. But the time factor is decisive and the Australian world at any rate would not be content to wait or to pay for graduates who required a minimum of six to eight years' training before setting about the business of earning a living.

Research

The picture assumes a much gloomier tone when we proceed to consider the position of that all-important university function—research. Lack of resources and the consequent over-burdening of staff with teaching duties have combined with our isolation from the main centres of original work to restrict the activities of our postgraduate schools to a deplorable extent. There has been a constant pressure on the part of our better younger workers to take advantage of the superior facilities available in Great Britain and America, and the resulting adverse balance of trade in brains has been causing concern for some time past. There is no lack of first-rate raw material in the country: good work is done in bits and pieces in all the universities and the successes gained abroad by Australians in all fields leave no room for contradiction. But the volume of work that can be achieved under existing conditions is not such as to make university research the educational and social force that it ought to be, and still less to make it a means of attracting to Australia first class brains from the other side of the world.

There are, however, two recent developments which afford some belief that better days are coming. One is that the Federal Government has trebled the annual grant to universities for research in physical and social science and there are hopes that the total available may shortly be further increased to £140,000. The other is the foundation of the National University at Canberra and the provision for it of funds—some £375,000 a year—on a scale which will make the establishment of first-rate research schools feasible. The new university is to restrict itself to start with to research only, and steps are being taken to set up four institutes to work in Physical and Medical Research, Social Science and Pacific Relations. No appointments have as yet been made but negotiations are in active progress.

There has been much criticism of this decision which was sprung upon the Australian people with little or no previous discussion. It has taken the obvious lines that it would have been much wiser to spend the money on building up strong schools in the existing universities and that Canberra, which has been unkindly described as 'Six Suburbs in search of a City,' is no place in which to isolate research workers at the present stage of its development. Against this it can be said that the centralisation of available funds is much more likely to produce a really attractive foundation than their piecemeal dispersal and that the kind of society which will develop around it is exactly what is wanted to make Canberra into the real capital city of a great Commonwealth which it ought to be. In any case the decision has been made and critics must make the best of it. Existing universities can derive nothing but profit from the new institution provided that those in charge of it realise that research cannot flourish *in vacuo* and that the rapid development of research schools throughout Australia is an essential prerequisite to their own success.

There must obviously be the closest co-operation between Canberra and its sister universities not only in research but, it may be hoped, in teaching as well—co-operation which the very advanced and efficient internal air services of Australia render entirely feasible. Above all, the new foundation does hold out real hopes to the younger generation of Australians that it will now be possible to enter upon a career in research without the urgent and expensive necessity of certainly a period and possibly a life spent abroad. The importance of this for both the individual and the nation can hardly be exaggerated.

The future

It has been impossible in an article of restricted length to do more than touch on a few aspects of the whole picture. Those who administer universities in these days find it difficult to face the future with equanimity. It is no longer possible to dream of the unexpected millionaire who at one wave of his magic wand will remove the wrinkles from a Vice-Chancellor's brow. We have to deal more and more with the unpredictable politician. But I have hopes that he will gradually follow the example of Great Britain and America which are both pouring money into their universities on a long-term basis as the best of national investments in a difficult world. If and as our poverty vanishes, so too will our isolation; which from the point of view of those who make or mar universities—their teachers—is the greatest single obstacle to that real progress which we all desire.

Note

1 Excluding books and equipment.

21

Excerpt from
THE AFRICAN UNIVERSITY
IN DEVELOPMENT

Asavia Wandira

Source: A. Wandira, *The African University in Development*, Johannesburg: Ravan Press, 1977, pp. 8–36.

The Jones Colleges

Two events separated by nearly fifty years symbolise the beginning and intensification of conflict over the roles of the university in Africa. The first of these was the appointment of the Phelps-Stokes Commission under the chairmanship of Dr Jesse Jones. The Commission reported on education in West, South and Equatorial Africa in 1922 and two years later produced a separate report on education in East and Central Africa. The second event was the holding in 1972 of a workshop on emerging issues confronting African Universities in the 1970's. Held in Accra under the umbrella of the Association of African Universities, the workshop produced a report a year later edited by Dr T. M. Yesufu. Both events were preceded by periods of dissatisfaction with University education and its role in African development.

Inspired by the desire to see their countries develop and vindicate the African race in the search for parity with Europeans, educated English-speaking West Africans had for nearly a century advocated the establishment of a university in West Africa. The names of Dr James Africanus Beale Horton of Sierra Leone, Professor Edward Wilmoth Blyden of Liberia, Casely Hayford of the then Gold Coast and Dr Benjamin Nnamdi Azikiwe of Nigeria are associated with these early initiatives. The beginnings of success came with the establishment of Fourah Bay College (1876), Achimoto College, Accra (1927) and the Higher College, Yaba, Nigeria (1934). Elsewhere the demand for higher education led to the beginnings of such education at Makerere College, Uganda (1922), and the Gordon Memorial College and the Kitchener School of Medicine, Khartoum (1924). In a different category but also owing its beginnings to early African agitation for higher education, was Fort Hare College which opened its doors in 1915 as the 'South African Native College'.

The problem of the apex

In the early years of their establishment, the Jones Colleges (as they were sometimes called) faced two difficult conceptual problems. The first arose out of the necessity to synchronise the stage of university development with the stage reached by the secondary education system. The problem may be put in the form of a question:

> In relation to the educational systems universities served, what was to have first genesis: a well developed secondary school system or a well developed university?

Another aspect of the same problem concerns the levels and standards to be demanded by the university:

> Should university entrance and university standards be geared to the standards of a poorly developed secondary school system or must they be set at some pre-conceived level apart from and irrespective of the school system?

The second conceptual problem concerns the relationship between the university as an institution and similar institutions in the world:

> Having regard to their international standing, should new universities be allowed to depart from existing internationally recognised models of university structures and operations and to seek an identity of their own?

The difficulty of reaching a concensus on these problems is illustrated by the controversy that greeted the 1933 recommendations of the British Advisory Committee on Education in the Colonies. The committee recommended that selected institutions in the colonies should be developed to university status. In West Africa, British officials argued that such a development would be premature as the secondary school systems were insufficiently developed to support a viable university (Nduka Okafor (1971–84)). This argument was sustained in spite of the fact that Oxford and Cambridge had flourished long before a sound secondary school system had been developed in England (Ashby (1964:15)). What universities should do in the service of an educational infra-structure that is insufficiently developed, remained an unresolved problem.

In more recent times, experimentation with mature entry schemes, preparatory, preliminary or pre-entry courses and other mechanisms have given universities opportunities to bridge the gap between secondary and higher education levels. Now and in the past, however, few universities are prepared to revise their concepts of the hallmarks of entrance to university degree courses. The tendency to regard university levels and methods apart from those of the secondary school system has continued. Bridging mechanisms and the rest of the educational system must produce the kind of candidates who will profit from university education as determined by the university itself.

The choice before a university serving an inadequately developed secondary school sector is clear. As the institution awarding the highest and most prestigious qualifications, it stands at the apex of the educational system. Its admission requirements and, indirectly, its final examinations and final standards, can be related to a gradual development of the educational system as a whole or they can be fixed at a pre-determined level corresponding to what the university regards as international standards. The one choice results in a fluctuating apex of the educational system. The other choice results in a fixed apex determined by considerations outside the educational system. In the pioneering years of its development and in the struggle to establish an adequate and competitive pool of university entrants, every university is faced with a choice between these two conflicting conceptions of the apex and its relation to educational development.

In the case of the colleges established after the Jones Commission, the conflict in the conception of the apex remained a real dilemma. One particular example illustrates the efforts of an institution to reach a compromise between a fixed and a fluctuating apex. In 1937, a Commission, appointed by the British Secretary of State for the Colonies to inquire into Higher Education in East Africa and popularly known as the De La Warr Commission, recommended the development of Makerere College in Uganda as the University College for East Africa, to be raised to full university status soon afterwards. Accepting that the secondary school system in East Africa was inadequately developed, the Commission (1937:118–19) boldly declared:

> We are aware of the present very flimsy foundations of primary and secondary education upon which such institutions will need to be based, and realise the possible risks of too rapid advance and of a top heavy structure. Nevertheless, we are convinced that the material needs of the country and the intellectual needs of its people require that such risks as there may be should be taken.

The Commission (1937:60–1) recommended the award of Makerere diplomas in medicine, agriculture and teacher education in the first instance. As soon as possible, however, Makerere was to enter temporary arrangements for the award of the London external degree. An East African School Certificate would be established with standards comparable to those of the British School Leaving Certificate.

These recommendations illustrate the effort of the Commission to come to terms with conflicting concepts of the university as the apex of the educational system. The apex would be allowed to fluctuate but for a temporary period before British standards were to be established. Significantly, this approach was opposed by a minority of the De La Warr Commission (1937:127) which argued in favour of a steady rise of Makerere standards 'partly of its own force and partly by pressure from below as the schools improve.' Clearly, the Commission did not fully resolve the conceptual conflict even though its Report gave impetus to the development of Makerere. The conflict continued right through the later years of the college's development to university status. The Faculties of Arts, Social Sciences, Science and, later, Agriculture, elected to enter candidates for the London external degree. The final awards of the Faculties of Medicine and Education and of the School of Fine Arts remained college awards until the establishment of the University of East Africa in 1962. The problem of the apex had not been resolved.

The philosophy of adaptation

Another conceptual problem besetting the early years of university development in Africa arose directly out of the recommendations of the Phelps-Stokes Commission Reports (1922, 1924). The Commission successfully argued the necessity for educational adaptation before the transference of western education to the colonies. Following the Commission's Reports, Britain established an Advisory Committee on Education in the colonies to work out the necessary policy guide lines and in 1925 issued a White Paper accepting educational adaptation as an official policy. How were the imperatives of this policy to be met in the case of higher education in the colonies? The search for an answer is reflected in the 1933 Report of the Advisory Committee on Education. The Report, devoted to higher education in the colonies, drew attention to the discrepancy between the policy of educational adaptation and the fact that the growing demand by Africans for higher education was being met (for those able to afford it) by sending candidates to European and American universities. Such an arrangement, the Report pointed out, was unsatisfactory as the universities in question were intended to serve the needs of Europe and America. Logically the policy of educational adaptation suggested the need to meet the demand for higher education in selected institutions that would be developed to university standards in the colonies themselves. The Committee recommended that the proposed universities be grouped together and associated with the University of London, in much the same way as Birmingham,

Manchester, Leeds, Liverpool and Reading had entered into special relations with London.

The 1933 deliberations of the Advisory Committee did not lead to immediate action. In the case of East Africa it required another Commission, that of De la Warr (1937), to recommend the development of Makerere as the University College of East Africa. As from 1940, Makerere became a College of Higher Education for the region and in 1949 entered into special relations with London. In the case of West Africa, discussion of the possibilities of establishing a West African university went on for over a decade. The establishment of the University Colleges at Ibadan and Legon had to wait for the post-war period. Okofa Nduka (1971:85) points to the then British policy which favoured colonies getting only those amenities for which they could pay. If universities were to be established, who was going to pay for them? It was not until there was growing recognition of the responsibility of Britain to develop its colonies that British resources were set aside on a large scale for the development of universities. The way for this to happen was cleared by the acceptance of the Colonial Development and Welfare White Paper of 1940. Thereafter University Colleges developed according to the arrangements described in the paragraphs that follow.

Meanwhile, let us note that the policy of educational adaptation as interpreted by the Advisory Committee on Education in the Colonies, posed the same conceptual conflicts as did the problem of the apex. Adaptation was good. But then, standards were to be secured in association with the University of London. What the left hand offered, the right hand seemed to take away. A university that followed a policy of adaptation had to consider, as did the Advisory Committee, whether or not links with an external university framework would hinder its innovative role. Alternatively, it had to consider whether the advantages of links outweighed the potential constraints which such links imposed upon innovative efforts

The Asquith Colleges

Following the new British policy on colonial development, a Commission on Higher Education in the Colonies was appointed under the chairmanship of Mr Justice Asquith. The Commission's Report (1945) became the basis of university development in the decade or two preceding the independence of African colonies and their universities. For this reason it is worth looking at some of its recommendations in detail.

The Commission reaffirmed the need for the early establishment of university colleges in those colonies that did not already have them. In order to ensure quality and recognition of degrees, the Commission recommended the granting of London University degrees to candidates from the colonial colleges in a special relationship scheme with London. The essential features of the scheme were to be:

(i)   the establishment of direct and easy co-operation between the academic boards of the colonial colleges and the Senate of the University of London;

(ii)   the institution of a regular system of consultation between the authorities of the University and the staffs of the colleges upon questions of syllabus and examination requirements;

(iii)   the promotion of personal contact between the external examiners appointed by the University and the teachers in the colleges in part by visits of examiners to the colleges;

(iv)   the participation of members of the staff of the colleges in the actual work of examining their own students.

It is worth stressing that the Asquith Commission saw the 'special relationship' scheme as the best way of securing adherence to the policy of educational adaptation while at the same time ensuring international recognition of the degrees granted by the colonial institutions. Support for the scheme would come from an Inter-University Council for Higher Education created for the purpose of encouraging and channelling co-operation in such matters as staffing and technical assistance between British universities and the new colleges. The Commission recommended that an appropriate part of the funds becoming available under the Colonial Development and Welfare Act should be earmarked for the development of the university colleges.

The gold standard of learning

Commenting on action following the Asquith Commission Report, Ashby (1966:233) points to the speed with which its major recommendations were implemented. The Inter-University Council for Higher Education was set up in 1946 and between that year and 1949 special relationships had been established with colleges in the Sudan, West Indies, Nigeria, Gold Coast and Uganda. Later, university colleges in Salisbury, Nairobi and Dar-es-Salaam were admitted into special relationship with London University. British universities provided men and advice under the scheme. The British Government found the money for development. Ashby (1966:234–5) adds the following significant comments:

> Both standards and curricula were anchored to those of the University of London, under the guidance of a senate committee to deal with special relationship. Of the many contributions which the University of London has made to higher education in the British Commonwealth, the achievements of this Committee are undoubtedly the most important. 'On the one hand, the link with the University of London ensured that degrees in the colleges in

special relationship would be on the gold standard of learning; this has been of inestimable benefit to the African people. Indeed Britain's greatest gift to higher education in Africa has been to demonstrate to Africans that they can compete successfully on their own soil with undergraduates in England. In 1960, for instance (the last year before the links with the University of London were loosened), some 300 students in East and West Africa sat for degree examinations of the University of London. Eighty percent of them passed. This percentage pass was about the same as that in the same year for internal candidates of the university. Within ten years the colonial colleges had earned their hallmarks of excellence. Their graduates carried away the modern equivalent of *ius ubique docend.*

On the other hand, the link with the University of London was one of partnership, not merely of patronage. Teachers in the colonial college took part in examining. London examiners visited the colonial colleges; they became familiar with, and inevitably interested in, the problems of teaching and research in Africa and the West Indies . . .

Moreover, the University of London was prepared to admit, within the framework of its degree structure, substantial modifications in syllabus. In biology courses, African plants and animals took the place of European ones. Papers in African history and geography were introduced. The university consented even to examine students in subjects not within its ordinary repertoire: the study of government, for instance, was incorporated into the degree structure at Ibadan and the study of East African legal systems into that in Dar-es-Salaam. By the mid 1950's nearly 300 special syllabi had been approved by the University.

Ashby (1966:239) rightly points to the encouragement London gave the Asquith Colleges to cultivate research. The special relationship enabled staff members to work for the Ph.D. of London as internal students. Research topics which could not have been pursued in Europe were undertaken at the colleges. Tropical disease, social anthropology, freshwater biology, African religion, African history and African archaeology all benefited from this policy.

At the same time, however, there were disadvantages in the special relationship scheme. Ashby (1966:243) describes some of them. While the University of London generously encouraged adaptation in the content of curricula, it was 'uncompromising in resisting any departure from the pattern of the degree.' Only minor adaptations were in fact possible. As a consequence, in some African universities students could graduate without 'an objective and scholarly understanding of the society from which they themselves have come' and their education was not always seen by those paying for it 'to be relevant to Africa's needs for high level man-power.' Many Africans pursued courses of study traditional to Oxford or Cambridge and without 'visible and obvious relevance' to their future employment.

Thus the Asquith scheme of special relationship, designed to secure the London 'gold standard of learning,' had built-in potential for conflict with the earlier policy of adaptation. The justification for adaptation lay in the need for visible and obvious relevance to the needs of students and the communities from which they came. To fulfil this criterion there had to be a ready understanding of the needs and aspirations of students and their communities as well as a readiness to make frequent changes to meet them. This, as Ashby points out, could not easily be accommodated within the uncompromising degree structures of London. It is not inevitable, of course, that adaptation should conflict with standards. Contents and structures can change while at the same time retaining the same or demanding higher standards. Conflict arises when the frequency of change required by adapta-tion appears to threaten the continued recognition of the degree by agents outside the university system.

More fundamentally, however, adaptation as a policy for university development in Africa, was itself an inevitable source of conflict. It assumed that Western concepts of education had to be adapted, and thus left no room for other choices. Eventually the time was bound to be reached when Africans would define other starting points for themselves and for adapta-tion, other priorities for university development. This is what makes adaptation, linked to the London gold standard of learning, such a poten-tial source of conflict. Nhonoli (1973:174), of the University of Dar-es-Salaam, put it this way:

> When we consider the role of the African university in the 1970's we must define the objectives and functions in the light of a univer-sity in a country where more than 80 per cent of the inhabitants cannot read or write. We must decide what relevance it has to the society it purports to serve, and recognise the potential conflict between these functions and the concept of international standards and equivalence.

Colleges off the gold standard

In spite of the potential conflict in the Asquith model of colonial univer-sities, it is likely that it might have endured much longer than it did, had African independence not produced a further cause for conflict. True, the special relationship was never envisaged as a permanent arrangement. The Asquith Commission had specifically foreseen its temporary nature and had laid down conditions which had to be fulfilled before the colonial colleges could assume full university status. For instance, college staff needed some years of experience of university work; the conditions of work at the colleges had to be such as permitted the pursuit of research; and there had to be a substantial number of students who had satisfactorily completed degree courses fairly evenly spread among the various faculties. But these conditions were being stipulated against the background of gradual change envisaged by even the most optimistic advocates of colonial development. The special scheme was bound to conflict with the surge of nationalism impatient for change.

Independence for the colonies, starting with Ghana in 1957 and dominating the first half of the 1960's, created a situation in which special relationships had to be re-examined, loosened and eventually ended. In the first instance, political independence brought under question *all* relationships with the mother country and made some of them anachronistic. Could special relationships with the University of London, forged within the colonial era, survive the upsurge of nationalism? Secondly, with independence, university institutions became accountable to their new nations. How could they reconcile their new status with continuing obligation to the University of London? Thirdly, the pressures of independence meant that universities had to be ready to respond more quickly and flexibly than the workings of special relationships had granted. The independence of the university colleges became as much the logical outcome of the policy of adaptation and special relationship as it was the inevitable end of the decolonisation process. The Asquith Colleges had to become fully-fledged independent universities in their own right.

Accordingly, the University College of Khartoum which had enjoyed special relationship with London since 1947 became the University of Khartoum in 1956, the year of Sudan's independence. The University of the Gold Coast, which had been admitted into special relationship in 1948, assumed the new title of the University College of Ghana on the independence of Ghana in 1957 and four years later became the University of Ghana. The University College of Ibadan, which had been admitted into special relationship in 1948, became the University of Ibadan in 1962, two years after the independence of Nigeria. Makerere University College entered special relationship with London in 1947 to be followed by the University College of Nairobi in 1961 and the University College of Dar-es-Salaam in the same year. The three colleges became the constituent colleges of the University of East Africa launched in 1963 by the three East African countries following the independence of Tanzania in 1961, Uganda in 1962 and Kenya in 1963. The dramatic Unilateral Declaration of independence effected by Rhodesia in 1965 resulted in the establishment of the University of Rhodesia and the end of eight years of special relationship with the University of London. Independence inevitably led to a new status for the universities.

The Yesufu Universities

Awareness of the need for accommodation between the university and the priorities, challenges and urgencies of Independence, found expression in a workshop held under the auspices of the Association of African Universities in Accra, Ghana, from 10 to 15 July 1972. The Workshop theme *Creating the African University: Emerging Issues of the 1970's* reflected the search for an African Identity which had led to the formation of the Association itself and the desire to:

> formulate a new philosophy of higher, particularly university, education for Africa, in the hope of evolving institutions that are not only built, owned and sited in Africa, but are of Africa, drawing inspiration from Africa, and intelligently dedicated to her ideals and aspirations.
>
> (Yesufu 1973:5)

The Workshop called for a fundamental redefinition of the role of the university. Ajayi's (1973:11) definition of a university as a group of scholars and students living together as a community and claiming a large measure of autonomy was regarded as 'highly inadequate in the African context.'

> Some felt that universities in Africa as they had developed in the 1960's were hardly more than White Elephants and flashy symbols of modernisation: ivory towers occupied by a minority elite, expensively educated, and as expensively continuously maintained, at the expense of the vast majority of the population, with whom they have little in common.
>
> (Yesufu 1973:39)

Universities could not be allowed in the name of academic freedom to remain 'indifferent to the prevailing poverty and squalor that surround them.' The Workshop concluded:

> What seemed to be required, therefore, was a new working definition of university, which would signify its commitment, not just to knowledge for its own sake, but to the pursuit of knowledge for the sake of, and for the amelioration of the conditions of the common man and woman in Africa. The African university must in the 1970's not only wear a different cloak, but must also be differently motivated. It must be made of a different and distinctive substance from the traditions of Western universities, and must evolve a different attitude and a different approach to its task. The truly African university must be one that draws its inspiration from its environment,

not a transplanted tree, but growing from a seed that is planted and nurtured in the African soil.

(Yesufu 1973:40)

The Workshop rejected as irrelevant 'the ideas, structures and curricula which were copied for the university in Africa from the metropolitan countries.' It was not enough to tinker with imported forms — 'a fundamentally different conceptualisation of the university idea' was called for. In the light of these requirements, the role of the *truly African university* in the 1970's was analysed into six major functions (Yesufu 1973:42):

(a) *Pursuit, promotion and dissemination of knowledge*-
The emphasis being on practical knowledge 'immediately useful to the generality of people, and therefore, locally oriented and motivated.'
(b) *Research* — with priority given to research into local problems that will contribute to the amelioration of the life of the ordinary man and the rural poor.
(c) *Provision of intellectual leadership* — involving 'not only research and acquisition of knowledge, but its wide and effective diffusion, so as to light the beacons by which governments, industry, commerce and the rural population can plan and execute meaningful programmes of economic and social development,' the university seeing itself as 'the servant, not master of the people.'
(d) *Manpower development* — not just graduates who have tended in the past to be 'highly academic and generalist' but 'skilled personnel' including middle-level manpower in whose production the university must participate.
(e) *Promoting social and economic modernisation* — by setting examples of how 'divisive and centrifugal tendencies' can be arrested and removed and by accepting 'the challenge and the primary role in promoting social cohesion, and setting examples in the establishment and operation of democratic institutions.' Universities must 'break the chains of tradition which bind them within the walls of the campus and involve themselves with the social milieu.' University research workers must be more than 'mere purveyors of knowledge'. They must become 'extension workers as well', helping small-scale traders, artisans and farmers 'to improve upon their ancient and inefficient methods of production and economic organisation'.
(f) *Promoting intercontinental unity and international understanding* — accepting 'a responsibility to pursue research, disseminate knowledge and take all other necessary action which will emancipate the African continent from the prevailing shackles of ignorance, break

down the barriers of artificial isolation imposed by colonialism, as well as the natural barriers of language and cultural separation.'

Clearly, the Yesufu model of University development is not only different in conceptualisation from those advocated by the Jones and Asquith Commissions, it is vastly expanded in role and responsibilities. It is this expanded vision of the university which links the Accra Workshop with the expanded models of education discussed by the Swaziland National Association of Teachers to which reference was made at the beginning of this essay.

The crux of the matter is whether this expanded vision of the role of the university eliminates the conceptual conflicts found in earlier models or indeed in contemporary visions of the general role of education. What chance has the Yesufu model to resolve conflicts in the African University of the future? Alternatively, if conceptual conflicts do or must continue, in what way can their negative effect on the role of the university in development be minimised? To a discussion of these questions we now turn.

Continuing conceptual diversity

Perhaps nothing illustrates the continuing conceptual diversity within African Universities better than the three speeches made by the chief officers of the new University of Botswana and Swaziland (successor to the University of Botswana, Lesotho and Swaziland) at its first graduation ceremony held at Kwaluseni, Swaziland, on 14 October 1976. The Rector of the University College of Botswana (1976:4–6) spoke of the importance of relevence in the teaching and research of the new university, particularly that relevence which would contribute to the amelioration of the life of ordinary men. He declared:

> The challenge is to build a strong university of the future which will be academically sound and relevant to the needs of the individual, his family, society and the nation. We are committed to the concept of a university for national development.

Further:

> We have confidence in the future of our university; we believe that the university will provide for the manpower needs of Botswana and Swaziland; yet at the same time university teaching must be such that it will have an influence on the acquisition of certain psychological, social and cultural attitudes implicit in development and that these attitudes should help promote the following in the individual, his family, the community around him and the nation as

a whole: rational thought, organisation, enterprise, the habit of saving, technical and economic inventiveness, aesthetic taste, co-operation, social and civic awareness, active participation in political life and a deep belief in progress, these qualities in turn to have an influence on health, emotional stability, family life, national unity and identity, international understanding and the economic development of the country.

The Rector of the University College of Swaziland (1976:3–4) stressed the importance of parity of esteem between the two Colleges of the University and the need for them to achieve international recognition:

Mr Chancellor, with the break-up of what was formerly UBLS whose degrees and diplomas were recognised throughout the Commonwealth and further afield, sharp and critical eyes will be focussed on the degrees and diplomas of the new University of Botswana and Swaziland. It will have to prove itself as did its predecessor. Not only that: whether we like it or not, whether we say it or not, comparisons will be drawn between the University College of Botswana and the University College of Swaziland. Nothing, I repeat, nothing would be more painful than if it were said tomorrow that the least prepared students of the former UBLS are those on either the Botswana or the Swaziland campus of the new University. It is not only the students who will be hurt by this, it is also their parents, governments and other sponsors and, in the final analysis, the nation as a whole.
At this moment in time our two colleges that constitute the joint University have the necessary staff with appropriate qualifications and experience to ensure the continued recognition of our degrees and diplomas.

The Chancellor of the University of Botswana and Swaziland (1976:2–4) recalled the importance of continuity and traditions in universities, particularly those traditions that ensure good teaching and learning. Universities have the burden of ensuring that they avoid those discontinuities that had become commonplace in other walks of life. But, the Chancellor stressed, concern for continuity and tradition must be balanced by an even greater concern for something new. Schools and universities have always been the symbol of the new, of changing times and of the things desired by the people of Swaziland. He hoped the mystique of the university as a source of something new and novel will never completely disappear — 'I express the hope that our University will always remain at the frontiers of knowledge and will bring to society those ideas far and near which society would not have got without the University.' The University Colleges have to live up to the expectations of society, growing and finding new and meaningful working relationships with their communities. 'Nothing gives our countries greater pleasure than to see our Colleges and University grow in service to the community beyond their walls, standing in the midst of that community for something which is not already there.' He emphasised:

> This growing relationship between the University and the Community has other dimensions. We are used to the cry for high-level skilled manpower and the need for the University to be in the forefront of supplying that manpower. Very often, however, our desire to get our manpower arithmetic right has obscured far more important questions such as the nature of the service graduates are called on to render. Often our concern has been to find men and women to slot into existing vacancies. How well suited that service is to discharge its present and future obligations is sometimes forgotten. It is my hope that university involvement with its immediate community will gradually introduce other perspectives of service. The university and its products must surely be expected to take part in discussions which could lead to a transformation of that service, a redefinition of the main direction of service and new visions of future paths of progress. University involvement in the discussion of the worrying issues of our times and university expertise in the definition of alternative strategies in tackling those issues, are things which our new and transformed University must consider as a new and special kind of service to the community.

The different conceptions of the priorities of the new African university were thus clearly indicated in the speeches of its chief officers. It would be easy to say that the new university must pursue all those priorities, since they are all urgent and are not necessarily in conflict. Unfortunately, this would be unrealistic. University resources are not unlimited and soon give rise to the need for orders of priorities. In establishing priorities, conflicts of interest and emphasis begin to emerge.

Unfortunately, conflicts cannot be eliminated by the adoption by the new African university of the Yesufu model. That model itself has serious built-in areas of conflict. It reserves for the university an intellectual leadership role, especially in the light of prevailing illiteracy of the majority of the population, and the relative inexperience of public and other functionaries. It is careful to warn that the university should not adopt a patronising attitude in its dealings with the mass of the population and must see itself as the servant, not master of the people. Nevertheless it would be foolish to assume that humility would automatically remove conflict. The university is likely to find that there will be other leaders and agencies in society that will resent its intrusion. Similarly, in trying to meet its other role, that of promoter of social and economic modernisation as required by Yesufu, the university increases areas of contact with the community and thereby increases the potential for conflict with its leaders. This, as we shall argue, need not by itself lead to tragedy for the university. It would be wrong, however, to foresee increased social commitment without the possibility of role conflict.

We are forced to conclude that Yesufu has added one more model of university development without necessarily removing the conflicts internal to the university and its role in the educational system or external to the university and its role in development. Further, in any one university, however new, one will find other models co-existing with Yesufu. Academic staff recruited from other countries will bring with them their own conceptions of the role of the university. They may sometimes be heard discrediting the conceptions they find as too colonial, traditional, or alternatively, too radical, novel or particularistic. Similarly, indigenous academics who have studied elsewhere will bring back with them new insights into the workings of universities and may sometimes show an impatience with what exists. Any attempt to defend what exists, particularly in terms of the gold standard of learning, comes to be associated with custom and tradition, with excellence without relevance, and with concepts that must go. Conceptual diversity and conflict is as much a problem of the small and new university as it is of the old and well-established university. The small and new is tempted to follow well-trodden paths to international recognition, to the annoyance of the critics; 'while the old and prestigious university is sometimes more fascinated with keeping learning in good measurable, controllable order than with recalling its fundamental goals.' (Commission on Non-Traditional Study sponsored by the U.S.A. College of Entrance Examination Board and the Educational Testing Service 1974:2)

The Yesufu model is unlikely to end conflict over the role of the University in development for an even more fundamental reason. It derives its force from the optimistic presumptions implicit in modern writings about the expanded roles of education and the power of schools to build a new social order. This optimism exists without questioning whether increased social commitment on the part of universities will pay off (however defined) more than their more traditional engagement. Above all, the optimism exists without asking whether the institutional and attitudinal changes, as well as budgetary considerations, necessary for an amelioration of the conditions of the poor man do not depend on policies and political decisions far removed from the university teacher or researcher. Paradoxically, an innovative university may find that the society it wishes to serve will not finance a university engaged in heavy social commitments without immediate evidence of a pay off. Yet many of the benefits promised by Yesufu are long term and difficult to quantify. The dilemma of the Yesufu model is that a poor country, short of funds, may be unwilling or unable to finance the innovative university it needs. To break this vicious circle by resort to external assistance, may well introduce the dangers of irrelevant ties and strings. The future of the Yesufu model is in the melting pot.

Conflict resolution

Up to now, discussion has centred upon the description and analysis of selected historical examples of situations in which conflicts over conceptions of the role of the university in development seemed inevitable. These situations have ranged from the philosophy of educational adaptation resulting from the Jones Commission recommendations of the early 1920's to contemporary assumptions about the expanded role of education and the effort to create a separate identity for the African University. As most African universities are beset by one or other of these examples of conflict, it seems appropriate to ask whether it is desirable or possible to resolve or minimise conflict in universities. Alternatively, it seems also necessary to ask if it is possible that out of the apparent inevitability of conflict in universities, will arise a new appreciation of the role of the university in African development.

Reaction varies to the continuing conceptual conflicts as to the role of the university in African development. Firstly, there are those who defend and glamorise conflict and its expression as a necessary element in any university. They argue that universities are places where diverse and, often, opposing views are held. They are also places where the free expression and defence of those views must be allowed. To eliminate the clash of opinion from the university, is to take away a prerequisite for the very success of university education. The uninhibited pursuit of truth is the essence of university education. If scholars disagree about what the truth is or how to ascertain it, they must be free to say so. This includes clashes over the workings of the university as an institution. To maintain an atmosphere in which views about the workings of the university can be expressed in confidence and without fear of victimisation is a prerequisite of impartial and uninhibited inquiry. Thus the Chairman of the Commission of inquiry into Makerere University Affairs (1976), was heard to state:

> A University can only flourish if freedom of expression prevails. If this cherished principle cannot be precipitated in the favourable climate of a Commission of Inquiry, the fate of the University may be doomed.

For understandable reasons, therefore, there may be expected to be much sympathy in universities for the defence of the freedom to inquire and follow truth wherever it might lead.

Yet academics ought to be aware that certain styles and modes of expression, taken for granted inside the university, could be totally misunderstood and could hinder communication with bodies outside the university. To persons unused to handling vigorous, diverse and clashing opinion on any one issue, the inability of university men to express any common view about vital matters of public concern is a weakness for which they cannot be forgiven. Men of words locked in debate and unable to come to any conclusion over matters in which they are supposed to be the experts, do not impress men of action. Unless universities can convince such men of action of the necessity to examine all sides of the question before decision making, they may well find themselves locked out of the decision-making process and unable to influence development in their country or, indeed, their own university.

The second reaction to conflict in university is one which resigns itself to the inevitability of conflict and calls for its better management. All development, it is argued, inevitably involves tension and universities must learn to live with it. The existence of a conflict or crisis in the country or the university must be expected. The role of university staff lies in adjusting themselves and their institution to a crisis atmosphere. 'These things happen. We must learn to take them.' Sometimes, the attitude of resignation is followed by withdrawal into the apparent safety and protection of academic autonomy and the ivory tower. It is argued that, after all, there is enough to do inside the university without inviting trouble from outside. Yet, as events in some universities have indicated, resignation and withdrawal can postpone, but only temporarily, the final hour of reckoning. Academic autonomy can be overridden and the ivory tower bulldozed by those who do not respect their university.

Sometimes resignation to conflict has been followed by alarm and fear that conflict will destroy the very fabric of the university. The academic community has been reminded of its special position and responsibility in society. University men, it is argued, are the most educated and privileged of men. They must show by example of good behaviour what a model community can live like, settling all differences rationally, through the consultative channels of the university, and in good temper. It is unbecoming that differences should be carried outside the walls of the university or be conducted in public. For, it is argued, those who hold power outside the university will take alarm at what appears to be internal dissensions in the university and, under the guise of saving it from destruction, will be tempted to intervene. They will thus find justification for unorthodox methods of silencing, elimination or liquidation of dissenting voices in the university.

University staff who have lived through periods of strain in their institutions will be the first to recognise that there are times and degrees of conflict in universities that give cause for genuine alarm. At such periods, academics, like members of other communities going through similar strains, may be expected and called on to exercise restraint in the expression of their opinions. Equally, however, it must be asked whether the resolution of conflicts in universities does not sometimes call for restraint on the part of critics outside of the university, a readiness to examine all sides of the question before judgement and an effort to understand the other party. Hasty action on the part of outside authorities could paralyse an institution and render it incapable of playing that development role which the country needs.

The plea for restraint on both sides is made in spite of the difficulties involved and in the belief that it creates the atmosphere for conflict resolution which we discussed before. For the third reaction to conflict in a university surely lies in positive initiatives and strategies on the part of the university and the community it serves, to resolve or minimise conflict and so release energies for development. This approach might include any or several of these elements:

(i)   The identification of fields of conflict and deliberate efforts taken to resolve them. This applies whether the conflicts be internal or external to the university. Among devices for conflict identification and resolution are face to face discussions between persons championing different concepts, ad hoc committees, visitations and inquiry committees to which evidence can be submitted.

(ii) The setting up of permanent machinery for conflict resolution. Examples might include Union/Management Committees, Joint Planning Committees with members drawn from universities and agencies involved in particular development projects or areas, representation of governmental agencies on internal university committees and representation of university on government committees, etc.

(iii) Planned change and development programmes which spell out clearly the patterns and strategies of change to be expected and anticipate fields of conflict, providing adequately for their resolution. Examples of this might include development plans and finance negotiated between government and university, with appropriate mechanism for review and orders of magnitude within which adjustments may, by mutual consent, be effected.

(iv) Efforts to narrow in advance the areas of conflict, by spelling out in advance and if necessary incorporating in legal form, the roles of each agency with whom the university is collaborating in any enterprise. For instance, Ashby (1965:7) suggests conflicts over university autonomy might be minimised by the insertion of entrenched clauses in University Acts in the same way as federal constitutions have entrenched clauses to ensure reserved areas of autonomy for different bodies in the federation. By the same token, governments that wish to increase their superintendance of university affairs might do so through legal means and spell out their intentions in advance. The Makerere University, Kampala, Act 1970, Article 35, gives extensive powers to

341

the Minister of Education, while the University of Nairobi, Act 1970, Articles 19 and 20, spell out in great detail government powers of superintendance over the finances of the university.

(v) Efforts to develop the art of negotiation, mutual tolerance and the capacity to compromise. This applies to university personnel and those from outside the university who might together work in conflict situations. Young academics often have an idealistic image of university and of the rationality that should govern its operation. They are often frustrated by the cut and thrust of university and power struggles which bear no relation to the rational model. The same idealistic image may be carried to the outside world where factors that govern decision-making may be far from those known to the academic. It stands to reason that such academics should be sensitised to the realities of the conflict situation in which they might be asked to work. Similarly, high-level negotiators on behalf of government or other agencies might be assisted to appreciate the peculiarities of universities and their particular modes of operation. Here is an enormous area for education which sharpens the sensitivity of man and assists him to consider other men and points of view.

Conclusion

It remains for us to consider whether the existence of problems in the conception of the university and its role in development should be a matter for regret. It is, of course, preferable that the energies of a country and of all its institutions should be directed toward the solution of the most urgent problems of the nation. On the other hand, the new nations of Africa and their universities have yet to define and implement conceptions of universities which they will wish to cherish for years to come. In such circumstances, it is not entirely a matter for regret that universities and the societies they serve should be engaged in heated dialogue. After all, conflict resolution in university is part of the process of national integration which Mazrui (1969:105) discusses so eloquently. The process goes through at least four stages. First the different groups of the nation barely co-exist. Then contacts between them are established and increased. They gradually learn to compromise and to live together. Finally the different groups of the nation coalesce into a single nation. He remarks:

> Where conflict plays a crucial part in moving from a relationship of contact to a relationship of compromise and then from compromise to coalescence, it is the cumulative experience of conflict-resolution which deepens the degree of integration in a given society. Conversely, unresolved conflict creates a situation of potential disintegration. The groups within the society could then move backwards

from a relationship of, say, compromise, to a relationship of hostile contact.

One could even argue that internal conflict within a country is inherently disintegrative. Yet, paradoxically, no national integration is possible without internal conflict. The paradox arises because while conflict itself has a propensity to force a dissolution, the resolution of conflict is an essential mechanism of integration. The whole experience of jointly looking for a way out of a crisis, of seeing your own mutual hostility subside to a level of mutual tolerance, of being intensely conscious of each other's positions and yet seeing the need to bridge the gulf — these are the experiences which, over a period of time, should help two groups of people to move forward into a relationship of deeper integration. Conflict-resolution might not be a sufficient condition for national integration, but it is certainly a necessary one.

So be it with the universities of Africa. In their present endeavours to find a new role in the development of their nations, they may well increase areas of conflict within and outside their walls. This by itself need not lead to despair. Let their efforts to resolve conflicts be attended with success and let (in Mazrui's words) the 'cumulative power of precedent' in overcoming crises sharpen their capacity to discover areas of mutual compatibility within their nations. Let their awareness of 'reciprocal dependence' generate a realisation that they must work together with agents of change in society rather than fight them. Let social agencies discover in the university a companion in arms. As their efficiency in the arts of conflict resolution and negotiation increases, let the African universities find their place in the development of an integrated and independent continent.

The future of the African University lies in its ability to handle both conflict and development at the same time.

References

Ajayi, J. F. A. 1973: 'Towards an African Academic Community', p.11 in *Creating the African University: Emerging Issues of the 1970's*. Oxford University Press, Ibadan.
Ashby, Sir Eric. 1964: *African Universities and Western Tradition*. Oxford University Press, London.
1966: *Universities: British, Indian, African*. Weidenfeld & Nicholson, London.
British Government. 1937: [De la Warr Report] *Higher Education in East Africa: Report of the Commission appointed by the Secretary of State for the Colonies*. HMSO Col. No. 142, London.
1945: [The Asquith Commission Report] *Report of the Commission on Higher Education in the Colonies*. HMSO CMD 6647, London.
Guma, S. M. 1976: Rector, University College of Swaziland, Graduation Address, 14 October, Mimeographed.

Makosini, Prince. 1976: (Address by the Chancellor, University of Botswana and Swaziland, 14 October.) Mimeographed.

Mazrui, A. A. 1969: *Violence and Thought*. Humanities Press.

Nduka, Okofa. 1971: *The Development of Universities in Nigeria*. Longmans, Ibadan.

Nhonoli, A. M. 1973: 'The University of Dar-es-Salaam' in *Creating the African University: Emerging Issues of the 1970's*. Oxford University Press, Ibadan.

Setidisho, N. O. P. 1976: Rector, University College of Botswana, Graduation Address, 14 October. Mimeographed.

Uganda Government. 1976: *Commission of Inquiry into Makerere University Affairs: on Proceedings, Procedures and Problems*. Chairman's Opening Address. Mimeographed.

USA College Entrance Examination Board and Educational Testing Service 1974: *On Non-Traditional Study: Diversity by Design*. Jossey-Bass Publications, London.

Yesufu, J. M. 1973: 'Emerging Issues of the 1970's', pp. 42–44 in *Creating the African University: Emerging Issues of the 1970's*. Oxford University Press, Ibadan.

22

UNIVERSITY EDUCATION
IN FREE INDIA[1]

S. R. Dongerkery

Source: *Universities Quarterly* V (1950–1): 72–9.

The Report of the University Education Commission is a remarkable document. It is, without doubt, the most authoritative and comprehensive treatise on the subject of university education in India that has appeared in print since the publication of the Calcutta University Commission's Report in 1919. That report dealt with almost all important problems of secondary and university education, and included a study of the organization and working of Indian universities. The Report of the Central Advisory Board on Post-War Educational Development (1944) was concerned with the general educational policy of the Government of India, and university education naturally occupied a comparatively small portion of it.

The rapid increase in the number of the Indian universities, the shifting of the emphasis in university studies from arts to science, the greater attention paid to technological training and the growing importance of the research activities of university teachers and students, which followed in the wake of the First World War, changed the face of university education in India, as in the rest of the world, during the last thirty years. The Second World War, the achievement of India's independence, the partition of the country and the resulting problem of displaced persons hastened the need for a "complete and comprehensive enquiry into all aspects of university education and advanced research in India". With the advent of independence, it became imperative for India to remould her educational policy as one of the first steps in her national progress. The appointment of the Universities Commission, headed by Dr. S. Radhakrishnan, did not therefore come a day too soon.

Unanimity in the Commission

The task before the Commission was formidable, and the speed and success with which it completed that task call for the highest praise. Considering the variety, complexity and magnitude of the problems it had to tackle, it is even more remarkable that the conclusions embodied in the report were unanimous. These conclusions cannot but carry great weight as the considered opinions of a body of ten eminent educationists with varied experience in different fields of academic work.

The Commission points out that India's independence demands a wider conception of the duties and responsibilities of the universities in the country, which are now called upon to provide leadership in politics and public administration, in industry and commerce, and in the professions. The subjects of study must be taught as parts of a connected curriculum, and the universities must never lose sight of the social order for which they are educating the young men and women who go to them.

One of the outstanding features of the report is the distinct service the Commission has rendered to university education by giving the teacher the place which, though due, has been denied to him hitherto in the educational structure. To quote its words: ". . . the teacher is the corner stone of the arch of education, he is no less, if not more, than books and curricula, buildings and equipment, administration and the rest". He must, of course, be of the right kind, namely, one who has a vivid awareness of his mission, who not only loves his subject but also those whom he teaches.

It is, of course, understood that only those with the best qualifications will be selected for teaching appointments in the universities and colleges, and that no one would normally be appointed a professor unless he had established his reputation for scholarship, possessed wide interests and was capable of inspiring his colleagues as well as his students. In the ordinary course, no one would reach this enviable position in the teaching hierarchy until about the age of 45 years. Only the best men and women, irrespective of province or country, should be appointed to university chairs, as in America and England.

The task of the schools

The Commission places its finger on the weak spot in the educational machinery when it asserts that any university reform will remain ineffective unless the level of secondary education is so raised as to furnish the necessary foundation for a sound university system. Secondary schools need strengthening by improving the quality of the teachers employed in them. Up to this point every one will agree with the Commission, but when it recommends that the standard of admission to universities should be the present Intermediate examination, to be taken after the completion of full

12 years of study at a school and an intermediate college, one may feel justified in taking a different view, especially as the Commission itself concedes that "a real, strong, well-staffed 4-year intermediate college, as envisaged by the Calcutta University Commission, hardly exists anywhere in India". It would be easier to raise the standard of admission to the universities by improving the teaching in the secondary schools than by transferring the intermediate classes from degree colleges to secondary schools, and perpetuating an evil complained of by the Commission. When the system of intermediate colleges has admittedly been a failure in the United Provinces, there is no justification for extending that system.

The Commission's recommendation that the duration of both pass and honours degree courses should be increased from two to three years is not likely to be accepted without demur by the Indian universities. Having regard to the average span of life in this country, and the economic condition of those who seek university education without financial assistance from the State, it would be putting an unbearable strain on most parents to compel them to maintain their children at the university for one additional year. There is, in any event, no cogent reason for extending the duration of the pass course, which aims only at a good general education. The honours course may, perhaps, admit of a year's extension, as it is taken by the more ambitious type of students, and the number of such students being naturally smaller, the poorer among them may well be helped with scholarships and even maintenance grants from the provincial budget. The Commission will, no doubt, find greater support for its recommendation that the standard at the degree examinations should be raised.

According to the report the low standards of teaching and achievement in affiliated colleges are attributable to overcrowding in class rooms and laboratories. The remedies suggested are: an upper limit of 1,500 on the admission to all colleges, improved methods of instruction, compulsory tutorial classes for undergraduates, larger library grants, better designed lecture rooms and laboratories, and encouragement of the book-buying habit among teachers with moderate means by small grants, conditional on equal contributions by themselves. No special comment is called for on the content of the first degree courses in arts and science, except that religious education may be cut out with advantage. The recommendations for greater uniformity in the regulations for the masters' degrees and the introduction of a *viva voce* test for the Ph.D. degree are welcome.

Agriculture, industry and the professions

The only sections of the chapter on Professional Education which call for special attention are those on Agriculture and Engineering and Technology. The facts and figures given in these sections make us painfully conscious of the backwardness of our education in these important branches. We are told that facilities for training and post-graduate research in agricultural science in the whole of India are available for only 166 students, and that there are hardly any facilities for training in soil survey or soil conservation in our country, despite its predominantly agricultural character. India has only 17 agricultural colleges with about 1,448 students, as against 70 universities and colleges in the U.S.A., with a total of about a million students, which are maintained with the help of the Federal and the State governments. Each Land-Grant college in the States, where agricultural courses are taught has an experiment station, with branch stations and field laboratories in many cases.

The Thomason Engineering College at Roorkee (1847) was the first engineering college to be established in India. It was never affiliated to a university, though its diplomas have been considered equivalent to university degrees. With the establishment of the Calcutta, Bombay and Madras Universities, the engineering colleges at Sibpur, Poona and Guindy came into existence, but until very recently, none of them provided courses in mechanical or electrical engineering. To the Benares Hindu University goes the credit for being the pioneer in starting degree classes in these subjects and in metallurgy. It has been estimated that, during the next ten years, India will need about 2,700 engineers, architects, metallurgists and chemical technologists a year as against the present annual output of about 1,130. The defects in our system are due to the lack of the most modern electrical equipment in our colleges, meagre financial assistance, and the failure of the present courses to provide a general education coupled with specialised instruction in business administration, labour problems and industrial finance. The Commission recommends a four-year course with an additional year of practical training, and organized teaching for the Master's and the Doctor's degrees to make India independent of foreign experts for research work and design. It is rightly opposed to the idea of segregating technical training from other branches of higher education and of raising the status of technical institutes to that of independent universities. Viewed in this light, the conversion of the Roorkee Engineering College into an independent university appears to be a retrograde move.

The recommendation that a degree course either in Arts or in Science should be a pre-requisite, and that this should be followed by three years of study for the degree of Bachelor of Laws is certain to lead to considerable hardship, if the arts or science degree can be taken only three years after passing the Intermediate examination. Normally, no one, under this scheme, would be able to begin the practice of the legal profession until he had completed 24 years of age. This is too late, seeing that the usual period of waiting at the bar before practice comes to a lawyer ranges from 8 to 10 years.

The limit of 100 annual admissions recommended for medical colleges, the provision of a minimum of 10 beds per student in hospitals attached to these colleges, and a compulsory "internship" for one year as a resident medical

348

house officer are conditions essential for maintaining a proper standard of medical education. The Commission has further recommended that the heads of departments in charge of the clinical units should be full-time professors with considerable experience, and that they should be assisted by part-time clinical teachers. The report recommends the reorganization of post-graduate teaching in medicine on the lines suggested by a Conference held in Madras on January 1st, 1949, between the Vice-Chancellors and the representatives of the Medical Faculties of the Universities and of the Government of India to consider the entire subject of post-graduate medical education.

One cannot, however, help expressing one's disappointment that the Commission has not made any specific suggestions with regard to the reorganization of the courses of instruction in medical subjects in the light of recommendations made by the Goodenough Committee (1944), the Bhore Committee (1946) or the Medical Curriculum Committee of the British Association (1948). It is surprising that no reference to the important recommendations of these Committees occurs anywhere in the report. One would have expected to find something said about the need for humanizing medical education by taking cognizance of the human relationships and social responsibilities of the doctor, and also about the psychological aspects of medicine.

The language question

The chapter on the Medium of Instruction is very important. It gives useful information on the principal languages and literatures of India and their relative potentialities. The Commission observes that the scientific vocabulary is fast becoming international and that in a number of sciences the terms used in English, because of its international position, may be considered as international. It advocates the desirability of adopting these terms in the Indian languages. It also expresses the "hope that the federal language will be the language of inter-provincial intercourse, of all societies and institutions of all-India character, and of business and commerce." It concludes that Hindi is the only alternative to English as the federal language, and that to enable every region to take its proper share in the federal activities as well as to promote inter-provincial understanding and solidarity educated India will have to be bi-lingual, and pupils at the higher secondary and university stages will need to know even three languages: the regional language, the federal language and English.

The examination system, as we know it, calls for reform. What is wrong with our examinations is not so much the method of conducting them as the attitude of the teacher, the student and the public towards them. An educational system dominated by examinations kills all initiative in the teacher and the taught. The British system of university education has not done away with examinations, and yet no one condemns it as fatal to all initiative, or as productive of corruption. The reason is that the British university student does not look upon the passing of examinations as the be-all and end-all of his student career. The attitude of Government and other public employers is mainly responsible for the undue importance which is attached by the public to examinations in India. The Commission does not advocate the abolition of all examinations, but suggests that they be made objective by the removal of all subjective elements in their administration and assessment. No doubt, the insistence by employers on a university degree as the minimum requirement for even minor posts in the administration, or in business, has been the main cause of the evils of cheating, corruption and favouritism that have crept into the examination system. Examinations must be a test of achievement and progress and a mode of finding out the aptitude of students for a course of instruction rather than a passport to employment.

The next steps

The question, in the meanwhile, is how far the interim recommendations should be acted upon. The Commission suggests special State examinations for recruitment to government service to which even persons without a degree may be admitted, credit for classwork, to the extent of a third of the marks allotted to a subject and compartmental examinations, subject-wise and time-wise. The system of credits for class-work is liable to abuse on the part of college authorities, who may not always be free from the canker of rivalry or the equally harmful motive of favouritism, and no amount of supervision on the part of a university could eradicate these evils. The association of internal with external paper-setters and examiners is a sufficient guarantee against lack of correlation between examination and teaching. Compartmentalization of examinations would encourage cramming, complicate the examination machinery and lead to disintegration of connected or allied courses of study, thus defeating the very aims of a general education. The admission of non-graduates to public service examinations may, to some extent, keep university examinations free from corrupt influences, but it will positively lower the efficiency of the public services which need men with a sound general education.

The report lays emphasis on the need for a physical check up of university students at stated intervals, and physical training for all such students, excepting the medically unfit. All the Indian universities will welcome the suggestion that the Central Government should take over the entire responsibility for the administration of the National Cadet Corps, and detail officers and men for instruction in the universities, as the present dual system, with divided responsibility between the Centre and the Provinces, is highly unsatisfactory. All praise is due to the Commission for pricking the bubble of so-called compulsion for social service by pointing out that it is a contradiction in terms, and that it is more in keeping with a totalitarian regime than with the idea of a democratic constitution.

In the chapter on Finance the Commission points out the danger that lurks in the specious argument that until primary and secondary education have spread all over the country university education should wait for its share of financial assistance, for the very basis of primary and secondary education depends on the simultaneous expansion of university education. Further, university education has a very important part to play in the industrial and economic development of the country, in the efficiency of its services and in its defence and foreign relations. Government must, therefore, give substantial grants to universities for buildings, equipment, libraries, hostels, salaries of staff, scholarships and fellowships and, in particular, for encouraging post-graduate work and research and technical and professional education.

The report favours the idea of freedom in the planning of new universities. It urges Government to give financial aid to all institutions which substantially contribute to the economic, intellectual, cultural and spiritual life of India, even though they may not conform to an accepted norm. The financial responsibility of Government is bound to increase as private benefactions decrease with the changes in our social structure. No new university should be encouraged unless it is free from communal exclusiveness, provides an all-round education and maintains a high standard of instruction. Another valuable suggestion made by the Commission is that hereafter new universities should be established by charter to be granted by the Head of the State, on the recommendation of the University Grants Commission, and that a period of probation should be insisted upon before the conferment of university status on an educational institution is made permanent.

The report of the University Education Commission contains a lucid exposition of the aims and objects of university education, a comprehensive review of the present situation in India and many valuable suggestions for the future course of its development with reference to India's immediate and ultimate needs in the context of her freedom. It represents a piece of solid work, worthy of the names of the signatories to the document. It is a joint product to the making of which some of the best minds of the East and the West have combined to contribute. Here and there one sees unmistakable traces of the influence of the American and British educational experts who worked with their no less eminent Indian colleagues, an influence which is all to the good and demonstrates that East and West can meet on common ground in the field of higher education and combine to rear an edifice worthy of the best traditions of the Oriental and the Occidental cultures.

Note

1 A full length review of the Report of the University Education Commission (India) (1949) published by the Manager of Publications, Delhi.

23

GENERAL FEATURES AND PROBLEMS OF HIGHER EDUCATION

Fahim I. Qubain

Source: F. I. Qubain, *Education and Science in the Arab World*, Baltimore: Johns Hopkins University Press, 1966, pp. 48–60.

Most of the modern universities in the Arab world are of comparatively recent origin. A large number of them came into being only after the Second World War. During the last ten years, total enrollment in these institutions of higher learning more than trebled, while enrollment of women increased more than five times. In 1950/51 there were a little over 46,000 students. By 1959/60 this figure had increased to more than 141,000. Again in 1950/51 there were about 4,000 women students. By 1959/60 their number had increased to over 22,000.

There are two systems of higher education: the traditional Muslim institutions for the training of religious leaders, Muslim judges, and Arabists, and the new modern universities patterned mostly after French, British, and American experience. In the Muslim institutions, the curriculum is mostly traditional and based on the writings of the great Muslim masters of the Middle Ages. Although some modern studies have been added, these were in the nature of accidental accretion, rather than a planned process of change to meet the requirements of modern life. The two types—vastly different from each other in aims, content, methods, and organization—exist side by side and present a dichotomy which has not as yet been resolved. The two systems produce personalities which are different from each other in mentality and approach to life. Aside from the sweeping reorganization of al-Azhar, which took place in 1961, no serious attempt has been made to rationalize the two systems.

Administration

Most Arab universities are operated by the state. The two American and the two Jesuit universities are private organizations independent of government control, either of their countries of origin or the host countries. To this extent, they enjoy a considerable measure of autonomy. The state universities are usually under the ultimate control of their respective ministries of education. In Egypt for instance, the minister of higher education is the *ex-officio* president of all state universities. The rectors are called *mudirs* (literally, directors).

The internal affairs of the university are administered by a university senate (or council) headed by a president or rector. The rector is usually appointed at the nomination of the university senate, the recommendation of the minister of education, the approval of the government cabinet, and confirmation through a royal or a presidential decree. He usually has the rank of a cabinet minister. The rector is responsible for the administration of the educational, administrative, and financial affairs of the university and for the execution of all the laws and regulations that apply to it. The rector is usually assisted by a vice-rector and a secretary general. The vice-rector assists his chief in all responsibilities and duties and takes his place during his absence; the secretary general is responsible for administrative and financial affairs, including the maintenance of buildings, equipment, and properties.

The university senate has the responsibility for laying down the rules and regulations that govern virtually all aspects of university life. Among many others, these include determining the syllabi and curricula, admission regulations, examinations, appointment, promotion, transfer, and dismissal of teachers, preparing the budget, administering university funds, granting degrees, constructing and renovating buildings, and regulating student life, including rewards and penalties. Senior faculty appointments and promotions, however, are subject to the approval of the minister of education and sometimes even the cabinet. Also, in some cases, decisions of the university senate require the approval of the minister, while in others, the minister has the right to object, but must show cause.

The university senate is usually composed of the rector as chairman and the following as members: the vice-rector, the deans of the various colleges, a representative from the ministry of education, and two or three distinguished persons from public life who are knowledgeable in educational affairs and are appointed by the minister of education. The college deans are usually selected from among the professors of the colleges to which they belong and are appointed by the minister at the recommendation of the rector. Below the senate is the college council, responsible for determining the rules and regulations that govern all aspects of life in the college, as well as administering its affairs. It is composed of the dean as chairman, and the vice-dean, department chairmen, and usually one professor from each department, in most cases chosen by rotation for a two-year period. In most cases, the university senate has the right to nullify the decisions of the college council.

From the above brief survey, two central features of university administration in the Arab world emerge. Through various legal and administrative devices, the state reserves to itself ultimate control over and interference in every aspect of university affairs. In actual practice, however, the university authorities are left to their own devices within the general framework of government policy, and they enjoy a considerable measure of *de facto* autonomy. Usually, except when a serious question arises, decisions of the senate are approved as a matter of routine procedure.

The second significant feature of internal university administration is that it is almost exclusively controlled by the rector, the deans, and, to a lesser extent, teachers with professorial rank. The first two are the most important figures. Junior members of the faculty—which means those who are young and have fresh and new ideas—have little or no voice whatever.

Organization

With few exceptions, one of the main features of university organization in the Arab world is extreme decentralization and lack of coordination. Each college, and indeed sometimes each department within the same college, is a world unto its own. Each maintains its separate teaching staffs, courses, laboratories, libraries, and its students may not register for courses in any other college. There may even be separate, unconnected departments of the same subject within a university.

Two historical factors contributed to this type of university organization. First, when higher education began to develop, it was greatly influenced by and has largely followed the organizational pattern of European universities—mainly French and British. Second, and probably more important, is that the establishment and development of separate professional colleges preceded that of the universities. This is especially true of Egypt and Iraq. Most of the universities came into being largely through the incorporation of existing colleges into a university structure. By the time this development took place, however, the separate colleges had already established traditions, facilities, and identities of their own and vested interests and privileges which they were most reluctant to give up. Centralization and consolidation would mean at least some loss of funds, professorships, and control over some facilities.

A third important factor is related to the physical location of different colleges in the same university. Most universities have begun to develop unified campus layouts only recently. Otherwise, the various colleges were (and in some instances still are) scattered throughout the city at considerable distance from each other. This contributed not only to a sense of "spiritual distance" and "isolationism" among the various colleges but also made it necessary for each college to be a self-contained and self-sufficient unit in its teaching staff and facilities.

Clearly, a certain degree of consolidation—especially among colleges such as science, medicine, engineering, and agriculture—would be valuable. The benefits would be considerable financial savings, fuller and better utilization of instructional manpower, less duplication of facilities and equipment, maintenance of a measure of uniformity in standards, greater exchange of ideas, and better planning. For instance, most of these results would be achieved if instruction in basic science courses were to be centralized in certain departments, instead of being duplicated again and again in various departments of various colleges. Students throughout the university would receive instruction in the required basic course in the same department, by the same teachers, with the same curriculum, and in the same laboratory or laboratories.

Curricula

Although Arab university education is patterned after Western models, no single style prevails in all the universities, or for that matter, among different colleges in the same university. For instance, the faculties of law in most universities are patterned after the French system because of the prevalence of the Napoleonic Code in the Arab world and because a large number of the teaching staff was trained in French universities. On the other hand, many colleges of medicine and engineering follow the British model. The American universities, as is to be expected, follow the American pattern. An extreme case is the University of Baghdad. There, the Colleges of Arts, Science, and Medicine follow the British pattern; the College of Agriculture, the American; the College of Law, the French; and the Colleges of Engineering and Education a mixture. In some cases even different departments in the same college follow different patterns. Thus, for instance, within the College of Arts of Cairo University, the Department of Arabic Language and Literature is French and al-Azhar inspired, while the Department of Geography follows the British model, probably because most of its professors were graduated from British universities.

It is quite evident that, due to the difference in tradition and sources of inspiration, there is no uniform system of higher education in the Arab world. This is not necessarily a disadvantage. Not only does it make for a certain richness, but also out of this conglomeration may develop a new pattern resulting from the integration of traditional Arab studies with the various Western models. For the time being, however, certain urgent problems require solution in the immediate future. Among these are the following.

355

Adaptation of the curricula to local needs. For the most part, the curricula used in the universities were borrowed wholesale from Western sources with little or no critical evaluation. Western textbooks (or books based entirely on Western sources), references, and illustrations are used. Little of this material is adapted to local, national, and regional needs. There are reasons for this: most of the teachers received their advanced education in the universities of the West, many of them in the post-Second World War period, and the latter are still comparatively young. They have not as yet acquired the self-confidence that comes with long years of experience.

General education versus specialization. Since the universities, faculties, and departments follow a variety of Western patterns, there is little agreement among them on the concept and function of higher education. The organization of curricula and the requirements for degrees differ greatly. Faculties following the British and French models require much more specialized study and a greater degree of concentration in preparation for the bachelor's or *License* degrees than those following the American model, which emphasize general education and only a moderate degree of concentration. These variations are causing a problem of recognition with universities granting general degrees being regarded as having lower standards. Most state universities and the Jesuit Université St. Joseph at Beirut emphasize specialization, while the two American universities (Beirut and Cairo) emphasize general education.

Integration of science and arts. Related to the above problem is the question of the unity of knowledge and the ability of a student registered in one field to take courses in another. In French universities, the faculties of arts and science are completely separate from each other, so that a student in the arts faculty has great difficulty being able to take science courses as part of his requirements for a degree. In British universities, while science and arts faculties may be part of the same "university college," the requirements are such as to prevent, for all practical purposes, a student from taking courses outside his own faculty.

Most Arab state universities follow the European pattern in this respect, not from considered judgment and evaluation of the merits of the case, but mostly from the early predominance of European influence. A case is that of the Colleges of Arts and Science at the University of Baghdad. In 1949 the College of Arts and Science was established. By design this institution was organized as covering both fields to allow the student more freedom of choice. As the years went by, however, the two faculties gradually drifted apart, until in recent years they finally developed into two separate colleges. Today, only the American universities combine the two fields and allow the student a degree of choice.

Graduate study and research. For all practical purposes, universities in the Arab world are still transmitters rather than producers of knowledge. Their main function has been the training of students on the undergraduate

356

level. Comparatively speaking, very little graduate work and research is undertaken.

Graduate programs were started in most universities only recently. Most of the state universities in Egypt today grant the Ph.D. and master's degrees. The two American universities at Beirut and Cairo, as well as the universities of Damascus and Baghdad, have recently started graduate programs in some fields for the master's degree. Throughout the area graduate programs are still in the embryonic stages, and their total enrollment is nominal as compared with undergraduate enrollment.

The same can be said of faculty research. Until recent times, virtually all the instructor's time was devoted to the training of students. There was a tendency to regard the university as not "getting its money's worth in services" if the instructors devoted some time to research. Fortunately, this attitude has virtually disappeared. The universities today are increasingly sponsoring research through moral encouragement, financial support, and making facilities and equipment available.

The development of graduate study and research and the training of advanced specialists are indeed great opportunities for the universities in the Arab world. Virtually every field of knowledge is either unexplored or insufficiently explored—natural phenomena and resources (flora, fauna, minerals, rock formation), the social and behavioral sciences, the humanities, and the arts. The list is nearly inexhaustible.

Aside from the academic value of research—and aside from the fact that there is something wrong with a university that continues year after year merely to borrow from rather than contribute to world knowledge—the development of graduate study, research, and the training of advanced specialists has now become of special practical urgency, since many of the Arab countries have launched programs to develop their natural and human resources and aspire to a higher material, cultural, and spiritual life. While some reliance on advanced study abroad is not only desirable but enriching, such exclusive reliance as usually exists has the disadvantages of prohibitive costs and limiting the number of students that can be trained, as well as a multitude of cultural and political problems. Moreover, in this age of science and technology, research is the mainspring of scientific and industrial development. Any country that does not create the facilities and intellectual climate for such research, no matter how many universities it can claim, will always remain behind advanced countries.

Staffing

Another critical problem facing the universities in the Arab world today is the question of competent staff, for it has a direct bearing on the quality of instruction and research and on the kind of contribution the universities can make to Arab life.

Since most of the universities are comparatively new, they have not as yet developed from within themselves well-trained scholars for instruction and research. As a result, almost all of them had to resort to recruiting foreign staff at all levels from full professor down to laboratory technician. This was largely the case at Cairo University during the early days of its formation—the 1920's and 1930's. It is still true of many universities in the area. As might be expected, the American universities employ a comparatively large number of Americans. The universities of Libya and Saudi Arabia rely very heavily on teachers from other parts of the Arab world.

Those staff members who are not foreign are largely nationals who received their advanced training abroad. Some studied abroad at their own expense, especially those from Lebanon and Jordan. The vast majority went at state expense, particularly those from Egypt, Iraq, and to a lesser extent from Syria, where literally thousands did so.

In earlier years, a person who possessed a doctorate was considered to have reached the acme of learning. He therefore found it comparatively easy not only to find an appropriate teaching post, but also quickly to climb the professional ladder. Today, however, many universities require the doctorate as a minimum qualification for an instructor. This is particularly true of the state universities in Egypt. The universities of Damascus and Baghdad are moving in that direction.

In the recruitment of competent local staff the universities face the serious problem of the salary scale. While industry has begun to show some signs of competing for specialists, as yet the most serious competitor is usually the government. In most universities, members of the teaching staff are legally regarded as civil servants, and their salary scales are incorporated as part of the salary scale of the civil service.

Raiding also causes trouble. Since trained manpower is comparatively limited, members of the university staff tend to be lured into government service, either on their own initiative or at the invitation of the government. Government service may be more attractive because it offers higher pay, promotion, prestige, the opportunity to do practical work, or a combination of all these allurements. As soon as a professor attains a certain prominence in his field, he is likely to be taken away and placed in charge of a government department. For instance, over the past twenty to thirty years, many of the most able professors at Cairo University left their posts to become ministers, under secretaries and directors general in the government. This process continually drains away the most able members of the university staff and places a heavy strain on the universities and the quality of instruction.

The recruitment of foreign staff poses another problem. Since modern higher education in the Arab world is fundamentally of foreign origin, it was only natural for the various governments to import foreign teachers to introduce and develop the various branches of knowledge. Gradually many of the universities became more and more independent of foreign help, as the number of scholars among their own nationals increased progressively. The need, however, continues to be considerable, especially in two principal areas: first, to fill vacancies in certain disciplines where no local specialists are available; second, to attract high level scientists and scholars to help in the development of graduate and research work. The need to fill vacancies applies mostly to younger colleges and universities and is most pronounced in the various fields of natural science, mathematics, and technical subjects. To a lesser extent, it arises in the social and behavioral sciences. The need for high level scholars is greatest in those universities attempting to attain a high quality of instruction and to develop graduate study and research. Given the youth and inexperience of large numbers of the staffs, foreign scholars are still needed. Some difficulties are encountered, however, in attracting foreign scholars. First is the world-wide shortage of high level specialists and the progressively increasing demand for their services. Second is the problem of paying adequate salaries to attract them. Third, most universities in the Arab world do not offer permanent contracts to foreign scholars but only term contracts until such time as the post can be filled by a native.

Able scholars in established foreign universities are naturally reluctant to leave their posts and their research in order to take up temporary positions at universities where they would be comparatively cut off from the world of science, not only in terms of physical distance, but also because of the lack or inadequacy of research facilities and the lack of stimulation from colleagues of equal calibre working in the same or related fields. Additionally, most universities are reluctant to grant long leaves of absence to members of their teaching staff.

Expansion and admission

It was mentioned previously in this chapter that enrollment in the higher institutions of learning in the Arab world more than doubled, and in some cases trebled, during the past ten years. This expansion has not always been healthy. In some cases it has been impulsive, with little or no prior planning, and too often subject to public and political pressure.

It is not implied here that there is no need for expansion. Indeed, the contrary is true. The facilities for higher education in the Arab world come nowhere—both quantitatively and qualitatively—near meeting the numerous needs of the area. Expansion, however, must be based on study and planning, considering manpower requirements, as well as adequate buildings, staff, and equipment. These conditions have rarely been met in the public universities, for the pressure of students has often been too great for them to resist.

A classic case of wasteful and unbalanced expansion is the fantastic mushrooming of student enrollment in colleges of arts—but particularly commerce and law—all over the Arab world, far beyond any imaginable need of any single country or the area as a whole. In fact, many of the graduates finally wind up as ordinary clerks in government or business offices or find no employment. Generally speaking, the expansion of these colleges has been accompanied by lowering of standards, and many of their graduates are of mediocre abilities. At the same time, there has been a rather spectacular expansion in pure and applied science training, both in facilities and enrollment. Generally speaking, these colleges attract and admit the better qualified students.

There are two processes by which students find their way to higher institutions of learning: the socio-economic process and the meeting of formal academic requirements.

No study has ever been made of the socio-economic composition of the student body in the universities and colleges of the Arab world. However, there is overwhelming *prima facie* evidence that the majority of these students are drawn from the urban or urbanized middle class and from the upper and wealthy strata of society. Thus, primarily for economic reasons, children of farmers and workers are comparatively few in higher education. This socio-economic selection begins to operate at even lower levels. For instance, a secondary school student who may be good university material may drop out and thus be deprived of a university education purely for economic reasons. In addition, the fact that most universities are located in big metropolitan centers tends to favor the selection of the city student who can continue to reside with his family, the only visible direct costs being any tuition fees and a few other incidentals. In contrast, a student from a rural area would have to bear the costs of transportation, room and board, usually new clothes, and so on, in addition to the difficulties involved in communicating with an organization from a distance. In recent years all state universities have abandoned tuition fees. In addition, some provide free room and board (Baghdad and Libya), while those in Egypt provide various forms of financial aid. All this has tended to ameliorate the situation somewhat and to democratize higher education.

The second process of selection is the formal academic requirement. In all state universities and colleges, the secondary school certificate provides the minimum requirement for admission. In addition, some colleges require a special selection of subjects, a certain average in all subjects, and high grades in certain subjects. Generally speaking, the admission requirements of science colleges are much more stringent than those of colleges of arts, law, and commerce. The universities have exercised hardly any influence on the curricula of secondary schools in the Arab world comparable to that exercised, for instance, by the College Entrance Examination Board in the United States. In this respect the Arab university seems to exist in a world of its own, giving only a very vague notion of how the secondary school student should be trained to attain standards to qualify him for university education. It can probably be argued with some justification that the contrary is true, that the pressure of graduates from secondary schools has forced the state universities to lower their standards.

Equipment

Most Arab governments have been more than generous to their universities. They take great pride in developing them and provide extensive funds for buildings and equipment. However, scientific equipment especially is expensive and in some universities, particularly those in less prosperous countries, such equipment is woefully inadequate and the need is acute. As important as the problem of funds is that of intelligent procurement. In some cases, expensive scientific equipment is ordered out of catalogues by unqualified or inexperienced persons. When it arrives, it is found to be unsuitable and is either inefficiently used or left to deteriorate. In the words of a prominent Arab educator: "Fitting the equipment to the need without lavishness has been one of the main difficulties. As to planning and equipping research laboratories, it is even more difficult."

Perhaps even more serious is the problem of service and maintenance. Because almost all scientific equipment has to be imported from abroad, the technicians to repair these machines are often simply not available, and expensive machines may have to be discarded and reordered for this reason alone. Thus the establishment of workshops to repair such scientific equipment and the training of technicians to service them is of critical importance and would result in substantial savings, as well as removing many of the snarls and bottlenecks from research work.

Finally, there is a critical shortage of qualified laboratory technicians. The need for a program to train such personnel is urgent not only for the universities, but also for development in industry, agriculture, and medicine.

Maintenance and support personnel

While the universities have been on the whole generous in providing funds for buildings, equipment, and teachers, they do not, generally speaking, make adequate provisions for maintenance, support, and administrative personnel. The administrative staff in most universities is very limited in numbers. Any matter involving office work usually results in endless waiting and delays. Record keeping is often so haphazard that when such records are needed they are often unavailable. Most faculty members below the professorial rank are provided with little or no office space. Secretarial help is woefully inadequate. The instructor is forced to spend a considerable part of his time doing routine administrative or paper work. Little attention is given to the maintenance of buildings, grounds, and equipment. Because of this, far too often beautiful new buildings soon acquire a rather delapidated and seedy look and deteriorate at a rapid rate.

University education and social mobility

Unlike the case in the West, modern higher education in the Arab world did not develop slowly side by side with, and was not the outcome of, the natural process of intellectual, cultural, and material growth of society. In a sense it was imposed from above by the respective governments to meet specific needs for specialized manpower. Thus the development of higher education was not motivated by the "quest for knowledge" but largely by the need for specialists. This is especially reflected in the salary scales of the various Arab governments, most of which have been constructed on the basis of educational degrees rather than on ability to perform a certain job.

In a society which until recent years was rather rigidly stratified, the university degree has now become the passport and the key to economic and social advancement. It opens doors and opportunities which otherwise would be entirely closed. Although the desire for knowledge per se is no doubt an important factor among many students, for others, particularly those with a middle or lower class background, the driving force is largely a desire for economic security and social recognition.

24

MODELS OF THE LATIN AMERICAN UNIVERSITY

Orlando Albornoz

Source: Joseph Maier and Richard W. Weatherhead (eds) *The Latin American University*, Albuquerque: University of New Mexico Press, 1979, pp. 123–34.

At the beginning of the century, the River Plate Basin was the most conspicuous zone of dynamic economic expansion and stable political development in Latin America. Mexico began its civil war and revolution, while the other Latin American countries, struggling to find some way of creating viable nation states, were frequently falling under dictatorial governments. It is not surprising, then, that the intellectual epicenter of the university reform movement was located in Uruguay and Argentina. The *reforma* was successful insofar as the concept of university autonomy was embraced and members of the university community won the right to govern themselves and to select those who would govern them without governmental interference. Democratization of the university, in the sense of opening its doors to all classes and extending educational opportunities to all citizens, remains an ideal. Only in the more advanced nations, however, does a relatively high degree of opportunity exist. In the more traditional societies the university is still an institution open only to the elite, in somewhat the same manner as the colonial university (not being equipped philosophically or materially to accept the masses).

In these societies, there had not been a middle class large enough to make sufficiently insistent demands for higher education as a form of public service. One of the major factors in university reform in Argentina was the increase in the size of the student population and the emergence of student organizations. At the University of Buenos Aires, the students in the faculties of medicine, engineering, and law set up their own organizations between 1900 and 1905. These soon became instruments through which students could voice their opinions, exert pressure, formulate demands, oppose administrative policies, and hamper university operations. In 1903, the students in the Faculty of Law organized a strike because the university authorities ignored their petition for relatively mild reforms. As the strike progressed, the students became more adamant and increased the items on their list of reforms; before the imbroglio was over, the National Congress and even the president were involved in trying to return the university to its normal operations. By 1905, the students in the Faculty of Medicine were organizing a series of demonstrations to protest the procedure for granting a *cátedra*.[1]

World War I and the influence of positivist and evolutionary ideas had eroded the traditional attitudes toward the sciences. Centers of scientific research were founded, opening new perspectives on teaching and training. Intellectual life took on a new vitality because of the increased production and circulation of books and because of visits from distinguished intellectuals who traveled to Buenos Aires to lecture. The nation's population had swelled enormously (especially because of immigration from Italy), the economy was rapidly expanding, and the political scene had been remade by the entry of newly organized special interest groups, labor unions, and political parties representative of the urban middle classes. Much the same process was happening elsewhere in Latin America, but only where the political game had been opened to the new claimants and where the economy was a productive engine for social change could the reform movement have a lasting effect on higher education. Even today one finds countries where the reform has not been fully introduced.

Alfredo Palacios, Alejandro Korn, and José Ingenieros, the intellectual luminaries who had done so much by their writings to bring Argentina to the front rank of the Hispanic literary world, enthusiastically supported the movement. Argentina's claim to leadership was based also upon a good system of communications with Europe and the United States, an active printing industry, and two of the most prestigious and influential newspapers in the Spanish-speaking world.

Although more than five hundred miles inland and surrounded by mountains, Córdoba nevertheless felt the reverberations of intellectual activity in Buenos Aires—something the conservative leaders of Córdoba disliked and feared. By 1917, Córdoba was a city divided; liberal, socialist, and anarchistic ideas had filtered into Córdoba and quickly found advocates.

The University of Córdoba was a typical university of its time, with 1,500 students and the three traditional faculties of law, medicine, and engineering. At the end of 1917, the students of medicine had begun to protest a decision by the university authorities to close a student dormitory. It was but a short step to make demands for changes in the university's administration. On March 14, 1918, the students of medicine formed what they called the Committee in Favor of Reform in cooperation with students from the other faculties. The committee then called a strike on June 21 and took the position that the strike would remain in effect until the students' demands were satisfied. On the same day the *Córdoba Manifiesto* was issued; it has become the Declaration of Independence for all Latin American students. From this moment, the university situation in the provincial town was a national problem of international significance.

> Men of a free republic, we have just shaken off the last chains which shackled us to a monarchic and monastic domination—and this situation in the twentieth century! We are determined to speak the truth frankly and boldly. Córdoba has been redeemed. We have given our country one more freedom and we have removed a point of dishonor. The pain which yet endures is the freedom yet to come. We have not erred, our hearts tell us so. We are on the eve of revolution, the tocsin for all America has sounded!

This opening paragraph of the *Manifiesto de la Juventud Argentina de Córdoba a los Hombres Libres de Sud-América* sets the tone of the entire message to "all our comrades [*compañeros*] in Latin America."[2] The *Manifiesto* goes on to say that

> The university has been until now a refuge for the mediocre, a sinecure for the ignorant, an asylum for the invalid, and, even worse, a place in which every form of tyranny could be preached and practised. The university is thus the exact image of a decadent society, a senile man who will neither retire nor die.

The students were determined to remove what they called "the archaic and barbarous" exercise of authority within the university. They felt that authority was used to uphold a sham dignity and a false competence and that it had turned the house of study into a stronghold of tyranny. The Córdoba rebels demanded "a genuine democracy and a form of government where sovereignty is vested primarily in the students," because

> The dominant characteristic of youth is its heroism. It is disinterested and pure. It is not yet contaminated with the errors of age. The young can make no mistake in choosing their teachers. Adulation and self-seeking find no response among the young. The young must be allowed to select their teachers and superiors for, certainly, their choice will meet with success. Henceforth, the republic of the university will have as its teachers only those who are makers of souls, creators of truth, beauty, and goodness.

Throughout the reform movement there runs a strong antireligious bias, concentrated upon the Jesuits, whom the students accused of opposing the *reforma* because they knew that when it triumphed, it would spell the end of "the menace of clerical control of education."

The reform movement awakened public opinion to the anachronistic mechanisms and procedures of the traditional colonial university. The labor movement looked sympathetically upon the students' demands and it was no mere romantic assumption at the time to see the students, the intellectuals, and the workers joining forces in one common interest—democratizing society. This ideal remains alive, but only intermittently has it been translated into reality.

The immediate impact of the reform movement was felt first of all in those countries near Argentina—Uruguay, Chile, Bolivia, and Peru. Alfredo Palacios visited Bolivia and Peru in 1919. Students in Argentina and Chile pledged themselves to a common course of action in 1920. In the same year, Argentinian students, led by Gabriel del Mazo, and Peruvian students, headed by Víctor Raúl Haya de la Torre, signed agreements that had the purpose of internationalizing the Córdoba demands. In 1921, Haya de la Torre went to Argentina specifically to study the implications of the *Córdoba Manifiesto* and to meet with the student leaders. Of greater significance in the long run was the International Student Congress, held in Mexico City in the same year. Students from the United States, Europe, Asia, and many parts of Latin America attended. The Congress urged the adoption of fundamental reforms, such as student participation in the government of a university, academic freedom, and free tuition. They proclaimed themselves in favor of developing closer and more fraternal bonds with the proletariat by means of university extension. They called for an effective internationalism that would unite all peoples in an "international community" and expressed their strong opposition to militarism, dictatorship, and imperialism.

In Medellín in 1922 and in Bogotá in 1924, Colombian students proclaimed their allegiance to the *Córdoba Manifiesto;* in 1923 Cuban students did so in a national meeting. In Venezuela, university students led the opposition to the Gómez dictatorship waving as their banner the principles of the reform movement.

The international organizations developed by the students did not have enough force or following to affect the structure of the university. Governmental intervention in university affairs is so frequent that the pattern seems to be more repressive than libertarian. The struggle for students' rights—the basis of the *Córdoba Manifiesto*—has occupied the center of the stage on which the university controversy has been acted out, and its impact has been greatest in the national universities. The private university has been relatively unaffected.

The Córdoba reform did not bring about any immediate changes in the structure of the Latin American university. It remained oriented toward the traditional studies of medicine, law, and engineering, incorporating humanities and philosophy, which reflected a strong French influence. Until 1945 the university continued to function in the buildings erected in the colonial period, which sometimes, as in the case of Mexico City and Buenos Aires, were scattered inconveniently about the city. An old concept of university life newly applied, the *cité universitaire*, was to create a new university ecology and spawn the new urban complex known as *la ciudad universitaria*. The selection of a piece of city land for the location of a university, the principal national university, was perhaps the first measure taken by Latin American governments to promote the growth of higher education, committing heretofore untapped resources to the university. After 1945 the demographic pressure of students who had received primary and secondary schooling on a massive scale could no longer be ignored. New social groups, previously denied the opportunity of higher education, were now waiting restively at the threshold of the university. With no junior colleges, trade schools, or technical training centers, the university was obliged to accept the newcomers who had no other place to go.

The construction of a *ciudad universitaria* sought to fulfill the traditional concept of a university community in which professors and students living together in the same place would achieve—by means of dialogue, conviviality, and a degree of isolation from the outside—the ideal of the full growth of the individual's intellectual capacities. The *ciudad universitaria* was thus generally located at a site somewhat distant from the center of the city.

By 1950, the idea of the *ciudad universitaria* had come into its own. The most impressive example was the Universidad Nacional Autónoma in Mexico City, a striking architectural expression of Mexican art through which the nation intended to show its pride in indigenous creativity. The Universidad Central de Venezuela in Caracas was conceived along the same lines, although in this case the inspiration was found in contemporary France and not in national art. Bógota, Quito, São Paulo, and Brasilia followed the same pattern. In the 1960s the Central American countries had undertaken the construction of a new university, partly inspired by Mexico City's *ciudad universitaria*. In Argentina and Chile, however, the national universities continue to operate in the more traditional separate quarters.

The university city, as the site for a republic of the intellect, would have had undeniable success if the human resources and the process for recruiting talent in a national and democratic manner had been given as much attention as the physical facilities. The growing number of students has come close to cancelling out the effort to reduce the student-classroom ratio. The huge buildings planned as libraries remain unused as such for want of books to fill the shelves. At its present stage of development, the *ciudad universitaria* has dramatized the contrast between the possibilities of the physical plant and the potentialities of its inhabitants. In many countries the concentration of university buildings in one spot seems to have caused more problems than it has solved. Although conflicting class schedules and the isolation of the separate faculties have to some extent been overcome, the *ciudad universitaria* has also made possible an increase of student political activity stirred up by political parties and other pressure groups.

As new trends have appeared in the private sector, there have emerged two types of the private model of the university: the Catholic university and the technologically oriented university modeled after its North American counterpart. The latter has also grown as an offshoot of the national model, with the possible intention of offering itself as an alternative to the national university. Two significant examples of the technological university are to be found in the Tecnológico de Monterrey (Mexico), a private organization, and in the Universidad de Oriente (Venezuela), a governmental organization.

The North American research-oriented university is to the Latin American university what the German university was to U.S. colleges around 1900. The spread of industrialization, the influence of the United States, and the needs of the more progressive sectors of society, both private and public, required trained personnel equipped to carry out the plans of social and economic development. Thus, the U.S. model has had almost no competition and has become, like the Soviet university, a new model of higher education. The research-oriented university in Latin America gets aid from the industrial sector in each country and from the United States and international organizations to a greater extent than the national universities. The latter often receive less financial help because their students and professors, sometimes in large numbers, constitute a political opposition that appears threatening to those who might otherwise be willing to lend support to them.

Although Catholic universities were weakened by the liberal and positivist crusade from the late eighteenth through the last part of the nineteenth century, the greatest assault upon them came with the expulsion of the Jesuits in the eighteenth century.[3] A recent resurgence of the Jesuits, however, has coincided with the establishment of numerous Catholic universities, most of which are run by them.

Catholic universities began to appear in significant numbers with the opening of the Pontificia Boliviana in Medellín in 1936 and the Universidad Javeriana in Bogotá in 1937. These two, along with the Pontificia Universidad Católica in Chile founded in 1888, are among the most prestigious Catholic universities in Latin America. The Universidad Pontificia of Peru was created in 1949 as a national university enjoying the same legal status as other national universities. By the end of the 1950s some fifty Catholic universities had been opened in Argentina, as well as one in Caracas in 1953 and one in Paraguay in 1959. Even in Mexico, a Catholic university began functioning in 1963. The academic structure of the Catholic universities is oriented toward traditional matters and less concerned with research than are the national universities; there is less social awareness on their campuses than in the universities financed by public funds.

The Universidad Católica de Nuestra Señora de Ascunción, which may serve as an example, consists of a community of professors, students, and graduates under the authority, tutelage, and protection of the Church. It is an institution of higher education whose purposes are: (1) to preserve, transmit, and deepen the spiritual inheritance of humanity in its three dimensions—moral, scientific, and technical; (2) to provide religious instruction that conforms with the doctrines and precepts of the Catholic Church; (3) to provide proper training in the liberal and technical professions; and (4) to contribute to the study and dissemination of the sciences and the arts and to stimulate an inquiring spirit of mind among its members in the pursuit of knowledge in all areas.

Generally speaking, more than half of all Latin American students are in the national universities. The significance of students in the private institutions cannot be judged by numbers alone, however; the quality of private education and the later influence of their graduates in society have brought a significant increase in the role of the private sector vis-à-vis the public sector.

One has the general impression that all students attend a country's largest university, such as UNAM in Mexico City or the Universidad de Buenos Aires. These are, indeed, two very large institutions, each with over 80,000 students in some kind of attendance (twenty-five percent in each are part-time students or are pursuing some form of preuniversity studies). It should be remembered, however, that the small provincial university with a few thousand students and very limited resources is the typical university.

To elaborate on these generalizations, it may be helpful to describe a real university situation in Colombia. The National University, set in the national capital, is the oldest and biggest of all Colombian universities. Located in the heart of the downtown area and set within the limits of the *ciudad universitaria*, it is nationally and internationally the most important of Colombia's universities. Because of the diversity of its student body, it represents a microcosm of Colombian society, drawing students from all the social strata and geographical areas of the country. The Javeriana, which represents the typical private denominational university, recruits its students mainly from families that have a strong identification with the Catholic church. These students are more politically conservative and come from the upper classes. The Universidad Libre is a small school dedicated to teaching and careers in the law and education; it has a strong working-class or labor-elite orientation and is regarded as a center of radical politics. The Universidad de los Andes is an example of the newer private university, with a small enrollment of mostly upper-class students, academically oriented toward the modern professions, with an emphasis on economic development and urban planning. The university in Popayán, in the south of Colombia, is a small and traditional institution reflecting the life of the provincial capital and devoted to the teaching of such conventional subjects as medicine, law, and civil engineering.

Colombia's student population is younger in the private universities than in the public ones: at the Universidad de los Andes sixty-five percent are under twenty; at the National forty-seven percent are between nineteen and twenty-one; and at the Universidad Libre, some seventy-five percent are between the ages of twenty-two and thirty. Forty percent of the students at the Javeriana are women, while in Popayán only nine percent are women. In the other universities the proportion of men to women is four to one. The ratio reflects the position and participation of women in Latin American society—women still have little effect on public affairs except through family ties or church affiliation.

In general, students attending private universities have experienced a longer period of residence in a large city and have a better acquaintance with city life-styles than students at public universities. The newer arrivals to the city tend to go to the national universities, whether located in the national capital or in the provinces. For example, eighty-six percent of the students at the Javeriana come from cities with populations greater than 100,000, as do thirty-six percent at the National University, and fifty-eight percent at the Universidad Libre. Those coming from places with less than 20,000 inhabitants account for thirty-five percent of the students at the Universidad Libre, fifteen percent at the Nacional, eight percent at the Javeriana, and three percent at Los Andes. Thus, private universities tend to have more urbanized students than public universities except for those like the Libre, which recruit their students from the working classes.

In addition, we find that there is a greater proportion of part-time students in the public universities. Only ten percent of the students at Los Andes are engaged in any type of gainful employment, compared with sixty percent at the Libre and twenty percent at the Nacional. The Javeriana is much like Los Andes and the University at Popayán is closer to the Nacional in this sense. In other words, more students from the working classes go to the public national or provincial universities than to the privately organized universities, and working students obviously have less time for their studies than do full-time students.

There is a correlation between the size of the student's family and the type of university he attends. Smaller families tend to send their sons to private schools. In some families the older brother will enter the labor market directly, without any higher education, having in mind the support of his younger brother or brothers in their studies. The younger son or sons are thus seen as the main hope of the family for ascending the social scale, higher education being thought of as one of the best means for achieving upward social mobility.

A student's outlook and conduct are affected by whether or not he lives with his family. Students attending private universities are typically under family control or influence. In Bogotá only ten percent of those who attend private institutions live on their own, in contrast with thirty-five percent at the public universities.

The public universities located in the larger urban centers become sites of greater political controversy and student participation than do the provincial and private universities, even when these are in populous urban areas. Thus, approximately fifty-five percent of the students at the Nacional, seventy-five percent at the Libre, and fifty-two percent of those at Popayán had joined in a strike or a demonstration in the late 1960s and early 1970s, while the corresponding percentage at private universities stood at about five percent. Much the same situation prevails with the influence of political parties in the universities. The public universities are more politicized and more ideologically oriented than are the private or technically oriented schools such as Los Andes. Fourteen percent of the students at Los Andes admit to participating actively in political party affairs, compared with forty-five percent at both the Nacional and the Javeriana—the former leaning leftward and to nonreligious stances and the latter rightward and to more religious justifications of political opinions and activities.

The religious universities, almost all Catholic institutions, possess a doctrinal body of ideas that gives them ethical and philosophical criteria enabling them to validate and legitimize any situation. The matter of academic freedom does not arise because the ideological codes of the church have already prescribed what is permissible to teach in the classrooms. While the religious universities have some secular concerns, such as the training of professionals, they are ruled by an idea that is essentially extraacademic—the preservation and diffusion of the faith. These universities ordinarily do not experience crises that demand a definition or redefinition of fundamental principles or of the direction and purpose of the university.

In the national and public universities ideological controversy and partisan conflict are frequent. The students bring an ideological heterogeneity and speak more often in terms of Latin America and of national matters than at private universities. Academic freedom is a more likely subject of dispute.

The private universities manage to retain a greater amount of autonomy and self-governance than the national universities. The aims of the national university may be at odds with those of the state—the Latin American university is an integral part of the political scene—while the private universities are more in accord with the goals of society and lack a direct political role. National universities frequently identify with, or join the ranks of, opposition groups against the government in power. The instances of cooperation between national universities and the government are usually rare and short-lived, except during the brief euphoria following the fall of a dictator.

The private universities have no effective system of *cogobierno*. They are operated like private enterprises; decisions are made at the top, and while students and faculty may influence decisions, they do not participate in the decision-making process. On the other hand, the system of governance at the national universities does provide for the joint participation of the administration, professors, and students in decision making—at least in theory. *Cogobierno* affects administrative and academic matters equally, and the failure to differentiate between technical and academic functions embroils the university in conflicts and tensions.

The characteristics of the Latin American university are such that no university, no matter how much it differs from the general pattern, can escape the structural limitations inherent in a developing area. The role of the university is more distinct, as an element of development, to the extent that the area is able to agree upon common social and political goals, principally in the matters of economic and social development.

Notes

1 See Tulio Halperin Donghi, *Historia de la Universidad de Buenos Aires* (Buenos Aires, 1962).
2 The Córdoba Manifiesto is easily available in Spanish. For an English translation, see *University Reform in Latin America: Analyses and Documents*, edited by International Student Conference (Leyden, 1961).
3 See Magnus Mörner, ed., *The Expulsion of the Jesuits from Latin America* (New York, 1965).

25

THE PAST AND FUTURE OF ASIAN UNIVERSITIES

Twenty-first century challenges

Philip G. Altbach

Source: P. G. Altbach and Toru Umakoshi (eds) *Asian Universities: Historical Perspectives and Contemporary Challenges*, Baltimore: Johns Hopkins University Press, 2004, pp. 13–32.

Asia is notable for its size and its diversity. Asia accounts for a majority of the world's population and for several of the world's most dynamic and fast-growing economies, as well as some of the weakest. In higher education, Asia has not traditionally been a leader in research or innovation. In the coming decades, however, Asia will experience massive higher education expansion—indeed, a majority of the world's enrollment growth will take place in Asia. Further, Asian economies will increasingly demand university-trained personnel to ensure the success of sophisticated economies. Research and development will inevitably become more important to Asian countries.

This essay concerns higher education trends in Asia from India and Pakistan to China and Japan. While Asia's diverse academic systems do not lend themselves to easy generalizations, there are some common elements as well as shared experiences. We are seeking to understand the challenges that face Asian universities in the 21st century, when institutions will need to be part of the international knowledge system and play a central role in meeting national educational needs. Universities are part of the global system of science and scholarship while at the same time being rooted in their own societies. The coming period will be one of considerable potential and looming problems for higher education in the region.

This essay will look at both the potentials and the challenges in broad terms, for it is impossible to fully analyze all of Asia in this essay (Postiglione & Mak, 1997). The focus will be on such topics as expansion, competition, and quality, as well as the role of research and the links between higher education and society in the Asian context. The central reality of the past several decades as well as the coming period for most Asian countries is expansion and coping with the effects of massification on higher education. Although much of this analysis revolves around the implications of expansion, several Asian countries face declining populations and the accompanying problems of likely contraction of the academic system. Between 1980 and 1995, enrollments in developing countries increased from 28 million to 47 million—a significant part of that growth taking place in Asia (Task Force, 2000, p. 27). Asian higher education will continue to expand rapidly, in large part because some of the largest Asian countries—such as China and India as well as Vietnam, Cambodia, Pakistan, Bangladesh, and several others—now educate relatively small proportions of their young people at the postsecondary level and face immense pressure to meet the popular demand for access and the economic needs of modernizing economies. Vietnam, for example, educates around 6 percent of the university age cohort, while Cambodia has half that proportion in higher education (Task Force, 2000, pp. 104–107). India educates around 10 percent. China has recently boosted its enrollment rate to 15 percent and now has the largest number of students in postsecondary education in the world—having recently passed the United States in total enrollments, although the United States is educating well above half of the relevant age group.

Academic institutions have always been part of the international knowledge system, and in the age of the Internet they are increasingly linked to trends in science and scholarship worldwide. All Asian nations—even the largest and best developed, such as Japan, China, and India—remain largely peripheral internationally (Altbach 1998, pp. 133–146). The major Western universities retain scientific and research leadership. As Asian universities grow in stature, they will need to become able to function in a highly competitive academic world. All of the elements of academic life, including research, the distribution of knowledge, the students, and the academic profession, are part of an internationally competitive marketplace. Without doubt, the immediate future holds considerable challenges for Asian higher education, as it does for higher education in the rest of the world.

Historical perspectives: colonial and postcolonial patterns

Contemporary Asian higher education is fundamentally influenced by its historical traditions. No Asian university is truly Asian in origin—all are based on European academic models and traditions, in many cases imposed by colonial rulers, and in others (e.g., Japan and Thailand) on voluntarily adopted Western models (Altbach & Selvaratnam, 1989). The fact that all Asian universities began as foreign implants has played a central role in how academic institutions have developed—with regard to academic freedom, institutional autonomy, the relationship of the university to society, and other factors.

It is significant that no Asian country has kept, to any significant extent, its premodern academic institutional traditions. Most Asian countries had pre-Western academic institutions—the Confucian academies in China, the traditional *pathashalas* or *madrasahs* in India, and similar institutions in Vietnam, Cambodia, Thailand, and elsewhere were largely destroyed or abandoned as Asian countries began the process of modernization beginning in the 19th century. In India, for example, British academic practices came to dominate the system, although traditional patterns were never entirely eliminated (Ashby, 1966; Basu, 1989). Today, there are a small number of institutions providing education in traditional fields, such as ayurvedic medicine, but they are largely organized along Western lines.

The imposition of academic models by the colonial powers has had a profound impact. The British academic model was imposed on all of the countries that were under British colonial rule, and it remains a powerful force in such countries as India, Pakistan, Bangladesh, Sri Lanka, Malaysia, Hong Kong, Nepal, and several others. Even where the British model has been largely jettisoned, such as in Singapore, elements of it remain evident, and ties with the United Kingdom remain strong. Because of the extent of British colonial rule in Asia, the British model is probably the most important foreign academic influence in that whole region.

Other European colonial powers also exported their university ideas to Asia: the French in Indochina (Vietnam, Cambodia, and to a lesser extent Laos), the Dutch in the Dutch East Indies (Indonesia), Spain and, after 1898, the United States in the Philippines, and Russia in the central Asian republics that were part of the Russian Empire and then the Soviet Union. Japan began its role as a colonial power at the end of the 19th century, and it had an active higher education policy in Taiwan and Korea, its main colonies. It is worth noting that, with the exception of the Americans in the Philippines, the other (European) colonial powers were not enthusiastic exporters of higher education. Even the British, in whose colonies higher education was the most developed, did not spend a great deal of effort or money in fostering universities. Indeed, the role of indigenous populations in establishing Western-model universities during the colonial era deserves more emphasis.

It is also worth noting that, with few exceptions, the colonial powers did not dismantle existing indigenous higher education institutions. Rather, Western-style universities proved more popular because they were tied to the colonial administration and to emerging economic interests. Indigenous schools were simply left to atrophy. An exception to this generally laissez faire approach was Japan, which had a more activist educational policy in Korea and Taiwan and actively repressed local institutions of higher education (Lee, 2004).

The European powers felt that the implantation of higher education in their colonies would introduce a subversive institution. They were correct in this assumption since Western-educated intellectuals produced by the universities were everywhere the leaders of independence movements, and the universities themselves were important intellectual centers involved in the development of nationalism and dissent. Perhaps the most dramatic example of the impact of Western-educated university graduates is Indonesia, where the very concept of the Indonesian nation with a common language was created by a small group of intellectuals trained both at home and in the Netherlands. Despite the reluctance of the colonial authorities, there was a need for small groups of Western-educated people, literate in the language of the colonial administration, to staff the civil service and provide midlevel administration. The pressure for expansion came almost entirely from local people seeking the opportunities provided by a Western academic degree, and in some cases the colonial powers permitted modest expansion to meet these demands.

The role of Christian missionary work in the development and expansion of higher education in Asia is also significant. Missionaries devoted much effort to establishing higher education institutions to foster conversions to Christianity. In much of Asia, the establishment of early academic institutions was due to missionary work. This was especially the case in India, China, and Korea, where Christian organizations were among the early founders of colleges and universities, although in most Asian countries missionaries had less success in converting people to Christianity. A significant exception to this rule is the Philippines, which is majority Roman Catholic as the result of centuries of Spanish colonial rule. The Spanish colonial authorities gave the Catholic Church the full responsibility for higher education. South Korea also has a large Christian minority. Missionaries generally had the support of the colonial authorities although from time to time, as in India, there were disagreements concerning higher education policy. In some parts of Asia, Christian universities and colleges remain an important part of the academic landscape.

There are important common elements in the European colonial model in Asia. In all cases, instruction was offered exclusively in the language of the colonial power. Universities in the British colonies functioned in English, in the Dutch East Indies in Dutch, in Korea and Taiwan in Japanese, in the Philippines in English, and so on. The widespread use of European languages in higher education has had a profound impact on the development of higher education. It has been difficult, in some Asian countries, to use local languages in higher education—Indonesia is an example of a country that made an early and effective shift from a European language (Dutch) to an indigenous language (Cummings & Kasenda, 1989). Neighboring Malaysia had more difficulty changing from English and is now restoring some English to the higher education system. South Asia retains English as one of the languages of instruction. The Asian countries that were not colonized—e.g., Japan, China, and Thailand—did not adopt European languages. Thus, in much of Asia, the impact of colonial languages on academic development has been, and continues to be, central to higher education.

The colonial powers placed restrictions on the academic institutions they established in Asia—government control was strict and academic freedom limited. The purpose of the colonial universities was to train a loyal civil service and a small number of medical doctors, lawyers, and others to serve the colonizers—not to establish universities in the full autonomous sense of the term. Thus, the colonial university did not have all of the characteristics of the metropolitan model. This historical tradition of subservience and of a lack of full autonomy and academic freedom created problems for the emergence of modern universities in postindependence Asia.

It is also important to examine those Asian countries that were not colonized. Japan and Thailand are the most significant examples. China, while never formally colonized, was strongly influenced by Europeans, and also by Japan, along the coast where higher education became the most entrenched. In all of these cases, the noncolonized Asian countries chose Western academic models rather than relying on indigenous intellectual and academic traditions. In the second half of the 19th century, Japan and Thailand established Western-style academic institutions after careful consideration. In the Japanese case, the new Meiji regime adopted the German academic model with some influences from the United States as the pattern for the new universities. After some discussion concerning the appropriate language of instruction, during which the minister of education advocated the use of English, Japanese was chosen as the medium of instruction. In Japan, Thailand, and China, governments established Western-style higher education to assist in the process of modernization and industrialization.

Upon attaining independence, no Asian country chose to break with the academic models imposed by the colonial powers. Other links with the universities in the former metropole were also retained. In the former British colonies, English was retained as a medium of instruction to varying extents. As mentioned, Malaysia, which moved to Bahasa Malaysia a few years after independence, has recently reintroduced English to some extent in its universities. Indonesia was the largest country to shift the language of education, introducing Bahasa Indonesia immediately following independence. Korea and Taiwan stopped using Japanese and moved to Korean and Chinese, respectively. In the decade following the 1949 Communist revolution in China, a variety of Western patterns yielded to the Soviet academic model (Hayhoe, 1996). For different reasons and at different times, China and the central Asian republics, once part of the Soviet Union, found the Soviet model to be inappropriate. China dropped it a half century ago, while the central Asian nations are now in the process of change.

As Asian academic systems have grown and matured, countries have not been inspired to develop new indigenous academic models. Rather, Asian countries have looked abroad for ways to expand and improve their universities. For the most part, the United States has provided the ideas and forms for academic development. There are several reasons for this "Americanization" of Asian higher education. The U.S. academic system is the largest in the world—the first to cope with the challenges of enrollment expansion. The United States also has the largest and most advanced academic research system. Moreover, many Asian academic and political leaders studied in the United States and absorbed American academic ideas during their student years.

Asian academic systems carry the baggage of their historical past. The legacy of colonialism linked universities to government and gave considerable power to governmental authorities over higher education. Even in countries without a colonial past, notably Japan and Thailand, the impetus for the establishment of modern universities came from government. Asian universities have shallow roots in the soil of their countries—the norms and values of academe are perhaps less well entrenched than in many Western nations. On this point, however, it should be remembered that German universities voluntarily succumbed to Nazi authority despite their rich historical tradition. Still, historical traditions play an important role in all social institutions— and no institution is more influenced by history than universities.

The Asian economic miracle

Nowhere in Asia have the early stages of contemporary economic development been dependent on higher education. Even in those countries that have achieved impressive rates of growth and have joined the ranks of the industrialized world—Japan, Taiwan, South Korea, China and to some extent Thailand and Malaysia—development has not been based on knowledge industries or on higher education. The underpinnings of economic growth are varied. The typical pattern was industrialization based on an inexpensive labor force, with a basic education and literacy skills, and a reliance on exporting relatively unsophisticated manufactured goods or the products of heavy industry. In some cases, raw materials (such as oil and rubber in Malaysia) or agricultural products were added.

Significant investment in education did play a role, but the focus was on primary and to some extent secondary education to provide the workforce for the emerging industries with the appropriate literacy and skills. The countries that had the most success—Japan, South Korea, Taiwan, and in recent years China—invested heavily in basic education and achieved very impressive gains in literacy and other educational skills. The South Asian countries, which invested less in education and still have much lower literacy rates, have done less well economically.

Higher education was not emphasized during the initial phases of industrialization, and most Asian academic systems remained small, enrolling a modest percentage of the age cohort. The universities largely served the elites, and there was only limited demand from other sectors of the population. Governments invested little in higher education. In a number of countries, private universities became an important part of the system (Altbach, 1999).

As a middle class developed, as a growing segment of the population acquired some wealth, and as literacy levels and secondary schooling became more widespread, demand grew for access to higher education. For much of East Asia, these trends occurred in the 1980s and have continued today. Other parts of the region have moved more slowly. Moreover, in a few places, such as India, expansion was not directly linked to economic development. Universities and other postsecondary institutions were established to serve this growing demand, often in the private sector, given the frequent unwillingness of government to invest in higher education. Almost everywhere in Asia, university expansion was driven by demand from the increasingly articulate emerging middle classes and those seeking upward mobility in society. Only later, as governments recognized the role of postsecondary expansion in economic development, did the public sector invest significantly in higher education.

As countries such as Japan, South Korea, Taiwan, Singapore, and others developed, their economies became more sophisticated and wages rose, and they were no longer competitive with lower-wage economies. They realized that they had to develop more sophisticated industries and a service sector to remain competitive. In short, they were forced to move toward becoming "knowledge-based economies"—and higher education was seen as a key factor in national economic survival.

Investment in academic institutions and in a research infrastructure is taking place in many Asian countries, although the pace of investment and expansion varies considerably. Japan transformed itself first, starting in the 1960s, and it was followed by Taiwan, South Korea, Singapore, with Malaysia, Thailand, and others following somewhat later. Governments took more interest in higher education, and increased expenditures for both expansion and research. Although government expenditure on higher education in much of Asia remains modest by international standards, it grew during this period of expansion. Asia had the advantage of an active private higher education sector that paid for much of the expansion. Some Asian countries, including Cambodia, Laos, Burma, and to some extent Vietnam, remain at an early stage of economic development, with higher education still given a low priority.

One of the most interesting examples linking higher education to new economic policies has been Singapore (Tan, 2004). Singapore, which has had until recently no private higher education sector, kept enrollment rates modest in its two universities. As the country redirected its economic growth strategies to such high-tech areas as biotechnology, medical and financial services, and related fields, there was a recognition that a larger proportion of the population needed academic qualifications. Academic institutions have been expanded and a growing segment of the age cohort is enrolling in postsecondary education. Singapore is developing links with some of the best universities abroad, and for the first time, private initiatives in higher education are being permitted. Malaysia now has a national policy of encouraging high-tech development, and is linking this strategy with targeted higher education expansion.

The regional giants, China and India, after developing their economies in a fairly traditional pattern, now have elements of both "old" and "new" economic policies, and their higher education systems are adjusting in different ways to the new realities. While China has achieved much higher literacy rates and more impressive economic growth than has been the case for India, both countries are faced with the challenge of adapting their academic systems to meet the demands of growing numbers for access while ensuring that at least a part of the system serves the needs of a high-tech economy. Both countries show that it is possible to have at least a part of the higher education system operate at very high levels of quality and are involved with the international knowledge system. Such schools as the Indian Institutes of Technology and the key Chinese universities are examples of the best-quality academic and research institutions. India met the demand for access by permitting privately owned but government-subsidized colleges to expand, which has resulted in a decline in the overall quality of the academic system China now seems to be moving in a similar direction, encouraging the private sector (which receives no government funding) to absorb demand for access and expanding enrollments in many of the public universities without commensurate increases in funding.

Higher education will inevitably become more central as Asian economies become more technology based, more heavily dependent on informatics, and more service based. Japan and Singapore have already been transformed into postindustrial information-based societies. China and India have moved partly into this realm, as have South Korea, Taiwan, and Malaysia. All these countries have recognized the importance of higher education in this transformation and are moving to ensure that at least part of the university system is prepared to function in the new environment. Japan's current structural reforms of the national universities are aimed in part at ensuring that higher education institutions will be prepared to play an active role in building the new economy. China is also in the process of ensuring that some of its top universities will have the training and research capabilities to assist in the economic changes needed for a research-based economy. Other Asian nations that recognize their role in a knowledge-based economy are, in different ways, developing university structures that can serve the new economic realities. Poorer Asian countries—Cambodia and Burma are examples—have yet to grapple with these changes. Still others, such as Thailand and in the future perhaps Pakistan, have yet to think seriously about higher education's role in a changing economic structure.

As much of Asia moves toward a more sophisticated economic base, universities will become more central to the economy, research will receive more attention, and closer links will evolve between the universities and the economy. While the initial phases of Asian economic success did not depend on higher education and technology, it is clear that the next stages will rely on the universities for both training and research. Japan, Taiwan, and South Korea have already recognized this, and China and Malaysia are adapting to current realities. Other countries will inevitably recognize the importance of higher education for the next phase of development.

The challenge of massification

The central reality of higher education almost everywhere is the expansion in student numbers that has taken place since the 1960s. Worldwide, between 1975 and 1995, enrollments doubled, going from 40 million to over 80 million. While growth has slowed in many industrialized countries, expansion continues in the developing nations, and will remain the main factor in shaping academic realities in the coming period. The pressures for expansion will be most significant in the countries that still educate a relatively small portion of the age group—under 15 percent—and in Asia this includes such major nations as China, India, Indonesia, Bangladesh, Burma, Vietnam, Cambodia, Pakistan, and others. Most industrialized nations educate from about 35 and to more than 50 percent of the age group—in Asia, only South Korea, Japan, and Taiwan have achieved this proportion, with Thailand, the Philippines, and Singapore catching up rapidly. These patterns of enrollment in Asia do not reflect the growing international trend to provide postsecondary education to "nontraditional" students—those who are older but have either missed out on an academic degree or who require additional skills for their jobs or professions. This so far underserved segment of the population will also demand increasing access in the coming years.

Expansion is an inevitable and irresistible force. Ever-growing segments of the population demand access to postsecondary education because they know that it is necessary for social mobility and for improved salaries and standards of living in most societies. Countries need larger numbers of university-educated workers to support knowledge-based economies. As more young people gain access to secondary education, they naturally gravitate to higher education, having gained the qualifications to gain entry to universities. In addition, as a middle class grows in size and in political influence, it will also demand access to higher education. Few countries

381

have been able to resist the social demand for access, and none can permanently block it.

Almost all Asian countries are currently coping with the implications of continuing expansion. This pressure makes it difficult to focus on other things—improving quality, upgrading research, enhancing the salaries and working conditions of the professoriate, among others. The inevitable result of expansion has been the development of differentiated systems of higher education, with institutions serving different roles and with varying levels of support and prestige. The traditional university remains at the pinnacle of a hierarchy, but is no longer the main postsecondary institution. An overall deterioration of quality is also a result of massification. In most countries, there continue to be high-quality universities that maintain traditional academic standards and a commitment to research, but many of the institutions lower on the hierarchy offer an education that is more modest in quality—and in prestige as well. As in other parts of the world, mass higher education means a differentiated academic system, with major variations in quality, purpose, and orientation. Massification drags down the overall quality of the academic system as it creates a more diversified academic system.

The challenges are considerable. Two of the most important are funding the expansion and providing necessary physical facilities. The problem of funding is particularly acute for two reasons. Not only is it difficult to find public resources to support ever larger numbers of students, but there has also been a basic change in thinking in many countries concerning who should pay for higher education and other public services. Led by the World Bank and other international agencies, countries increasingly argue that higher education is mainly a "private good" serving the needs of individuals and less a "public" or social good. Therefore, the thinking is that the "user"—students, and perhaps their families—deserve to pay a significant part of the cost of higher education. This has led to the imposition of tuition and other fees for higher education in most Asian countries. Indeed, there may be no Asian country, with the exception of North Korea, that does not charge tuition. The two factors of a simple lack of sufficient public funds and a new perspective on higher education have combined to instigate a major rethinking of the financing of higher education as a private good in Asia. Even in countries that adhere to a socialist economic system—such as China and Vietnam—tuition has been introduced.

While it is not possible to fully analyze the nuances of the public vs. private good arguments here, it is clear that an effective higher education system will recognize that both are part of the academic equation. While it is certainly the case that earning a degree is a significant advantage to the graduate in terms of income and in other ways, it is also true that universities provide a considerable public good to society. Not only are there public benefits accruing from the individual graduate (such as a heightened civic consciousness and the ability to pay higher taxes because of higher earnings), universities provide other benefits to society: they are repositories of knowledge through their libraries and other databases and they provide the basic and applied research that can help with development.

The private sector in Asian higher education

Another central reality of massification is increased reliance on private higher education institutions (Altbach, 2000). Private higher education is the fastest-growing segment of postsecondary education worldwide. In Asia, private institutions have long been a central part of higher education provision. In such major countries as Japan, South Korea, Taiwan, the Philippines, and Indonesia, private universities enroll the majority of students—in some cases upwards of 80 percent. The large majority of Indian students attend private colleges, although these are heavily subsidized by government funds. The private sector is a growing force in parts of Asia where it was previously inactive—China, Vietnam, and the central Asian republics are examples.

In general, private universities are found at the lower end of the prestige hierarchy in Asia. There are a few exceptions of high-quality private universities, such as Waseda, Keio, and a few others in Japan; De La Salle and the Ateneo de Manila in the Philippines; Yonsei in Korea; and Atma Jaya in Indonesia. Generally, private institutions rely on tuition payments, receive little funding from public sources (although in Japan and several other countries some government funding is available to the private sector), and have no tradition of private philanthropy (in part because the tax structure does not reward private donation to nonprofit organizations such as universities), and as a result are unable to compete for the best students. However, the private sector plays a central role by providing access to students who would otherwise be unable to obtain academic degrees.

It is useful to disaggregate the Asian private higher education sector because of the significant differences among institutions and the divergent roles they play in society. As noted, there are a few very prestigious private universities in the countries in which a private sector operates. In some cases, these institutions are sponsored or founded by religious groups—largely but not exclusively Christian. Sophia and Doshisha in Japan, Yonsei and Sogang in South Korea, Santa Dharma in Indonesia, Assumption in Thailand, and De La Salle and Ateneo de Manila in the Philippines are examples. These universities are typically among the oldest in their countries, and they have a long tradition of training elite groups. Another category is the newer private institutions, often specializing in fields such as management or technology, established with the aim of serving a key but limited market with high-quality academic degrees. The Asian Institute of Technology in the Philippines and its sister institution in Thailand and the new Singapore

Management University are examples of such schools. These prestigious private universities have been able to maintain their positions over time and rely largely on tuition payments for survival.

Most Asian private universities serve the mass higher education market and tend to be relatively nonselective. Many are small, although there are some quite large institutions, such as the Far Eastern University in the Philippines, which has a large student population and was for a time listed on the Manila stock exchange. Some are sponsored by private nonprofit organizations, religious societies, or other groups. Many are owned by individuals or families, sometimes with a management structure that masks the controlling elements of the school. This pattern of family-run academic institutions has received little attention from analysts and is important to understand as it is a phenomenon of growing importance worldwide. Even in countries that do not encourage for-profit higher education institutions, family ownership has become an established phenomenon.

The emerging for-profit sector is a growing segment of private higher education in some Asian countries. In 2002, China passed legislation that permits private higher education institutions to earn an "appropriate" profit. Two for-profit higher education patterns have emerged in India: several quite large and successful postsecondary trade schools and a number of colleges (mostly focusing on professional and medical training) that charge high fees and are intended to provide a return on investment to investors although their legal status has come into question. While a number of Asian countries have not as yet opened their doors fully to for-profit higher education, there are already semi-for-profit enterprises operating, and before long this trend will prevail.

Many Asian countries have long experience in managing large private higher education sectors, while others are seeking to establish appropriate structures. The main challenge is to allow the private sector the necessary autonomy and freedom to establish and manage institutions and to compete in a differentiated educational marketplace, while at the same time ensuring that the national interest is served. In India, where the large majority of undergraduate students attend private colleges, these institutions are largely funded by the state governments, and are closely controlled by the universities to which most are affiliated. University authorities, for example, determine and administer examinations and award academic degrees, stipulate the minimum qualifications for entry, and supervise the hiring of academic staff. Japan and South Korea have a long tradition of rigidly controlling the private institutions—going to the extent of stipulating the salaries of academic staff, the numbers of students that can be admitted, approving the establishment of new departments or programs, and supervising the appointment of trustees. In recent years, these two countries have moved toward allowing private institutions more autonomy and freedom. Other countries have imposed less strict supervision.

As in other parts of the world, private higher education is expanding throughout Asia, and the countries that are moving toward a large private sector would be well advised to look at the experience elsewhere in Asia for guidance. There is a dramatically growing private sector in China, with more than 500 private postsecondary institutions, most of which are not accredited or approved by the government. Vietnam and Cambodia also have rapidly growing private sectors, as do the central Asian nations. The challenge will be ensuring that the emerging private sector is effective, well managed and serving national goals.

Distance higher education

Of the world's 10-largest distance higher education institutions, 7 are located in Asia—in Turkey, China, Indonesia, India, Thailand, South Korea, and Iran. These institutions have enrollments of more than 100,000 each. A variety of distance methodologies are used to deliver academic programs. These institutions, which are all public universities, were established to meet the growing demand for higher education, especially in regions not served by traditional academic institutions.

The potential for expansion of distance higher education is fuelled by a variety of trends. Access to technology is rapidly expanding in many Asian countries, which enables growing numbers of people to take advantage of distance delivery programs. Distance institutions can reach students in places without traditional universities—a relevant factor in much of Asia, where transportation is difficult and people lack the funds to relocate to study in major urban areas. Distance higher education, as developed in the Asian context and in most developing areas, is less expensive to deliver than are traditional academic degree programs. Distance higher education does not require the facilities needed for traditional academic institutions—a considerable advantage in the light of greatly increased demand and relatively limited existing universities.

While claims are made that Asian distance universities are providing an acceptable level of academic quality, there have been few evaluative studies. It is likely that foreign providers will seek to enter Asian markets, especially if the academic doors are forced open should Asian countries enter into agreements under the General Agreement on Trade in Services, a part of the World Trade Organization (Altbach, 2002).

Trends and challenges

Asian higher education faces considerable hurdles in the coming period. While there are significant differences among Asian countries in size, historical patterns of academic development, wealth, and other factors, it is nonetheless possible to highlight trends that are common to most of the

385

region. Since the problems are similar, it may be useful for countries to examine the experience of other Asian countries rather than always looking toward the West for answers to pressing questions of higher education development. The following issues seem to be of special relevance for Asian academic development.

Massification

The challenges of mass higher education have been considered in this essay. It remains a central reality for most of Asia (Japan and South Korea are exceptions, with their well-established academic systems and falling populations). Massification will place continuing strains on public funds, and at the same time will shape academic decision making. Massification requires differentiated academic systems able to serve different segments of the population and fulfill different purposes—with varying levels of funding and resources.

Access

Directly related to mass higher education is the question of access—providing higher education opportunities for all sections of the population able to take advantage of them. In most Asian countries, educational opportunities lag behind for women, rural populations, the poor, and some minority groups. It will be a challenge to provide access to previously disenfranchised groups.

Differentiation

Mass higher education requires a clear differentiation of goals and purposes among academic institutions so that resources are efficiently managed and the various purposes of higher education served. This means that there must be a coordinated system of higher education loosely managed by an authority that has both power and responsibility for a system of higher education. Such a management arrangement need not be under the direct control of the state but can be a joint effort by public authorities, the academic community, and others. Systems require clear definitions of institutional goals and responsibilities, as well as appropriate funding. The private sector should be treated as part of the national higher education system. Small as well as large countries will necessarily need to develop such systems because even small populations will need a range of academic preparation to meet the new economic realities.

Accreditation and quality control

Large academic systems require transparency in terms of quality of academic programs and institutions and assurance that minimum standards are being met. This is necessary not only to provide students with appropriate information about institutions but also to ensure that public resources are being effectively spent. It is sometimes argued that the market will ensure effective quality control. While the market might ensure the quality of some products, it will not be effective for higher education because the measurement of quality is complex and far from obvious to students or to employers. Accreditation and quality control arrangements can provide this information and can ensure that appropriate standards are maintained. There are many models available, and these can be adapted to specific Asian circumstances—some accreditation systems are supervised by government while others are the responsibility of the academic system itself, other nongovernmental organizations, or a combination of several stakeholders.

Research

Not all universities need to be focused on research—for example, most American universities are mainly teaching institutions—but almost every country needs some universities that engage in top-quality research in relevant fields or that at least are able to interpret research done elsewhere. This does not mean that countries with out the financial resources or infrastructure need to have a full-fledged research university, but all need to have at least some academic staff capable of interpreting and using research. Supporting research universities is neither easy nor inexpensive. Yet, for most countries, it is necessary, for research is at the heart of the modern knowledge-based economy. Further, only universities can engage in basic research since this requires a long-term commitment and resources that industry cannot support. While a few Asian countries adopted the Soviet-style "research institute" model, most have realized that universities can better serve as the basis of a culture of research.

The academic profession

At the heart of any university is the academic profession. Yet, in many countries, the professoriate is in crisis—inadequately paid and suffering from ever higher workloads and low morale. In order to attract the "best and brightest" to academe, appropriate conditions must be created. In many Asian countries, there is too little evaluation of academic work—an evaluation system is needed that combines attractive working conditions and accountability that ensures productivity by the professoriate. Current trends toward a part-time teaching force (as is common in Latin America) contribute to a lack of professional commitment to academe. Research-oriented universities especially need a highly motivated and well-trained professoriate. In many Asian countries, few university teachers hold advanced academic degrees. An essential part of ensuring the necessary conditions for teaching and research is the presence of an academic environment based on academic freedom and an appropriate balance between autonomy and accountability for the professoriate. The academic profession requires careful attention and support in a modern university system.

Globalization and internationalization

Universities worldwide are becoming part of a global academic environment, and this has implications for Asian universities. Distance education and information technology are parts of globalization—students, staff, and academic institutions themselves are affected by the ease of communication and the access to information provided by IT. Academic programs offered through distance education from abroad will have some impact on Asian countries as well. These are new realities that will require careful planning and adjustment in each system. Students and staff are increasingly part of an international academic community. Asian students are by far the largest group of students studying abroad worldwide, and more Asian scholars now work outside their own countries. The flow of academic talent is from Asia to the industrialized West for the most part (although Australia and Japan are also attractive destinations for Asian students and staff). India and China are the largest "exporters" of students and probably of staff as well, and Malaysia, South Korea, Taiwan. Hong Kong, and several other Asian countries also send significant numbers of students abroad. There is also a need for Asian universities to incorporate knowledge from abroad —and again the bulk of knowledge is imported from the "metropolitan" academic systems of the West. Asian academic systems cannot insulate themselves from the global academic system and will need to adjust positively to it.

Transnationalization

Related to globalization is the trend for academic institutions and other education providers from one country to offer degrees or other academic programs in another country. Asia is already the largest world market for such transnational educational enterprises, and this phenomenon will grow rapidly. Malaysia is probably the world's largest transnational market at present. China has recently opened its doors to foreign providers, and other countries will no doubt follow down this path. In most cases, academic institutions from the industrialized nations, and especially from Australia and the United Kingdom, with the United States beginning to become involved, open branch campuses or develop partnerships or other arrangements in an Asian country. In some cases, distance methods are used to deliver all or part of the educational degree or other programs. The implications of transnational higher education enterprises are as yet unclear, for local higher education markets, quality, accreditation, and control of higher education.

Conclusion

Asian universities are shaped by their historical traditions and have to face the complex realities of the 21st century. They enter this new era from a position of some weakness. With the exception of a few Japanese universities, Asian academic institutions are seeking to catch up with their counterparts in the West in an environment where entering the "big leagues" is both difficult and expensive. Yet, many Asian countries have some features that work to their considerable advantages as well. Well-educated populations, traditions of scholarship, and a high respect for learning are part of virtually every Asian society. Asian countries also have the opportunity to shape their relatively new university systems to meet the needs of the 21st century in ways that the more entrenched universities of the West may have difficulty doing. What is clear is that universities are an essential part of the knowledge economies of the future. Unless they are able to build effective universities that can educate a growing proportion of the population while competing globally for research and knowledge products, Asian countries will be doomed to peripheral status.

References

Altbach, P. G. (1998). Gigantic peripheries: India and China in the world knowledge system. In P. G. Altbach (Ed.), *Comparative higher education* (pp. 133–146). Greenwich, CT: Ablex.

Altbach, P. G. (1999). *Private Prometheus: Private higher education and development in the 21st century.* Westport, CT: Greenwood.

Altbach, P. G. (Ed.). (2000). *The changing academic workplace: Comparative perspectives.* Chestnut Hill, MA: Center for International Higher Education, Boston College.

Altbach, P. G. (2002). Globalization and the university: Myths and realities in an unequal world. *Seminarium* no. 3–4, 807–836.

Altbach, P. G., & Selvaratnam, V. (Eds.). (1989). *From dependence to autonomy: The development of Asian universities.* Dordrecht, Netherlands: Kluwer.

Ashby, Eric. (1966). *Universities: British, Indian, African.* Cambridge: Harvard University Press.

Basu, Aparna. (1989). Indian higher education: Colonialism and beyond. In P. G. Altbach & V. Selvaratnam (Eds.), *From dependence to autonomy: the development of Asian universities* (pp. 167–186). Dordrecht, Netherlands: Kluwer.

Cummings, William K., & Kasenda, Salman. (1989). The origins of modern Indonesian higher education. In P. G. Altbach & V. Selvaratnam (Eds.), *From dependence to autonomy: The development of Asian universities* (pp. 143–166). Dordrecht, Netherlands: Kluwer.

Hayhoe, Ruth. (1996). *China's universities, 1895–1995: A century of cultural conflict.* New York: Garland.

Lee, Sungho H. (2004). Korean higher education: History and future challenges. In P. G. Altbach & T. Umakoshi (Eds.), *Asian universities: Historical perspectives and contemporary challenges.* Baltimore, MD: Johns Hopkins University Press.

Postiglione, G. A., & Mak, G. C. L. (Eds.). (1997). *Asian higher education: An international handbook and reference guide.* Westport, CT: Greenwood.

Tan, Jason. (2004). Singapore: Small nation, big plans. In P. G. Altbach & T. Umakoshi (Eds.), *Asian universities: Historical perspectives and contemporary challenges.* Baltimore, MD: Johns Hopkins University Press.

Task Force on Higher Education and Society. (2000). *Higher education in developing countries: Peril and promise.* Washington, D.C.: World Bank.

26

CHINESE HIGHER EDUCATION

The legacy of the past and the context of the future

Weifang Min

Source: P. G. Altbach and Toru Umakoshi (eds) *Asian Universities: Historical Perspectives and Contemporary Challenges*, Baltimore: Johns Hopkins University Press, 2004, pp. 53–83.

Universities in China have undergone dramatic changes in recent years, including rapid expansion of enrollments, structural reforms, and quality improvement. Many of the national universities have the goal of becoming world-class institutions and have made significant progress. These changes in Chinese higher education have taken place in the context of an expanding Chinese economy, which has maintained an average annual GDP growth rate of 8 percent for the past two decades. The implementation of economic reforms and an open-door policy have helped the Chinese economy to become more integrated into the international economy. Chinese higher education has increased its degree of interaction with universities in other countries and now functions as part of the international academic community. To understand the challenges universities in China will face in the future, it is necessary to examine their historical development and current realities.

Overview

The current Chinese higher education system is one of the largest in the world, with more than 3,000 universities and colleges—including 1,225 regular full-time universities and colleges, 686 adult higher education institutions, and 1,202 new private universities and colleges. The system encompasses 13 million students and over 1.45 million staff members, 554,000 of whom are faculty members. The predominant public sector enrolls about 12 million students and the recently developed private sector about 1 million students. The public sector consists of two major components: regular higher education, which includes 7.19 million students, and adult higher education, which includes 4.55 million students. Regular higher education institutions comprise universities with both undergraduate and graduate degree programs and short-cycle (two- or three-year) colleges without degree programs. Adult higher education institutions include television-based universities offering a variety of programs, workers' universities for training and upgrading employees, peasants' universities for training and upgrading farmers, colleges of management for training and upgrading administrators and Communist Party cadres, educational colleges for school teachers and administrators, and independent (private) correspondence colleges.

Adult higher education is provided in both part-time and full-time programs, some of which offer bachelor's degrees. They usually have no advanced degree programs. Table 1 provides statistics on China's higher education system.

In 2001, among the total enrollments at regular higher education institutions, students majoring in engineering accounted for 34.6 percent, in the humanities 15.5 percent, in management 14.2 percent, in the sciences 10 percent, in medicine 7.4 percent, in law 5.4 percent, in education 5.2 percent, in economics 5.0 percent, and in agriculture 2.6 percent. Engineering majors have accounted for the largest proportion of students since the 1950s and are still the largest single group at present. Currently, the number of

Table 1 The Chinese Higher Education System, 2001.

Type of Institution	No. of Institutions	No. of Students
Graduate education institutions	728	393,200
Graduate programs at universities	411	371,600
Graduate programs at research institutions	317	21,600
Undergraduate education institutions	3,113	12,880,900
Regular[a] higher education institutions	1,225	7,190,700
Universities	597	5,212,000
Short-cycle colleges	628	1,978,700
Adult higher education institutions	686	4,559,800
TV universities	45	400,300
Workers' colleges	409	351,100
Peasants' universities	3	800
Management training colleges	104	153,900
Educational colleges	122	304,400
Correspondence colleges	3	15,500
University-run adult higher education programs		3,333,800
Private higher education institutions	1,202	1,130,400

Source: Department of Development and Planning, Ministry of Education of China, 2002.
[a]Regular higher education institutions comprise universities with both undergraduate and graduate degree programs and short-cycle (two- or three-year) colleges without degree programs.

students in management, law, economics and other applied fields is increasing rapidly, while enrollments in the basic sciences and the humanities are declining, in response to the labor market (Ministry of Education, 2002).

Historical perspectives

Indigenous higher education

China's long higher education tradition evolved along with Chinese civilization. The earliest Chinese state was established in the Xia dynasty (about 2200 B.C.). From the beginning, Chinese culture attached great importance to education, as recorded in ancient Chinese writings: "To establish a nation state, education should come first." "A man without education cannot be a knowledgeable and moral man." These values and this belief system have exerted significant influence on Chinese people's character, thinking, and behavior for thousands of years down to the present time. For example, one of the current national policy goals is to invigorate the country through education and science.

Chinese higher education originated as early as 1100 B.C. during the Zhou dynasty and was called *pi-yong*. During the Han dynasty (206 B.C.– A.D. 220); higher education institutions were called *tai-xue*, which means "institutions of higher learning," and were attended by more than thirty thousand students during the dynasty's most prosperous time at its main campus in Changan, the capital city (Wang *et al.*, 1994). During the Tang dynasty (A.D. 618–907) and afterward, Chinese universities were called *guo-zi-jian*, a type of higher education institution established for the children of royal families and senior officials. The content of learning was drawn mainly from the classical texts of Confucian teachings, which were also the dominant contents of the imperial examinations for senior civil service positions.

In addition to these ancient universities established by the Chinese state, which continued to exist until the late nineteenth century, private universities also flourished in ancient China. Confucius (551–479 B.C.) introduced private higher education in China during the Eastern Zhou dynasty, at a time when state institutions were becoming weaker. It was recorded that Confucius had more than three thousand students. It became fashionable to run private learning institutions during this time, and many leading scholars at different schools operated their own institutions. When speaking of ancient private institutions of higher learning, one must mention *shu-yuan*. These institutions started to appear during the Tang dynasty (A.D. 618–907), when they were first established in both the state and private sectors as places for collecting books. *Shu-yuan* were not places for teaching and learning initially but gradually developed into private academies or scholarly societies, as alternatives to official higher education institutions, eventually becoming a dominant type of private university throughout the country during the Song dynasty (A.D. 960–1279). *Shu-yuan* played an important role in ancient Chinese higher education and continued to function until the early twentieth century. As Ruth Hayhoe suggests, the *shu-yuan* of ancient China may have been similar to the medieval universities of Europe (Hayhoe, 1989). In short, indigenous higher education in China had a long tradition going back three thousand years, encompassing both public and private sectors of higher learning. However, constrained by feudalism, traditional Chinese higher education was only able to develop slowly.

Modern universities and the European model

Although the indigenous tradition had a significant impact on Chinese higher education, modern Chinese universities developed from the European model. This process involved a long and even painful interaction with the West after the Opium War in 1840, when the Western powers opened China's doors by gunboats. This opening made Chinese intellectuals aware of Western advancements in science and technology and of the backwardness of China, which they in their conceit viewed as the "Central Kingdom" of the world. The impact of the European university model on China worked through three major channels: the establishment of Western missionary colleges in China, the study-abroad programs for Chinese scholars and students begun in the late nineteenth century, and the modernization efforts of Chinese reformers.

As the Western powers gained the right of entry into China, the introduction of the Western university model on Chinese soil took place. Many foreign groups tried to create higher education institutions in China, including French Jesuit missionaries, American Protestants with the cooperation of British and Canadian colleagues, and German industrialists. By 1949, there were twenty-one universities run or subsidized by foreigners, including such influential institutions as Yenching University in Beijing and St. Johns University in Shanghai. Among the total of 205 higher education institutions in the country, foreign universities accounted for about 10 percent and enrolled about ten thousand students. The higher education models introduced by the missionaries and other foreign groups influenced the development of modern higher education in China, but they were "largely peripheral to the mainstream education reforms being engineered by a modernizing Chinese leadership. They did not look to missionary efforts for inspiration in their reforms, but visited or sent delegations to the nations whose educational institutions were of interest and modeled their reforms directly on foreign experience" (Hayhoe, 1989, pp. 36–37).

One of the important ways in which the European university model influenced Chinese higher education was the study-abroad programs for Chinese scholars and students. Seven years after the 1840 Opium War, three young students—Rong Hong, Huang Kuan, and Huang Sheng—followed their teacher, Samuel Robinns Brown, to the United States for university studies in 1847, the first Chinese to do so. Rong Hong received his bachelor's degree from Yale University and returned to China in 1854, becoming the very first Chinese person to have received a university education in a foreign country. Through the efforts of Rong Hong and others, in 1872 the Chinese government decided to send a group of 120 students to the United States, initiating the country's first official study-abroad programs. This was followed by programs that sent students to the United Kingdom and continental European countries. In the wake of increased Japanese influence in China, many Chinese scholars and students went to Japan, where they experienced the European university model with a Japanese imprint. In the late nineteenth and early twentieth centuries, more than ten thousand Chinese students studied in Japan. They would constitute a significant phenomenon in Chinese higher education. A large proportion of the returned students worked in the Chinese higher education system as teachers, researchers, and administrators, becoming a driving force in the development of Chinese universities.

One of the modernization efforts introduced in China after the Opium War was the movement to adopt the Western university model and to promote the learning of Western science and technology as a response to foreign aggression. From the 1860s to the 1880s, Western-style military and naval academies and foreign-language institutions were established in China. In 1898, as one of the major reform strategies, Capital Metropolitan University—the predecessor of Peking University—was established by the state. It was the first modern national comprehensive university in China and became a milestone in the development of the Chinese higher education system.

According to 1902 educational reform legislation, Peking University was regarded as the leading institution of higher learning in China, and it was expected to provide leadership for all schools in the country. However, in the context of the corrupt and weakened feudal Qing dynasty, modern Chinese universities were constrained from further development. Peking University achieved little during its first ten years. A new institutional environment and new leadership for Chinese higher education were needed. It was during the presidency of Cai Yuanpei that Peking University became the first truly modern Chinese university. Cai Yuanpei had studied in Germany from 1908 to 1911. After the Revolution of 1911, the provisional government established by Sun Yat Sen appointed Cai Yuanpei as the first minister of education in China. Drawing on his experiences as a student in Germany, he introduced the European university model to China through his involvement in formulating the 1912 education reform legislation. In 1917, after his return from his second period of studies in Germany and France, Cai Yuanpei was appointed as the president of Peking University (Hayhoe, 1989). As president of the university, he promoted institutional autonomy and academic freedom. He also emphasized arts and sciences, instead of ancient classics, as core curriculum areas, patterned after the Western university model.

In 1922, new educational reform legislation was implemented that reflected the greater influence of American university traditions. The American 6-3-3-4 schooling system—that is, six-year primary school, three-year junior high school, three-year senior high school, and four-year college—was adopted in 1922 as the basic system of teaching and learning. This schooling system functioned until 1949 and currently retains a strong impact on education in China. Since China suffered from continuous foreign invasions and civil wars before 1949, the economy was extremely backward, people were very poor, and higher education had developed slowly. By 1949, China had only 205 higher education institutions—124 public universities and colleges, 21 missionary universities and colleges, and 60 private universities and colleges (including short-cycle colleges), with a total enrollment of 117,000 students.

Soviet influences in the early 1950s

After the founding of the People's Republic of China, the central government took over and nationalized all higher education institutions. All private universities and colleges were brought under the jurisdiction of either the central or provincial government by 1952. During this period, missionary-based universities and colleges, which represented the foreign educational presence and influence in China, were regarded as perpetrators of Western cultural imperialism. Thus they were shut down and their academic components were merged into the public universities. For example, Yenching University's College of Arts and College of Sciences were merged to become Peking University; the Department of Education became Beijing Normal University; and the Department of Chemical Engineering became Tianjin University. St. Johns University's Department of Architecture became Tongji University; the medical programs became Shanghai Second Medical College; and engineering departments became Shanghai Jiaotong University.

After all universities and colleges became state-run institutions, the higher education system was then reorganized and restructured according to the Soviet model. The reorganization was based on the belief of the leadership that the higher education system, as one part of the superstructure of the society, should be integrated with the economic base of the country. Since China was engaged in building a socialist, centrally planned economy, it would need to change its higher education system accordingly. Thousands of Soviet experts were sent to China in all fields to assist the country in developing the planned economy. Large numbers of Soviet scholars came to teach at Chinese universities and colleges, and Soviet educational administration specialists provided assistance with structural reforms of universities.

Many Soviet curricula, course syllabi, and textbooks were translated into Chinese and widely disseminated and used in China. As in the Soviet system, the policy objective in China was to bring all higher education institutions under the leadership of the government. National unified instructional plans were implemented at all colleges and universities throughout the country, so that the higher education system would closely serve the manpower needs of a centrally planned economy. Indeed, the reorganization following the Soviet model promoted higher education development in China and contributed to the industrialization and development of the centrally planned economy of the 1950s.

China's adoption of the Soviet model meant that specialized higher education institutions were established and that the Chinese higher education system became more departmentalized and segmented under different central-line ministries. For example, Beijing Agricultural University came under the jurisdiction of the Ministry of Agriculture, Beijing Forestry College under the Ministry of Forestry, Beijing Chemical Engineering College under the Ministry of the Chemical Industry, Beijing Metallurgy College under the Ministry of the Metallurgical Industry, Beijing Geology College under the Ministry of Geology, Beijing College of Mines under the Ministry of the Mining Industry, and so on. There were a total of about sixty ministries in the central government, each operating its own higher education institution. Existing universities and colleges also became more specialized. Some comprehensive universities became specialized engineering institutes, and their schools of arts and schools of sciences were removed. Some comprehensive universities retained their identities—for example, Peking University—although its Agriculture College was moved out to form Beijing Agriculture University and its engineering departments were transferred to other specialized technical institutes.

Along with the Soviet higher education model, the Soviet-oriented research system was also adopted in China with the establishment of the Chinese Academy of Sciences (CAS), which formed an independent national research system with hundreds of research institutes throughout the country. The major research function of the country was carried out by these institutes, which were separate from the Chinese higher education system. Large amounts of research funding went to the CAS instead of to the universities. The institutional structure of the Soviet research model, which separated research from the teaching of young people, significantly reduced the research capacity of Chinese universities, resulting in wastage of scarce human, physical, and financial resources. For example, while Peking University had a strong Department of Mathematics, the CAS established another large institute of mathematical research nearby in Beijing; and while Peking University had a strong Department of Chemistry, the CAS set up a research institute in chemistry next door to the university. Although since the late 1950s many Chinese scholars and professors have recommended closer cooperation between the Chinese universities and the CAS and better integration of teaching and research, the CAS is still functioning independently of the universities. When the CAS received a larger share of national research funding, research universities would get a smaller piece of the pie. The legacy of the Soviet research system has had a very strong impact on the Chinese higher education system, especially in terms of the development and strength of the country's research universities.

Among the far-reaching influences of the Soviet higher education model in China were departmentalization, segmentation, overspecialization, and the separation of teaching from research. These traits shaped the structure of the contemporary Chinese higher education system until the 1990s, even though they were criticized during the late 1950s and attacked during the Cultural Revolution that lasted from 1966 to 1976. They became the main targets of higher education reform during the transition from a centrally planned to a dynamic market economy.

The great leap forward, 1958–1960

With the adoption of the Soviet model, the Chinese government had formulated and implemented the First Five-Year Plan for Economic and Social Development (1953–1957), which formed the basis for a national manpower plan. A higher education development plan was also implemented. Students represented products in a centrally planned economy, and the plan introduced national unified instructional plans, syllabi, and textbooks. It was a very rigid system. In 1958, after the completion of the First Five-Year Plan, the Chinese government launched a nationwide mass movement for economic development—the Great Leap Forward for Socialist Construction. The plan triggered the so-called Great Leap Forward in Higher Education, which lasted approximately three years. The policy objective was to increase significantly the number of universities and colleges and expand higher education enrollments to match the ambitious economic growth plan.

This great leap forward deviated somewhat from the rigid Soviet model. It reflected the impetuosity of the Chinese leadership with regard to economic and educational development but was also a reaction to the regimentation, overspecialization, and fragmentation of knowledge in the Soviet system. During the period, the number of higher education institutions increased from 229 in 1957 to 1,289 in 1960. Within 3 years, more than 1,000 new universities and colleges were established and total enrollments increased from 441,181 to 961,623. Such a dramatic expansion caused many problems for the Chinese higher education system in the 1960s, such as those of low efficiency and quality. These problems, together with the worsening of the Sino-Soviet relationship and serious economic austerity in the country starting in the early 1960s, led to a readjustment of higher education development policy. Accordingly, in 1961 the Ministry of Education cut down the number of higher education institutions and consolidated the newly established small universities and colleges. In three years (1960–1963), the total number of institutions had decreased from 1,289 to 407. From 1963 to 1965, Chinese higher education emerged from the period of hectic expansion and difficult reorganization, and by 1965 both the quality of instruction and institutional efficiency were improved.

The Cultural Revolution

Only a few years after the Chinese higher education system was put on track toward steady and healthy development from 1963 to 1965, the so-called Cultural Revolution broke out in 1966. It was a nationwide political movement that had a profound impact on Chinese higher education. Universities and colleges were attacked as places disseminating ideas that combined Soviet revisionism, Western bourgeois ideologies, and traditional feudalism. The Cultural Revolution negated almost everything in the existing higher education system, including Chinese academic traditions, Western academic influences, and the Soviet academic model. Universities and colleges were stopped from enrolling undergraduate students for more than four years, and no postgraduate students were enrolled for twelve years. The national college entrance examinations were abolished, and many universities and colleges were closed down. After 1970, some higher education institutions started enrolling "worker-peasant-soldier students" based on political criteria with no consideration of academic qualifications. Not only did the quality of instruction deteriorate, student numbers also declined dramatically. Total enrollments decreased from 674,400 in 1965 to 47,800 in 1970. These developments resulted in a serious shortage of well-educated specialized manpower. The reasons for the Cultural Revolution and its policy objectives were political rather than educational. The higher education sector was the most severely afflicted area in the society.

In the thirty-year period from 1949 to 1978, higher education in China was forced to undergo dramatic changes along a tortuous and circuitous path of development. The period included the takeover from the previous authority, nationwide adoption of the Soviet model in the early 1950s; the Great Leap Forward and the educational revolution from 1958 to 1960; retrenchment, readjustment, reorganization, and consolidation from 1961 to 1963; and steady improvement of the system from 1963 to 1965. Finally, this period also included the unprecedented destruction and serious shrinking in size of the higher education system during the so-called Cultural Revolution from 1966 to 1976 and gradual recovery from 1976 to 1978. It is important to note, however, that the overall operational framework of Chinese higher education as of 1979 was still characterized by the central planning model that had been adopted from the Soviets in the early 1950s.

This is the key to understanding the contemporary realities of the reform process that started in the early 1980s.

Issues and realities

From the 1980s up to the beginning of the twenty-first century, Chinese higher education has been characterized by a series of reforms. The economic transition, the fast-growing market economy, the rapid development of science and technology, and the increase in individual income levels and living standards stimulated increasing demands for higher education. Education was considered the strategic foundation for economic success given the growing recognition of the need for well-educated manpower, especially high-level specialized personnel. Priority was given to university development, and the Chinese higher education system has expanded quickly over the past twenty years. Total enrollments at higher education institutions in China rose from about 1 million in the early 1980s to about 13 million in 2001. Obviously, the structure of the old higher education system based on a centrally planned economy could no longer fit in with the new reality. Dramatic changes took place in the higher education sector.

The economic transition in China that began in the 1980s coincided with rapid advancements in science and technology, especially the revolution in information and communications technology, that have led the world into a new age of the knowledge-based economy. As knowledge-based institutions, universities have been called on to play a central role in economic development. Furthermore, the knowledge-based economy is international by nature. Capital, production, management, market, labor, information, and technology are organized across national boundaries, which has resulted in a strong tendency toward globalization. China's entry into the World Trade Organization (WTO) is a part of this process. Cross-cultural interactions, exchanges of students and faculty members, joint teaching and research programs, and academic communications, especially over the Internet, have formed an ongoing and irreversible internationalizing trend in higher education, providing further impetus from the outside world toward Chinese higher education reform.

Structural reforms

While policies for economic transition and openness were being implemented, the structure of Chinese higher education in the early 1980s was basically unchanged from the one that took shape in the context of the centrally planned economy of the 1950s. It was in the context of central planning that the governance and administrative system of Chinese higher education originated and evolved. The central government instituted the national socioeconomic development plan and corresponding manpower plan, according to which the State Planning Commission and the Ministry of Education jointly formulated a higher education development plan that included the number and types of institutions and students needed, student quotas for each sector and each province, the distribution of student enrollments by field of study, and institutional enrollment quotas by discipline and specialty. According to the specific manpower requirements, higher education institutions devised their curricula. Students were usually trained in very narrow specializations. Graduate job assignment plans were designed by the government according to the manpower plan of each central-line ministry and province. The system was highly centralized, and universities, attached to governmental agencies, were simply part of the state-planned system. This centrally planned system continued to function all the way to the mid-1990s. In 1995, among the 358 national-level universities and colleges, 35 belonged to the Ministry of Education (State Education Commission, 1996), and 323 universities and colleges were under the jurisdiction of 61 central-line ministries, such as the Ministry of the Electronics Industry, the Ministry of the Metallurgical Industry, and the Ministry of Agriculture. The higher education system was compartmentalized and segmented in structure. Obviously, such a higher education system based on central planning could not fit in well with the new market economy.

As the economic sector has taken the lead in initiating reforms, dramatic changes have taken place in the human resources sector, which is closely related to higher education. In the newly developed market economy in China, it is market supply and demand rather than government planning that plays the basic role in resource allocation and utilization. The labor market plays the key role in determining human resources development and allocation. In such a system, higher education institutions need to gear their programs to meet the human resources needs of the labor market. This does not mean that all teaching and research should be shaped only by market forces, but it does mean that the human resources requirements for socioeconomic development, as signaled by the labor market, will be of primary importance to universities. The Chinese higher education system, which used to be part of the centrally planned economy, must be reformed.

The labor market now influences the wage structure of graduates by level and type of education, and thus the expected benefits of higher education as well as the demand for higher education opportunities. In terms of labor market performance, the relative competitive advantage of graduates with certain types and levels of education will serve as feedback to the universities. For example, if graduates in a given field are in oversupply, their competitive advantage in the labor market will be reduced. Student demands for this field will decline, and universities will adjust their programs and enrollment policies accordingly. This is exactly what is happening in China today. However, the market is not omnipotent—nor is it a panacea—and market failure also occurs from time to time. Thus, the state still has a very important role to play in this market-oriented environment.

The government uses a number of channels to influence, supervise, and coordinate the higher education system. Government actions range from setting the country's macroeconomic policies that will help to determine labor market needs and employment and wage policies in the public sector defining national priorities and funding relevant educational programs, to developing an accreditation and quality control system for higher education institutions, to establishing a legal infrastructure for both protecting and regulating the operation of colleges and universities.

The process of institutionalizing the new framework of higher education involves changes in governance and administration, the government/university relationship, the legal status of higher education institutions, university autonomy, and the focus on socioeconomic development and labor market demands. Much has been accomplished with regard to these reforms in recent years, and the new framework of higher education is now gradually replacing the old one.

As mentioned earlier, the national-level universities and colleges were under the jurisdiction of the sixty-two different ministries (State Education Commission, 1996), while the provincial universities and colleges belonged to the corresponding provincial-line departments. However, with the development of a market economy, after graduating from a university belonging to a specific line ministry, a student might well find a job in a completely unrelated field through labor market mechanisms. As more and more graduates found their own jobs in the labor market instead of through job assignments handled by the ministry, the manpower plan of the central-line ministries failed. The recent reforms have focused on restructuring the Chinese higher education system through mergers of universities or collaborative arrangements among higher education institutions that breach the existing boundaries between the different ministries.

Between 2000 and 2003, hundreds of universities and colleges were reorganized. For example, Beijing Medical University under the Ministry of Public Health merged with Peking University, which is under the Ministry of Education. Interestingly, until the early 1950s, Beijing Medical University was the medical school of Peking University. The medical university was separated from the comprehensive university and brought under the jurisdiction of the Ministry of Public Health in the 1950s when the Soviet higher education model was adopted. Similarly, in Hangzhou City, Zhejiang Province, Hangzhou University, Zhejiang Agriculture University, and Zhejiang Medical University, under different jurisdictions, were merged into Zhejiang University, which is under the Ministry of Education. Hangzhou University used to be the School of Sciences and Arts of Zhejiang University, Zhenjiang Medical University used to be the medical school of Zhejiang University, and Zhejiang Agricultural University used to be the agricultural school of Zhejiang University. These entities were all separated from Zhejiang University and brought under the jurisdiction of different ministries and departments in the 1950s, under Soviet influence.

Thus, in some cases, the current structural changes are, to a certain extent, a restoration of the university structure that existed before the Soviet model was adopted. From 1993 to 2001, 708 universities and colleges were reorganized into 302 institutions through the elimination of the line ministries' control over higher education institutions in China. The structure of the Chinese higher education system was changed dramatically.

Reforming the curriculum

Changing the modes of teaching and learning is at the core of the reforms. Policies concerning curriculum and instruction evolved since the 1960s following the rationale of the centrally planned economy. This was a system in which students were enrolled, trained, and positioned as products of the centrally planned economy. Higher education was characterized by over-specialization. In the mid-1980s, before the period of reform, higher education in China was divided into more than 1,400 narrow specialties. For example, instead of a general program in mechanical engineering, there were specialties in light industry machinery, heavy industry machinery, chemical industry machinery, public works machinery, petroleum industry machinery, metallurgical industry machinery, agricultural machinery, mining machinery, and so on. Students were usually locked into narrow specializations, with little freedom to decide what to learn in school and what to do after graduation, which restricted their ability to respond to the new realities created by changes in technology and the economy. Even in a centrally planned economy this overspecialization resulted in a wastage of skills and expertise. For example, a survey of one hundred thousand college graduates in the late 1980s showed that more than 40 percent of them held jobs unrelated to their professional training (Guizhou Institute of Educational Research, 1988).

With the transition to a dynamic market economy under way, the rapidly changing needs of the labor market and advancements in science and technology stimulated a call for a more competitive and adaptive labor force. Therefore, it is imperative for China to implement reforms to broaden the specializations of students to increase their flexibility in the labor market. The reforms have emphasized expanding the knowledge base by changing the curriculum. Since the mid-1980s, fields of specialization have been broadened: for example, the overspecialized machinery programs have been folded into a more general mechanical engineering program. Interdisciplinary studies have been encouraged to provide students in the humanities and social sciences with basic knowledge in science, mathematics, and informatics. Likewise, students in science and engineering would acquire basic knowledge in the humanities and social sciences to help them understand how best to put what they learn at school in the service of the development needs of the country. The total number of specialties was reduced from more than 1,400 in the mid-1980s to about 200 in 2003. Further reforms in this direction are still under way. For example, at Peking University in Beijing, experimental classes have been created under the special "Yuanpei programs," in which students are enrolled not in academic departments such as physics, chemistry, or mathematics but rather in the general arts and sciences programs, with a much broader curriculum. After two years of studies in general education programs, students gradually become more focused on specific academic fields. This is a reversal of the overspecialization of the Soviet model.

Curriculum reforms were coupled with reforms in the teaching and learning process. The shift in emphasis went from the memorization of factual knowledge to the cultivation of students' ability in creative and critical thinking, problem solving, information acquisition and generation, and intellectual independence. The economic transition and the knowledge revolution dramatically changed the way of teaching and learning. Reforms in teaching and learning have not only encouraged students to acquire the existing knowledge, they are also encouraged to develop the ability to explore and anticipate what will happen in the future. Thus more heuristic and participatory methods of teaching were adopted. The current understanding in Chinese higher education is that young people should not be trained for short-term jobs but helped to develop the ability to cope with new challenges throughout their lives. Universities should not only educate the younger generation intellectually, but also tend to their moral, physical, and aesthetic development. Graduates should not be viewed simply as products but rather as well-educated members of future generations. These changes represent the mainstream of the current curriculum and instruction reforms in Chinese higher education. However, these reforms are unevenly implemented among different universities and colleges. In the leading national universities, new curricula and teaching and learning approaches were adopted more quickly because of their strong and more qualified faculty and better facilities, while in some of the local colleges in remote areas, reforms proceeded slowly because of inadequate human, physical, and financial resources.

Higher education finance

Stimulated by the soaring societal and individual demand for higher education, Chinese higher education enrollments have expanded rapidly over the past twenty years. However, the increase in state appropriations for higher education could not keep up with the growing costs, leading to serious financial constraints for universities and colleges. Although the cost of salaries and fringe benefits accounted for an increasing share of the total budget, faculty income was still relatively low in the 1980s and 1990s. There also was a shortage of nonsalary funding for the teaching and learning infrastructure, which resulted in understocked laboratories and libraries. Many universities lacked the necessary equipment and funds for upgrading obsolete facilities (Min, 1990). Obviously, without successfully tackling the financial constraints, the Chinese higher education system could not sustain a healthy development and upgrade its quality to meet international standards. Thus systematic reforms in financing higher education were implemented.

An effort was made to change the structure of government spending to benefit education. Despite the increase in state appropriations to higher education since the early 1980s, public expenditure on education in China remains relatively low by international standards. In the late 1990s, China was spending less than 3.5 percent of its gross domestic product (GDP) on education, as compared with an average of 6 percent in developed countries and 4 percent in other developing countries. A decision was made by the central government to increase appropriation to education at all governmental levels at a rate higher than the rate of increase of revenues. Allocations per student and teacher salaries were increased for direct teaching and learning purposes. The central government decided to increase allocations to education by one percent over the previous year continuously for five years between 1999 and 2003. Thus in 2003, the central government's budgetary allotment for education had increased by 5 percent. In the higher education sector, total government spending increased from 54.5 billion RMB yuan (U.S.$6.7 billion) in 1998 to 111.4 billion RMB yuan (U.S.$13.6 billion) in 2001, doubling in three years. Similarly, average teacher salaries increased impressively.

Developing a cost-sharing and cost-recovery system represents another major reform in the financing of higher education. Under the centrally planned economy, the Chinese higher education system did not charge students any tuition. It also provided students with free dormitory housing and stipends for food and other expenses, which amounted to about 20 percent of total recurrent costs. Chinese universities started to charge tuition and fees as one of the strategies to address their financial difficulties, gradually institutionalizing the concept that the expenses of higher education should be paid in part by those who benefit from higher education. At the same time, student loan and scholarship programs have been set up for students from needy families to address the equity issue. This policy became both necessary and feasible because of dramatic changes in national income distribution stemming from the transition in the economy. Along with the increasing willingness and capacity to pay on the part of students and their families, tuition levels gradually rose. At present, more than one-fifth of the total operational budgets of Chinese higher education institutions is covered by tuition and fees. In 2000, of the Chinese higher education system's 98.3 billion RMB yuan (U.S.$12 billion) in total recurrent expenses,

21.7 billion RMB yuan (U.S.$2.64 billion) came from tuition and fees paid by students.

One of the significant changes in financing higher education in China since the mid-1980s has been to allow universities to make use of their human capital resources and capacities in science and technology to generate revenue for themselves. This is one of the promising strategies for increasing the resources devoted to higher education. The revenue generated by universities themselves has increased remarkably since 1985, when higher education institutions were given the autonomy to do so. Universities generated funds through research contracts with industry, technical consulting work with businesses, training and educational services, and fund-raising activities. Many universities established foundations and development offices to seek contributions from alumni, other individuals, and businesses. Some universities, such as Peking University and Tsinghua University, even set up foundations as charitable corporations in the United States.

Chinese universities also generated revenues by incubating spin-off companies. For example, Peking University is home to the largest university-affiliated high-tech company in China—the Founder Corporation—which markets its innovations in computer-laser technology to the newspaper typesetting and publishing industry. In 2002, the company had a business volume of 14.5 billion RMB yuan (U.S.$1.8 billion). Although it was established outside the university structure as an independent legal entity, the Founder Corporation supported the university, providing research funding for the advancement of computer-laser technology and submitting a certain proportion of its net profit as royalties to the university. In recent years, 15 percent of Peking University's operational budget was supplied by its affiliated companies. Chinese universities also secure more and more of their research funding from the proceeds of their business ventures—increasing from 1.4 billion RMB yuan (U.S.$0.25 billion) in 1990 to 17.3 billion RMB yuan (U.S.$2.1 billion) in 2001. In 2000, of the 98.3 billion RMB yuan (U.S.$12 billion) in total recurrent expenditures of the Chinese higher education system, 57 percent came from state appropriations, 22 percent from tuition and fees, and the remaining 21 percent from revenue generated by the universities themselves. At present in China, some universities, such as Peking University and Tsinghua University, generate more than 50 percent of their total revenues.

Universities are also being encouraged to improve institutional management and thereby turn a relatively high-cost system into a more cost-effective one. This change was achieved by the internal reorganization of universities—rearranging small departments, broadening specialties, eliminating duplication in programs—to make more effective use of staff and physical resources. The teacher-to-student ratio was increased from 1:3 in 1983 to 1:16 in 2001. Arrangements were made for institutions or departments to share expensive equipment, faculty, and other resources. One cost-savings approach was to achieve economies of scale by consolidating small institutions into larger ones as well as by breaking down some departmental boundaries, as mentioned earlier (Min, 1991). The average enrollment at Chinese universities and colleges increased from less than two thousand in 1990 to over four thousand in 2001.

Promotion of the private sector

Although public higher education has expanded quickly, the unmet demand for higher education in China is still immense. Enrollments at higher education institutions in China comprised less than 3 percent of the college age cohort in the early 1980s, but that figure had risen to 14 percent by 2002. However, the demand for higher education is rising much faster than the rate of higher education expansion. Constrained by the limited resources available for higher education development, the Chinese government implemented policies to promote private institutions. In August 1993, an important document, the Provisional Stipulations for the Establishment of *Minban* Higher Education Institutions, was issued. *Minban* (non-state-run) universities and colleges are actually private institutions, as defined internationally.

The goal of this policy is to mobilize more resources from the private sector to accelerate higher education development. Since the early 1990s, local private institutions have mushroomed, financed by tuition fees, donations, and income generated by training programs, consultation, and technical services. Initially, Chinese private universities and colleges were usually small in size with flexible curricula. Their generally short-cycle vocational programs served as important complements to the public higher education system. However, the private institutions quickly grew and matured, some becoming very large and competitive. For example, Xi'an International University—a private comprehensive university established in 1992 in Xi'an City, Shaanxi Province—now has ten colleges and 21,000 students, modern teaching facilities that include a satellite digital transmission system, a multimedia computer network, a campus on-line network, a computer center, an audiovisual teaching center, and a considerable number of laboratories. Xi'an International even established international links with universities in the United States, the United Kingdom, Australia, and Canada. Currently, private universities and colleges number 1,202, and enroll 1.13 million students. It is important to note that when China adopted a Soviet-based centrally planned economy in the early 1950s, all private universities and colleges were converted into public institutions. During the transition from a centrally planned to a dynamic market economy, private institutions reemerged and have contributed significantly to the human resource development of the country.

Currently, there are over one thousand private universities and colleges, most with only two- or three-year study programs. To a certain extent, they are the equivalent of community colleges or trade schools in the United States. At present, only about 5 percent of these institutions have been officially accredited by the National Committee for the Establishment of Higher Education Institutions, and their diplomas are recognized by the Ministry of Education. In December 2002 the 31st session of the Standing Committee of the Ninth People's Congress adopted a new law to promote private education in China. This law gives private schools and universities the same legal status as public institutions and guarantees their autonomy. It also stipulates the evaluation procedures and legal guidelines that private institutions must follow. The legislation represents the official recognition that private universities serve the public interests. Private universities and colleges will be expected to grow more quickly, account for an ever larger proportion of higher education enrollments, and play an increasingly significant role in Chinese higher education.

World-class universities

The economic transition has been accompanied by dramatic technological changes. The rapid advancements in science and technology, the knowledge explosion, and the revolution in information technology have transformed the international economy. A country's capacity to generate, accumulate, deploy, and utilize knowledge and information becomes crucial for development. As knowledge-based institutions, universities play a critical role in a country's economic growth and social development. Universities are involved in knowledge generation, processing, dissemination, and application through their teaching, research, and service to industries and communities. Thus, if knowledge is the fuel of the new world economy, universities are one of the engines driving economic development in the twenty-first century (Castells, 1991). The Chinese government has, therefore, formulated policies not only to expand the higher education system but also to upgrade the quality of the leading national universities to world-class status. Increased funding was allocated to selected universities, such as Peking University and Tsinghua University. Special funding was also allocated to some other national universities to help them to upgrade and strengthen specific disciplines and academic programs. The rationale was that limited resources should not be thinly spread out but rather concentrated on some priority institutions or academic programs in selected universities.

As knowledge generators, world-class universities are usually also the leading research institutions. For this reason, the research function has been reemphasized in Chinese universities. In the early 1950s, when the Soviet model was adopted, research was separated from the universities, and the CAS was established to conduct research. Since the 1980s, there has been a growing recognition of the importance of combining teaching and research at universities, especially at the leading national universities with postgraduate programs. Universities were required to be both centers of teaching and centers of research. Integrating teaching and research is considered a major strategy to update curricula and improve instructional quality, as well as enhance research. At universities, both research and publication in international scholarly journals are being promoted as part of the effort to achieve world-class status.

World-class universities also need to establish worldwide contacts. China's implementation of policies of reform and opening up were based on the principle that no country can develop and prosper if it isolates itself from the rest of the world—especially in the information age. For Chinese universities to achieve world-class status, they need to be integrated into the international academic community. As reforms integrated China into the global economic system, Chinese universities also become more internationalized. Approximately 450,000 students and scholars have gone to study abroad in the past twenty years, more and more international academic exchange programs and joint research programs have been set up, and numerous international education conferences and workshops are held each year in China. With the introduction of information technology, especially computer networks such as CERNET (China Education and Research Network), which is interconnected with the Internet, the pace of international communication and collaboration in higher education has accelerated. Internationally oriented programs account for an increasing proportion of the curriculum. These programs—such as international studies, foreign languages, international relations, international economics, international business, international politics, history, and international law—have become very popular at Chinese universities. At the same time, more and more international students are coming to study in China.

To create world-class universities has been the ideal and goal of several generations of Chinese educators over the past one hundred years. When Cai Yuanpei was appointed as the president of Peking University in 1917, he certainly had such a vision in mind. In the current period of higher education reform and development, Chinese educational leaders in both the government and the universities have tried to realize this goal. However, being pragmatic in approach, they are aware that the limited resources mean the system can only afford to lift a small number of universities to world-class status in the near future. Thus, the Chinese Ministry of Education has made it clear that China will initially seek to promote fewer than ten universities in their struggle to reach world-class status, with top priority going to Peking University and Tsinghua University. It is expected that these leading Chinese universities will be able to serve as locomotives to help raise the standards of the higher education system as a whole in China.

Enhancing faculty development

Faculty are key to reforming the curriculum and the teaching and learning process, as well as to upgrading Chinese universities to world-class status. Great efforts have thus been made to strengthen the faculty. Of the 1.45 million employees in Chinese higher education, about 554,000 are faculty members. In general, the academic profession is well respected in traditional Chinese culture. However, the prestige of university teachers was destroyed in the mid-1960s during the so-called Cultural Revolution.

From the 1970s to the 1990s, the incomes of faculty members were relatively low. While basic salaries of university faculty were comparable to those of other professionals with similar educational qualifications, faculty remuneration was lower because of larger bonuses given to employees in companies, especially in joint venture firms. The government and universities have sought to raise faculty prestige and income with additional state appropriations and revenue generated by the universities themselves. From 1998 to 2001, the average annual income of university teachers in China doubled, going from 12,000 RMB yuan (U.S.$1,500) to 24,000 RMB yuan (U.S.$3,000)—an increase that raised faculty salaries above the average income levels in the country. The government also spent 114.4 billion RMB yuan (U.S.$14.3 billion) to improve teachers' living conditions. Fifteen billion square feet of new faculty housing was built between 1994 and 2001 (Li, 2002). At present, the morale of university teachers is high in China, and the academic profession has become an attractive occupation for young scholars.

Currently, the Chinese higher education system is composed of full professors, (9.5 percent), associate professors (30.3 percent), lecturers (35.2 percent), assistant teachers (19.1 percent), and instructors (6 percent). (Lecturers are the equivalent of assistant professors in the U.S. system; assistant teachers are the equivalent of teaching assistants, but they are also full-time employees of the university.) At some of the leading national research-oriented universities, senior faculty members account for a much larger proportion of the total. For example, at Peking University, senior faculty members including both professors and associate professors account for more than 70 percent of the total faculty. Among faculty members, 46.4 percent are below the age of 35 years, showing the effect of recent heavy recruitment of faculty due to the rapid expansion of higher education. About 39.8 percent of faculty members are between 36 and 50 years of age and about 11.4 percent between 51 and 60. This latter age group is also relatively small, showing the generational gap of quality faculty that occurred as a result of the destruction of higher education during the Cultural Revolution. Because the retirement age for lecturers and associate professors is about 60 and for full professors about 63, only 2.2 percent of faculty are over age 61. Female faculty account for an increasing proportion of faculty in China, increasing from 10 percent in 1950 to almost 40 percent in 2001 (Ministry of Education, 2002).

Traditionally, faculty members were trained mainly at domestic higher education institutions, especially at national universities with graduate programs. Since China did not have an academic degree system until the 1980s, only about 30 percent of all faculty members hold postgraduate degrees. Along with the implementation of reforms and open-door policies, many internationally trained scholars with advanced degrees joined the university teaching force, which improved the quality of faculty and enhanced the international links with the world academic community. As part of the current higher education reform, more faculty members have been sent abroad for advanced studies. Chinese university faculty have increased their international links through academic exchange programs, international conferences, study tours, and joint research projects with foreign colleagues and international academic and professional organizations. These activities play an important role in improving Chinese scholarship and in enabling Chinese scholars to contribute to academic development internationally.

Trends and challenges

Chinese universities have undergone rapid expansion and dramatic changes. Enrollments have increased quickly. In 1998, about 1.08 million new students were admitted to universities and colleges, while in 2002 that number had increased to 3.49 million. It is anticipated that by 2005 total enrollments will reach 15 million and that the enrollment rate will exceed 15 percent of the college age cohort (Chen, 2002a). According to demographic projections, the college-age population will continue to grow quickly, reaching its peak in 2008. As a result, higher education will continue to face great pressure to expand, driven by the fast-growing economy, the rapid rise in family income and living standards, and the huge unmet demand from the 85 percent of college-age young people who currently are not enrolled in higher education institutions. This ongoing trend will lead to a series of challenges for the Chinese higher education system.

Maintaining and improving quality

The quality of higher education is always a major issue almost everywhere in the world, and Chinese higher education is no exception. Some of the leading national research universities that did not overexpand enrollments paid sufficient attention to improving quality while marching toward world-class status. Thus their quality level in both teaching and research was raised. However, the quality of many local universities and colleges was negatively affected by the rapid expansion of enrollments and overcrowding, which has made it difficult to sustain quality inputs such as the number of qualified faculty and staff, curriculum development and program upgrading, laboratory facilities, and library books. If these issues are not addressed properly, the quality of Chinese universities could deteriorate.

It is imperative for China to enhance supervision and quality assurance of higher education institutions, especially with regard to the accreditation and regulation of the newly mushrooming private universities and colleges. Since faculty quality is the key to quality education, serious measures need to be taken to improve and enhance faculty development. During the rapid expansion, large numbers of teachers were recruited and promoted. Some of them were short on academic qualifications and teaching experience, and some of the older generation of teachers were held back by social changes and unable to keep up with the rapid advances in science and technology. Thus, one of the challenges for Chinese universities is to develop in-service training programs to allow faculty members to improve their teaching skills and update their knowledge. Another task is to set stricter academic standards for faculty appointments and promotions and to attract capable young academics to join the university teaching force. A project entitled "Enhancing Higher Education Quality" was initiated by the Department of Higher Education in the Ministry of Education and was implemented in 2003 as part of a major effort to tackle quality problems in Chinese higher education.

China is a large country with a huge higher education system consisting of more than three thousand institutions; quality levels vary across institutions. The Chinese government has adopted various policies that gave priority support to certain key national universities. For example, the "211 Higher Education Project" initiated in 1995 gave additional special funding to one hundred selected universities. The "985 World-Class University Project," which was initiated in May 1998 during the centennial celebration of Peking University, gave more concentrated support to a smaller number of national universities to upgrade their academic levels to world-class status. As a result, higher education institutions in the future will be more differentiated, with a few national research universities at the top. The leading national universities should function as national "centers of excellence." They are expected to serve as the engines that drive the whole Chinese higher education system to a higher level. It will be a challenge for these key institutions to upgrade themselves and at the same time help to improve the quality of local institutions.

Regional disparities

The Chinese economy has grown rapidly over the past 20 years, but the rate has varied greatly among different provinces across the country. For example, in 1980 the per capita GDP in Shanghai was 2,738 RMB yuan (U.S.$1,190), while in Guizhou it was only 219 RMB yuan (U.S.$95). By

2001, Shanghai's per capita GDP had risen to 37,382 RMB yuan (U.S.$4,600) and was 12 times higher than that of Guizhou.

The increasing regional economic disparities were accompanied by regional disparities in higher education. For example, in 2001, for every 10,000 people in the population 169 were registered higher education students in Beijing; 112 in Shanghai; and 12 and 17 in Guizhou and Qinghai, respectively. The unmet demand for higher education in the underdeveloped provinces was huge. For example, in 2000, only about one-fourth of the young people who applied to higher education institutions and took the entrance examinations were admitted in some of the poorer provinces. Not only was the difference in quantity large, the difference in quality was even more significant. All the top-ranking national universities—such as Peking University, Tsinghua University, Fudan University, Shanghai Jiaotong University, Nanjing University, and Zhejiang University—are located in the economically more developed provinces and municipalities, while the less-developed provinces of Guizhou, Qinghai, Xinjiang, Henan, and Shanxi have no key national universities. The uneven development and growing regional disparities in higher education have become critical issues and have attracted the attention of the national leadership. One of the policies instituted gave high priority to developing the western part of the country. Each of the leading national universities in the more developed areas was required to twin with a university in a less-developed province and to provide substantial support to the provincial university. The assistance included helping them with respect to increased enrollment capacity, curriculum development, donation of equipment, and faculty development. To improve university management the national universities sent capable administrators and teachers to the twinned campuses and brought teachers and administrators from the provinces back to the universities in the developed areas for further training and upgrading. For example, Peking University sent an excellent administrator to its twinned university, the Xinjiang Shihezi University, to serve as vice-president, as well as providing teachers and equipment. These university-twinning programs have been in existence for two years and have been effective in reducing the regional disparity in higher education. However, given the very nature of the decentralized market economy, the uneven growth in GDP among different provinces, and the corresponding decentralized financial system—which was called "each province cooks its dinner on its own stove"—regional disparities will remain as one of the major challenges facing China.

Changing patterns of access

In China, the distribution of higher education opportunities and public investment in higher education used to be very unequal among different social groups. These inequities have lessened with the economic reforms and development and the expansion of higher education enrollments. For example, according to the 1991 City and Township Household Survey, college-age young people from the poorest 20 percent of households accounted for only 2.3 percent of higher education enrollments in China, while those from the richest 20 percent of households accounted for 55.6 percent of higher education enrollments. The enrollment rate for the highest-income families was 24 times higher than that of the lowest-income families. During the 1990s, access patterns changed for the better. In 2000, college-age young people from the poorest 20 percent of households accounted for 9.5 percent of total higher education enrollments in China, a significant increase from 10 years earlier. Students from the richest 20 percent of households accounted for 30.1 percent of higher education enrollments, a 25.8 percent reduction since 1991 (Ding, 2003).

In 2001, female students accounted for 42 percent of total enrollments, a higher percentage than before. The improved access is one result of the expansion of higher education, as well as the introduction of financial aid programs for students from low-income families. For example, in 2002, the Ministry of Education and the Ministry of Finance initiated a new national scholarship program with an annual allocation of 200 million RMB yuan (U.S.$25 million) that provides outstanding students from low-income families with stipends for living expenses. The program also stipulates that scholarship recipients should receive tuition exemptions from their universities.

Although access to higher education has improved to a certain extent, it remains a serious challenge for China. In 2000, the enrollment rate for the 20 percent of highest-income families was still three times higher than that for the lowest-income families. Furthermore, since the higher education system is becoming increasingly differentiated, more college-age young people from higher-income families are likely to attend the leading national universities than those from lower-income families, which creates equity issues within the system. This is another kind of access issue that China will need to tackle in the near future.

The employment of graduates

Before the 1980s, university and college graduates in China were treated like products of the centrally planned economy. They were assigned jobs upon graduation by the government, which determined where they should go and what they should do, in a top-down process. With the economic transition, the occupational prospects of graduates were shaped by the labor market. With the government no longer responsible for job assignments, graduates have to find jobs on their own. To do so, they must respond to the needs of a rapidly changing labor market. The rapid expansion of the higher education system meant that more than 3 million university students graduate each year—more than the labor market can absorb at once. Recently, it has become difficult for some students to find jobs upon graduation, especially those from local colleges and from overspecialized colleges—some of which are holdovers from the centrally planned economy. Unemployment will become a more serious issue in years to come as more young people graduate from universities.

The issue is mainly structural in origin. Among current higher education institutions, a large proportion still have highly specialized curricula. The students are locked into specialized fields, which makes them less flexible and adaptive to technologically induced changes in the workplace and to labor market needs in a rapidly changing economy. The result is often a mismatch between narrowly trained graduates and the manpower needs of the labor market. University graduates prefer to seek employment in large cities or the coastal regions, even though the job market is relatively tight, avoiding the remote areas in the interior that have a serious shortage of university graduates. To tackle the issue of unemployed graduates will require broadening fields of study, thereby increasing students' flexibility and adaptability. Universities will also need to establish closer links with industries and other sectors of society, as well as developing better communication and interaction between students and potential employers. More autonomy should be given to higher education institutions to adjust their enrollment patterns so as to reduce the mismatch between the supply and demand of university graduates.

Consolidating the reforms

Chinese universities have just undergone a dramatic reform process. Restructuring higher education required eliminating excessive government control over institutions and granting universities more autonomy in the management of programs and resources (Communist Party, 1985). The ongoing challenge will be to deepen the reforms and consolidate and institutionalize the implemented changes. Extending greater autonomy and decision-making power to universities and colleges will make them more innovative, creative, and responsive in the development process. Another crucial strategy is to continue to multiply and diversify the sources for financing higher education. The structure of higher education needs to be differentiated by levels and fields of learning so that the system is better able to meet the country's social and economic needs. Another area requiring comprehensive reform concerns the faculty in the areas of appointments, promotions, professional development, and the introduction of more effective incentive mechanisms. The establishment and development of private universities should continue to be encouraged, and more effectively monitored, to expand the provision of higher education. Finally, it is imperative to construct and enact a legal infrastructure to better protect and regulate universities and colleges, while increasing institutional autonomy.

Facing the challenge of the WTO

China's entry into the WTO will definitely have a strong impact on both the economy and the higher education system, bringing both opportunities and challenges. With the further opening up of the economy, the country will become more integrated into the global marketplace and face increased competition. Thus, Chinese universities need to produce a more qualified labor force in order to enhance the country's economic competitiveness.

Chinese universities will also be facing increased competition. In keeping with the educational commitments China made to the WTO, no restrictions will be placed on foreign countries' recruitment of Chinese students to study abroad, and foreign universities will be allowed to operate in China with Chinese partners. There will be more students and teachers flowing across national borders (Chen, 2002b). As a result, more high-quality Chinese students and teachers might be attracted to foreign countries or to foreign universities operating in China. It should also be noted that with the entry of more foreign companies into China, more high-level Chinese professionals may decide to leave the academic profession for higher-paying positions in corporations. Western thought patterns, values, and belief systems will accompany international trade and investment, resulting in new challenges for traditional Chinese values in education. China's entry into the WTO will further strengthen the trend toward internationalization in Chinese higher education. How to become an integral part of the international higher education community and at the same time keep their own cultural identity will also be a challenge for Chinese universities in the years to come.

Conclusion

The current reforms and future trends within Chinese higher education are the logical and inexorable consequences of the past. Just as the future will be shaped by current reforms and developments, the reforms since the late 1970s were the inevitable and logical responses to the failure of the centrally planned system adopted from the Soviet Union in the 1950s. The adoption of the Soviet model grew out of the international social, economic, and political context surrounding the founding of the People's Republic. It also should be understood that the Soviet model of higher education was implanted in China on a foundation built on several thousand years of Chinese cultural and educational tradition and more than a hundred years of Western higher education influence.

Recognizing the dysfunctional nature of the Soviet system and the changing international environment, in the early 1980s China made the historic choice to implement new reform policies and to open up to the outside world. The reforms have lasted for more than twenty years, leading China into the twenty-first century with the new characteristics and challenges discussed in this chapter. Some of these reforms and reorganizations are simply a restoration of the Western-influenced university model that pre-dated the introduction of the Soviet system—such as the merger of Beijing Medical University back into Peking University and the consolidation of four universities into the new Zhejiang University. Some of the reforms are innovations generated by the demands of the current domestic and international context. It takes a dynamic perspective to understand current developments in Chinese higher education and the system's historical roots.

References

Castells, Manuel. (1991, June 30). "University system: Engine of development in the new world economy." Paper presented at the Worldwide Policy Seminar on Higher Education Development in Developing Countries, Kuala Lumpur, Malaysia.

Chen, Zhili. (2002a, October 17). Historical accomplishments in education reform and development (in Chinese). *China Education Daily*, 1–3.

Chen, Zhili. (2002b, January 9). The impact of WTO on Chinese education and research strategies (in Chinese). *China Education Daily*, 2.

Communist Party of China, Central Committee. (1985). *Decision on educational reform* (in Chinese). Beijing: Beijing Foreign Language Press.

Ding, Xiaohao. (2003, February 7). "An examination on higher education equalities in China." Paper presented at the International Conference on Chinese Education, Teachers College, Columbia University.

Guizhou Institute of Educational Research. (1988). *Investigation of the effectiveness of the Guizhou education system* (in Chinese). Guiyang City, China: Author.

Hayhoe, R. (1989). China's universities and Western university models. In P. G. Altbach & V. Selvaratnam (Eds.), *From dependence to autonomy: The development of Asian universities* (pp. 25–61). Dordrecht, Netherlands: Kluwer Academic.

Li, Lanqing. (2002, May 10). "Implementing strategics of developing China through science and education and promoting higher education reform and development" (in Chinese). Paper presented at the National Conference for Educational Awards, Beijing.

Min, Weifang. (1990, October). The mode of expansion and cost-effectiveness of Chinese higher education (in Chinese). *Educational Research*, *129*, 39–49.

Min, Weifang. (1991). Higher education finance in China: Current constraints and strategies in the 1990s. *Higher Education*, *21*, 151–161.

Ministry of Education. (2002). *Statistical yearbook of Chinese education 2002* (in Chinese). Beijing: People's Education Press.

State Education Commission. (1996). *Statistical yearbook of Chinese education, 1995* (in Chinese). Beijing: People's Education Press.

Wang, B. *et al.* (1994). *Introduction to the history of Chinese education*. Beijing: Beijing Normal University Press.

27

JAPANESE HIGHER EDUCATION

Contemporary reform and the influence of tradition

Motohisa Kaneko

Source: P. G. Altbach and Toru Umakoshi (eds) *Asian Universities: Historical Perspectives and Contemporary Challenges*, Baltimore: Johns Hopkins University Press, 2004, pp. 115–43.

While Japan narrowly escaped colonization, it had to build a modern nation strong enough to survive in a world dominated by Western imperialism. To do so, it had to introduce Western technologies and institutions in every sphere of society. Higher education was one of the critical areas on which the growth of the nation depended.

Initially, the government introduced Western models of higher education through trial and error. These early developments gradually led to growing popular demand for higher education, requiring the government to modify the system and eventually deviate from Western models. After World War II, Japan introduced various aspects of the American model, which later underwent considerable transformation during the years of expansion. The selective introduction of Western models and their adaptation through dynamic interactions between market forces and government policies have been the leitmotif throughout Japanese higher education history. In the twenty-first century, Japanese higher education appears to be entering a new phase—probably with yet another variation of the leitmotif.

Where did those dynamics originate and how did they evolve over time? What are the consequences of such a pattern of development, and what are the future challenges in the twenty-first century? How can Japan respond to those challenges? These questions, which the Japanese are asking themselves, form the focus of this chapter.

Table 1 Phases of Development in Japanese Higher Education.

1870	Institutional buildup
	Early institutions of higher education University of Tokyo (1877) Imperial University of Tokyo (1886)
1910	System integration
	1918 higher education law Establishment of private universities Two-sector, two-tier system Expansion of enrollments
1950	Postwar reform and massification
	Postwar education reform New universities (1947) Rapid expansion of enrollments (1960–1975) Stabilization Current cost subsidy for private institutions (1976)
1990	Structural reforms

Historical perspectives

The history of Japanese higher education spans over 130 years and can roughly be divided into three periods: institutional buildup, system integration, and postwar reform and massification—each covering about forty years. (See Table 1.)

Institutional buildup

Prior to the Meiji Restoration, the history of higher education in Japan had been long but thin. Institutions of higher learning existed for religious or administrative leaders, but their size and scope of learning were limited. Moreover, Japan did not develop a mandarin class as in China or Korea that would have required some form of advanced learning. In the early nineteenth century, popular demand for education started to rise among lower-class Samurai and the emerging urban merchant and artisan class. In response, various types of schools began proliferating from lower to advanced levels, raising the literacy rate substantially. However, most of the schools were small and lacked systemic links between the lower levels and higher education. Lacking the modern institutions to organize the latent demand into a national education system encompassing basic to advanced levels, Japan would have to wait until the Meiji Restoration.

After the Meiji Restoration of 1868, the new government introduced modern social institutions in Japan. The earliest design of the education system resembled that of France, where "university" signified not only a higher learning institution but also the whole national school system. Thus, the early University of Tokyo was designed not only as a place of higher learning but also as the administrative body for the national education system. The highly structured model of public education must have appealed to the leaders of the fledgling nation. In a development closely resembling the French *grandes écoles*, a number of government departments established their own ministerial schools for advanced and specialized studies: the Ministry of Law, for example, had its own law school, and the Ministry of Industries had its college of engineering.

After ten years of trial and error, however, this model was basically abandoned. The Napoleonic model of public education was too rigid to allow for the gradual implementation of a system of education. In higher education, it proved to be more efficient to consolidate the places of advanced learning into a single institution. The University of Tokyo was reestablished in 1877 as the central institution for advanced learning, and the early ministerial specialized schools were gradually integrated into this newly established university.

How this new university should be managed was not a trivial question. The government naturally tried to control it as an administrative unit of the Ministry of Education. At the university, however, academics started demanding autonomy as a number of them returned from studying in Germany, bringing along the idea of academic autonomy. It should be noted that in the latter half of the nineteenth century the German model strongly influenced higher education reform in France and in the United States. Moreover, it also became evident that the government could not closely control specialized teaching and research. Greater autonomy was gradually given to the university (Terasaki, 1979). In 1886, the University of Tokyo was reorganized into the Imperial University of Tokyo and positioned as the center for learning and research, with a substantial degree of autonomy given to the institution as a whole and to the professors. Nevertheless, this did not completely follow the German model. In contrast to German universities, which consistently resisted the pressure to incorporate practical subjects, the Imperial University had a College of Engineering as one of its original five colleges and soon added a College of Agriculture (Ben-David, 1977). In this respect, Japan adopted forms common to Scottish and American universities (Nakayama, 1989).

Besides the Imperial University—the center of academic research and learning—other types of schools were established for training the midlevel professional workforce. These institutions were focused on providing technical education that could be attained in a relatively short period, and at lower cost, than was possible at the university. Unlike the university, these specialized schools did not require students to have advanced ability in foreign languages, for all the instruction took place in Japanese. These schools constituted one of the significant segments of the prewar higher education system.

Significant numbers of educational institutions were established not by the government but rather by groups of citizens, teachers, or missionaries. Prominent institutions included Keio, founded by a leading social activist and author; Waseda, founded by political leaders and journalists; and Doshisha, founded by a Christian missionary. Some of these private institutions had high academic standards and called themselves universities. However, they were only given the legal status of specialized schools by the Meiji government, whose policy was to dominate institutions of higher learning and research.

System integration

By the beginning of the twentieth century, after the stage of institutional buildup, Japan had embarked on an initial stage of economic growth. By World War I, the national school system had nearly been established and primary education almost universalized. Enrollment at secondary schools had increased, and the demand for access to higher education started expanding. Meanwhile, the government increased the number of specialized schools as a means of supplying a technical workforce with fewer resources and less time than would be the case through the university. Private bodies also established specialized schools to meet the increasing demands for higher education. By the turn of the century, the entrance and graduation requirements of specialized schools had been standardized.

Against this background, during World War I the government organized a blue-ribbon council to discuss basic reforms in education. Various changes were later put into effect. Most important, from the perspective of higher education, was the 1918 higher education law, which allowed private foundations to establish universities. The private university was thus granted legitimacy as a formal sector of the higher education system.

Through these reforms, higher education in Japan became a two-sector, two-tier system. The two sectors consisted of the national (public) and private sectors. The two tiers consisted of universities, which required three years of preparatory education at "higher schools" after completing secondary school, and specialized schools, which admitted students directly from secondary school. With a few modifications, this structure characterized the pre–World War II higher education system. Amano argues that the two-tier and two-sector system in the prewar period eventually provided the basis for massification in the postwar period (Amano, 1986).

With this framework in place, higher education in Japan kept growing up until World War II. The number of imperial universities increased to seven, and the system included a substantial number of national colleges with university status. There were also a number of private universities. By 1940, the number of universities had increased to 47, with an enrollment of almost 82,000 students. Specialized schools, both public and private, had increased in number to 200 by 1940, enrolling some 141,000 students. Japanese higher education was already on the threshold of the mass stage of higher education.

Postwar reform and massification

After Japan's defeat in World War II, the Japanese education system was transformed drastically under U.S. occupation. The prewar school system that was divided into academic and vocational tracks, beyond the primary level, was transformed into a single-track system following a 6-3-3-4 sequence. This change removed a significant institutional barrier to meeting the demand for higher education. As a result of the integration of the two tiers, the universities' preparatory schools (higher schools) and many high-quality specialized schools were transformed into new universities. It was through this process that the number of universities increased substantially, thus creating the basis for expansion from the supply side.

The government faced serious difficulties, however, in securing the necessary financial resources in a devastated economy. The highest policy priority was directed toward consolidating the new national universities. To secure enough resources, financing the national institutions was integrated into the national budget. Financial autonomy given to the prewar imperial universities was curtailed through this process. For their part, meanwhile, private institutions were left without public support.

Toward the end of the 1950s, the economy began showing signs of a steady recovery, eventually accelerating the pace of growth into the 1960s. Rising income levels and expectations for future expansion of employment resulted in an unprecedented increase in popular demand for higher education. On the supply side, government policies concentrated the limited resources available for higher education on qualitative upgrading of the national universities and colleges, rather than on their quantitative increase. The frustrated demand arising from this gap had to be satisfied by expanding enrollments in the private sector of higher education. By the end of the 1960s, the private sector accounted for three-quarters of total enrollments. Total enrollments at four- and two-year institutions increased from 708,000 in 1960 to 2,086,000 in 1975, representing almost a 3-fold growth in just fifteen years. Over the same period, the participation rate increased from 8.2 percent to 27.1 percent. Japan thus jumped from the elite to the mass stage of higher education.

By the mid-1970s, the explosive expansion came to an end, reflecting partly a deceleration in economic growth and partly a shift in higher education policy. At the same time, the government set up "specialized training schools" as a new type of institution in postsecondary education. During the 1980s, many private proprietary schools were converted to this type of school. In the 1990s, participation in four-year institutions increased again primarily due to the shrinking excess demand arising from the decline of eighteen-year-olds.

Today, the level of participation in Japanese higher education ranks among the highest in the world. In 2002, 39 percent of eighteen-year-olds entered four-year institutions of higher education. If enrollments at two-year junior colleges and specialized training schools are included, more than 60 percent of the college age cohort received some kind of education beyond senior secondary school. Private institutions constitute by far the largest segment, accounting for more than 70 percent of undergraduates at four-year institutions and 91 percent at two-year institutions. About one hundred national universities, while enrolling a quarter of undergraduate students, play significant roles in research and graduate education. The remaining 3 percent of undergraduates are enrolled in municipal, or local, public institutions.

The dynamics of development

The history briefly sketched above is characterized by the dynamic interaction between market forces and the higher education system as a social institution. The dynamics can be analyzed in terms of the interaction between the demand and supply of higher education, the strategy of the government, and the formation of boundary and internal differentiation of the higher education system.

Demand-supply interaction

The development of higher education can be interpreted as the product of the dynamic interaction between supply and demand of higher education in the social and economic contexts. In most European countries, the supply and demand for higher education expanded only gradually. In its long history since the Middle Ages, higher education started expanding only in the latter half of the nineteenth century in close relationship with the growth of industries and the power of modern states. At the time the West was experiencing the first wave of modern expansion, Japan introduced its first institutions of higher education.

When it was introduced, higher education was a completely alien institution in Japan—the values of Western knowledge, and the benefit to individuals, were still unclear to most of the population. Higher education was not necessarily an obvious choice among the wealthy urban merchants or landlords. It was rather among the lower-class samurai, who had lost their traditional status and jobs, that aspirations for higher education started to grow.

As modernization progressed, however, higher education rapidly became an attractive alternative for ambitious young persons. Modernization in Japan implied the creation of a small island of the modern sector that promised high wages and good working conditions in the vast ocean of low-productivity agriculture. Given the disparity, competition over employment in the modern sector became increasingly intense. Moreover, Japan as a latecomer to industrialization was able to import modern industrial organization and technology as a complete set, which could be effectively taught in schools. Under these circumstances, recruitment of employees in the modern sector was closely linked to the requisite educational background. The benefits of higher education in Japan thus exceeded those experienced in the West at a corresponding stage of development, creating aspirations, or even a "fever," for higher education. This is what Ronald Dore (1976) called the "late development effect."

As the rising popular demand for higher education gained momentum, political pressure to expand opportunities for higher education mounted. In response, in the 1910s, the government finally ushered in the educational reforms mentioned earlier. Nonetheless, the extent of the demand for higher education was constrained by the small size of the middle class with sufficient resources.

After World War II, postwar reforms and economic development introduced significant changes in Japan. The renewed ideal of democracy, together with the decline of the prewar urban middle class and landlord class due to hyperinflation and land reform, produced a society much more egalitarian in ideology and in actual income distribution. Moreover, the steady growth in family income in the 1960s allowed more families to have sufficient financial capacities to send their children to institutions of higher education. Hence, for a large proportion of the population a middle-class lifestyle, including white-collar occupations and higher education, became something obtainable for the children. It was also expected that the demand for college graduates would grow in subsequent years. These factors combined to induce the phenomenal expansion in popular demand for higher education.

The government, preoccupied with the need for qualitative improvement, was reluctant to allow for the expansion of supply. Popular demand for more places in higher education, however, eventually won the political battle. At the beginning of the 1960s, the then ruling Liberal Democratic Party opted for a less stringent policy on the expansion of private institutions (Pempel, 1978). That induced a tremendous proliferation of private institutions and rising enrollments in the private sector. Private institutions responded to this change quickly. Many existing universities added new faculties and acted to increase their "prescribed size of enrollment," even admitting students beyond the set limit, to gain financial stability. Numerous new institutions were established, and they eventually followed the same pattern as the older ones. The private sector of higher education thus achieved a tremendous quantitative expansion, but that induced sharp qualitative disparities between the public and the private sectors. Against this background, the government implemented a series of policies around 1975, basically reversing the laissez-faire policy of the previous fifteen years. It introduced the "current cost subsidy to private institutions," which allowed the government to subsidize a portion of current costs at private institutions. At the same time, the government moved to restrain the expansion of private institutions. These measures were expected to improve educational conditions at private institutions and to diminish the disparity between national and private institutions.

Since 1975, the participation rate at four-year universities showed a slight decline for males and unchanging numbers for females. These trends were due in part to the stagnating demand for higher education and in part to the government policy of limiting the supply of places in universities. The policy of reducing enrollments at four-year institutions was compensated by the introduction of special training schools, which the government established to provide vocational training for two or three years after high school. The special training schools soon attracted a substantial number of students, enrolling almost 30 percent of high school graduates. In the 1990s, the enrollment rate at four-year institutions started increasing again.

During this period, the changes in the demand for higher education constituted the major driving force. Higher education policies dealt mainly with the problem of how to respond to the demands. The effectiveness of government policies lay in its ability to restrain or allow the private sector to respond to the demands.

The government and the market

The developments described above created the basic landscape of Japanese higher education: a large private sector enrolling three-quarters of undergraduate students. This situation, however, created a strain between the government and private institutions.

While the concept of *private* institutions of higher education was evidently influenced by the American system, it was at the same time deeply rooted in the power structure of Meiji Japan. The Meiji regime, as a confederation of old feudal states, won the downfall of the Tokugawa Shogunate militarily to acquire power and tax revenues; it justified its power as the agent for building a modern nation strong enough to compete against the West. Nonetheless, there was a sizable middle class of landowners and urban merchants that were excluded from the social networks dominated by the Meiji government, and this group had considerable wealth, influence, and intellectual capital. Moreover, the ideology of democracy had a significant impact on the society. Despite its popular image as a powerful monolithic state dominated by the military and the bureaucracy, the Meiji regime had to be responsive to the demands from various segments of the society.

The national education system was not only the means of introducing modern culture and technology, but also a way of integrating the whole nation and consolidating the power of the government. The University of Tokyo, later the Imperial University, was put at the apex of this system to attract talented young people who would, with their critical skills and knowledge for nation building, serve the state and the government. Meanwhile, a few private institutions had a substantial pool of talent and supporters among the urban middle class, landlords, and political dissidents. Some other private institutions served a large number of students who wanted more accessible opportunities for higher education. Whereas government policy was to restrict the title of "university" to those established by the government, political support for private institutions remained substantial.

Naturally, the dual structure including both public and private sectors engendered serious conflicts. The complexity of the relationship between the government and private institutions can be seen in some of the newspaper articles in the early Meiji period concerning tuition levels at the national institutions of higher education (Kaneko, 1992). Supporters of private institutions denounced the unequal treatment of national and private institutions and demanded subsidies for private institutions as well as an increase in the tuition at the national institutions. To this, a person on the government side stated candidly: "if the tuition levels are raised, the applicants to national institutions will decrease, which implies that the pool from which to choose talented young people will shrink" (Editorial, 1989). The national institutions and the private ones were indeed competing not only for government resources but also for talented applicants.

The system integration achieved by the 1918 higher education law can be seen as a major compromise between these two forces. After the law was enacted, the government raised the tuition level at national universities, thus allowing the private universities to raise tuition rates and secure enough revenue. In very subtle ways, the government had sought a political balance between the national and private sectors.

After World War II, the legal authority of the government over private institutions was curtailed substantially under a new Constitution that extolled freedom of speech and belief. Even though the education law stipulated that private schools, as a part of the national education system, be under the jurisdiction of the Ministry of Education, it was practically impossible for the ministry to regulate any private university. The only avenue left for the ministry was the "establishment permission" process by which each new institution was assigned a prescribed enrollment size based on the "university establishment standards" that specified necessary educational standards concerning teaching staff, facilities, and curriculum. Existing institutions were also required to go through this process whenever they wished to add faculty or increase their prescribed enrollment size. Even though the ministry was deprived of the legal power to penalize institutions that admitted students beyond their prescribed enrollment size, the institutions with excessive enrollment would face difficulties if they were to go through the establishment permission process for expansion. Since private institutions, especially the newer ones, constantly tried to expand their enrollments in order to gain financial stability, this process worked effectively as a way of putting the behavior of private institutions under the control of the Ministry of Education.

In fact, the enormous expansion of the private sector in the 1960s took place after the Ministry of Education, under mounting political pressure, issued an ordinance to the effect that some of the requirements in the establishment permission process could be applied more leniently than before. Following this subtle procedural change, the enormous expansion took place and the ministry lost practical control over the size of enrollments and the quality of education. For the next fifteen years, the private sector kept expanding.

After the rapid economic growth of the 1970s, Japanese society shifted its attention toward social and individual well-being, and government policies headed in the direction of a "welfare society." At the same time, the negative consequences of the demand-led expansion in the 1960s were exposed and, as the campus disputes erupted around 1970, caught the attention of the public and the political parties.

Under these circumstances, government subsidy to private institutions was subsequently formalized in 1975 as the current cost subsidy of private institutions. The current cost subsidy was introduced initially to alleviate strained financial conditions at many private institutions after campus strife, making it possible for private institutions to raise tuition. However, by the end of the 1970s, the subsidy accounted for a quarter of the revenues at private institutions. At the same time, the government initiated the policy of gradually expanding the national universities and colleges in regional areas and beginning to establish "new concept" universities. If these policies had continued, the role of government contributions to higher education finance would have substantially expanded, eventually altering one of the basic characteristics of Japanese higher education. By the end of the 1970s, however, the fiscal conditions had deteriorated due to the accumulating deficit, forcing the government to cut back its expenditures.

The current cost subsidy significantly changed the relationship between the government and the private sector. Even though there was no explicit legal action, introduction of the subsidy led to the understanding that the establishment of new institutions could be constrained on the grounds of fiscal condition. Moreover, the current cost subsidy was based on a formula according to which exceeding the prescribed enrollment size works as a strong negative factor. In extreme cases, the subsidy could be revoked altogether. These procedures created a strong incentive for institutions to reduce excess enrollment.

Moreover, since in practice the regime made it extremely difficult for new institutions to be established, competition among institutions over students became less threatening, allowing the existing institutions to raise their tuition levels. Private institutions, being able to reap benefits from the monopolized higher education market, showed little resistance to restrictions on their freedom. Under this monopolized and protected market, many private institutions increased their tuition levels while slightly reducing enrollments. Through these measures, they could lift their level of selectivity while securing financial stability. Meanwhile, the government succeeded to an extent in improving the educational quality of private institutions. It was ironic, however, that the government subsidy, initially targeted at lessening financial burden on students' families, resulted in tuition increases.

The above analysis indicates that relations between the government and the higher education market have never been stable. This phenomenon has been one of the most critical factors in determining the direction of change and has therefore always been at the center of controversy concerning higher education in Japan.

Segmentation and differentiation of the system

In the first phase of higher education development, the boundaries of the system were unclear as there were many institutions with various levels of instruction and admissions requirements. As discussed earlier, through system integration around the time of World War I, the higher education system was given a legal definition with respect to the outer boundaries and internal segmentation. The higher education system consisted of two tiers (universities and specialized schools) and two sectors (public, both national and local, and private). The combination produced four segments, and each of them developed its own mission. Through the subsequent years prior to World War II, each of the four segments underwent a significant expansion. In the first segment of national universities, the number of imperial universities, which were centers of excellence in research and education, had increased to seven by World War II. A number of colleges of technology, medicine, and commerce were added to this segment. On the other end, the fourth segment, private specialized schools, was established at the margins of the higher education system, responding to the popular demand for accessible opportunities of higher education. Between the two segments were public specialized schools and private universities. While institutions in these two segments were diverse in prestige and selectivity, many of them had their own niche with respect to field of training, relation to the labor market, or link to the region.

The postwar reform removed the distinction between the university and nonuniversity tiers, while leaving in place the public and private sectors. In subsequent years, this reform left two policy issues unresolved: one was the persistent pressure for revival of a nonuniversity tier, and the other was the development of a hierarchical structure among four-year institutions in terms of selectivity and status.

When higher education institutions were integrated in principle into a single tier of four-year institutions, one exception remained—junior colleges, which provided the associate bachelor's degree after two years. Initially, there was a provision to allow a small number of former specialized colleges to operate before they had met the conditions to become new four-year universities. Some junior colleges, however, found strong market demand especially among young women, who had fewer employment opportunities than did male graduates of four-year institutions. Consequently, the number of private junior colleges increased over time, especially during the period of expansion in the 1960s. In the 1980s, about 24 percent of eighteen-year-old women were enrolled in junior colleges. In the 1990s, however, women began shifting to four-year institutions.

Since the 1950s, industrial leaders had been demanding that specialized schools be revived by creating polytechnic-type institutions. Despite strong resistance from the Ministry of Education, which insisted on maintaining the single-tier principle, "higher specialized schools" were created as a type of secondary school. They admitted fresh graduates from junior high schools and trained them for five years, implying that the last two years corresponded to higher education. The demand for this type of institution, however, failed to expand in subsequent years.

The third case was the creation of special training schools in the mid-1970s. As mentioned above, these schools were created at the time of the shift to a stringent policy on the expansion of four-year universities. Special training schools were expected to absorb some of the unmet demand. In subsequent years, the demand for this type of education expanded rapidly—by the 1980s about one-fifth of eighteen-year-olds, both male and female, were enrolled in the special training schools. Most of these institutions were private, and they quickly responded to skills required by a changing labor market.

Among four-year universities, the most significant development was the sharp differentiation among institutions with respect to selectivity and prestige. To an extent, the hierarchical structure reflected the one that existed in the prewar period. The position of each institution in the hierarchy reflected its history—the old imperial universities tended to be at the top and the old private specialized schools at the bottom. It should also be noted that, unlike their French or German counterparts, Japanese national universities were not required to enroll all the qualified students; each institution had the right to select its students. Moreover, unlike in the United States, a substantial proportion of institutions were concentrated in a few metropolitan areas, which weakened geographical distribution as compared to hierarchical differentiation.

During the postwar expansion the hierarchy developed even further: newly established institutions provided the bottom of the hierarchy, followed by still newer institutions. Meanwhile, traditionally prestigious institutions further enhanced their reputations by limiting admissions to raise their selectivity. Midlevel institutions, once they were financially secure, tried to raise their selectivity by restricting admissions.

The hierarchy in terms of selectivity was reinforced through the link between higher education institutions and business firms. Large business firms with abundant capital were able to invest in newer technology and in human capital, through on-the-job training, thus achieving significantly higher productivity—as well as higher wage and fringe benefits—than smaller firms. Moreover, large firms developed lifetime employment in the postwar period. In this sense, the labor market was segmented also, according to corporate size. It was thus natural for college graduates to seek employment in large firms.[1] The larger firms preferred graduates of selective institutions— if not for their superior education then for the academic competence shown by their success in entrance examinations. Meanwhile, graduates from less selective institutions had to seek employment in smaller firms. It was therefore natural for high school graduates to make every effort to get into the most selective institutions.

Under these circumstances, the selectivity of institutions became one of the most significant signals of desirability. Typically, people tried to get into the most selective of the institutions to which they might be admitted. With every student competing fiercely according to this tactic, the examination system became increasingly accurate in matching academic ability and institutional selectivity. This, in turn, induced employers to favor graduates from prestigious institutions to a greater extent.

Entrance examinations thus had a dual role: first, in selecting those individuals who would earn a college diploma and, second, matching individual applicants with individual institutions. This dual role took on greater significance in the late 1970s and 1980s. Not only did the government take policy steps to control expansion, but many private institutions also reduced the number of entrants in order to raise their status in the hierarchy. Meanwhile, criticisms of excessive competition led to the creation of a standardized examination that can be used as a substitute for, or a complement to, the entrance examinations given by individual institutions. Ironically, however, the standardized examination had an unexpected effect: it provided students with information as to their standing in the national distribution of achievement scores. To this, the education system added information about likely the cut-off level for each individual institution. Thus, students were given more accurate information to identify the most selective institution to which they were likely to be admitted. The position of a college in the hierarchy became an even better predictor of the graduate's academic competence, giving business firms more reasons to recruit students from selective institutions. This self-propelling trend brought about various negative effects that will be discussed later.

Issues and realities

The dynamic developments discussed above had various structural consequences, which have to be rectified before Japan positions itself for the future. At the same time, new factors—demographic structure, the trend toward a knowledge society, globalization, and marketization—pose serious challenges.

Legacies from the past

In retrospect, the development of higher education in postwar Japan was indeed a significant achievement. Among other things, it provided the opportunity for higher education to a large segment of the population. Enrollment expansion itself worked as a great equalizer of educational opportunities. In the prewar period, when the participation rate at the tertiary level stood well below 10 percent, higher education opportunities were limited to a selected few, mostly from upper- and upper-middle-income families in urban areas and from landowners in rural areas. Access to higher education was beyond the imagination for the vast majority of the population. The postwar expansion of higher education changed this picture drastically. The participation rate at the tertiary level rose to 50 percent by the late 1970s, and to 60 percent by the early 1990s. In the process, the gender gap declined significantly; by the mid-1980s, the female participation rate in postsecondary education actually surpassed the male rate. Higher education is entering a universal stage. The differences among income classes with respect to enrollment had been kept relatively low (Kaneko; 1989; 1997). In addition, the expanded system succeeded in supplying a sufficient number of graduates to the growing economy.[2]

Still, it is evident that the process of expansion entailed serious problems. One of the most serious issues has been the quality of undergraduate instruction. Even though the rapid expansion naturally resulted in the entry of less academically able students, faculty members remained committed to the traditional concept of teaching. According to the Humboldtian idea of freedom of learning and *Bildung*, professors are supposed to influence students by demonstrating the spirit of rigorous academic pursuit; students need to be left in solitude, struggling to capture the truth by themselves. Yet, the academic and mental readiness of the student body changed significantly as more and more students entered colleges. Moreover, the hierarchical structure among institutions created its own problem. Institutions at the lower end of the hierarchy experienced low morale among faculty and students. Even more important, the prestigious institutions had their own problem: since the students knew that they would be recruited by business firms not on the basis of what they learned at the university but rather on the basis of their performance on the entrance examination, their motivation to study was limited. This situation provided good excuses for faculty members not to invest their time and energy in education. The strange combination of the Humboldtian ideal of freedom of learning and a hierarchically segmented labor market created a structural obstacle to any effort toward the qualitative improvement of education. Given that the only element of relevance to society was not education but rather the *selection* of elites, it is no surprise that universities suffered from a serious morale problem.

Another fundamental issue was the relationship between the public and private sectors. Even though national and private institutions served the same purpose of providing higher education and undertaking research, the financial support from the government differed significantly. The levels of current cost subsidy to private institutions had been stagnating since the 1980s due to financial constraints. While the tuition level at national institutions had been steadily rising to lessen the difference from the levels at private institutions, tuition levels at private institutions kept rising. As a result, the tuition at national institutions continued to be only half the tuition charged by most private institutions. Private institutions have criticized the disparity in family contribution as unjustifiable. Moreover, relatively selective private institutions have lost potential students to national universities due the difference in tuition levels. For less selective institutions facing potential financial difficulty, an increase in the amount of government subsidy was an acute necessity. In any case, inevitably, the differential treatment of private and national institutions has become a serious political issue.

Demographic shift and universalization

A significant factor affecting the future of higher education is demographic shift. As a result of a decline in the birthrate in the 1980s, the population of eighteen-year-olds will decline dramatically from 2.0 million in 1994 to 1.2 million in 2010. The supply-demand gap is now gradually diminishing, and it will eventually be reversed. There will be redundant capacities at the universities, and any high school graduate will be allowed to enter a university insofar as he or she is willing to pay the cost. In that sense, it appears as if universalization of higher education is going to be realized in an unexpected context.

How the demographic shift will affect the universities depends on a few factors. If the proportion of eighteen-year-olds who enroll in four-year institutions keeps growing to compensate for the decline in the cohort size, then the number of entrants to higher education institutions will remain the same. In fact, as the cohort size of eighteen-year-olds started declining, the participation rate at four-year institutions increased from 30 percent in the late 1980s to 40 percent at the beginning of the twenty-first century. However, the degree of decline is of such magnitude that enrollment rates will have to keep rising even farther to 60 percent if the number of entrants is to remain constant. That increase seems to be unlikely—from 2002 to 2003 the participation rate stagnated at around 40 percent. Meanwhile, signs of insufficient demand have already appeared. Since 2000, a few two-year institutions have been forced to close due to insufficient student numbers. In the spring of 2003, almost one-quarter of private four-year institutions admitted less students than their prescribed enrollment size. It is anticipated that, except for a small group of prestigious institutions, many private institutions will have to reposition themselves to survive in the age of insufficient demands. This is a radical departure from the past, which saw only a few cases of closure of higher education institutions over fifty years.

Equally important, this change will shift the relation between the government and private institutions. As pointed out above, the chronic excess demand has been one of the major factors that defined the development of higher education in Japan. Against this backdrop, the government was able to use establishment permission as an instrument to sustain a minimum level of educational conditions and, presumably, quality of instruction. As excess demand disappears and the prospect of institutional expansion diminishes, the government will lose its leverage over private universities.

Marketization, globalization, and the knowledge society

At the same time as the demand and supply structure undergoes a significant shift, the social and economic contexts of higher education are changing their shape in terms of the future.

One significant factor is the advent of *marketization*. Aside from the financial crisis brought about by exponential increases in social spending, the ideological tide of "neoliberalism" has been acquiring considerable momentum in Japan as elsewhere in the world. Whether or not one accepts the new ideology, it appears to be the case that the increased diversity and complexity of modern society and its needs have made centralized decision making and control less effective. It is thus argued that many social services provided directly by the government should be moved to the realm of the market for the sake of efficiency. This argument can be applied directly to higher education. The basic premise underlying the role of government in higher education has been that government is the best agent to satisfy the various needs of the whole society. This premise, however, appears less plausible when social activities become increasingly diverse and industrial development less predictable. Meanwhile, the financial resources that the government can provide to higher education are shrinking. The government appears to be losing the ideological and fiscal wherewithal to be the sole or primary agent mediating the exchange between society and the university.

A second factor is the coming of what might be called the *knowledge society*. Knowledge has assumed an increasingly central role in society. Fierce competition over technical innovation has caused research and development to become critically important for success in the market. The creation and transmission of knowledge, which has been the central task of the university, is going to assume the central role in the economy. It does not imply, however, that society will become more generous to the present universities. On the contrary, society will more likely criticize universities' ability to respond to the challenges facing them. Since the required knowledge may be very different from traditional academic knowledge, universities will face serious difficulty in responding to those needs. In fact, knowledge is produced and transmitted in various forms and at various locations, often outside the university. Even basic research takes place in business firms that have been developing the capability to produce knowledge and make a profit from that activity. The university no longer enjoys a monopoly in the production of advanced and specialized knowledge.

The third factor is *globalization*. Given the lower barriers to international trade, financial capital and production equipment can now move easily from one country to another, making it possible for many countries to participate in the production of sophisticated goods. The relative strength of a nation's economy, or its competitiveness, rests on the ability to create and accumulate knowledge. At the same time, the direction of economic growth has moved from manufacturing to the service sector and the production of human services based on various kinds of knowledge. For many countries, maintaining a high level of competitiveness in international trade appears to be essential for economic well-being or even for survival; in order to foster competitiveness the knowledge transmitted and created by the university is essential. Moreover, the services rendered by the university are becoming increasingly mobile. Not only do students move across national borders, but the universities are also moving across borders to recruit students. E-learning technology makes it possible for universities to offer courses overseas. In a word, there are growing global markets for higher education.

These arguments can be made anywhere in the world, but they cause a particularly acute sense of crisis in Japan. The marketization argument threatens the delicate balance between the government and private sectors of higher education, as that relationship has been a controversial one ever since the creation of higher education in Japan. If the underlying agenda of the knowledge society lies in the increased involvement of research and education in the market, then the Humboldtian principle of academic freedom and abstract academic pursuit that has constituted the backbone of Japanese research universities will have to be questioned. With the advent of globalization, Japan is threatened on the one hand by China and other low-wage countries in the market for manufactured goods and on the other by the United States and other English-speaking countries in the trade of services, including higher education. In both spheres, the competitiveness of Japan has to be questioned. There is a growing awareness that the former social and economic structure that enabled Japan in the past to succeed in catching up to the West may be losing ground in the face of those new trends. Japanese society has to find a new mechanism for growth, in which higher education must assume a critical role.

Trends and challenges

The sense of crisis and awareness of the need for reform grew in the 1990s, resulting in various reports from government councils. Some of their recommendations were followed by a series of government policy initiatives in the 1990s and in the early twenty-first century, while others are still awaiting further debates to decide their fate. The reform initiatives are focused in three directions: reconstruction of the linkage between the university and the economy, qualitative assurance and improvement, and a shift away from government involvement.

Linkage with the economy

Reconstruction of the linkage between higher education and the economy is the goal in both education and research. In education, the policy so far has been directed toward expansion of graduate education as the place for training and retraining highly professional workers. Providing lifelong employment, business firms raised skill levels among their workers not only through formal training but also by exposing workers to various tasks in the workplace or by on-the-job training. This has been particularly effective in providing workers with the knowledge and skills relevant to their work (Aoki & Dore, 1994). In recruiting new workers, employers tended to evaluate recruits' basic ability to absorb on-the-job training, rather than their possession of specific knowledge or skills mastered at university. However, it is argued that, with the advent of globalization and rapid technological innovation, this pattern of skill formation will lose its effectiveness. With constant technological innovation and shifts in demands, skill requirements keep changing rapidly, making on-the-job training less effective. At the same time, the demographic shift requires the mobilization of a middle-aged and older labor force. All these factors point to the need for advanced education and training for the young people and adult workers. From this perspective, expansion of graduate programs at universities appears as the logical approach.

In fact, expansion of graduate schools had already been taking place since the 1970s in such fields as engineering and pharmacology. By the end of the 1980s, about one-third of new graduates with bachelor's degrees in engineering went on to graduate programs. In other academic fields, however, graduate programs remained essentially places for training academics. Against this background, in 1988 the University Council, which was established by the Ministry of Education as the central body to outline the basic policies on higher education, released its first report, entitled "Toward a Flexible Graduate Education System," on advanced professional graduate education (Daigaku Shingikai, 1988). To induce greater flexibility and variety in graduate education, the report suggested a few changes in chartering standards, some of which had direct relevance with regard to retraining working college graduates. Following the report, in 1989, the Ministry of Education revised the "chartering standards for graduate education," relaxing requirements concerning class schedules, entrance requirements, and full-time residency.

In 1991 the University Council recommended a two-fold increase in the enrollment in graduate programs by 2000. Following the government initiatives, a number of graduate courses were set up with curricula targeting the training of professionals. Many private institutions established graduate programs in the social sciences and humanities. As it turned out, the goal set by the University Council was achieved at least numerically: enrollment in master's programs increased from 62,000 in 1990 to 143,000 in 2000. Another development was the creation of graduate professional schools. In 2002, the Central Education Council, a government body, proposed creation of professional graduate schools. Meanwhile, the Ministry of Law started reexamining the national examination system for legal professions. More than forty graduate law schools started enrolling students by 2004. There are proposals to assign schools of medicine, currently one of the undergraduate faculties, the status of professional graduate schools.

These developments, however, do not necessarily imply that graduate education has actually become a significant route for retraining adult workers, as the University Council originally intended. Except for the recruitment of engineers, businesses still tend to prefer new undergraduates from selective institutions over those with graduate degrees. This forms a contrast with the situation in Korea, Taiwan, and China, where master's degrees are gaining significance in the labor market. The future development in Japan will be contingent on changes in the labor market.

The university-industry linkage through research has attracted attention since the end of the 1990s. In retrospect, it is ironic that in the 1980s, when the robust performances of the Japanese manufacturing industry alarmed the West, the strong ties of Japanese universities with industry was seen as one of the critical factors supporting its strength. Typical arguments held that Japanese universities were inclined toward applied, rather than basic, research while free-riding on the basic research in American and European universities, and that through close cooperation with universities Japanese manufacturers were able to reap the benefits. In the United States and the United Kingdom, these arguments resulted in a series of policies to fortify the role of higher education institutions in economic development. However, the tide reversed in the 1990s, when the American economy started a steady recovery. The success was attributed to the close collaboration between universities and industry, and the businesses created around universities, as typified by what happened in Silicon Valley.

These stories started making an impact in Japan when the "bubble economy" burst in the 1990s, suddenly undermining Japanese confidence in the economy's competitiveness. Japan had to develop new arenas of industry, and the universities were expected to play critical roles in this respect. From this perspective, however, Japanese universities were found to have critical shortcomings: the cooperation with industry tended to rely on informal and closed relations between a particular laboratory in a university and a particular section of a large manufacturing company. This particular pattern had been created partly because of strong resistance within the university, in the tradition of academic freedom, against university-industry cooperation. Japanese universities thus needed a transparent institutional framework and incentive systems that would induce a creative combination between potential supply of knowledge and the demands of the market.

On these matters, the Ministry of Education issued a series of policies in the 1980s and 1990s—including such measures as financial incentives for joint research programs between universities and industries and the creation of "university-industry cooperation centers" at selected national universities. In 1998, the Diet passed a law aimed at encouraging technology transfer from higher education institutions to industry through the establishment of a "technology licensing organization" for universities. The law also stipulated procedures on the ownership of patents. Since 2000, the government has taken measures to allow faculty members at national universities to serve in private firms on a part-time basis. Meanwhile, the Ministry of Economy, Trade, and Industry (previously the Ministry of International Trade and Industry) has become active in promoting university-industry cooperation. The plan is for there to be one thousand venture business firms established by university faculty members by 2004; the number actually had already reached five hundred by May 2003. Moreover, the reorganization of national universities into more independent bodies is expected to make them more aggressive in pursuing industry-university collaboration. How these measures will work, however, remains to be seen.

Excellence, evaluation, and quality assurance

The second focus of the reforms was to control the quality of higher education and research—promoting excellence and ensuring minimum standards, while developing forms of evaluation.

As "excellence in research and education" became a politically popular catchphrase in the 1990s, a series of government actions were undertaken along these lines. The initiatives included increases in scholarships and other forms of financial support for graduate students and young researchers and in the funding of research projects. In 1997, the government passed a law that allowed universities to employ academic researchers in fixed-term appointments, which had been illegal in the postwar period—when Japanese employees were given strong protection. This measure was aimed at promoting mobility and competition among young researchers. In 2001, the Ministry of Education proposed a "structural reform plan in higher education" that proposed the designation of thirty leading research universities as Japanese centers of excellence by international standards. Faced with the criticism that selection of such institutions would be practically impossible, the ministry revised the plan as the "21st Century Centers of Excellence Plan." Under this plan, the ministry will help set up and finance about two hundred "centers of excellence," in ten fields of research, at national and private universities. The competition for the grant, which started in the summer of 2002, received wide attention not only among universities but also from the media.

Japanese achievement in basic science is in fact improving. According to an international comparison of publication in academic journals in 2003, two Japanese institutions appeared among the top 10 (the University of Tokyo ranked second and the University of Kyoto sixth) and five in the top 20. Japanese scholars won the Nobel Prize for three consecutive years. However, the extent to which these records are attributable to government policy is unclear. Moreover, it is ironic that the Japanese public is now more concerned with the economic value of research.

Significant developments have been made concerning university evaluation. In postwar Japan, there have been two mechanisms for quality assurance: one is the aforementioned establishment permission by the government, and the other is accreditation by the Japan University Accreditation Association. The latter, however, has been criticized for being too lenient on the member institutions and therefore ineffective in assuring quality. Consequently, the establishment permission process remained practically the sole mechanism to maintain the quality of higher education institutions. Over the years, standards for the establishment of universities, on which the permission process is based, became increasingly involved and detailed to accommodate different types of higher education institutions. There were criticisms that the myriad standards tended to thwart any initiatives to experiment with new approaches in undergraduate education. Responding to these criticisms and the trend of deregulation, the Ministry of Education substantially simplified the standards in 1991. At the same time, the revised standards required institutions of higher education to undertake self-evaluation. This logically brings about the need for effective external evaluation and assessment.

In response to this need, as well as to the increasingly strong claims for accountability in cost and performance, the University Council recommended establishment of a government agency for evaluation of the national universities. Subsequently, a National Institute for University Assessment and Academic Degrees was established in 2000. With more than one hundred staff members, it is probably the world's largest evaluation agency. Since 2001 it has been undertaking annual rounds of evaluation—a massive exercise involving several hundred evaluators. The methods and results of evaluation have received mixed reviews from the universities.

A more fundamental issue is quality assurance for the entire higher education system, including private institutions. It was mentioned above that the establishment permission process, together with current cost subsidy, has been the major vehicle of quality control. This approach will inevitably lose its effectiveness, however, due to the inevitable oversupply of places. Moreover, there has been increasing pressure from the United States and other countries through World Trade Organization (WTO) negotiations to open the higher education market for overseas institutions. Japan needs to establish a transparent framework for assuring minimum standards for Japanese institutions to protect the system from domestic and foreign degree mills. In 2002, the school education law was amended to add a clause that stipulated that all universities have to be accredited by at least one of the government-recognized accrediting bodies. The accrediting body can be a private foundation, a government body, or even a private corporation. Through this scheme, the Ministry of Education obtained explicit legal authority, albeit indirect, over the operation of private institutions for the first time in the postwar period.

Deregulation

The third area of reform is deregulation and marketization. After Japan went into a serious economic stagnation in the mid-1990s, the pervasive political ideology moved toward the reduction in the role of government in economic and social activities, either in the form of regulation or by direct involvement. On the agenda of the reforms along this line, higher education assumed a central position for its symbolic value.

Starting in the last decade of the twentieth century there has been steady movement toward deregulation. It was mentioned above that the standards for establishment were considerably simplified. In addition, the regulations and requirements concerning higher education have either been cut back or abolished altogether. For example, the requirement of at least twelve years of schooling before entering institutions of higher education is no longer enforced, allowing some students to "jump" to university before completing high school. It is also possible now to enroll in graduate programs after three years of undergraduate coursework. Requirements concerning university facilities have been substantially reduced. One area of deregulation that remains controversial is the inclusion of for-profit higher education institutions in the national system of education. Under the current school education law, only nonprofit "school juristic persons" can establish legally defined *schools*, including higher education institutions. Many proponents of deregulation are now proposing to remove this requirement. When the Economic Advisory Council under Prime Minister Koizumi proposed its "action plan" in 2002, legalization of for-profit universities was listed among the prioritized issues. While this proposal met staunch opposition from the minister of education, the issue has not yet been resolved.

One reform that has already brought about concrete changes is incorporation of the national universities, which were considered legally as government organizations, even though they had been given substantial autonomy in academic matters. The governance and finance of the national universities have been criticized internally as inflexible and externally as inefficient and unresponsive to the changing needs of the economy and society. Moreover, as mentioned above, there has been a strong sense of resentment among private institutions about the privileged status of national institutions.

In 1996, the government under Prime Minister Hashimoto placed restructuring of government organizations high on the political agenda. The reform was to encompass every part of government, including higher education. "Privatization" of the national universities was frequently mentioned in government committees. Under the subsequent government of Prime Minister Obuchi, the legal status of the national universities was formally changed to that of "independent administrative agencies," serving a public function but organizationally independent from the government. Subsequently, a committee of experts—including representatives from the national universities—issued a report in the summer of 2002 providing the basic outlines of the new body, the National University Corporation (NUC). In 2003, the NUC law was passed in the Diet, and each of the national universities became a National University Corporation in the spring of 2004.

Under this law, the NUC will be an independent entity legally separated from the government, governed by a president and an executive board, in consultation with the academic board and the administrative board. The president will be selected by the selection committee and appointed by the minister of education. The government provides a subsidy to the NUC based on a prescribed formula, and the NUC administers the budget according to an accounting system similar to that of private firms. The subsidy will be determined in the framework established by the six-year "middle-term goals and plan" approved by the minister.

A variety of criticisms have been raised against this scheme. One of the major concerns is the unusually strong power concentrated in the hands of the university president. The president, together with the executive board members whom he appoints, makes basic decisions, acting as the chief executive. There is no internal organization, such as a board of trustees as in private institutions, to supervise the president and his staff. The Ministry of Education will retain decisive power in approving the midterm goals and plan that would bind the administration legally and fiscally. Meanwhile, the traditional authority given to the faculty body or academic council may be curtailed substantially.

Since many of the internal procedures for decision making are left for individual institutions to design, the actual practice of governance may turn out to be less radically centralized than the law appears to stipulate. At least, it will take some time before the new system of governance and finance takes root. How these changes will affect the organizational behaviors of the national university is unclear, but it is likely that the national universities will become more aggressive in acquiring their own standing in the market and, as a result, become more divergent in their identity and mission. That will inevitably recall the persistent issue of the validity of differences in mission between public and private institutions.

Conclusion

Unlike some Asian countries, Japan was not forced by colonization to adopt a single model of higher education from the West; instead, it was able to select, through trial and error, institutional arrangements from various models. Dynamic interaction between demand and supply took place, eventually resulting in transformation of the institutional framework. In this latter process, Japan shares a common pattern with many Asian countries.

Because of the "late development effect," popular demand for higher education expanded at relatively early stages of development, to create chronic excess demand over subsequent periods. Countries have varied widely, however, with respect to the timing and magnitude of the expansion in demand, and the government's power and resources to control the market. In former English colonies, the governments typically resisted market forces. In contrast, in Japan the government allowed, and relied on, the private sector to absorb the excess demand. Similar patterns were observed in such East Asian countries as Korea, Taiwan, and the Philippines.

The Japanese approach made it possible to extend access to higher education to a large segment of the population and to provide the necessary volume of manpower critical for economic development. The negative consequences include a number of issues. Governmental control over the quantity and quality of higher education eventually had to be severely limited. The disparities between the public and private sectors in terms of cost levels to be borne by families created a sense of unfairness. Another problematic consequence was the development of a hierarchy among higher education institutions, which created a mechanism that persistently undermined efforts to improve the quality of instruction.

At the beginning of the twenty-first century, Japan is trying to rectify the problems created as a result of past developments in higher education. At the same time, emerging social and economic trends are causing new challenges. In order to respond to these challenges, Japanese higher education is trying to reshape itself in various ways. That raises a number of critical issues, the most fundamental of which is the role of government in higher education. Thus, Japan has to reexamine the basic premises underlying its higher education system throughout its history.

Notes

1 For more detailed discussion about in-firm training, see Kaneko, 1992, p. 52.
2 For a detailed discussion and evaluation of the supply and demand of college graduates in the postwar period, see Kaneko, 1992.

References

Amano, Ikuo. 1986. Educational crisis in Japan. In William K. Cummings *et al.* (Eds.), *Educational policies in crisis* (pp. 23–43). New York: Praeger.

Aoki, Masahiko, & Dore, Ronald. (1994). *The Japanese firm: Sources of strength*. Oxford: Oxford University Press.

Ben-David, Joseph. (1977). *Centers of learning*. New York: McGraw-Hill.

Cummings, William K. (1980). *Education and equality in Japan*. Princeton, NJ: Princeton University Press.

Daigaku Shingikai (University Council). (1988). *Daigakuin Seido No Danryakuka Ni Tuite* (Toward a flexible graduate education system). Tokyo: Author.

Dore, Ronald P. (1976). *The diploma disease: Education, qualification, and development*. Berkeley: University of California Press.

Dore, Ronald P., & Sako, Mari. (1989). *How the Japanese learn to work*. London: Routledge.

Editorial. (1989, January 25). *Yomiuri Shimbun*, 2.

Kaneko, Motohisa. (1989). *Financing higher education in Japan*. Hiroshima, Japan: R.I.H.E., Hiroshima University.

Kaneko, Motohisa. (1992). *Higher education and employment in Japan*. Hiroshima, Japan: R.I.H.E., Hiroshima University.

Kaneko, Motohisa. (1997). Efficiency and equity in Japanese higher education. *Higher Education*, *34*(2), 165–181.

Nakayama, Shigeru. (1989). Independence and choice: Western impacts on Japanese higher education. In P. G. Altbach & V. Selvaratnam (Eds.), *From dependence to autonomy: The development of Asian universities*. Dordrecht, Netherlands: Kluwer Academic.

Pempel, T. J. (1978). *Patterns of Japanese policy making: Experiences from higher education*. Boulder, CO: Westview.

Terasaki, Akio. (1979). *Nihon ni okeru daigaku jichi seido no seiritu* (Emergence of university autonomy in Japan). Tokyo: Hyouronsha.

28

HIGHER EDUCATION AND SCIENTIFIC DEVELOPMENT

The promise of newly industrializing countries

Philip G. Altbach

Source: P. G. Altbach *et al.* (eds) *Scientific Development and Higher Education: The Case of Newly Industrializing Nations*, New York and London: Praeger, 1989, pp. 3–29.

The development of research capability, the education of specialized personnel needed for research and the academy, and the building of the infrastructure needed for a scientific and research enterprise are highly complex matters. Yet, scientific development is a very important aspect of nation building, especially for Third World countries seeking to enter the mainstream of contemporary technology and commerce. This chapter considers the many ramifications of the development of science in the Third World, focusing on four key newly industrializing nations. Malaysia, Singapore, South Korea, and Taiwan are among the wealthiest and most successful of Third World countries.[1] They have made impressive economic strides and have stressed higher education as well. All four countries have emphasized a high-tech future and have been concerned with scientific development. These nations are important not only because they are a growing economic force in Asia and worldwide but because they are the vanguard of Third World progress and their experiences may be useful for other countries.

We are concerned here with a nexus of factors in the process of scientific development and our reflections are necessarily broad. A special emphasis is placed on the role of higher education in the process of scientific growth. This emphasis is especially relevant for Third World nations because virtually all of the scientific infrastructure in most of these nations is located in the universities. Academic institutions are not only the location of much of the scientific research that is done but these institutions also employ the largest proportion of scientists. As in all countries, universities also provide training for scientists. Thus, academic institutions stand at the center of the research network in all countries, and they play a particularly key role in the Third World.[2] Academic science relates to the wider world of industry, government, and the public. Professors are frequently involved in applied research, and are often funded by industrial or governmental bodies. They do consulting outside academe.

A variety of forces have an impact on scientific development. This chapter points out some of these factors. Contemporary science is an international phenomenon, and Third World science is particularly dependent on the international knowledge network. Language is a perplexing issue for Third World science and affects scientific development in the Third World. English, the current international scientific medium, is the language of choice in order to take advantage of current worldwide knowledge. Yet, when an academic system functions in a language like Bahasa Malaysia or Korean, language problems emerge. Another aspect of the internationalization of science is what might be called the "scientific disspora" that affects many Third World nations. Significant groups of scientists from Third World countries work in the industrialized nations, and frequently maintain close ties with their home countries. These scientists often help scientific development in their countries significantly by serving as links. The question of foreign training also enters into the international equation. In the four newly industrializing nations under consideration here, the large majority of the top scientists were trained abroad. The flow of students abroad continues and a degree from a Western univeristy is a distinct advantage. The impact of foreign study is considerable.

Malaysia, Singapore, South Korea, and Taiwan are among the most successful of the countries of the Third World. Education and technology have played a role, but it is fair to say that, except for Malaysia, which has relied on export of natural resources and agricultural products, economic growth in these countries has been based on relatively "low tech" industrial development with a base of low labor costs and an efficient workforce. Singapore has also benefitted from its position as the world's second busiest port. However, all of this is changing as these four countries are moving to more sophisticated industries and are developing independent scientific bases. Higher education and science will play an ever greater role in these nations. With their efficient and increasingly well educated labor forces and export-oriented industries, they will be powerful competitors for years to come. They may also yield valuable lessons for other Third World nations in terms of strategies for development. Our concern here is for the role that higher education and science play in development and especially in gaining some insights into how the universities function in these newly industrializing countries.

The international knowledge system

It has frequently been noted that Third World nations, however prosperous, are part of an international knowledge system that places them at a disadvantage since the system is controlled in many respects by the advanced industrial nations. The major universities and research laboratories are located in such key countries as the United States, Britain, West Germany, France, the Soviet Union, and a few others. These countries spend the bulk of the world's R&D funds. They are the home base to the major publishers of books and scientific journals. They produce the largest number of patents and their discoveries and innovations dominate world science and technology. The research agendas of these countries dominate world research. Many scientists and scholars from the Third World are educated in the advanced industrialized nations and maintain ties with their metropolitan centers. These factors necessarily tie Third World nations into the international knowledge system and make them dependent, to a significant extent, on "imported knowledge."

The implications of an international knowledge system for all countries at the periphery of the system, including many of the smaller industrialized nations (but especially for the Third World), are considerable. The small scientific communities of these newly industrializing nations haven't the personnel, equipment, or funding to maintain a world-class scientific infrastructure. Advanced training in most fields inevitably has to take place in the metropolitan nations. There is pressure on scientists to publish their findings in international journals, which are seen to be more important—and more prestigious—than local journals. Local scientists also desire access to a wider international audience for their work. Key research findings are almost always imported and the major basic work is done elsewhere. Scientists look abroad for insights. There is a sense that the most important scientific research is being done elsewhere and as a result there is often seen the position among both scientists and those in universities and government who set standards and make judgments on career advancement that local work is less important. There is something of a paradox at work—much attention is paid to the fostering of indigenous scientific institutions while at the same time foreign science is given the most prominence and the highest prestige. There are also practical implications of peripherality. Expensive scientific equipment must be imported. Researchers must frequently travel abroad to keep up with the latest work in their fields and to maintain contacts with the "invisible college" of researchers in any field of study. The research orientation of Third World scientists is often seen as less important in international circles. In sum, these scientific systems must constantly worry about keeping up with developments abroad—developments that inevitably place Third World science at a disadvantage.

Despite the basic structural disadvantages of peripherality, the countries with which we are concerned here have made impressive strides toward developing an indigenous scientific base and have made major financial and resource commitments to scientific development. They recognize that they will never be fully independent of the major centers, which now include

445

Japan. They are, nonetheless, convinced that local scientific development can contribute not only to a mature and productive academic system but also to scientific innovations that will be useful to domestic industry and technology. Such development can also produce the personnel needed not only for research but for enhanced high-tech industrial growth. In these countries, it is possible to observe scientific development that remains part of an international knowledge system but at the same time has increasingly strong local roots that have been nurtured by government and academic policies and by funding for indigenous scientific development.[3]

The language issue

The language of science, instruction, and scholarship is a key issue for Third World universities and is directly related to the international knowledge system. The four countries considered in this essay reflect different approaches to language policy and higher education, and it is worth briefly discussing how the complex issue of language has been dealt with in these rapidly developing nations. English is the main international language of science. A large proportion of the international scientific literature (both formal and informal) and most of the informal scientific networks function in English. All four of these countries are greatly influenced by English in terms of higher education and research and all four have somewhat differing approaches to language issues. Indeed, there is a kind of language policy continuum evident among the countries.

In Singapore, all postsecondary education—and most education at primary and secondary levels as well—is in English and in some ways there is no "language issue" since English is the langauge of instruction and research. All scientific journals in Singapore are published in English. The Singapore government feels that Singapore must be a direct part of the international economy to survive and that English is a key ingredient in that participation. In Singapore, English is the only language of science and technology. The other three countries have a more complex approach to language issues in education and science. In all three, an indigenous language is the medium of instruction in education, including higher education. Efforts have been made to adapt indigenous languages to scientific purposes and to ensure that vocabularies are appropriate for academic and scientific purposes. All three countries used foreign languages for higher education as well as governmental administration prior to independence and provide some useful examples for other Third World nations faced with problems of linguistic adaptation.

English was the colonial language of both Malaysia and Singapore and these two countries are very interesting examples of divergent language policies.[4] While Singapore has retained English as the medium of education, government and commerce, Malaysia slowly shifted to the national language, Bahasa Malaysia for all purposes, changing the medium of instruction in the universities in the 1970s.[5] Malaysia has paid considerable attention to providing textbooks and other educational materials in Bahasa Malaysia and has made impressive gains. Scholarly journals now appear in the language, and in most fields there are adequate materials for undergraduate instruction. For advanced learning and research, however, English remains a necessity in Malaysia and there has been concern by Malaysian scholars that the standard of English has declined so that graduate study and international collaboration is jeopardized. A government-funded agency, the Dewan Bahasa dan Pustaka (Language and Literature Agency) has commissioned many textbooks at all levels of education and has otherwise stimulated writing and publication in the national language. Several of Malaysia's universities have sponsored scholarly journals and publish scholarly books in Bahasa Malaysia. The problems are serious and include very high costs for translation and publication for a small market—Malaysia's total population is under 15 million and there are about 60,000 students and some 6000 academic staff in the nation's tertiary institutions. There is also a shortage of translators and authors. Senior scholars continue to publish in English for international publication. Despite the problems, Malaysia has taken seriously its commitment to develop Bahasa Malaysia as an adequate medium for education and research. It is, however, likely that scientific progress has been slowed because of the emphasis—and resources—placed on the development of the national language.

Taiwan and Korea share a similar colonial history. For more than a half century, Japan was the colonial power and imposed Japanese as the sole medium of instruction in higher education. Japan was responsible for the establishment of modern universities in both countries; although during the colonial period access to these institutions by Taiwanese and Koreans were limited. Japanese colonial domination ended in 1945 and the medium of instruction shifted to Chinese in Taiwan and Korean in Korea. The arrival of the Nationalist Government from mainland China on Taiwan, and later the impact of the United States, meant that the Japanese influence was quickly diluted. For Korea, a particularly bitter colonial experience under the Japanese hastened the replacement of Japanese influence—again the United States became the major model. In both countries, while indigenous languages became the media of instruction, English became the main language of contact with the outside world. While Korea established scholarly journals in Korean, Taiwan chose, at least in the sciences and technological fields, to publish academic journals in English so that they would have a significant international circulation. In both Taiwan and Korea, there is a range of postsecondary textbooks available at the undergraduate level, but advanced training in the sciences requires knowledge of English and many of the materials used, including graduate-level textbooks, are in English. In both countries, professors are expected to publish their research in English for promotion in the better universities. The situation in the humanities and social sciences differs somewhat and there is a greater proportion of work done in indigenous languages. Korea and Taiwan are interesting examples of Third World development, since they were the two major colonies of Japan. Their postindependence experiences have not been easy—both have been involved in conflicts with neighboring countries. The use of indigenous languages for higher education combined with a reliance on English for more advanced work have been successfully carried out. Korea, with a population more than twice that of Taiwan, has done more to entrench the local language as a scientific medium, complete with journals. Taiwan, on the other hand, has used English even for internal purposes as the major language of advanced science and research.

Singapore chose to use English as the only language of higher education and research, as well as commerce and government. This decision was made because policymakers felt it important to tie the nation firmly to the international knowledge network and the international marketplace. It was also recognized that Singapore, as a small country with a Chinese majority in a region dominated by Malays, could best rely on English as its main means of communication. Singapore has had no problems with providing textbooks or other research materials in its university, but virtually all of the materials used are imported from the United States, Britain, or occasionally, Australia. Singaporean scholars write exclusively in English for publication either in the small number of local scholarly journals or for international journals. The use of English in higher education has meant that expatriate teachers could be used and close to half of the teaching staff at the National University of Singapore is foreign. Policymakers have welcomed foreign academic staff, feeling that it is necessary to be in the meanstream of international ideas and that expatriates could contribute to the country's cosmopolitanism.

All four countries function in an international scientific system dominated by English and all have made adjustments to this fact. Korea has the most successful scientific infrastructure that operates significantly in Korean, including journals and other publications. Malaysia also has made major efforts at indigenization but there are shortages of scientific materials of all kinds. In Taiwan, while teaching is done in Chinese, most advanced research materials, including textbooks, are in English. For a long period, Taiwan's flaunting of international copyright rules made the unauthorized reproduction of English language books and journals inexpensive and easy.

All four countries rely on the international scientific community for validation of research excellence and productivity by academic scientists. Publication in international journals, mainly in English, is a key ingredient for promotion in all countries although it has somewhat differing weights, with less stress in Korea and Malaysia than in Singapore or Taiwan. The stress on international publication and international recognition of scientists in these countries helps to tie the local scientific communities not only to the English language as a means of communication but also as to the norms and values of a broader scientific culture. This may have advantages in terms of linking the local community to the frontiers of sciences but may also separate science from local concerns and local technological problems. These four countries exhibit somewhat different approaches to language and to the broader issue of involvement with the metropolitan scientific community. It is, however, fair to say that all are very much a part of this broader community and are greatly affected by it.

The scientific diaspora

All four countries have strong ties to the metropolitan scientific communities in ways that have been discussed above. An often ignored but crucially important link are scientists and scholars who live and work in the United States or other metropolitan nations. For Taiwan and Korea, the numbers are quite large and the Korean and Taiwanese overseas scientific community is very important for research and technology and for the broader direction of academic life. For all four countries, the majority of doctoral degree holders have been trained overseas. For Taiwan and Korea, a majority of the students who have gone overseas to study, mostly at the graduate level, have not returned home directly after completing their degrees. Many of these doctoral degree holders obtain good jobs in the United States or other countries and advance rapidly in their careers overseas. Some have been opposed to political trends at home and have chosen to remain abroad. There are very likely more Korean and Taiwanese scientists and engineers working abroad than at home, although there are no reliable statistics and there is a significant flow back and forth. Many fewer Singaporeans and Malaysians have remained abroad, although many Chinese Malaysians have emigrated in recent years, feeling that government policies favoring the indigenous *bumiputeras* (Malays) were opposed to their long-term interest. Overall, both employment prospects and living conditions have been more favorable in Singapore and Malaysia than in Taiwan and Korea.

There is no doubt that there has been a significant brain drain from Korea and Taiwan during the past three decades. But the situation is much more complex than it would appear on the surface. Indeed, the literature relating to the migration of workers—skilled and unskilled—has recognized that migration may not be an entirely negative phenomenon in the contemporary world.[6] In the case of highly trained scientific personnel from the newly industrialized countries, the migration of talent is a complex matter. For the most part, scientists migrated for two main reasons—working conditions were better abroad and it was possible to pursue scientific research in Western universities more easily than at home and opportunities and salaries were better overseas. As Korea and Taiwan have expanded and improved their universities and research laboratories and as industry has grown and can absorb more research personnel, opportunities and working conditions have significantly improved. It can be argued that in the absence of satisfactory opportunities at home, it might be appropriate for skilled personnel to remain abroad.

Members of the Third World scientific diaspora often contribute to scientific development at home even while living abroad. Most scientists have family ties at home and return for visits frequently. They often work with local researchers and enterprises, serving as paid consultants or sometimes as informal guides. They are important links between the local scientific and research community and the international scientific community. They speak the local language and know local conditions. They are able to translate scientific innovations into local conditions better than anyone else. In a real sense, they are bridges between cultures and technologies. Multinational firms often utilize the services of foreign-trained local personnel in their work in the Third World.

In the present circumstances, there is a two-way migration of talent. A significant number of Asian scientists who have worked abroad are returning home to take positions in both academe and industry. In some cases, these individuals planned to remain abroad for only a few years for the experience, but in many instances, improved conditions at home have lured them back. It is possible that political liberalization in both Taiwan and Korea have played a role as well. There is also, of course, some out-migration. A significant proportion of the foreign students from these countries continue to remain abroad, although the percentage is probably down. Even when abroad, these professionals frequently remit funds to their relatives at home. Further, they sometimes invest in local industry and commerce, often in high-tech development.

Scientists and researchers from Third World nations who choose to work outside of their borders are often not a complete loss to their country of origin.[7] Many do not spend their entire careers abroad and return home permanently after a period of time. Others return from time to time. These peripatetic professionals are an increasingly important part of the international flow of knowledge. There are "push" and "pull" factors involved in the decision to migrate—and later to return. Professional opportunities, family ties, chances for high incomes, availability of scientific equipment and laboratories, political tensions, immigration rules, and other factors are all part of the decision-making process. Some Third World countires have tried to keep their highly skilled personnel while others have permitted easy migration. Industrialized nations also have differing approaches to the immigration of highly trained personnel. In general, however, despite protestations concerning the importance of Third World skills remaining at home, industrialized nations relax immigration restrictions when they need the skills offered by the immigrants. Some Third World countries seem to produce a large number of well educated emigrants while others do not. Korea and Taiwan, as well as India, Pakistan, and the Philippines, and other nations have traditionally had a large out-migration. Malaysia and Singapore have not. Countries like Indonesia and Thailand, with fewer opportunities at home for highly trained professionals, have nonetheless had a relatively modest out-migration.

The point of this discussion is that the migration of highly trained professionals is a matter of considerable complexity. A scientist from a Third World nation working abroad may in fact be participating in the scientific culture of his or her native country in terms of maintaining contacts, working with local scientists, and reporting on the latest developments. Many work in more than one country during their careers. Some contribute articles to local journals while working abroad. And a few invest not only their skills but sometimes money in their native country. There is a kind of scientific diaspora that functions effectively as a means of communication and helps to ensure that countries like Taiwan and Korea have quick access to the latest developments in the metropole.

Foreign training

Asia is by far the largest exporter of foreign students to the industrialized nations and all four of the countries discussed here contribute significant numbers of foreign students.[8] Indeed, Taiwan, Korea, and Malaysia are all among the top ten countries sending students to the United States—and the numbers are still increasing. While it is not possible in this essay to deal comprehensively with the complex issues relating to overseas study, it is important to focus on the role of foreign training as it affects higher education and research development in the newly industrializing nations.[9] As noted, foreign-trained academics and scientists constitute a significant proportion of the total numbers in these four countries—perhaps a majority. This is certainly the case in the upper ranks of the universities, among senior administrators and policymakers in higher education, and among the most productive researchers. Thus, those who are shaping both higher education and scientific development in the newly industrializing nations have been trained abroad.

The impact of foreign education is considerable and has been touched on earlier in this essay. It is our purpose here to focus on how foreign training affects the academic and research systems of the newly industrialized nations. The reasons why these four nations—and most Third World countries—have sent students and sometimes professionals abroad for higher education are straightforward. In almost all academic fields, the most advanced training facilities, the best libraries, and the most distinguished scholars are located in the major Western nations. Students go abroad to obtain this training

451

because it is not available at home. In addition, foreign degrees have a certain prestige value. Foreign degree holders generally obtain the needed expertise and those who return home obtain places in industry or the academy.[10] Foreign training ties degree holders to an international scientific community, with both the positive and negative implications of those ties.

Foreign-trained scientists and academics sometimes have problems of readjustment to the norms and values of their societies and their home institutions. They may be impatient with the pace of change or with academic systems that have a great deal of respect for seniority. They may be reluctant to work on locally relevant research topics, since this research may not be at the cutting edge of international science and may not be publishable in internationally circulated journals. The training that they receive abroad may not be entirely relevant to domestic concerns and may be partly dysfunctional in some ways. As the four newly industrializing nations considered here move quickly to the international mainstream, readjustment problems become less serious. For most scientists, there seems to be a reasonable fit between an international scientific orientation and local issues and needs.[11]

Foreign training is a necessary element of the creation of a pool of scientific personnel in the Third World and will remain so for the foreseeable future. These countries simply will have have the capacity to train personnel to the highest international levels. The cost of providing the laboratories and other facilities needed for advanced scientific training and research is beyond the resources of Third World nations. Further, given the small size of the academic communities in most of these countries, it would probably be unwise to make the investment even if resources were available. Indeed, the cost of building up a scientific infrastructure continues to increase, thus making it ever more difficult for Third World countries to catch up. For all of these reasons, foreign training, with its pluses and minuses, will remain an integral part of advanced training for these newly industrializing countries, as well as other Third World nations.

The traditional universities

Universities in developing countries have come under considerable criticism for their lack of relevance, their high cost, and their elitism. Much of this criticism has come from those who do not understand the nature of the contemporary university. Further, despite any shortcomings, the universities are the main institutions for training scientific personnel and, in most countries, for conducting research. It is, therefore, of special importance to understand how academic institutions work. The contemporary university is a Western institution wherever it exists. With the exception of the Al-Azhar in Egypt, there is no functioning Third World academic model.[12] Universities that have grown in the sometimes not entirely hospitable soil of the

Third World are transplanted institutions. They are meritocratic institutions in societies that sometimes have not completely accepted meritocracy. In many countries, they stem from a colonial past that has been rejected. They are seen as elitist institutions in Third World societies that have in many cases adopted the rhetoric of egalitarianism. Perhaps most important, they are highly developed, very complex institutions that are fragile. It is not possible to order a university to change rapidly and still have it keep its academic ethos—an ethos that seems to be necessary for quality research and training.[13] It is necessary for there to be an informal agreement between the university and the state with regard to the goals of development and the appropriate role of higher educational institutions in development. In our four countries, it seems that more or less workable arrangements have been made to ensure that academic institutions function as fairly independent entities while at the same time contributing to the goals of development.[14] Debates concerning the traditional autonomy that universities need, on the one hand, and accountability to funding agencies for overall goals, and how the very substantial funds that government provides to universities are spent, continue. Academic institutions must recognize that they play an important and often quite sensitive role in their societies. On the other hand, governments must recognize that in order for universities to function effectively, they must have a significant degree of autonomy and freedom.

Universities, particularly in the Third World, are pulled in many different directions, creating tensions and impossible demands. It must be kept in mind that very few of the world's universities are primarily research institutions. This distinction is held by only a small number of the most distinguished academic institutions and even these universities have a major responsibility for teaching as well as research. Third World universities were established as teaching institutions primarily by colonial authorities interested in training a loyal civil service and staffing an educational system.[15] Research was a secondary matter and was, in general, not encouraged. Further, Third World universities were not mainly focused on technology but rather on such professional fields as law as well as the traditional arts and sciences subjects. Generally, Third World universities tend to resemble, in terms of the patterns of enrollments, administrative structures and facilities like the middle-ranking public comprehensive universities in the United States or perhaps the newer "plateglass" universities in Britain rather than the elite institutions such as Oxford or Harvard. Creating research-oriented institutions in the newly industrialized nations is, for these reasons among others, a difficult and time-consuming process.

Governments seek to have academic institutions conform to their wishes. Frequently, the universities are unable and sometimes unwilling to adjust. The governance processes of an academic institution are cumbersome and the best universities are characterized by a great deal of autonomy for academic staff. Thus, rapid changes in policy and orientation are difficult. Universities are frequently hotbeds of political and social debate and often dissent. They function best with a significant degree of academic freedom, and this often means toleration for a variety of opinions and sometimes dissent on campus. Many Third World countries, including from time to time the four newly industrializing nations under consideration here, are reluctant to permit a wide latitude of academic freedom on campus and tensions ensue. It is also likely, although there is no convincing data, that academic excellence and efficiency is diminished as academic freedom is violated. At a more mundane level, governments demand accountability for expenditures and seek to ensure that academic institutions provide the training and research programs that governments feel are needed. Sometimes, it is possible to conform to these demands—in other cases it is not. Third World universities are fairly new and do not have the entrenched power of tradition to fall back on in their relations with governments. They are often less sure of their own goals and foci. Thus, they are in a less favorable position than universities in the West to resist pressures—and at the same time the pressures are often immense.[16]

In Singapore and Malaysia, the British established a university in 1949 which provided medical education and training in the social sciences and humanities—and very little else. This university was located in Singapore (a branch was later set up in Kuala Lumpur) and served British possessions in Malaya. It was not until well after independence and into the 1970s, that higher education was expanded dramatically in both countries. The emphasis in both Malaysia and Singapore has been on science, technology, and in fields like management training, although Singapore has been more oriented toward science and technology. From the beginning, local universities were unable to serve the demands of the growing middle classes for higher education and also the needs of rapidly expanding economies (although in Malaysia there was a downturn in both the economy and in the demand for first-degree graduates in the late 1970s) and thus many students went overseas for study—including a significant number at the first-degree level.

At the present time, there is one university in Singapore that is supported by several polytechnical institutions. The National University of Singapore has an enrollment of 14,150 of which 5056 are in science and engineering. This academic system serves a city-state with a population of 2.6 million. The National University is well funded and the government has made it clear that it expects the university to be up to an international standard. Indeed, it has recruited a large number of expatriate staff in part for this reason. Facilities, including the library and science laboratories, are excellent. In fields emphasized by government planners, such as computer science and biotechnology, facilities are outstanding and resources abundent. In terms of its physical plant, the National University of Singapore is a world-class institution. Its research output and the productivity of its academic staff are also of a high standard, although it is unlikely that the university can compete with the world's top-ranking institutions. Teaching loads for most academic staff are relatively high. Singaporean staff are relatively young and are drawn from a very small pool of talent. Despite high salaries and favorable living and working conditions, the university does not attract the most prominent expatriate professors. Singapore is somewhat away from the international academic mainstream, which is a disadvantage in attracting foreign staff. Further, few expatriates are given tenured appointments and there is a sense of insecurity among them. In recent years, there have also been cases of nonrenewal of contracts of expatriate staff because they have displeased government officials by their writings. On the other hand, the National University of Singapore, because it uses English as the sole language of research and teaching, has closer international ties than most other universities in its region. The university has placed its greatest stress in recent years on science and technology and the science and engineering faculties, along with mangement, have grown rapidly. The university has also tried to build ties with local industry through the Singapore Science Council and other means. Government authorities have encouraged these contacts, and in Singapore's highly planned environment this has meant considerable success. The basic structure and focus of the university, however, is quite traditional and pressure to increase enrollment, which has resulted in increased stress on teaching, has limited the amount of time and energy available for university-industry collaboration.

Malaysia has a more complex higher education system, with five universities enrolling about 38,000 students (another 22,000, or 37% of the total enrollment study abroad). The proportion of science and engineering has increased significantly in the past few years to around one-quarter of the total graduates. In recent years the universities have been faced with considerable challenges regarding rapidly increasing enrollments to meet popular demand and government policy, rapid expansion in the number of institutions (the growth in enrollments over a period of more than a decade has been 14% annually), compliance with government policy to increase the number of indigenous (bumiputera) students in higher education, and the change in the medium of instruction from English to Bahasa Malaysia. These pressures have placed great strains on the universities and have probably been responsible for the relatively low rate of research productivity when compared to higher education institutions in the other three newly industrialized countries considered here. Nonetheless, Malaysian academics are involved in research and promotion depends on research productivity and publication. The organization of the Malaysian universities was traditionally British although there have been some moves to organize higher education in a more American direction in recent years. The Malaysian universities remain predominantly teaching institutions, with relatively high teaching loads and continuing pressure to expand enrollment. While all of the five universities offer a full range of degree programs, the new institutions have specific foci—in science and technology, agriculture, and, for the newest university, the Universiti Utara Malaysia, management studies. Malaysian authorities have in recent years been concerned about an overproduction of arts and social science first degree graduates and there have been efforts, not entirely successful, to reduce enrollment in these fields. The shift in the medium of instruction placed great strain on the educational system and particularly on the universities. Instructors, many of whom were not very fluent in Bahasa Malaysia, had to orient themselves to teaching in the language, which had an inadequate vocabulary for academic purposes. Textbooks were unavailable and had to be prepared. Despite these difficulties, the Malaysian higher education system in general functions effectively and is moving in a more research-oriented direction. Academic journals in Bahasa Malaysia have been established.

Korean higher education stems from two rather different roots. American missionaries established academic institutions, including a medical school, in the late nineteenth century and higher education had a specific American orientation until the period of Japanese domination, between 1910 and 1945. The Japanese established their own university and at the same time hindered the operation of existing academic institutions. The Japanese Keijo Imperial University was modelled exactly on universities in Japan and, unlike the existing institutions that used Korean as the language of instruction, Japanese was the sole medium. Enrollment of Koreans was limited (the majority of students were Japanese). After World War II, U.S. influence was again strong and after a period of reconstruction following the Korean War, higher education expanded rapidly, generally using the U.S. model for the organization of higher education institutions. By 1986, there were 111 colleges and universities enrolling 992,233 students and with 28,224 faculty members. However, 70 percent of the institutions are private and the large majority of these have little interest in research or publication. There are, in addition, 69,962 students in a variety of graduate schools working on advanced degrees. Again, the majority (78%) of these students are in private institutions, where there are considerable variations in quality. Korean higher education has long had a science and engineering orientation, and currently more than 40 percent of the enrollments at the undergraduate level are in these areas. At the higher levels of the academic system, there is a considerable emphasis on research and publication, but for the majority of the academic system and particularly in the low-status private universities and colleges, the system is very much oriented to teaching. In this respect, the hierarchy of the Korean academic system is somewhat similar to that of the United States. Korea has the largest academic system of the countries considered here—it enrolls about 31 percent of the relevant age cohort, compared to 54 percent for the United States, around 20 percent for Japan and West Germany, 12 percent for Singapore and 21 percent for Taiwan. It has moved from an "elite" system to a "mass" orientation to higher education. The establishment in 1971 of the Korea Advanced Institute of Science and Technology (KAIST) as a high level training and research institution has added a dimension to Korean higher education. KAIST has around 2000 graduate students and an academic staff of 142 and provides the best quality training and research in the country. Korean higher education has always (except for the Japanese period) been conducted in Korean and there is an active scientific system, including journals and scholarly books, in Korean. Among the countries considered here, Korea has the most successful indigenous language publication system, although graduate students and even undergraduates in some fields must rely on texts and other materials in English. Korean professors, particularly in the sciences, publish some of their work in English for international journals, but a significant amount also appears in Korean. Because of its size and scope, it is somewhat more difficult to generalize about the Korean university system. In many respects, it is similar to the U.S. academic system in its diversity, organizational pattern, and variations in quality and orientation.

Taiwan shares with Korea a period of Japanese colonial domination which ended in 1945. The Japanese established the first university in Taiwan. While it functioned in Japanese and had a majority of students from Japan, it provided the first opportunities for higher education to Taiwanese and was welcomed. After World War II, the Nationalist (Kuomintang) government retreated from mainland China to Taiwan and brought with it higher education institutions and policies. A final and very important influence on Taiwan higher education came from the United States, where many students in Taiwan went to study and which provided considerable advice and assistance to Taiwanese higher education. Taiwan has close to 200,000 university students and 11,325 faculty members. The growth in both student enrollments and the number of institutions has been dramatic. The number of universities, for example, has grown from four in 1950 to 28 in 1986. Forty-five percent of the students major in science or engineering fields. As in Korea, the majority of students attend private universities, where standards vary and there is not much research orientation. The public sector is the prestigious element of the higher education. In the public universities, academic staff is expected to do research and to publish. In the sciences and engineering, most of this publication is in English so that an international audience can be reached. In these disciplines, journals published from Taiwan tend to be in English rather than in Chinese (the situation is different in the arts and social sciences, where local scholarly journals are generally in Chinese). Advanced level students must read textbooks in English, although all teaching is done in Chinese throughout the academic system. Academics, mainly in the public institutions, find it fairly easy to obtain research funding from the National Science Council although the grants tend to be fairly small. The public universities are fairly well equipped for research and in fields that have been stressed as national priorities, such as biotechnology and some fields of engineering and computer science, facilities are excellent. Taiwanese scholars tend to look to the United States for academic models and norms of research.

There are some generalizations that are possible concerning these four highly successful academic systems. Although historical circumstances, cultural factors and languages differ, there are some common elements. In all four countries, universities have been favored institutions. They have been provided, for the most part, with needed resources. The professoriate is well paid and a prestigious occupation. In all four countries, there have been significant foreign influences on higher education—influences that remain strong today. The colonial heritage is important—with British and Japanese influence still distinguishable in higher education. The more recent impact of the United States is very significant in all four countries but is more pronounced in Taiwan and Korea. All four countries have expanded postsecondary education dramatically in the past decades, and all have increased resources to pay for this expansion for the most part. Nonetheless, the strains caused by expansion have been considerable—particularly in terms of high teaching loads and an insufficient number of well trained academics, especially at the senior levels. There have been pressures on the universities to contribute to research and to orient this research to areas considered relevant to expanding and increasingly technologically based economies. All four countries have pushed their universities in a technological direction—and all have a higher proportion of their graduates in science and engineering fields than, for example, the United States or Britain. There have been tensions between government and university authorities concerning the direction of change, the speed of change, and the issues of autonomy and accountability, while the universities have survived and government officials in general understand that universities are not equivalent to other public agencies. Overall, these new academic systems have made very impressive progress. They have, in general, an academic ethic that stresses research. Teaching is of a high standard and the challenges have generally been handled with responsibility. In Korea and Taiwan, there is considerable variability among academic institutions, with the premier public universities most closely resembling metropolitan institutions. Malaysia and Singapore have more uniform standards in their academic institutions, perhaps reflecting their British backgrounds.

The research infrastructure

Considerable progress has been made in developing research facilities in these four countries and substantial resources have been devoted by governments to building up research capacities. It is useful to point to several specific research trends in our four countries before generalizing about the development of scientific research in newly industrializing countries. Without question, the bulk of research done in each of the four countries is done in the universities, although all four have also devoted funds to nonuniversity research. Much of the university-based research is not specifically funded by government or other sources and is part of the regular responsibilities of the academics.

In Singapore, there is overall coordination of research by the Science Council, which works closely with government departments and with academic scientists. The government had identified several areas for emphasis and special funding—fields that are intended to contribute to Singapore's economic future. These include biotechnology, electrical engineering, and computer science. In addition, since Singapore sees itself as a major financial center, it has expanded the Faculty of Management at the National University to provide the needed personnel and expertise. Research initiatives have taken place either within the structure of the National University or with strong university connections. For example, the Institute of Systems Science, located on the campus, focuses on computer applications and related matters. Singapore has devoted considerable funding to research and development in the areas that have been identified as key priorities. Funds have been given to the university and in a few instances to other agencies. The Singapore government has also worked hard to ensure that the many high-tech multinational corporations that have manufacturing facilities in the country also set up research facilities there. These efforts have met with only limited success. Because Singapore is a small country with a very small scientific community and because it has a tradition of centralized direction of effort in many spheres of the economy and society, there has been careful coordination of research priorities and facilities. In 1984, the government established a science park to attract high-tech companies and to encourage R&D. Thirty-four R&D related organizations have settled in the park, 29 of which are from the private sector, while several are multinational corporations. The technologies in the park are mainly biotechnology and biomedical sciences, computer software and hardware, and chemical-related products. With its 1300 academic staff and advanced scientific facilities, the National University is the largest scientific agency in the country. University-industry collaboration has been a priority for the university. It has engaged in a number of special manpower training programs with industry and has engaged in many research projects relating to local industrial needs. University academic staff frequently act as consultants, with the encouragement of university authorities.

Singapore has devoted considerable attention as well as resources to the development of scientific capability because the country sees itself dependent on technology and commerce for its survival. The university, the science ark, the university-related research facilities and specific programs to encourage R&D efforts are at the heart of Singapore's efforts. There has been a recognition that a small country must assess its scientific priorities carefully and invest only in areas that fit its perceived needs.

Science and technology has traditionally been less of a priority for Malaysia than for Singapore although Malaysia has recently placed considerable stress on scientific development. Further, Malaysia has long had specialized research institutions related to the country's major agricultural products—especially rubber and palm oil. Well funded government sponsored laboratories have operated for several decades focusing on these products. Malaysia has recently promulgated a science plan that stresses fostering high-tech industries as well as taking advantage of the country's rich natural resources as a base for further industrialization. While there has been recognition that university staff constitute the largest number of scientific personnel in the country, there has been less emphasis placed on utilizing the university for applied scientific research. The universities have been busy expanding, changing the language of instruction, and dealing with the problems relating to that change, and in general working out the problems of rapid development. The situation is now changing, however, and there are signs of increased concern with the use of higher education institutions for research and development. The growth of the Science University in Penang has been important in this regard as has been the establishment of an Institute for Advanced Study at the University of Malaya, the nation's premier academic institution. As Malaysia has built up a technological base—the country is now a major producer of relatively low-tech computer chips and related products and as developed a significant manufacturing sector—R&D will become more important.

Korea and Taiwan are both larger countries which have developed impressive export-based industrial sectors in the past two decades. The base of their industrial strength has not been in high technology but rather in the efficient use of established processes combined with a skilled and relatively low-paid labor force. Now, as their economies mature, considerable attention is being paid to the development of a scientific infrastructure that will permit these countries to compete technologically. There is recognition that as wage rates rise, as competition from other Third World nations such as Bangladesh and Sri Lanka increases, and as some of their customers, including the United States, place restrictions on unlimited exports, there is a need to diversify the economy. Both countries have promulgated detailed science plans and have provided funding for their implementation. There are some important structural differences between Korea and Taiwan that have an impact on R&D development. The existence in Korea of very large corporations such as Daewoo, Hyundai, and Lucky-Gold Star, which have significant financial and technological resources, means that there can be significant private sector contribution to R&D. Taiwan, in contrast, is characterized by a large number of relatively small firms that in general do not have the resources to invest in R&D. Thus, the government has played a more important role.

Korea's interest in R&D development goes back to the mid-1960s. The Ministry of Science and Technology was established in 1967 and it has established a number of research institutes in fields such as energy, metals, electronics and telecommunications. It has also helped to coordinate private sector R&D development and has worked to ensure that collaboration between industry and universities takes place. The Technology Development Promotion Law of 1972 has provided significant incentives for private sector industry to invest in R&D. Unlike the other countries considered here, a high percentage (44%) of R&D personnel are located in private companies while 38 percent are in universities and colleges. Further, only 15 percent of Korea's R&D personnel focus on basic science fields such as physics, biology, or chemistry. The large majority are in applied engineering. Private firms account for 65 percent of the R&D spending in Korea—a sharp contrast to the other three countries, where most R&D funding comes from public sources. One of the main government initiatives in science and technology development was the establishment of the Korea Advanced Institute of Science and Technology (KAIST), which is intended to function as a focus for editing elite scientists and leading the national R&D enterprise. The top universities in the country also have an important role in the science infrastructure. They train most R&D personnel and academic scientists conduct all of the basic science research. There have been efforts to articulate the universities with industrial R&D and this has yielded some success. There has also been some criticism of academic scientists for their fairly low rate of publication in international journals. The Korean model of science development is rather different from the other countries considered here. Whether Korea will be successful in the long run relying mainly on the private sector for the development of its scientific research capability remains to be seen.

Taiwan has taken a strong interest in the development of a strong research infrastructure. The National Science Council (NSC) established in 1959, is the main funding and coordinating body. A series of national science and technology conferences have been held to coordinate activities and ensure a momentum. Two main agencies are involved in scientific research—the universities and the Academia Sinica (AS), a body similar to the Academy of Sciences in the Soviet Union. The AS operates 30 research institutes, most located on its campus in Taipei. Much of the work of the AS institutes is basic, but there is some collaboration with industry and research on applied topics. The universities also engage in a significant amount of research as well, both applied and basic. Research is limited mainly to the major public universities in Taipei and its vicinity and is unusual in the private institutions, which are mainly devoted to undergraduate teaching. The NSC provides research grants to scientists in all fields (including the social sciences and humanities) on a competitive basis and has a sufficiently substantial budget so that funding is not too difficult to obtain. However, the grants tend to be fairly small and thus large scale research efforts are unusual with NSC assistance. There is also relatively little collaboration between the institutes of the Academia Sinica and the universities. Taiwan has for a considerable period of time placed stress on the development of research capability and the establishment of a scientific infrastructure. The recent growth of the Science-Based Industrial Park, which is located close to several key public universities in the suburbs of Taipei, attempts to involve academic researchers with the expansion of private high tech industry. The bulk of funding for R&D has come from government sources. Private industry has been slow to invest in research, in part because most companies are small and cannot afford such expenditure. The government has been willing to provide funding, particularly in high-tech areas such as biotechnology, computers and several engineering fields, where it feels there will be a significant pay off in terms of export-linked industrial development.

All four countries have placed significant emphasis on the development of scientific infrastructures. Their approaches are related but there are some significant variations. Malaysia and Korea have come later to a recognition of the importance of scientific research for development. Korea has relied more on private sector industry to fund and conduct research than the other countries. All of the countries, however, have placed considerable stress on the involvement of universities in the enterprise and all recognize that academic institutions are the key training places for scientific personnel. And all of them, since the 1970s, have made significant expenditures of funds and energy to ensure that there is an adequate base for R&D. All have tried to coordinate activities and all have developed national science plans to help guide developments.

Research in small scientific communities

Some of the problems of research in these four countries are common to research systems in any small country, regardless of level of economic development. The scientific and academic communities in these countries are small and both the institutional and resource base for research are similarly limited. These scientific communities will inevitably be dependent on larger scientific communities in other countries, and particularly in the metropolitan centers. In Korea, the largest of the countries considered here, there are fewer than 29,000 academics in all of the country's universities and research institutes with only 9500 in the public institutions, where most of the research is done. In Taiwan, the total number of academics is 8300, with 5200 in the research-oriented public institutions. Malaysia has fewer than 6000 academics and Singapore boasts a bit more than 1500. When divided into the various academic disciplines, the communities of academics are quite small.

Fully self-sufficient research communities are not possible in such small academic environments. This is particularly the case when there is only a limited amount of scientific literature available in the language used in the country. In Bahasa Malaysia, for example, there is virtually no basic scientific literature—the current generation of Malaysian academics (along with the very limited research community in Indonesia) is basically creating a new literature in the national language. The Korean academic community, despite its fairly successful efforts to develop a viable scientific communications network in the Korean language, relies for the most part on foreign publications for new knowledge. In the long run, it is possible that a fully autonomous research network in Chinese may emerge as the People's Republic of China develops its research institutions. However, this is a long way off and it is significant that Taiwan has chosen to use English as the main means of scientific communication rather than to pioneer a network in Chinese.

It is necessary for small research communities to forge relationships with other research groups to form a viable network for communications and expertise. In general, the relationships are between the various peripheries and a metropolitan center. It is significant that all four countries considered here look to the industrialized world for scientific sustenance, and largely to the United States. While there is some collaboration between Singapore and Malaysia, reflecting traditional ties, and Taiwan now looks to Japan for some research guidance, there is very little regional collaboration. This is typical of Third World scientific communities. Where regional cooperation has been tried, as in the University of East Africa experiment in the 1960s, it has in general been unsuccessful. However, there are also some common forces. The use of English as a major scientific language in all four countries is a major advantage. The various programs of the Association of Southeast Asian Nations (ASEAN) might be expanded, at least in concept, to include other Asian countries. The four countries have some common problems, including the need to share scientific information. It might well be that regional cooperation could build a stronger consciousness of scientific independence in a world dominated by the metropolitan centers. It might be possible to establish scientific journals throughout Asia that could have an international standard of excellence, thus building confidence and providing an outlet for research and communication.

The challenges facing small scientific communities are, however, daunting and are by no means limited to Third World or newly industrializing nations. Scientific communities in countries like Canada, Sweden, and Belgium tend to rely on their larger neighbors for basic scientific direction and for innovations in most scientific fields. They increasingly use one of the metropolitan languages (English or French) for scientific communication and publication. These countries indicate that it is possible to have a strong and active scientific community in a small country but that autonomy is very difficult indeed and that the scientific agenda tends to be set from the outside, even where local scientific traditions are centuries old.

463

The role of scientific research in newly industrialized nations

How is science used in these four countries? Does it play a role in development and in the expanding economies? Three of these nations—Taiwan, Korea, and Singapore—take scientific research very seriously and see it as an important contributor to future development. However, there is relatively little evidence to date that indicates that indigenous scientific research has contributed significantly to the impressive progress made. It would seem that development has been based on established industrial processes, imported technologies or, as in the case of Malaysia, the export of natural resources.

The situation, however, shows signs of rapid change. The example of Japan may also be relevant. The four countries considered here currently play a role that Japan had a decade or more ago—as producers of relatively low-tech products that require a skilled, poorly paid workforce, owing in part to low wages and also to efficient manufacturing techniques. As Japanese wages increased, Japan looked for increasingly more sophisticated products to produce and began to emphasize R&D as both a government priority and as a responsibility to industrial firms. Japanese R&D now ranks among the world's best and many Japanese innovations, both basic and applied, have resulted in new patents and products. Japan is now a major scientific power in its own right.

These four countries have a long way to go to catch up to Japan—and as noted earlier, their small size creates serious problems. However, all of them are taking R&D more seriously. All except Malaysia have paid careful attention to planning for science and identified key foci for scientific R&D. There is a recognition that R&D is an important part of a necessarily high-tech future. These countries are now experiencing increasing wages and their products will inevitably become more expensive on world markets. They also see nations like Thailand, Indonesia, and Bangladesh, with even lower wages, becoming industrialized. Singapore made a conscious decision to increase the wages and also the overall skill levels of its workers so that they could play a key role in an international service economy and in highly skilled manufacturing. Research in fields like computer engineering and biotechnology has been emphasized as part of this thrust. So far, research initiatives have come from government and not from industrial firms. The Singapore government, however, has encouraged multinational firms to locate research facilities in Singapore and has offered incentives for this purpose. It is not clear what the results will be.

Korea and Taiwan face some difficult decisions if they wish to strengthen high-tech industry and have indigenous research contribute to this development. While there has been a recognition that research is an important element in future economic development, there has been little movement by the traditional industries to build R&D capability themselves or to contribute

464

to other efforts for research development. Korea is a partial exception, but even in Korea the contributions of industry have been modest.

These four countries stand at a crossroads in terms of the user of research for development and economic growth. They face a variety of policy decisions that will determine how research will be used. Even at this early stage, there are some interesting differences among the four countries, indicating that there is more than one approach.

The role of the university

Universities inevitably have a key role in scientific research in any country and it is likely that they will play an even more crucial role in these four nations. They are, first and foremost, existing institutions with libraries, laboratories, and highly skilled personnel.[17] They have a research tradition and orientation. In these four countries, the universities have moved to stress not only research and publication as a means of recognition and promotion through the academic ranks but have also developed foci in key areas of science and technology. Particuarly in the elite sectors, universities in these four countries are more oriented toward the sciences and technology than universities in Western countries. Contrary to the colonial models from which they emerged, these academic institutions have become very much oriented toward technological development, due largely to patterns of resource allocation in the past two decades.[18]

Universities are the key source of training for technologically skilled manpower. As industry becomes more sophisticated, it needs a larger supply of well educated personnel. The universities provide this personnel. New specializations in such fields as management, computer technology, economics, and others, have contributed the skills needed for development. The universities are therefore providing the rank and file personnel for sophisticated economic development. They are also educating small numbers of research workers who have a higher level of skills who may remain within the universities as teachers and researchers (frequently after advanced education overseas) or go into government or industry in positions of considerable authority.

Because universities have the basic infrastructures for research, they are easy to turn to for assistance. Scholars in the biological sciences can be asked to work on biotechnology issues, for example. New facilities can be built and incentives offered to scholars to work on interdisciplinary subjects. In Singapore, new research facilities have been located on the campus of the National University. In Taiwan, the location of the Science-Based Industrial Park is near two of the nation's best technologically oriented universities and helps to foster close relations. It is generally easier to utilize university staff and facilities in the development of new research initiatives than to build entirely new facilities. Further, it is often the case that the universities have the only qualified staff in many scientific fields and it would be difficult to obtain the necessary expertise without academic cooperation.

Academic institutions also have some disadvantages from the viewpoint of applied R&D. Academic scientists are often more interested in "basic science" and in the issues that have a broader theoretical relevance to the international scientific community than to the applied concerns that are directly relevant to industrial development. They may sometimes be reluctant to shift their research concerns. The academic freedom to engage in research is a significant strength for the long-term development of the university and the best researchers, but it is a potential problem when seeking to harness academic talent for applied research. Universities tend to value research that has theoretical importance and that relates to broader issues. Highly applied work is sometimes held in low esteem. Universities are also teaching institutions—the emphasis on teaching tending to be greater in developing countries—and the sometimes heavy teaching loads of academic staff may interfere with concentration on research. Academic structures may inhibit interdisciplinary arrangements or directly working with private sector firms or even government agencies. The very independence of the university, which is one of its most strongly held values, may make it difficult to motivate in directions desired by government or industry.

Despite these drawbacks, universities are the most important sources of scientific research in these four countries and they are likely to remain so. There are increasingly close links to government and industry in terms of research and the incentives provided by government to ensure the cooperation of the universities have generally been successful. Universities offer unparalleled flexibility so that academic personnel may vary their responsibilities among teaching and research functions. Graduate students may be used as research workers at relatively low salaries. University staff have international contacts so that they can keep in touch with scientific developments in the larger learning centers. There is an increasing recognition, even in countries like the Soviet Union, which has traditionally separated advanced research done in the Academics of Science from the universities, that there are drawbacks to this arrangement. Universities, in short, offer the resource base, flexibility, and orientation that serves research well.

However, if universities are to serve their full potential, governments must recognize both their strengths and weaknesses. A kind of treaty between the universities and government needs to evolve so that academic institutions will have appropriate autonomy while at the same time they will recognize the need to participate in the process of development. Universities in these four countries have done a very effective job of balancing the often quite severe pressures of external authorities for expansion, and in some instances political conformity and an orientation toward the sciences with a commitment to academic values. But the struggle has not been easy and there is a

466

need to recognize that universities are unusual and rather fragile institutions that not only require adequate funding but also a considerable degree of autonomy.

Conclusion

Taiwan, South Korea, Singapore, and Malaysia are at a crucial turning point in their development. They have achieved an impressive level of economic growth in the past several decades. They have also built up impressive academic infrastructures that are poised to engage in research. Future economic growth will depend, at least in part, on R&D and on the harnessing of technology. The question is not whether R&D will be an important part of the economic future of these countries but how it can be used and what precise direction it will take. Small steps have been taken to ensure that R&D is fostered.[19]

Yet, the challenges are considerable. How can small scientific communities such as those in four countries build up the necessary expertise and the appropriate critical mass? What are the appropriate institutional arrangements? How can the current links with metropolitan R&D and academic communities be effectively used? Does the brain drain constitute an unmitigated disadvantage or are their positive considerations? What are the best policies for building up the needed infrastructures and orientation toward applied research? How can the traditionally autonomous academic institutions be constructively involved?

These and other questions may seem daunting, but they are an indication that science in general, and R&D in particular, in these four important countries are at a point of take off. The questions concern the nature of scientific development and the relationship of academic science to applied research. The challenges are considerable, but there is a reasonable assurance that there will be sustained scientific growth and that both R&D and the universities will contribute to this development.

Notes

I am indebted to Drs. William Cummings, Thomas Eisemon, and Sungho Lee for their comments on an earlier version of this essay.

1 This chapter is based on data presented in Philip G. Altbach, Charles H. Davis, Thomas O. Eisemon, S. Gopinathan, H. Steve Hsieh, Sungho Lee, Pang Eng Fong and Jasbir Sarjit Singh, *Scientific Development and Higher Education: The Case of Newly Industrializing Nations* (New York: Praeger, 1989).
2 Joseph Ben-David, *Fundamental Research and the Universities* (Paris: Organization for Economic Cooperation and Development, 1968).
3 Michael Moravcsik, *Science Development: The Building of Science in Less Developed Countries* (Bloomington, IN: International Development Research Center, 1973).

4 S. Gopinathan, "Higher Education and the Indigenization Response: The Cases of Singapore and Malaysia" (unpublished Ph.D. dissertation, SUNY Buffalo, 1986).

5 Singapore is an interesting case study. It has four official languages for its population of 2.5 million—English, Chinese, Malay, and Tamil. Although Malay has been designated as the "national language," English is used for all postsecondary education (and the bulk of primary and secondary schooling), for all governmental business, for commerce, and for the legal system.

6 "Voluntary Servitude: Asian Migrant Workers," *Economist* 308 (September 10, 1988), pp. 21–24.

7 Some Third World nations export professionals to other developing countries. There are, for example, large numbers of Indian teachers, scientists, and engineers working in Africa, the Middle East, and other parts of Asia, either under specific contract or as migrants. Palestinian professionals are important in the Arabian Gulf states.

8 William K. Cummings, "Going Overseas for Higher Education: The Asian Experience," *Comparative Education Review* 28 (May, 1984), pp. 241–57. See also William K. Cummings and W. C. So, "The Preference of Asian Overseas Students for the United States: An Examination of Context," *Higher Education* 14 (August, 1985), pp. 403–23.

9 For an extensive analysis of foreign student issues see Elinor Barber, Philip G. Altbach, and Robert Myers, eds., *Bridges to Knowledge: Foreign Students in Comparative Perspective* (Chicago: University of Chicago Press, 1984). See also Philip G. Altbach, "The Foreign Student Dilemma," *Teachers College Record* 87 (Summer, 1986), pp. 590–610.

10 At the present time, none of the four countries has any problem in absorbing into the economy advanced degree holders trained abroad, although there is some unemployment of first degree holders in Malaysia. This was not always the case as both Korea and Taiwan had problems in employing all graduates, and this contributed to the brain drain. Many other Third World nations have serious problems of unemployment of advanced degree holders and while foreign-trained individuals often have an advantage, there are difficulties.

11 These countries have less serious problems than many other Third World nations because their academic and research systems more closely resemble those of the metropolitan centers and research issues are often related to those which are current in the international scientific community.

12 For further discussion of these issues, see Philip G. Altbach, *Higher Education in the Third World: Themes and Variations* (New York: Advent Books, 1987).

13 Edward Shils, *The Academic Ethic* (Chicago: University of Chicago Press, 1982).

14 Philip G. Altbach, "Academic Freedom in Asia: Learning the Limitations," *Far Eastern Economic Review* (June 16, 1988), pp. 24–25.

15 For a perspective on the British experience, see Eric Ashby, *Universities: British, Indian, African* (Cambridge, MA: Harvard University Press, 1968).

16 Western academic institutions have not always been able to resist societal pressures. The German universities did not put up strong resistance to the demands of the Nazi authorities in the 1930s—and in part as a result have never regained their academic preeminence. In the United States, many universities did not strongly defend academic freedom during the McCarthy period in the 1950s, although the most prestigious institutions were generally more vigorous than smaller and less affluent campuses.

17 Joseph Ben-David, op. cit.

18 For perspectives from Latin America on the role of higher education in research, see Hebe M. C. Vessuri, "The Universities, Scientific Research and the National Interest in Latin America," *Minerva* 24 (Spring, 1986), pp. 1–38 and Osvaldo Sunkel, "Underdevelopment, the Transfer of Science and Technology and the Latin American University," *Human Relations* 24 (No. 1, 1970), pp. 1–18.
19 See Eugene Garfield, "Mapping Science in the Third World," *Science and Public Policy* 10 (No. 3, 1983), pp. 112–127.